Personal Financial Planning

The McGraw-Hill/Irwin Series in Finance, Insurance, and Real Estate

Stephen A. Ross
Franco Modigliani Professor of Finance and Economics
Sloan School of Management
Massachusetts Institute of Technology
Consulting Editor

FINANCIAL MANAGEMENT

Adair
Excel Applications for Corporate Finance
First Edition

Benninga and Sarig
Corporate Finance: A Valuation Approach

Block and Hirt
Foundations of Financial Management
Eleventh Edition

Brealey, Myers, and Allen
Principles of Corporate Finance
Eighth Edition

Brealey, Myers, and Marcus
Fundamentals of Corporate Finance
Fifth Edition

Brooks
FinGame Online 4.0

Bruner
Case Studies in Finance: Managing for Corporate Value Creation
Fifth Edition

Chew
The New Corporate Finance: Where Theory Meets Practice
Third Edition

Chew and Gillan
Corporate Governance at the Crossroads: A Book of Readings
First Edition

DeMello
Cases in Finance
Second Edition

Grinblatt and Titman
Financial Markets and Corporate Strategy
Second Edition

Helfert
Techniques of Financial Analysis: A Guide to Value Creation
Eleventh Edition

Higgins
Analysis for Financial Management
Eighth Edition

Kester, Ruback, and Tufano
Case Problems in Finance
Twelfth Edition

Ross, Westerfield, and Jaffe
Corporate Finance
Seventh Edition

Ross, Westerfield, and Jordan
Essentials of Corporate Finance
Fifth Edition

Ross, Westerfield, and Jordan
Fundamentals of Corporate Finance
Seventh Edition

Shefrin
Behavioral Corporate Finance: Decisions That Create Value
First Edition

Smith
The Modern Theory of Corporate Finance
Second Edition

White
Financial Analysis with an Electronic Calculator
Sixth Edition

INVESTMENTS

Bodie, Kane, and Marcus
Essentials of Investments
Sixth Edition

Bodie, Kane, and Marcus
Investments
Sixth Edition

Cohen, Zinbarg, and Zeikel
Investment Analysis and Portfolio Management
Fifth Edition

Corrado and Jordan
Fundamentals of Investments: Valuation and Management
Third Edition

Hirt and Block
Fundamentals of Investment Management
Eighth Edition

FINANCIAL INSTITUTIONS AND MARKETS

Cornett and Saunders
Fundamentals of Financial Institutions Management

Rose and Hudgins
Bank Management and Financial Services
Sixth Edition

Rose and Marqui
Money and Capital Markets: Financial Institutions and Instruments in a Global Marketplace
Ninth Edition

Santomero and Babbel
Financial Markets, Instruments, and Institutions
Second Edition

Saunders and Cornett
Financial Institutions Management: A Risk Management Approach
Fifth Edition

Saunders and Cornett
Financial Markets and Institutions: An Introduction to the Risk Management Approach
Third Edition

INTERNATIONAL FINANCE

Beim and Calomiris
Emerging Financial Markets

Eun and Resnick
International Financial Management
Fourth Edition

Kuemmerle
Case Studies in International Entrepreneurship: Managing and Financing Ventures in the Global Economy
First Edition

Levich
International Financial Markets: Prices and Policies
Second Edition

REAL ESTATE

Brueggeman and Fisher
Real Estate Finance and Investments
Twelfth Edition

Corgel, Ling, and Smith
Real Estate Perspectives: An Introduction to Real Estate
Fourth Edition

Ling and Archer
Real Estate Principles: A Value Approach
First Edition

FINANCIAL PLANNING AND INSURANCE

Allen, Melone, Rosenbloom, and Mahoney
Pension Planning: Pension, Profit-Sharing, and Other Deferred Compensation Plans
Ninth Edition

Altfest
Personal Financial Planning
First Edition

Crawford
Life and Health Insurance Law
Eighth Edition (LOMA)

Harrington and Niehaus
Risk Management and Insurance
Second Edition

Hirsch
Casualty Claim Practice
Sixth Edition

Kapoor, Dlabay, and Hughes
Focus on Personal Finance: An active approach to help you develop successful financial skills
First Edition

Kapoor, Dlabay, and Hughes
Personal Finance
Eighth Edition

Personal Financial Planning

Lewis J. Altfest, Ph.D.
Pace University

McGraw-Hill
Irwin

Boston   Burr Ridge, IL   Dubuque, IA   Madison, WI   New York   San Francisco   St. Louis
Bangkok   Bogotá   Caracas   Kuala Lumpur   Lisbon   London   Madrid   Mexico City
Milan   Montreal   New Delhi   Santiago   Seoul   Singapore   Sydney   Taipei   Toronto

PERSONAL FINANCIAL PLANNING

Published by McGraw-Hill/Irwin, a business unit of The McGraw-Hill Companies, Inc., 1221 Avenue of the Americas, New York, NY, 10020. Copyright © 2007 by The McGraw-Hill Companies, Inc. All rights reserved. No part of this publication may be reproduced or distributed in any form or by any means, or stored in a database or retrieval system, without the prior written consent of The McGraw-Hill Companies, Inc., including, but not limited to, in any network or other electronic storage or transmission, or broadcast for distance learning.

Some ancillaries, including electronic and print components, may not be available to customers outside the United States.

This book is printed on acid-free paper.

1 2 3 4 5 6 7 8 9 0 CCW/CCW 0 9 8 7 6

ISBN-13: 978-0-07-253640-9
ISBN-10: 0-07-253640-3

Editorial director: *Brent Gordon*
Publisher: *Stephen M. Patterson*
Executive editor: *Michele Janicek*
Editorial coordinator: *Barbara Hari*
Executive marketing manager: *Rhonda Seelinger*
Lead producer, Media technology: *Kai Chiang*
Project manager: *Gina F. DiMartino*
Production supervisor: *Gina Hangos*
Lead designer: *Matthew Baldwin*
Media project manager: *Ellyn Zydron*
Senior supplement producer: *Carol Loreth*
Cover design: *Chris Boyer*
Typeface: *10/12 Times Roman*
Compositor: *International Typesetting & Composition*
Printer: *Courier Westford*

Certified Financial Planner Board of Standards, Inc., is a professional regulatory organization based in the United States of America that fosters professional standards in personal financial planning so that the public has access to and benefits from competent and ethical financial planning. They can be reached at (888) 237-6275, or on the Web at www.cfp.net. CFP® Certification Exam Questions © 2004, 1999, 1996, 1994 CFP Board. Used with permission.

Library of Congress Cataloging-in-Publication Data

Altfest, Lewis J.
   Personal financial planning / Lewis J. Altfest.
      p. cm.
   Includes index.
   ISBN-13: 978-0-07-253640-9 (alk. paper)
   ISBN-10: 0-07-253640-3 (alk. paper)
   1. Finance, Personal. 2. Financial planners. I. Title.
HG179.A4484 2007
332.024—dc22   2005056228

www.mhhe.com

To my wife Karen. Her success as a financial planner after receiving a Ph.D. in an unrelated field made her inputs particularly valuable in constructing this text. Perhaps more importantly, through her ability to balance a career and dedication to our children and the quality of our lives together, she created an environment that made this book possible.

About the Author

Lewis J. Altfest, Ph.D., CFP, CFA, CPA, PFS

Lewis J. Altfest has balanced a career in financial planning and investing with one as an associate professor of finance. He began as an accountant working for a then "Big 8" accounting firm and became a Certified Public Accountant. After some shorter-lived ventures, he joined the Wall Street firm of Wertheim and Co. in its investment research department. He held similar positions with Lehman Brothers and Lord Abbett & Co.

At Lord Abbett & Co., an investment management firm, he rose to become Director of Investment Research, Chief of Long Range Strategy, and a general partner of the firm. At the same time, he began seriously pursuing a Ph.D. and teaching part-time. It was at Lord Abbett that Lewis Altfest decided to focus on helping individuals instead of institutions. He wanted to become the "Consumer Reports of Financial Planning," that is, to provide unbiased financial and investment advice and to dedicate himself to instructing students and the public on financial matters.

In 1982 he established a financial planning and investments firm along with another individual and in 1983 incorporated a firm performing the same activities by himself. At about the same time, he joined the faculty of Pace University as Associate Professor of Finance.

His wife, Karen C. Altfest, joined him in business shortly thereafter (his son some 20 years later) and together they have established a multi-person financial and investment advisory firm, L.J. Altfest & Co. Inc., located in New York City.

Dr. Altfest has been active in financial planning industry matters for over 20 years, interacting with other planners nationwide, and has been an original member and a member of the board of directors of the National Association of Personal Financial Advisors and served on the board of directors of the IAFP New York Chapter, the predecessor of the Financial Planning Association, and on the board of the Educational Foundation of NAPFA as well.

Over the past 20 years, Dr. Altfest has been named to Best Planners in the United States lists by *Money* magazine, *Worth Magazine, Mutual Funds Magazine,* and *Medical Economics*. Dr. Altfest's firm has been named among Bloomberg's "Top Wealth Managers" for the past three years.

At Pace University he has been active in many pursuits, including serving on the university's employee benefits committee and chairing the finance department's recruitment and tenure committees. He has published academic research papers in financial planning and investing and has two other books, *Introduction to Business* (Harper and Row) and *Lew Altfest Answers Almost All Your Questions about Money* (McGraw-Hill), which he co-authored with his wife. His most recent research paper is "Personal Financial Planning: Origins, Developments and a Plan for Future Direction," *American Economist,* published in 2004.

Dr. Altfest participates in many professional and academic associations today, including the FPA, NAPFA, CFA Institute, and AICPA, and is an original member of the Academy of Financial Services. His advice and research have been quoted in such media as the *New York Times, The Wall Street Journal, Newsweek, US News and World Report, Fortune, BusinessWeek, Money Financial Advisor, Financial Planning, Investment News, Bloomberg Wealth Manager,* and *Bottom Line,* and he has written a monthly column for *Medical Economics* for over a decade. He has appeared on CBS, ABC, NBC, CNN, CNBC, and others. He has been named an Alumni of the Year by CUNY Graduate Center, where he received his Ph.D. degree.

You can catch him on Saturdays and Sundays relaxing on the deck of his weekend home, alternately doing work, talking to Karen, and gazing at the birds on the treetops, which one of his clients assured him would add years to his life.

Preface

GOALS OF THE BOOK

Personal Financial Planning is designed to be used for the study of personal finance and financial planning from a planner's perspective. This text goes beyond the traditional personal finance texts to teach students how to do actual financial planning and integrates the theory and practice of personal finance.

This book incorporates a theory of personal financial planning that demonstrates the similarities and differences between personal and business finance and integrates the entire body of financial material presented. It is intended to utilize the theoretical contributions over the past half-century, particularly modern portfolio theory, to elevate the level of presentation. At the same time, its goal is to remain easy to understand and useful in real life.

Experienced financial planners and other professionals looking for a one-volume reference to the planning field from a practitioner's perspective, or who may be considering pursuing the Certified Financial Planner™ (CFP®) certification should find the book appealing. Those who would like to plan their own financial future in a comprehensive way also should find the text informative. Consequently, instructors of education courses, whether for general or CFP® certification preparation purposes, may consider the text's practical combination of planning facts, analysis, and frequent step-by-step instructions attractive.

THEMES

This text is unified by a few themes. One is that the household resembles a business and can profitably use its financial techniques. Another is that decisions for the household, for you, include all operations and all assets and obligations. In other words, decisions are ultimately made on an integrated basis. Whether we are engaged in investment activities or mapping retirement plans, we are performing household operations that fall under personal financial planning's mandate.

Our personal financial planning objective is effective household operations that we achieve through logical, businesslike financial procedures. Households whose activities are financially efficient have the foundation for personal goal achievement. This approach is covered in more detail in Chapter 4.

ORGANIZATION

In keeping with its practical emphasis, *Personal Financial Planning* is largely ordered around the parts of a financial plan. Its parts all funnel into the final section, "Integrated Decision Making." The approach is illustrated in Figure A.

Many of the chapters that require active planning use a full or modified process-oriented approach that takes the student through the methodology point by point. This approach not only provides an easy-to-follow structure; it also better prepares financial planning majors for more advanced material to come.

FIGURE A
Sections of the Book

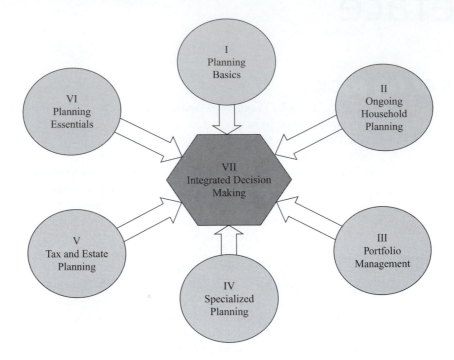

Content

Personal financial planning is an unusually broad discipline that requires knowledge of topics ranging from mathematics to human interaction. Not coincidentally, there is an introductory chapter in Part One that presents virtually all the mathematical material needed in simple fashion with solved examples for each step. It is a feature of the book that all new concepts are followed by examples using generic calculator solutions where possible and Excel-based solutions in the text and on the Web site.

The human side of the process, which is often overlooked, is presented in Chapter 3 in the sections that stress communications and goal setting. Human actions are expanded on in a separate chapter, "Behavioral Financial Planning" (Chapter 19), which presents the latest thinking on the topic. Practical examples of its contributions are given in each major area of personal financial planning.

In keeping with the practical nature of the text there is a final chapter, "Completing the Process," that truly explores the finishing process. To the author's knowledge, this is the only textbook to cover PFP integration and overall decision making in detail. The chapter could have been called simply "Completing the Financial Plan." However, it essentially does more, indicating how certain tools and practices demonstrate the comprehensive nature of PFP and improve the completion process. It is this integration that requires overall decision making that differentiates personal financial planning from personal finance and from other professions that offer financial advice.

Personal finance and investments courses alike tend to treat financial investments as the centerpiece of investment material. There are other assets, namely human-related and real assets, that importantly enter into decision making. In Chapter 8, "Nonfinancial Investments," these investments, often given less emphasis, are described and analyzed in detail.

The text has two review chapters in Part Six, "Planning Essentials." The background chapter includes economics and other material intended to provide those without a proper background, or students in need of a review, with a quick upgrading in usable knowledge. The investment chapter presents descriptive material on stocks, bonds, and mutual funds.

Personal Financial Planning is the only text that covers every topic required in the new Academy of Financial Services (AFS)–CFP Board guidelines for the first course, and each subject in the CFP Board's newly revised topic list[1] of general principles of financial planning for the exam. It is an appropriate method of presentation for all students, not just financial planning majors. Professors who desire further descriptive coverage, including those who prefer broader CFP® certification preparation information, will find special chapters for that purpose as well. Suggested course outlines for various instructional approaches are detailed in the Instructors Manual found on the book's Web site.

Features

There are a number of features throughout the chapters to help bring the text material to life.

- **Chapter Goals**

  The goals of each chapter are stated at the beginning of that chapter. They are most often expressed in action-oriented terms to emphasize the usefulness of the material in daily situations.

- **Dan and Laura opening case**

  A key feature is the use of a single case study that is developed throughout the text. Each chapter starts with a relevant sentence or two from that chapter's event. Significantly at chapter's end, Dan and Laura's day-to-day problems are stated and answered from a financial planning practitioner's point of view. This ongoing case study also reviews the chapter's material and places it in a broader context. The case permits the student to understand how the chapter's material can be applied to real-life situations and experience the information-gathering process as a professional interviewer would. Reviewers have said that this case study, which is deeper than a typical academic one, is more interesting and closer to a student's own experiences.

- **Real Life Planning**

  Almost every chapter starts with a minicase called "Real Life Planning." It sets the stage for the educational material to follow. Students have found these "stories," largely based on the author's own experiences with clients and told in a nontechnical manner, an interesting, easy-to-relate-to way to begin the chapter.[2]

- **Key terms**

  Key words are presented in boldface to highlight terms and concepts that are emphasized.

- **Practical Comments**

  Practical Comments are often used to underscore the situations in which real human actions differ from the way the book tells you it should be done. These highlighted boxes' recommendations, given to meet the issues at hand, carry the tone of a financial planner who has dealt extensively with these circumstances himself.

- **Tables and figures**

  Tables and figures have been placed throughout the text. Wherever useful, the tables have presented a summary of factual material in an easy-to-refer-to manner.

- **Examples**

  As we mentioned, there are many examples given, particularly in mathematical and more-difficult-to-describe concepts. Special efforts are made to provide an answer for every type of problem, often including an explanation of why a particular step is taken.

---

[1] First test date: November 2006.

[2] Certain material has been altered in part to protect the identities of the people who are discussed.

- **Excel and calculator examples**

  Excel is explained and solutions are given for all appropriate problems in the appendix to the text and on the Web site. In addition, calculator solutions are provided on a generic pictorial basis in the body of the text where possible, thereby allowing any financial calculator to be used to solve those problems. Where problems are more complex, keystrokes of two leading calculators, the HP12C and the TI BAII Plus, are illustrated right in the example.

- **Comprehensive Financial Plan**

  An actual comprehensive financial plan is provided on the Web site. It is based on the Dan and Laura case study presented by chapter, but this time in a more compact manner after final decisions have been made. Students should gain an appreciation for how an actual financial plan looks and, together with chapter presentations, how it is developed.

There are many end-of-chapter study tools to be used for self-study, and/or homework:

- **Chapter Summary**

  The salient points of the chapter are placed here. Together with the goals section and key terms, it can guide the student into a better understanding of the chapter's points.

- **Key Terms list with page references**

  This feature provides in one place a useful compendium of important terms introduced in the text.

- **Web sites**

  Selected Web sites indicate where additional information can be obtained.

- **Questions and Problems**

  A select list of questions is presented representing a mixture of factual and evaluative matters. The problems stress mathematical computation as a practical exercise of the chapter's numerical material.

- **CFP® Certification Examination Questions**

  An unusually broad list of former CFP® certification examination questions is provided. These demonstrate selected areas of emphasis for those contemplating taking the exam. They also present many practical questions that require students to demonstrate knowledge of the chapter's topics.

- **Case Application and questions**

  There is a second case study, called Case Application, that is similar in approach to the first one about Dan and Laura. However, instead of having a solution given in the text, this one is to be prepared and submitted by the student and/or discussed in class.

- **Student Financial Plan**

  Instructors who wish to schedule a term project for students doing a financial plan for "clients" can do so. In my experience of over 20 years teaching PFP to matriculating undergraduate and graduate students, this assignment is very popular. The knowledge derived from the two case studies in each chapter and the full financial plan on the Web site enable students to prepare their plans well.

There are also a Glossary and Suggested Readings at the end of the book.

SUPPLEMENTS

Online Learning Center

www.mhhe.com/altfest

The Online Learning Center contains the following assets which are password-protected for instructors only:

- *Instructor's Manual.* Includes solutions for end-of-chapter questions, problems, and case studies.
- *Test bank.* Word files containing 30–40 questions, including true-false, multiple choice, and essays, prepared by Aron Gottesman, Associate Professor of Finance, Pace University.
- *PowerPoint slides.* PowerPoint slides for each chapter to use in classroom lecture settings, created by Aron Gottesman, Associate Professor of Finance, Pace University.

Acknowledgments

My personal thanks to all academic reviewers. Each contributed importantly to the final copy. Their knowledge of the material and understanding of what it takes to communicate it effectively significantly enhanced the book.

Haseeb Ahmed
Johnson C. Smith University

M. J. Alhabeeb
University of Massachusetts

Mike Barry
Boston College

Conrad Ciccotello
Georgia State University

Sheran Cramer
University of Nebraska—Omaha

Karen Eilers Lahey
University of Akron

Kay N. Johnson
Penn State University—Erie

J. Jeffrey Lambert, CFP®
University of California—Davis Extension

Jennifer LeSure
IVY Tech State College in Indianapolis

Ann Perkins
North Dakota State University

Bruce L. Rubin
Old Dominion University

Deanna Sharpe
University of Missouri—Columbia

David Sinow
University of Illinois

Michael Snowdon
The College for Financial Planning

Gene R Stout
Central Michigan

Don Taylor
The American College

Kenneth M Washer, CFP®
Texas A&M University—Commerce

Glenn Wood
Winthrop University

I am grateful to the following professionals who read individual or multiple chapters and offered their helpful comments. They verified facts, pointed out discrepancies, added to the material presented, and otherwise contributed to a more polished product.

Roy Ballentine, CFP®
Ballentine, Finn & Co., Inc.

Janet Briaud, CFP®
Briaud Financial Planning, Inc.

Gayle Buff, CFP®, CFA
Buff Capital Management

Alfred C. Clapp, Jr.
Financial Strategies & Services Corp.

Larry Copperman
Steve Aronoff PC

David Drucker, CFP®
Fieldstone Financial Management Group, LLC

Louis Feinstein
Louis I. Feinstein, CPA, PC

Linda Gadkowski, CFP®
Beacon Hill Financial Educators, LLC

Harvey M. Goldfarb
All Risk Insurance Agency, Inc.

Gary Greenbaum, CFP®, CFA
Greenbaum and Orecchio, Inc.

Roy Komack, CFP®
Family Financial Architects, Inc.

Mary A. Malgoire, CFP®
The Family Firm, Inc.

J. Michael Martin, CFP®
Financial Advantage Inc.

Ed O'Hanlon
Kieffer & Hahn LLP

Tom Orecchio, CFP®, CFA
Greenbaum & Orecchio, Inc.

Morton Price
Cowan Liebowitz & Latman

Alan Romm
Independent Broker

Bruce Ross, CFP®, CLU, ChFC

Ronald Rutherford, CFP®
Rutherford Asset Planning, Inc.

Suzette Rutherford, CFP®
Rutherford Asset Planning, Inc.

Harry Scheyer, CFP®, CPA/PFS
Pinnacle Financial Advisors LLC

Bob Veres
Inside Information

Henry Wendel, CFP®
Wendel Financial Planner & Investment Advisor

I would like to thank my colleagues at Pace University who assisted me by providing constructive suggestions, including Michael Szenberg, Ron Filante, Aron Gottesman, Qi Lu, Jouahn Nam, Alan Tucker, and P. V. Viswanath. I am also grateful to my graduate assistants over the term of this project. One in particular stands out. Oktay Veliev not only was extremely helpful in production aspects treating the book as if it were his own but was responsible for many of the creative diagrams and software examples.

Finally, I am grateful to members of my professional staff. Ekta Patel, Dawn Brown, and Michael Prendergast were of material assistance as were administrative staff members Helen Cummings and Marina Bletnitsky. However, three others stand out. The first is Karen C. Altfest, who provided a strong contribution in overall advice and chapter reviews. The second is Paul Palazzo, who made a major contribution to the case study and helped in several other areas. Lastly, I want to thank Dr. C. A. Fenster for his constructive suggestions, pedagogy, and continuing support in the strategy and execution of this book.

It is my hope that this book will contribute to the further development of personal financial planning and enhance the stature of the discipline, the instructors who teach the course, and the professionals who practice its fundamentals.

Lewis J. Altfest

(LJA@Altfest.com)

Brief Contents

* Located online at www.mhhe.com/altfest

Contents

Chapter 9
Financial Investments 224

Chapter 10
Risk Management   254

Personal Financial Planning

Part One

Planning Basics

---

1. Introduction to Personal Financial Planning
2. The Time Value of Money
3. Beginning the Planning Process

In the first section, Planning Basics, you will learn the preliminaries necessary to perform personal financial planning. Chapter 1 is an overview of the entire PFP process and details the segments of a financial plan. It also introduces a case study that we will develop throughout the book. Unlike many other case studies you may have come across, this one provides the solutions using the facts developed by a financial planning practitioner.

Chapter 2 examines the time value of money, one of the basic ideas in finance. It supplies you with virtually all the mathematical techniques you will need to perform the calculations required throughout the book. Chapter 3 begins the planning process with what can be called its initial stages. These include goal setting, data gathering, and understanding how to communicate with others.

With these topics under your belt, you will be prepared for the financial planning activities that lie ahead.

Chapter One

Introduction to Personal Financial Planning

Chapter Goals

This chapter will enable you to:

- Understand what personal financial planning (PFP) is and how it works.
- Place goals at the head of the PFP process.
- Develop familiarity with PFP's financial and personal frameworks.
- Understand the specific role of financial planning and the financial plan as a comprehensive integrated process.

Dan and Laura, both age 35, were recently married. Each works, Dan as a systems engineer and Laura as a schoolteacher. They feel they have major decisions concerning their lives that they want to make, including questions about the cost and timing of children, purchasing a house, and maintaining a "great" lifestyle. They have heard that personal financial planning might be helpful. Dan and Laura know little about finance and nothing about planning, so they set an appointment with a financial planner to find out about it. Their questions are basic: What is personal financial planning? How can it help us achieve our goals? Can we do financial planning ourselves? Their immediate concern is the debt they are accumulating. (To be continued at chapter's end.)

Real Life Planning

Linda stepped into the advisor's office looking awkward. She appeared to be unsure she belonged there. Linda wasn't the advisor's typical client. She was a young messenger for a national package delivery firm who had occasionally delivered items to the advisor's previous office location. She arrived in her uniform without an appointment. Her face showed that she was troubled by something and needed an answer right then.

The advisor ushered her into his office, offered her a soft drink, and discussed some things they had in common. When she seemed more at ease, he asked why she had come in. She said her husband was thinking of purchasing a second house and renting it out. She, on the other hand, was against doing this. It would require almost all of their nonretirement savings for just the down payment and they would have to take on significant additional mortgage debt besides. She said she could not stop thinking that if this investment soured, it could ruin their savings, expose their existing investment in their home to risk, and, most importantly, jeopardize their plans to raise a family. Linda said that the dispute was seriously affecting their relationship and she and her husband fought constantly over this outlay. She asked the advisor what he thought of the investment for them.

The advisor did some data gathering. Both husband and wife had full-time jobs that provided moderate sources of income. They seemed to have sound financial operations that generated significant savings each year, and they had accumulated a decent sum. Both liked their work and had opportunities to advance and raise their income. They planned on working until full retirement in their existing jobs even if the government pushed back the retirement age for full Social Security.

They had no debt outstanding except for their mortgage. Their insurance and other benefits were covered by their employer and they had purchased additional life insurance on their own. Like many young people, they hadn't gotten around to making a will.

Their goals were not complex. They wanted to start a family within a few years and to continue what was from the advisor's perspective a relatively modest but comfortable lifestyle. She said they didn't want to worry about their financial future.

The advisor then focused on the real estate investment. He asked her the purchase cost of what turned out to be another house in their neighborhood. A quick calculation indicated they could make a significant annual sum by renting it out after expenses, including interest on debt borrowed and maintenance costs. The advisor asked if she was confident of the figures and she said yes, she had knowledge of both projected rental income and costs. Her husband was handy and would supervise the project. The advisor asked about the outlook for the neighborhood and was told it was one for people with modest incomes but was becoming popular with younger, more affluent urban dwellers.

The advisor then thought about what he wanted to say to Linda. Often his recommendations incorporated two factors, a blend of what was financially best and wherever feasible what the client's preferred alternative was. In this case he believed there was no conflict between the two approaches. The husband was not an irrational risk taker. Purchase of the house made financial sense. What remained were Linda's concerns.

He decided to find out if she had a low tolerance for risk or just needed some advice and support in an area she was fearful of. He told her that while any investment contained risk, and that he had not had time to analyze their situation in depth, this investment seemed sound. If her figures and appraisal were correct, her husband should be commended for his enterprising thoughts. The investment income from the property could replenish their savings fairly quickly. Moreover, it could bring them closer to realizing their financial goals.

The smile that broke out on her face, and her more relaxed manner, told the advisor that all she needed was some confidence in the idea. He gave her the names of some mutual funds to invest in when their cash was reestablished and advised her to make an appointment with a lawyer to draw up a will within two weeks. He told her to review the real estate investment and her savings each year after it was bought. The advisor declined any money for this "engagement." He said the satisfaction he got from being helpful was pay enough.

As he accompanied her out, he realized that he had performed the major steps in the financial planning process. Both he and Linda had established that the planning scope was to discuss the real estate investment. However, in order to render proper recommendations, he had to gather data, establish goals, and analyze a broad range of information.

In fact, in the space of a very short time he had composed a kind of financial checkup with selected elements of a mini-financial plan for someone with a fairly simple financial life. He had concluded that the couple was on the right financial path. He made some recommendations and included some implementation steps that extended the original scope. The whole process was done over a moderately longer than normal lunch period, completed just in time for his next scheduled client.

OVERVIEW

Personal financial planning (PFP) is a practical activity whose objective is to help achieve your goals. This chapter provides an introduction to planning and begins with a look at the overall planning setting including why PFP is important, its history, and its placement within the finance field.

The chapter moves on to the heart of planning, describing the fixed process that is used to increase the chance for reaching the objective. The planning process is what defines the profession of personal financial planning. The financial plan itself is discussed with an emphasis on its comprehensive integrated approach.

Finally, the chapter discusses financial planning as a career and the practice standards that planners must adhere to.

Thereafter, the Dan and Laura financial plan is introduced, which will serve a unified case study for each chapter in the book. You should find it useful in helping you understand how actual planning is performed.

Knowing how financial planning operates as described in the chapter will serve as a useful backdrop for the information and techniques to be introduced throughout the book. More importantly, knowledge of this information and utilization of the PFP process should result in better decision making and improvement in outcomes. In other words, it can provide material help in achieving the goals you set out.

WHY IS FINANCIAL PLANNING IMPORTANT?

Financial planning is important because we live in a fast-paced world in which an ever-increasing number of financial alternatives are presented to us. At the same time, information through all kinds of media, including the Internet, is available to help us make selections. Making wise decisions enables us to achieve our goals. Financial planning, which includes gaining insight into the efficient way to perform a task and then handling it in a logical, disciplined way, enables us to further our objectives.

Understanding personal financial planning and being comfortable with our own planning efforts have important benefits for society as well. They allow us to dedicate our full efforts at work to the job at hand. They also may make us more effective at that job since the household and the business approach many problems in the same way, and many personal financial planning techniques are useful in work-related situations.

THE HISTORY OF PERSONAL FINANCIAL PLANNING

Personal financial planning (PFP) has existed for many years. Until well into the twentieth century, however, it was generally restricted to very wealthy people who were advised by their lawyers, accountants, registered representatives, insurance agents, investment advisors, or bankers.

Around 1970, these services began expanding to a larger population. Many middle class people had the discretionary income and desire to seek help with the growing complexity of financial instruments and services. The new personal financial planners developed as professionals who could provide solutions to a range of financial problems and coordinate the activities of their clients' other advisors.

Money magazine, established in 1972, and later a wide variety of additional publications and other media helped inform the broad population in financial planning matters and in the usefulness of consulting financial planners.

CHARACTERISTICS OF FINANCE

In this and the following two sections, we will place PFP within an overall setting for the finance field. **Finance** deals with the management of funds, money issues. Individual businesses and government all have concerns over use of funds. We can say that finance is a practical field of study that is based principally on cash flow. **Cash flow** is the amount of money made available for use. Finance is concerned with such variables as

1. **Markets.** Places where tangible goods and financial instruments like stocks and bonds are bought and sold.
2. **Capital.** The real, financial, and human-related assets that are generated by individuals and organizations or bought and sold in the marketplace.
3. **Market structures.** The economic operations of the business, the government, and the household that facilitate the purchase and sale of items.
4. **Market value.** The market-established worth of a product or a financial instrument.
5. **Fair value.** The inherent worth of nonmarketable assets based on cash flow, risk, and the time value of money principles
6. **Cash flow.** The economic operation of the organization based on the cash it generates.
7. **Risk.** The uncertainty of outcomes.
8. **Investments.** Placing cash flow into assets designed to improve an organization or to provide future funds for consumption.

In an academic program, finance is generally broken down into courses on personal finance and business finance, with second-level courses such as investments analysis and portfolio management, capital markets, and capital budgeting. We will discuss all items above as they pertain to personal finance and personal financial planning. Let's begin with personal finance.

PERSONAL FINANCE

Personal finance can be defined as the study of how people develop the cash flows necessary to support their operations and provide for their well-being. **Household finance,** the subject of Chapter 4, is the study of how a household and the people in it develop the cash flows necessary to support operations and provide for the well-being of its members.

Basic finance tools such as the time value of money, cash flow analysis, investment models of behavior, and risk analysis form the backbone of personal finance and personal financial planning. They will be discussed in this and subsequent chapters. As we will see, there are also a wide variety of other disciplines that have a significant role in the practice of personal finance and PFP. Some of these are listed below.

Discipline	Explanation
Microeconomics	The study of single units in the economy. It helps us understand how people and households allocate scarce resources.
Macroeconomics	Looks at the functioning of the entire economy or a major section of it. Economic conditions often have a strong influence on household actions.

(Continued)

(Concluded)

Discipline	Explanation
Accounting	Provides some of the analysis and record-keeping structures employed.
Law and taxation	Presents the rules and regulations in many PFP areas in general and in taxation in particular.
Mathematics and statistics	Yields logical thinking and appropriate measurement of household operations.
Business and government	Business provides a benchmark for selected household activities; government can change the planning environment—for example, altering regulation of the household and PFP.
Psychology and sociology	PFP extends beyond logical actions to behavioral ones. Behavioral actions are human responses such as emotional reactions. These two disciplines help in understanding how people act as distinct from how they should act.

PERSONAL FINANCIAL PLANNING

Personal financial planning can be thought of as the analysis and decision-making extension of personal finance. Basically, PFP must satisfy four broad categories of personal-finance decisions: consumption and savings, investments, financing, and risk management.

PERSONAL FINANCIAL PLANNING PROCESS

Personal financial planning can be defined as the method by which people anticipate and plot their future actions to reach their goals. When we engage in financial planning, it is usually to solve a problem or to structure a plan for the future. In either case, we go through the following decision-making process:

1. Establish the Scope of the Activity

Establishing the scope answers the question: How broad an area are we analyzing? For financial planning practitioners, it defines the specific services that they will provide.[1] For example, are we concentrating on saving money for a down payment on a home or are we examining the entire financial planning process?

2. Gather the Data and Identify Goals

In order to solve the problem, we must gather certain information. We accumulate data on household financial assets and information on income and expenditures. In addition, we develop information on limiting factors such as health, time available, and tolerance for risk.

A person or household can have many types of goals at any point in time. Goals that arise from values differ by household. The underlying goal, however, is to have the highest standard of living possible. The time devoted to work and types of leisure activities and expenditures will vary with each individual.

3. Compile and Analyze the Data

We funnel the data received into the balance sheet, the cash flow statement, and any other statements that are relevant. After that is done, we proceed to analyze the statements and establish the client's overall financial position. What are the resources that are available?

---

[1] When a financial planner is involved, according to the Practice Standards established by the CFP Board, this scope would include the range of services to be provided, how the planner is compensated, how long services will be provided, and so forth. Instead of terming this first step "Establish the Scope of the Activity," the CFP Board calls it "Establishing and Defining the Client-Planner Relationship."

Practical Comment   Why People Seek Financial Planners

Most people focus on financial planning for themselves because they have a particular problem or goal in mind. As financial planners are aware, the majority of clients don't come in asking for a review of their finances or a financial plan. Just as most patients, particularly younger patients, come to a doctor with a symptom and not for a check-up, we can say that most clients come to a planner with a "financial hurt."

Some of the most common reasons for the visit and the broad categories of financial planning they fall into are

Reason	Principal Category
1. Inability to save properly.	Consumption and saving
2. Need to resolve a debt problem.	Financing
3. Desire to improve investment returns.	Investing
4. Desire to retire comfortably on time.	Consumption and saving[2]
5. Discomfort with present risk profile.	Risk management

[2] Incorporates other areas as well.

The financial hurt and the category it falls into give rise to a financial planning process for solving it. Often other financial categories are drawn into the process. The result is that, frequently, the single financial hurt results in a more comprehensive look at the person or household. The financial planning process and the financial plan that often provides the solution for the "hurt" is presented here.

For example, does the balance sheet suggest a safe level of borrowing or does the household have a high level of debt? If there is a great deal of debt, does the cash flow indicate that paying it off may be a problem in the future? All major parts of financial planning are considered and any special needs included.

4. *Develop Solutions and Present the Plan*

There are often many different ways to solve a problem. There are a host of products that are available and many alternative services or practices to call on. For example, if the client's goal is to save more money, it can be done simply by placing more money in a savings account, purchasing a whole life insurance policy instead of a term one, or buying a bigger house with a larger mortgage whose paydown each month could be considered a form of saving.

The best solution is usually the one that solves the problem at the lowest cost. In the case of the savings problem above, the lowest cost solution, assuming it is followed, would probably be simply to make regular deposits into a savings account.

5. *Implement*

Implementation is the action step. It is taking the best solution and putting it into practice. Although this may sound simple, for many people it is difficult to accomplish. This may be due to simple inertia or the action steps may be painful to carry out (saving money, for example).

6. *Monitor and Review Periodically*

All planning procedures are subject to change. Incomes change, life situations change— some people get married, a portion of those get divorced, and many have children. In addition, individual goals may need to be altered as a person ages. The environment we live in

FIGURE 1.1
Personal Financial
Planning Process

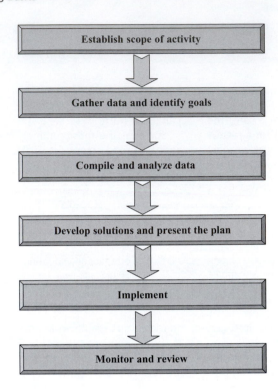

changes as well. Therefore, all planning procedures must be monitored for material changes and reviewed periodically to ensure they remain up to date. This process is summarized in Figure 1.1.

THE FINANCIAL PLAN

The **financial plan** is a structure through which you can establish and integrate all your goals and needs. It therefore can be the practical embodiment of the financial planning process and the tool to assist in its implementation. It may take the form of a detailed written document—particularly if you consult a financial practitioner. It is then often referred to as a **comprehensive financial plan.** Alternatively, it could be summarized on a single sheet of paper, even written on the back of an envelope, or could just exist in the head of the person in charge of the household's financial affairs. The key decision is a commitment to the financial planning process, including its analytical component. In other words, the financial plan is an organizational tool that can aid in financial planning.

Parts of the Plan

The plan can be separated into 11 parts, each of which is explained briefly below.

1. *Establishing goals.* **Establishing goals** involves deciding on your priorities not only for living today but for the rest of your life. It is the reason the plan is made. Therefore, all the other parts of the plan follow this one. We will describe goals more fully in Chapter 3.

2. *Analysis of financial statements.* **Financial statements** provide a current picture of your financial condition. They present the resources that are available to fund your goals. As mentioned, financial statements include a balance sheet, a cash flow statement, and other relevant statements.

Practical Comment Elements of a Financial Plan

In common usage, a financial plan is sometimes viewed by the public as a written document to answer their needs and not as a rigorously defined document. As we have seen, most people come to a financial planner for a solution to one or two problems and not for a comprehensive solution. Consequently, they may view, for example, an investment review or a retirement plan as a financial plan. A financial plan has a defined minimum scope, which is detailed in this section. As discussed, when prepared by a financial planner, the document is often referred to as a comprehensive financial plan.

The use and form of this document will vary considerably among financial planners. Some use it to form the basis of an ongoing relationship. Others employ it at the end of an extended process of looking at client activities. Some make it a highly detailed document; others summarize it in a few pages. Unless any planning document is geared to the individual and deals with all relevant factors of a client's financial life, it will not be as useful as it could be. Said differently, whether engaging in financial planning orally, in summary form, in a segmented plan—one that focuses on just one or a few areas—or in a comprehensive financial plan, the key is to incorporate all the relevant client factors and gear recommendations to the individual needs of the client.

3. *Cash flow planning.* In **cash flow planning,** household income and expenditures and other cash flows are compiled and analyzed. The goal is to plan income and expense flows so that work, cost of living, savings and investment, and financing issues interact in an optimal way to provide the highest returns possible.

4. *Tax planning.* **Tax planning** is the practice of attempting to minimize unnecessary tax payments to the government. It is done through application of allowable tax deductions, credits, and other forms of tax benefits.

5. *Investment planning.* Through **investments** we enable our net cash flows to grow as rapidly as possible, subject to our tolerance for risk. Generally households have a portfolio of human, real (ones you can touch), and financial assets to consider in the investment process.

6. *Risk management.* The objective of **risk management** is to control the level of risk and consequently of loss for each significant household asset and for the entire portfolio of assets. It involves implementation of certain risk-modifying practices and consideration of products such as insurance.

7. *Retirement planning.* **Retirement planning** is focused on household saving and investing decisions that allow individuals to retire at the age and lifestyle that they desire. Ideally, the process for this goal, which for many people has a high priority, starts early in the establishment of the household.

8. *Estate planning.* **Estate planning** generally deals with planning for yourself and others while you are alive and for current and former members of your household and other people or institutions upon your death. It usually involves a combination of legal, tax, and personal wishes for other members of the household. In addition, it involves planning for future household members such as children, particularly when the monetary goal for accumulation of assets at the time the last member of the household dies is greater than zero.

9. *Special circumstances planning.* **Special circumstances planning** is a miscellaneous category to handle other goals and activities. Examples include planning for elderly parents, special needs for children, marital or divorce planning, or business planning as it pertains to personal financial planning.

Practical Comment Integration

Financial planning is more than the sum total of individual goals for each section. Household resources are limited. Integration looks at goals and resources as a whole and at how actions in one part of the plan can affect other areas. For example, money saved in a pension plan can increase investment sums, reduce retirement planning and estate planning needs, and, of course, result in fewer resources available for spending today.

Integration presents a reality check on what can or cannot be achieved, which in turn can result in a modification of certain financial planning goals. It is an action that should be taken before each decision has been made. A comprehensive plan incorporates integration in that its parts are coordinated. Sometimes the word *holistic* is used to refer to the integrative approach. Although it isn't a section in the financial plan, integration can be thought of as the final step, and it will be the subject of the final section of the book.

10. *Employee benefits.* **Employee benefits** are the forms of compensation other than salary. The objective is to understand and integrate the best mix of employer and independently funded products, services, and other planning mechanisms. Where applicable, employee benefits can be provided as a separate section but are often listed under the other relevant sections of the plan, an approach that we will follow.

11. *Educational planning.* **Educational planning** is preparing financially for the outlays for educating adult and children members of the household. Most commonly, expenditures are for college and graduate school. The objective is to have sufficient monies prior to the expenditure utilizing all appropriate tax-advantaged mechanisms.

The parts of a financial plan are presented in Figure 1.2. Note that goals are placed at the top because they are the reason for the plan. Analysis of financial statements follows as a prerequisite of the active financial planning segments. Integration is presented toward the bottom of the figure since it serves to ensure that the goals in each section can be accomplished.

The example below provides a practical example of the entire financial planning process and of the parts of a simple financial plan.

FIGURE 1.2 **Parts of a Financial Plan**

Example

The following situation demonstrates one fairly common financial issue and the process and outcome for dealing with it. Elliot and Marsha went to a financial planner with a specific goal: to save money for the down payment on a home. They had wanted their own home for some time but always seemed to spend all their money each week. The planner went through the six-step financial planning process to assist them with their needs. First, he established that planning would be limited principally to their down payment goal but that he would make other comments that might be helpful to them.

He then began the data-gathering process. He learned that they were recently married; both worked and spent all of their available monies on what they described as enjoying themselves. Elliot and Marsha had little in the way of assets other than their income earning ability. Their overall goals were clearly to continue to enjoy life today and to acquire a home.

He mentally went through all the parts of a financial plan in connection with his analysis of the data. Where appropriate, he asked the couple questions. Elliot and Marsha had a significant combined income and modest liabilities. The planner decided that cash flow planning would be the key to the work today. He compiled their incomes and nondiscretionary living expenses. The remaining money would be sufficient for the couple to accumulate enough for a down payment to purchase a home in two years, yet enable them to continue most of the activities they enjoyed today. There didn't seem to be any material tax planning issues aside from the tax benefits available through home ownership.

A preliminary discussion indicated there weren't any employee benefits topics that seemed appropriate for this project. Investment analysis would enter in two ways. The first was to decide where the projected savings would be placed. The second was to incorporate investment information in deciding on the specific home to be purchased. The couple were fairly careful in their personal activities. They had a moderate tolerance for risk, had insurance (including term insurance at work), and didn't want to consider additional sums or types at the present time.

Both Elliot and Marsha had 401(k) pension plans at work that they weren't contributing to. Retirement planning was a low priority for them at this time. Estate planning was even more remote and neither had a will. There were no specialized planning issues.

The advisor decided that a simple two-page written document would be sufficient for them given their goals, situation, and the resources they wanted to allocate to the planning process. It would embody the solutions to their needs in the form of a list of recommendations. He repeated the goals and scope of the project. They included

1. A recommended savings amount per person per paycheck. The amount was to come directly out of the paycheck to ensure compliance. A cash flow statement demonstrated that the purchase of a home was possible in two years.

2. An investment approach that was highly conservative. Savings were to be placed in money market funds or bank certificates of deposit (CDs), given how soon the accumulated sums were to be used.

3. A recommendation that the couple begin retirement savings as soon as their home was purchased. If possible, each would contribute the maximum amount to a 401(k) account.

4. A recommendation that each establish a will as soon as possible. The advisor offered to give them the name of some qualified attorneys.

The advisor reviewed all parts of the plan and was satisfied himself that the recommendations were integrated and met the needs of the engagement and of the couple's overall goals. He presented the written document and discussed it with them. He stressed the importance of the recommendations and that no document was worthwhile unless it was implemented. All three set dates for each implementation step. The advisor told them to monitor their progress in savings and to update the document whenever material changes in circumstances occurred such as a large raise or a desire to retire earlier. They set a date for a review in one year and then a more detailed one when they began looking at actual homes. At that time, the investment characteristics and, if necessary, affordability issues would be considered.

A diagram of the origins of personal financial planning that summarizes selected material in the chapter is presented in Figure 1.3.

FIGURE 1.3   Origins of Personal Financial Planning

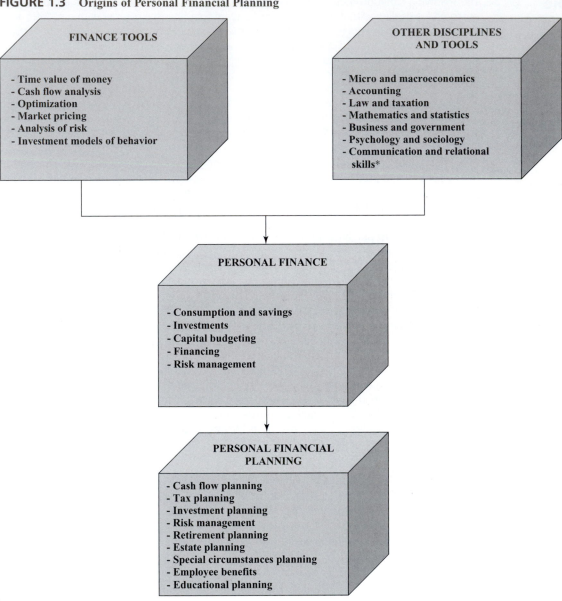

FINANCE TOOLS

- Time value of money
- Cash flow analysis
- Optimization
- Market pricing
- Analysis of risk
- Investment models of behavior

OTHER DISCIPLINES AND TOOLS

- Micro and macroeconomics
- Accounting
- Law and taxation
- Mathematics and statistics
- Business and government
- Psychology and sociology
- Communication and relational skills*

PERSONAL FINANCE

- Consumption and savings
- Investments
- Capital budgeting
- Financing
- Risk management

PERSONAL FINANCIAL PLANNING

- Cash flow planning
- Tax planning
- Investment planning
- Risk management
- Retirement planning
- Estate planning
- Special circumstances planning
- Employee benefits
- Educational planning

*Discussed in Chapter 3.

FINANCIAL PLANNING AS A CAREER

The Financial Planner

Financial planners are the professionals who practice personal financial planning. They generally provide that service to people who wish to improve their financial activities. For example, a person might consult with a financial planner in structuring an investment portfolio or in preparing adequately for retirement. While other financial people also may give advice in limited areas, a financial planner should always look at a client's overall financial situation before making recommendations. That is, **financial planners** are people with designations, education, or experience who are trained to perform the procedures described in this chapter.

The formal training to become a financial planner began in 1972 when the College for Financial Planning offered education leading to the CFP® or CERTIFIED FINANCIAL PLANNER™ certification. In 1985 the CFP Board of Standards was established to regulate CFP® practitioners.[3] In January 2000 the two largest financial planning membership organizations—the Institute of Certified Financial Planners and the International Association for Financial Planners—merged to establish the Financial Planning Association, a national organization of 30,000 financial planners.

The CFP® certification indicates that a person has been educated in all major facets of financial planning. Designees must take at least five courses[4] in financial planning including course material on investments, risk management, retirement and employee benefits, estate planning, and taxation. They are then required to pass a comprehensive examination and must have at least three years of practical financial experience before qualifying for the designation.

Types of Financial Advisors

A variety of people offer personal financial planning advice today.[5] They include not only people who identify themselves as independent financial planners, but also accountants, lawyers, trust officers, registered representatives, insurance agents, investment advisors, and employee benefit specialists at corporations. In addition to the CFP-related associations (FPA, Board of Standards), there are the National Association of Personal Financial Advisors (NAPFA) for fee-only advisors, whose members are called NAPFA-Registered Financial Advisors; the American College, for insurance agents and others who can receive the Chartered Financial Consultant (ChFC) designation; the American Institute of Certified Public Accountants, for Certified Public Accountants (CPAs) who receive the Personal Financial Specialist (PFS) designation; and CFA Institute, which offers the Chartered Financial Analyst (CFA) designation for people who specialize in investments. All but CFA designation have a broad educational requirement in financial planning.[6]

As of 2005, there were more than 500,000 people providing financial planning services of some sort. Approximately 48,000 held the CFP® certification, with more than 190 colleges and universities throughout the United States providing CFP Board–approved educational courses.

What a Planner Does

A financial planner is capable of helping people with virtually all of their major financial activities. These activities are embodied in the operating areas of the financial plan. It is necessary to be knowledgeable about all areas because solutions to client problems, even if pertaining to one activity, must take into account the client's entire financial situation. However, a large number of financial planners specialize in one or a few financial planning areas.

---

[3] Originally it was called the International Board of Standards for Certified Financial Planners.

[4] Often including one introductory course.

[5] The term **financial advisor,** often used by people offering financial advice, has different meanings to different people and groups. To some the term means a more sophisticated financial planner. To others it connotes anyone who provides financial advice to a person. In this book, we will use financial advisor in its latter broader meaning, except for the background sections that describe a financial planning practitioner.

[6] An explanation of overall practice standards is provided in Appendix I at the end of the chapter and a detailed description of CFP Board Practice Standards is given in Chapter C on the Web site.

Below are examples of the activities that financial planners commonly help people with:

- Constructing a comprehensive financial plan.
- Selecting an overall asset allocation and individual investments.
- Establishing and implementing risk management–insurance parameters.
- Structuring and planning household cash flows.
- Eliminating debt difficulties.
- Helping plan for retirement.
- Setting up an estate plan.
- Developing goals.
- Reducing taxes through planning, products, and structures.
- Becoming knowledgeable about financial matters.

Example

The role that a financial planner plays is somewhat similar to that of a doctor. The doctor may be a general practitioner (GP), a professional who is familiar with most common patient medical problems. Where the ailment is less common or could otherwise benefit from a more concentrated focus, the person is referred to a specialist. Often the GP maintains the role of the patient's principal medical advisor.

Many doctors specialize in a particular type of medicine. While their patients come to them for a particular ailment, they must be familiar with the workings of the entire body. That is true because the symptoms may come from their specialized area, but the cause may lie elsewhere.

You may see a financial planner for a comprehensive financial checkup or financial plan, as you would a doctor for a comprehensive physical checkup. Or you may have a particular concern to discuss. In each case the overall state of the person's health, whether it be financial or physical, must be kept in mind.

For many reasons, including being involved in challenging rewarding activities, personal financial planning is a popular career path with a growing number of students selecting it as an undergraduate or graduate major. One broad survey that evaluated PFP's characteristics ranked it third highest of all careers in the country.[7]

Back to Dan and Laura

The following case study will be developed throughout the book with the relevant material presented at the end of each chapter. Both the facts and interpretation of each meeting will be presented through the eyes of the financial planner doing the advising.

BACKGROUND—FIRST INTERVIEW

Dan and Laura, who became my clients in January 2006, came into my office. They brought along their new baby son, Brian. Laura mentioned that since Brian was so young she was reluctant to leave him in anyone else's care. A discussion about Brian seemed to help both of them unwind. We then proceeded to talk about both of their backgrounds. Laura, 35, grew up in a comfortable middle-class neighborhood, the only child of an owner of a successful sporting goods store. She was raised in a home in the suburbs and had all the comforts she wanted. She went to a private, all-women's college where she majored in English. She took a position as a public school teacher when she graduated. She is currently on a pregnancy leave of absence arising from Brian and is unsure when she will return to work.

[7] Les Krantz, *Jobs Rated Almanac,* 6th ed. (Fort Lee, NJ: Barricade Books, 2002).

I noticed that Laura's body language seemed relaxed and natural. Even though her baby started to cry from time to time, she maintained her participation in the proceedings. In contrast to Laura, Dan still did not seem to be completely engaged. His face seemed strained, his eyes half closed when he spoke, and his arms were folded. I decided to turn my attention to him.

Dan, 35, is one of four children in his family. His mother and father both immigrated to this country. Household finances were very tight. Both parents worked, and Dan's father often had two low-paying jobs. Dan remembers the time that his Dad was laid off and they were almost forced to take a smaller apartment in which Dan would have slept in the living room with his brother. Despite that trouble, Dan described his family life as happy. He described himself as always having been a "worrier" when it came to money. Dan worked part-time as a teenager and went to a state university where he borrowed the entire sum for room and tuition. He studied computer science in college and is currently working as a systems engineer for a computer service company. His job involves above-average risk since he works for a firm on a multiyear project but could be terminated after it is over. On the other hand, he is well compensated for his efforts.

In fact, the immediate reason that Dan and Laura came to see me was that they had $20,000 in credit card debt. The reason they accumulated this debt was higher household expenses and a desire not to touch their marketable investments. They wanted the debt eradicated as soon as possible. I made a mental note that the debt seemed inconsistent with Dan's worries about money but decided not to discuss this until later. I told them that I would create a debt repayment plan, but first I wanted to collect some data on their accumulated assets, other liabilities, and goals. The fact that Dan was able to discuss his background and his concern about his debt and that I treated the problem in a matter-of-fact way seemed to lift his spirits. He became more relaxed, turned directly to the table, and even smiled once or twice.

The couple had accumulated about $10,000 in pension assets, $34,000 in money market funds, $103,000 in stocks and stock funds, and had $2,800 in a checking account. More broadly speaking, they had $3,000 in current assets and $147,000 in marketable investments. They owned two used cars worth $6,000 each. Their furniture and fixtures were valued at $7,000. Dan had a stamp collection worth about $1,000, and Laura had jewelry worth $4,000. In addition to $20,000 in credit card debt, they had a total of $46,000 in student loans and $20,000 in loans from parents.

Next we turned to the couple's goals. Their most immediate goal was to lift the pressure created by their debt. They believed that their current lifestyle was fine and saw no need to raise it. They wanted to have one more child. As Laura said, she always felt lonely as an only child, while Dan liked having siblings and thought that Brian would want one too. They believed their current two-bedroom apartment was sufficient for one child but wanted to own their own home. They wanted their insurance checked for adequacy. They were placing money in retirement savings accounts but felt that it wasn't diversified properly.

Dan and Laura had ambitious retirement goals. They wanted to be financially independent by age 55. In retirement they wanted to maintain their current lifestyle and thought their costs would stay the same as when they were working. In addition, they wanted each child to be left $100,000 in inflation-adjusted terms. Finally, their objective was a plan that laid out their goals, indicated whether they were realistic, and, if so, would provide guidance in achieving them.

I explained to them that they had basically described the function and scope of a financial plan. I indicated that the recommendations would reflect their goals and what I believed they should focus on.

Laura mentioned that given her preoccupation with her baby, she would prefer frequent meetings by topic to in-depth interviews. I gave them a questionnaire to help them focus and to obtain further financial information. The goals, time frame, and cost were set. At just that moment, Brian started to cry loudly and the first meeting was over.

I decided to prepare each section of the financial plan discussed after each meeting, and I told them I would send a draft subsequent to the session for them to examine. I recognized that parts of the plan would have to be revised once the total costs of their goals were compared with current and future cash inflows. The introduction to financial planning could be completed right now.

Personal financial planning is the process of supervising your financial activities so that you can meet the goals you have set out. In order to accomplish those goals, it is helpful to construct a financial plan. This document will look at your goals overall, compare them with your current and future resources, and establish a plan for attaining them. In addition to outlining your goals and current assets, the plan consists of the following active areas: cash flow planning, tax planning, investments, risk management, retirement planning, estate planning, educational planning, employee benefits planning, and special circumstances planning, sometimes incorporated in other sections for all else that is financially relevant.

Let me explain the financial planning process for you. After our preliminary interview we have established the scope of the activities to be completed. In your case, as mentioned, it is a full financial plan. Based on that engagement, we will gather the data and identify goals. I have already provided you with a copy of my questionnaire to supplement the data gathered in our face-to-face meeting.

After that process is completed, we will accumulate and analyze the data. It will be comprehensive, encompassing all major parts of the plan as already indicated and any others we decide are important. At that point we will develop solutions. The solutions will be integrated, meaning they will combine all parts, giving you what we arrive at as the best use of your money.

Given your preference, each part will be discussed separately. Nonetheless, we will have a completed financial plan presentation at the end of the process and a meeting to go over it. Planning does not end there. The plan will have to be reviewed and updated periodically.

We will construct your financial plan with your goals in mind. As indicated, we will discuss and I will develop each part of the plan separately. I will explain why I make my recommendations in enough detail so that you can provide me with your reactions prior to the final integration stage for completing the plan.

We are off to a good start, and I look forward to helping you achieve your goals.

Summary

The chapter introduces personal financial planning (PFP) and its process for your preliminary examination.

- PFP is the method by which people anticipate and schedule their future activities to reach their goals. It is the action stage of personal finance.
- PFP is a six-step process that begins with establishing the scope of the activity and ends with monitoring and reviewing the plan as set out.
- The financial plan is a practical structure for achieving the goals set out. A comprehensive financial plan incorporates all relevant financial areas including cash flow, tax, investment, risk management, retirement, estate, special circumstances, employee benefits, and educational planning.
- Financial planning is a growing career opportunity that helps people in a wide variety of their financial pursuits.

Key Terms

capital, *5*
cash flow, *5*
cash flow planning, *9*
comprehensive financial
plan, *8*
educational planning, *10*
employee benefits, *10*
establishing goals, *8*
estate planning, *9*
fair value, *5*

finance, *5*
financial advisor, *13*
financial plan, *8*
financial planner, *12*
financial statements, *8*
household finance, *5*
investments, *5, 9*
market structures, *5*
market value, *5*
markets, *5*

personal finance, *5*
personal financial
planning, *6*
retirement planning, *9*
risk, *5*
risk management, *9*
special circumstances
planning, *9*
tax planning, *9*

Web Sites

http://www.cfp.net
CFP Board
This is the Web site of CFP Board of Standards, the institution that offers the CFP exam. It provides information about the CFP exam and related courses, the financial planning profession, and information on finding a CFP® practitioner. The site also contains links to request a free kit on financial planning and report a complaint against a CFP® practitioner.

http://www.fpanet.org
Financial Planning Association (FPA)
This is the Financial Planning Association's home page. It features financial resources for financial planners and people interested in earning the CFP® certification. You can also find a link to the *Journal of Financial Planning,* the CFP® practitioner's journal.

http://www.napfa.org
National Association of Personal Financial Advisors (NAPFA)
NAPFA, set up exclusively for fee-only financial planners, has a Web site that contains links for both the public and professionals. Among featured services are finding a fee-only financial planner, consumer tips, press releases, member resources, and career center.

http://www.finplan.com
Financial Planning
Comprehensive information for the major parts of a financial plan is provided. You can get insights about what a financial plan is all about.

Questions

1. Why did it take until the 1970s for the field of financial planning to begin?
2. Why does personal financial planning involve other disciplines as shown in Figure 1.3? Give some practical examples of their use.
3. What are the differences between financial planning and a financial plan?
4. Describe the personal financial planning process and relate it to planning procedures.
5. Contrast a segmented and a comprehensive financial plan.
6. Describe some similarities and differences between a financial planning practitioner and a physician.
7. Why is integration so important in financial planning?
8. List and discuss the parts of a financial plan.

9. Sam went to a financial planner who proceeded to give him written recommendations in all areas of financial planning. Is that a financial plan? If not, what might be missing?

10. What does a financial planner do?

11. Name some common financial problems planners deal with.

**CFP®
Certification
Examination
Questions
and Problems**

1.1 You receive a phone call from someone you have *not* spoken to recently. The caller is excited, having just heard that a brand new mutual fund is positioned to deliver large gains in the coming year. The caller wishes to purchase shares of the fund through you. Keeping in mind the stages of the overall personal financial planning process, which of the following questions that address the first two stages of financial planning should you ask?

1. What are your goals for this investment?

2. What other investments do you have?

3. What is your date of birth?

4. Do you want dividends reinvested?
    a. (1) and (3) only
    b. (2) and (4) only
    c. (1), (2), and (3) only
    d. (1), (2), and (4) only

1.2 Arrange the following financial planning functions in the logical order in which these functions are performed by a professional financial planner.

1. Interview clients, identify preliminary goals

2. Monitor financial plans

3. Prepare financial plan

4. Implement financial strategies, plans, and products

5. Collect, analyze, and evaluate client data
    a. (1), (3), (5), (4), (2)
    b. (5), (1), (3), (2), (4)
    c. (1), (5), (4), (3), (2)
    d. (1), (5), (3), (4), (2)
    e. (1), (4), (5), (3), (2)

Case Application

BACKGROUND—FIRST INTERVIEW

Brad and Barbara arranged to come in to see me. They were both young college graduates and arrived wearing jeans and T-shirts. I soon found out they were recently married and lived with Brad's parents, Richard and Monica, in the basement of the parents' house. They paid for all of their own expenses. Brad's parents got along extremely well with Barbara and treated her as one of their children.

Recently Brad's parents seemed to be arguing all the time and their relationship had deteriorated. When they weren't arguing, they were whispering to each other. Both Brad and Barbara had overheard some of their conversations and it seemed to be about money and investing. Brad was very close to his uncle Tim and asked his advice. He suggested that they recommend that their parents see a financial planner.

Tim thought Brad and Barbara should meet the planner prior to discussing it with their parents. He had one in mind, the advisor. He said that Brad's parents were both educated and unusually open in their discussions. Brad and Barbara should relay to the parents their concerns, and the fact that it was beginning to affect their own lives. He said that they should suggest handling the financial concerns as a family problem that could be worked out together, one that could bring the four of them closer. He was sure they would respond favorably.

In fact their uncle was correct. My meeting with Brad and Barbara was very constructive and I gained insight into the parents. Thereafter, Richard, the father, called and made an appointment. Interestingly, he mentioned that Brad and Barbara had some financial issues themselves. While the detailed planning was to be done for the parents, the engagement also would cover any planning that Brad and Barbara wanted done.

Richard walked tentatively into my office early one evening. He glanced around nervously and closed the door behind him. I could sense that there was no need for small talk. Richard wanted to tell me his story. Richard, age 58, told me he had grown up in a small town and had married the high-school prom queen. He described Monica as a sweet and caring wife, as beautiful at 54 as she was at 18. He indicated that she would be devastated by his news. He became choked up, and we paused for a minute.

The news was that he had lost $200,000 in a speculative investment. He mentioned that his $550,000 in retirement assets was down to a current figure of $350,000. He asked me to help them without telling his wife of the loss. I told him that if I took on an assignment that involved two people, there would have to be honesty all around. He mentioned again that he thought she would be devastated. My response was that even if we hid it, the true story would come out eventually anyway. I thought that he and Monica should come in next and we would start the process.

At our next meeting, Richard came in first, and we waited for Monica. She entered the room, a tall, elegant woman with a ready smile. We engaged in some small talk, and after a time I announced that Richard had something to say. When he broke the news, she was not as frail and sensitive as Richard feared. She was visibly shaken but said their recent arguments over money had made her suspicious. She then asked how we could "make it up." I indicated I would help but first wanted some particulars.

Richard was a lawyer who worked in the entertainment industry. When he got out of college, he wanted to be a rock star, but his parents persuaded him to do something "more substantial." Monica had gone to a state school and majored in English. She did a little writing but spent most of her time raising her children when they were young and the rest of it since in community activity.

They had married when Richard finished college and Monica graduated from high school. Their graduation ceremonies took place on the same day, but fortunately they were able to make both. They had two children, the elder son Brad and a younger daughter Stacy. Both were married, but Stacy and her husband were separated, and they were helping her pay her bills.

They indicated they were saving about $20,000 a year gross, but admitted that vacations and special expenditures came out of that pool.

They wanted to retire when Richard turned 65. In retirement, they wanted the same lifestyle that they currently had. They did mention that it didn't have to be in the high-cost metropolitan region they lived in then; it could be in a retirement community in Arizona. They wanted to make sure that Stacy was given at least $10,000 per year in income once they passed away. They had approximately $200,000 in life insurance on Richard's life. They wanted a total review of their assets and to examine the sensibility of that age 65 retirement.

I looked around and Richard seemed relieved and Monica had fully recovered.

Case Application Questions

1. What do you think of Brad and Barbara seeking help for Brad's parents?
2. What prompted Richard to seek assistance? Was it only because of Brad and Barbara?
3. What type of financial plan seems appropriate for Richard and Monica?
4. Why do you think Monica didn't react more negatively to the financial news?
5. What might the loss tell you about Richard?
6. Do you think the financial planner should have met privately with Richard? Why?
7. Complete the introductory section of the financial plan.

Appendix I

Practice Standards

Practice standards are the methods by which professionals establish acceptable ways of performing their occupation. They are particularly important for financial planners because of the significant role that financial advice often has for the achievement of client goals. In addition, complying with proper practices can be a defense against litigation in the event of loss and adhering to high principles can reduce the chance of getting sued. Finally, well-thought-out and executed practice standards can differentiate a true professional from the array of people who may call what they do financial planning.

Practice standards begin with establishing the client relationship and extend to gathering data; analyzing the client's financial situations; developing and presenting recommendations made; and providing for implementation and monitoring. A detailed presentation of CFP Board Practice Standards, along with its Code of Ethics, is provided in Chapter C on the Web site.

Chapter Two

The Time Value of Money

Chapter Goals

This chapter will enable you to:

- Develop a working understanding of compounding.
- Apply time value of money principles in day-to-day situations.
- Calculate values for given rates of return and compounding periods.
- Compute returns on investments for a wide variety of circumstances.
- Establish the effect of inflation on the purchasing power of the dollar.

Dan and Laura e-mailed and asked if they could set up a meeting to discuss some problems that had come up. I noticed the stern look on Dan's face as they walked in. They were having a disagreement that they said was about paying government taxes early. Laura wanted Dan to claim seven dependents on his withholding form at work. That would, of course, lead to greater available cash during the year. I suspected that their argument was not only about early payments and the time value of money, but also about their different beliefs about spending cash.

Real Life Planning

Vivian had an ever-present wide smile and looked 10 years younger than her age. This was true even though her husband had died when their children were young, and she had raised them by herself while holding down a full-time job.

Her children were all grown now and on their own. As she explained it, they had met and decided to recommend that she see a financial planner. They wanted someone to review the performance of their mother's account. The same financial advisor had managed that account for 25 years. He was such a "nice fellow" and she was one of his first accounts. He had done "so well by me," she said; he had invested the $200,000 proceeds from her husband's life insurance policy, putting it all into stocks, and turned it into $500,000 today. Moreover, she was able to save $5,000 each year and now that sum invested in stocks with the same broker was worth $150,000. She didn't know why her children wanted her account reviewed.

The advisor was shocked by the results. They indicated a return of 3.7 percent annually for the lump sum and 1.5 percent annually for the yearly deposits. He asked Vivian a second time whether there were any withdrawals that had been made and was told no.

During that 25-year period, stocks with the same risk characteristics had increased 12 percent a year. If she had earned a market rate of return, her $200,000 lump sum would now be worth $3,400,000 and her $5,000 deposits would have grown to $667,000.

The advisor decided not to tell Vivian that her current combined accumulated retirement sum of $650,000 could have been worth over $4,000,000 today. It would have been too upsetting. He would mention that only if she failed to grasp how poorly she had done.

Instead he discussed basic time value of money concepts with her. He explained how compounding over extended periods of time can make weak results look favorable. He said that the $300,000 gain from the lump sum was one such instance and that calculating the compounded rate of return was the appropriate approach to use. He told her that many people made mistakes in decisions because of these compounding distortions. He indicated that her results were very weak and that average results could have placed substantially more money at her disposal today. In fact, the results were so weak that in inflation-adjusted terms, her returns were negative. In other words, instead of growing, her sums, in purchasing-power terms, were worth less than at the time they were originally deposited.

The advisor indicated that he was using standard time value of money concepts for lump sums and annuities. They were objective calculations that could speak for themselves. He then handed over those calculations. Vivian looked at them, then stared straight at the advisor and asked, "What do we do now?"

This chapter will enable you to understand time value of money concepts. You will be able to calculate returns yourself, often simply, as, for example, in Vivian's case.

OVERVIEW

Financial planning entails making decisions from choices presented. Among the alternatives are spending today versus saving for the future, selecting one investment over another, or deciding on the future amount of money needed for retirement. All of the choices use time value of money principles to solve for the correct decision. Without them you couldn't compare the choice of $1.00 today with $1.20 in, say, six years.

In this chapter we will examine the time value of money, its major principles and methods. We will start with compounding, then discuss finding the present value, the future value, the discount rate, and annuities. You will learn about how important differing rates of return and time are to compounding, how to handle irregular cash flows, as well as the effect of inflation on figures and serial payments.

The next time someone offers you a choice of income payments over, say, three years, or higher payments over four years, you will be able not only to speak definitively about the best choice but also to compute the values for each alternative. The overall objective, then, is for you to be able to use time value of money techniques whenever appropriate to make correct PFP decisions.

BASIC PRINCIPLES

The **time value of money** can be defined as the compensation provided for investing money for a given period. In sum, under the time value of money, your money has different values at different points in time. If you were offered the choice of $1,000 today or $1,000 two years from now, you would opt for the money today. That is because you could invest the money and in two years have much more than the original $1,000. Some years ago, a bank offered traveler's checks at no charge. It wasn't a gift. The bank knew that people hold traveler's checks for a period of time before spending a portion of them and then cashing the remainder in. In the meantime, before returning the money, the bank could use your capital—in effect borrowing from you—to invest temporarily and earn income.

In other words, your money has increased in value over a time period. Although the money lent to the bank was the same amount as the money repaid to you when the traveler's checks were cashed in, the bank found the transaction attractive because of the possibility of earning a return during the interim period.

Compounding

Compounding is the mechanism that allows the amount invested, called the principal, to grow more quickly over time. It results in a greater sum than just the interest rate, or rate of return on your investment, multiplied by the principal. Once we compound for more than one period, we receive not only interest on principal but interest on our interest. In our multiplication, we add 1 to the interest rate to get the end-of-period value.

For example:

1. One-period compounding:

   Principal beginning of year: $2,000
   Interest rate: 10%

$$\text{Principal end of Year } 1 = \$2{,}000 \times (1 + \text{Interest rate})$$
$$= \$2{,}000 \times (1 + .10)$$
$$= \$2{,}000 \times 1.10$$
$$= \$2{,}200$$

2. Two-period compounding:

   Principal beginning of year: $2,000
   Interest rate: 10%

$$\text{Principal end of Year } 2 = \$2{,}000 \times (1 + \text{Interest rate}) \times (1 + \text{Interest rate})$$
$$= \$2{,}000 \times 1.10 \times 1.10$$
$$= \$2{,}000 \times 1.21$$
$$= \$2{,}420$$

Were it not for the compounding, or interest on interest, we would have taken a simple interest rate for two years, $1 + .10 + .10 = 1.20$:

$$\$2{,}000 \times (1.20) = \$2{,}400$$

The difference between $2,420 and $2,400, $20, represents the interest on interest. If we compound for long periods of time, the interest on interest can amount to a huge sum. Think of a small snowball rolling down a snow-covered mountain. As it moves along it gets larger, not primarily because it is placing snow on the original small snowball but because it is placing snow on top of an ever-larger snowball. That is the equivalent of interest on interest. By the time the snowball hits the bottom of the mountain, it can become a boulder capable of crushing anything in its path.

Native Americans were paid $24 for Manhattan Island in the year 1626. If they had placed that money in a blend of bond and stock investments returning 8 percent a year, they would have had almost $112 trillion by the year 2005. They would have had enough money to buy the Brooklyn Bridge and probably all the buildings that could be seen from the top of it.

Let's do a calculation using that $2,000 investment that shows the effect of compounding at a 10 percent interest rate for five years. Notice in Table 2.1 that the compounding

TABLE 2.1
Impact of Compounding—Investment of $2,000

Year	Beginning Principal	Ending Principal	Simple Interest Income	Compound Interest Income	Compounding Contribution
1	$2,000	$2,200	$200	$200	$0
2	$2,200	$2,420	$200	$220	$20
3	$2,420	$2,662	$200	$242	$42
4	$2,662	$2,928	$200	$266	$66
5	$2,928	$3,221	$200	$293	$93
Total			**$1,000**	**$1,221**	**$221**

contribution has gone from $20 at the end of two years to a cumulative sum of $221 by the end of five years.

Note that the total contribution of compounding over simple interest at the end of five years is $221, which is more than one year's worth of simple interest. The cumulative gain turns out to be over 60 percent of the beginning principal as compared with 50 percent for simple interest. A comparison of simple interest relative to compounding for a cumulative 5-year and 20-year period is given in Figure 2.1.

At the end of 30 years, the amount of simple interest would be insignificant relative to the compound interest. This is illustrated in Figure 2.2.

Using a Financial Calculator

In many of the problems that follow, you could receive your answer by looking up a compounding factor in a financial table, but that is hardly efficient. There are many fine calculators that can perform the operation for you. In fact, all financial calculators generally use the same basic keystrokes. They often have special keys to calculate the time value of money and perform many other financial operations.

FIGURE 2.1
Comparison: Compound Interest versus Simple Interest

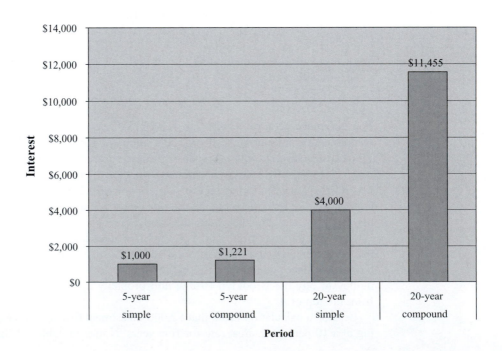

FIGURE 2.2 **Comparison: 10 Percent Interest—Simple versus Compound**

Five special keys—N, I/Y, PV, PMT, FV—allow you to solve all the simple time value calculations in this chapter.[1] They are presented in Figure 2.3 below.

N   = The number of years or compounding periods

I/Y   = The rate of return on an investment or discount rate

PV   = Present value

PMT = Periodic payment

FV   = Future value

We will use a form of this "all calculator" diagram to solve for all simple time value type problems throughout the book. Basically, as you will see, you enter all the inputs and press the key for the variable you are solving for. Unfortunately the calculators diverge in their approach to more complex financial problems.[2] In these instances, we have selected two leading financial calculators—the HP12C and the TI BA II Plus—for which we will supply the individual keystrokes. In Appendix II to this chapter, you will find details on performing the same calculations in Excel.

Present Value

The **present value** of a sum is its worth at the beginning of a given period of time. We may be offered an amount of money in the future and want to know what it is worth today. In other words, we want to know its current value. In financial terms, we call this being given the future value and having to solve for the present value. The amount is obtained through discounting that future value by an appropriate discount rate. In effect, discounting is like compounding in reverse. Just as you may have been surprised at how large a

[1] Note that HP12C uses *i* instead of I/Y notation.

[2] Our complex problems are mostly IRR, which will be explained later in this chapter, and NPV, which is explained in Chapter 8.

FIGURE 2.3
Financial Calculator
Keystrokes

sum of money grew through compounding over many years, you may have the same response to the results of discounting. However, in this case, your surprise would be at how small the present value is relative to the future value when discounting occurs over many years.

The formula is

$$PV = \frac{FV}{(1 + i)^n}$$

Note: In entering figures or receiving solutions, remember to record cash received as a positive figure and cash payments as negative ones. For the HP12C, mark the negative amounts with the keystroke $\boxed{\text{CHS}}$ while for the TI BA II Plus use $\boxed{+/-}$. Always remember to clear the financial register before starting a new problem (HP12C—press the keystroke $\boxed{\text{f}}$ and then $\boxed{\text{FIN}}$; TI BA II Plus—press $\boxed{\text{2nd}}$, $\boxed{\text{RESET}}$, and $\boxed{\text{ENTER}}$). Also keep in mind that depending on the procedures you follow (for example, the number of decimal points entered), your calculation may differ slightly from the example provided. Generally, those differences are not important.

Example 2.1   What is the present value of $3,270 to be received one year from now if the discount rate is 9 percent?

$$PV = \frac{3,270}{(1 + .09)^1}$$
$$= \$3,000$$

Calculator Solution

Inputs:

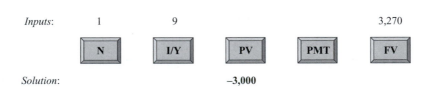

Solution: −3,000

> *Note:* The present value figure is negative since $3,000 would have to be paid today to receive $3,270 in the future.

Example 2.2   What is the present value of $223,073 to be received 50 years from now if the interest rate is 9 percent (see Figure 2.4)?

$$PV = \frac{223,073}{(1 + .09)^{50}}$$
$$= \$3,000$$

Calculator Solution

Inputs: 50   9   223,073

Solution: −3,000

FIGURE 2.4
Present Value

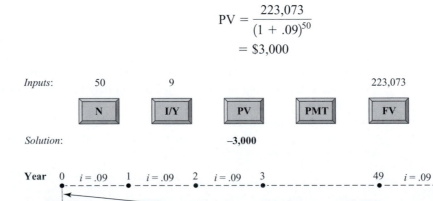

FIGURE 2.5
Future Value

Year   0 $i = .05$ 1 $i = .05$ 2 $i = .05$ 3   ....   4 $i = .05$ 5

$-\$7,000$ $\$8,934$

Future Value

Future value is the amount you will have accumulated at the end of a period. The sum accumulated is dependent on the amount you invested at the beginning of the period, the interest rate, and the number of years and compounding periods involved.

It is given by the following formula:

$$FV = PV(1 + i)^n$$

Example 2.3

If you were to deposit $7,000 in a certificate of deposit for five years earning 5 percent annually, you would have $8,934 accumulated at the end of the period (see Figure 2.5).

$$FV = 7,000 \times (1 + .05)^5$$

**Calculator
Solution**

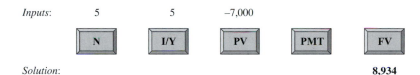

Inputs: 5   5   −7,000

N	I/Y	PV	PMT	FV

Solution: **8,934**

The future value of a lump sum is simply the present value equation given in the previous section rewritten.

The future value of a sum compared with its present value depends to a great extent on the rate of return on the investment. Clearly, the higher the rate of interest, the greater the sum you accumulate at the end of the period. Given the power of compounding, a relatively small difference in the rate can make substantial differences over longer periods of time.

Figure 2.6 shows these differences.

FIGURE 2.6
**Future Value at
Alternative Rates of
Return**
(Payment of $1,000
for 20 years)

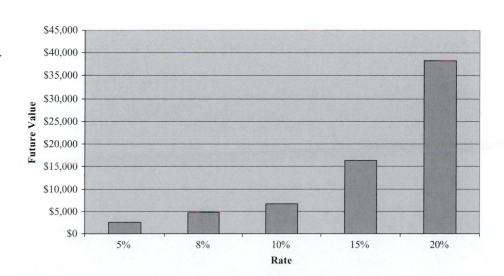

SENSITIVITY TO KEY VARIABLES

The interest rate for compounding or discounting and the number of time periods are the key variables for determining accumulated sums given a fixed amount deposited. As you will see, a shift in either compounding time or interest rate, even when relatively modest, can have a material effect on final results.

In the following sections, we demonstrate that sensitivity in our description of the use of the rule of 72, compounding periods, and discount rates.

The Rule of 72

The rule of 72 provides us with a simple way to establish the difference that the return on an investment makes in accumulating assets. It tells us approximately how long it takes for a sum to double. It is given by the following formula:

$$\text{Years to double} = 72/\text{Annual interest rate}$$

Example 2.4

Compare how quickly money would double at (a) an 8 percent annual rate of return and (b) an 18 percent annual rate of return.

a. 8%

$$\text{Years to double} = 72/8$$
$$= 9 \text{ years}$$

b. 18%

$$\text{Years to double} = 72/18$$
$$= 4 \text{ years}$$

In other words, it would take more than twice as long for the 8 percent investment to double as it would for the 18 percent one. If $1,000 were deposited in the 8 percent investment, it would be worth $2,000 in about nine years, while by year 9 the 18 percent investment would be worth $4,435.

Compounding Periods

The number of compounding periods tells us how often interest on interest is calculated. Generally, it involves the number of times that compounding occurs per year. The more often interest on interest is calculated, the greater the investment return. For example, if you were offered yearly compounding for your $1,000 deposit at an 8 percent rate for 10 years, you would have $2,159. If, in the same example, you were offered quarterly compounding, you would receive $2,208.

In your calculations, assume yearly compounding unless told otherwise. To obtain an approximation of the sum for more frequent compounding, divide the yearly interest rate by the number of compounding periods per year and multiply the number of years you compound by the number of compounding periods per year. Thus:

Yearly Compounding

$$FV = PV \times (1 + i)^n$$

$n = $ Number of years

Multiperiod Compounding

$$FV = PV \times \left(1 + \frac{i}{p}\right)^{n \times p}$$

$$p = \text{Number of compounding periods each year}$$

$$FV = 1{,}000 \times \left(1 + \frac{.08}{4}\right)^{10 \times 4}$$

$$= 1{,}000 \times (1.02)^{40}$$

$$= 2{,}208$$

Calculator Solution

Compounding yearly:

Inputs: 10   8   −1,000

N	I/Y	PV	PMT	FV

Solution: **2,159**

Compounding quarterly:

Inputs: 40   2   −1,000

N	I/Y	PV	PMT	FV

Solution: **2,208**

Discount Rate

As mentioned, the **discount rate** is the rate at which we bring future values back to the present. Generally, it is obtained by taking the rate of return offered in the market for a comparable investment. It is sometimes called the present value interest factor (PVIF) in discounting and can be referred to by other terms, depending on the calculation being performed. The higher the discount rate, the lower the present value of a future sum. There are a variety of reasons why discount rates may be higher or lower, which we will discuss in Chapters 8 and 9. One reason is the inflation rate. Typically, the higher the rate of inflation, the higher the discount rate. If the discount rate is 6 percent in a relatively low-inflation environment such as the United States, $40,000 promised in 10 years will have a present value of $22,336. That same amount promised in a high-inflation economy such as Australia's in the 1980s might have a discount rate of 9 percent. In that country, $40,000 promised in 10 years would have a present value of only $16,896. If you want to solve for the discount rate, you can do so by again moving around terms in the same formula:

$$(1 + i)^n = \frac{FV}{PV}$$

Example 2.5

Susan has promised to pay Paul $40,000 in nine years if he gives her $20,000. What discount rate is Susan using?

$$(1 + i)^n = \frac{FV}{PV}$$

$$(1 + i)^9 = \frac{40{,}000}{20{,}000}$$

Inputs: 9   −20,000   40,000

Calculator Solution

N	I/Y	PV	PMT	FV

Solution: **8**

Periods

The number of compounding periods is the last variable in the formula you solve for. For example, you may be asked how long it will take for $10,000 to reach $19,672 if the rate of interest is 7 percent.

$$(1 + i)^n = \frac{FV}{PV}$$

$$(1 + .07)^n = \frac{19,672}{10,000}$$

Calculator Solution

Inputs:

	7	−10,000		19,672
N	I/Y	PV	PMT	FV

Solution: **10**

ANNUITIES

Annuities are a series of payments that are made or received. You may make a series of payments to reduce and finally eliminate a loan. Alternatively, you may make an investment that entitles you to receive a stream of income over the rest of your life. In this chapter, we will be concerned with ordinary annuities, which are level streams of cash flow over a period of time.

All the approaches to solving the problems that we used before can be used here. The difference is that the formulas must accommodate multiple cash flows instead of a single one. Let's do one.

Future Value of an Annuity

$$FVA = PMT \times \frac{(1 + i)^n - 1}{i}$$

FVA = Future value of an annuity

PMT = The annual payment made at the end of each year by the investor to the account

Example 2.6

Jack and Alice want to deposit $3,000 at the end of each year to accumulate money for a college fund for their daughter, who was just born. They expect a return of 7 percent on their money. How much will they have at the end of her 17th year (see Figure 2.7)?

$$FVA = 3,000 \times \frac{(1 + .07)^{17} - 1}{.07}$$

Calculator Solution

Inputs:

17	7		−3,000	
N	I/Y	PV	PMT	FV

Solution: **92,521**

FIGURE 2.7
Future Value of an Annuity

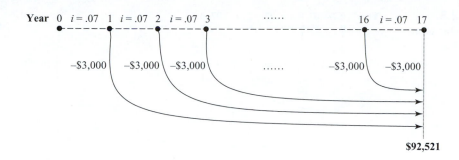

Year 0 $i = .07$ 1 $i = .07$ 2 $i = .07$ 3 ...... 16 $i = .07$ 17

−$3,000 −$3,000 −$3,000 ...... −$3,000 −$3,000

$92,521

Regular Annuity versus Annuity Due

Usually, it is assumed that payments are made at the end of the period. When annuity payments are made at the end of the period, the annuity is called an **ordinary annuity** or regular annuity. When payments are made at the beginning of the period, the annuity is called an **annuity due.** An annuity due gives you one extra year of compounding for payments made. For the calculator solution to have payments at the beginning of the period, set the calculator in the BEGIN mode (HP12C—press the keystroke [g] and then [BEG]; TI BA II Plus—use the following sequence: [2nd] [BGN] and [2nd] [SET]). For purposes of avoiding mistakes, always remember to switch back to the END mode once you are done with the BEGIN mode calculations. Unless you are told otherwise, assume payments are made at the end of the period.

Present Value of Annuity

$$PVA = \sum_{t=1}^{n} \frac{PMT}{(1 + i)^t}$$

$$PVAD = PVA \times (1 + i)$$

$$= \left[\sum_{t=1}^{n} \frac{PMT}{(1 + i)^t} \right] \times (1 + i)$$

PVA = Present value of an annuity

PVAD = Present value of an annuity due

$\sum_{i=1}^{n}$ = Sum of a series of payments starting with the present period (time period 1) and extending to time period n (generally the end of the period)

Example 2.7

Maria was offered annuity payments of $6,000 at the beginning of each year for 30 years. The discount rate was 7 percent. What should she pay (see Figure 2.8)?

$$PVAD = \left[\sum_{t=1}^{30} \frac{6,000}{(1 + .07)^t} \right] \times (1 + .07)$$

$$= \$79,666$$

FIGURE 2.8
Present Value of an Annuity Due

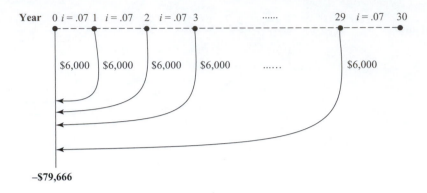

Year 0 *i* = .07 1 *i* = .07 2 *i* = .07 3 ...... 29 *i* = .07 30

$6,000 $6,000 $6,000 $6,000   ...... $6,000

−$79,666

Calculator Solution

Set the calculator in the BEGIN mode.

Inputs: 30   7   6,000

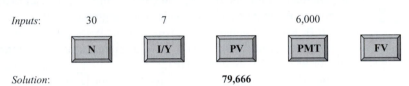

| N | I/Y | PV | PMT | FV |

Solution: 79,666

Rate of Return on an Annuity

Here we know all the cash inflows and outflows for our annuity streams and solve for the rate of return. Varda was offered an annuity of $8,000 a year for the rest of her life for a payment currently of $100,000. She and the insurance company assume she has a 20-year life expectancy. What is her anticipated return on the policy?

$$\text{PVA} = \sum_{t=1}^{n} \frac{\text{PMT}}{(1 + i)^t}$$

$$100,000 = \sum_{t=1}^{20} \frac{8,000}{(1 + i)^t}$$

Calculator Solution

Inputs: 20   −100,000   8,000

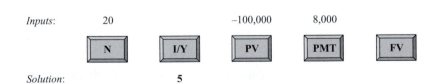

| N | I/Y | PV | PMT | FV |

Solution: 5

Periodic Payment for an Annuity

We solve for a periodic payment to decide how much we have to pay, assuming a level payment each period. A common type of periodic payment is a loan.

Example 2.8

Fred took out a $25,000 loan, which he promised to fully retire after eight equal yearly payments. The interest rate on the loan is 8 percent. When interest and principal payments are combined, how much will be paid annually?

Calculator Solution

Inputs:

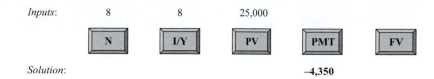

8	8	25,000		
N	I/Y	PV	PMT	FV

Solution: −4,350

Perpetual Annuity

A **perpetual annuity** is a stream of payments that is assumed to go on forever. One example of this type of annuity is a preferred stock. A preferred stock's value emanates from its dividend, which is generally level and in theory is paid forever. The calculation of the present value of a preferred stock is simply the dividend divided by the appropriate interest rate.

$$PVA_p = \frac{PMT}{i}$$

PVA_p = Present value of a perpetual annuity

Example 2.9

John was considering purchasing a preferred stock paying $5 per share annually. The market interest rate for that type of stock was 9 percent. How much should he pay for the preferred?

Solution

$$PVA_p = \frac{5}{.09}$$
$$= \$55.56$$

IRREGULAR CASH FLOWS

In the sections on time value of money, we have performed calculations based on either lump sums or multiple payments of the same amount of money. But in many instances the payments are for differing amounts. We can call these differing payments **irregular cash flows.**

Often, the procedure for solving problems with irregular cash flows is to bring all inflows and outflows to the beginning of the period. In essence, each cash flow will be a separate subproblem with a different number of compounding periods. The solution will be to add up all the subproblems, as diagrammed in Figure 2.9. Fortunately, you can solve this problem in one step by using multiple registers of the calculator.

Example 2.10

Manny had an investment that would supply him with $5,000 in year 1, $4,000 in year 2, $3,000 in year 3, and $1,000 in year 4. He wanted to know how much he should be willing to pay for that investment today if he wanted to earn 10 percent on his investment. (See Figure 2.9.)

Calculator Solution

General Calculator Approach	Specific HP12C			Specific TI BA II Plus		
Clear the register				CF		
	f	FIN		2nd	CLR Work	
Enter initial cash outflow	0	g	CF₀	0	ENTER	↓
Enter cash inflow Year 1	5,000	g	CFᵢ	5,000	ENTER	↓ ↓
Enter cash inflow Year 2	4,000	g	CFᵢ	4,000	ENTER	↓ ↓
Enter cash inflow Year 3	3,000	g	CFᵢ	3,000	ENTER	↓ ↓

(Continued)

General Calculator Approach	Specific HP12C	Specific TI BA II Plus
Enter cash inflow Year 4	1,000 g CF_j	1,000 ENTER ↓ ↓
Enter the discount rate		NPV
	10 i	10 ENTER ↓
Calculate the net present value	f NPV	CPT
	10,788	10,788

INFLATION-ADJUSTED EARNINGS RATES

Earnings is the amount received, and the earnings rate, the return on assets held. **Inflation,** the rate of increase in prices in our economy or in specific items, can distort earnings results. For example, we may receive $2,000 a year in dividends from stocks today. Those dividends are projected to grow 3 percent a year. Overall inflation, meanwhile, is expected to increase by 5 percent a year. That means the inflation-adjusted return on stocks in the form of dividends will decline each year. We call the inflation-adjusted return on assets the **real return.**

The real return on assets contrasts with the **nominal return.** The nominal return and nominal dollars are the figures we are used to seeing. They are based on the actual number of dollars received, not those adjusted for inflation.

When the nominal number of dollars goes up but the value in real dollars goes down, those dollars can purchase fewer goods and services. As a result, we have had a decline in purchasing power terms.

We can calculate the real return:

$$ RR = \left(\frac{1 + r}{1 + i} - 1 \right) \times 100 $$

where

RR = Real return

r = Investment return

i = Inflation rate

When multiplying by the real return to get a new cumulative sum, we use the real growth rate, which is equal to $\frac{1 + r}{1 + i}$.

We will employ the real return frequently in capital needs analysis in Chapter 18.

FIGURE 2.9
Present Value of Series of Irregular Payments

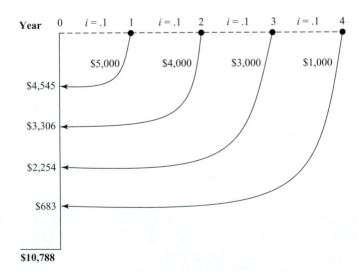

Example 2.11   Brad was about to retire. He wanted to live on the return on the $500,000 savings he had accumulated and leave the entire amount to his children. The $500,000 provided him with $35,000 this year, which is growing 3 percent annually. Inflation is projected to rise 5 percent per year. Calculate the amount of cash he has available to spend currently as well as how much he will receive in nominal and real dollars over the next five years.

$$\text{Cash available} = \$35,000 \text{ this year}$$

$$\text{Nominal return Year 1} = 35,000 \times (1 + \text{Nominal growth rate})$$

$$= 35,000 \times 1.03$$

$$= 36,050$$

$$\text{Real return Year 1} = 35,000 \times \text{Real growth rate}$$

$$= 35,000 \times \left(\frac{1 + 0.03}{1 + 0.05} \right)$$

$$= 35,000 \times 0.9810$$

$$= 34,335$$

Years	0	1	2	3	4	5
Nominal dollars	35,000	36,050	37,132	38,245	39,393	40,575
Real dollars	35,000	34,335	33,683	33,043	32,415	31,791

Calculator Solution

Sample calculation for = real dollars Year 5

$$\text{Real return} = \left(\frac{1.03}{1.05} - 1 \right) \times 100 = -1.9048\%$$

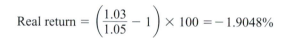

Inputs:	5	−1.9048	−35,000		
	N	I/Y	PV	PMT	FV
Solution:					**31,791**

Brad's situation is deteriorating each year. That is because the growth rate of his income is 3 percent while the inflation rate is 5 percent. More precisely, as this solution shows, his returns are declining 1.9048 percent in real terms annually. Each year, while his cash amounts in nominal dollars are going up, in real dollars they are dropping. Consequently, his dollars will be able to purchase fewer and fewer goods over time. If he cannot raise the returns on his assets so that they are more in sync with the inflation rate, he will have to accept either a lower standard of living or a reduced amount to be left to his children, even in nominal terms.

INTERNAL RATE OF RETURN

The **internal rate of return (IRR)** uses time value of money principles to calculate the rate of return on an investment. It obtains that rate of return by combining all cash flows including cash outflows (usually initial outlays to purchase the investment plus any subsequent losses) and cash inflows (generally, the income on the investment plus any proceeds on sale of the investment). The IRR is the discount rate that makes the cash inflows over time equal to the cash outflows. We will discuss the IRR and a related measure, the NPV, more extensively in Chapter 8. A simple example of the IRR and the keystrokes to solve it is given in Example 2.12.

Example 2.12

Lena had a stock that she purchased for $24. She received dividends one and two years later of $0.80 and $0.96, respectively, and then sold her investment in year 3 for $28. What is her IRR?

Calculator Solution

General Calculator Approach	Specific HP12C		Specific TI BA II Plus	
Clear the register	f	FIN	CF	
			2nd	CLR Work
Enter initial cash outflow	24	CHS g CF₀	24	+/− ENTER ↓
Enter cash inflow Year 1	0.80	g CFⱼ	0.80	ENTER ↓ ↓
Enter cash inflow Year 2	0.96	g CFⱼ	0.96	ENTER ↓ ↓
Enter cash inflow Year 3	28	g CFⱼ	28	ENTER ↓ ↓
Calculate the internal rate of return	f	IRR	IRR	CPT
	7.7%		7.7%	

The IRR was 7.7%.

ANNUAL PERCENTAGE RATE

The **annual percentage rate,** or **APR,** is an adjusted interest on a loan. The Federal Truth in Lending Act mandates that this rate be disclosed on all loans so that consumers can compare the rates offered by different lenders. The APR incorporates many costs other than interest that make its rate different from the one included in a lending contract. For example, the APR on a 7 percent mortgage loan would be greater than 7 percent because of such items as loan processing fees, mortgage insurance, and points.

By comparing these costs, we may find that two loans that each has a 7 percent interest rate may have different APRs of, say, 7.10 percent and 7.25 percent respectively. There are other costs in connection with that same loan that are excluded from the APR such as attorney fees, home inspection fees, and appraisal fees. Where those non-APR costs in alternative loans materially differ, they should be included in decision planning.

The APR is best used to compare similar types of loans for similar periods of time. For example, if you were to compare a 15- and a 30-year mortgage, the results, given the same closing costs, would differ because those costs are spread over different periods of time, thereby distorting your comparison. Adjustable rate mortgage comparisons can be more complicated since their costs can depend in part on other factors such as the benchmark rate determining future expense.[3]

The benchmark figure must be used carefully, and it is a good idea to separate all costs from alternative lenders and compare them as well as noting their relative APRs.

Now that you know and appreciate time value of money principles, you can use them to help make financial decisions. Since all operating parts of financial planning employ financial calculations, these principles and formulas will come in handy.

---

[3] The benchmark is the specific market-developed rate that determines how much the borrower will pay. See adjustable rate mortgages in Chapter 7.

Back to Dan and Laura

TIME VALUE OF MONEY

Our next meeting was scheduled to be on cash flow planning. However, Dan and Laura e-mailed to ask if they could have one on some specific problems that had come up. I, of course, agreed, and, when they came into the office, I noted the stern look on Dan's face. They had had a disagreement. Ostensibly, it was about tax payments. Laura wanted Dan to claim seven dependents on his withholding form at work because they always received a large refund when their return was filed. That action could, of course, lead to greater deductions and therefore greater available cash during the year but a potential tax payment on April 15. It doesn't change the ultimate cash outflow but does change its timing and therefore involves time value of money. I suspected that their disagreement would not only be about tax payments and the time value of money but also about their differing beliefs about spending money.

Sure enough, when I asked why she wanted to do it, Laura said so that they would get more money to spend currently. Dan couldn't see why they would want to jeopardize their already precarious current cash position. There was the possibility of underpayment, which would result in a large disbursement when the final tax return was due. He said they could end up with even greater credit card debt to finance the tax payment if Laura spent all the cash available during the year. Laura didn't see the problem. She said, "We aren't paying any more to the government under this approach." Both wanted my opinion of this practice.

Dan mentioned that he had received an offer to purchase a bond for $15,000 that would pay back $50,000 in 30 years with no interest in the meantime. He thought that sounded attractive. Laura said she saw a study that said $1,000 invested in stocks 75 years ago adjusted for inflation would be worth more than 50 times that of a comparable investment in bonds. Is that true, and, if so, shouldn't they put all of their money in stocks? They then started to criticize each other's beliefs about the appropriate level of risk.

I had often seen disagreements erupt at meetings concerned with constructing a financial plan. I decided to deal with it directly, early in the planning process. It could make subsequent meetings more productive.

I told them that emotionally charged differences of opinion sometimes took place at financial planning meetings. I believed that in part they came from the stress of having to think about long-term factors and make decisions concerning them. Of course, the fundamental reason was the differences in personalities and beliefs. I assured them that virtually all the decisions they made could be modified or changed later. I mentioned that I found it ironic that many people selected mates who were dissimilar in certain traits from themselves, and could complement their own "weaknesses," but later came to criticize those very traits. I told them I thought that Dan's innate conservatism offset Laura's aggressive investment posture and that his desire to protect household finances as shown by the income tax withholding issue and anxious demeanor blended well with Laura's more laid back convenience-oriented approach. I reminded them that in my experience people seldom selected mates that were exactly like themselves.

That talk seemed to ease the tension, and we moved on to the last point. Laura's mother had been offered an annuity in which she would deposit $200,000 and receive $15,530 a year over her expected 23-year life span. Laura was already familiar with the advantages and disadvantages of an annuity, and she just wanted to know what the rate of return was and whether I considered the return attractive.

The questions you have raised all, to varying degrees, have to do with the time value of money. The literal meaning of this term is that money given or received has a value. The value is generally what you could earn on that sum by investing it in marketable securities. Rather than further describing time value principles, I suggest you read a basic finance textbook or more simply a good manual on the use of a financial calculator. I recommend the HP12C or the TI BA II Plus. Given your desire for information on how I arrived at my financial decision and not knowing whether you already have a financial calculator, I will provide generic calculator keystrokes. I'll handle the calculations first and the question on withholding at the end.

Compounding for an investment involves not only interest on an original sum but interest on interest. If we receive compound interest for an extended period of time, the interest on interest takes on increasing importance. Over longer periods, interest on interest can actually dwarf the original sum. Compounding can make it difficult to make an accurate assessment of the return on an investment without calculating it. Sometimes what looks like a great return isn't.

I believe that the proposal that Dan has is an example of something that looks like a good investment, but isn't. Dan is being offered a zero coupon bond, which just means that all interest and principal are paid at maturity. The fact that he will more than triple his original sum over time makes it look attractive. However, we can reject this investment with a simple calculation.

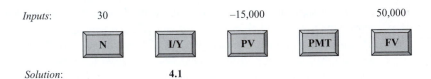

Inputs: 30   –15,000   50,000

Solution: **4.1**

That rate of return of 4.1 percent compares with U.S. government bonds for that same period of 5 percent. We don't even have to incorporate risk (the bond being offered is of a medium-quality business) or take into account the negative tax consequences of this type of bond in a nonpension account. This bond is not attractive.

The example Laura presented is an illustration of how compounding can make a huge difference in returns over time. The returns she expressed were over a 75-year period. They were adjusted for inflation. I will assume 11 percent per year for stocks and 5.5 percent per year for bonds and 3 percent for inflation.

The real return for stocks and bonds is the return after adjusting for the negative effect of inflation. It is given by the following formula:

$$\text{Real return} = \left(\frac{1+r}{1+i} - 1\right) \times 100$$

For stocks:

$$\text{Real return} = \left(\frac{1.11}{1.03} - 1\right) \times 100$$

$$= 7.77$$

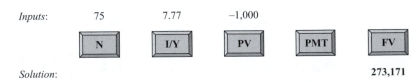

Inputs: 75   7.77   –1,000

Solution: **273,171**

Compounding $1,000 for 75 years at the real return for stocks is $273,171.
Similarly, calculating the real interest rate and compounding for bonds yields $4,230.

$$\text{Real return (bonds)} = \left(\frac{1.05}{1.03} - 1\right) \times 100$$

$$= 1.9417$$

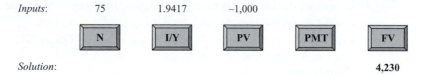

Inputs: 75   1.9417   −1,000

Solution: **4,230**

As can be seen, it is true that alternate compounding rates can make an enormous difference and that the stocks did do more than 50 times that of bonds. Whether stocks or bonds or, more likely, a combination of the two is appropriate for you will be left to our discussions on investments.

Your mother's rate of return on her annuity can be calculated as follows:

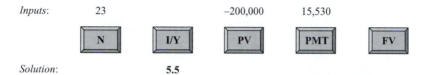

Inputs: 23   −200,000   15,530

Solution: **5.5**

The 5.5 percent return on investment offered does not seem attractive relative to the 5 percent return on U.S. government bonds. While the government bond will repay principal at the end of 23 years, the annuity does not provide any principal, only interest payments. Your mother should either seek another estimate or place her money in something else.

Finally, you have a difference of opinion on how to handle tax withholding. For Laura, as indicated in this write-up, money over time has worth. The money you give to the IRS early could be invested in a money market fund or some other investment that would provide you with some income. So Laura is correct that from a financial standpoint, overwithholding is inefficient.

Yet, many people overwithhold. They may do this to avoid an abrupt payment on tax day, April 15. Alternatively, they may use overwithholding to structure themselves so that they can feel they are receiving an unexpected bonus from Uncle Sam that they can then spend. These are nonfinancial human reasons. I have explained the advantages and disadvantages as I see them. Whether you want the financial sacrifice for the sake of the comfort and structure provided by overwithholding is up to you.

Let me end with a personal note that may not be part of many financial planners' written documents but that you have asked me to include whenever I thought it useful. Money matters, like many others in life, can result in differences of opinion. Given my earlier remarks to you, you have an idea of how I feel. Basically, you can run your monies separately, with differences in assets selected, tax withholding rules, and a host of other decisions. Or, as most couples do, at least for first marriages, you can compromise so that both people make meaningful sacrifices. You should both verbalize your differences and try to reach a settlement of the issues and go forward together in financial matters. If you would like my input on any specific financial problem, please let me know.

Summary

The time value of money is one of the basic ideas in finance. As such, it is very important that you understand how to use it in decision making.

- The time value of money enables you to make correct decisions when current or future amounts need to be established or when deciding which alternative is best. It allows impartial comparison of past or future performance or values.
- Cumulative sums are highly sensitive to the number of compounding periods and to the rate of return used. For example, using the rule of 72, it will take 12 years for a sum to double in value when the rate of return is 6 percent, but only 4 years when the rate is 18 percent.

- In making decisions it is essential to know the present value, the future value, the discount rate for lump sums, and similar figures for annuities.
- Real rates of return are those adjusted for inflation. There is an exact formula given in this chapter that can be approximated by subtracting the inflation rate from the indicated return.
- The internal rate of return (IRR) is the one most commonly used to compare the return on investments that have differing inflows and outflows over time.

Key Terms

annual percentage rate (APR), *36*
annuities, *30*
annuity due, *31*
compounding, *23*
discount rate, *29*

future value, *27*
inflation, *34*
internal rate of return (IRR), *35*
irregular cash flows, *33*
nominal return, *34*

ordinary annuity, *31*
perpetual annuity, *33*
present value, *25*
real return, *34*
time value of money, *22*

Web Site

http://www.teachmefinance.com
Time Value of Money
This Web site covers concepts such as the time value of money, future values of uneven cash flows, annuities, perpetuities, techniques involving cost of capital calculations, cost of capital budgeting, and a host of other things.

Questions

1. What is compounding and why is it important?
2. Why is knowledge of the time value of money useful?
3. Explain the terms PV and FV.
4. What rate is most often used for time value of money calculations?
5. If the discount rate on a proposed investment is raised, what happens to its present value? Why?
6. Which one will provide a greater FV: a lump sum today or the comparable amount in periodic payments deposited over time? Why?
7. Give explanations and examples of regular annuity versus annuity due.
8. What is rate of return and why do we use inflation-adjusted return?

Problems

2.1   What is the present value of a $20,000 sum to be given six years from now if the discount rate is 8 percent?

2.2   What is the future value of an investment of $18,000 that will earn interest at 6 percent and fall due in seven years?

2.3   Jason was promised $48,000 in 10 years if he would deposit $14,000 today. What would his compounded annual return be?

2.4   How many years would it take for a dollar to triple in value if it earns a 6 percent rate of return?

2.5   Marcy placed $3,000 a year into an investment returning 9 percent a year for her daughter's college education. She started when her daughter was two. How much did she accumulate by her daughter's 18th birthday?

2.6   Todd was asked what he would pay for an investment that offered $1,500 a year for the next 40 years. He required an 11 percent return to make that investment. What should he bid?

2.7   Ann was offered an annuity of $20,000 a year for the rest of her life. She was 55 at the time and her life expectancy was 84. The investment would cost her $180,000. What would the return on her investment be?

2.8   How many years would it take for $2,000 a year in savings earning interest at 6 percent to amount to $60,000?

2.9   Aaron has $50,000 in debt outstanding with interest payable at 12 percent annually. If Aaron intends to pay off the loan through four years of interest and principal payment, how much should he pay annually?

2.10   What is the difference in amount accumulated between a $10,000 sum with 12 percent interest compounded annually and one compounded monthly over a one-year period?

2.11   What is the difference in future value between savings in which $3,000 is deposited each year at the beginning of the period and the same amount deposited at the end of the period? Assume an interest rate of 8 percent and that both are due at the end of 19 years.

2.12   Kenneth made a $20,000 investment in year 1, received a $5,000 return in year 2, made an $8,000 cash payment in year 3, and received his $20,000 back in year 4. If his required rate of return is 8 percent, what was the net present value of his investment?

2.13   John had $50,000 in salary this year. If this salary is growing 4 percent annually and inflation is projected to rise 3 percent per year, calculate the amount of return he will receive in nominal and real dollars in the fifth year.

2.14   Becky made a $30,000 investment in year 1, received a $10,000 return in year 2, $8,000 in year 3, $11,000 in year 4, and $9,000 in year 5. What was her internal rate of return over the five-year period?

Case Application

TIME VALUE OF MONEY

Richard e-mailed that he and Monica differed about the impact of his extra spending over the past 15 years. He calculated it at about $3,000 a year. He said the total cost of $45,000 was well within his capability to make up. Monica said the cost was much greater and asked that they compute it. They were offered an investment of $20,000 that would pay $70,000 in 20 years. They want to know if they should take it. Finally, there is an annuity that Richard could sign up for at work. It would cost $100,000 at age 65 and provide payments of $8,000 per year over his expected 17-year life span. He wants to know if it is attractive. The appropriate market rate of return on investments is 7 percent after tax.

Case Application Questions

1. Calculate what the $3,000-per-year deficit, had it been invested, would have amounted to at the end of the 15-year period.

2. Explain to Richard what compounding is and how it affected the cumulative amount received in question 1.

3. Calculate the return on the proposed $20,000 investment and indicate the factors entering into your recommendation to accept or reject it.

4. Indicate the expected return on the annuity and whether it should be accepted or rejected.

5. Construct an explanation of the time value of money for the financial plan using your answers to questions 1 through 4 in this part of the financial plan to help you communicate the time value information to Richard and Monica.

Appendix II

Serial Payments

Serial payments are payments received or given that increase by a constant percentage each year. The constant percentage will often be linked to the inflation rate, with other potential figures including the rate of growth in a financial investment or in salary. Savings is a good example of how we can use serial payments effectively. As you will see in the example below, developing a required sum over an extended period by saving a constant amount each year may not be practical. That is because our salaries go up over time, making it more practical to save an increasing amount as we continue to work. Serial payments are a method of handling such a situation.

Another example is a growing annuity. The amount we receive as an annuity may increase at a constant percentage. For example, a disability policy may provide for a 5 percent increase in payout each year upon becoming disabled. The intention there is to cushion the effect of inflation.

Here is the formula for serial payments:

Steps

1. Calculate the real return. Use the formula given earlier:

$$RR = \left(\frac{1+r}{1+i} - 1 \right) \times 100$$

Percentage value should be converted to decimal value.

2. Develop the base first-year payment.

    a. First find the cumulative real return, which is the sum of all years' real returns. The real return of one particular year is the sum of 1 plus the real return calculated in part 1, and this sum is raised to the power of the number of periods to conclusion of the serial payment.

    Mathematically, it is

$$CRR = (1 + RR)^n + (1 + RR)^{n-1} + (1 + RR)^{n-2} + \cdots + (1 + RR)^{n-n}$$

    where

    CRR = Cumulative real return

    RR   = Real return in decimal value

    n = Number of periods to conclusion

    b. Divide the desired ending value expressed in current dollars by the calculated CRR to obtain the base first-year payment (FYP).

$$FYP_b = \frac{CST}{CRR}$$

    where

    CST = Cumulative sum in today's dollars

    FYP_b = First-year payment beginning of year

3. Multiply the first-year payment by 1 plus the inflation rate for each year beyond the first.

$$YP = FYP \times (1 + i)^n$$

4. If the amount required is to be paid at the end of the year, multiply each payment by 1 plus the inflation rate.

$$YP_e = YP_b \times (1 + i)$$

    where

    YP_e = Yearly payment at end of year

Example 2.A1.1   Dan wanted to save $50,000 in today's dollars as a down payment on a house. He expected to have the money available in four years. His income was growing, which would make it possible to save larger and larger amounts as he drew closer to the down payment date. He decided to have his yearly savings go up by the rate of inflation. He wanted to know how much he would have to save each year to reach his goal, assuming that inflation was 3 percent, his investment return was 5 percent, and payments would be made at the end of each year.

$$RR = \left(\frac{1.05}{1.03} - 1\right) \times 100 = 1.9417 \quad \text{(percentage value)}$$

$$RR = 0.019417 \quad \text{(decimal value)}$$

$$1 + RR = 1 + 0.019417 = 1.019417$$

$$CRR = (1.019417)^{(4-1)} + (1.019417)^{(4-2)} + (1.019417)^{(4-3)} + (1.019417)^{(4-4)}$$

$$CRR = (1.019417)^3 + (1.019417)^2 + (1.019417)^1 + (1.019417)^0$$

$$= 4.1180$$

$$FYP_b = \frac{50,000}{4.1180}$$

$$= \$12,141.82 \quad \text{at the beginning of year}$$

$$\text{FYP}_e = 12141.82 \times (1.03)$$

$$= \$12{,}506.07 \quad \text{at the end of year}$$

Successive payments rising by the rate of inflation multiplied by 1.03 were $12,881.25, $13,267.68, and $13,665.72.

Year	Required Total Payments	Number of Compounding Periods	Returns on Payment at 5 Percent	Required Down Payment Sum
1	$12,506	3	$1,971	$51,500
2	$12,881	2	$1,320	$53,045
3	$13,268	1	$663	$54,636
4	$13,666	0	$0	$56,276
	$52,321		$3,955	$56,276

Note that the required sum at the end of the period is $56,276, not $50,000. That is because inflation has increased the required sum. In other words, $56,276 is $50,000 in real (inflation-adjusted) terms at the end of four years. When added up, the required payments are also greater than $50,000 and would have been even larger if not for the investment return on the first three years' deposits. When the required payments are combined with interest on those payments, they add up to the required down payment sum.

Appendix II

Excel Examples*

We have already discussed how you can solve the financial problems using a financial calculator. In this appendix you will learn how to use Excel to solve the problems presented throughout the chapter.

ANNUAL COMPOUNDING

We will calculate the principal resulting after one-period and two-period compounding. Notice the difference when we compound for more than one period. (See Figure 2.A2.1)

Building This Model in Excel

1. **Inputs.** Enter the input data in the ranges **B6:B8** and **B15:B17**.
2. **Compounding.** We use the formula for annual compounding to calculate the principal at the end of the compounding periods:

Principal end of compounding period = Principal $\times$ (1 + Interest rate)$^{\text{Number of years}}$

- **One-period compounding.** Enter **=B6*(1+B7)** in cell **B9.** This is a one-year period, and we don't put a power to the expression in the parentheses because it is 1.
- **Two-period compounding.** Enter **=B14*(1+B15)^2** in cell **B17.** This time we use the power of 2 for the two-year period.

PRESENT VALUE

We will calculate the present value of a single cash flow in two ways: using the formula for present value of a single cash flow and using the built-in Excel function PV.

* Adair, Troy A., *Excel Applications for Corporate Finance,* Burr Ridge: McGraw-Hill/Irwin, 2005, and Craig Holden, *Excel Modeling in Investments,* New Jersey: Prentice Hall.

FIGURE 2.A2.1
Excel Model for One-Period versus Two-Period Compounding

	A	B	C	D	E
1	**Annual Compounding**				
2					
3	**One-Period Compounding**				
4					
5	**Inputs**				
6	Principal beginning of year	$2,000			
7	Interest rate	10%			
8	Number of years	1			
9			=B6*(1+B7)		
10	**Principal end of Year 1**	$2,200			
11					
12	**Two-Period Compounding**				
13					
14	**Inputs**				
15	Principal beginning of year	$2,000			
16	Interest rate	10%			
17	Number of years	2			
18					
19	**Principal end of Year 2**	$2,420	=B15*(1+B16)^2		

Example 2.A2.1   What is the present value of $223,073 to be received 50 years from now if the interest rate is 9 percent? (See Figure 2.A2.2.)

Building This Model in Excel

1. **Inputs.** Enter the input data in the range **B4:B6**.

2. **Present value using the formula.** Enter **=B4/(1+B5)^B6** in cell **B9.** We use the following formula to calculate the present value of a single cash flow:

$$\text{Present value} = \text{Cash flow}/(1+\text{Discount Rate})^{\text{Number of periods}}$$

3. **Present value using the Excel PV function.** The Excel PV function has five parameters:

$$PV(rate, nper, pmt, fv, type)$$

The first parameter *rate* is the discount rate per period (year, month, day, etc.), *nper* is the number of periods, and *fv* is the future value of the cash flow; *pmt* and *type* are used to handle annuities, which we will discuss later. In this case, we put 0 for *pmt* and nothing for *type,* which Excel takes as 0. The *type* parameter has two values—0 and 1—which indicate whether the cash flow occurs at the end (0) or at the beginning (1) of the period. The Excel PV function can be used to calculate the present value of a single

FIGURE 2.A2.2
Excel Model for Present Value of a Single Cash Flow

	A	B	C	D	E
1	**Present Value of a Single Cash Flow**				
2					
3	**Inputs**				
4	Future cash flow	$223,073			
5	Discount rate	9%			
6	Number of years	50			
7					
8	**Present Value Using the Formula**				
9	Present value	$3,000	=B4/(1+B5)^B6		
10					
11	**Present Value Using the Excel PV Function**				
12	Present value	$3,000	= −PV(B5,B6,0,B4)		
13					

FIGURE 2.A2.3
Excel Model for
Future Value of a
Single Cash Flow

	A	B	C	D	E
1	Future Value of a Single Cash Flow				
2					
3	Inputs				
4	Amount deposited	$7,000			
5	Interest rate	5%			
6	Number of years	6			
7					
8	Future Value Using the Formula		=B4*/(1+B5)^B6		
9	Future value	$9,381			
10					
11	Future Value Using the Excel FV Function				
12	Future value	$9,381	=−FV(B5,B6,0,B4)		
13					

cash flow, the present value of an annuity, and the present value of a bond price. We put a negative sign in front of the PV function because otherwise it returns a negative result. Again, this is somewhat irritating, but it is the way of handling that problem.

$$\text{Enter} = -\text{PV(B5,B6,0,B4) in cell B12.}$$

Notice that we get the same result ($3,000) both ways.

FUTURE VALUE

We will calculate the future value of a single cash flow in two ways: using the formula for future value of a single cash flow and using the built-in Excel function FV.

Example 2.A2.2 If you were to deposit $7,000 in a certificate of deposit for six years earning 5 percent annually, how much would you have accumulated at the end of the period? (See Figure 2.A2.3.)

Building This Model in Excel

1. **Inputs.** Enter the input data in the range **B4:B6.**
2. **Future value using the formula.** Enter **=B4*(1+B5)^B6** in cell **B9.** We use the following formula for calculating the future value of a single cash flow:

$$\text{Future value} = \text{Cash flow} \times (1 + \text{Interest rate})^{\text{Number of periods}}$$

3. **Future value using the Excel FV function.** The Excel FV function has the same format and parameters as the PV function, except for the fourth parameter, which is *pv*:

$$FV(rate, nper, pmt, pv, type)$$

The built-in FV function can be used to calculate the future value of a single cash flow, the future value of an annuity, and the future value of a bond price. Again, we put a negative sign in front of the FV function so that the future value result will be positive. Enter **=−FV(B5,B6,0,B4)** in cell **B12.**

Notice that again we get the same result ($9,381) using both methods.

SOLVING FOR THE DISCOUNT RATE

Sometimes we come across problems that we have to solve for the discount rate. There is no closed-form solution for that particular problem, but Excel makes our work easier by offering a built-in function that will solve for the discount rate. The function Rate has the following format and parameters:

$$Rate(nper, pmt, pv, fv, type, guess)$$

All the parameters were defined earlier except for *guess,* which refers to your optional first guess at the correct answer. Generally, you can omit it.

FIGURE 2.A2.4
Excel Model for Solving for the Discount Rate

	A	B	C	D	E
1	**Solving for the Discount Rate**				
2					
3	**Inputs**				
4	Present value of a cash flow	$20,000			
5	Future value of a cash flow	$40,000			
6	Number of years	9			
7					
8	**Discount Rate Using the Excel Rate Function**				
9	Discount rate	8%			
10			=RATE(B6,0,−B4,B5)		

Example 2.A2.3   Susan has promised to pay Paul $40,000 in nine years if he gives her $20,000 now. What discount rate is Susan using? (See Figure 2.A2.4.)

Building This Model in Excel

1. **Inputs.** Enter the input data in the range **B4:B6.**
2. **Discount rate using the Excel Rate function.** Enter **= Rate(B6,0,−B4,B5)** in cell **B9.** We put 0 for the second parameter, *pmt,* because it is used for annuities. The trick here is that the function works only when the present value and future value have opposite signs. This is the reason we put a negative sign in front of the present value. While irritating, this step is necessary to get the proper result.

SOLVING FOR THE NUMBER OF COMPOUNDING PERIODS

Sometimes we come upon problems that we have to solve for the number of compounding periods. That particular problem has no closed-form solution. However, Excel makes the calculation easier because Excel has a built-in function that solves for the number of periods. This function, Nper, has the following format and parameters:

$$\text{Nper}(rate, pmt, pv, fv, type)$$

We already know the definition of all the parameters.

Example 2.A2.4   How long will it take for $10,000 to reach $19,672 if the rate of interest is 7 percent? (See Figure 2.A2.5.)

Building This Model in Excel

1. **Inputs.** Enter the input data in the range **B4:B6.**

2. **Number of periods using the Excel Nper function.** Enter **=Nper(B6,0,−B4,B5)** in cell **B9.** Again, we use a negative sign for the present value in order to get the proper result.

FIGURE 2.A2.5
Excel Model for Solving for the Number of Compounding Periods

	A	B	C	D	E
1	**Solving for the Number of Periods**				
2					
3	**Inputs**				
4	Present value of a cash flow	$10,000			
5	Future value of a cash flow	$19,672			
6	Interest rate	7%			
7					
8	**Discount Rate Using the Excel Nper Function**				
9	Number of years	10			
10			=NPER(B6,0,−B4,B5)		

FIGURE 2.A2.6
Excel Model for Future Value of an Annuity

	A	B	C	D	E
1	**Future Value of an Annuity**				
2					
3	**Inputs**				
4	Payment	$3,000			
5	Discount rate	7%			
6	Number of years	17			
7					
8	**Future Value Using the Formula**		=B4*(((1+B5)^B6−1)/B5)		
9	Future value	$92,521			
10					
11	**Future Value Using the Excel FV Function**				
12	Future value	$92,521			
13			=−FV(B5,B6,B4,0)		

FUTURE VALUE OF AN ANNUITY

We will calculate the future value of an annuity in two ways: using the formula for the future value of an annuity and using the built-in Excel function FV.

Example 2.A2.5   Jack and Alice want to deposit $3,000 at the end of each year to accumulate money for a college fund for their newborn daughter. They expect a return of 7 percent on their money. How much will they have at the end of the 17th year? (See Figure 2.A2.6.)

Building This Model in Excel

1. **Inputs.** Enter the input data in the range **B4:B6.**

2. **Future value of an annuity using the formula.** We use the following formula for calculating the future value of an annuity:

$$\text{Future value} = \text{Payment} \times (((1 + DR)^{NP} - 1)/DR)$$

where

DR = Discount rate

NP = Number of periods

Enter **=B4*(((1 + B5)^B6 − 1)/B5)** in cell **B9.**

3. **Future value of an annuity using the Excel FV function.** Except for future value of a single cash flow, the Excel FV function can be used to calculate the future value of an annuity. The format of the function in this case is

$$FV(rate, nper, pmt, 0)$$

FIGURE 2.A2.7
Excel Model for Present Value of an Annuity

	A	B	C	D	E	F
1	**Present Value of an Annuity**					
2						
3	**Inputs**					
4	Payment	$6,000				
5	Discount rate	7%				
6	Number of years	30				
7						
8	**Present Value Using the Formula**		=B4*((1−(1+B5)^(−B6))/B5)*(1+B5)			
9	Present value	$79,666				
10						
11	**Present Value Using the Excel PV Function**					
12	Present value	$79,666				
13			=−PV(B5,B6,B4,0,1)			

We put 0 for the fourth parameter because we don't have a cash flow at the beginning of the period; hence, the present value is 0. We put a negative sign in front of the FV function so that the future value result will be positive.

Enter **=−FV(B5,B6,B4,0)** in cell **B12**.

Notice that we get the same result ($92,521) both ways.

PRESENT VALUE OF AN ANNUITY

We will calculate the present value of an annuity in two ways: using the formula for the present value of an annuity and using the built-in Excel function PV.

Example 2.A2.6   Maria was offered annuity payments of $6,000 at the beginning of each year for 30 years. The discount rate was 7 percent. What should she pay now? (See Figure 2.A2.7.)

Building This Model in Excel

1. **Inputs.** Enter the input data in the range **B4:B6**.
2. **Present value of an annuity using the formula.** We use the following formula for calculating the present value of an annuity:

$$\text{Present value} = \text{Payment} \times ((1 - (1 + DR)^{-NP})/DR) \times (1 + DR)$$

We add the last part, $(1 + DR)$, because payments are made at the beginning of each year. In our case, we have an annuity due. Basically, the formula for the present value of a regular annuity is

$$\text{Present value} = \text{Payment} \times ((1 - (1 + DR)^{-NP})/DR)$$

Enter **= B4*((1 − (1 + B5)^(−B6))/B5)*(1 + B5)** in cell **B9**.

3. **Present value of an annuity using the Excel PV function.** Except for the present value of a single cash flow, the Excel PV function can be used to calculate the present value of an annuity. The format of the function in our case is

$$PV(rate, nper, pmt, 0, 1)$$

The format of this function is similar to the format of the function for the future value of an annuity, except for the fifth parameter. If you recall, the PV and FV functions have five parameters, the last of which is *type*. In our case, we set the *type* parameter to 1 because payments are made at the beginning of each year. If we have a regular annuity, when the payments are made at the end of the period, we put nothing for *type*, which Excel takes as 0.

FIGURE 2.A2.8

Excel Model for Comparing Various Nonannual Compounding Periods

	A	B	C	D	E	F
1	**Nonannual Compounding**					
2						
3	**Inputs**					
4	Present value	$1,000				
5	Annual rate	8%				
6						
7	**Comparison of Various Nonannual Compounding Periods**					
8						
9	**Frequency**	**Periods per Year**	**FV**	=−FV($B$5/B10,B10,0,$B$4)		
10	Annual	1	$1,080.00			
11	Semiannual	2	$1,081.60			
12	Quarterly	4	$1,082.43			
13	Bimonthly	6	$1,082.71			
14	Monthly	12	$1,083.00			
15	Biweekly	26	$1,083.15			
16	Weekly	52	$1,083.22			
17	Daily	365	$1,083.28			

FIGURE 2.A2.9
FV as Compounding
Frequency Increases

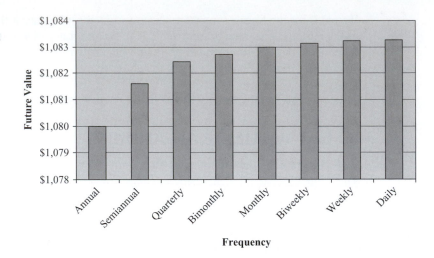

NONANNUAL COMPOUNDING

We've already discussed the annual compounding at the beginning of this appendix. Now we will focus our attention on nonannual compounding. We know that investments pay cash flows not only annually but also semiannually, quarterly, monthly, daily, and so on. Nonannual compounding deals with periods shorter than a year. As you will see, Excel can handle the nonannual compounding.

Example 2.A2.7   What is the future value of $1,000 if the annual interest rate is 8 percent and we have various frequencies of compounding: annual, semiannual, quarterly, bimonthly, monthly, biweekly, weekly, and daily? (See Figure 2.A2.8.)

Using the results obtained, we build a graph that shows how the future value of an investment increases as frequency of compounding increases (see Figure 2.A2.9).

Building This Model in Excel

1. **Inputs.** Enter the input data in the range **B4:B5.**
2. **Future value of the investment for various compounding periods.** First we construct the table, filling out the data for frequency and corresponding number of periods per year. Then we calculate the future values of our investment for various period lengths in the range **C10:C17**. Recall the formula for nonannual compounding:

$$\text{Future value} = \text{Present Value} \times (1 + (\text{DR}/m))^{N \times m}$$

where

N = Number of years

m = Number of periods per year

Using this formula, we make the necessary changes in the parameters of the FV function. The interest rate is divided by the number of periods per year.

Enter = **− FV($B$5/B10,B10,0,$B$4)** in cell **C10** and copy it down to cell **C17.**

Note that the more frequent the compounding, the higher the future value.

Chapter Three

Beginning the Planning Process

Chapter Goals

This chapter will enable you to:

- Start the financial planning process smoothly.
- Determine how human behavior influences the PFP process.
- More easily ascertain personal goals that people have.
- Employ the data-gathering process in common planning situations.
- Improve your communication skills.
- Develop desirable interviewing and counseling techniques.

This meeting with Dan and Laura was set up to further discuss personal goals that both seemed anxious about and to go over the data-gathering questionnaire they had filled out. Dan, who liked the way I handled our first meeting, asked if I would give him some tips on successful communication and interviewing techniques. He was having difficulty establishing rapport with an important new client.

Real Life Planning

Albert walked in with his mother. He wasn't the advisor's typical client. A tall, thin boy dressed in hip-hop jeans and a T-shirt, Albert looked like a teenager. The expression on his face said, "What am I doing here?" The advisor wondered how he was going to communicate with this person, given their differences in age, interest, and culture.

The advisor introduced himself to both Albert and his mother, made eye contact with the boy, and smiled. He offered soda and chocolate chip cookies, which had been placed at the center of the table. He had chosen his office, which had a small round table instead of the large one in the conference room that had the advisor at the head, because he thought it would be more personal and friendly.

The advisor was already familiar with many of the facts that Albert's mother had discussed with him over the phone. The boy had been in the back seat of a car whose driver was drunk, and the car had crashed into another one coming from the opposite direction. The boy had sustained injuries to his brain and nervous system. The injuries were not apparent but could possibly limit his functioning and therefore his job opportunities in the future.

The legal settlement had come to $400,000 net of lawyer's fees. Albert's mother had placed the money in a bank account two years ago. Now Albert was almost 18, the age at which he would have full control over the proceeds. His mother had encouraged him to seek assistance.

A glance at Albert told the advisor a great deal. His arms were folded, he leaned sideways far back in his chair, and he spoke softly without feeling. To the advisor, it meant that he was uncomfortable being there. His mother was about to say something when one glance from Albert resulted in her complete silence for the rest of the session.

The advisor tried to break the ice by asking what Albert's interests were. He said, "Having fun." When asked what things provided him with fun, he said hanging around with friends and driving "cool" cars. It was clear that he was beginning to relax. They started to talk about his future. He wanted to join the Army and develop a trade. The advisor decided not to bring up the difficulty his injury might pose in being accepted. He began to see another side to Albert that was more mature and interested in his own well-being. The advisor explained how the income on the invested sum, if handled properly, could supplement his job-related cash and raise his standard of living. The advisor told him it also would be available if he became seriously ill. Albert nodded slightly.

The advisor decided further questioning would add little and could alienate the boy. Life insurance was out of the question, tax planning was not a serious concern outside of investments, cash flow planning would be taken care of through living with his mother for the time being, and retirement and estate planning would seem like it came from another planet. Besides, the advisor was being retained for investment advice.

The advisor simply asked what Albert would like to do now that the money would be available. He said he would like to have a huge party that would go on for 24 hours. The next question was how much he thought the party would cost. He said $7,000. The advisor asked, "Is that all?" He replied that he would like a new red BMW convertible. The advisor asked what model and the cost. His face broke out in a smile as he mentioned the model and the cost—$60,000.

The advisor mentioned that he could see how both items could be a lot of fun. Looking at it from the boy's point of view, the advisor asked whether, if the amount was given to him, Albert would be amenable to having the balance of the money being set aside for his financial future. He nodded, and the advisor went over his plan for diversifying his investments according to Albert's tolerance for risk. The next day, $67,000 was wired into a checking account and the balance to an investment account at a financial institution.

The advisor thought about the reasons for what he considered a successful outcome. He decided it was because he had listened to Albert's feelings, attempted to be nonjudgmental about his preferences, and looked at his situation from the boy's perspective. The advisor was able to establish himself as an authority on related matters and develop a rapport with Albert. Summing it up, he was able to communicate with Albert.

OVERVIEW

The first step in the financial planning process is to identify household goals and needs. This is usually accomplished through data gathering. It is important that proper communication and interview techniques take place at that time to ensure a firm beginning to the work to be done. This chapter deals with establishing such goals, data gathering, and the communication techniques that bring about sound planning. It details the role behavioral finance and personality differences play in the process.

BEHAVIORAL FINANCE

Finance is typically viewed as a highly structured discipline. People are taught the one right way to perform financial operations. Generally, the idea is to make logical decisions with the goal of receiving the largest amount of money possible. This approach can be characterized as the "ideal" person performing as a machine producing the maximum cash flow.

In reality, of course, people do not act like machines. They act like human beings. They have many shortcomings and differ from each other in many respects, including preferences. **Behavioral finance** can be defined as the concentration on actual human actions in financial matters. **Behavioral financial planning** has a more proactive definition. It strives to understand and improve people's decision-making abilities so that they can more easily achieve the goals they set. Behavioral finance and behavioral financial planning are discussed more fully in Chapter 19.

So, as we can see, personal financial planning is a very practical activity. It must analyze how people actually act to help them come closer to how decisions should be made. Knowledge of people's behavior patterns and how they influence PFP are required parts of curriculums such as the CFP®. PFP must take into account a variety of differences among people. In the next section, we examine some of these behavioral differences.

Cultural Background

To some extent, our actions are influenced by our culture, the social, ethnic, and religious backgrounds that contribute to our beliefs, material possessions, values, and goals.

Peer groups—groups of friends and associates with similar backgrounds—are those people against whom we measure ourselves. Together, they help create the personality characteristics and attitudes that determine the lifestyle that we have established for ourselves. For example, one peer group may stress outward signs of achievement, such as material possessions, while another may emphasize balanced living or intellectual self-realization.

The Life Cycle

Age is also a strong influence on our interests and preferences, as we can see by considering the life cycle in terms of age categories. Three are proposed here. The age range for each category described can vary, depending on age at marriage and having children, time of retirement, as well as type of lifestyle. Thus, the ranges given below are somewhat arbitrary. Longer life expectancy, improved health, and increased options have all created changes in self-perception and this, in turn, affects both preferences and interests.[1]

Young: 18–42

For the young, planning often takes a back seat, at least until they establish lasting personal relationships. When young, people tend to place great emphasis on their current standard of living and fairly often on their career advancement. Thus, savings is sometimes given lower priority. Risk tolerances often can be high. When marriage and children are on the horizon, the major concern is on accumulation of real assets for a home and its possessions, and on life insurance to protect other household members. Borrowing to purchase these assets, and sometimes to finance graduate education, is fairly common.

Middle Aged: 43–67

For many people, the onset of middle age is an occasion for increased planning, particularly in regard to saving for retirement. With middle age may come better-defined parameters for careers and a more consistent cost of living. The home and its possessions and the car may have already been improved upon. Financial assets are accumulated and expended for children's educations and increased sums saved for retirement.

Debt as a percentage of assets generally declines for two reasons: Debt on the home is being paid off and real and financial assets have grown, so that would make the debt percentage go down even if total debt had remained stable. In middle ages, risk taking tends to decline. For some the use of whole life insurance now replaces cheaper term-life insurance.

---

[1] The approach taken is one for traditional couples. Clearly, people who remain single, or who choose not to have children, or who otherwise differ will have an alternative pattern.

Once people have funded their children's college obligations, their annual savings often increase markedly. They also begin to think more seriously about estate planning.

Seniors: 68 and Beyond

It is a mark of change in our society that the term *senior* has replaced *old* to describe people in this age bracket. Often, seniors go through a period of active retirement, perhaps maintaining some part-time job, followed by a slower pace. Accumulation of wealth during youth and middle age gives way to spending down of assets. Risk tolerance declines sharply, and so does the use of debt. Thoughts about taking care of others through estate planning are given a high priority. Tax rates may decline and help contribute to a decline in cost of living where uninsurable medical and elder-care costs are not excessive.

Family

Your family background can have a strong pull on how you establish your lifestyle. Those who have had a happy childhood and a strong family bond may continue the patterns set by their parents. Others who have not may move in the opposite direction. Some people feel birth order is another influential factor, with the eldest child more likely to be conservative, following the parents' point of view, with the younger children more likely to become more creative and rebellious.[2]

Personality

Your **personality** is the sum total of all the attributes—emotional, mental, etc.—that distinguish you from other people. In PFP, we can view it narrowly as those innate traits we have based on how we were born or are currently "built."[3] For example, given the same trying event, one person may be highly emotional, another more analytical; one more confident, another more anxious; one more independent, another a delegator.

Our personality affects our tolerance for risk, which influences our planning actions. It along with other factors helps create our values, which determine our goals. Financial planning based on differing goals is discussed in Chapter 19.

Finally, behavioral finance covers human weaknesses. One of the most fundamental is lack of knowledge of the subject matter, a common problem in financial planning. Ways to meet these weaknesses are developed in Chapter 19.

In sum, the characteristics we have listed are covered under a broader definition of behavioral finance, one that goes beyond a focus solely on emotions. These characteristics are important in both understanding ourselves and assessing others. Some may contribute to shortcomings that we will want to overcome to reach our financial goals. Others may result in our having goals that are different from a singular emphasis on money achievement. Before we deal with goals, and data gathering, we should understand the importance of communication in relating to others professionally, to other household members, and even as an aid in understanding ourselves.

SOME PRINCIPLES OF COMMUNICATION

Communication is very important in any activity we undertake in life. Often it is not good enough to be honest, knowledgeable, and concerned. We must be able to have others believe that we possess the required traits so that we can be successful in the task we have set out for ourselves or the relationship we wish to establish.

---

[2] Frank Sulloway, *Born to Rebel: Birth Order, Family Dynamics, and Creative Lives* (New York: Vintage Books, 1997).

[3] A broader definition would include environmental factors as well.

FIGURE 3.1
Nonverbal
Communication

Source: http://www.clipart.com.

Communication can be defined as the ability to transmit a message successfully to another person. That success is indicated by having someone receive and understand your message in the manner you intended it to be conveyed.

Communication is more complex than you may think initially. **Verbal communication** is a way of transmitting our thoughts and emotions through the spoken word. When you speak, you communicate in many ways. One way is through the content of the message. We can call that content the **verbal message**. The verbal message often contains specific information. It also can convey a message that extends beyond the specific information. For example, the tone of voice and intensity, the passion with which you speak, also convey information, but that information is nonverbal.

Through **nonverbal communication** you transmit your thoughts and emotions without or in addition to the words you use. Whether intentionally or unintentionally, your facial expressions, body movements, hand gestures, use of eye contact—even the way you dress or the appearance of your office—can transmit a message. For example, through your **body language** you may communicate an entirely different message than the one you're speaking about. Thus, folding your arms across your chest and other tight gestures and facial expressions may convey a lack of receptivity, even though you nod your head in agreement. This is illustrated in Figure 3.1.

A movement of your body toward the speaker in a relaxed manner may signify interest in or assent to the idea being discussed while a shift back in the seat away from the speaker with loss of eye contact could indicate the opposite reaction. Should your voice rise in tone it often conveys a strong feeling about a subject. In contrast, a weak vocal response could signify a lack of interest in or conviction about what is being discussed.

As is shown in Figure 3.1, clearly a person who expresses agreement with a message in a free, animated way, with eyes focused on the other person, is more likely to receive, process correctly, and agree with the content of that message.

There are many reasons for communicating with another person. You may want to express your opinion or feelings about a matter. You may wish to convey some specific facts. In some instances, it is not the message itself that is your goal, but the desire to develop a relationship with another person. If you are acting as an advisor, your intent can fall in any of those categories, as well as to persuade someone to hire you or to follow your advice. Whatever the reason, it is generally much more effective to conduct the meeting face to face. In each instance given, there are important skills that you can develop.

Listening

Listening has many facets. It allows you to gather the information that you are interested in. It enables you to develop an understanding of the other person's thoughts and feelings beyond the facts given. Very importantly, it can transmit your interest in the person or the topic at hand.

Some rules that can help you to become a more effective listener are

1. Focus your full attention.
2. Do more listening than talking.
3. Try not to be judgmental; instead, be understanding.
4. Try to get into the other person's way of thinking.
5. Keep your responses to the topic being discussed.
6. Try to respond occasionally. Wherever possible, speak positively about the person's strongly held beliefs.
7. Look for the principal points of the topic from both your own and the speaker's points of view. Acknowledge your understanding of the topic from time to time.

Showing Empathy

Empathy is attempting to place yourself in the other person's position—trying to identify with what he or she is experiencing—his or her thoughts, feelings, and attitudes. It means listening, understanding, feeling, and communicating with increased sensitivity to someone else's perceptions. Showing empathy has the potential to help you not only establish a relationship with a person but also provide more expert advice.

Establishing Trust

Trust is the belief that you can rely on someone or something to perform as expected. Creating trust in financial planning comes from expertise—having a strong educational background and experience in a given area. In addition, it is generated by being truthful, by putting aside potential conflicts of interest and acting in the best interests of that person. Presenting a confident manner and appearance also helps. Finally, trust comes from attention—demonstrating your particular understanding and concern for the other person.

When trust in another person is present, communication and effective planning can proceed more smoothly. The person believes the result will be more predictable with a much reduced chance of a loss or an otherwise disappointing outcome.

Example 3.1

The advisor knew many marketing representatives from financial services firms. They all had products to offer him, some attractive, some not, and the representatives varied in their degree of effectiveness in presenting the advantages of their offerings. When they came in, the advisor was polite, yet aware of the generally narrow sales focus of the representative.

Dennis, a marketing representative for a major mutual fund company, was different. He asked to spend some time with the advisor to learn about his operations and goals for the future. At that meeting, the representative was very attentive and interested, asked for elaboration of certain points, and seemed to understand the advisor's approach thoroughly. He conveyed knowledge, genuine interest, and even an empathy for certain problematic situations.

Surprisingly, when asked how his firm's products fit the advisor's investment goals, Dennis said he would rather devote the time to a focus on helping with the advisor's overall business operations. A discussion of products could come later in the relationship. By the end of the meeting, the advisor was impressed. He was no longer wary of the interchange and made a mental note to give careful consideration to any recommendations Dennis would make. He asked himself what it was that distinguished Dennis from many other representatives. He concluded it was that Dennis truly listened and was focused on the advisor's best interests.

INTERVIEWING

The client interview can be the first activity performed in the financial planning process. It is at this meeting that goals are talked about and often established, and data gathering begins. The interview process often has another purpose. Many advisors offer a free initial interview. This meeting allows the clients and the advisor to establish whether they wish to work together and to begin the relationship.

Fortunately, the interview process allows both relationship screening and data gathering to take place at the same time because both focus on client interests. This interview process calls upon the communication and listening skills and the establishment of trust necessary for a strong relationship.

To be successful, the interview process must have certain ingredients.

Preplanning

Advisors should set out the purpose of the meeting. The topics to be covered should be selected in advance and an outline of the questions to be asked should be prepared. The interview room should be neat and free from distraction. Any background on the person should be reviewed to help direct the question and to help establish rapport. Advisors should review effective techniques. For example, they should plan for desirable communication techniques such as a reality check at key points to ensure that the client, not the advisor, is doing most of the talking. Advisors must acknowledge that effectiveness often arises from clients believing they have a personal relationship with the advisor. Thus, it can be more important to foster the relationship than to demonstrate competence over and over again.

Beginning the Interview

The interview should begin by making the client feel comfortable and relaxed. It may involve "small talk" that has nothing to do with the topics to be discussed but places the person at ease and, if possible, establishes rapport and common interests. The planner should mention the purpose of the interview, perhaps the approach and topics to be discussed, and invite two-way communication that is as frank as possible.

The Substance of the Interview

To place the client in the right framework for the rest of the interview, the substance of the interview should begin with a simple question. Generally, a variety of types of questions will then be asked. Open questions are those that permit answers that can go in any direction—for example, "What interests you in your life?" or "What are your goals?" Closed questions are shorter and ask for a specific answer, such as "How much money are you making currently?" or "Do you expect to go to graduate school?"

Primary questions are the first ones in a new area—for example, "How much life insurance coverage do you have?" or "Do you have a listing of your investments?" Probing questions seek to develop further information about a primary question—for example, "What types of life insurance do you own and why?" or "What does money mean to you?"

Leading questions are those that bring a client toward an intended answer. Asking someone if he or she would like a better-performing investment portfolio or "Are you satisfied with your financial planning?" can lead that person toward hiring an advisor.

There should be several advisor questions seeking elaboration and, wherever possible, verbal exchanges that stress client interests. Interruptions of any type other than for clarification should be discouraged.

Advisors should focus on listening to the client's answers to their questions. These answers should give rise to additional questions. By paraphrasing answers, advisors can confirm that they are on the right track for proceeding. Although client interviews need structure, a certain flexibility is called for. When a client's verbal answer and body language seem to conflict, further questioning is needed. It is often advisable to let clients continue their line of thought even though the answer may range over several topics—the underlying motivation and character of the client can come out in that reply. As mentioned, it is often best to be nonjudgmental about the client and to develop genuine interest and empathy in the exchange.

Advisors should refrain from such counterproductive questioning techniques as allowing their questions to roam widely without establishing informational goals and structure, not using the time allotted efficiently, or allowing meetings to extend beyond schedule without good reason, which can be frustrating to both client and advisor. In addition, avoid being either too shallow or too detailed in information gathering or too direct in the line of questioning, not adjusting for sensitive subjects. Finally, make sure the meeting isn't too structured with the line of questioning entirely preplanned, in which client wishes are not accounted for and information uncovered is not developed.

Example 3.2   John was an excellent financial planner. He was bright, well qualified, and cared about his clients. However, his interviews were inevitably too long and he did not read the client's frustration with the extra time being spent. After he adhered to an average limit on a first interview with some questions handled later in the process or eliminated, and as he became more aware of his client's body language, he developed into a more effective questioner.

Conclusion

Every meeting should have a conclusion. It may happen through covering all questions intended or through an advisor's indication that the time is drawing to a close. One signal may be asking whether there is anything else that should be covered at the meeting. The advisor should sum up the points covered during the meeting and establish a date or other plan for action.

FINANCIAL COUNSELING

Financial counseling can be asked for at all stages of the planning process. At the beginning of the process, planners often are asked what type of service is called for. Interim assistance also may be requested. For example, a financial planner may suggest that clients not make any further investments with available cash until a specific part or all of the planning is completed. Counseling involves providing support for people. Interviewing is an integral part of the process; it helps frame the problems, interests, and background information required.

Financial counseling can be defined as the mechanism for assisting people in making their financial decisions. In contrast, financial advising is sometimes considered making the decisions for the client.

The thought in counseling, then, is to provide more personalized service, perhaps including nonfinancial support, with the ultimate decisions in the hands of the client. As a practical matter, counseling and advice often are combined, with little distinction made between the two.

Effectiveness in providing counseling has many elements, a number of which we have already discussed. These include providing a structured presentation that is simple to understand. The advice should not be abstract, but tailored to the interests of the person. Feedback should be asked for at all points during the presentation or exchange.

When clients show some resistance to the advice, the planner should attempt to understand fully the cause of the resistance and, where appropriate, persuade the clients that their ways of viewing the matter aren't accurate or in their interest. The planner should give specific reasons as to why this is so.

Practical Comment   Counseling versus Advising

Often in financial planning, the difference between counseling and advising can have more to do with the personality of planners than with their backgrounds or even their use of a financial plan. Some planners view themselves as assisting people in making their decisions. They can be extremely sensitive to people's needs, with financial rules taking a back seat. Other planners view themselves as experts whose advice is correct and should be followed in all instances.

Many planners find themselves somewhere in between. They follow rules about the best financial advice but are flexible in their recommendations and bend those rules to accommodate client desires. Clients themselves can often determine through their initial interview which type of person they are dealing with and select the advisor that best suits them. Of course, many advisors are able to accommodate themselves to the style the client prefers, which can be an attractive trait. Despite the differing types of planners, many end up giving a combination of advice and counseling as circumstances dictate, which may be why the term advisor is often used to encompass both.

Alternatively, it may be best to change the advice. Sometimes when resistance is received, all that is needed is just listening and acknowledging your understanding of the client's point of view. Frequently, "venting" or just talking about the situation is the client's only intention. Resistance that occurs either through words or body language should generally be dealt with politely but discreetly, with a question about where the difficulty comes from.

Example 3.3   Doug was conducting an interview with a new client. The person was about to retire and had a choice of taking pension monies in the form of a lump-sum distribution or an annuity of yearly payments for life. Doug stressed the benefits of a lump sum, which he believed would provide greater income over the longer term. He noticed that the client's face tightened when he mentioned this and that the client spoke of the safety of an annuity. He then checked himself, recognizing that perhaps he had let his own interests in providing ongoing investment advice, should the lump-sum option be taken, color his thinking. He immediately shifted his approach, presenting the benefits of an annuity to a person with a low tolerance for risk.

Receptivity to points being made is often increased by having rapport with a client and by the client's recognition that the planner's advice can be trusted. Empathy, perceiving things from the client's point of view, and value-free judgments also can help. Thus, advisors should be aware of their own biases and ask themselves whether their advice is extending beyond hard financial practices and the client's wishes to their own preferences. If so, the question should then be whether the planner's preferences are in the client's best interests.

Whenever possible the planner should make strong efforts to hold the client in positive regard and to demonstrate that in interactions. At the same time the planner must be genuine since true feelings are often given away in communications such as body language. If the client feels the advisor is not genuine the entire relationship which is based on trust can be undermined. At a minimum any unfavorable judgments should be set aside for the balance of the consultation.

GOALS

Goals are the results you would like to achieve. The financial planning activities undertaken are based on stated goals. In this chapter, we provide a broad overview of the topic. In Chapter 19 we deal more extensively with life planning—a goals-oriented approach that extends beyond money issues to strategic matters for verification and realization of life-time objectives.

How are our goals established? The answer depends in part on which discipline you choose.[4] A sociologist is concerned with the study of groups, so it should not be surprising that sociologists believe our goals are influenced by the way we were raised by our families and other groups of people in our environment. A sociologist might theorize that we strive to maintain our status relative to our peer groups—our friends, families, and business associates.

In contrast, a biologist might say that, to some extent, we are programmed through our genetic makeup to strive for certain objectives. The psychologist who studies motivation might assume that the underlying goal of most human behavior is to have as many pleasurable experiences as possible.

Clearly, different people get pleasure from different activities. Some work to achieve the most money or fame. Others strive to allocate the greatest proportion of their life to leisure activities or to have fulfilling personal relationships. Moreover, our goals can change over time. For example, some goals have a life cycle component. We may want to play as hard as we can when in our 20s and strive to relax by a pool in our 70s.

Economics translates goals into utility (pleasure) terms and then attempts to quantify them in objective terms. It does this by placing a dollar value on them. Quantifying goals helps to bring scientific measurement to the discipline. Finance also expresses most things in money terms. For example, in financial terms, the goal of business is to make the most money possible, subject to a given level of risk.[5]

To demonstrate the wide array of interpretations depending on discipline, consider the following analysis of possible reasons for having a child:

1. Sociologically, it is what the group is expecting you to do.
2. Biologically, it is an inner need that has to be fulfilled.
3. Religiously, it is what is expected by a higher power.
4. Psychologically, it provides happiness.
5. Economically and financially, it can be considered a major long-term overhead cost similar to a capital expenditure, or the need to have someone to care for you in old age.
6. In ordinary terms, having a child can be viewed as a way to form a lasting, enjoyable, emotional relationship.

At first glance, the economics and finance approach might seem somewhat narrow and unfeeling. Economists and finance people know that they are simplifying human motivations by translating them into common dollar terms. But doing so permits scientific measurement to go forward and enables us to gain additional insight into how human beings operate and how to improve their operations.[6] Since this is a financial text, in most instances we will use a finance business approach. Here we will take a broader perspective, as in the discussion that follows.

Approaches to Goals

There are other ways of presenting goals. For example, the psychologist Abraham Maslow believes that people first try to satisfy their basic, or physiological, needs—food, shelter,

---

[4] For a review of how other disciplines approach goals, see Michael Jensen, *Foundations of Organizational Management Strategy* (Cambridge, MA: Harvard University Press, 1998).

[5] Publicly owned companies' goal is to maximize the stockholder wealth figure that combines profit and risk.

[6] For a discussion of simplifying assumptions, see George Stigler and Gary Becker, "De Gustibus Non Est Disputandum," *American Economic Review* 67, no. 2 (March 1977), pp. 76–90.

Practical Comment Goals and Standard of Living

This book often uses the term **standard of living** as finance's practical implementation of the word *money* or it uses *economic well-being*. The goal of financial planning is to help achieve the highest standard of living possible. Standard of living has two meanings. In strict financial parlance, you've seen, it means making the most money possible. In more common usage, it can mean attempting to achieve an attractive balance of life's factors.

Financial planners know that their clients' goals extend beyond just acquiring material items. For example, they don't often recommend that a client take a permanent second job to earn more money.

They rely heavily on financial numbers because that is frequently what they are hired to do and because money often has a strong place in overall goal achievement.

Yet many financial planners manage to blend money with other goals. In this second, broader meaning, standard of living is a relative term that depends on individual values. In this instance, the term *quality of life* is perhaps closest to the meaning of standard of living. The goal, especially when material comforts have been achieved, can be one of satisfaction with lifestyle and accomplishments.

and clothing. If these are taken care of, people move on to satisfy their need for safety. The next level involves social needs, such as the need for belonging. If people have enough resources, they attempt to satisfy their higher needs. These would include the need for esteem, both self-esteem and esteem from others. The highest-level need, according to Maslow, is for self-actualization, which involves achieving your personal goals in life. Figure 3.2 shows an illustration of Maslow's hierarchy of needs in a pyramidal form.

On a more pragmatic level, a person might establish three levels of goals in each part of the financial plan: minimum goals, satisfactory goals, and higher-level goals. If you didn't reach your minimum goals, you would be distinctly disappointed. Satisfactory goals are those that you target and would be pleased to attain. Higher-level goals, if you achieved them, would give you pleasure beyond your expectations. For example, your satisfactory goal may be to live in an attractive home in a good neighborhood in the suburbs. Your minimum goal would be to rent an apartment in a similar neighborhood. Your higher-level goal

FIGURE 3.2
Maslow's Hierarchy of Needs

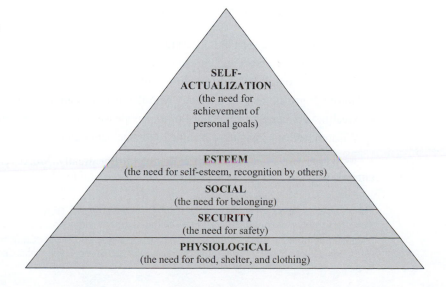

SELF-ACTUALIZATION
(the need for achievement of personal goals)

ESTEEM
(the need for self-esteem, recognition by others)

SOCIAL
(the need for belonging)

SECURITY
(the need for safety)

PHYSIOLOGICAL
(the need for food, shelter, and clothing)

Practical Comment   Analysis of Goals

Goals may not always come to mind easily. You may need to think them through. Sometimes what you think of as your goals are just short-term considerations. For example, you may seek professional assistance to help save for a car; your real goal, however, may be to establish a savings structure to allow you to maintain the same lifestyle both before and after retirement. At other times, your goals and needs may be in conflict. Your goals—continuing to spend, for example—may be unrealistic, whereas the consequences—taking on debt—suggest a different need and course of action.

would be to have a luxurious vacation home in addition to the suburban house. The approach is termed the money ladder.[7]

Goals can be separated into three time frames. Short-term goals are those you intend to achieve within one year—for example, being more selective in purchasing goods and appliances that may not be needed, or saving for a vacation. Intermediate goals are to be completed in one to four years—saving for the down payment on a car or a home, for example. Long-term goals are those you expect to accomplish in five years or more. Examples would include saving for a child's college education and having enough money to retire comfortably.

The list below is one financial planner's method of helping you select the life values that are important to you. He suggests that you choose three to five of these items and rank order them.[8]

Life Values
- Achievement: to accomplish something important in life
- Aesthetics: to be able to appreciate and enjoy beauty for its own sake
- Authority: to be a key decision maker directing priorities
- Adventure: to experience variety and excitement
- Autonomy: to be independent, have freedom
- Health: to be physically, mentally, and emotionally well
- Integrity: to be honest and straightforward, just and fair
- Friendship: to have close personal relationships, share with family and friends
- Pleasure: to experience enjoyment and satisfaction from activities in which I participate
- Recognition: to be seen as successful, receive acknowledgment for achievement
- Security: to feel stable and comfortable with few changes or anxieties in my life
- Service: to contribute to the quality of life for other people
- Spiritual: growth to have harmony with the infinite source of life
- Wealth: to acquire an abundance of money/possessions; to be financially independent
- Wisdom: to have insight, to be able to pursue new knowledge

As you can see, people's goals in life can differ greatly. Moreover, your goals can be altered over time by practical experiences—for example, the degree of your success in

---

[7] Lewis J. Altfest and Karen C. Altfest, *Lew Altfest Answers Almost All Your Questions about Money* (New York: McGraw-Hill, 1992). A variation of this approach is used in Chapter 20, Appendix III.

[8] Adapted from Ken Rouse, *Putting Money in Its Place* (Sedona, AZ: Rouse Companies, 1994), pp. 56–57. Latest edition published by The Rouse Companies, Inc., 30 Stone Greek Circle, Sedona, AZ 86351. www.lifefocus.com <http://www.lifefocus.com/>.

reaching previous objectives and your attraction to new ideas. Many people who are comfortably middle class find that money goals diminish in importance as they age. We will examine the issue of goals further in Chapter 19.

DATA GATHERING

Data gathering is accumulating the information that is needed to perform personal financial planning objectives. Therefore, before beginning our tasks, we must establish the particular goals that determine the type of planning to be done. For example, an investment review will require much more specialized and less extensive material than a comprehensive financial plan.[9] We also must ascertain needs where they differ from goals and develop a sense of priorities among goals and needs.

The data to be received may be in the form of written documents or through questioning of other advisors retained by the client such as an accountant, lawyer, and insurance representative or in the filling out of an appropriate questionnaire. Where the work is being performed for others, an interview of the person or couple is a highly significant part of the process. We will look at interviewing procedures for financial planners in the next section.

The categories for information for a comprehensive financial plan or comprehensive review follow the major parts of a plan. Even with a **segmented financial plan** (one that covers a limited specialized portion of all financial activities), the household's overall financial condition should be established. Some of the key areas and information needed are outlined in Table 3.1.

The interview and data-gathering process have other objectives as well. At this time, we want to establish how financially sophisticated the clients are. For example, are they able to understand the workings of common financial instruments such as stocks and bonds? Can they distinguish the risks of various investment alternatives? Do they know the differences among the various types of life insurance?

A preliminary assessment of their risk tolerance can be established. It may just be a self-assessment of risk preference either overall or relative to the "average person." Risk should be viewed not only in terms of investment—stock and bond risk—but also in terms of overall household risk, including such things as need for insurance, and personal practices and career goals.

Toward the end of data gathering, the advisor should be aware of any factors that distinguish this situation from others. For example, is there a particular focus on client education or on providing children who have severe learning disabilities with lifetime support? Will there be a particular difficulty in obtaining reliable revenue and operating cost figures? Do the clients have particular personal problems such as excessive gambling, drinking, or perhaps excessive spending habits?

Full data gathering can take some time. At the completion of the interview and preliminary data gathering, however, the advisor is ready to indicate, based on client interests and needs, what he or she thinks is the appropriate scope of the engagement and indicate what the cost will be.

Alternatively, an hourly rate will be established, sometimes with a minimum and maximum cost indicated. In some cases, a flat fee is provided for a fixed service. The client ultimately decides, generally in consultation with the advisor, whether the scope indicated should be accepted or modified. Getting the specific terms of the engagement clear, what is included, what is not, is very important.

[9] Sometimes establishing goals is a part of the preliminary data-gathering process. The approach may be to ask some preliminary questions that help develop the scope of the work, then develop the specific goals. Detailed data gathering then follows. Alternatively, goals may come out of an advisor's comprehensive review and assessment of needs or from modifying preexisting goals.

Practical Comment   Tolerance for Risk

Risk tolerance can sometimes be a difficult item to assess. People may have different responses depending upon such factors as the criteria used, their financial sophistication, the way the question is framed, and the investment climate at the time. The advisor had one client who described his investment risk tolerance as moderately aggressive; when pressed, the client indicated that the security he associated with that risk tolerance was a certificate of deposit.

Behavioral variables often enter. People commonly change their long-term risk tolerance based on shorter-term investment performance. They also

may ignore such basic concepts as the higher the return sought, the higher the risk of the investment. For example, when asked to provide relative ratings from 0 to 100 for what was most important to them, including safety of principal and high returns, a significant number of clients put 100 for both.

Wherever possible, advisors should use a variety of criteria in determining risk tolerance, including the client's current practices; where a client's responses are inconsistent or not logical, press further. We'll consider this topic in more detail in Chapter 9.

TABLE 3.1   Selected Data Gathered for Comprehensive Financial Plan

Source: Ross Levin, *The Wealth Management Index* (New York: McGraw-Hill, 1996).

Type	Selected Information Needed
Background of household members	Personal information: name, number, and ages of household members; educational attainment; type of job; personal traits and beliefs; advisory services used; and so on.
Balance sheet	Current assets and liabilities.[1]
Cash flow planning	Current projected income and expenses, both for daily items and for capital outlays.
Income tax planning	Income tax return for the past year and perhaps the past three years.
Debt	Existing home mortgages,credit cards and credit lines, such as home equity loans.
Investments	A detailed list of bank, brokerage, mutual fund, and other investment accounts and specific holdings. Current market value and projected outlays for home and details of other investments. Establishment of investment risk tolerance.
Retirement planning	Retirement accounts and retirement savings. Rates of inflation and rates of return, retirement goals, government benefits.
Estate planning	Copies of wills and trusts. Establishment of titling of assets. Intended gifting policies and those for estate distribution at death.
Risk management	Copies of all insurance policies. Intended insurance coverage. Other risk management procedures. Determination of overall household risk tolerance.
Employee benefits	Copies of description of all company benefits. Amounts and investment alternatives for pension plans.
Family planning	Current number of household members. Marital and children planning versus household members today.
Educational planning	Types of plans and amount of assets in place. Prospective costs for college and, in the case of children, the amount or percentage to be funded by the parent.
Specialized planning	Description of particular planning needs for the individual household.
Other	Health, possible inheritances, broader family responsibilities and obligations, personal nonfinancial problems.

[1] Pro forma future statements will come out of planning procedures.

Practical Comment   Steps in the PFP Process

Notice that the initial steps in the financial planning process can sometimes be shifted. Traditionally, setting the terms of the engagement is thought of as being performed first, followed by the goals, and then data gathering. From a legal standpoint, this approach is correct.

Where there is no fixed service being offered, however, the advisor may not know what is needed and what the cost will be. Many advisors, of course, offer free initial consultations, whose purpose is to establish not only the particulars of the engagement but also whether the two parties desire to work together.

What can happen, therefore, is a preliminary or even fairly detailed session on goals and data gathering prior to establishing contract terms. Certain goals then can come out of data gathering. Once the contract is signed, the goals are often examined in greater depth, and more detailed data gathering begins.

With data gathering, goals, and needs established, at least preliminarily, and a time horizon determined to satisfy each, you are able to move to how the household operates, and the ways that financial planning activities can help. In analyzing each part of the plan, always keep in mind the overall goals. That process is sometimes referred to as where we want to be, as compared with where we are now. The activities given in the next sections of the book will provide the building blocks for how to get there.

Back to Dan and Laura

DATA GATHERING, GOAL SETTING, AND COMMUNICATION

This meeting with Dan and Laura was set up to further discuss personal goals that both seemed anxious about. They also brought with them what they said was the completed questionnaire. Both were enthusiastic about the coming planning process. They thought that the advisor had handled the initial interviews very well.

Dan said he particularly liked the way I had moved the meetings along smoothly and handled their recurring differences of opinion easily. He said he was having difficulty communicating with an important new client and would like me to give him some tips on successful communication and interviewing techniques after discussing goals.

Thank you for your kind comments about our initial interviews. I will strive to meet your expectations. Before I discuss communication matters, let me mention that data gathering is an arduous, detailed process. I know that filling out the questionnaire is not fun. However, it must cover all parts of the financial plan and anything financial that you care to add.

The questionnaire you sent back was not complete, and I frankly thought you hadn't given it your full attention. The questionnaire encompassed a large part of the information that I will need to process. Since a financial plan can only be as good as the figures and forethought that goes into it, I am asking you to review it again—this time more carefully. If you have any questions about it, please let me know. If you prefer, we can sit together while you fill it out. Now, let me turn to goals.

Goals can be looked at in specific money terms. For example, how much will it cost for a vacation or a down payment on a home? Goals also can be viewed in terms of completion over a time frame—for example, short versus long term. For some people, goals change with income or education so that basic goals are transformed into the fulfillment of higher needs, such as self-esteem and self-actualization.

Finally, the process of setting goals can be expressed in minimum, satisfactory, and higher-level forms—often based on how hard we want to work and sacrifice today's standard of living for tomorrow.

Your financial plan will provide the best way for you to achieve your goals. It is goals that motivate you to plan your financial future in an orderly way. As indicated to me in our first meeting and the one we just had, your goals are as follows:

1. To get out of credit card debt and student loans as soon as possible.
2. To be less concerned about the future by planning now.
3. To have two children and maintain the standard of living you have today.
4. To purchase a house in the not-too-distant future.
5. To be financially independent by age 55.
6. To have your insurance needs examined.
7. To provide money to have both children go to college.
8. To leave $100,000 to each child in your will.
9. To develop an overall asset allocation for your investments.

We will construct your financial plan with these goals in mind. As you requested, I will develop each part of the plan separately. I will explain why I made my recommendations in enough detail so that you can provide me with your reactions prior to the final integration stage for completing the plan. Be aware that goals are often modified as more information on financial capabilities becomes available. Therefore, we are likely to return to this subject.

Dan, as far as communication and interviewing strategy are concerned, I made use of many established techniques in your first interview. I attempted to make my office very quiet and hospitable for frank discussions. Our first conversation was not related to business; rather, it was designed for us to get to know each other and establish a relationship. The questions that followed were simple and open-ended so that I could become familiar with your interests and personalities.

I was very much aware of your gestures and facial expressions. Laura, yours were very natural and free of tension. Dan, your face and folded arms suggested that you were not comfortable with the process of open communication or perhaps with me. That is why I spoke to you in depth first. Perhaps the singular thing I did to win you over and make you relax was to listen intently. You may have noticed my comments and gestures, which sought elaboration and expressed a nonjudgmental approach to what I was hearing.

I knew right away that the two of you had different opinions. I listened to you both and tried to empathize with what I heard. In other words, I tried to look at your problems from your own perspectives. I have found that if I do that, both parties with conflicting opinions believe they have had a hearing, are taken seriously, often sympathetically, and are then ready to engage in open communication.

Although it is early in the process, I tried to counsel you and to provide support for you making your own decisions. My comments were simple and clear and encouraged feedback on how I was doing. Later on I will continue to counsel you, but I also will express my opinions as an advisor, which I believe you want me to do.

You may notice that our first interview had a beginning, a substantial content-contained body of discussion, and a conclusion with my summation of what was covered and what the next steps would be.

Dan, I believe that if you follow these steps, particularly the ones that concern listening and focusing on your client's needs ahead of your own, you will do just fine.

I hope this helps.

Summary

Communication, data gathering, and goal setting are interrelated topics. Our objective is to begin the planning process smoothly so that goal establishment and data gathering occur correctly and the required information is received. This involves

- Understanding the particular needs and behavior of the people for whom planning is to be done. They differ because of such variables as culture, age, family background, and personality.
- Developing sound communication skills such as reading body language, listening carefully, and placing yourself in the other person's shoes.
- Establishing trust by being knowledgeable and honest and acting in the best interests of the client.
- Preplanning your interviewing procedures. Start by making the person feel comfortable, cover the topics intended, and have a conclusion that includes summing up and establishing the next step in the planning process.
- Goals are the focal point of PFP. There are normally many types of goals, and these depend, to a great extent, on a person's life values.
- Data gathering is developing the information necessary to perform PFP. Each area of the plan contributes.

Key Terms

behavioral finance, *53*	empathy, *56*	standard of living, *61*
behavioral financial planning, *53*	financial counseling, *58*	trust, *56*
body language, *55*	nonverbal communication, *55*	verbal communication, *55*
communication, *55*	personality, *54*	verbal message, *55*
data gathering, *63*	segmented financial plan, *63*	

Questions

1. Define behavioral finance.
2. How does behavioral finance differ from quantitative finance?
3. Contrast the interests of young people and seniors.
4. Explain what nonverbal communication means.
5. Why is listening important in the financial planning process?
6. Name four techniques helpful in becoming a good listener.
7. How do you establish trust?
8. Why is preplanning for an interview important?
9. What are some attractive interviewing techniques?
10. How does financial counseling differ from financial advising?
11. How should resistance to a question or recommended course of action be handled?
12. Why are goals important for financial planning?
13. List some of the broad financial goals of people with whom you will come in contact.
14. Break down some financial planning goals by parts of the financial plan into minimum, satisfactory, and higher-level components.
15. What does standard of living mean to you?
16. Contrast financial and personal interpretations of financial planning.

17. Are goals more short-term or long-term oriented? Explain your answer.

18. How is Maslow's hierarchy of needs related to income?

19. What is data gathering?

20. Why is data gathering important?

21. Name two pieces of data that are needed in each of the six financial planning areas.

22. Which types of data should be gathered at the initial interview and which should be left for future meetings?

Case Application

DATA GATHERING, GOAL SETTING, AND COMMUNICATION

Brad and Barbara made an appointment to see me concerning their own financial situation. They were a newly married couple in their early 20s. Barbara came from a family that had children early in their lives; the women were full-time mothers until their children were in college. Barbara had no career ambitions of her own and wanted to have children. Brad was an artistic person who had graduated with a BA in English. He was thinking of a career in the arts but didn't yet know which area. He wanted time to pursue the alternatives and have children later, when he was in his 30s. They seemed to get along well and showed unusual understanding of their and their spouse's personalities.

Case Application Questions

1. As a planner, what communication techniques would you review to prepare for the meeting with Brad and Barbara?
2. How would you open the interview?
3. Assuming you didn't know any of the information above, what data-gathering questions would you ask?
4. Assuming you knew the information above, how would you question the couple about their goals?
5. Would you take sides on their differing goals? Why?
6. What approach would you use for the meeting? Would you be closer to a counselor or to an advisor?
7. Suppose that before the meeting, Brad and Barbara said they weren't sure that you were the right person for the position and that they might interview others. How would that influence the interview process? Give some examples.
8. Suppose you found yourself doing most of the talking. What might that mean? What would you do?
9. How would you end the meeting?
10. What are their goals?
11. What type of information would you ask them for in their first meeting?
12. Assume you were doing a financial plan for Brad and Barbara. Complete the goals section of the financial plan.

Ongoing Household Planning

This section discusses basic household operations. As a help to that discussion, Chapter 4 presents financial planning theory with its two major themes: the household enterprise with its businesslike characteristics and decision making that integrates all assets and obligations. You will learn that the household produces goods and services and generates a kind of profit. Keep in mind that the goal of the household enterprise is to operate as productively as possible. Doing so leads to the highest standard of living you can achieve. PFP's mandate is to help make that happen.

Chapter 5 details financial statements analysis. By constructing and analyzing financial statements, you are able to make an appraisal of where you are financially at the time. The statements also can be financial projections used to help point the way toward necessary future actions. Methods of developing financial statements and evaluating the results are both discussed.

Chapter 6 presents cash flow planning. Cash flow is the resource generated that is used in virtually every personal financial planning activity. When we are operating efficiently, we generate the highest cash flow possible, given time and risk limitations. The focus in this chapter will be on savings, a difficult process for many, and on financial ratios, several of them cash flow–generated, that help determine our financial health.

Chapter 7 describes debt and the ways it is and should be used in the household. For many, debt through the use of credit cards has become a normal household function for obtaining cash and effecting ordinary transactions. The advantages and disadvantages of credit card debt will be presented.

Knowledge of daily household operations and planning for them, as presented in this section, will set the stage for more sophisticated analysis throughout the book.

Chapter **Four**

Household Finance

Chapter Goals

This chapter will enable you to:

- Apply household finance and its economic and financial underpinnings to improve your personal financial planning (PFP).
- View the household as a functioning enterprise.
- Start to apply business thinking to PFP.
- Put into use in personal financial decision making cost of time and life cycle theory principles.
- Differentiate various types of household outlays.
- Begin to understand personal financial planning theory and total portfolio management (TPM).

Dan and Laura were intrigued by their friends' comment: They said the key to their financial success was that they ran their household as a business. Dan liked the idea of operating the household in that way and wondered if there was any theory of personal financial planning. Laura didn't understand why her husband was interested in all that "theoretical stuff." Wasn't financial planning just a straightforward process?

Real Life Planning

Henry

Henry was a sports star known for his talent and temperament. He was a "control freak," unable to delegate all but the most technical matters to others. Henry's first meeting with the advisor was held in Henry's sports car in the parking lot after a game.

Unfortunately, Henry was as frugal and unschooled in personal financial matters as he was flamboyant and sophisticated in sports. He would write all checks himself and could never find the time to pay his bills when they were due. Unopened bills lay on his floor. He never reconciled his bank statement, and sometimes large sums of money lay dormant in non-interest-bearing bank accounts.

The advisor told Henry to think of himself as running a business enterprise. The main asset of his business was his own revenue-generating ability through competing in games and serving as a spokesman for various products. His expenses were the food, clothing, shelter, and other costs necessary to keep his own household operating smoothly and healthily. The remaining cash flow would be used for fun activities and savings to continue to generate revenue for the time when his athletic abilities would no longer be in demand.

The advisor said that Henry was missing out on two opportunities. The first was the opportunity to earn greater sums by investing his money judiciously and through handling day-to-day financial functions properly. It would require money to hire the proper financial people to help him with this. While his operating costs would rise, his enterprise would likely provide greater returns for use after athletic retirement. The second opportunity was the chance to eliminate his fear of the future. The advisor would provide a financial plan that would detail ways to both raise his quality of life today and protect him in the future. The advisor had already concluded that these goals were achievable.

To take advantage of these opportunities, Henry would have to relinquish some control to others, although he would still be in the financial driver's seat. The advisor told Henry that, in effect, there was a cost to the time he was devoting to his household activities. He could use the time freed up to earn more money or to relax more. Henry didn't immediately say whether he was retaining the advisor. Instead he turned on the ignition, drove out of the parking lot, and, when he got to the highway, launched into a broader discussion of his financial concerns. The advisor took notes and thought of the challenge associated with setting Henry on the right financial path.

The Walkers

The advisor got to know his clients, the Walkers, just after Jim had become a doctor and taken a position in a medical practice. Jim and Carmen had met in graduate school on their way to academic careers. They married, and Jim abandoned his aspirations for an academic career, deciding to enroll in a medical school instead. When it came time for Jim to start his own practice, Carmen was placed in charge of developing the right resources, systems, and location for it. She had no experience in setting up a medical practice; hers was a liberal arts background. Nonetheless, she approached each aspect of the project as if it were an area of graduate study, and she did an excellent job.

With Jim handling the patients and Carmen the back office, while their family lived upstairs, the practice developed a strong following. Carmen was up to the task of making sure that the household ran efficiently as well. If there was an ideal way to run it, the advisor thought, she had perfected it. Carmen generated cash flow for savings in an environment where people who were less focused would not have succeeded. The household budget was not elaborate, but its details were ingrained in her head. Jim helped with the important decisions, and his insights often carried the day.

Given her dual role in running a business and a household that included their child, Carmen had very limited time and much to do. When the advisor asked Carmen how she was able to simultaneously run a practice and a household, she thought for a second and said it was simple: she ran both the practice and the household as businesses with personal attention not only to her child but to Jim's patients as well.

OVERVIEW

Personal financial planning didn't emerge full blown from a shell. This chapter traces the development of household finance and personal financial planning theory. We will begin by establishing that the household is the proper organizational structure for an individual's financial activities. We will then look at the economic theories that have led to the household financial approach. You will learn about the cost of time and how household outlays can be separated into two parts: maintenance and leisure.

With the above material as background, we will discuss the household as an enterprise with similarities to a business. Household finance as an approach that embraces the entire book is then described and linked to personal financial planning. A theory of personal financial planning with its active arm, total portfolio management, extends and completes the chapter.

Knowledge of these topics will enable you to have greater insight into PFP and its integrated core, and to increase your understanding of the material to come in future chapters. It also can result in your making better decisions in practice.

THE HOUSEHOLD STRUCTURE

The household represents an organizational structure that unites its occupants. We are interested in the household structure because it can best describe the combined financial actions of its occupants. Just as structure or form affects a business, so too the form of a household can affect its financial operations.[1] The household also can provide an opportunity for logical decision making by its members, which is, of course, a principal goal of personal financial planning and of this book.

The household can be described as a structure for one or more people who live in the same home. This definition is very broad and can include people who share nothing other than the same roof.[2] A similar definition is often used by the U.S. Census Bureau, which publishes many economic statistics by household.

For our purposes, a more meaningful definition of **household** is an organization of one or more people who share a dwelling and share financial and other resources intended for the well-being of its members.[3] This definition requires more involvement and sharing to qualify as a household when there are multiple members. In other words, the household is the principal organization intended to handle the financial and other personal activities of one or more people and to foster achievement of their goals.[4]

The household comes in many organizational forms, which, as with a business organization, influence its financial, legal, and tax situations. For example, financial efficiencies can result from a multiperson household through reduction in income fluctuation, specialization of tasks, and economies of scale. If two people work, they reduce the risk of a cutoff in income in the event of sickness or job layoffs. Specialization in household activities can be completed more quickly and with higher quality. Sharing of fixed costs for shelter and other goods offers greater economies of scale. This thought is reflected in saying, "Two can live as cheaply as one."

A breakdown of alternative household structures and their effect on financial, legal, and tax matters is presented in Table 4.1.

Over the past half century, the composition of households in the United States has changed. For total households, the percentage of stereotypical nuclear families—married couples with children—has declined; the nuclear family now accounts for a little less than 25 percent of all households. Households with single divorced members and those with no prior marital relationship have increased in number. As we saw in Chapter 1, from a strictly

---

[1] Many introductory texts in business finance incorporate a description of a business structure, and the CFP curriculum requirement does as well.

[2] John Taylor, *Principles of Microeconomics,* 2nd ed. (Boston: Houghton Mifflin, 1998), p. 13.

[3] For a discussion of qualifications for a household, see W. Keith Bryant, *The Economic Organization of the Household* (Cambridge: Cambridge University Press, 1995).

[4] In traditional economic theory, all members of the household are assumed to have interests identical to those of the overall household (Paul Samuelson, "Social Indifference Curves," *Quarterly Journal of Economics* 70, no. 1 (February 1956), pp. 1–22), or the outcomes are as if they did (Gary Becker, "Altruism in the Family and Selfishness in the Market Place," *Economica,* n.s., 48, no. 189 (February 1981), pp. 1–15). Thus, it is possible to speak of household and individual interests interchangeably—a procedure that, for the most part, we will follow in this book. In the book's final two chapters, however, we will consider an alternative view. Any alternative view of household interest that does not incorporate a one-voice theory can be considered roughly similar to an approach that does not align worker and owner interests in a business in its traditional goal of maximization of profits.

TABLE 4.1   Household Organizational Summary

Type of Household	Financial Benefits	Taxation	Legal	Life
Single person	Few	Can be an advantage for income taxation[1]	No responsibility for others	Limited to person
Married persons	Specialization Economies of scale Possible reduction in risk of income fluctuation	Can be a disadvantage for income taxation	Marital responsibilities set by the government	Limited to last surviving spouse
Unmarried persons	Specialization Economies of scale Possible reduction in risk of income fluctuation	Can be an advantage over married persons for income taxation	Few legal responsibilities unless set by contract recognized by state or local municipality	Last surviving member
Above types with children	None extra	Extra tax deduction—favorable tax treatment for single-adult head of household in income taxation	Additional responsibilities set by state	Last surviving adult member

[1] In some income circumstances, the opposite is true—for example, getting married is an advantage over staying single.

economic standpoint, the single-adult-person household, with or without children, can be a less efficient organization than a household that has more members. The above-noted average growth of the single-adult-household category (including households with children) may be one reason that household savings in the United States have declined in recent years.[5]

Consider the comparison of household formations in Table 4.2.

In sum, we have identified a structure, the household, for individuals in their personal activities that is broadly equivalent to the structure of the business in its operating activities. Instead of having a corporation, partnership, or individual proprietorship, we have households of one person, or multiple people, married or unmarried, with or without children.

[5] Martin Browning and Annamaria Lusardi, "Household Savings: Micro Theories and Micro Facts," *Journal of Economic Literature* 34, no. 4 (1996), pp. 1797–855.

TABLE 4.2   Household Formations

Source: U.S. Census Bureau, http://www.census.gov.

Year	Average Size	Total Households (in thousands)	Family Households		Total Nonfamily Households (in thousands)
			Married—Families (in thousands)	Other Families (in thousands)	
1950	3.37	43,554	34,075	4,763	4,716
1960	3.33	52,799	39,254	5,650	7,895
1970	3.14	63,401	44,728	6,728	11,945
1980	2.76	80,776	49,112	10,438	21,226
1990	2.63	93,347	52,317	13,774	27,257
2000	2.62	104,705	55,311	16,715	32,680
2001	2.58	108,209	56,592	17,175	34,442
2002	2.58	109,297	56,747	17,581	34,969
2003	2.57	111,278	57,320	18,276	35,682
2004	2.57	112,000	57,719	18,497	35,783

This structure, which implies more logical thinking for people and shared goals for multi-person households,[6] is one of the building blocks for household finance and personal financial planning theory.

THEORY: AN INTRODUCTION

Theory underlies the personal financial planning process. However, theories don't usually give a complete representation of how people act. In many cases, the assumptions made seem unrealistic. Theory leaves out parts of reality in order to simplify key points that will help us understand deeper aspects of behavior. Without theory, the generally recognized activities of personal financial planning—cash flow and tax planning, investments, risk management, retirement and estate planning—would be thought of solely as a mechanical process. With theory, we can attempt to explain why people do what they do. Moreover, theory can enable us to think more logically and to make sound decisions, both of which can lead to higher cash flows. Let's begin with the basic economic theory of choice and work our way to the theory of financial planning.

THE THEORY OF CONSUMER CHOICE

Household finance had its roots in economic theories. Perhaps the simplest approach is the theory of consumer choice. The **theory of consumer choice** describes the method through which people select goods and services to satisfy their needs.

Today, a great number of goods and services are offered to consumers. However, we don't have enough resources to purchase them all. How do we decide which items to buy? The answer is that each person has certain preferences. Those preferences come from the **utility**—a term used in economic theory to quantify satisfaction—that an item presents. We often use two terms in connection with economics and financial matters: maximization and optimization. These terms refer to the mechanism through which individuals obtain the highest possible satisfaction from an activity. Faced with a host of preferences and limited resources, we make purchase decisions designed to maximize utility. In other words, we attempt to optimize—we try to use our resources to get the most satisfaction we can.

People select goods and services from those made available in the marketplace by grouping them into consumption bundles and ranking the bundles in order of attractiveness. For example, you could oversimplify what you intend to spend money on by separating them into alternative combinations of food, clothing, shelter, and "fun" items. Your choice of the most attractive combination is called your **consumption bundle.** Attractiveness is measured by satisfaction in relation to price. Our wealth gives us the limit on the amount we can consume. This limit is called our **budget constraint.** We naturally select the bundle that provides us with the greatest enjoyment given our budget constraint.

Our selections are made not only for this year but for future periods as well. Savings allow us to consider the wide range of multiyear consumption bundles. Savings in the theory of choice represent future spending. Our choices in a more realistic multiyear time frame are made by considering all current and future consumption bundles as compared with current and future wealth.

---

[6] Martin Browning, Francois Bourguignon, Pierre-Andre Chiappori, and Valerie Lechene, "Income and Outcomes: A Structural Model of Intrahousehold Allocation," *Journal of Political Economy* 102, no. 6 (December 1994), pp. 1067–096.

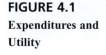

FIGURE 4.1
Expenditures and
Utility

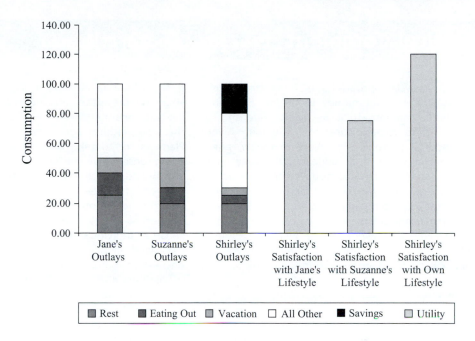

Example 4.1

Shirley was always very serious. She came from a large family that had few resources. She was forced to go out to work and set up her own household after graduating from high school. She attended college at night. While her friends spent all the money they made, she managed to put away some money for the future.

Shirley had just completed a course in microeconomics and thought about her spending options in theory of choice terms. Her best friend, Jane, had an expensive apartment and loved to entertain and eat out. Most of her spare money went for those activities. Another friend, Suzanne, had a moderate rental apartment but spent all her cash left over on vacations. All three were making the same amount of income and, aside from the expenses above, spent about the same money.

Shirley looked at Jane's consumption bundle and found it appealing. She was also drawn to Suzanne's interesting vacations. However, she made a decision to save 10 percent of her salary per year to ensure that later on in life she would not be placed in her parents' weak position. She chose a modest but cozy apartment, ate out once a week, and took a moderately priced vacation each year. Given her budget constraint, she had chosen the consumption bundle that pleased her the most.

In Figure 4.1 you see the differences in expenditure pattern and their utilities according to Shirley's lifestyle preference. Be aware that utility is subjective and the utility associated with similar activities will vary by person. Notice that while expenditure levels for all three friends are the same, from Shirley's perspective, one has the best mix in her lifestyle terms. On the right-hand side of Figure 4.1, you see Shirley's evaluation of her lifestyle and the lifestyles of her two friends.

THE LIFE CYCLE THEORY OF SAVINGS

The **life cycle theory** of savings, as formulated by Franco Modigliani,[7] economics and finance professor, builds on the theory of choice. It shifts from the theory of choice's hard-to-measure utility to concrete money terms. Like many economics and finance theories, the life cycle theory assumes that utility can be measured in money terms. It also presents a specific theory about how people actually make decisions. It says that our spending decisions are based not on the amount of income we currently earn but on the total amount we

---

[7] Franco Modigliani, *The Collected Papers of Franco Modigliani,* vol. 2, *The Life Cycle Hypothesis of Saving* (Cambridge, MA: MIT Press, 1980).

Practical Comment   Life Cycle Approach Evaluated

The pure life cycle approach has many shortcomings. It doesn't provide for money to be left for non-household members such as adult children. It assumes that expenditures can remain level throughout a person's life when, in reality, age-specific expenses such as educational outlays for children and high medical outlays for the elderly make that extremely difficult. Moreover, it doesn't account for uncertainty in projecting future incomes and expenses and the desire of some to have a standard of living that varies by age instead of being level throughout our lifetimes. Besides, many young people can't borrow enough money to achieve this level standard of living.

Why then do we study a life cycle model? First, it may be the foremost specific economic model taught that shows how people behave. Perhaps more importantly, it serves as a formative model for personal financial planning. Financial planners encourage people to think beyond their current incomes and to set goals for the future. Often these

goals include an increase in standard of living for young people as their incomes rise and, as the model indicates, maintenance of a level standard of living through middle age and perhaps retirement. Planners try to take uncertainty into account by being conservative in their projections about returns and providing for emergency funds. Their projections of future needs can fairly easily accommodate age-specific and other "bumpy expenditures" and a sum left to others at death.

On an individual basis, it doesn't matter to planners whether people desire a level, increasing, or decreasing standard of living. Planning can handle it. Planners also know that in their deliberations, people vary in the weight they place on current income and expenses versus projections for these items over their life cycle. Nonetheless, the life cycle model, with its stress on forward thinking and planning based on it, is a highly useful guide to the way many people do, and perhaps more people should, act.

expect to earn over our life cycle. According to this theory, once we have established our lifetime resources, we try to maintain a constant level of expenditures throughout our life cycle. In other words, we try to maintain the same standard of living over our lives.

The life cycle approach has great significance for households. It says we are not impulsive consumers who spend all the money that we generate. Instead, we are planners whose actions extend beyond our current resources and pleasurable activities to our future needs and assets. The simple form of the theory assumes, as does the theory of choice, that risk and inflation are not present and that people act logically to pursue their goals.

According to life cycle theory, borrowing generally takes place early in the household's life, when income is low. In that way, people can raise their consumption expenses and then

FIGURE 4.2
Demonstration of Life Cycle Theory

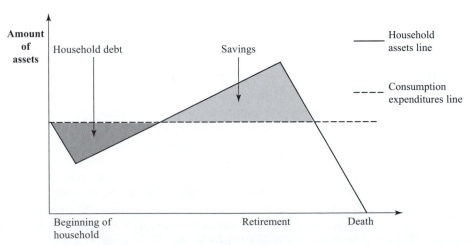

attempt to even them out over their lives. Then, as the income rises, people pay off their debt and save for retirement. In retirement, when work-related revenues have stopped, savings are steadily liquidated to maintain their cost of living. At death there are no assets remaining. In essence, the goal is to "die broke."

The life cycle theory is illustrated in Figure 4.2. The formula for calculating the life cycle model is provided in Appendix III.

THE THEORY OF THE FIRM

It may seem strange to read a brief discussion of business in the middle of a chapter about the household, but, as we have said, we will soon be looking at some of the many ways in which household and business activities are related.

According to the economic theory of the firm, the **firm** or business is an organization that produces goods or services. It purchases inputs—raw materials, labor, and capital in their respective markets—to produce its offerings. The goods it offers are sold to households at a price established in the marketplace outside its control. Therefore, the business concentrates on revenues (output level) and costs (inputs). It does so to find the optimum level of production that provides the highest profits.

Maximization of profits, then, is the firm's goal. It achieves its goal through making intelligent decisions on its use of its funds for the basic materials needed during production and in its mix of production investments. Its workers, including top management, help make those daily operating and investment decisions. Its operating costs are split into those that are fixed and those that vary with the level of production. Profits are revenues minus fixed and variable costs, which can be called **nondiscretionary** and **discretionary expenses.** Remember this broad model as we begin to examine household operations.

THE COST OF TIME

The theory of the firm describes choices in money terms. Gary Becker, an economics professor,[8] employed a money framework to develop a theory of the cost of time. Households and the people living and working in them are limited, as we have seen, in the amount of money they can spend. People also are limited in the time they have available. As we all know, there are only 24 hours in a day.

Fundamentally, our time can be viewed as being spent either in work-related or leisure activities. How do we decide how much time to devote to each? We compare the utility we receive from leisure time with that from the money we receive from work time. The fewer leisure hours, the greater their pleasure; the higher the wage rate, the more enticing further work time is since it can purchase additional goods and services that we enjoy. Obviously, the preference for work over leisure or vice versa at any level will vary from one person to another. (For a further explanation of leisure, see Appendixes I and II.)

Of course, not all work is for pay. For example, we work around the house cleaning up and we allocate time to get to work. Neither pays us any money, but we must perform these activities. We perform other activities, or work-related tasks, because they can be viewed as making us fit for work.

When we engage in any activities that don't provide us with money, we can say we have an **opportunity cost of time.** The opportunity cost of time is the amount of money we could have made if we had worked instead.[9] Normally, this cost of time would be our

---

[8] Gary Becker, "A Theory of Allocation of Time," *Economic Journal* 75, no. 299 (1965), pp. 493–517.

[9] The opportunity cost of time can be extended as well to those not working at the maximum level of income.

hourly wage or its equivalent.[10] By placing a money value on our nonearning time, we can better evaluate efficiencies in many areas. For example, it can help us in making decisions about working at home by doing housework ourselves versus working longer hours for pay and hiring someone else to perform certain household duties. Or it can simply help us recognize that our leisure time is valuable and measurable.

Example 4.2   John, who earned $25 per hour after deducting tax and transportation expenses, worked four eight-hour days instead of five. He chose to bicycle through the countryside on Fridays. His cost of time for the fifth day was $200 ($25 per hour × 8 hours). Clearly, the pleasure from bicycling exceeded that wage rate or he would have worked that fifth day.

THE HOUSEHOLD ENTERPRISE

We can now begin to put these economic theories to use. According to traditional economic theory, the household is merely a supplier of labor to business and a purchaser of its goods. But it is more than that: in fact, in many ways, the household resembles a small business.

The household produces goods and services for its own consumption.[11] It does this by combining items purchased with the time it takes to process them. For example, it "manufactures" cooked food to consume through combining raw materials bought at the supermarket, an oven, and the production time spent preparing and cooking that food. The household product manufactured is the meal to be eaten.[12] The cost is that of items purchased plus the opportunity cost of the time.

We can extend the classical household production approach to include those items created for consumption by others. We combine business-related costs such as business attire with long-lasting capital goods expenditures such as an automobile to transport us to a destination with our time at work. The resulting product manufactured, our services, is sold in the marketplace for a salary or hourly fee.

In fact, the household can be viewed as producing goods and services 24 hours a day. Some add directly to revenues. Others support revenues if only through keeping us healthy and ready to provide our best during the time we allocate to work. The rest of our time and money is devoted to activities that we enjoy doing.

The structure we are describing can be called the **household enterprise.** An enterprise can be defined as an entity that engages in certain tasks for an end result. When people refer to an enterprise, they often think of a business, which is organized to handle a specific task—to make as much money as possible for its owners. The household enterprise attempts to run the household as efficiently as possible in order to provide as much time and money as possible for pleasurable activities.

The broader form of household production is presented in Figure 4.3.

THE TRANSITION TO FINANCE

Thus far we have dealt primarily with economics. That is because, in the past, economics has been the principal provider of broad-based information about household resources. Historically, the information was descriptive, a series of recipes for good household practices, sometimes called "home economics." Becker's work in the 1960s made home

---

[10] Becker, "A Theory of Allocation of Time."

[11] William A. Lord, *Household Dynamics: Economic Growth and Policy* (New York: Oxford University Press, 2002), p. 286.

[12] Becker calls these products *commodities*.

FIGURE 4.3
Household Production: Establishment of Household Goods and Services

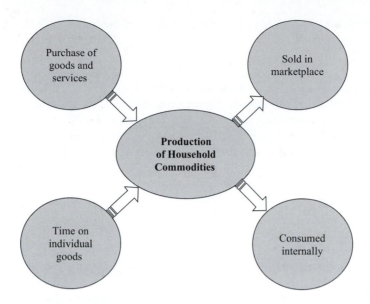

economics more scientific through introducing the cost of time and household production for internal use.[13]

Finance has lagged behind economics in this area. There is no integrated theory of household finance or personal financial planning. Most work in finance has concentrated on marketable securities such as stocks and bonds and on research on businesses and financial markets.

This book sets forth an integrated theory of personal financial planning. We actually started the process by presenting the household as a leisure-seeking enterprise. In establishing this theory, we view items in a financial rather than an economic framework. Although the line between the two can sometimes be blurred,[14] finance places greater or exclusive emphasis, relative to economics, on the following four factors that are relevant to our discussion:

- *Practicality.* Finance places more stress on practicality in its analysis.
- *Cash flow.* Finance describes most processes in tangible money terms.
- *Portfolio solution.* A portfolio is a grouping of assets. Finance is able to look at how those assets interact so as to provide an integrated solution to a problem.
- *Risk-return analysis.* Finance more often incorporates risk in decision making and can offer outcomes in combined risk-return terms.

We start by expressing the household in financial terms. Given finance's emphasis on cash flow, and the cost of time not being an actual cash charge, we reserve its use in the book for relevant decision making.

HOUSEHOLD FINANCE

Household finance is the financial counterpart of the household enterprise. It can be viewed as personal finance placed in an organizational framework. The household is the structure that reflects all the financial activities of its members. Financial planners know this to be true from experience, as financial advice is not usually requested on a person-by-person basis. Instead, personal financial planning is typically performed on an overall household basis. The goal of

[13] Becker, "A Theory of Allocation of Time."

[14] Especially concerning finance and financial economics.

household finance is to have the cash flows of the household's members managed as efficiently as possible, given the household's financial and nonfinancial objectives.

The household has three types of day-to-day financial activities: revenue production, overhead costs, and leisure outlays. The most common revenue-producing activities are jobs and investment income. **Overhead costs,** which we can call **maintenance costs,** include those that directly support employment such as commuting costs and business lunches; housing-support costs such as mortgage interest and utility expenses; and personal support costs such as eating, nonbusiness clothing, and personal care. They can be perceived as fixed costs, at least over the short term. **Leisure outlays** are defined broadly to include all nonwork, nonoverhead-related items. These may include eating out, watching television, playing tennis, and even shopping if the shopping is not for necessities.

According to classical economic theory, all consumption expenditures are generally grouped together. In household finance, however, we can be more precise. We particularly want to distinguish between maintenance and leisure costs. It is fairly easy to differentiate between them, at least for simple items. Maintenance costs are made for necessities. Leisure items provide us with utility, which, as we noted, is another word for satisfaction.

Given our financial orientation, this distinction is important. We want to spend as little time and money as possible on overhead-related items. Few people get pleasure from washing the dishes. As far as most of us are concerned, the more time and money we can spend on leisure activities the better. Of course, the choices of types of activities and whether they are time- or money-intensive will vary by person.[15]

The remaining household activities are not day-to-day ones. They include capital expenditures, other types of investments, and debt financing. **Capital expenditures** are cash outflows that provide household operating benefits over an extended period of time. A washing machine and a car are two examples.

We want to separate capital expenditures because including these often expensive cash outflows together with daily costs can distort our analysis of the financial performance for the year. Additionally, merging them could result in failing to recognize the extended-period worth of the purchases for our household. Because they have ongoing worth, capital expenditures are a form of investment. Other investments, most commonly financial investments such as stocks and bonds, also are treated separately.

Borrowing money or paying it off also can distort financial performance if we don't segregate it. It is of little use to say you have $5,000 more cash in the bank this year than last if you haven't paid attention to the fact that your credit card debt is up by $7,000 during that period.

The balance of your funds is those not being used or planned for use in current operations. This free cash flow can be saved and invested for future purposes, and is often where investments in stocks and bonds are placed.

THE HOUSEHOLD AS A BUSINESS

By now, those who are familiar with businesses will recognize that the household is managed in many ways like a business and that household finance is similar to business finance. Both have revenues and operating expenses. Both have assets and make capital expenditures that help improve operations. Each has a goal. The goal of a business is to earn as much profit as it can.[16] The goal of a household is to maximize utility.

Much is made of the difference between household and business goals. Many people would object to limiting household goals to the business goal of making the most amount of money possible. Yet, few would disagree with the view that money is one of the significant

[15] Sometimes there is more than one reason for purchasing an item. This topic is discussed in Chapter 8.

[16] Or, more precisely, to maximize shareholder's equity, particularly in the case of a publicly owned company.

Practical Comment Incentive to Operate Efficiently

It is important to recognize that households, like businesses, have great incentives to operate efficiently. The more productively household members utilize revenues and maintenance expenses, the more money and time they have to participate in discretionary activities they enjoy. Interestingly, this is true regardless of their own value system about how many hours they work and whether they prefer active leisure or just reading a novel. Nor does an emphasis on efficiency necessarily detract from the pursuit of nonfinancial objectives. In fact, it could enhance the ability to achieve them.[17]

[17] A difference between a household and a business is that the household supervises leisure outlays whereas business responsibility stops with the payment of dividends. Given its supervision of leisure outlays, household operations could be said to have a pure business side and a personal side. The words *pure business* are sometimes used because, even in its leisure activities, the household can benefit from business practices such as purchasing leisure equipment at the lowest possible cost.

factors in achieving personal goals. The relative importance of money, of course, will vary by household.

Our approach—segregating daily outflows into maintenance and leisure expenditures—can help to identify the similarities between a household and a business. As we have seen, maintenance expenditures are household overhead expenses and are equivalent to business operating expenses.

The household's resemblance to a business can extend to profits and dividends. Business profits that get paid out to owners for their choice of use are called dividends. Household cash flows after overhead charges are the equivalent of business profits. The amounts of these cash flows paid out to household members to be used in any way they wish resemble business dividends. You can think of leisure outlays as dividends for our efforts.

Viewing the household as a business implies that its activities are more complex and its decisions more logical than many people acknowledge. It is true that instead of making a correct financial decision, people may respond emotionally. But so do businesspeople. Nor can one or two household members bring the same depth of knowledge to a topic that a specialist at a large corporation can. Household members are largely generalists.

As we shall see, however, household members often make the right choice. They have an advantage over many businesses because they are able to make a decision quickly and integrate all relevant facts, which a complex organization may find difficult. This ability of the household's "owners" to make decisions rapidly without going through various levels of management and employees improves their ability to use an overall portfolio decision-making approach. This approach will be explained later in this chapter.

Our use of sophisticated business techniques that help measurement can assist the household in making more logical and better-informed decisions. The similarities between the household and a business are shown in Figure 4.4.

MODERN PORTFOLIO THEORY

Modern portfolio theory (MPT) has a key place in personal financial planning. MPT, as introduced by Harry Markowitz, a finance professor, helped turn corporate finance and investments from mere words into an operating theory.[18] As is true of many theories, it has proponents and critics that can point to real-life inconsistencies.

[18] Harry Markowitz, "Portfolio Selection," *Journal of Finance* 7, no. 1 (March 1952), pp. 77–91; and Harry Markowitz, *Portfolio Selection—Efficient Diversification of Investments* (New York: John Wiley & Sons, 1959).

FIGURE 4.4   Household versus Business Financial Process

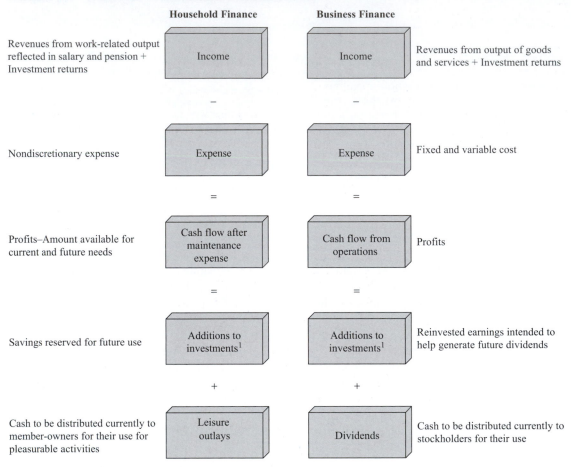

[1] Net of addition to or repayments of debt and, in the case of Business, any additional equity financing as well.

Three key principles of the theory are given here. The first is that investments should be viewed as part of a portfolio, not individually. It is how the pieces fit together that counts.

Second, in making a decision about whether to purchase an investment, don't analyze return alone; analyze return in relation to risk. According to MPT, the higher the risk, the higher the potential return.

A third principle of MPT is that overall risk is influenced by the degree of diversification among assets in the portfolio. The more dissimilar the assets are—that is, the lower the correlation among them—the lower the risk for the portfolio. For example, McDonald's and Microsoft, when combined in a portfolio, will provide greater diversification than a combination of Ford and General Motors. These principles and their relationship to personal financial management will be discussed at great length in Chapters 9 and 16.

Finally, keep in mind that MPT is generally limited to marketable financial investments such as stocks and bonds.

THE THEORY OF PERSONAL FINANCIAL PLANNING

Having discussed existing theories and having presented some new ideas, we are now in a position to put everything together and construct a theory of financial planning. It will be expressed as a series of statements that serve as building blocks for the theory.

1. *PFP goal.* Personal financial planning can have many goals, but overall it is to enjoy the highest standard of living possible. It is equivalent to the theory of choice's maximization of utility.

2. *The life cycle approach.* Life cycle theory provides an appropriate model of individual actions. It says that people plan for future events using current and future financial resources with the objective of smoothing fluctuations in their standard of living.

3. *Household structure.* The household is the appropriate structure through which to analyze one or more people and their goals and operations.

4. *The household enterprise.* The household acts as an enterprise. It manufactures goods and services for internal and external use. Its objective is to become as efficient as possible.

5. *Household finance.* Household finance is the financial component of the household enterprise. It represents the structural counterpart of personal finance. In its financial function, it converts household efficiency into achievement of the highest cash flow possible, given the time allocated to work-related activities. In performing operating tasks, the household in many ways resembles a business.

6. *The household portfolio approach.* The household can be viewed as a portfolio, an accumulation of assets and liabilities. Decisions concerning these assets and liabilities are made on an integrated basis by household members. From a household finance standpoint, it can be expressed as a portfolio that uses a modern portfolio theory approach, but with a broader grouping of assets.[19]

7. *The portfolio solution.* The goal in financial terms is to manage the portfolio as productively as possible. This is done through allocating resources in the proper weighting to the most attractive investments. In other words, its objective is to get the highest return for the risk we are willing to undertake.

8. *PFP goal achievement.* Personal financial planning is the analysis and implementation arm of household finance. By generating the highest cash flow possible, household portfolio optimization satisfies the PFP goal of enjoying the highest attainable standard of living.

Put most simply, the theory of financial planning views the household as a financial enterprise that uses a portfolio risk-return framework to provide solutions to financial planning goals. Using this theoretical approach transforms home economics into household finance.

As previously stated, a suitable theory can lead to logical thinking, thereby creating greater cash flows. A theory is even more helpful when its approach can be applied in real-life circumstances without a large number of assumptions, simplifications, and modifications. A practical approach to the theory is the subject of our next section.

TOTAL PORTFOLIO MANAGEMENT

Total portfolio management (TPM) is the active arm of personal financial planning theory. The household has many assets it can call on to help it earn money. Your financial assets such as stocks and bonds represent one category. Your earning power in your employment is another. For people who are owners, not renters, their home is a significant asset. The household equipment you purchase to save time and money and to provide pleasure is another.

Certain obligations are also relevant to TPM. The easiest to identify are financial liabilities such as mortgages and credit card debt. We can call maintenance a fixed-expenditure obligation as well because we have no choice but to satisfy this obligation. After all, if we

---

[19] Including liabilities, which in theoretical terms can be viewed as negative assets.

don't pay our utility bill, buy food, or put gasoline in our car, we don't have the foundation to live the lifestyle we have established for ourselves.

As mentioned earlier, these assets and obligations form a portfolio—our household portfolio. The returns we receive on this portfolio, our revenues less our overhead expenditures, are our "profits." Our household financial projections of revenues and expenses are made on a longer-term basis as broadly structured by life cycle theory. Since we cannot predict the future precisely, our projections are subject to unexpected occurrences, which we can call *risk*.

TPM's focus, then, is to provide the highest return possible for the household portfolio, given our resources and risk preferences. All household assets work together toward this same goal. The TPM approach attempts to select the best mix of assets to achieve this objective. As we saw earlier, the greater the degree of diversification among assets, the lower is the household's risk. Of course, the higher the return on the portfolio, the higher the standard of living household members can enjoy.

TPM provides specific ways of solving household problems, which we present in the final part of the book. However, TPM is not dependent on the validity or lack of appropriateness of any one practical interpretation of its principles. It is the veracity of the overall approach that counts most.

The TPM approach is unique because it uses all household assets and obligations. Other financial models are generally limited to marketable financial assets alone. They may be appropriate for their purposes. However, people think about all their assets and obligations in making important household decisions, and financial planners do so in making their recommendations.

BEHAVIORAL FINANCIAL PLANNING

Behavioral finance is the human side of money. Much of the information you will be given in this book teaches you the right way to plan. It suggests how people should act; how they actually do act can be very different, of course. For example, sound financial planning often advises that you begin to save money for retirement as soon as you start working. The dollars saved then are much more "high powered" for accumulation purposes than identical amounts saved later in your life.

Yet many young people do act very differently; they postpone retirement saving, preferring enjoyment today to what they perceive as a distant concern. When the decision to spend today is caused by imperfect mental processing of information and later regretted, behavioral financial planning enters into consideration.

The approach of **behavioral financial planning** is to educate and establish practices that close the gap between actual and ideal planning, thereby bringing people closer to their own goals. More broadly speaking, behavioral financial planning can also provide insight into and help foster achievement of nonfinancial goals. Many of the practical comments throughout this book concern behavioral issues, and there is a separate chapter on this topic in the final part of the book.

This material is presented early in the book to familiarize you with several of its themes. They help to integrate the separate financial planning topics. The concepts presented here are a road map to understanding the rest of the book. Each chapter that follows relates its subject to overall household operations and, where appropriate, to TPM. The final section of the book will integrate all the material presented and Chapter 18 will describe TPM in detail.

Figure 4.5 presents a summary of personal financial planning theory. In this form, TPM is integrated into PFP theory and a few steps in the building process have been slightly modified or combined.

FIGURE 4.5
Summary of Personal Financial Planning Theory

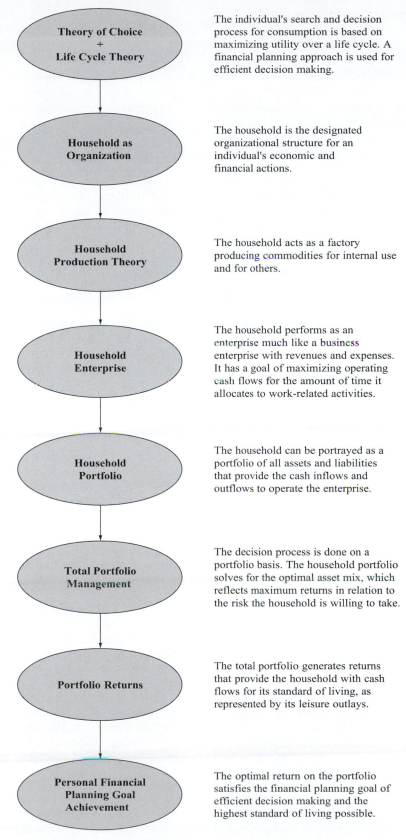

Theory of Choice + Life Cycle Theory

The individual's search and decision process for consumption is based on maximizing utility over a life cycle. A financial planning approach is used for efficient decision making.

Household as Organization

The household is the designated organizational structure for an individual's economic and financial actions.

Household Production Theory

The household acts as a factory producing commodities for internal use and for others.

Household Enterprise

The household performs as an enterprise much like a business enterprise with revenues and expenses. It has a goal of maximizing operating cash flows for the amount of time it allocates to work-related activities.

Household Portfolio

The household can be portrayed as a portfolio of all assets and liabilities that provide the cash inflows and outflows to operate the enterprise.

Total Portfolio Management

The decision process is done on a portfolio basis. The household portfolio solves for the optimal asset mix, which reflects maximum returns in relation to the risk the household is willing to take.

Portfolio Returns

The total portfolio generates returns that provide the household with cash flows for its standard of living, as represented by its leisure outlays.

Personal Financial Planning Goal Achievement

The optimal return on the portfolio satisfies the financial planning goal of efficient decision making and the highest standard of living possible.

Practical Comment PFP Theory—A Practical Modification

The separation of outlays into maintenance and leisure is important to the theory of financial planning. It closely approximates the business division of expenses, profits, and dividends. The goal of life cycle planning is to achieve a smooth standard of living figure that is based on leisure, not total, outlays. Use of this planning approach allows TPM to solve for leisure outlays, which, in theory, are the pure measure of economic well-being.

As an alternative to the separation of expenditures into maintenance and leisure, two other terms are commonly used in finance: *nondiscretionary*

and *discretionary expenses.* Through distinguishing between these two expenses, depending broadly on whether we do or don't have control over them,[20] we capture much of the essence of the original terms without the need for a more strict separation. Under this practical approach, the nondiscretionary and discretionary categories are both considered operating costs. The idea of discretionary expenses as separate pleasure-producing items is maintained.

[20] At least over the shorter term. Of course, we have more control over many items over the longer term.

In sum, we have two approaches. The first approach, which uses maintenance and leisure, is consistent with pure financial planning theory and presents a more straightforward, logical approach to household finance. The second approach, which uses a nondiscretionary and discretionary approach, is more practical.

Because this is a practical text, we will generally use the nondiscretionary and discretionary approach for the balance of the book (e.g., for cash flow statements). We will be careful to retain the basic thought that only certain outlays qualify as pleasure-producing ones. PFP, whose ultimate goal is maximization of utility, has an obligation to call attention to the maintenance-leisure separation so that planning can be effective. For example, a perceived need for a dependable means of transportation actually may be a cover for a pleasure-producing new car. For a further discussion of PFP theory issues, see Appendix III.

In Example 4.3, a practical application of TPM is shown.

Example 4.3

Jan and Jen wanted advice on doing the best they could with their assets. They had $225,000 in stocks and $80,000 in bonds. They had a home worth $200,000 and were thinking of trading up to a new one costing $350,000. Jan worked in the back office of a stock brokerage firm and earned $100,000 a year; Jen was a manager with a local real estate company and earned $75,000 a year. They had $90,000 left in mortgage debt and about $120,000 in overhead expenses. They described their tolerance for risk as aggressive.

They were referred to an investment manager by a couple with whom they were close. The investment manager had performed some investment services for the couple with which they were satisfied. The investment manager told them that he practiced modern portfolio theory. He took into account their tolerance for risk and entered their stocks and bonds in a portfolio model. The output was a reshaping of their stock and bond portfolio with recommendations on specific purchases and sales. The investment manager indicated he had optimized their portfolio using the best market-based investment methods. Jan and Jen wondered why he didn't include their current and proposed real estate investments. They noted that they had the same mix of stocks and bonds as their friends. Although both couples had a similar overall risk tolerance, the other couple held relatively safe employment in contrast to the much more risky positions held by Jan and Jen.

They went to see a financial planner whose services encompassed comprehensive planning and who practiced total portfolio management. He told them he would include all their assets and major debt in his recommendations. He took into account their securities, real estate, and projected life cycle job-related income. He proposed an asset allocation and encouraged them to purchase the more expensive home because the projected returns would be favorable and would further diversify them, thereby reducing their overall risk. He provided a stock and bond breakdown and specific recommendations.

The planner mentioned that his recommendations included reduction in the allocation to stocks because Jan's job at the stock brokerage firm could be affected by a decline in the stock market. A similar relationship between the home and Jen's job was incorporated in calculations of the overall portfolio. The planner told them that the relationships among these factors, which he called their correlations, reduced household diversification and therefore raised its risk. He explained that because of this he had raised the bond allocation.

The planner recommended a figure for overall living costs going forward based on the long-term returns on this total portfolio. His figure included portfolio risk and represented the highest possible living cost given their tolerance for risk.

Jan and Jen found the planner's approach and recommendations attractive. The advice was clearly based on their own personal characteristics. The financial planner had taken into account all their assets, not just stocks and bonds. They particularly appreciated that both financial planning and investment management were integrated in one seamless operation. They decided to proceed with the recommendations and to use this planner for all their future work.

Back to Dan and Laura

HOUSEHOLD FINANCE

Dan and Laura had called and asked for an appointment. I thought to myself that previous discussions about financial planning and the form it had taken evidently had been insufficient. Both still seemed to be concerned about their financial future. They wanted an instant solution to their problems, while I was offering a methodical financial plan. The trigger for a disagreement between them was a casual comment by a couple with whom they were friendly. The couple had no financial concern; they just ran their household like a business.

Dan liked the idea of operating the household as a business and asked if it could be related to his college economic training. Dan vaguely remembered his economics professor discussing home economics and wanted to know if financial planning could be related. Was there any theory of personal financial planning? Or was it just a series of financial facts?

Laura, on the other hand, didn't understand why her husband wanted to know all that "theoretical stuff." Wasn't financial planning just a straightforward process? Wasn't the "cost of time" to which she had heard Dan repeatedly refer just theoretical jargon? After all, no money passed hands. Didn't theory provide a mental headache without any useful result? She asked if they should just concentrate on the facts and the ways of reaching correct decisions and forget about economic principles and financial planning theory.

By this time, Dan and Laura were glaring at each other. I wondered whether this fight was really about another more serious dispute they were having. Or perhaps they were just tense, given their current financial difficulties. It obviously didn't help that baby Brian cried intermittently as the discussion progressed. I decided to end the meeting and promised to get back to them soon. That seemed to break the mood, and they left holding hands, with Brian in a baby carrier that was attached to Dan's shoulders.

Both of you have raised interesting and important questions. Before I begin to answer them, let me say that it is not unusual for couples to differ in their take on planning and problems. Dan appears to approach problems conceptually. People who do this start with the broadest possible view and gradually narrow to the specifics. Laura, on the other hand, is very practical and wants to get to the solution as quickly as possible. It is often an advantage to have both viewpoints when tackling a problem.

Let's start with an explanation of your friends managing their household as a business. We know that in some respects our perception of a household is far from the image of a business. That is principally because the household represents more than just money factors. For example, a multiperson household can represent affection and common interests and a commitment to stay together. But, as you know, our interest is principally financial.

Wherever possible, we attempt to express things in dollar terms. It should come as no surprise to you that even a business can extend beyond money interests. For example, workers may seek to further their interest sometimes to the detriment of the business, and sometimes closely held business owners have goals other than just maximizing profits.

Looking at the household as a business means treating household actions in a carefully thought-out way so that you get the "biggest bang for your buck"—in other words, trying to work hard in order to receive large wages. It means treating household internal operations with thought, weighing whether to perform them yourself or get machines or people to substitute for you. You would do so if it would free up enough valuable time for work or leisure to make it worthwhile. Keep in mind that the greater the cash generated after overhead expense in the time allotted to work-related activities, the greater number of choices you will have. It's clear that your friends have picked up on that approach and its benefit.

Dan, personal financial planning has grown out of home economics. Finance is more practical and uses more advanced analytical tools than the old home economics. There is no established personal financial planning theory yet, but I will propose one. In it, all your resources and your risk preferences will work together in one portfolio to provide efficient decision making and the highest cash flows to achieve your goals. Of course, that is why we are doing this financial plan for you. Household finance is the term that can express your overall financial activities and personal financial planning is the strategic-results-oriented process to achieve them.

Laura, you're right that theory alone will not achieve your goals. But theory can help you understand why we are doing what we do and which tools to use to solve your problems. I agree that theory is of little use to you currently unless specific practical steps are taken that result in progress toward your objectives. I know you would prefer action, but in your case a more systematic step-by-step approach is best. The first action steps will come soon.

As far as the opportunity cost of time is concerned, it is true that no money passes hands when we calculate it. However, it could result in cash flow if you chose to replace your work at home with time in the workforce. The cost of time forces us to recognize that time has value as well, whether in work-related cash flow or leisure terms.

Permit me to again reiterate that both of your approaches to planning have merit. You will learn more about the process and about financial planning theory and its offshoot, total portfolio management, as we go along. I will provide a recommended portfolio incorporating total portfolio management principles at the end of the financial planning process, when all separate planning activities are integrated.

Summary

Household finance and PFP theory reflect the basic thought that a household can be perceived as a business and include all resources in making its decisions. Specifically:

- The household is the organizational structure that incorporates all of a person's or group's financial activities.
- The household signifies logical financial actions and, in the case of several members, it draws their personal financial planning objectives together.
- The household is a functioning enterprise. Its stress on having efficient operations and generating the highest cash flows for the time allocated to work is analogous to a business.
- Household finance is the financial counterpart of the household enterprise. It represents a person's entire financial life. Its origins are in economics and financial concepts such as the theory of choice, life cycle theory, the cost of time, the theory of the firm, modern portfolio theory, and risk-return analysis.

- The opportunity cost of time provides a dollar amount for time spent on nonmoney-producing activities. Assigning a value to time makes it easier to include it in planning and decision making.

- The life cycle theory of savings has strongly influenced personal financial planning. It maintains that people include thinking about their future in their actions today. The strict form of the theory says that people try to even out their resources over their lifetime. However, the approach can allow for more flexible interpretations.

- Household outlays can be separated into nondiscretionary and discretionary outlays. We try to minimize nondiscretionary outlays, or overhead expenses. Discretionary outlays provide us with pleasure, and we strive to increase the money and time connected with them.

- Personal financial planning theory is an integrated overall approach to decision making for household finance. It uses total portfolio management as its underpinning. TPM says that all household assets are included in decision making. The best mix of those assets will lead to the largest cash flow possible within risk and time allocated to this task. This optimal mix satisfies the personal financial planning goal of achieving the highest standard of living possible.

Key Terms

behavioral financial planning, *86*
budget constraint, *76*
capital expenditures, *82*
consumption bundle, *76*
discretionary expenses, *79*
firm, *79*
household, *74*

household enterprise, *80*
household finance, *81*
leisure outlays, *82*
life cycle theory, *77*
modern portfolio theory (MPT), *83*
nondiscretionary expenses, *79*

opportunity cost of time, *79*
overhead costs (maintenance costs), *82*
theory of consumer choice, *76*
total portfolio management (TPM), *85*
utility, *76*

Questions

1. Define the household in financial terms.
2. What makes the household the financial structure for the individual?
3. List some of the advantages and disadvantages of various organizational structures for the individual.
4. How do people choose their goods?
5. How are spending decisions made under the life cycle theory of savings?
6. What does life cycle theory say you should have in savings at the end of the household's life? Is that practical? Explain your answer.
7. Define the term *opportunity cost of time*.
8. Since the cost of time is a noncash charge, why is it important?
9. What makes the household an enterprise?
10. How do finance and economics differ in emphasis?
11. Describe household operations under household finance.
12. Why is it important to differentiate among the various types of household expenditures?
13. Outline the similarities and differences between a household and a business.
14. What is the importance of the theory of financial planning?

Case Application
HOUSEHOLD FINANCE

Richard and Monica asked if they could come in to discuss an issue. At that meeting, Monica seemed worried, and Richard slunk back in his chair. Monica said Richard was having second thoughts about going ahead with the financial plan. He wanted to know what the specific benefits of financial planning were. As far as he was concerned, he said, people's planning took place one paycheck at a time. I could tell by Monica's way of explaining this that she disagreed. She asked for my help in dealing with this problem.

Case Application Questions

1. What do you think is the difference in philosophy between the two?
2. How does the life cycle theory enter the discussion?
3. Based on the original interview and this one, how can looking at the household as a business help?
4. What are the benefits of financial planning for these people?
5. Write up your explanation to their issues and your recommendation.

Appendix I

Leisure Time

Our discussion of leisure time will include how we use the opportunity cost of time to measure leisure as well as how leisure-time decisions relative to work decisions are made. Doing so can help us reach better financial conclusions.

First, let's briefly review. From a classical economic standpoint, we can define *leisure time* activities as expenditures on goods and services that provide utility. If we take into account the opportunity cost of time, we can define *leisure outlays* as expenditures on goods and services plus time spent on activities that provide utility. The combination of expenditures and time form a *leisure commodity*. For example, buying a ticket to a movie plus the time spent watching it result in a leisure commodity. So we can think of leisure as time and money spent on things we enjoy doing.

The view of leisure as a commodity that includes an opportunity cost of time has an important benefit: the ability to include all costs, not just cash expenditures, in computing leisure outlays. Having a fairly gauged standard for calculating leisure outlays allows us to place utility on a plane we can more easily understand and measure in economic and financial terms.

We generally cannot calculate total utility per person, but we are able to analyze marginal utility at equilibrium. *Marginal utility* is the pleasure we get from one additional unit of an item we consume. *Equilibrium* is the state at which two forces—in this case utility and goods purchased—are in balance. At equilibrium, the marginal utility or pleasure from each good or service relative to the price we pay for the good or service is equal. At the same time, the ratio of marginal utility to price for each leisure good is equal to the benefit in cash flow (to be spent on future utility) relative to the cost in displeasure from one additional hour of work. In other words, if we call our benefits-to-cost ratios relative values, in equilibrium all of our marginal actions provide us equal values. If they didn't, we would alter the selections. The equation can be expressed as

$$\frac{MU_x}{P_x} = \frac{MU_y}{P_y} = \cdots = \frac{MU_n}{P_n}$$

where

MU	= Marginal utility
P	= Price in resources of each and time
$x, y, \ldots n$	= Leisure goods

We will illustrate the method of measuring leisure costs and taking those costs into account in affirming our equilibrium analysis.

Example 4.A1.1   Jack spends $10 a visit three times a week renting a tennis court. He plays tennis for one hour each time. He earns $12 an hour in his job. Therefore, his cost of time is $12 for each visit. He goes to the theater once a month, which costs him $34 for each three-hour sitting. Jack decides to set up a utility scale that starts at 100 units. The money he earns by working provides him with 132 units of pleasure per hour. He estimates that the theater gives him 770 units of pleasure each week. In contrast, tennis gives him 242 units of pleasure for each day. He wants to know whether he has a logically placed equilibrium between tennis and theater outlays and whether he should replace leisure activities with additional work.

At equilibrium:

$$\frac{MU_{TE}}{P_{TE}} = \frac{MU_{TH}}{P_{TH}} = \frac{MU_{W}}{P_{W}}$$

where

MU_{TE}	= Marginal utility of a unit of tennis
MU_{TH}	= Marginal utility of a unit of theater
MU_{W}	= Marginal utility of an hour of work
P_{TE}	= Cost of a unit of tennis
P_{TH}	= Cost of a unit of theater
P_{W}	= Cost of an hour of work

Since

$$\begin{aligned} \text{Marginal price of tennis} &= \text{Cash outlays} + \text{Cost of time} \\ &= \$10 + \$12 \\ &= \$22 \end{aligned}$$

and

$$\text{Marginal utility of tennis} = 242$$

$$MU_{TE} = 242$$
$$P_{TE} = 22$$

$$\frac{MU_{TE}}{P_{TE}} = \frac{242}{22} = 11$$

$$\text{Marginal price of theater} = \text{Cash outlays } + \text{ Cost of time}$$
$$= \$34 + \$36$$
$$= \$70$$

and

$$\text{Marginal utility of theater} = 770$$

$$\text{MU}_{\text{TH}} = 770$$
$$P_{\text{TH}} = 70$$

$$\frac{\text{MU}_{\text{TH}}}{P_{\text{TH}}} = \frac{770}{70} = 11$$

$$\text{MU}_{\text{W}} = 132$$
$$P_{\text{W}} = 12$$

$$\frac{\text{MU}_{\text{W}}}{P_{\text{W}}} = \frac{132}{12} = 11$$

Jack spends over three times as much money for the theater as for one game of tennis. However, the utility per unit of cost of 11 is the same for tennis and the theater. Jack has selected his leisure activities properly. His benefit-to-cost ratio for work is equal to that for leisure activities. He should not alter his labor-leisure ratio because Jack is at equilibrium.

Note that any leisure item considered would have as its benchmark comparison the utility in earning cash from one more hour of work.

Our analysis can be extended so that we can compare decision making among individuals for the same leisure opportunity. A person with a low cost of living and great satisfaction from "doing nothing" will have a consumption pattern different from that of a person who enjoys "keeping up with the Joneses."

Example 4.A1.2   Kate and Evelyn are computer programmers, both employed by the same company. Each earns $35 an hour and works 2,000 hours a year. Both are offered some additional work on Saturdays at $50 an hour. Kate has a modest cost of living and spends Saturdays with her family. She rejects the additional pay, even at $50 an hour, as insufficient to compensate for the pleasure of relaxation and family interaction. Therefore, her marginal utility for current leisure exceeds $50 an hour. Kate has actually requested a reduced four-day work schedule. Evelyn, who has a high cost of living and would like to retire at age 55, accepts the Saturday offer thinking that her leisure time today is less important than the consumption of leisure time starting at age 55. Her marginal utility for current leisure is less than $50 an hour. Notice that each is optimizing her own choices or bundles of consumption commodities.

Our discussions using the cost of time have enabled us to take a seeming intangible, consumer satisfaction, and describe it in money terms. In this way we are able to mainstream leisure into the financial decision-making process. By using dollars to describe leisure alternatives, we can accommodate virtually any lifestyle including one that emphasizes keeping dollar earnings to a minimum.

In other words, the marginal utility of leisure can help us come to better personal financial planning conclusions concerning work and leisure, including which leisure activity to select. It can do so by incorporating time as well as cash outlays in the decision framework and placing a cost on each.

Equilibrium analysis is provided in Appendix II. Table 4.A1.1 presents how the average man and woman spend their time.

TABLE 4.A1.1
Time Allocation for Men and Women, 1981 (hours per week)

Source: Adapted from Thomas Juster and Frank Stafford, "The Allocation of Time: Empirical Findings, Behavioral Models, and Problems of Measurement," *Journal of Economic Literature* 29, no. 2 (June 1991), pp. 471–522, (Table 1, p. 475).

	Men	Women
Market work[1]	44.0	23.9
Housework	13.8	30.5
Total work	57.8	54.4
Personal care[2]	68.2	71.6
Leisure	41.8	41.9
Adult education	0.6	0.4
Social interaction	14.9	17.6
Active leisure	5.6	4.2
Passive Leisure	20.8	19.8
Total time	168.0	168.0

[1] Includes 3.5 hours for men, 2.0 hours for women commuting.
[2] Includes 57.9 hours of sleep for men and 59.9 for women.

Appendix II

Equilibrium Analysis: Labor and Leisure Hours

The assumption of constant labor and leisure hours makes decision making for the household simpler to describe and quantify. Clearly, in a business, the goal is to earn the most money possible. We can call its objective the maximization of cash flows. The business will produce and expand as much as possible as long as it is profitable to do so. Equilibrium is set and they stop when the revenue they get from an extra unit of output exactly equals the cost of producing that unit. Similarly, equilibrium is set and households want to maximize their operating cash flow given a certain amount of time devoted to work. They stop working when the benefit they get from an extra hour of work revenues equals the cost in forgone leisure pleasure. The difficulty is in fixing the amount of work time.

For example, if a person were to receive a raise in salary, the labor-leisure ratio cannot be precisely determined. Higher pay could result in more hours worked since it would be more financially rewarding. Economists call that "the substitution effect." Alternatively, the raise could lower the hours worked and increase leisure time because, if the same income is desired, it can now be received with less work effort. Economists call this the "income effect." The household's choice will depend on the marginal utility of work versus that for leisure, given the higher income. The process was described in Appendix I.

By assuming no change in overall labor or leisure hours, we can express the outcome in exact dollars. A $10,000 increase in after-tax salary is equal to a $10,000 rise in cash flow from operations. A fixed labor-leisure ratio highlights internal household operations. It suggests a focus on making the household operate as efficiently as possible.

Many people work in one job in which their salary and work hours are determined. The emphasis then is entirely on household efficiency. The focus is similar to the business focus on efficient operations. Think of it as an eyewear store in a shopping mall in which the prices of a visit and a pair of glasses are set by the market. By mall contract, the store can stay open only for 12 hours a day, and it is currently at capacity—that is, the store is unable to accept more than its current volume of clients each day. Therefore, the store can generate higher cash flows only by becoming more efficient in its operations.

As a practical matter, although the fixed labor-leisure assumption makes outcomes clearer to measure, the assumption is not necessary. The point is that the household will attempt to operate as efficiently as possible and maximize its operating cash flows both before and after a change in incomes and at whatever labor-leisure ratio it establishes.

Appendix III

The Life Cycle Theory of Savings

The classical approach to savings comes from Modigliani in his *life cycle theory of savings*.[21] As we saw, for Modigliani, consumption decisions are based not on the amount of income we generate currently, but on the amount of income we expect to earn over our life cycle. Household income may fluctuate from year to year, but we seek to maintain a constant standard of living throughout our lifetime.

According to this theory, the value of all household assets is assessed at a given point in time. Assets are separated into work-related and other assets. The stream of work-related income is brought back to the present using a market-provided discount rate to establish an asset value. Other assets, assumed to be marketable assets that are owned by the household, also are evaluated. We then plan to consume the income and principal from those assets in a way that will result in level expenditures over our lifetime.

Given the desire for level expenditures over our life cycle, we might create negative savings in life by borrowing money when income is low; then, as our income rises, pay off the debt and save for retirement. In retirement, when our work-related revenues have stopped, savings would be liquidated steadily to maintain our cost of living.

At death no assets would remain. The implication is that a change in one year's income—for example, a large bonus received—will not alter our spending habits. Spending patterns will only be changed by a permanent shift in expectations of future income.

The Modigliani life cycle formula is

$$c = \frac{y + (N - t) \times y^e + a}{L_t}$$

$$\text{Current consumption} = \frac{\text{Current income} + \left(\text{Expected retirement age} - \text{Current age} \right) \times \text{Projected yearly income} + \text{Current assets}}{\text{Remaining life span}}$$

where

c = Current consumption

y = Current income

a = Current assets

t = Current age of the household

y^e = Projected yearly income

N = Expected retirement age

$(N - t)$ = Expected remaining earning span in years

L = The life span

L_t = $L - t + 1$ = Remaining life span at age t

---

[21] Franco Modigliani and Richard Brumberg, "Utility Analysis and the Consumption Function: An Interpretation of the Cross Section Data," in K. Kurihara, ed., *Post-Keynesian Economics* (New Brunswick, NJ: Rutgers University Press, 1954); Franco Modigliani and Richard Brumberg, "Utility Analysis and Aggregate Consumption Function: An Attempt at Integration," in A. Abel, ed., *Collected Papers of Franco Modigliani*, Vol. 2 (Cambridge, MA: MIT Press, 1979).

For a variant on the theory, called "the permanent income hypothesis," see Milton Friedman, *A Theory of the Consumption Function* (Princeton, NJ: Princeton University Press, 1957).

The formula indicates that consumption is developed by taking current income y, plus the value of total future income $(N - t) \times y^e$, plus the value of current assets a, and dividing the sum of the three by the remaining life span in years. Put more simply

$$\text{Current consumption} = \frac{\text{Current income} + \text{Projected future income} + \text{Current assets}}{\text{Remaining life span}}$$

By dividing all our income and assets by the number of years we have remaining, we arrive at the maximum consumption we can afford. This model assumes that we know many variables such as the date of death with certainty. The critical underlying assumption of the model—that consumption today is not related to current but projected future life cycle income—is illustrated in Example 4.A3.1.

Example 4.A3.1   Jamie, 35, worked as a medical resident for Techno Corporation. She made $45,000 a year but knew that she would make $90,000 a year in real terms starting next year as a full-fledged physician and thereafter; she had $255,000 in assets accumulated today. Assume Jamie knew she would work until age 65 and die at age 84 and that the discount rate was equal to the growth rate in future salary. Therefore, her salary can be considered flat over time. Assume Jamie would not be eligible for Social Security payments. What will her cost of living be?

$$c = \frac{y + (N - t) \times y^e + a}{L_t}$$

$$= \frac{45,000 + (65 - 35) \times 90,000 + 255,000}{84 - 35 + 1}$$

$$= \frac{45,000 + 30 \times 90,000 + 255,000}{50}$$

$$= \frac{3,000,000}{50}$$

$$= \$60,000 \text{ per year}$$

Notice that her cost of living is not significantly dependent on her current salary; it is related to her current assets and projected lifetime income. Jamie's cost of living throughout her lifetime has to be adjusted to plan for 20 years of expected retirement with no income at retirement time other than the amount accumulated from prior investments.

Appendix IV

Divisions

As we have seen, household operations consist of generation of revenues, household expenses in support of revenues that include basic human needs, and outlays of time and money on pleasurable activities. We can call them *divisions*. The first division can be termed the *production* division. It produces the resources the household needs to sustain itself and includes the expenses that support it. The second division can be termed the *distribution* division. It spends resources on things that we enjoy doing.

This setup is not unlike a business that has multiple divisions. Use of it can shed light on the idea of the leisure dividend. Like a business, the household declares a dividend. However, business operations stop with the payment of the dividends. The household's activities are broader and include decision making on how the dividend is spent.

The household enterprise uses business techniques in both production and distribution activities. Both want to be as efficient as possible in pursuing their objective. Money generated from the production division not reserved for future use is paid to the distribution division in the form of a cash outflow, a dividend. The distribution division records it as revenues available to spend. When the two divisions are consolidated, the production outflow and the distribution inflow drop out.

What we are left with on a total household basis is revenues less overhead costs from the production division and outflows on leisure activities from the distribution division. In common, financial parlance, broadly speaking, overhead costs and leisure outlays are called nondiscretionary and discretionary expenses. We will generally use that terminology throughout the book.

However, we will retain the idea of a dividend. It helps focus on the difference between the two types of expenses, one for a necessity and the other for a pleasurable activity. The leisure dividend is far different from a maintenance cost. That is why in this book we have generally called leisure an outlay instead of an expense.

Chapter Five

Financial Statements Analysis

Chapter Goals

This chapter will enable you to:

- Recognize the importance of financial statements to PFP.
- Produce and evaluate a balance sheet.
- Construct a cash flow statement.
- Compare finance and accounting-based techniques.

Laura dropped in while her mother was taking care of baby Brian one afternoon. She said she felt uncomfortable about her lack of understanding of financial statements. She said sheepishly that she didn't know what a balance sheet and a functional cash flow statement were. Could I help?

Real Life Planning

Todd and Julia were a young couple whose lifestyle was on a fast track. Todd was a lawyer with a nonprofit company and enjoyed his work for it. Julia was a writer whose novels were only modestly successful. They entertained lavishly and were known in their small town for the parties they had.

Neither Todd nor Julia had large work-related incomes. Julia's parents had both passed away at an early age and had left her a significant-sized inheritance. When the advisor interviewed them, it became apparent that they had no idea about their finances. When asked about their yearly savings, they said they were strong savers but didn't know the amount. Then they mentioned that they had a home equity loan and borrowed money and paid off debt all the time; sometimes they sold some of the securities from Julia's inheritance to pay off some debt. They wanted to do even more entertaining and asked how much they could afford.

The advisor decided to begin by constructing a balance sheet and cash flow statement. The balance sheet showed that they had assets that chiefly consisted of a house worth $400,000 and securities from the inheritance amounting to $250,000. They had no idea what the market value of these securities was. The advisor asked the amount of the original investment and found out it had been $450,000.

The decline in investment assets despite a favorable stock market was surprising and the advisor made a mental note to use it as a check against the results of the cash flow statement. However, nothing prepared him for the $410,000 combined mortgage and home equity line on the house. In effect, the couple had no equity in their home even though their original mortgage was for much less. The only reason the home equity line was extended for so much money was that Julia's assets were pledged as collateral against the loan.

The cash flow statement disclosed a large negative cash flow each year. Their negative cash outflow from operations was made up through both additional borrowing and liquidation of securities.

The advisor showed them the balance sheet and cash flow statement. The balance sheet indicated what their assets, liabilities, and net worth were now as compared with two years ago. It confirmed that their assets had declined and their obligations were higher now.

Julia mentioned that their net cash flow was positive in recent years. She asked, "Why the concern?" The advisor explained that the only reason for the positive amounts was the combination of asset liquidation and increased borrowing. Their true operating figures a few lines up on the cash flow statement showed large deficits. If they continued the way they were going, they would run out of money before too long.

Both Todd and Julia were visibly shaken. Todd mumbled that he had no idea things were so bad. The advisor was not surprised. In his experience, many people were financially unsophisticated and did not even know what a balance sheet and cash flow statement were for. He wondered what percentage balanced their checkbooks.

He spent some time educating them in basic finance, presented options, and recommended that they be placed on a budget. They said little and left.

Three weeks later, all three sat down again. Todd and Julia said that their plans for future parties would be scaled down sharply. Todd was looking for a new position with a law firm that would pay considerably more money. Not so surprisingly, they wouldn't adhere to a detailed budget but agreed to hard figures for debt reduction and cash savings. They called it their financial diet. We scheduled the next meeting, and I noted they had their old enthusiasm back. When given some financial knowledge, in part through examining financial statements, and keeping to a financial regimen, even a loosely structured one, positive things could happen.

OVERVIEW

Financial statement analysis is a key part of the planning process. Our objective often is to make a preliminary assessment of the financial health of the household early in the data-gathering process. With some experience, we may be able to obtain a rough indication of assets and liabilities accumulated. We should then draw up an accurate balance sheet as part of the planning process.

The second financial statement we are usually interested in is the one that presents the household's cash flow. Cash flow is at the heart of PFP. It is difficult for many to balance current living needs and preferences with savings. The cash flow statement tells you how you are doing today and sets the stage for any steps that need be taken to alter future activities. A projected cash flow statement can provide further structure and insight.

This chapter shows you how to construct both statements and discusses related issues.

THE BALANCE SHEET

The **balance sheet** is a statement of financial position at a given point in time. When describing personal statements it is often referred to as the **statement of financial position.** It consists of all your assets, your liabilities, and your net worth. The first assets listed are generally current assets. **Current assets** are those that are expected to be or can be converted into cash in the current year. Included are checking account, money market funds, and refunds due such as those on catalogue purchases. **Marketable investments** are those that are traded publicly—for example, stocks and bonds. Retirement investments that are not available for current use are treated separately. Real estate typically refers to the home while **household assets**—a car, furniture, and appliances, for example—are those used in day-to-day household activities. Other assets are a miscellaneous category that can include such things as jewelry and art.

The most prominent asset for the household is typically the future income stream of its wage earners, called **human assets.** Because they cannot be sold, however, human assets are not usually placed on balance sheets. **Human-related assets** is a broader term that includes other forms of resources in addition to human assets that are omitted from the balance sheet. The term *human-related* is used because the value is derived from human-related work efforts or human relationships. Included are pension plans that pay out yearly income upon retirement such as Social Security or company pensions. Expected gifts or inheritances based on relationships are a further example.

Liabilities are items the household owes. They are placed on the right-hand side of the balance sheet. Credit card debts, taxes outstanding, and mortgage debt are all liabilities. They too can be split into current and long term, based on whether they are due within one year or beyond that period. The mortgage payment due within the year is expressed as a current liability.

Household equity, another name for **household net worth,** is the difference between its assets and liabilities. It is intended to show how much the household is worth at that point in time. Household equity can be relatively small or even negative when household members are young and college debt and other obligations are high. Net worth generally increases as the marketable investment portion rises. The process of generating net worth is shown in the simple example below, Example 5.1.

Example 5.1

Tricia had a $20,000 savings account, owned a car valued at $12,000, and owed $9,000 that she had borrowed to help finance the car. Calculate her net worth and explain the process.

Assets	$32,000
Liabilities	(9,000)
Net worth	$23,000

Although Tricia has assets of $32,000, there are obligations against those assets of $9,000. Consequently, her net worth, the equity she has built up over time, is $23,000.

The balance sheet has many formats. A common one is shown in Table 5.1. Example 5.2 uses that balance sheet.

Example 5.2

Shirley had $500 in cash, $12,500 in stock, and $2,500 in bonds and owned a car worth $12,000. She had $2,000 in credit card payments, an education loan of $8,000 with payments not due to begin for three years, and a mortgage loan of $144,000 with $5,000 due this year. She owned a home worth $175,000, furniture and fixtures of $3,000, appliances with a value of $4,000, and jewelry of $5,000. She expects to pay her mortgage and other obligations from current year's earnings. Her balance sheet is shown below.

Household Balance Sheet 12/31/06

Assets		Liabilities	
Current Assets		**Current Liabilities**	
Cash	$500	Credit card payment	$2,000
Total Current Assets	$500	Current portion mortgage loan	$5,000
		Total Current Liabilities	$7,000

(continued)

(Concluded)

Household Balance Sheet 12/31/06

Assets		Liabilities	
Marketable Investments			
Bonds and bond funds	$2,500	**Long-Term Liabilities**	
Stocks and stock funds	$12,500	Mortgage loan	$139,000
Total Marketable Investments	$15,000	Education loan	$8,000
		Total Long-Term Liabilities	$147,000
Real Estate			
Home	$175,000		
Total Real Estate	$175,000	**Total Liabilities**	**$154,000**
Household Assets			
Autos	$12,000		
Furniture and fixtures	$3,000		
Appliances	$4,000		
Total Household Assets	$19,000		
		EQUITY	
Other Assets			
Jewelry	$5,000	Household equity	$60,500
Total Other Assets	$5,000	**Total Equity**	$60,500
Total Assets	**$214,500**	**Total Liabilities and Equity**	**$214,500**

A summary and explanation of balance sheet items appears in Table 5.2.

TABLE 5.1
Household Balance Sheet 12/31/06

Assets	Liabilities
Current Assets	**Current Liabilities**
Checking accounts	Credit card debt
Money market funds	Other current debt
Refund due on returned clothing	Current portion
Total Current Assets	**Total Current Liabilities**
Marketable Investments	**Long-Term Liabilities**
Bonds and bond funds	Mortgage
Stocks and stock funds	Other long-term debt
Total Marketable Investments	**Total Long-Term Liabilities**
Pension Assets	**Total Liabilities**
401(k) plans	
IRAs	
Total Pension Assets	
Real Estate	
Home	
Total Real Estate	
Household Assets	
Autos	
Furniture and fixtures	
Total Household Assets	
Other Assets	**EQUITY**
Jewelry	
Stamp collection	Household equity
Total Other Assets	**Total Equity**
Total Assets	**Total Liabilities and Equity**

TABLE 5.2 Balance Sheet Items Explanation

Category	Definition	Examples
Assets		
Current assets	Those intended to be liquidated within the year.	Checking accounts, tax refunds, merchandise refunds not yet received.
Marketable investments	Financial assets that can be turned into cash.	Stocks, bonds, mutual funds.
Retirement investments	Financial assets in individual or company plans.	Stocks, bonds, mutual funds.
Real estate	Property attached to land. Generally, the land and property on it are given a combined valuation.	Home, investments in other property.
Household assets	Assets used in household operations.	Car, furniture, household, appliances.
Other assets	A miscellaneous category.	Jewelry, stamp collection, etc.
Liabilities		
Current liabilities	Those expected to be paid within the current year.	Those expected to be paid currently, taxes due, current portion of mortgage on house.
Long-term liabilities	Due beyond the current year. When there are few, they may be clustered together.	Mortgage, home equity loan, long-term credit card debt, amounts owed to parents.
Equity		
Total equity	Generally a one-line category representing net worth.	Combined assets less combined liabilities.

THE CASH FLOW STATEMENT

The **cash flow statement** is perhaps the single best measurement of the financial performance and therefore the health of the household. It does so by representing how much cash has been generated over a period of time. When describing personal statements it is sometimes referred to as the **statement of cash flow.** All household operations that require financial resources are included. The word *flow* indicates that it measures results between two periods, say between the end of last year and the end of this year.

The cash flow approach contrasts with that of the balance sheet, which provides figures as of a period of time—for example, as of the end of this year. The amount of water in a pond is constant at any point in time like a balance sheet, whereas a stream has water entering and leaving like a cash flow statement with change measured by the strength of its flow from the beginning to the end of the period.

The cash flow statement is fairly simple to understand and measure. Your cash generated is the difference between the cash you started and ended the period with. As you might expect, it is determined by totaling the sources of cash—your cash inflows—and subtracting from it the uses of cash—your cash outflows. For example, revenues you received from your job are a source of cash while rent you have paid would result in an outflow of cash.

Under our household finance approach, which entails running the household as a business, we can benefit from a detailed cash flow statement. We can call that document a **functional cash flow statement.** This functional statement separates cash flows by type of household activity. There are basically three types: operating, financing, and investment activities. Investments are separated into capital expenditures, which are shown separately, and financial investments, which are grouped last with remaining cash flows, which is our period savings figures.

Use of a functional cash flow statement permits a clearer description of household results for the period and an easier comparison with other periods. It is structured as a blend of the business income statement and its cash flow statements. Not so incidentally, the cash flow statement for a business is also separated by function. The major parts of this household functional cash flow statement—operating activities, capital expenditures, financing activities, and savings—are discussed below.

Practical Comment   Cash Flow and Debt

People sometimes get confused by debt's impact. They believe that repayment of debt is a good practice, which is of course true; however, they confuse lower debt with having higher cash flow for that period. The cash flow statement focuses on cash only. Borrowing $10,000 has the same effect on cash as earning a $10,000 after-tax bonus. That is why it is best to treat debt in a separate section and to look beyond the bottom line cash number. By doing so, we can judge operating performance before the sometimes substantial influences of increases or repayments of borrowings. A closer examination of that section would show that although debt repayment is often regarded as a positive development, it remains a negative cash flow item.

Operating Activities

Operating activities are the day-to-day financial functions of the household. This part of the household functional statement closely resembles a business income statement. The principal difference is that the household statement is recorded on a strict cash basis while the business one includes noncash items.

The operations segment can be segregated into cash inflows and outflows that we will call income and expenses. Income consists of salary, investment returns, and other sources of operating cash. Expenses can be divided into nondiscretionary and discretionary items. Nondiscretionary expenses are the household's overhead items such as interest expense, rent, household, food, clothing, and taxes.[1] These are largely fixed costs: We cannot alter them easily, particularly over shorter periods of time. Discretionary expenses are those you choose to make, principally because you get pleasure from them. Examples are entertainment, eating out, and vacation outlays.

The difference between income and expenses is cash flow from operations.

Capital Expenditures

Capital expenditures are outlays on household-related matters that provide benefit beyond the current year. They are a form of investment, as we will see in Chapter 8. Included are such items as cars, furniture, fixtures, and appliances. We want to display them separately because these cash outflows don't occur regularly, so to include them with other costs could distort the operating figures.

For example, a comparison of this year's operating cash flow with last year's would be clearer if it excluded a $20,000 payment to buy a car. The purchase of a car is a once in, say, five-year occurrence. By placing it in a separate section of the cash flow statement, we can more easily compare this year's operating activities with last year's. In addition to their positioning on the cash flow statement, the individual capital expenditures, particularly if they are large, also are placed as assets on the balance sheet.

Financing Activities

Financing activities are the cash flows that come from changes in debt. Borrowing money has a favorable impact on cash flow because it increases the cash available. Repaying debt has a negative effect on cash flow because it reduces cash resources.

Additions to, or subtractions from, debt are reflected in the total debt outstanding, placed as liabilities on the balance sheet.[2]

---

[1] Taxes are sometimes shown as a separate category below nondiscretionary and discretionary expenses.

[2] Capital expenditures are also a form of investment, but, in people's thinking and in practice, they are segregated from financial investments on the cash flow statement.

Savings

Savings is the cash left over after our operating, capital expenditure, and debt activities. It is also known, for financial statement purposes, as **cash flow,** representing prior cash inflows minus cash outflows. Investments that are not in the form of capital expenditures are treated as part of the savings section. Thus, savings placed into vehicles such as stocks is handled here.[3]

Savings can be outlaid for specific purposes such as retirement or a down payment on a home. The amount of cash available after such targeted investing is called **net cash flow.** Net cash flow is the bottom line on the cash flow statement. It is the savings available for further investing or for spending in the next period.

When the net cash flow figure is negative, it can be due to targeted investing. Alternatively, the figure may be positive only because of borrowing during the period. When there is a significant negative net cash flow figure before targeted investing, or a positive one only because of borrowing, further analysis and possibly changes in household operations may be called for.

Savings applied to investing such as amounts for stocks and bonds add to the amount shown under marketable securities in the balance sheet. Savings left in cash are included under cash at period-end on the balance sheet. Balance sheet cash at the end of the period less cash at the beginning of the period equals net cash flow on the cash flow statement for that time frame.

A functional cash flow statement is provided in Table 5.3.

Traditional Household Cash Flow Statement

In practice, many people currently use a cash flow statement that groups all inflows and outflows together and makes few or no distinctions between flows based on operating, capital expenditures, and debt repayment. In that statement, paydown of debt and interest payments are lumped together and income tax payments are often placed at the bottom, just before the net cash flow figure. This approach, which we can call a **traditional cash flow statement,** ends up with the same net cash flow figure; its advantages are simplicity and custom. However, it is less useful as an analytical document for financial planners and individuals. This type of cash flow statement, using the same categories that appear in Table 5.3, is shown in Table 5.4.

---

[3] Keep in mind that interest on the debt is not placed in the finance section. It is a nondiscretionary overhead cost. It must be paid until the debt is retired. Interest expense is not included on the balance sheet.

TABLE 5.3
Functional Cash Flow Statement

	2006	2007	2008	2009	2010
Operating Activities					
Income					
Salary					
Business					
Investment					
Other					
Total Income					
Expenses					
Nondiscretionary					
Housing upkeep					
Health care					
Insurance					
Interest					
Alimony					
Food					

(continued)

	2006	2007	2008	2009	2010
Operating Activities					
Expenses (continued)					
Clothing					
Transportation					
Personal					
Taxes					
Total Nondiscretionary Expenses					
Cash Flow before Discretionary Activities					
Discretionary					
Recreation/entertainment					
Personal					
Vacations					
Gifts and charitable contributions					
Hobbies					
Interest					
Other					
Total Discretionary Expenses					
Cash Flow from Operating Activities					
Capital Expenditures					
Discretionary					
Nondiscretionary					
Total Capital Expenditures					
Financing Activities					
Total repayments					
Additional debt					
Total Financing Activities					
CASH FLOW					
Targeted for retirement					
Targeted for other					
Net Cash Flow					

	2006	2007	2008	2009	2010
Income					
Salary					
Business					
Investment					
Other					
Total Income					
Expenses					
Mortgages and property taxes					
Housing upkeep					
Food					
Clothing					
Health care					
Transportation					
Insurance					
Recreation and entertainment					
Vacations					
Hobbies					
Gifts and charitable contributions					
Contributions to pensions					
Net additional debt proceeds					
Capital expenditures					
Interest					
Other					
Taxes					
Total Expenses					
CASH FLOW					

Practical Comment Estimating Expenditures

People often have problems portraying their actual expenditures accurately:

1. Generally they underestimate their expenses. In budgeting, they think of those continuing expenses that they can remember and often exclude less frequent expenditures. The problem can be overcome by using software programs detailing records of expenditures, or through hard copies of records of checks paid and actual bank and investment account cash deposits and withdrawals. The simplest way to find out whether the estimation of past expenses is generally accurate is to use records of last year's actual savings. By recording take-home (after-tax) income plus other cash inflows and subtracting the amounts deposited into savings accounts, you can obtain actual cash expenditures. We

know that often estimated expenses will be materially lower than actual ones. An "other" category representing the balance between the two should be established and generally carried forward in projections of future expenses.

2. Many people and some programs blur or eliminate the distinctions between assets and liabilities, income and expenses, and cash inflows and outflows. For example, their cash flow statement includes repayment of debt, treating it inaccurately as an expense. There are many who view it as such. The paydown of mortgage debt increases the projected net cash you would receive on the sale of a home and therefore your net worth. As we've seen, mortgage debt is best placed under a financing category on a functional cash flow statement.

In Table 5.5 you see the differences between a functional cash flow statement and a traditional one, followed in Example 5.3 by a practical example of the use of a functional statement.

TABLE 5.5
Household Statement of Cash Flows

	Traditional Statement	Functional Statement
Calculates net cash flows properly	Yes	Yes
Develops separate operational income statement	No	Yes
Resembles business cash flow statement	No	Yes
Segregates capital expenditures and financing activities	No	Yes
Separates nondiscretionary and discretionary costs	Sometimes	Yes
Handles revenues properly	Yes	Yes
Is more simple	Yes	No
Is more informative	No	Yes

Example 5.3 Spencer had the following statistics for the past two years. Construct his functional cash flow statement and calculate his cash flow for the year.

	Last Year	This Year
Salary	$120,000	$140,000
Investment income	4,000	3,000
Discretionary expenses	45,000	55,000
Nondiscretionary expenses	50,000	52,000
Capital expenditures	10,000	18,000
Debt—increase/decrease	8,000	(13,000)
Retirement investments	$12,000	$14,000

SPENCER
Functional Cash Flow Statement

	Last Year	This Year
Income		
Salary	$120,000	$140,000
Investment income	4,000	3,000
Total Income	$124,000	$143,000
Expenses		
Nondiscretionary	$50,000	$52,000
Discretionary	45,000	55,000
Total Expenses	$95,000	$107,000
Cash Flow from Operations	$29,000	$36,000
Capital Expenditures	($10,000)	($18,000)
Financing Activities	8,000	13,000
Cash Flow	$27,000	$5,000
Retirement investments	($12,000)	($14,000)
Net Cash Flow	**$15,000**	**($9,000)**

As you can see, Spencer had a positive cash flow of $15,000 last year and a negative one of $9,000 this year. The $9,000 negative figure is somewhat misleading, however. The functional statement allowed us to see that cash flow from operations actually rose from $29,000 to $36,000 in the new year. It was the increase in capital expenditures and, most important, the paydown of debt this year, in contrast to the increase in borrowings last year, that led to the negative cash flow figure. As we discussed, the reduction in debt this year is actually favorable.

FINANCIAL STATEMENT PRESENTATION

Financial statements are intended to make the household's financial circumstances as clear as possible. A number of situations call for either the separation of figures on the statement or, more frequently, footnotes to them. Some typical areas that require separate treatment, often involving taxation matters, are discussed below for the balance sheet and the cash flow statement.

Balance Sheet

Retirement Assets

Retirement assets that are in pension accounts typically consist of marketable assets such as stocks and bonds.[4] They should be listed separately for two reasons. First, unlike personal ones, retirement assets often cannot be turned into cash immediately or at least not without penalty. For example, many firms impose limits on taking money from pension plans, and the government generally imposes a 10 percent penalty on qualified pension withdrawals prior to age 59½.[5]

---

[4] Pensions by companies or the government that provide guaranteed income at retirement generally are not listed on the balance sheet.

[5] Several exceptions to the 10 percent penalty on premature distributions exist, including distributions because of permanent/total disability, payment for health insurance premiums while unemployed, purchase of a house (a penalty-free withdrawal of up to $10,000 for first-time home buyers), distributions made to you after you separated from service and you are over age 55, receipt of money as part of substantially equal payments for your lifetime, distributions required as part of a qualified domestic relations court order (QDRO), and money withdrawn for educational purposes or for widows or others aged 59½ or over.

The second reason is that normal withdrawals from pensions are taxable. It can be useful to know what pensions would be worth on an after-withdrawal, after-tax basis. Where such withdrawals are scheduled to be made over a relatively short period of years, it is helpful to footnote the potential impact of taxation.

Life Insurance

Much life insurance has no current value or a low cash value relative to its face amount. If there is a significant cash value, it belongs on the balance sheet. The face value, the amount to be paid in the event of death during the period the policy is in effect, should be given in a footnote.

Taxation and Unrealized Appreciation

Investment assets are expressed on the balance sheet at their current value. It is useful for a footnote to the balance sheet to give their cost individually or, if there are many assets, a total cost figure. In that way, the effect of taxation on the gain upon ultimate sale can be estimated.

Liquidation Cost

Whenever we expect the proceeds from sale to be materially lower than the value placed on the balance sheet, it is a good idea to footnote the amount of liquidation costs and net proceeds. For example, if a large amount was placed in an asset that had an 8 percent redemption fee and there was a reasonable chance for liquidation, the footnote could say "subject to an 8 percent redemption fee."

Cash Flow Statement

The footnotes here often provide further information on special charges for the year. For example, the housing category could footnote a large $3,000 repair on a home. Where the other category is used for all miscellaneous expenses, the footnote could explain the substantial components of that category year by year.

PRO FORMA STATEMENTS

Pro forma statements are statements that include projections. The two statements we have been concerned with in this chapter, the cash flow statement and the balance sheet, both can include projected amounts. The previous tables that showed functional and traditional cash flow statements and provided for future-year figures in addition to current-year actuals were therefore, in part, pro forma. A written household budget and a statement providing projected retirement or insurance needs are also examples of pro forma statements.

We include projections in a statement to better anticipate needs, to forecast resources to meet those needs, and to adjust our plans accordingly. For example, our projections of a need to renovate our home over a period of years at a cost of $50,000 can lead to its focused attention in our savings rate and living costs.

Pro Forma Cash Flow Statement

There are two principal approaches to making projections for a cash flow statement: the common rate and the separately estimated rate or amount.

Common Rate

The common rate is the rate of annual increase that many household expenses share. As financial planners know, that increase is often based on an assumed future inflation rate. In the absence of specific information to the contrary, this rate is employed for much of the anticipated revenue and the majority of projected increases in expenditures.

Separate Rate

Certain inflows and outflows cannot be estimated by using a projected rise in inflation. Increases in salaries, particularly among younger workers, will be projected using a separate rate. Investment income can be projected based on an assumed return. Insurance costs are based on contractual rates, and mortgage interest and principal payments also are stated in the contract. Lumpy outlays[6] or capital expenditures may be preplanned at a set amount. On the other hand, certain child costs including those for college will be established in current terms and may rise at a rate that differs from inflation.

In Table 5.6 you see a breakdown of common projections.

[6] Those that don't occur in a steady yearly stream.

TABLE 5.6
Projected Cash Flow Statement

	Explanation for Projections
Operating Activities	
Income	
Salary	As separately estimated or rate of inflation
Business	As separately estimated or rate of inflation
Investment	Assumed rate of return
Other	
Total Income	
Expenses	
Nondiscretionary	
Housing upkeep	Rate of inflation
Health care	Rate of inflation
Insurance	Per contract where fixed; otherwise, rate of inflation
Interest	Per debt outstanding
Alimony	As stated
Food	Rate of inflation
Clothing	Rate of inflation
Transportation	Rate of inflation
Personal	Rate of inflation
Taxes	Based on separate tax calculation
Total Nondiscretionary Expenses	
Cash Flow before Discretionary Activities	
Discretionary	
Recreation/entertainment	Rate of inflation
Personal	Rate of inflation
Vacations	Rate of inflation
Gifts and charitable contributions	Rate of inflation
Hobbies	Rate of inflation
Interest	At stated rate
Other	Rate of inflation
Total Discretionary Expenses	
Cash Flow from Operating Activities	
Capital Expenditures	
Discretionary	As separately estimated or rate of inflation
Nondiscretionary	As separately estimated or rate of inflation
Total Capital Expenditures	
Financing Activities	
Total repayments	Per contract
Additional debt	As separately estimated
Total Financing Activities	
CASH FLOW	
Targeted for retirement	As stated
Net Cash Flow	

Practical Comment   Concern about Projections

Projections frequently need to be thought through carefully. Often people say that they are satisfied with their current lifestyle and they project flat real expenditures. Nonetheless, their expenses tend to increase with their income even if their income rises at a faster pace than inflation. In other cases, they project a decline in expenditures with the intention of generating additional savings. Many, confusing a wish with future reality, never accomplish this.

Also, projections for capital expenditures and other large nontime outlays on such items as auto-mobiles, furniture, home repair, weddings for children, large appliances, or trading up in homes are often left out. Systematically overstating cash flows can have a significant effect on yearly cash flow planning and, more important, on assumed periodic saving for retirement. When future yearly net cash flows are projected to be materially higher than in the past, a more sober appraisal of future funds that will be made available may be called for.

Pro Forma Balance Sheet

The balance sheet can be a more difficult statement to forecast than the one for cash flows. That is because some of its figures include the impact of cash flows and outflows on them. For example, the investment account will include not only the growth rate on existing assets but the deposit of new savings. Liabilities will include the impact of cash inflows to reduce the amount outstanding or the absence of cash flow, which results in a larger debt figure. For this reason, projected balance sheets are used less frequently than those for cash statements.

FINANCE VERSUS ACCOUNTING

Finance and accounting have alternative ways of presenting transactions and results. Accounting employs GAAP, or generally accepted accounting principles. Most large businesses use GAAP accounting. Often the difference between finance and accounting lies in the importance placed on cash.

GAAP versus Household Accounting

Businesses and households have different ways of recording transactions. Household accounting is similar to a basic finance principle: Changes in cash generally determine results for a period. Business accounting is more sophisticated. It utilizes GAAP. Under GAAP the business attempts a proper matching of revenues and expenses. Its goal is a fair presentation of business results for a period—say, a year. Its results can involve cash and noncash items for a particular period.

A simple example may be instructive (see Example 5.4).

Example 5.4

Under household accounting, a person receiving a two-week $3,000 cash advance at year-end 2004 would have a $3,000 higher figure in the household cash flow statement for 2004. It wouldn't matter that the money wasn't earned until the work was completed in 2005. On the other hand, a business receiving a $3,000 advance from a customer would not treat the money received as income until the following year. It would wait until it had expended the costs—say $2,500 in 2005—necessary to complete the customer transaction.

By following GAAP procedures, business results for 2004 wouldn't look exceptionally good with $3,000 higher profits. Similarly, 2005 would not have lower profits due to the costs of production without any revenues against it. The business accounting process would record a

$500 profit ($3,000 revenues − $2,500 costs) matching revenues and expenses in 2005 when the transaction was completed. That reporting procedure is followed even though the cash was received in 2004, one year earlier.

Household results for a period are provided on a cash flow statement, whereas business results are given on an income statement. For information on an income statement for businesses, see Appendix I. In sum, business accounting under GAAP attempts to report income and expenses, whether or not in cash, for a fair presentation. For household reporting of results for a period, only cash matters.

Capital expenditures are outlays that have benefit for more than the current period. We've seen that households often combine them with other outflows on the traditional cash flow statement. Businesses capitalize them as assets on the balance sheet instead of expensing them on the income statement.[7]

Depreciation is the projected reduction in asset value due to wear and tear or obsolescence. It is a tax-deductible expense on the business income statement. Since the decline in asset value did not involve a cash transaction, it is not recorded on the household's cash flow statement.

Finally, GAAP generally requires that businesses record transactions on the balance sheet at original cost less accumulated depreciation. Households generally record assets at their fair market value.

Consider Example 5.5.

Example 5.5

Sally and Henry bought identical cars. Each paid $24,000 for their assets. Sally used the car for business purposes, to travel to clients. Henry used it personally to transport his family. Sally took $7,200 of depreciation[8] on the car in the first year. According to GAAP methods, the tax deduction on $7,200 created a $2,400 tax benefit for Sally. Show the difference between Sally's business and Henry's personal treatment of the transaction assuming that the car had a fair market value of $26,000 at the end of the year.

	Sally—Business Treatment		Henry—Household Accounting Treatment
Income statement	$7,200 pretax depreciation $2,400 tax benefit $4,800 deduction in net income		Generally there is no separate income statement.
Cash flow statement	Noncash depreciation of $7,200 added to net income to obtain cash flow from operations. Capital expenditure section will reflect $24,000 outflow.		$24,000 cash outflow placed on statement.[1]
Balance sheet	Original cost Less accumulated depreciation Net amount on balance sheet	$24,000 7,200 $16,800	Recorded at $26,000 fair market value.

[1] On regular statement grouped with other cash charges; in functional statement included under capital expenditures.

Recording Transactions

In Table 5.7 you see a summary of the differences between business and household methods of recording transactions as well as the definitions of various financial statement items.

---

[7] The business would use accruals amounts due and amounts owed business accounts, which have the effect of aiding the matching of revenues and costs.

[8] Depreciation amount equals 30 percent of the car's depreciable basis or purchase price.

TABLE 5.7 **Recording Transactions: Business versus Household**

Item	Explanation	GAAP Business	Finance
Balance sheet	Assets and liabilities at a given point in time	Based on original cost	Based on current fair market value of assets
Performance for period	Cash flow statement giving operating performance for the period	A proper matching of revenues and costs for the period in an income statement	Cash inflows and outflows only in a cash flow statement without regard to proper matching
Revenues	Sale transactions	Recorded when fairly represents a transaction	Recorded when cash is received
Expenses paid	Cost transactions	Recorded as necessary for proper matching with revenues	Recorded when cash is disbursed
Profits	Earnings for period	A "fair" presentation of results for the period	No exact equivalent; replaced by cash inflows minus cash outflows
Capital expenditures	Outlays providing extended-period benefits	Capitalized as asset on balance sheet, not as an expense on income statement	Recorded as outflow on flow statement; recorded at fair market value on balance sheet
Depreciation	Amount an asset has declined in value for the period	Recorded as an expense on income statement based on original cost; deducted from asset on balance sheet	Not recorded
Asset value on balance sheet	The assigned worth of an item at a point in time	Recorded at original cost less depreciation	Recorded at fair market value

Back to Dan and Laura
FINANCIAL STATEMENTS ANALYSIS

Laura dropped in one afternoon while her mother was taking care of baby Brian. She said she felt uncomfortable about her lack of understanding of financial statements. She heard Dan speaking to a couple they were friendly with about their balance sheet and my promise to do a functional cash flow statement and the wife nodded knowingly. She said, sheepishly, she didn't know what each was. Could I help by sending her some information on them?

Laura I'm glad you were forthright about your lack of knowledge of balance sheets and cash flow statements. The truth is many people are not that familiar with each. Let me see if I can enlighten you in brief fashion.

As we learned, financial planning is a process that sets goals. But goals cannot be set abstractly. Instead, they must be set in connection with resources. The *balance sheet* indicates the resources that are available. It is a statement of assets, liabilities, and household equity at a point in time. **Assets** are those items that have value to the household going forward. Assets are placed on the left-hand side of the balance sheet. They can be separated into *current assets* and **long-term assets.** Current assets are those that are likely to be consumed within the year, while long-term assets extend beyond a one-year time frame.

The balance sheet is separated into current assets, marketable investments, retirement investments, real estate, household assets, and other assets such as household overhead and leisure time. The most prominent business asset for the household is typically the future income stream of its wage earners, called *human assets*.[9] But since human capital cannot be sold, it is not usually placed on balance sheets. Other business assets could be a computer or business car. Marketable assets might include stocks and bonds. Retirement assets are, of course, segregated for use when you are no longer earning a salary. Real estate will be your home. Household assets might include a car, a refrigerator, a television, a VCR, a stereo, a boat, and so on.

Liabilities are items the household owes. They are placed on the right-hand side of the balance sheet. Credit card debts, taxes payable, and mortgage debt are all liabilities. They too can be split into current and long term based on whether they are due within one year or beyond that period.

Household equity is the difference between assets and liabilities. It is intended to show how much the household is worth at that point in time. Household equity can be relatively small or even negative when household members are young and generally increases as their marketable investment portion rises.

Net working capital is a figure reached by subtracting current liabilities from current assets. It represents the cash that will become available over the next 12 months to pay liabilities that will fall due over that period. Consequently, a strong balance sheet will have a positive net working capital.

Balance Sheet

Your current financial condition as shown in the statement below is fairly positive. Your biggest strength is having $147,000 in marketable assets. On the negative side, you have $27,000 in current liabilities and only $3,000 in current cash. When your long-term liabilities of about $59,000 are added in, your net worth is a positive $88,000. In addition, both of you have strong future income prospects and they are not included as assets in the current statement. The only negative is a weak net working capital position if we exclude your money market funds under marketable investments as you like us to since you don't want to dip into them. Excluding those assets, your current liability will exceed your current assets.

[9] For a discussion of human capital, see Theodore W. Schultz, "Capital Formation by Education," *Journal of Political Economy* 68, no. 6 (December 1960), pp. 571–83; and Gary Becker, "Investment in Human Capital: A Theoretical Analysis," *Journal of Political Economy* 70, no. 5 (October 1962), pp. 9–49.

Assets		Liabilities	
Current Assets		**Current Liabilities**	
Checking accounts	$2,800	Credit card debt	$20,000
Refund due on returned clothing	200	Educational loan—current	7,000
Total Current Assets	**$3,000**	**Total Current Liabilities**	**$27,000**
Marketable Investments		**Long-Term Liabilities**	
Money market funds[1]	34,000	Educational loan—LT portion	39,000
Stocks and stock funds	103,000	Loan from parents	20,000
Total Marketable Investments	**$137,000**	**Total Long-Term Liabilities**	**$59,000**
Pension Assets		**Total Liabilities**	**$86,000**
401(k) plans	6,000		
IRAs	4,000		
Total Pension Assets	**$10,000**		
Household Assets			
Autos	12,000	**EQUITY**	
Furniture and fixtures	7,000		
Other	5,000	Household equity	88,000
Total Household Assets	**$24,000**	**Total Equity (Net Worth)**	**$88,000**
Total Assets	**$174,000**	**Total Liabilities and Equity**	**$174,000**

[1] Not considered part of the current assets because the amount won't be used currently. Instead, it is set aside under marketable investments for long-term use.

The important thing to recognize is that your balance sheet is currently fairly strong. However, it doesn't reflect your human assets, your future earning ability. With the proper care, these human assets will bring about an even stronger future financial position.

The cash flow statement is sort of an income statement for the household. However, it is broader than a business income statement. It includes not only cash inflows such as job-related income and day-to-day expenses, but also capital expenditures—larger outlays for items that last for more than one year—and debt indicating whether borrowings have increased or declined for the year. A functional cash flow statement separates the above categories to make it simpler to analyze them.

Once cash outflows are deducted from cash flows, we receive net cash flow for the year. That is the amount of cash that you have increased or decreased for the year. Under the finance disciplines approach, cash is often the focus and is most easy to identify. All you do is look at your cash at the beginning of the period and compare it with the end-of-period figure. The difference should be net cash flow for the year.

I hope that is of help. If there is anything you would like to ask, contact me or we'll talk about it at our coming cash flow planning meeting. At that time, I will show you your cash flow statement.

Summary

Financial statements can provide an objective way to assess your financial condition.

- The balance sheet provides your assets, liabilities, and equity at a given point in time.
- The cash flow statement serves as a kind of income statement for the household that indicates how well it is operating, but its coverage is broader than an income statement for a business.
- The cash flow statement can be divided into operating, capital expenditures, debt, and net cash flow figures.
- Finance focuses on actual cash generated while accounting attempts to match income and expenses even when cash is not received or paid.

In forming a balance sheet, finance uses fair market value; accounting uses original cost.

Key Terms

assets, *113*
balance sheet, *100*
capital expenditures, *104*
cash flow, *105*
cash flow statement, *103*
current assets, *100*
depreciation, *112*
financing activities, *104*
functional cash flow statement, *103*

household assets, *101*
household equity (household net worth), *101*
human assets, *101*
human-related assets, *101*
liabilities, *101*
long-term assets, *113*
marketable investments, *100*
net cash flow, *105*

net working capital, *114*
operating activities, *104*
pro forma statements, *109*
savings, *105*
statement of cash flow, *103*
statement of financial position, *100*
traditional cash flow statements, *105*

Web Sites

http://www.studyfinance.com/lessons/finstmt
Financial Statements
This site provides an introduction to financial statements and financial statement concepts.

http://www.onlinewbc.gov/docs/finance/fs_intro.html
Financial Statements
This site offers a tutorial for understanding the basics of financial statements. The tutorial presents the different parts of a balance sheet and income statement and introduces financial ratios and indicators of financial quality.

http://www.hoovers.com
Hoovers Online
This site provides an online database for company information including financial statements and stock performance.

http://www.sec.gov/edgar.shtml
SEC's EDGAR
This is the link to the Security and Exchange Commission's EDGAR (electronic data gathering, analysis, and retrieval system) database where SEC filings on a company's financial performance and other operating information such as 10-Ks and 10-Qs are posted.

Questions

1. What is a balance sheet? Why is it important?
2. Why segregate a balance sheet by type of asset and type of liability?
3. What is a cash flow statement and why is it important?
4. Detail the sections of a functional cash flow statement.
5. Contrast a functional and a traditional cash flow statement.
6. Is an increase in debt a plus or minus from a cash flow standpoint? Explain.
7. What is a pro forma statement? What is its use?
8. Outline some expenses of a pro forma statement that cannot use inflation to project their growth and indicate what rate should be used.
9. Contrast the views of finance and accounting on recording operating results.
10. In your opinion, which presents results more fairly, finance or accounting? Explain.
11. What are reasons that a person may have a poor net cash flow yet be considered to be in good financial health?

CFP® Certification Examination Questions and Problems

5.1   A client provides a current balance sheet to the financial planner during the initial data-gathering phase of the financial planning process. This financial statement will enable the financial planner to gain an understanding of all of the following *except*

a. Diversification of the client's assets.
b. Size of the client's net cash flow.
c. Client's liquidity position.
d. Client's use of debt.

5.2   A cash-basis taxpayer includes income from a service business when

a. The services are performed.
b. The client is invoiced for the services.

   c. The client's check is deposited in the bank.

   d. The client's check is received.

5.3 The estimated value of a real estate asset in a financial statement prepared by a Certified Financial Planner licensee should be based upon the

   a. Basis of the asset, after taking into account all straight-line and accelerated depreciation.

   b. Client's estimate of current value.

   c. Current replacement value of the asset.

   d. Value that a well-informed buyer is willing to accept from a well-informed seller where *neither* is compelled to buy or sell.

   e. Current insured value.

Case Application

FINANCIAL STATEMENTS ANALYSIS

The Balance Sheet

Richard called and said that he had compiled a list of assets and would send it. It came a few days later. His assets included a home worth $300,000, approximately $350,000 in securities, two cars worth $40,000 with loans of $15,000 against them, and other assets including jewelry $5,000, art $5,000, and furniture $7,000. He and his wife had money market funds of $2,000 and a bonus due of $5,000 net in taxes and credit card payments due of $12,000. Their house had a $130,000 mortgage.

Case Application Questions

1. Construct the balance sheet.
2. Does it look substantial?
3. Would you tell Richard and Monica that it was strong? Why?
4. Complete the balance sheet section of the plan.

Appendix I

Income Statement

An income statement reports on profits for a fixed period of time. A publicly held business often identifies net income for a quarterly or yearly period. The household statement of profitability can be said to be provided under the cash flow statement, particularly under the functional cash flow statement.

As discussed in this chapter, business reporting under GAAP is more complex, which necessitates a separate income statement.

An income statement can take many forms depending on the industry or reason for its compilation, but it often can be separated into the following parts:

Parts of Income Statement	Explanation
Sales	Provides all the inflows that give the company its inflows from direct operating activities for the period. Often called "Revenues," which are transactions for goods and services sold to customers.
Cost of Goods Sold	These are outlays that are directly related to the goods and services sold to customers. For example, a beverage company would include such items as the glass or aluminum container and the cost of the beverage ingredients.
Gross Profit	This is the sales less the cost of goods sold. It indicates how much profit has been generated before other necessary costs are deducted.
Selling, General, and Administrative Expenses	These are the costs that are outlaid to help support operations. They include such items as sales or marketing expenses, salaries, rent, and research and development costs.
Other Expenses	This category includes interest expense and miscellaneous expenses such as nonrecurring write-offs.
Pre-Tax Income	Profits for the period before taxes.
Tax	Tax expense to be paid to the government based on profits.
Net Income	The benchmark for determining profits for the period. It is revenues less all expenses.

Notice that outlays for capital expenditures and inflows or outflows for debt borrowings or repayments are not included. These are included in a separate cash flow statement along with one figure from the income statement: net income.

Chapter Six

Cash Flow Planning

Chapter Goals

This chapter will enable you to:

- Apply cash flow analysis to household finance.
- Treat cash flow planning as a central activity in PFP.
- Utilize budgeting techniques effectively.
- Develop savings approaches.
- Employ financial ratios as an evaluation method.

Dan and Laura had a problem. They were operating on two tracks: Dan was saving money and at the same time Laura was spending it. The net impact on the household was unfavorable. Something would have to be done fairly quickly.

Real Life Planning

The advisor was asked by clients of his to see their daughter and her husband. The clients were conservative people who pronounced themselves "depression babies," which meant they grew up in a poor economic climate in the 1930s when a dollar really had to be stretched. They felt their daughter's family was irresponsible, that they were spending money on things they couldn't afford and not saving a penny. Would he see them? The parents would pay for the visit.

Eileen and her husband Phil were a young couple with two children. She was a teacher, he a social worker. They lived on relatively modest incomes and had high special costs for their children. When the advisor met with them, they appeared to be vaguely depressed, perhaps because they knew why Eileen's parents had suggested the visit. Their living costs did not seem extravagant to the advisor, and the "splurging on a vacation" mentioned by her parents turned out to be a $1,000 trip to a local resort town, all costs, even children outlays, included.

The advisor thought to himself this wasn't the first time there was a difference in financial approach between parent and child. People of the parents' generation often saved automatically due to fear of the unknown while the children's generation was often more optimistic about the future and needed a reason for saving. In addition, Eileen, if she stayed at her current job, would receive a government pension, which would help cover retirement needs.

The advisor asked them if they would like to have their own home instead of the inexpensive apartment they lived in. They said very much but that it wasn't possible given their current finances. They said they were stuck in their current small apartment. The advisor thought they were not only stuck in an apartment, they seemed stuck in a rut.

The advisor asked whether, if he could make it feasible, they would like to own a home now. For the first time their faces brightened and they looked at each other and said yes. He explained how it could involve some sacrifices and that they would all work together on them.

The couple mentioned they had no savings at all. The advisor mentioned that he would speak to Eileen's parents about helping fund a down payment and made a mental note to assure the parents that they could afford it. The advisor looked over at Phil, who then volunteered to ask his parents. Both sets of parents agreed to help.

The advisor and the couple worked on some areas that could be cut back modestly. Phil mentioned that he could offer therapy sessions in the basement of a home if it had a separate entrance. A cash flow statement with its current breakeven payment was constructed and a pro forma one for a budget with higher income; higher after-tax housing-related costs, particularly mortgage costs; and lower other expenses was drawn up. The figures fit.

With some direction by the advisor on affordability and the bidding process, a house was selected. It turned out to be close to Eileen's parents' home, a great advantage to all of them. The next time the advisor saw Eileen and Phil, they talked about how grateful they were.

The advisor smiled and said to himself, that is what makes financial planning so worthwhile. It wasn't the compensation, which was modest. It was the ability to positively affect people's lives. To the couple, the advisor was almost a magician, producing a home where none seemed possible. To the advisor, he had set people on a new course; they now had both a new investment and a higher quality of life. He wished cash flow planning for household goals was as simple for all his other clients.

OVERVIEW

Cash flow is the heart of personal financial planning. Cash flow is literally the amount of cash generated from household activities. It includes those items that produce cash flows such as our jobs and those items that utilize them such as our living costs. The reason cash flow planning is often the first part of financial planning to be analyzed is simple. Cash flow underlies all major household decisions.

Thus cash flow has the same status that food does for the individual or energy does for business. It is the lifeblood of household activities. A good supply of cash flow will enable households to operate and plan for the future. A poor supply of cash flow provides you with few or no choices: you are constantly trying to catch up with your obligations. Often a weak cash flow arises from poor planning and control of expenditures.

All parts of a financial plan must incorporate cash flow considerations. After all, financial planning deals with how we allocate limited resources. Whether we are deciding how much to spend on finishing the basement or the amount to put away for retirement, cash is involved.

In this chapter, we will concentrate on one segment of the financial plan: current operating needs. We will briefly discuss lifestyles. We provide reasons for saving and sound budgeting techniques. Cash flow planning is a matter of projecting sources of cash and household uses of it, thereby determining available cash flow both for targeted savings needs and for generating free cash flow. When targeted savings are planned properly, free cash flow can be used for additional spending today, invested for future spending, or put aside to reduce household risk.

As part of the planning system, purchasing power, emergency funds, liquidity, and marketability are discussed. A step-by-step description of the budgeting process is then provided. The chapter ends with a presentation of financial ratios, which are an objective way of helping determine financial health.

The chapter's planning objective, then, consists of three parts: for you to recognize the importance of cash flow to achieving goals, to learn how to identify savings problems, and to establish what can be done in practical terms to overcome these problems.

CASH FLOW PLANNING AND CURRENT STANDARD OF LIVING

Cash flow planning refers to the scheduling of current and future cash needs to achieve household goals. Cash flow planning can include such objectives as supporting a current lifestyle, paying off credit card debt, and saving for a vacation. More sophisticated and long-term goals that can be achieved through cash flow planning could include reducing tax liabilities and planning for retirement.

When we discuss cash flow planning, we are interested in what we do with our money. Lifestyles vary significantly. Some people live simply; the identities and goals of others involve spending on visible signs of achievement and status. In very basic terms, we have a choice between spending and saving.

To spend is to add to our standard of living today. To save is to provide for future needs. Establishing how people differ in the way they spend their money is generally not of concern to advisors; people typically have no difficulty in spending. However, many people have difficulties in generating the amount of savings they need, despite a host of good reasons for doing so. Example 6.1 discusses lifestyles and spending and savings strategies. It is followed by a fuller exploration of savings, often the focus of households and advisors alike.

Example 6.1   The Smiths and the Joneses were two couples who lived on different sides of town. The Smiths lived in a big house financed mostly through debt and had many obligations connected to it. The Joneses lived more modestly than the Smiths. The Smiths never seemed to have enough money, and one day Mr. Smith had to ask his firm for an advance because he didn't have enough money to pay to park his car downtown adjacent to his company headquarters. Mr. Jones, who made less money, let his cash flow dictate his spending policies. He always had a number of spending alternatives because he always generated a positive cash flow.

Reasons for Savings

In reality, there are a number of reasons for savings. We start with the classical, pure life cycle motive:[1]

1. *Pure life cycle motive.* To provide monies to even out differences in earnings over time. A key motivation is to build up resources for retirement when work-related earnings are no longer available.

2. *Investment motive.* To take advantage of investment opportunities that can make achievement of our financial goals easier.

3. *Down payment motive.* To provide monies for the down payment or full purchase of longer-lived assets such as durable goods or educational expenditures.

4. *Precautionary motive.* To provide a fund to cover future uncertainties such as fluctuating income, sickness, inflationary effects on expenditures, and so forth.

5. *Improvement motive.* To sacrifice today so that your future lifestyle can improve.

6. *Independence motive.* To fund sufficient money to be able to be financially independent after working to a certain age. You may not want to retire but to derive pleasure from a sense of independence, power, and prestige.

7. *Bequest motive.* To accommodate funds to provide for nonhousehold members whether they are children, friends, relatives, or charities.

---

[1] Adapted from Martin Browning and Annamaria Lusardi, "Household Savings: Micro Theories and Micro Facts," *Journal of Economic Literature* 34, no. 4 (1996), pp. 1797–855, which in turn was adapted from J. Maynard Keynes, *The General Theory of Employment, Interest and Money* (London: MacMillan, 1936).

Practical Comment   Steady Savings

Steady savings has an underappreciated advantage. It allows you to dollar cost average into investments. Dollar cost averaging signifies buying securities steadily, thereby obtaining a price that averages out its highs and lows. To people, it can signify not worrying so much about timing purchases. To advisors, it can help overcome a tendency to stay out of investment for a period of time, and some believe for the wrong period of time.

8. *Hoarding motive.* The ability to accumulate investments with no intention of converting them into purchases in the future. In effect, pleasure comes from the accumulation of money itself or the power and cachet that having it brings.

People don't usually calculate the amount of money they need to save and then do it. Instead, many need assistance. Below we describe several ways to help people save by improving budgeting practice.

FORMAL AND INFORMAL BUDGETING

Budgeting is a method of planning current and future household cash flows to determine needs and adhere to desirable allocations of resources. There are two types of budgeting techniques: formal and informal.

Informal budgeting involves less detailed ways of planning, sometimes as simple as just thinking about household planning such as a down payment on a car. The majority of budgeting planning is done this way. In general, many people dislike formal budgeting, which involves specific household figures enumerated in detail. They find it time-consuming and will do so only when highly motivated.

When budgeting is formal and reflects all categories of household expenditures, usually in the form of a document, it is said to be a **household budget.** The budget is a type of pro forma cash flow statement with a purpose. Because little can be done about fixed expenses, budgeting tends to focus on discretionary items.

By thinking about and writing down the amount planned for each category, households have several goals. Some of them include prioritizing outlays based on household preferences and needs, reducing or eliminating impulsive purchases that may be regretted later, not being caught short of cash funds, and saving enough money for future needs and contingencies.

In theory, saving is a mechanical process. You decide how much savings you require to fulfill your objectives and then you mechanically implement the plan. In reality, human behavior intervenes. We know that many people have trouble saving money. That can be true even in higher-income households that some would say have the resources to save comfortably.

Detailed written budgets when not established by very organized people are often a means of establishing structure for those who need it. They may be drawn up in response to special circumstances such as planning for a large outlay, material debts, or a general inability to save.

The budget, then, can become a detailed framework for the future. The projected figures are compared with actual ones once the time period being measured has been completed. Where there are notable differences, the reasons for them are analyzed and subsequent budget figures may be adjusted or household spending patterns altered to bring actual performance in line with projections. Consider the case of Dorothy in Example 6.2.

Chapter Six *Cash Flow Planning* **123**

Practical Comment How to Increase Savings

People may intend to save but find themselves with no money left at the end of the pay period. This lack of effectiveness can be overcome in several different ways.

SIMPLE STRUCTURAL APPROACH

- Treat savings as another expense. Write a check to savings each period at the same time that fixed monthly expenditures are paid.
- Alternatively, have cash automatically wired to a separate savings or investment account when the payroll check is deposited.
- Develop a budget—a detailed list of income and expenses with planned expenditures limited to accommodate a desired amount of savings.

PROVIDE MOTIVATION: "THE BUCKETS APPROACH"

People find it easier to save when they have a concrete goal in mind. It is simpler to motivate savings when there is a direct connection between savings and the goal. Therefore, a slush fund for total savings is not as effective as separate accounts for each need. These accounts can be called "buckets," with one bucket for retirement, one for children's college education, another for a down payment on a house, and so on.

ELIMINATE OPTION TO SPEND

When keeping to a savings pattern even with structure proves difficult:

- Place money in accounts that have penalties for early withdrawals such as pension accounts, tax-deferred annuities, or life insurance policies.
- Alternatively, contract for a house and undertake large monthly mortgage payments. Aside from potential appreciation on the home, the savings

will come from accelerated paydown of debt, which leads to increased equity in the house.

REDUCE TEMPTATION

Buying on impulse can undermine savings efforts. To overcome this:

- Stay away from stores that result in greater spending than needed.
- Carry credit cards only for planned expenditures and for vacations. Try to use cash as much as possible.

MINIMIZE DISCOMFORT

People are reluctant to cut back on current spending because they can perceive limiting spending as resulting in a decline in their standard of living. They are more agreeable to savings based on future increases in income. Therefore, success in saving can occur by having people save a fraction of the extra money obtained from raises before the new money enters the spending stream.

OTHER REASONS FOR NOT SAVING

There can be reasons other than a lack of discipline that account for why people don't save. They may not have a strong ability to correctly visualize the long-term future or estimate future revenues or current savings needs. Or they just may prefer greater spending today rather than in the future. They may feel that their life span is uncertain and, therefore, assured spending today provides more pleasure. Alternatively, they may value simpler, less costly pleasures when they retire and want more material ones now. When choices are made rationally, there is little that should be done. However, a financial planner can explain the repercussions of not saving in visual factual terms that are often persuasive even for people who have the spend-for-today mindset.

Example 6.2

Dorothy had a problem. She planned to save some money each month. At the end of each month, however, she found herself a few hundred dollars further in credit card debt. She set up a rough budget for the year. As you can see, at the end of the year, the actual figures were different:

	Budgeted	Actual	Difference
Salary	$66,000	$66,000	$0
Nondiscretionary expenses	(43,000)	43,000	0
Discretionary expenses	(15,000)	(25,000)	(10,000)
Repayment of debt	(3,000)	2,000	(5,000)
Retirement savings	5,000	0	5,000
Net cash flow	0	0	0

Practical Comment   Conservative Projections of Income

Financial planners are aware that in order to be conservative, some people hold salaries level in making projections. Where projections extend over a number of years, extreme distortions can occur rather than incur in cash flow by doing so. Often, the solution is to express revenues and expenses in current dollars and then, as we saw, increase these items where appropriate each year by the inflation rate. When that is done, statements are generally more accurate. Such steps can help deal with **purchasing power risk,** the risk of having your money decline in what it can buy over time due to inflation.

Dorothy looked at the difference between budgeted and actual figures. Her discretionary expenses were well above budget. As a consequence, she was not able to save any money and in fact went further into debt. She decided to set up an item-by-item household budget. She made what she thought were realistic projections. Her cash flow statement provided for both savings and repayment of debt. She vowed that she would not spend a single new dollar in the new month unless the prior month's actual cash flow met expectations.

There are a number of items that need to be considered when establishing pro forma budgeting operations in general or a detailed household budget.

Purchasing Power

Purchasing power is the amount of goods and services a fixed sum of money will buy. Because of inflation, a single dollar is expected to buy fewer and fewer goods the longer the time period before purchase.[2] In making projections of salaries and household costs, inflation must be taken into account.

Emergency Fund

In making cash flow projections, it is important to have liquid assets. We want the ability to turn assets into cash quickly without a high transaction cost or loss of principal. Cash flow projections are subject to the risk of unexpected circumstances; we may need unplanned-for cash quickly. Often such cash comes from a liquid emergency fund set up specifically for that purpose.

There are many reasons why we may need to use an emergency fund. For example, we may unexpectedly be laid off in our jobs or receive a lower-than-anticipated bonus. Alternatively, our costs may rise due to health or extensive repairs to the house or car.

The amount that you place in an emergency fund will depend on the degree of risk you face and the availability of your borrowing alternatives. Risk would be higher for a one-wage-earner household when the person works in the fickle entertainment industry than when two people work in more stable industries. Other considerations in a decision on the size of an emergency fund include projections of future free cash flow to be generated; the amount of debt outstanding; and the availability of other assets such as stocks and bonds to be tapped under serious circumstances.

Liquidity Substitutes

Businesses often prefer to keep as little in liquid assets as possible, consistent with their risk requirements. In that way, they can put their monies into higher-earning assets in their business. We saw that, similarly, households often desire to place their funds into higher-earning assets or can choose to spend a greater sum today. As an alternative, they have

---

[2] Of course, if our country were to undergo deflation—that is, a continuing decline in the rate of overall prices—the opposite would be true.

Practical Comment   Size of Emergency Funds

Figures for the size of emergency funds often range from three to six months. Given an ability to borrow money and to convert other assets into cash, the three- to six-month rule of thumb may be simplistic. Because there are a number of other factors to consider, they should be compared with the projected gain from holding a lesser amount of liquid savings and investing more money. As we discussed, the potential for higher return and the ready access to liquidity substitutes are probably among the major reasons that a large number of people hold less than a quarter or half year's living costs as an emergency fund. Many of these people maintain no emergency fund at all.

A reasonable approach may be to establish an emergency fund with liquid assets. The monies would come from savings with no debt used to generate the cash needed. However, the size of the emergency fund could be influenced by the access to debt or to longer-term investments in the event that the emergency was of great scope or duration.

liquidity substitutes. **Liquidity substitutes** are another way of raising cash, often in connection with unplanned-for developments. Two types of liquidity substitutes are debt and marketable securities.

The access to and use of debt is growing in the United States. Cash needed for shorter-term, smaller emergencies can be accessed through credit card debt, while larger cash resources needed for extended periods of time can be generated through bank debt—particularly home equity loans, where applicable. We will examine the advantages and disadvantages of using such debt in Chapter 7.

Marketable securities are publicly traded financial assets for which a current market value can be determined. Examples include stocks, bonds, and mutual funds. Marketable securities are typically easy to sell in order to raise cash. As we will see, however, they don't qualify as fully liquid.

Liquidity versus Marketability

Liquidity and marketability are related terms, but they don't have the same meaning. **Liquidity** is the ability to turn an asset into cash quickly at a reasonable transaction cost and without loss of principal.[3] Given this definition, money market funds would be liquid, but bonds would not since investment losses on sale of bonds are possible.

Marketability is the capacity to find a seller or buyer of an asset at its current value. An asset can be marketable but not liquid. Stocks and bonds have buyers and sellers at any time and thus are marketable but are not fully liquid since losses on sale are possible. As mentioned, when either asset is placed in a pension account, it has a market price, but there are often restrictions on sale. Even when it can be sold, the resultant taxation including penalties may render it illiquid. Finally, a traditional home in a popular location is marketable because a buyer can generally be found[4] at a fair price, but it isn't fully liquid since it will take time to find a buyer and to close on the house. And it also may require time for the seller to move to another residence.

Liquidity and marketability are both relative terms: Assets may be highly liquid or marketable (e.g., a money market fund) or fairly illiquid and nonmarketable (e.g., a modern home in a rural community of colonial homes with a declining population) or they can be somewhere in between.

---

[3] Note that this definition would differ from the accounting definition, which would emphasize the ability to turn an asset into cash without requiring that it be done at no loss.

[4] Although it may not be considered as marketable as a financial asset such as a stock.

Practical Comment What to Place in Emergency Funds

Although either stocks or bonds can easily be sold to raise cash, people can be very reluctant to sell something at a material loss. There are behavioral reasons for this, as explained in Chapter 19. In addition, the public often believes that securities have cyclical highs and lows in their valuation and that selling at a loss costs them money because the securities will "come back."

The practical compromise to the emergency fund versus higher-return securities can be to use marketable securities that don't fluctuate as much as stocks. These can include bonds, particularly those with shorter-term due dates, and bank certificates of deposit that can be exited with a modest interest penalty.

STEPS IN HOUSEHOLD BUDGET

With these separate issues that affect budgeting out of the way, the household budget can be constructed by following the steps described below.

Establish Budgeting Goals

People may have a variety of goals in establishing a budget. These include targeting savings for a particular expenditure such as a new home entertainment system, car, or vacation. On the other hand, savings may be needed for larger investment purposes such as the down payment on a home or for retirement. However, often a budget is just established because the household is in a negative cash flow situation and debt is accumulating. The goal then is to reverse the cash drain and repay the debt.

Whatever the immediate goal, the objective of the budget is to ensure that the household generates enough cash to meet household operating needs and over time to provide resources for emergency funds if current assets are insufficient. Finally, by providing hard numbers to household members, the budget can help to reduce inefficient spending.

Decide on the Budgeting Period

Budgets can be made weekly, bimonthly, monthly, or annually. The period can follow the natural income and spending cycle, which can be linked to how often a paycheck is received and when bills are paid. Many people pay bills on a monthly basis. For review purposes, this period of time represents a balance between too frequent and too little examination of actual versus intended results.

Calculate Cash Inflows

Cash inflows for budgetary purposes for working people are typically the amounts received from paychecks. Monies received from investments and nonrecurring sources should be displayed in a separate section or otherwise noted. The segregation of sources of cash is significant because, for active workers, the measure of savings for the period is often based on job-related inflows only. The cash from investments is for a separate purpose and including nonrecurring inflows can distort the figures.

To simplify matters, often after-tax inflows received from paychecks are used. Of course, when a person retires, investment principal and income payments should be incorporated as a primary source of revenues. Care should be taken to include anticipated raises in salary and increases in any Social Security payments.

TABLE 6.1
Average Annual Household Expenditures

Source: Adapted from Bureau of Labor Statistics, *Consumer Expenditure Survey, 2002,* http://www.bls.gov/cex/home.htm.

Item	Complete Reporting of Income			
	Total Complete Reporting	Lowest 20 Percent	Middle 20 percent	Highest 20 Percent
Average annual expenditures	**100%**	**100%**	**100%**	**100%**
Food and beverages	14	18	15	12
Housing	32	35	32	31
Apparel and services	4	5	4	5
Transportation	19	17	20	17
Health care	6	7	7	4
Entertainment	5	4	4	6
Personal insurance and pensions	11	3	9	15
Life and other personal insurance	1	1	1	1
Pensions and Social Security	10	2	8	14
Other*	9	11	9	10

*Other includes personal care products and services, reading, education, tobacco products and smoking supplies, and miscellaneous and cash contributions.

Project Cash Outflows

Outflows should be separated into nondiscretionary and discretionary items. Key categories should be separately stated. (See Chapter 5.) To get accurate projected amounts, checkbook status or software should be used as a guide for past figures whenever possible. When that is not possible, a significant miscellaneous category should be used for projections for unanticipated expenses, including those for unforeseen circumstances.

A typical percentage breakdown of expenses by income strata is provided in Table 6.1.

Compute Net Cash Flow

Net cash flow is simply projected cash inflows minus projected cash outflows. If investment income and nonrecurring items have not been separated yet, adjustments should be made to get a fairer comparison. The resultant figure should be net cash flow after adjustments, the amount that truly represents your cash generated during the period.

Compare Net Cash Flow with Goals and Adjust

At this point, projected cash flow figures should be compared with goals. When the figures show a shortfall, you must determine how the shortfall is to be eliminated. Basically, there are three ways to do this: find additional income, for example, by working overtime; cut back costs, which is the most common way; or change goals. Alteration in goals—say, by postponing savings—can, of course, undercut the reason for establishing the goal.

Review Results for Reasonableness and Finalize the Budget

This step assesses the reasonableness of projections. Do they seem realistic? Do they take into account inevitable nonrecurring expenses? The outcome may be an adjustment in projections and, in some instances, further cutbacks in expenses. At this point, the budget can be finalized.

Compare Budgeted with Actual Figures

Comparing actual with projected results is an important part of the process. Results seldom come out exactly as projected. Where there are differences, the reasons have to be ascertained. Four common reasons for differences are impulse purchases, income that differs from projections, unusual occurrences, and gifts. The insights developed as a result of this step should be incorporated in future projections. For example, a figure for nonessential purchases may be added to future expenditures.

FINANCIAL RATIOS

Financial ratios are a way of gauging the current state of the household's assets and operating activities. Frequently, figures from both the balance sheet and cash flow statement are used to develop the ratios. Comparisons are made with absolute standards of good performance and with relative results for that particular household over time.

Example 6.3   Len wanted to know whether he was saving enough money. He calculated his current savings as a percentage of total income and found that it was 6 percent. His planner had said that for someone Len's age, with his goals, 10 percent seemed appropriate. He then calculated his savings rates over the past two years and found they were 3 percent and 5 percent. Although Len was pleased that his savings rate was rising over time, he decided to redouble his savings efforts to reach the 10 percent standard.

Now we take a closer look at selected liquidity ratios and operating ratios. In Chapter 7 we will describe ratios that have to do with liabilities.

Liquidity Ratios

Liquidity, we said, is the amount of cash and the ability to turn assets into cash with relative ease and without loss of principal. We consider two ratios below: the current ratio and the emergency fund ratio.

Current Ratio

The word *current* generally refers to actions to be taken in the present year. It is here that day-to-day assets and liability transactions reside.

$$\text{Current ratio} = \frac{\text{Current assets}}{\text{Current liabilities}}$$

The current ratio measures your present resources available to pay current debts. This ratio should exceed 1.0x which means current assets are greater than current liabilities. Having less could represent an inability to pay debts when due. The ability to borrow money through credit card purchases and to delay payment on existing card debt has somewhat reduced the concern of running out of cash to pay current liabilities.

Emergency Fund Ratios

The emergency fund ratio measures how many months of living expenses can be supported by available liquid assets such as money market funds and savings accounts.

$$\text{Emergency fund ratio} = \frac{\text{Liquid assets}}{\text{Total monthly household expenses}}$$

Total emergency household expenses include all expected cash outflows, both nondiscretionary and discretionary outlays. Often a ratio of at least 3x is called for, signifying that three months of cash or perhaps other somewhat liquid, less volatile securities are available. But, as we discussed, there is no hard-and-fast rule as to amount. The greater the uncertainty for income and expenses, the higher the ratio.[5]

Operating Ratios

Operating ratios measure the overall costs of the household and its components as a percent of total income. We are interested in how these percentages change over time.

---

[5] Where a decline in income of extended duration is a significant possibility, marketable securities such as stocks and bonds could be included in the numerator along with liquid assets.

Households with expected declines in real income were more likely to have adequate emergency fund reserves. Also, financial planners on average recommended three months of living expenses be saved. See Y. Regina Chang, Sherman Hanna, and Jessie X. Fan, "Emergency Fund Levels: Is Household Behavior Rational?" *Financial Counseling and Planning Journal* 8, no. 1 (July 1997), pp. 47–55.

Nondiscretionary Cost Percentage

$$\text{Nondiscretionary cost percentage} = \frac{\text{Total nondiscretionary costs}}{\text{Total income}}$$

The nondiscretionary cost percentage provides the proportion of day-to-day overhead costs to total revenues. When this percentage changes significantly from year to year, we would look at the individual components of nondiscretionary costs to find the reason. Our goal should be to reduce the nondiscretionary percentage over time and doing this can represent a measure of efficiency in household activities.[6] The lower the percentage, the greater the amount available for discretionary costs and savings and investment.

Discretionary Cost Percentage

$$\text{Discretionary cost percentage} = \frac{\text{Total discretionary costs}}{\text{Total income}}$$

Discretionary costs represent the benefits of our household efforts. Assuming appropriate savings for the future, the lower the percentage of household fixed costs and the higher the percentage of optional expenses, the greater your satisfaction and standard of living.

Total Operating Percentage

$$\text{Total operating percentage} = \frac{\text{Total nondiscretionary costs} + \text{Total discretionary costs}}{\text{Total income}}$$

The total operating cost percentage[7] provides an overall measure of day-to-day household expenses. The percentage indicates how much of household revenues are being spent today on nondiscretionary and discretionary costs. It can serve as a control on expenses and as a guide to the amount available for capital expenditures and savings; the lower the percentage, the larger the amount available for these items.[8]

Payout Ratio

When applied to households, the payout ratio views discretionary outlays as a kind of dividend. As with a business, the household must decide how much of available cash flow to pay out today for enjoyable activities and how much to save.

$$\frac{\text{Discretionary}}{\text{payout}} = \frac{\text{Discretionary expenses} + \text{Discretionary capital expenditures}}{\text{Cash flow before discretionary expenses}}$$
$$\text{percentage}$$

Cash flows before discretionary expenses indicate the amount of money available over which household members have choices. The discretionary payout percentage combines discretionary expenses and capital expenditures for leisure items such as a television. It measures the percentage of available cash flow that is actually expended on all leisure outlays.

---

[6] Unless the increased overhead costs come from a pleasure-producing commitment such as interest on debt used to finance a vacation home.

[7] The formulas exclude capital expenditures. To include them could distort year-to-year comparisons. In multiyear groupings of cash flow statements, however, these capital items should be included. A case could be made for incorporating an imputed expense based on the rental value during the year or perhaps including the depreciation in the value of the capital expenditures each year in the expense ratio based on the useful life of the asset, but that would be closer to an accounting or economic as opposed to a finance approach.

[8] As well as for paydown of debt.

The higher the payout percentage, the lower the percentage going into traditional efficiency-enhancing capital outlays for the household and other forms of investment such as mutual funds. A high payout percentage can reflect a desire for a higher standard of living today as opposed to improved household efficiencies and a higher, more secure standard of living in the future.

Savings Percentage

Savings represents the amount set aside for expected outcomes such as retirement, emergencies, and improvements in your future standard of living.

$$\text{Gross savings percentage} = \frac{\text{Net cash flow} + \text{Targeted savings} + \text{Change in debt}}{\text{Total income}}$$

The savings percentage[9] indicates the total combined percentage of total income that is being put away for future needs. The amount expended to pay off debt is considered savings while an increase in debt reduces the savings rate.[10] The objective for saving will depend on individual circumstances and goals, but saving 10 percent of your gross income is often a desirable rule of thumb.

Back to Dan and Laura
CASH FLOW PLANNING

At our next meeting, it became even clearer that I was dealing with two different spending philosophies. Dan was more frugal, preferring to save to have monies available for future contingencies and to begin to fund retirement. Laura said her parents never gave having enough money a thought and everything worked out.

Laura enjoyed taking trips to the regional mall to purchase fairly expensive clothes for Brian and herself. Now that Brian was around and she wasn't working, she also took more time at the health club. Both she and Dan ate out and spent considerable money on entertainment, which created high baby-sitting bills as well.

The combination of the absence of Laura's salary, higher living expenses, and their intent not to touch the investments had produced the cash shortfall and the $20,000 in credit card debt. I noted that, in effect, they were operating on two tracks, with Dan saving money at the same time that Laura was spending it. Both knew the system had to change and invited my comments on how to do this. When I told them that it was important to determine when Laura might go back to work, she replied, "In five years."

Just before they left, Laura smiled and said sweetly that she would have difficulty subjecting her spending to a fixed written budget. Then, after thinking about it for a minute, she said unless it was absolutely necessary.

Cash flow planning is the scheduling of cash outflows to meet near and long-term resources. It is often at the heart of a financial plan. Generally, without cash flow, household goals cannot be met. Cash flow planning is particularly important for couples like yourselves. You have to establish the structure to live within your means. That entails saving enough money to fund your goals: these extend from buying a home, to educating your current and

---

[9] Employer contributions would be added to savings figures.

[10] Amounts for certain types of capital expenditure such as those that increase the value of investment property may be considered savings as well. One example might be renovation of a kitchen or bathroom that, in particular, can enhance the value of a house.

anticipated children, to retirement. Where cutbacks are called for, as they are here, it is important to retain those expenditures that each of you believes are particularly important for an enjoyable life.

You began running a cash flow deficit before borrowing this year after Laura stopped working. As you are aware, these deficits have to end. They must be replaced by saving. There are a number of areas that appear to be particularly suited to being examined and perhaps cut.

Clothing is treated as an overhead item called nondiscretionary expenses. However, it is clear that you spend more than is necessary to dress yourself adequately. In fact, the act of shopping and finding interesting items is an enjoyable leisure pursuit. Despite that observation, to simplify things, I have included all clothing outlays under the nondiscretionary category. Vacations and eating out are true discretionary expenses. I would point out that one year ago, all these expenses were considerably lower, which suggests that they could be reduced without dramatically affecting your lifestyle.

Laura, I believe cutbacks are absolutely necessary for you to realize your goals. In certain cases the figures even with cutbacks are not that different from those outlays you had last year. I have attached a schedule of cutbacks. Notice they are focused on delivered food, clothing (even though they are placed entirely under the nondiscretionary column for convenience purposes, both of them have a discretionary component to them), recreational and personal outlays, and vacations. If there is an objection to any area of cutbacks, substitute another that provides the same amount of savings.

Schedule of Cutbacks

	2006 Before Plan	2006 After Plan
Nondiscretionary		
Groceries	$ 5,800	$ 6,800
Delivered food	3,000	0
Total food	8,800	6,800
Dan's clothing	4,000	3,000
Laura's clothing	7,000	5,000
Baby's clothing	2,500	4,000
Total clothing	13,500	12,000
Discretionary		
Recreation/entertainment	$ 6,000	$ 3,000
Personal	6,500	4,000
Vacations	8,000	4,000
Total savings		**$13,000**[1]

[1] This figure is the sum of the cutbacks as represented by the differences between "After Plan" and "Before Plan" columns.

The result of these efforts will be to place you on a better financial footing, including an ability to continue making pension payments.

I recommend that, as a structuring mechanism and to put you in the "savings habit," you do the following:

1. Establish separate savings accounts for anticipated educational needs and contingencies. Placing these in separate "buckets" for each item can better relate savings to a tangible goal. It also can make you more reluctant to withdraw monies for nonessential needs. You are fortunate that Laura's parents have volunteered to gift you $65,000 provided it is used for the down payment on a home. One bucket down already.

2. You can begin funding these buckets immediately out of your marketable investments. As noted in the balance sheet section, you have $137,000 in marketable investments.

With Laura not working, you are projected to run a deficit of close to $90,000 over the next five years. We recommend that you set aside $90,000 in a bucket to cover those deficits. The remaining marketable securities can be used to create an emergency fund, begin a college savings bucket, or fund 401(k)/IRA contributions each year, since funds will not be available from Dan's salary.

3. Write a check to each account at the beginning of each of Dan's bimonthly pay periods. We project, however, that you will not be able to begin doing so until 2011. Not going beyond the remaining amounts in your checking account can be an important structuring tool.

4. Be aware of your spending habits, particularly in the area discussed. However, as long as you don't do it too often, reward yourself occasionally with a spending "treat" when you have accomplished savings-spending goals for a period of time.

Recognize that your cash flow concerns should ease considerably once Laura goes back to work. The cash flow statement is attached. It includes the purchase of a home next year. As I will detail later under nonfinancial investments, I believe the home to be an attractive investment now. I have included other capital expenditures that will be discussed in a separate meeting. This cash flow statement is likely to be revised as your other financial goals come into better focus. However, for now, notice the difference in cash flow between the before and after cutbacks columns.

Finally the statement includes projections for seven years as opposed to the three or four years I usually display. That is done for you to see the difference in cash flow beginning in year 6 when Laura goes back to work.

Projected Cash Flow Statement

Operating Activities	2006 Before Plan	2006 After Plan	2007	2008	2009	2010	2011	2012
Income								
Total compensation	$100,000	$100,000	$110,000	$121,000	$133,100	$146,410	$239,882	$258,352
Total investment income	4,000	4,000	4,000	4,000	4,000	4,000	4,000	4,000
Total other income (gift from parents)	0	65,000	0	0	0	0	0	0
Total Income	**$104,000**	**$169,000**	**$114,000**	**$125,000**	**$137,100**	**$150,410**	**$243,882**	**$262,352**
Expenses								
Nondiscretionary								
Rent	$15,000	$15,000	$0	$0	$0	$0	$0	$0
Property tax	0	0	2,500	2,575	2,652	2,732	2,814	2,898
Upkeep and insurance	2,000	2,000	3,000	3,090	3,183	3,278	3,377	3,478
Utilities	3,600	3,600	3,708	3,819	3,934	4,052	4,173	4,299
Furnishings/moving	1,000	1,000	12,530	1,061	1,093	1,126	1,159	1,194
Mortgage interest	0	0	17,219	17,066	16,902	16,727	16,538	16,336
Total housing	21,600	21,600	38,957	27,611	27,764	27,914	28,061	28,205
Insurance	2,050	5,950	7,090	7,183	7,278	7,377	7,478	7,582
Professional fees	0	4,000	1,030	1,061	1,093	1,126	1,159	1,194
Child care (baby-sitter)	3,000	3,000	3,090	3,183	3,278	3,377	6,956	7,164
Food	8,800	6,800	7,004	7,214	7,431	7,653	11,361	11,702
Clothing	13,500	12,000	12,360	12,731	13,113	13,506	13,911	14,329
Health care (out of pocket)	1,350	1,350	1,648	1,697	1,748	1,801	1,855	1,910
Transportation	4,500	4,500	5,408	5,570	5,737	5,909	9,564	9,851
Credit card interest	0	0	0	0	0	0	0	0
Income and payroll tax	25,080	25,080	23,917	27,209	30,835	36,956	71,900	78,410
Total nondiscretionary	$79,880	$84,280	$100,503	$93,458	$98,277	$105,617	$152,245	$160,347

Operating Activities	2006 Before Plan	2006 After Plan	2007	2008	2009	2010	2011	2012
Cash Flow before Discretionary Expenses	$24,120	$84,720	$13,497	$31,542	$38,823	$44,793	$91,636	$102,005
Discretionary								
Recreation/entertainment	$6,000	$3,000	$3,090	$3,183	$3,278	$3,377	$6,956	$7,164
Personal	6,500	4,000	4,120	4,244	4,371	4,502	7,535	7,761
Vacations	8,000	4,000	4,120	4,244	4,371	4,502	9,274	9,552
Gifts and charitable contributions	2,000	2,000	2,060	2,122	2,185	2,251	2,319	2,388
Hobbies	2,750	2,750	2,833	2,917	3,005	3,095	3,188	3,284
Total discretionary	$25,250	$15,750	$16,223	$16,709	$17,210	$17,727	$29,272	$30,150
Cash Flow from Operations	($1,130)	$68,970	($2,726)	$14,833	$21,613	$27,066	$62,365	$71,855
Capital Expenditures								
Purchase of home	$0	$0	$250,000	$0	$0	$0	$0	$0
Total educational expenses[1]	2,666	2,666	24,924	26,046	27,234	28,494	1,458	1,170
Household maintenance[2]	1,000	31,000	1,030	1,061	1,093	1,126	1,159	1,194
Leisure	2,000	2,000	2,060	2,122	2,185	2,251	2,319	2,388
Total capital expenditures	$5,666	$35,666	$278,014	$29,229	$30,513	$31,870	$4,936	$4,752
Cash Flow before Financing Activities	($6,796)	$33,304	($280,740)	($14,396)	($8,900)	($4,805)	$57,429	$67,103
Financing Activities								
Total repayments[3]	$6,463	$23,463	$5,783	$6,162	$6,567	$6,998	$7,458	$7,948
Mortgage	0	0	(237,500)	0	0	0	0	0
Additional credit card debt	0	0	0	0	0	0	0	0
Total financing activities	$6,463	$23,463	($231,717)	$6,162	$6,567	$6,998	$7,458	$7,948
Cash Flow	($13,258)	$9,842	($49,023)	($20,558)	($15,466)	($11,802)	$49,972	$59,156
Targeted for retirement	$0	$0	$0	$0	$0	$0	$18,000	$18,000
Targeted for college expenses	0	0	0	0	0	0	14,000	14,000
Net Cash Flow	($13,258)	$9,842	($49,023)	($20,558)	($15,466)	($11,802)	$17,972	$27,156

[1] Includes expenses for Laura's master's program and student loan interest.
[2] Includes $30,000 for Dan's new car.
[3] Includes mortgage, student loan, and credit card principal.

Finally, I have provided your financial ratios. They point to a fairly weak cash position and weak savings ratio. While the gross savings of 20 percent is high, it is due to the parental contribution. After our discussions, this weak cash flow situation should not be a surprise. However, following my advice will have a substantial positive effect on these ratios.

$$\text{Current ratio} = \frac{\text{Current assets}}{\text{Current liabilities}}$$

$$= \frac{3,000}{27,000} = 0.11$$

$$\text{Emergency fund ratio} = \frac{\text{Liquid assets}}{\text{Total monthly household expenses}}$$

$$= \frac{37,000}{8,336} = 4.44$$

$$\text{Nondiscretionary cost percentage} = \frac{\text{Total nondiscretionary costs}}{\text{Total income}}$$

$$= \frac{84,280}{169,000}$$

$$= 0.50 \times 100\% = 50\%$$

$$\text{Discretionary cost percentage} = \frac{\text{Total discretionary costs}}{\text{Total income}}$$

$$= \frac{15{,}750}{169{,}000}$$

$$= 0.09 \times 100\% = 9\%$$

$$\text{Total operating percentage} = \frac{\text{Nondiscretionary costs} + \text{Discretionary costs}}{\text{Total income}}$$

$$= \frac{100.030}{169{,}000}$$

$$= 0.59 \times 100\% = 59\%$$

$$\text{Discretionary payout percentage} = \frac{\text{Discretionary expenses} + \begin{array}{c}\text{Discretionary}\\\text{capital}\\\text{expenditures}\end{array}}{\text{Cash flow before discretionary expenses}}$$

$$= \frac{17{,}750}{84{,}720}$$

$$= 0.21 \times 100\% = 21\%$$

$$\text{Gross savings percentage} = \frac{\text{Net cash flow} + \text{Targeted saving} + \text{Change in debt}}{\text{Total income}}$$

$$= \frac{9{,}842 + 0 + 23{,}463}{169{,}000}$$

$$= \frac{33{,}305}{169{,}000}$$

$$= 0.20 \times 100\% = 20\%$$

Summary

Along with financial statement analysis, cash flow planning is often performed near the beginning of the financial planning process. Both help to set the tone for other areas to come.

- Available cash flow makes financial planning possible.
- Savings for future needs can be difficult for some and budgeting techniques can help bring about acceptable savings rates.
- There are a variety of methods that can facilitate savings, including a simple structural approach providing motivation, eliminating an option to spend, reducing temptation, and minimizing discomfort.
- Financial ratios can provide an objective assessment of specific segments of a household's financial condition.

Key Terms

budgeting, *122*
cash flow planning, *121*
financial ratios, *128*

household budget, *122*
liquidity, *125*
liquidity substitutes, *125*

marketability, *125*
purchasing power, *124*
purchasing power risk, *124*

Web Sites

http://www.investopedia.com
Investing Glossary
The site provides a general online investment dictionary. It also features financial ratio definitions and articles and tutorials regarding cash flow planning.

Questions

1. What is cash flow planning?
2. Why is cash flow planning so important?
3. List five reasons for saving.
4. Why do some people have difficulty saving?
5. Provide five methods for helping people to save.
6. Why do people construct a budget?
7. What is a liquidity substitute? When should it be used?
8. What is the difference between liquidity and marketability?
9. Why are financial ratios important?
10. Chris's current liabilities exceeded his current assets. He said not to worry; he could use his credit card if he needed extra funds. What do you think of this practice?
11. Maya had a low nondiscretionary cost percentage and a high discretionary one. Is that good or bad? Explain.
12. What are reasons that a person's gross saving percentage may be low while his or her net cash flow may be high?

Problems

6.1 April made $50,000 in year 1 and $60,000 in year 2. She had the following yearly outflows:

	Year 1	Year 2
Nondiscretionary	$25,000	$27,000
Discretionary	10,000	12,000
Capital expenditures	5,000	13,000
Debt repayment	0	6,000

6.2 Calculate April's operating cash flow and net cash flow for each year.

Using the following statistics, calculate Jackson's current and emergency fund ratios.

Current assets	$2,000
Current liabilities	$1,000
Liquid assets	$8,000
Marketable securities	$20,000
Monthly household	$6,000

6.3 Jamie had the following figures over the past four years.

	Nondiscretionary Cost	Discretionary Cost	Total income
Year 1	$56,000	$7,000	$60,000
Year 2	$54,000	$8,000	$60,000
Year 3	$52,000	$9,000	$60,000
Year 4	$50,000	$10,000	$60,000

a. Calculate the nondiscretionary cost percentage and what the change in the ratio demonstrates over time.
b. Calculate the discretionary cost percentage and what the change demonstrates over time.
c. Calculate the total operating cost percentage and what the change demonstrates over time.
d. Indicate what your recommendation might be.

6.4 Sharon had gross income of $120,000 and nondiscretionary expenses of $32,000. She also had discretionary expenses of $10,000 and her capital expenditures on leisure items were $5,000. What is her discretionary payout percentage?

6.5 Abby had the following statistics:

Net cash flow	$6,000
Nondiscretionary expenses	$35,000
Discretionary expenses	$8,000
Targeted retirement savings	$5,000
Repayment of debt	$2,000

Calculate the gross savings percentage.

CFP®
Certification
Examination
Questions
and Problems

6.1 Robert Smith asks for your help in preparing his cash flow statement. He tells you that his salary before taxes is $250,000 and that he has *no* mortgage on his home. Which of the following statements is true about Robert's cash flow statement?

a. The value of the home would be an income source since there is *no* mortgage.

b. The value of the home would be an asset.

c. The taxes on his salary would be a liability.

d. The taxes on his salary would be an expense.

6.2 Six months ago, a client purchased a new bedroom suite for $6,500. For purposes of preparing accurate financial statements, this purchase would appear as a(an)

1. use asset on the client's net worth statement.

2. investment asset on the client's net worth statement.

3. variable outflow on the client's historic cash flow statement.

4. fixed outflow on the client's cash flow statement.

    a. (1), (2), and (3) only

    b. (1) and (3) only

    c. (2) and (4) only

    d. (4) only

    e. (1), (2), (3), and (4)

Case Application

CASH FLOW PLANNING

Savings and the Cash Flow Statement

Richard came in with his cash flow statistics and very helpful notes on projections. His list included

Revenues	
Salary	$100,000
Investment income	$8,000
Outflows	
Home Related	$20,000[1]
Food	5,000
Clothing	8,000
Health care	6,000
Transportation	2,000
Personal	3,000
Recreation	4,000
Cars, entertainment	9,000
Hobby	1,000
Gifts and charitable contributions	2,000
Insurance	6,000
Taxes	26,000[2]

[1] Includes mortgage interest and principal payments, property taxes, home maintenance, and home insurance.

[2] Net of $3,000 allowable tax loss with $191,000 tax loss carryforward on original 200,000 loss.

He said to assume that his salary will rise 6 percent a year, and his investment income is 11 percent a year (the investment loss came a year ago). His expenses should rise 3 percent a year except for medical, which will grow at a rate of 6 percent yearly, and taxes, which will grow at about 7 percent a year.

Richard said he was not worried about the losses taken. He would make them up, but Monica insisted that they save additional monies. He wanted to know what I recommended to help him save. He said he knew Monica was secretly putting away part of her household money into an account in her own name.

Case Application Questions

1. Do you have an observation on their expenditures?
2. What might the conversation above tell you about Richard?
3. What might Monica's actions tell you about both Monica and Richard?
4. What recommendations would you have to help them save more?
5. Construct their cash flow statement for this year and the next two years.
6. What do the future cash flow figures indicate?
7. Complete the cash flow section of the plan.

Chapter Seven

Debt

Chapter Goals

This chapter will enable you to:

- Develop debt strategies.
- Understand the many facets of debt.
- Calculate and comprehend the rates charged on loans.
- Identify the factors that enter into selecting credit.
- Evaluate a fixed- versus a variable-rate mortgage.
- Specify the advantages and disadvantages of a credit card loan.
- Interpret debt financial ratios.

Dan hated the thought of debt, yet here he was owing $20,000 on credit cards. Laura was very blasé about the borrowings. Not only financial issues were involved in our deliberations. Their differing points of view on debt were affecting their personal relationship.

Real Life Planning

The advisor was faced with a new situation. Instead of presenting the results of his analysis to a couple in the privacy of his office, he was to broadcast it to millions of people. A major network had contracted with him to provide a financial plan for a young couple. The results would be taped and televised on a newsmagazine show in prime time. The couple agreed to have their financial situation aired, and the taping took place in the advisor's office.

When he analyzed the couple's financial situation, it became apparent that it was dominated by debt. The husband and wife both had comfortable jobs with moderate incomes. There was nothing moderate about their credit card debt, however. It had been climbing steadily and now stood at almost six months' combined salary for them. The advisor remembered what one financially unsophisticated college graduate called her student loan, which had a 7 percent rate. She had called it an "evil loan" because it continued to climb in the amount outstanding each year even though she had not borrowed any more money. This couple's loan at an 18 percent rate if unpaid would climb much more rapidly, doubling in four years.

When questioned about the use of credit cards, the woman said she wanted to live the "American dream." She said she was going to make a large amount of money in a key executive position. The spending beyond her current means was just a down payment on her future lifestyle.

The advisor thought about her comment. On the one hand, it reflected a valid economic approach. It was consistent with Modigliani's life cycle theory of spending and saving, indicating people's desire to even out their standard of living over their lives. On the other hand, there was no indication that either person was on a fast track since recent raises had been fairly modest. When asked in a follow-up interview about the modest raises and increasing debt, the woman repeated her comment about the "American dream" and expressed a great confidence in her ability to become important. When questioned separately, the husband, who had his own credit cards and spending pattern, merely said he wasn't worried.

The advisor had seen this pattern of spending and debt before, and it often led to financial difficulty and even bankruptcy. Modigliani or not, he decided to present the findings in a sober way. At the taping he did so. He mentioned the amount outstanding and the potential for bankruptcy, and then outlined a method of gradually clearing their debt. It turned out that neither person was aware of the debt the other had amassed. Each literally pointed a finger at the other as the source of blame. (The producer told the advisor at the time that everyone in the room knew that dramatic scene would definitely be aired.) Despite that animated moment, the advisor felt the woman was not buying into that part of the plan's recommendations.

Weeks after the show was aired, the advisor spoke to the woman to find out how implementation of the plan's recommendations was going. She mentioned she had taken a position as head of an office of a U.S. subsidiary that would take advantage of her bilingual abilities, at five times her former pay. Her debt strategy had paid off. The "American dream" had come true. The debt wasn't a problem after all.

The advisor thought about his cash flow recommendations. Were they inappropriate? He decided the answer was no. For every client like her, there were ten others who needed to hear the sobering advice. Perhaps he had failed to take into account the ability of the woman to utilize the power of a nationally televised show to market herself. In any event, it was enjoyable to see that the "American dream" was alive and well.

OVERVIEW

Debt arouses many feelings. To financial planners it often represents risk. Too frequently they see abusive use of credit leading to financial difficulties. They recommend that debt be limited to investment items such as the purchase of a home.

To consumers, debt represents opportunity. Borrowing money allows people to purchase items they don't have the current cash resources for. At its extreme, it can symbolize a preference for pleasure-producing goods today over consequences for the future—in other words, overspending.

This chapter, then, is about the many faces of debt. It considers how debt should be reviewed, when it is good or bad. It gives you ratios that indicate acceptable financing practices. It details how to obtain and maintain proper credit and calculate its costs, and it discusses the advantages and disadvantages of various financing alternatives. The chapter also will explain what to do when in financial difficulty and includes an evaluation of bankruptcy.

All these topics can be incorporated under the broader heading of debt management. Under household finance, the household enterprise can have spending needs that exceed its current resources. Borrowing presents a ready source of cash flow. Debt management leads to the proper utilization of financing alternatives for efficient household operations. Just as there is an appropriate amount of debt in a business capital structure, the household must decide how much debt it wants to contract for. The decision includes not only return alternatives but the household's tolerance for risk.

Borrowing helps by providing funds to raise your standard of living today or to make investments such as those for the house and its possessions or to contribute to the financing of a business. As you can see, debt is used for many purposes. It can allow you to enjoy a product that you could not yet afford to purchase outright. It may make it possible to balance the peaks and valleys in your spending pattern within each year such as when you borrow to fund high annual vacation expenditures. It also may help you even out your life cycle style needs or enable you to make an outlay for a significant capital expenditure or other investment opportunity. Borrowing theory is presented in Appendix I of this chapter.

In sum, borrowing is a tool that we use to accelerate consumption or to help finance investments. Our financial planning objective is to use debt wisely, selecting the lowest-cost source and proper amount of borrowing consistent with our goals and tolerance for risk. In order to do so, we will first examine risk more closely.

RISK AND LEVERAGE

As our discussion above indicates, debt is often associated with risk. The higher the debt, the higher the household's risk. People who have too much debt are said to be overleveraged. Few recognize that there are two types of leverage and two types of risk: operating and financial. Although much time is spent on this subject for business, it is often neglected for households. By explaining and distinguishing between operating and financial factors, we can better understand household risk and be more effective in planning for it.

Operating risk arises from uncertainties in connection with household activities. You may spend considerable time and resources investing in a job only to find that the company you work for has limited growth prospects. The washing machine you invested in may turn out to require constant repairs. The house you purchased may decline in value. In contrast, **financial risk** comes from the amount of debt outstanding relative to your assets. If your debt rises from 10 percent to 50 percent of your total assets, your financial risk has increased substantially.

Although frequently used to refer only to financial leverage, *leverage* can actually be separated into two components: operating and financial leverage. **Operating leverage** is the degree to which you have fixed costs in your budget that come from household operating functions. The greater the percentage of your nondiscretionary costs—high fixed costs that cannot easily and quickly be cut back—the greater your operating leverage. These nondiscretionary costs are ongoing obligations.[1]

When you have high fixed costs, a modest increase or decrease in your income can have a material impact on your free cash flow. For example, enrollment of a child in an expensive private college is a fixed cost that could give you significant operating leverage. A planned outlay on an expensive vacation would not increase your leverage since its cost could easily be cut back. The higher fixed costs are as a percentage of total costs, the greater your operating leverage.

Financial leverage arises from the amount of debt outstanding and its contribution to household fixed costs. The greater the amount of your interest expense and debt repayment commitments, the greater your financial leverage. As with operating leverage, when you have high fixed financial costs, a change in your income can have substantial effects on your free cash flow. For example, a decline in income can put you in great financial difficulty. Putting debt and financial leverage together, the larger the amount of debt, the greater the financial leverage, the higher the risk.

---

[1] They are treated as such in the pure form of total portfolio management. Capitalized nondiscretionary costs and financial debt are both employed in the intent to move toward the optimal asset allocation.

FINANCIAL LEVERAGE AND RETURNS

Financial leverage can increase potential rewards for the household. It can allow us to purchase and enjoy the benefits of a car or television set earlier. Many first-time homebuyers undertake significant financial leverage by making an expensive purchase of a dwelling. For example, 80 percent or more of the purchase price of a house may come from debt and 20 percent or less from personal savings. Should the home subsequently rise sharply in price, that financial leverage can enable the member-owners to make a high return on their household investment.

In sum, we have illustrated a basic financial principle. Undertaking additional debt has two effects: It not only raises risk; it also increases potential returns. We will expand on this risk-return concept in Chapter 9 on financial investments.

Example 7.1

Matthew has no savings and had borrowed $40,000 to finance a remodeling of the furniture and furnishings in his home and to buy a car. His income is $80,000 per year including an $8,000 bonus. In a good year for his company he can double the bonus, while in a poor year the bonus could get eliminated. Using the figures below, note the change in free cash flow given the same outlays but differing levels of income and indicate his degree of financial and operating leverage.

	Expected	Good Year	Poor Year
Income	$80,000	$88,000	$72,000
Nondiscretionary[1]	59,000	59,000	59,000
Discretionary costs	4,000	4,000	4,000
Cash flow before debt	17,000	25,000	9,000
Interest cost	7,000	7,000	7,000
Repayment of debt	8,000	8,000	8,000
Free cash flow	**$2,000**	**$10,000**	**($6,000)**

[1] Excluding interest.

Matthew has high financial leverage. A 10 percent increase in his income to $88,000 results in five times as much free cash flow: $10,000 versus $2,000. On the other hand, a 10 percent decline in his income could result in a $6,000 deficit and an inability to pay debts when due. The fact that he also has high operating leverage since most of his household costs are nondiscretionary gives him little room to cut back on his lifestyle to meet his debt repayment in the event of a bad year. High operating and high financial leverage could place Matthew in a potentially vulnerable situation.

From the household's standpoint, the amount of money it will borrow depends not only on the cost of borrowing in relation to the returns received but, as indicated, also on its member-owners' risk profile. The higher the tolerance for risk, the greater the amount of debt it will be willing to borrow.

DETERMINING SIMPLE INTEREST RATES

The **interest rate** is the cost for money borrowed. In order to make a proper borrowing decision, we need to know the interest rate being charged. To calculate the real interest rate, you need to know the time period for the loan and the actual amount of money that is made available. That calculation isn't always as simple as it looks. The difference in costs is exemplified by the following three alternatives for a $5,000 loan with a $600 yearly cost to borrow.

Practical Comment   Importance of the Reason for Borrowing

What you borrow money for counts. The approach presented here treats equally capital expenditures that generate higher cash flows and capital expenditures on leisure activities that may only result in increased pleasure. However, debt borrowed for items that increase household cash flows may be less risky. These cash flows provide resources to support future household operations. An example of a potentially attractive capital expenditure would be borrowing for education designed to materially increase your future job-related income. Another would be investing in a home. Borrowing to finance purchases of durable goods would be less attractive unless it led to significantly higher cash flows.

When expectations of materially higher future income are not realistic, substantial borrowing over a period of time to maintain or increase the household's current lifestyle is generally not considered desirable. This type of borrowing reduces household resources available to support its future lifestyle. Therefore, unless the borrowing is being used to smooth out yearly payments, an ongoing pattern of borrowing for such things as a vacation or fashion-right clothing may best be put off until it can be financed internally.

Interest Paid at the End of the Period

You obtain use of the money for the entire period, in this case for an entire year. The interest rate paid is given by the formula

$$\text{Interest rate} = \frac{\text{Interest paid}}{\text{Cash made available}}$$

$$= \frac{\$600}{\$5,000}$$

$$= 12\%$$

Interest Paid at the Beginning of the Period

When interest is deducted at the beginning of the period, the amount paid in interest is the same, but the cash made available is reduced.

$$\text{Interest rate} = \frac{\text{Interest paid}}{\text{Cash made available}}$$

$$= \frac{\$600}{\$5,000 - \$600}$$

$$= \frac{\$600}{\$4,400}$$

$$= 13.6\%$$

Installment Loan

Under an installment loan, repayments may be made in equal sums throughout the year. The key point is that the cash made available decreases constantly through the period of the loan. Assuming a one-year loan retired in 12 equal monthly installments of interest and principal of $466.67, the cash available would decline by that amount per month.

$$\text{Monthly installment} = \frac{\$5,000 + \$600}{12}$$

$$= \$466.67$$

The interest cost can be approximated by estimating the average amount of cash available, taking the amount at the beginning and the end of the period and dividing by 2.

$$\text{Interest rate} = \frac{I_P}{(CA_{BP} - CA_{EP})/2}$$

where

I_P = Interest paid

CA_{BP} = Cash available at the beginning of the period

CA_{EP} = Cash available at the end of the period

$$= \frac{600}{(5,000 - 0)/2}$$

$$= \frac{600}{2,500}$$

$$= 24\%$$

The actual cost can be calculated in the following manner:

Calculator Solution

Inputs: 12 5,000 −466.67

N	I/Y	PV	PMT	FV

Solution: **1.7882**

Press i = 1.7882% (Monthly interest)

$$\text{Annual interest} = 1.7882 \times 12 \text{ months}$$
$$= 21.5\%$$

The actual annual rate is 21.5%.

Annual Percentage Rate

The annual percentage rate (APR) must be given to borrowers under a federal law that requires lenders to provide an effective interest rate on consumer loans[2] and the total amount of finance charges. The APR includes all defined costs such as closing fees, points, and appraisal fees on mortgage loans on a time-weighted basis. It serves as a useful method for comparing costs on loan alternatives.

BORROWING FACTORS

Over the past decade, credit card use has become available to more households with higher combined total borrowing limits. At the same time, home equity loans have become easier to obtain and are being utilized more widely. The result has been greater credit availability to a wider cross-section of households. There are many issues that are involved when we borrow money. We will consider several of them below.

[2] Exceptions include margin loans on securities, loans over $25,000 not collateralized by real property, and loans from sellers' former occupants of houses.

Sources of Debt

Many financing sources are available to consumers. They differ by such factors as the interest rate charged, whether the interest cost is tax-deductible, whether the loan is secured by specific assets, and whether it is a closed-end or open-end credit loan. **Closed-end retail credit** is generally limited to a specific loan with a specific repayment schedule. One example is an auto loan. **Open-end credit** provides a loan limit that can be utilized for multiple purchases over a period of time. Part payments on scheduled retirements of debt owed may be allowed. An example of an open-end loan is a credit card loan.

Interest Rates Charged by Lenders

In theory, lenders should present an array of interest rates with the rate offered appropriate to the risk of nonpayment that the individual household presents. Instead there often appears to be one interest rate offered per lender. Loan applicants are placed into two risk classes,[3] with one rejected and the other accepted. The lender may be basing the interest rate on the average quality of the loans, with lenders who have lower-quality borrower pools charging higher interest rates. There is some indication that for certain types of loans, the interest rate charged may not be highly sensitive to changes in market rates.[4]

Types of Borrowers

The balance sheets, cash flow statements, and preferences for spending today differ for borrowers. The variation can be thought of as indicating two types of borrowers: unrationed and rationed.[5] **Unrationed borrowers** have sufficient internal cash flow and assets to be able to select the loan maturity offering the most attractive rates. When rates change, their decisions on amount, type, and repayment period for credit may change. **Rationed borrowers,** on the other hand, are short of internal cash flow and would like to borrow more credit at comparable interest rates than is available.[6] These borrowers, who are constantly seeking more funds, may have to take any payment terms offered.

Credit Standards

A number of items are used to assess whether credit should be extended to a household; these include the amount of income earned, the amount of debt outstanding, the history of timely repayments of debt owed, and whether the loan is secured by an asset such as the durable good being purchased.[7] We will return to this subject later in the chapter when we discuss credit reports.

---

[3] The approach may be a practical embodiment of Modigliani and Miller's risk classes. See Franco Modigliani and Merton H. Miller, "The Cost of Capital, Corporation Finance and the Theory of Investment," *American Economic Review* 48, no. 3 (June 1958), pp. 261–97.

[4] D. Brito and P. Hartley, "Consumer Rationality and Credit Cards," *Journal of Political Economy* 103, no. 2 (April 1995), pp. 400–33.

[5] Thomas Juster, "Consumer Sensitivity to the Price of Credit," *Journal of Finance* 19, no. 2 (1964), pp. 222–33.

[6] For an explanation, see David Cox,and Tullio Jappelli, "The Effect of Borrowing Constraints on Consumer Liabilities," *Journal of Money, Credit and Banking* 25, no. 2 (May 1993), pp. 197–213, and Eun Young Chah, Valerie Ramey, and Ross Starr, "Liquidity Constraints and Intertemporal Consumer Optimization: Theory and Evidence from Durable Goods," *Journal of Money, Credit and Banking* 27, no. 1 (February 1995), pp. 272–87.

[7] See Jane Bryant Quinn, *Making the Most of Your Money* (New York: Simon and Schuster, 1997), pp. 219–21.

Outcome

The outcome is that households often have a variety of borrowing alternatives at various interest rates. The ultimate selection is generally to take the lowest-cost alternative. This approach is consistent with centralized decision making; the decision is not necessarily made to link the borrowing to the item purchased but is usually made on an overall basis.

For example, a home equity loan may be used to finance the purchase of a car instead of an auto loan. As the amount of debt increases, the household will qualify for fewer loan alternatives and the cost of credit will increase. At some point, the cost of credit discourages further borrowing or, in some cases, it can reach the government-sanctioned limit of a 24 percent annual rate.

Long-Term versus Short-Term Debt

Short-term debt is money owed that is payable in a relatively brief period. For accounting purposes it is debt due within the current year, while in investment usage it is debt payable within three years. Examples of short-term debt are general credit card debt and credit extended by particular stores for purchases of clothing or durable goods such as a television.

Long-term debt involves financial obligations whose terms call for final payment to be made many years from now. While for accounting purposes it is any debt not due in the current year, it can be thought of as debt payable in four years or longer.[8] Examples are home mortgages, bank debt, and other loans such as those from friends and family members.

The length of the financing period should be matched to the size and benefits of the item creating the need for the borrowing. A house that serves as an investment will not normally be financed over a few years, while the purchase of clothing or short-lived household goods should not result in long-term debt. In fact, many would say that the use of credit for items other than capital expenditures should be limited to repayment within 30 days or for cyclical peaks in outlays to be paid off when demand for funds lessens, generally within the year.

Secured versus Unsecured Debt

Secured debt is borrowing that has a separate asset serving as collateral, to be sold by the creditor for repayment in the event the debtor is unable to do so. Examples of secured debt are a mortgage and an auto loan which are secured by the house or the automobile bought for which credit is extended. If someone cosigns for a loan, the loan can be thought of as secured since it obligates the cosigner to pay if the debtor does not.

Unsecured debt is borrowing whose repayment is based solely on the full faith and credit of the debtor. Of course, in the event of default the creditor can sue to recover the money owed.

Naturally, most creditors prefer secured debt since it lowers their credit risk, and they typically offer a lower interest rate for this type of loan. The disadvantage of a secured loan to the borrower is the greater probability that the asset will be repossessed in the event of financial difficulty.

There are many types of borrowings. We will discuss each of the major types, starting with real estate mortgages.

MORTGAGES

Mortgages are loans secured by real property. The U.S. government has placed a priority on housing availability and affordability for the average American. The government allows interest on debt used to purchase real estate to be deductible for income tax purposes.

---

[8] In investment usage a third category, intermediate-term debt, is employed which extends from three to ten years. Debt due beyond ten years is called long-term debt.

Deductions are allowable for up to $1 million of debt for the purchase of a house and up to another $100,000 in loans for any other purpose. Because these loans are tax-deductible and are secured by real estate, they are often the least expensive form of borrowing available to the average household.

Two publicly owned companies—the Federal National Mortgage Association (FNMA), known as Fannie Mae, and the Federal Home Loan Mortgage Corporation (FHLMC), called Freddie Mac—purchase mortgages from lenders like banks. Some people believe the U.S. government would step in to help these companies in the event of a severe financial difficulty for them, which may have allowed them to become very powerful in the mortgage lending business. The Government National Mortgage Association (GNMA), known as Ginnie Mae, provides the full faith and credit of the U.S. government as a guarantee of payment for buyers of bonds. The Federal Housing Authority (FHA) and the Veterans Administration (VA) insure selected mortgages against default. The net effect of these government-supported organizations is to broaden credit and offer it at a cheaper rate than might otherwise prevail.

Obtaining a mortgage allows you to purchase a property well before you would be able to through cash resources alone. As a borrower, you would go through the following process in making a loan.

Loan Process

The Loan Application

You fill out a loan application that includes such factors as current job, current income, bank accounts, and assets owned.

Assessment of the Borrower

Your characteristics and past history as a proposed borrower are appraised. Factors include household income in relation to size of loans; household assets, particularly marketable ones; other debt outstanding; and credit history. Whenever possible, it is a good idea to clear up any blemishes on your credit record well before applying for a loan.

Home Appraisal

Each house is generally given an appraised valuation based on the current market value. The amount of the loan is compared with the assessed valuation, with the lender often providing a maximum of 80 percent of the value of the home. Increasingly, a down payment of lower than 20 percent is available when the borrower purchases insurance against default and/or pays a higher interest rate.

Commitment

The lender finishes its credit screen and agrees to supply the agreed-upon sum to the borrower. Generally, the interest rate on the loan is not set until closing unless you pay an additional sum to lock it in at an earlier time.

Other

There are other factors and people who have a role in the real estate purchase and finance process. The buyer will inspect the home, probably with an expert, to identify potential problems such as structural ones. A title search and title insurance must be implemented and property insurance purchased. The Realtor, if any, who helped find and negotiate the price will be getting a commission. Attorneys in many respects coordinate the process, often with separate attorneys for the buyer, seller, and lender providing funds for the buyer.

TABLE 7.1
15-Year Mortgage Payment Model

Mortgage amount	$200,000
Annual interest rate	7%
Monthly interest rate	0.5833%
Loan term (in years)	15
Loan term (in months)	180
Monthly payment	$1,797.66
Annual payment	$21,571.88

Year	Total Payment at End of Year[1]	Principal	Interest
1	$21,571.88	$7,819.60	$13,752.28
2	$21,571.88	$8,384.88	$13,187.00
3	$21,571.88	$8,991.02	$12,580.86
4	$21,571.88	$9,640.98	$11,930.90
5	$21,571.88	$10,337.93	$11,233.95
6	$21,571.88	$11,085.26	$10,486.62
7	$21,571.88	$11,886.61	$9,685.27
8	$21,571.88	$12,745.89	$8,825.98
9	$21,571.88	$13,667.30	$7,904.58
10	$21,571.88	$14,655.31	$6,916.57
11	$21,571.88	$15,714.74	$5,857.14
12	$21,571.88	$16,850.76	$4,721.12
13	$21,571.88	$18,068.90	$3,502.98
14	$21,571.88	$19,375.10	$2,196.77
15	$21,571.88	$20,775.73	$796.15

[1]Mortgage payments for $200,000 at a 7 percent interest rate for 15 years (using payment schedule).

Closing

All parties to the purchase of the house meet, and all terms are set per contract including the interest rate, which is based on market factors at the time. The contract is signed, and title is passed to the buyer.

Points are fees paid to the bank to cover their administration fees. Borrowers are often allowed to reduce the interest cost on the loan by selecting the number of points they will pay at the time of closing. The greater the points, the lower the interest rate will be; sometimes there will be a one-quarter-point decrease in rate for each point paid at the time of closing. The points can be tax-deductible in the year the house is purchased for first-time financing of a home. Otherwise, they are deductible in equal amounts over the life of the mortgage.

The vast majority of mortgage loans are amortizing loans, as is true of most long-term consumer debt. This means both interest and principal are paid off over time. At the beginning of the term of the loan, the largest part of the payment is interest, but as principal is paid off and interest cost is reduced, a rising portion is applied to the paydown of principal. Toward the end of the mortgage, the overwhelming amount is usually applied to repayment of principal. The most common period for mortgages is 15 or 30 years. The breakdown of total cash outflow into payments of principal and interest is shown in Table 7.1.

The impact of mortgage payments on most households' cash flow tends to lessen over time. Incomes tend to rise, but mortgage costs often are fully or approximately level. Therefore, the household mortgage burden usually declines over extended periods. Moreover, as the portion of the monthly payment that is principal increases, the net equity in the house rises more quickly. Example 7.2 shows how to calculate monthly mortgage payments.

Example 7.2

Max just closed on a house and has taken out a 30-year fixed-rate mortgage for $200,000 at a 7.2 percent rate. What is the monthly mortgage payment?

Change annual rates into monthly figures.

	Amount	Explanation
Monthly interest rate	0.6%	$\frac{7.2\%}{12 \text{ months}}$
Number of compounding periods	360	30 years × 12 months

Calculator Solution

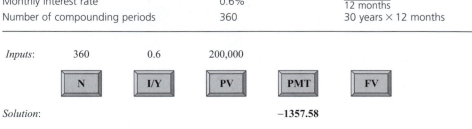

Inputs: 360   0.6   200,000

N   I/Y   PV   PMT   FV

Solution: **−1357.58**

Press PMT = ($1357.58)

Prepayments on Mortgage Debt

Prepayments of mortgage debt can be considered by any household generating the necessary cash flow to do so. For example, some households think about paying their mortgage every four weeks instead of monthly, which in effect results in one extra payment a year. Their goal is, of course, to eliminate their debt earlier.

The prepayment decision for mortgage or any other debt should be looked at as an alternative investment decision. The after-tax interest cost on the debt retired should be compared with the after-tax return on investment alternatives. For a fair comparison, prepayment and the investment alternative should have approximately the same risk, or the returns should be adjusted for difference in risk.

One other factor to consider is liquidity risk. Paying off debt can reduce the amount of money available in the event of an unforeseen need for cash. You can liquidate an investment in marketable securities within a few days, while in certain circumstances it can be difficult to borrow money—for example, if you lose your job.

Example 7.3

Alex was a conservative investor with a considerable amount of available cash. He invested all of his money in taxable bonds, which at the time were yielding 4 percent annually. He had a mortgage with a 6.5 percent interest rate. Alex was considering investing his current year's savings in the bonds. Then he realized that prepayment of his mortgage could be considered as an alternative investment vehicle.

Alex thought about the tax savings he would lose on the tax-deductible interest expense if he prepaid. On the other hand, investing in the bonds instead would subject him to taxation on the interest income received.

What it came down to was whether the interest saved on the mortgage exceeded the hurdle rate on investing in the marketplace with securities of approximately the same risk. He already had plenty of cash for emergencies. The 6.5 percent expense saving substantially exceeded the 4 percent hurdle rate, and he began prepaying the mortgage.

Types of Mortgages

Basically, there are two types of mortgages: fixed- and variable-rate mortgages. Each has distinct advantages and disadvantages.

Fixed-Rate Mortgages

Fixed-rate mortgages (FRMs) are those whose interest rate remains stable over time. They offer the certainty of a level rate of interest over the life of the mortgage. Because interest rates don't fluctuate, there is no interest rate risk[9] for the borrower.

---

[9] Except for the cost of refinancing.

Practical Comment Analyzing the ARM Rate

People sometimes place too much emphasis on the initial rate on ARMs, which can appear highly attractive. In fact, this rate is known as a teaser rate. What can be more important is the length of time the rate will be in effect and, even more significantly, the interest rate when the teaser rate expires.

The fully let-out rate, the rate after the teaser rate expires, is based on the current benchmark rate plus an add-on rate and is often the more meaningful one for decision purposes. For example, two mortgages may be similar in all respects except that one offers a 5 percent teaser rate for one year and then an adjustable rate benchmarked to the one-year U.S. Treasury plus 2.75 percent. The other has a 6 percent teaser but is then benchmarked to the one-year Treasury plus 1.50 percent. It is simple to conclude that the second, which saves 1.25 percent each year over the rest of the loan period, is more attractive.

Many homeowners are attracted to fixed-rate mortgages, which have two benefits. They lock in a rate of interest that will be unaffected by a rise in market rates. They also provide the opportunity to refinance should market rates decline. On the other hand, you pay a price for these benefits as the interest rate will generally be higher because of these benefits.

Adjustable-Rate Mortgages

Adjustable-rate mortgages (ARMs) are those whose interest rates to the borrower fluctuate yearly based on overall market rates of interest at the time. They are based on a benchmark rate of interest, such as the rates on one- or three-year U.S. Treasury obligations or the Federal Home Loan Bond Rate, which tends to be less volatile. The mortgage rate is equal to the benchmark rate plus an additional amount, often 1 to 3 percent.

Adjustable-rate mortgages often have lower rates of interest than fixed-rate mortgages over the term of the loan. To compensate for assuming the risk of fluctuations in interest rates, the borrower receives a lower rate. The most pronounced difference in rates occurs within the first three years, when borrowers are frequently offered below-market interest rates as an inducement to get them to take an adjustable-rate loan. The lower initial rate makes it easier for homeowners to qualify to purchase a larger house or larger loan. This is true because lenders tend to look at total interest costs in relation to household income in the first year of the loan.

The materially lower interest cost in early years can prove attractive for people who expect to move within a few years. You have the comfort of knowing that should interest rates decline, your cost will be adjusted down without the need to refinance. Fixed-rate loans often require significant costs to refinance. On the other hand, adjustable-rate mortgages are disadvantageous when rates rise. They don't allow you to lock into a rate, although it is possible to switch to a fixed-rate loan when you believe interest rates are low.

Many adjustable-rate loans provide interest rate limits called *caps*. The caps limit the increase for any one-year period and provide for a maximum rate that can be charged over the life of the loan. If rates rise sharply, borrowers of ARMs can be subject to negative amortization, which means that the monthly payment does not cover the higher interest cost. Consequently, the amount of the mortgage outstanding increases instead of declining.

In response to borrower concerns about interest rate fluctuations, many borrowers offer what can be termed a **hybrid ARM.** This is a mortgage that offers a fixed rate for a fixed period of years and then reverts to an adjustable rate.

TABLE 7.2
Summary of Mortgage Characteristics

	Fixed Rates	**Variable Rates**
Interest rate risk	Lender assumes the risk of increase in rates	Borrower assumes risk of increase in rates
Rates decline	Borrower can refinance when interest savings exceed fixed cost of refinancing	Rate changed automatically and declines on yearly benchmark date
Relative interest cost	Higher due to flat-rate guarantee and refinancing option	Lower due to borrower absorption of interest rate risk
Projected holding period	No material advantage or disadvantage	Can have advantages in cost if only holding for a few years due to benefits of teaser rate
Qualification for loan	More difficult than for ARM	Easier due to low initial teaser rate

Table 7.2 summarizes the advantages and disadvantages of the two types of mortgages.

Refinancing

Refinancing is an alternative when market rates decline. It is most often exercised by holders of fixed-rate loans. Holders of ARMs also may switch to a fixed-rate loan if they perceive the current fixed rate to be attractive. This would happen when rates are expected to rise. To determine whether it is profitable to refinance, the savings in interest cost over the term of the loan held is compared against the current outlay for refinancing. Refinancing costs including points, lawyer, title insurances, and so on are significant.

Thus, whether to refinance becomes a capital budgeting decision. In calculating the cumulative savings from refinancing, the possibility of selling the home and repaying the mortgage prior to the end of the mortgage period should be incorporated. The average period of residence in any one home is approximately five years,[10] in contrast to mortgages that are often for 15 or 30 years. Market declines in fixed-rate mortgages can make mortgage refinancing even more frequent.

Example 7.4

Elena has 15 years left on her 30-year fixed-rate mortgage, which has an 8 percent interest rate. She is thinking of refinancing as mortgage rates have declined to 7 percent. She has $140,000 left on her mortgage and would have to pay $3,000 to refinance. Assume it is all tax-deductible. Elena expects to live in the house for another seven years. She is in the 28 percent marginal tax bracket and can earn 6 percent after tax on an alternative use for the money. Should she refinance?[11]

	Amount	**Explanation**
Cost to refinance	$3,000	As given
Yearly tax-deductible amount	$200	3,000 ÷ 15 years
Yearly tax savings	$56	200 × 0.28
Yearly savings from rate decline	1%	8% − 7%
Yearly interest savings pretax	$1,400	140,000 × 1%
Yearly interest savings after tax	$1,008	1,400 × (1 − 0.28)
Savings		
Yearly tax savings	$56	
Yearly interest savings after tax	$1,008	
Total yearly savings	$1,064	

[10] Jason P. Schachter and Jeffrey J. Kuenzi, "Seasonality of Moves and the Duration and Tenure of Residence: 1996," Population Division Working Paper Series No. 69 (Washington: Population Division, U.S. Census Bureau, December 2002), http://www.census.gov/population/www/documentation/twps0069/twps0069.html.

[11] Calculation is approximate since, among other things, the savings in interest expense will decline as the mortgage does.

Calculator Solution[12]

General Calculator Approach	HP12C	TI BA II Plus
Clear the register		CF
	f FIN	2nd CLR Work
Enter initial cash outflow	3,000 CHS g CF₀	3,000 +/− ENTER ↓
Enter yearly savings	1,064 g CFⱼ	1,064 ENTER ↓
Enter number of years	7 g Nⱼ	7 ENTER ↓
Calculate the internal rate of return	f IRR	IRR CPT
	30%	30%

The 30 percent rate of return is attractive relative to the 6 percent investment alternative. Therefore, the mortgage should be refinanced. The loan value and interest rate savings will decline over the term of the loan. Consequently, this yearly savings is somewhat overstated. For a more accurate figure, use the breakdown of interest cost on the mortgage repayment schedule.

Home Equity Loans

A **home equity loan** is one that is secured by the house you own. In effect, it is a second mortgage, which means that it has a second priority on the house. In the event of nonpayment, the lender will have the proceeds remaining after the first mortgage holder is paid off. Because of this higher risk, the interest charged will be higher than that on a first mortgage. On the other hand, it is secured by a substantial asset, and homeowners are generally reluctant to default on the house they live in.

Therefore, the pretax cost of a home equity loan is still among the lowest available to the consumer. Moreover, the outlay for interest on the first $100,000 for single or married persons (or $50,000 if married and filing separately) of borrowing on a home equity loan is tax-deductible regardless of the purpose of the loan. Home equity loans for real estate activities are tax-deductible up to $1,000,000 for one property and $1,200,000 for two personal properties.

When substantial loan amounts are needed for work on the house or for other purposes, you may have a choice of taking out a home equity loan or refinancing the first mortgage for a larger amount. The two relevant factors in making such a decision are the interest rate on the mortgage outstanding and the amount by which the interest rate on the proposed home equity loan exceeds the current market rate on a new first mortgage.

It is often best to take out a home equity loan when the rate on your existing first mortgage is well below the market rate and the total sum of the original mortgage is large relative to the total amount of housing debt that will be outstanding after the additional borrowing.

Frequently, it is better for you to refinance when current rates are lower than those existing on your first mortgage. Although home equity loans may contain front-end closing costs, competition has sometimes compelled lenders to waive them.

Example 7.5

Martin and Kristin both had need for an additional $4,000 in cash and had to decide whether to refinance their existing mortgage to obtain a larger sum or to take out a home equity loan instead. The market rate on a new mortgage loan is 6 percent while one on a home equity loan is 7.5 percent. Martin has a 7 percent existing fixed-rate mortgage with $100,000 left on it, while Kristin has a 10 percent fixed-rate mortgage with $210,000 remaining to pay. Martin is probably better off with a home equity loan because of the low rate on his existing mortgage and thousands of dollars in closing costs to obtain a new first mortgage. Kristin, on the

[12] For an explanation of IRR evaluation of rates of return generated by it, see Chapter 8.

Practical Comment   Home Equity Loans and Retirement

Historically, the home has been one of the linchpins of a secure retirement. Often when people have reached their early 60s, the mortgage has been paid off, which reduces the cost of living in retirement. Moreover, when people sell their house to move to a smaller residence, or to a less expensive location, free cash is frequently generated in the shift.

By offering home equity loans, often without extensive paperwork, time, or cost, banks have made it convenient to use the house as a source of low-cost credit. The credit terms may be largely the same for a younger borrower whose income will rise and who will have many years to repay and for an older person with fewer years until retirement. The borrowing limits on a home equity loan are higher than those on a credit card since the lender has a secured asset.

While a homeowner could always have refinanced a first mortgage or taken out a second one,

the up-front processing cost and time to close made it attractive only for major additional borrowings. The home equity loan, on the other hand, can be used in ways that differ little from that of a major credit card. The result can be a slowly mounting accumulation of debt over time that reduces the equity in a home by the time the owner retires.

Therefore, the home equity loan in practice has advantages and disadvantages. It is usually the low-est-cost source of debt besides a first mortgage, with fairly easy access to it. At the same time, it reduces the benefit of the forced savings component of the house through paydown of debt over time. Consequently, for homeowners with weaker disci-pline and less foresight, the monthly repayment has the potential to erode their standard of living in retirement.

other hand, is better off refinancing rather than taking the home equity loan. She will save money on the new mortgage over the existing one. She would save four percentage points by refinancing a much larger sum than Martin's. The ability to save so much on her entire bor-rowings makes it the best choice for her.

Because a home equity loan is often the only loan that qualifies for a tax deduction, it is often the lowest-cost loan for those who qualify, and can be particularly useful in financing sizeable purchases of any type such as those for automobiles.

Home Equity Line of Credit

Closely aligned with a home equity loan is a home equity line of credit (HELOC). Instead of providing a fixed sum as a home equity loan does, a HELOC allows you to draw down part or all of a maximum amount as you wish. As with a home equity loan, it represents a second mortgage on your property. The advantages of a HELOC are the flexibility to take out only what you need and the ability to pay just interest, not principal, for an extended period of time.

The disadvantages of a HELOC range from a potentially higher level of interest and greater vulnerability to a boost in market interest rates because there may not be an inter-est rate cap as there is with an adjustable-rate mortgage (ARM). In addition, the lender is given the right to withdraw the line of credit periodically, which, if it happened, would necessitate either refinancing elsewhere or otherwise coming up with the funds, or risk los-ing your home.

A HELOC can be viewed as resembling a credit card that is secured by your home. It provides additional flexibility at a higher cost relative to a home equity loan[13] but a con-siderably lower after-tax cost when compared with a credit card loan.

---

[13] The APR for a HELOC cannot be compared with the one for a home equity loan since the compo-nents entering the calculations for the two differ.

CREDIT CARD DEBT

Credit card debt is the most common form of consumer loan debt in the United States. Credit cards can be distinguished from debit cards. Unlike credit cards, debit cards are not a source of additional funds through borrowing cash because purchase costs are automatically deducted from bank balances.

Credit card debt typically comes from purchasing consumer goods, although withdrawals for cash are permitted. If repayments are made within a grace period, say 25 days, no interest is charged. Thereafter, monthly interest is charged using varying methods that may be based on the previous month's closing balance or those sums outstanding, which more accurately reflect payments during the month.

Interest on credit cards is often offered at a high rate relative to interest on other consumer loans. Selected individuals with strong assets and credit histories may receive below-average credit card rates, but these still may be above that for many other consumer loans. Many advisors, including financial planners and accountants, view credit cards as an "evil lure," tempting people to spend more than they should and then charging them double-digit rates that can make it difficult to repay the loan. The public, on the other hand, uses them heavily. It can be instructive to identify the reasons why they are so popular.

First, credit cards can be utilized as a convenience card. As long as the money is paid off during the month, there is no interest cost; in effect, you receive free credit. Convenience for some also means using a card instead of carrying large amounts of cash and having to count out payments needed and receiving smaller cash sums as change.

Second, there is an advantage to credit cards in helping people structure their lives. Credit cards can be used to even out flows of expenditures without disrupting normal income and savings patterns. For example, normal monthly savings can continue while the bulge in summer vacation expenditure can be financed by credit cards and repaid over the next several months.

Third, credit cards can be employed as an alternative to holding larger cash balances. Large cash balances are used as a precaution against running out of liquidity in the event of unforeseen circumstances. Although the cost of credit card debt may be higher than that for investment alternatives, the fact that the debt is only used for part of the year for emergencies or for cyclical spending and is repaid promptly when cash flow permits[14] can still make it an efficient way to borrow. In this way, the ability to use credit cards can permit existing cash funds to be used for a full year at normal investment returns instead of at lower precautionary money market returns.

Finally, when credit card debt is compared with regular bank loans, the bank loans are more costly for amounts under a few thousand dollars when fixed costs and transaction costs are included. For larger amounts, credit card debt in some cases may still be attractive versus full-period loans if they are only outstanding for part-period peaks in expenditures.

In sum, credit cards do have significant advantages that can help account for their popularity. However, as the Practical Comment on the next page indicates, they have to be used with the personalities and behavior patterns of the people in mind.

MARGIN DEBT

Margin debt is money generally offered by securities dealers to help finance purchase of marketable investments such as individual stocks, bonds, and mutual funds. The securities serve as collateral for the loan. The maximum amount available for borrowing is set by the

---

[14] When not repaid according to the repayment schedule, a person's credit rating could be impaired.

Practical Comment Credit Cards and Personality

Given the advantages stated on page 153, despite the negative opinions among the financial press and many advisors, credit cards sometimes can be an efficient source of credit. Moreover, credit card statements, possibly in coordination with your checkbook, can be used as a fairly simple way to identify your total expenditures, easily separate them by type, and plan and execute monthly payments. In other words, credit cards have some distinct advantages in convenience of use and in structuring repayments.

Whether they are used efficiently or become an ongoing problem depends on the borrower's personality. Basically, there seem to be two types of people: savers and spenders.[15] Savers operate under the life cycle theory, putting away appropriate sums for retirement, unforeseen emergencies, and college expenditures for any children. They use credit cards as a rational financial alternative. Spenders may place the greatest emphasis on pleasure today. In economic terms, they have a high marginal rate of time preference.[16] Spenders may have difficulty putting away resources for the future, even when they recognize its importance.

Many spenders seek help through structure, including planned-out actions. For example, they may prefer that monies be withdrawn directly for retirement savings rather than have money pass through their hands. Credit cards can be the antithesis of what they need. Although credit cards can structure repayments, people must have the ability to follow through. Otherwise, the credit card represents an ongoing opportunity to spend without immediate consequence, wherever they go.

People also may deemphasize the cost of credit since it too has no current impact. Some spend up to the limits that companies offer. Ironically, these people may not be good candidates for a loan to consolidate their debt—for example, a home equity loan. They need the structure of being "maxed out" on their credit cards. It is because of such people that credit cards have developed negative connotations.

[15] N. Gregory Mankiw, "The Savers-Spenders Theory of Fiscal Policy," *American Economic Review* 90, no. 2 (May 2000), pp. 120–25.

[16] See Appendix I to this chapter for an explanation of the term.

Federal Reserve. It is 50 percent of the fair market value of the securities on margin upon original purchase and minimum 25 percent of the value of the collateral on an ongoing basis.

Because of the ease with which the lender can liquidate the collateral in the event of default, the margin rate is often among the lowest pretax rates available to the borrower. In addition, margin debt is tax-deductible up to the amount of taxable interest and dividend income for the year. The amount of interest expense that is greater than this income can be carried forward to the next year.[17] The deduction is only available for loans made for investment purposes. Therefore, a margin loan intended to finance a noninvestment item would not qualify.

OTHER SECURED DEBT

A loan that is secured by a valuable asset can have a relatively low rate. That asset can be liquidated by the lender to pay off the loan in the event of nonpayment. The most common example is an auto loan. In assessing auto loan rates, a credit subsidy by the manufacturer or dealer should be separated from interest rates for this type of loan. The rate can be a disguised discount on purchase of the automobile. If so, in some cases, a greater discount may be made available for cash purchase. When a cash purchase has no benefit for discount purposes, the subsidized interest rate can be very competitive. In the absence of a highly

[17] There is also the option of using capital gains income to offset taxable interest expense, but it will reduce the ability to use low tax rates on capital gains.

subsidized rate, when a home equity loan is available, it generally will be a less expensive way to finance this large capital outlay.

BANK LOANS

Bank loans can be made for purposes other than purchase of a home. They come in many forms and either are amortized over the life of the loan or are due by a specific date. Banks qualify borrowers by purposes of the loan, household income, and assets and credit history. Bank loans not made through credit cards can be lower than those for many other unsecured borrowings—particularly for qualifying borrowers who borrow significant sums.

CREDIT UNIONS

Credit unions, also called credit associations, are set up by individuals or companies that lend money to their members. In some cases, the rates are highly competitive, which can be attributed to such factors as the association's nonprofit status, the absence of marketing expenses, and, often, the above-average credit quality of its members.

PENSION LOANS

A loan against 401(k) or other pension assets can be taken if the employee plan permits it. Guidelines may be set by individual companies, but overall limits are 50 percent of the borrower's vested account balance or $50,000, whichever is less. The approach varies from assets withdrawn and interest costs paid directly to that employee's pension to loans against assets with monies paid to the company and pension assets staying intact. The time frame for repayments is generally stated, with maximum repayment dates set by the government, generally a maximum of five years. When repayment terms are not met, loans become distributions subject to income tax and potentially a 10 percent penalty tax. The interest cost to borrow is established by the employer and can vary from plan to plan.

LIFE INSURANCE LOANS

After certain life insurance policies are in existence for some time—for example, whole life policies—they can develop significant cash values. Those amounts can be borrowed in a process that is somewhat similar to that for loans from pension plans. However, repayment terms, if any, are less stringent than for pension plans. The rates for borrowing from cash value are stated in the contract. Sometimes taking out loans on policies can result in

Practical Comment   Loans from Friends and Relatives

Loans from friends and family are often fraught with risk. The problems are due primarily to different perceptions. Communication about the interest and repayment terms is often vague. For example, the borrower may assume that the loan will be paid off in a few years when he or she can afford to do so. From the same conversation, the lender may come away with the belief that the money will be repaid much more quickly, as soon as the borrower's liquidity problem has been resolved.

Each party may have a different point of view about whether such items as vacations come before or after repayment. Each may be uncomfortable with discussing the terms in what can be a combined business and personal transaction. When it becomes apparent that the two parties understand the loan terms differently, one or both may become frustrated, but the personal relationship may prevent them from speaking about it. The net outcome can sometimes harm that relationship.

To overcome the potential problem, it may be best not to borrow from people with whom you have a close relationship. When borrowing is to take place, it should be done in a strict businesslike way with the borrowing terms (including the interest rate) and repayment schedule established. An exception can be made for monies lent by parents to children, particularly for down payment on a new home. Here there is an emotional side to the loan including an attachment that extends beyond financial returns. The sum provided may not truly be a loan, but can be an advance against an estate distribution with repayment required only if the parents need the money. Where there is true loan intent, it too should be handled in a businesslike way.[18]

[18] Teri Agins, "When a Friend Asks for Money, Try Saying 'No,'" *The Wall Street Journal* (Eastern edition), August 6, 1985, p. 1.

lower assigned rates of return on the cash value of policies. Older policies at low rates can make attractive borrowing alternatives.

OTHER MARKET LOANS

There are a variety of loans available, including those from retail establishments to purchase their goods, from consumer finance companies to receive cash, and from pawnbrokers who require assets deposited as collateral. Their costs may be greater in part because the rate of nonrepayment of the debt may be higher than for, say, a bank loan.

EDUCATIONAL LOANS

College loans are often made based on need. The rates on these loans granted by the federal government or the college attended by full-time students can present an attractive alternative for those who qualify. A $2,500 tax deduction is available for student loans, but it is phased out based on modified adjusted gross income (MAGI) of $50–65,000 for singles and $100–130,000 for those filing joint returns. Mandatory payments are set up once income-producing activities begin.

LOANS FROM RELATIVES AND FRIENDS

Loans from relatives and friends can be a significant source of financing. Typically, the personal relationship is a factor in extending the loan. However, the loan itself must contain a market-related interest rate. If it doesn't, the loan can be considered a gift, and the borrower will not be able to deduct the interest paid.

TABLE 7.3 **Summary of Loan Alternatives**

	Type of Credit	Cost of Debt (pretax)	Tax Deductible	Cost of Debt (after tax)	Secured	Explanation
First mortgage	Closed end	Very low	Yes	Generally the lowest	Yes	Tax deduction limited to $1 million per home when purchased or redeveloped, $1.2 million per two homes
Home equity: Second mortgage Line of credit	Open end	Low	Yes	Very low	Yes	Maximum tax deduction limited to building cost plus $100,000 for all purposes[1]
Credit card debt	Open end	High	No	High	No	Other factors may reduce effective interest rate for noncontinuing debt
Credit association loan	Closed end	Low to medium	No	Low	No	
Bank loan	Closed end	Medium	No	Medium	Varies	
Pension loan	Closed end	Low to medium	Not for interest cost	Low to medium	Yes	
Insurance loan	Open end	Low to medium	Not for interest cost	Varies	Yes	
Educational loan	Open end	Low to medium	Yes[2]	Low to medium	No	
Loan from friends and relatives	Varies	Varies	No	Varies	Usually not	
Other loans: Finance company Pawnbroker etc.	Closed end	High	No	High	Varies	

[1] Actual tax deduction restricted to the amount of current real estate debt plus any new capital expenditures on the home and an additional $100,000 for all other purposes.
[2] Interest on educational loans is tax-deductible up to $2,500 per year.

OVERALL PROCEDURE

Once the money has been borrowed, the interest expense is generally considered a nondiscretionary cost in the cash flow statement, regardless of the purpose of the loan. For example, whether the borrowing occurred to purchase skis, food, a house, or common stocks, the interest expense related to these purchases becomes an ongoing nondiscretionary cost for the household.

A summary of the relevant characteristics of loan alternatives is presented in Table 7.3. Pay particular attention to the cost column. Wherever possible, it will typically be most beneficial to select the lowest-cost alternative.

CONTINGENT LIABILITIES

Contingent liabilities are potential cash outflows dependent on the occurrence of a possible event. For example, if you cosign for a loan with others, you will be obligated if they default. If you don't eliminate the ice on the sidewalk in front of your home, you may be vulnerable to a lawsuit if someone slips and is injured. Architects are fully aware of their vulnerability should faulty building design result in injury to people. When the likelihood of payment is high or the exposure very large and not covered by insurance or other practices, the amounts should be incorporated in debt considerations.

In the next part of the chapter, we will discuss important specialized topics in debt management. We will begin by explaining credit reports, move to consumer laws in finance, and then consider financial difficulties and bankruptcy. Our planning efforts are intended in part to minimize those difficulties. The last section on financial ratios provides ways of measuring our current status to help reduce financial difficulties and promote sound borrowing practices.

CREDIT REPORTS

Credit reports are the factual printout and evaluation of a person's creditworthiness. Your creditworthiness is developed using a scoring system. The higher your score, the more likely you are to receive credit and, in some cases, the lower will be the interest rate. Perhaps the most frequently used system is one developed by Fair Isaac Co. (FICO) for credit bureaus. Each major credit bureau has its own score based in part on FICO. The factors considered in scoring by the companies include

Factor	Explanation
Past credit history	The most heavily weighted item. No amounts-past-due disputes, charge-offs, bankruptcy to obtain high scores. In other words, it is not good enough to pay off your debt; you must repay it on time to receive a high score.[1]
Married	Higher score
Two wage earners	Higher score
Age	Being young or old gives you a lower score
Children	Higher score
Job	The more skilled the job, the more stable it is, the higher the score
Years at job	The longer, the higher the score
Having account book requesting loan	Higher score
Years at current residence	The longer, the higher the score
Years at previous residence	The longer, the higher the score
Current debt obligations	The lower the amount, the higher the score
Favorable credit history	
At bank granting loan	Very favorable for score
At any bank	Favorable for score

[1] The longer a past-due item is outstanding before being paid off, the worse the score.

Generally, the most important items in your score are your past payment history, the amount of money owed, when you last applied for credit, how long you have had credit, and the kind of credit. When credit scores skip, say from good to weak, borrowing rates can be altered.

As we have seen, at the present time credit is easier to obtain than it was 10 years ago, which has resulted in greater delinquencies. Good credit can be used as a screen for job applications and for insurance applications.

If you are rejected for credit, you have to be given a reason. If there is an amount in dispute, you have the right to explain the reason for it in 100 words and have the statement placed in your credit file.

There are three major credit bureaus: Equifax, Experian, and Trans Union. Each uses the FICO data to develop its scores. Since some credit providers subscribe and send credit information to only one or two bureaus, you can have different credit reports for each bureau. This can mean that if you have an important reason to check your credit, you may want to do so with all three bureaus. The credit report provides your credit history, any inquiries, and any relevant public information for a period of time, such as bankruptcy.

TABLE 7.4
**Improving Your
Credit Rating**

Steps	Explanation and Elaboration
Obtain and review a copy of your credit report	They are the logical beginning steps. See if report is correct and whether payments have been made on time. If not correct, write to credit bureau.
Pay all bills when due	Self-explanatory.
Reduce debt outstanding	The lower the debt, the higher the credit score. Do not consolidate debt.
Limit the number of credit cards outstanding	Having a few credit cards in force can increase your score; having many more can reduce it.
Plan future of credit	Limit credit outstanding—for example, by spacing cyclical purchases.

To obtain your credit report free,[19] you can order online,[20] call a toll-free number,[21] or send written requests.[22] Under federal law, you are entitled to receive one free credit report from each bureau for each 12-month period. In addition, you can get one free if you are denied credit, are unemployed and looking for work, think you have or may have been the subject of a fraudulent credit transaction, are on welfare, or have been told by a company that it will be reporting something negative about you to a credit bureau. Additional requests per year are available at a cost. Under Federal Trade Commission (FTC) guidelines provided in the Fair Credit Reporting Act, you can obtain a copy of your actual credit score and the way it was developed from any of the credit bureaus for a "fair and reasonable" fee.[23]

Taking the steps indicated in Table 7.4 can improve your credit rating.

For an explanation of consumer protection laws including those for credit cards, see Appendix II to this chapter. Privacy and identity theft are discussed in Appendixes III and IV respectively.

FINANCIAL DIFFICULTIES

Financial difficulties can be defined as problems in simultaneously supporting normal household operations and paying interest and principal on debt owed when due. These difficulties may be attributable to lower-than-expected earnings or layoffs, unanticipated costs, improper planning, investment setbacks, or simply unwise spending.

When a cash flow problem is just temporary, a partial liquidation of investments or a consolidating loan may be enough. Under a consolidating loan, the proceeds from one lender are used to repay many loans, such as debt outstanding from a variety of credit card sources. The terms of payment may be extended in time to allow better matching of cash flow availability in relation to interest and principal costs. In some cases, the total interest expense may be lower as well.

When the problem is more fundamental, either an additional source of revenues such as from a new or extra job must be found or a cutback in overall expenses must be implemented. The cutback can take place in selected significant costs such as entertainment, vacation, eating out, or, more extremely, housing. Alternatively, an across-the-board percentage reduction

---

[19] Implementation commenced December 2004 to September 2005 depending on the state you live in.

[20] The Web site for the credit report is https://www.annualcreditreport.com/.

[21] The toll-free number is 1-877-322-8228.

[22] The P.O. Box address is 105281, Atlanta, GA 30348-5281.

[23] See John Ventura, *The Credit Repair Kit*, 4th ed. (Chicago, IL: Dearborn Financial Publishing, 2004).

in costs can be effected. Typically, an operating budget should be monitored to ensure that it is adhered to. Often it is helpful to restrict the use of credit cards. If the problems are more pronounced, personal bankruptcy may be considered.

BANKRUPTCY

Bankruptcy is a way for people to lessen or eliminate the burdens of debt. It is executed under court proceedings and therefore has legal standing that protects you against creditor claims. The number of bankruptcy filings has risen over the past 20 years. In 1980 it was 331,264; in 1998 it was 1.44 million, while in 2004 it was close to 1.6 million (see Table 7.5).

There are two forms of personal bankruptcy: Chapter 7 and Chapter 13. Under a Chapter 7 proceeding, all existing debts are wiped out. Chapter 13 is more involved. Under Chapter 13, there is an extension in time to pay off debts and frequently a reduction in the amount of obligations. Although income taxes survive after bankruptcy, penalties for late payment of them are not imposed under Chapter 13. The criterion is "best efforts" to repay creditors; under this proceeding, something approaching normal household operations including living expenditures and household maintenance items (painting, etc.) is expected to continue. There is generally a three- to a maximum of five-year repayment period.

A bankruptcy proceeding is supervised by a bankruptcy judge and involves a private trustee appointed by a U.S. government trustee from the U.S. Justice Department. It is the private trustee's mandate to find as many creditor possessions as possible since payment is calculated on a fee-and-commission basis. The commission, contingent on the amount of assets found, provides incentive to uncover all assets.

TABLE 7.5
Bankruptcy Statistics

Year	Total Filings	Business Filings	Nonbusiness Filings	Consumer Filings as a Percentage of Total Filings
1980	331,264	43,694	287,570	86.81%
1981	363,943	48,125	315,818	86.78%
1982	380,251	69,300	310,951	91.78%
1983	348,880	62,436	286,444	82.10%
1984	348,521	64,004	284,517	81.64%
1985	412,510	71,277	341,233	82.72%
1986	530,438	81,235	449,203	84.69%
1987	577,999	82,446	495,553	85.74%
1988	613,465	63,853	549,612	89.59%
1989	679,461	63,235	616,226	90.69%
1990	782,960	64,853	718,107	91.72%
1991	943,987	71,549	872,438	92.42%
1992	971,517	70,643	900,874	92.73%
1993	875,202	62,304	812,898	92.88%
1994	832,829	52,374	780,455	93.71%
1995	926,601	51,959	874,642	94.39%
1996	1,178,555	53,549	1,125,006	95.46%
1997	1,404,145	54,027	1,350,118	96.15%
1998	1,442,549	44,367	1,398,182	96.92%
1999	1,319,465	37,884	1,281,581	97.12%
2000	1,253,444	35,472	1,217,972	97.17%
2001	1,492,129	40,099	1,452,030	97.31%
2002	1,577,651	38,540	1,539,111	97.56%
2003	1,660,245	35,037	1,625,208	97.89%
2004	1,597,462	34,317	1,563,145	97.85%

A bankruptcy proceeding stops evictions, default, foreclosure, and repossession actions for those notified, at least temporarily. Whether you will be able to keep your possessions will depend on the following factors:

- *The state you live in.* Most states mandate that a person in bankruptcy be left with a minimum amount of equity in a house, a car, and household possessions. The amount varies by state.
- *Whether assets are secured.* A secured asset is one in which other assets are pledged against a loan in case of default. For example, a house is pledged for a mortgage loan. In the event of default, the creditor often has a legal right to that asset regardless of bankruptcy. If loans are in good standing, the asset cannot be repossessed by that creditor.

As a practical matter, few homes, cars, or other, relatively inexpensive possessions are said to be repossessed in bankruptcy.

Not all obligations are affected by bankruptcy proceedings. In addition to income taxes, divorce-related issues such as alimony, child care, and property settlements remain, and so do obligations stemming from fraudulent representations. Student loans also carry on, except for those considered an undue hardship.

In 2005, the federal government passed the Bankruptcy Abuse Prevention and Consumer Act of 2005. The result of this act is expected to make it more difficult to file for bankruptcy, particularly for the more lenient Chapter 7 form. Some key features are

1. A means test is established. If you are in the top half in median income for people in your state and have income minus expenses of $100 a month or more, you must file under Chapter 13 and retire the debt over three to five years.
2. You must enroll in credit counseling and have a plan for repayment from an approved agency within six months of the bankruptcy filing.
3. The ability to keep pensions, IRAs, and prepaid tuition and college education plans has been affirmed.[24]
4. In Chapter 13, the bankruptcy judge has the discretion to reduce the amount to be paid by up to 20 percent of the total.
5. There are limits on the amount of debt for luxury items that can be expunged within a 60-day period of bankruptcy; cash advances within a 70-day period of that day are not eliminated.
6. Only $125,000 of interest in a homestead can be exempted if it was purchased within 1,215 days of the date of filing. Since some people seek debtor-friendly states, in order to take advantage of their generous exemptions from bankruptcy for homes in that state, you must have lived there for at least two years prior to filing.

The credit counseling and the more detailed bankruptcy filing requirements that will raise legal fees are believed will discourage bankruptcy filings.

As you can see, bankruptcy is a fairly involved procedure. It has many advantages and disadvantages, which we list below.

Advantages

1. Receive relief from financial burdens.
2. Eliminate worry and calls from creditors.
3. Can stop removal of some assets temporarily or permanently.

---

[24] If contributed at least two years before bankruptcy; if between one and two years, a maximum of $5,000 is allowed.

Practical Comment · When to Declare Bankruptcy

Bankruptcy is a serious step that will remain as part of a person's financial history for 10 years. Should it be considered? For some the answer is simple. For those who have a large obligation and are unable to pay it, there is no choice. At the other extreme are people who have a short-term liquidity problem. Their total debts don't amount to a great deal, but they are being pressed by creditors now and can't repay.

Those cash flow–strapped people should enter into negotiations with their creditors. Often an extension of terms or consolidation and perhaps even a reduction in amount due or interest cost can be worked out. For the person in debt, the threat of bankruptcy alone can be a persuasive negotiating tool. Hiring a financial planner or nonprofit credit counselor affiliated with the National Federation of Credit Counselors (NFCC) can help. In many cases, a detailed household budget should be implemented.

For others, bankruptcy is a kind of capital expenditure decision with strong pluses and minuses. The size of the loans, whether they are secured or not, local state policies, whether valuable assets will be taken, and ability to repay the loans are all factors that enter into financial consideration. The amount of current stress and its effect on your work and personal life should be weighed against the lessening but still existing social stigma and possible self-image difficulties after bankruptcy.

What it can come down to is whether you are willing and able to liquidate pension assets that may be insulated from creditors, cut back sharply on household expenditures for a time, or possibly take a second job. If there are emotional difficulties such as compulsive spending, the solution may be to seek help. These difficulties will not go away with bankruptcy.

Placed in a more simple framework, if you can pay off your creditors within three years, it is often best to avoid bankruptcy.

Disadvantages

1. Some assets may be taken.
2. There is a social stigma from bankruptcy. Bankruptcy information is a matter of public record.
3. It can result in rejection from a new job. Although discrimination because of bankruptcy is illegal, it could be difficult to prove.
4. It can contribute to poor self-image.
5. A guarantor of your debt will be personally liable to repay it.
6. The money for any preferred repayments, say for friends and relatives, that take place within one year prior to bankruptcy will have to be turned over to the trustee.
7. Bankruptcy involves costs including legal fees, an expense that is optional but generally recommended.

Given these distinct advantages and disadvantages, the analysis of whether to declare bankruptcy can take on aspects of an investment decision. The financial and behavioral issues in deciding a future course are discussed in the Practical Comment above.

FINANCIAL RATIOS

Financial ratios indicate the relative degree of financial risk the household has undertaken including the ability to pay off obligations when due. In other words, they can help tell you whether you are in or approaching a financial danger zone. There are two broad approaches to establishing that risk. The first is based on assets and the amount of debt outstanding relative to those assets. The second is based on cash flow and the amount of interest expense and debt repayments relative to those assets. Both are useful and, although the amount of debt outstanding is more often used by some as a benchmark of overall financial health, interest expense is more of a day-to-day cash flow consideration. The relevant ratios are listed below.

Mortgage Cost as a Percentage of Income

Mortgage debt is usually the largest obligation homeowners have outstanding. Mortgage payments, including real estate taxes and homeowner's insurance, are customarily expressed as a percentage of gross income. Lenders often use a 28 percent benchmark as a percentage of gross income as the limit to which they will extend credit. (They also add all other debt charges and limit the total to 36 percent of gross income.) However, the rate may be adjusted upward depending on circumstances such as living in a high-cost area such as the Northeast or the West Coast.

Installment Debt as a Percentage of After-Tax Income

Installment debt is the normal way of repaying credit card debt and other loans that are taken out for nonbusiness, nonmarketable investment purposes. Repayment of this debt is often compared with net salary (gross income minus taxes and other cash deductions from a paycheck). Keeping such debt under 20 percent of so-called take-home pay is often desirable—and a 15 percent limit is even more attractive. These benchmarks are particularly relevant when there are other types of debt outstanding such as mortgage debt.

$$\text{Installment debt, \%} = \frac{\text{Installment debt repayments}}{\text{Net salary}}$$

Total Debt as a Percentage of Income

Mortgage debt and related expense payments plus nonmortgage debt payments are combined and expressed as a percentage of net salary. Interest payments and real estate taxes are expressed on an after-tax basis with tax deductions assumed at the household's marginal tax bracket. As we have discussed, most nonmortgage debt is not tax-deductible and is therefore taken on a pretax basis. Total debt payments should be under 50 percent of net salary.[25] Where investment income is a substantial contributor to cash flow, it may be added on an after-tax basis to net salary.

$$\text{Total debt as percentage of income} = \frac{\begin{array}{c}\text{Total nonmortgage} \\ \text{interest and principal} \\ \text{payments}\end{array} + \begin{array}{c}\text{Total mortgage} \\ \text{interest } (1-t) \text{ and} \\ \text{principal payments}\end{array} + \begin{array}{c}\text{Real estate taxes } (1-t) \\ \text{and homeowner's} \\ \text{insurance expense}\end{array}}{\text{Net salary}}$$

where t = tax rate and $(1 - t)$ = expense presented on after-tax basis.

Debt Coverage Ratio

This ratio measures contractual debt and payments against household cash flows from operations. Thus, its benchmark is not take-home pay but the amount available after deducting normal household overhead expenses from take-home pay. It measures how much higher available cash flow is of interest and debt repayment cost. The higher the ratio, the safer the household is against negative unexpected occurrences.

---

[25] This figure differs from the bank screen for total debt of 36 percent in that it is based on after-tax, not pretax, income, and this formula expresses interest and real estate costs on an after-tax basis.

The ratio adds back after-tax interest payments since both pretax interest and its effect on lowering taxes were deducted to arrive at cash flow from operations.[26]

$$\text{Times fixed payments earned} = \frac{\text{Cash flow from operating activities} + \text{Interest payments}\,(1 - t)}{\text{Annual total interest and debt payments}}$$

Note: Cash flow from operating activities = cash flow after nondiscretionary and discretionary activities.

Debt as a Percentage of Total Assets

This ratio measures debt in relation to assets, not cash flow. It is difficult to develop broad benchmarks for warning signs of excess financial leverage. When people are young, they may place almost all their resources in a down payment on their home and borrow the rest. In that circumstance, debt may comprise 80 percent or more of their total assets. The ratio should decline over time since as people age other assets should accumulate, the home should appreciate, and the mortgage should be drawn down.[27] If debt payments become onerous, securities could be sold to help repay the debt. For people who are middle-aged or older, a debt figure of less than 50 percent of total assets may be desirable.[28]

$$\text{Debt as a percentage of total assets} = \frac{\text{Total debt}}{\text{Total assets}}$$

Current Ratio

The current ratio compares current assets with current liabilities. Since these are assets and liabilities that will fall due within one year, the ratio of the two can measure your ability to pay off your debts as they occur. However, as mentioned in the chapter, the use of credit card debt as an alternative to having high precautionary liquid savings has somewhat lessened the importance of this ratio.

$$\text{Current ratio} = \frac{\text{Current assets}}{\text{Current liabilities}}$$

With this knowledge of debt and ratios as background, you can address the Dan and Laura debt situation that follows.

Back to Dan and Laura

DEBT

The meeting we had on debt was somewhat charged. Dan hated the thought of debt. Yet here he was with $20,000 in credit card debt at 18 percent cost and about $46,000 in educational loans at 6 percent left over from his undergraduate days. Both he and Laura understood that the house, the car, and Laura's graduate school enrollment would require additional borrowings. Dan accused Laura of being too flip with money. He said that whenever they were short of capital, she was quick to flash a credit card, particularly for purchasing attractive clothes at the mall, and that she was oblivious to the thought that at 18 percent the cost was very high. Laura appeared very sensitive to the accusation. She said that Dan was very picky and that if they had followed his recommendations, they would be living in a one-bedroom apartment in a poor neighborhood, counting their pennies.

---

[26] The formula could be modified to include lease payments or all fixed obligations in the denominator under the assumption that they all must be funded or the household would run into difficulties.

[27] An alternative ratio would measure debt as a percentage of house plus liquid assets. Having a significant amount of total assets in marketable securities can serve as support for this formula.

[28] The asset to liability measure and a ratio measuring liquidity were the best predictors of insolvency. See Sharon A. DeVaney, "The Usefulness of Financial Ratios as Predictors of Household Insolvency: Two Perspectives," *Financial Counseling and Planning Journal* 5 (1994), pp. 15–24.

I was about to intervene. Their difference in point of view seemed to be affecting their personal relationship. Then both people caught themselves, looked at each other, and smiled. I had the feeling that they had been through this type of discussion many times before and that each appreciated that the other had a different point of view. Both were concerned about their debt and felt a little overwhelmed.

They wanted me to help them decide how to approach their financing needs. They indicated that Laura's parents were not charging interest on the loan to them and appeared willing and able to help them if they needed more capital—for example, to finance the purchase of a home. Laura mentioned that her parents viewed the loan as a gift and would apply the money against her share of her ultimate inheritance when her parents passed away. Significantly, I thought, Dan made no comment about this financing source.

Borrowing can be a positive or a negative force in financial planning. Borrowing for capital expenditures that improve income-earning abilities or for those that reduce ongoing costs can be highly effective. On the other hand, significant monies borrowed to support normal household expenditures over a period of time should be discouraged. It can lead to a dependence on debt and an ever-rising monthly interest and debt repayment schedule that can retard your financial planning. In other words, borrowing can make household operations more efficient more quickly, but it also can add to risk and potentially derail your plans.

Your own situation contains both "good" and "bad" use of debt. The borrowing that Dan made for college enabled him to obtain knowledge and a degree that substantially raised his projected lifetime income. The credit card debt you owe cannot be justified in terms of interest cost or probably even the reason for which the money was spent. Over the next several years until Laura goes back to work, your budget will have to reflect more limited income and higher child rearing and educational costs.

Here is my thinking. I understand that debt concerns were the reason you came to see me originally. I also know that the need to move on the recommended purchase of a home has only compounded the problem. The most attractive form of borrowing is home mortgage debt. Its cost is relatively low, and it is tax-deductible. I am going to recommend that you finance 95 percent of the cost of the home when you purchase it. That will result in your temporarily paying a higher interest rate to purchase insurance guaranteeing the lender repayment. That extra cost will exist until the combination of appreciation on the home and repayment of debt works the debt-to-home-value ratio down to a more reasonable level. Even with the extra cost, the home is still your best form of financing. If you can get your parents to cosign the loan indicating that they will pay the mortgage if you don't, you may be able to get the home at a regular interest rate.

Your parents' role should be able to provide you with the normal 20 percent down payment on the purchase of, say, a $250,000 home. Instead of helping to finance 20 percent of the home, they will finance 5 percent and contribute the remaining amount for Laura's tuition. Explain to them that you are doing this for tax reasons, as the cost to borrow on the home is lower than the cost to finance a nontax-deductible educational loan. Use your existing investments to repay the $20,000 of credit card debt due and $7,000 of other debt due. The approximate $65,000 gift from your parents should pay for the 5 percent down payment on the home, moving expenses, and half of Laura's tuition. It can only enhance the return on Laura going back to graduate school. The balance of educational costs in two or three years could be financed by liquidating a portion of your investments. Finally, it was nice that your parents decided to forgive your loan of $20,000 from them.

I believe that your use of credit cards as a form of debt should be limited. The cards should generally be paid off each month. In a few instances where you have a bulge payment, say for an unplanned expenditure, you can keep the debt outstanding for a few months. It may still be less costly than other forms of borrowing for short periods of time. However, if you don't have the demonstrated discipline to pay it off over a few months, then I recommend no credit card debt be taken out at all.

Keep Dan's existing college debt for now.

A summary of the transactions in today's dollars over a period of years is as follows:

Cash Inflows	
Sale of existing investments	$66,000
Parental gift	65,000
Total	$131,000
Cash Outflows	
Repayment of credit card and other current debt due	$27,000
Payment of graduate school costs	80,000
Down payment on home	12,500
Moving expenses	11,500
Total	$131,000
Net Cash Flow	**$0**

Summary

Debt is a financing tool that when used properly can enhance investment opportunities and provide earlier use of assets. When overused, it also can result in financial difficulties. The chapter details when and how you should use this tool.

- There are two types of leverage: financial and operating.
- Mortgages, which are a relatively low-cost way to obtain funds, come in fixed- and variable-rate forms.
- Credit card debt can actually be a favorable way to obtain funds, but too often it is used inefficiently.
- Consumer protection laws require safeguards and also mandate disclosures that can assist in maintaining favorable credit ratings.
- Bankruptcy is an alternative that creates opportunities but also has substantial negative ramifications.
- Financial ratios as given in the chapter provide objective benchmarks of financial health with regard to debt levels.

Key Terms

adjustable rate mortgage, *149*
bankruptcy, *160*
closed-end retail credit, *144*
credit report, *158*
financial difficulties, *159*
financial leverage, *140*
financial risk, *140*

fixed-rate mortgage, *148*
home equity loan, *151*
hybrid ARM, *149*
interest rate, *141*
long-term debt, *145*
margin debt, *153*
mortgage, *145*
open-end credit, *144*

operating leverage, *140*
operating risk, *140*
rationed borrowers, *144*
secured debt, *145*
short-term debt, *145*
unrationed borrowers, *144*
unsecured debt, *145*

Web Sites

http://www.bankrate.com
Borrowing
Sections on mortgages, home equity, automobile loans, credit card debt, personal loans, and bad credit are featured on this Web site. It also contains information about rates and trends and has credit and loan calculators.

http://www.interest.com
Mortgages
The Web site lets the consumer shop for mortgages and find a lender. It also has mortgage calculators; lets users track mortgage rates; and has sections on refinancing and other types of loans such as auto, home equity, and credit card.

http://www.abiworld.org
American Bankruptcy Institute
This site serves as an online resource for bankruptcy information and news. Bankruptcy statistics, education information, online newsletters and publications on bankruptcy, and a search tool for finding an attorney experienced in bankruptcy matters are provided.

http://loan.yahoo.com
Yahoo's Loan Center
The loan center offers information on mortgage, home equity, and auto loans and has an education section.

http://www.creditforum.org
Credit Forum
Information that spans topics including bankruptcy, credit scoring, credit factors, and credit reports and a dedicated section of credit Q&As are provided.

http://www.cccs.org
Consumer Credit Counseling Service (CCCS)
Adult education focused on debt management, budgeting, purchasing a home, and foreclosure prevention.

https://www.annualcreditreport.com/
Annual Credit Report
AnnualCreditReport.com is a centralized service for consumers to request annual credit reports. On this Web site, consumers can request and obtain a free credit report once every 12 months from each of the three nationwide consumer credit reporting companies: Equifax, Experian, and TransUnion.

Other Web sites offering online credit reports, credit improving tools, and advice include

http://www.equifax.com
Equifax

http://www.experian.com
Experian

http://www.transunion.com
TransUnion

Questions

1. What is debt's role in the household?
2. What is the difference between debt and fixed obligations?
3. What is the difference between debt and intangible liabilities?
4. Contrast operating risk and financial risk.
5. Why is operating leverage as it pertains to risk important?
6. Harry was deciding on the separation of outlays into nondiscretionary and discretionary. What advice would you offer him on the division as it relates to risk?
7. What is APR and why is it important?
8. List and explain the borrowing factors.
9. Contrast the strengths and weaknesses of a fixed-rate mortgage with those of a variable-rate mortgage.
10. Alexis wants to buy a large home relative to her income and thinks that she may not qualify for a mortgage for 80 percent of the price. She expects interest rates to rise and anticipates staying in the home for many years. Explain the strengths and weakness of fixed- versus variable-rate mortgages for her. Indicate which one you would select and why.
11. Why are adjustable-rate mortgages generally cheaper than fixed-rate mortgage loans?
12. When is a home equity loan better than refinancing a first mortgage?
13. Credit cards are a grossly inefficient way to borrow money. True or false? Explain and discuss their advantages.
14. Why borrow using secured debt?
15. Pension loans save you money because you pay yourself back. True or false? Explain.
16. Are loans from friends and relatives a good practice? Explain.
17. What borrowing mechanism provides the lowest cost? Why?
18. How can you improve your credit? Indicate the specific steps to do so.
19. Jeremy is in financial difficulty. He owes $5,000 and cannot pay it back now. Should he declare bankruptcy? Why? What do you think he should do?
20. In calculating the ratio times fixed payments earned, after-tax interest payments are added back in the denominator. Why?

Problems

7.1 Dorothy has the following projected cash flows: income, $65,000; fixed operating costs excluding interest, $44,000; variable outlays, $7,000; interest cost, $5,000; and repayment of debt, $6,000.

   Does Dorothy have high operating leverage? Calculate what a 15 percent higher and 15 percent lower income outcome would do to profitability.

7.2 John was given a choice of loans of $8,000 with the following characteristics.

   a. $1,200 in interest paid at the end of the period
   b. $1,200 in interest paid at the beginning of the period
   c. $1,200 paid equally over the period with part of the principal retired each month

   Calculate the interest rate paid. In part (c) calculate using both the approximate method and the actual cost method assuming a one-year loan retired in 12 equal monthly installments of interest and principal.

7.3 Melinda has a 15-year fixed-rate mortgage for $150,000 at a 6.5 percent rate. Calculate her monthly mortgage payments.

7.4 Martha has seven years remaining on her $160,000 mortgage, which has a 7.5 percent rate. She would have to pay $4,500 to refinance. Martha expects to live in the house for another five years. She is in the 33 percent marginal tax bracket and can earn 10 percent after tax on other uses for the money. If the mortgage rates have declined to 6.5 percent, should she refinance?

7.5 How much would a person save by borrowing money at 6 percent for a home equity loan versus 18 percent for a credit card loan. Assume a marginal tax bracket of 30 percent.

7.6 Given the following statistics, calculate the mortgage cost percent.

Annual mortgage interest	$9,000
Annual principal payment	2,000
Annual insurance and real estate taxes	8,000
Yearly gross income	120,000

7.7 Elena is in the 28 percent bracket and has the following real estate and non-real-estate-related costs.

Nonmortgage interest and principal	$4,000
Mortgage interest	15,000
Mortgage principal	7,000
Real estate taxes	8,000
Homeowner's insurance expense	2,000
Net salary	70,000

Calculate total debt as a percentage of income. Is it satisfactory?

7.8 Louis had the following cash flow items:

Cash flow from operations	$40,000
Interest payments	6,000
Total interest and debt payments	9,000

If Louis is in the 30 percent tax bracket, how many times are fixed payments earned?

**CFP®
Certification
Examination
Questions
and Problems**

7.1 The Moores recently found out that they can reduce their mortgage interest rate from 12 percent to 8 percent. The value of homes in their neighborhood has been increasing at the rate of 7.5 percent annually. If the Moores were to refinance their house with $2,000 in closing costs in addition to the mortgage balance ($120,056) over a period of time to coincide with their chosen retirement age in 22 years, what would the monthly payment be for principal and interest (closing costs are going to be added to the mortgage)?

a. $853.43
b. $895.60
c. $945.34
d. $967.86
e. $983.99

7.2 A young couple would like to purchase a new home using one of the following mortgages:

Mortgage no. 1: 10.5 percent interest with 5 discount points to be paid at time of closing
Mortgage no. 2: 11.5 percent interest with 2 discount points to be paid at time of closing

Assuming the couple could qualify for both mortgages, which of the following aspects should be considered in deciding between these two mortgages?

1. gross income
2. estimated length of ownership
3. real estate tax liability
4. cash currently available
   a. (1) and (2) only
   b. (2) only
   c. (2) and (4) only
   d. (4) only
   e. (1), (2), (3), and (4)

Case Application

DEBT

Part 1

Richard and Monica have diametrically opposite points of view on debt. Richard views debt as an opportunity to generate cash to make up for past investment losses. He has asked you whether he should remortgage his house and place the proceeds in the stock market. He says the present time may be appropriate to refinance since market rates for mortgage loans of 6.5 percent are well below his mortgage rate of 8 percent. He wants to use an adjustable rate that provides an even lower 4 percent rate for the first year with rates thereafter 2 percent above the five-year Treasury rate.

Richard would like a 30-year mortgage since he said he doesn't expect "to go anywhere" and the annual repayments would be low. He said he was thinking about buying a new car. While the existing one worked well, he was tired of it. If cash flows get tight, he is not at all averse to using credit card debt. He says that while credit card rates are high, the overall impact is not great and "people manage to pay money back." Monica has listened quietly to Richard with a pained expression on her face, occasionally shaking her head. She says she is afraid of taking on more debt and wants a budget to limit spending of all types.

Case Application Questions

1. What do you think of Richard's idea of borrowing to place money in the stock market?
2. Do you think the couple should refinance their mortgage?
3. Should they use the adjustable-rate mortgage offered?
4. What is your recommendation on a 30-year loan?
5. Should the couple buy a new car?
6. What do you think of Richard's view of debt?
7. Do you agree with Monica's point of view?
8. How would you treat the disagreement between Richard and Monica?
9. Complete the debt and future budgeting part of the plan.

Part 2

Brad and Barbara say they use credit cards all the time. They always intend to pay them off by the end of the month, but they often don't. In fact, their credit card debt has been rising recently.

Case Application Questions

1. Is this pattern common?
2. What is your recommendation?

Appendix I

Borrowing Theory: Risk and Equilibrium

In a world with perfect capital markets, one without risk, households can borrow or lend at the same rate. The alternative that fits the circumstance will be selected. People borrow when their capital budgeting opportunities or present consumption needs exceed their existing cash flow. Without risk in the marketplace, a household can borrow as much as it wants at a low risk-free rate. It would borrow up until the point that the return from capital expenditures or other forms of investment equaled the borrowing cost.

Of course, no such world exists. When risk and transaction costs are introduced, the framework changes dramatically. Now the cost of borrowing will be different than the return available on external investments such as marketable securities. What we pay for money we borrow depends on the amount of risk we undertake. The greater the uncertainty, the higher the market interest rate charged. We call the expense we pay in borrowing money the *cost of debt*.

Let us trace how debt is used under these circumstances. Whether the household will be saving and investing or alternatively will have a need to borrow funds will depend on its *marginal rate of time preference*. This marginal statistic is the rate that makes postponed future consumption expenditures accomplished through savings and investing equal in appeal to spending the money today. Each household has its own value systems, and therefore its own discount rate. Of course, the marginal rate will be influenced by the amount of cash flow that the household generates as well as its desire for additional goods.

The marginal rate of time preference will be compared with the cost of debt and the returns on internal and external investments.[29] Debt may be used for consumption when the cost of debt is lower than the marginal rate of time preference and for investment when the cost of debt is lower than the projected returns on investment.

What makes the analysis more complex is that investment consumption and borrowing patterns will be affected by the household's tolerance for risk and that tolerances can differ materially among households. For example, even without the need to borrow to buy a used dishwasher from a private party, one household may be willing to pay 50 percent of original cost while another, more fearful of the possibility of repairs occurring shortly after and therefore more risk-averse, would require a higher return on the durable good. Consequently, its member-owner might offer to pay 25 percent of original cost.

The impact of risk on consumption also would vary by household. We might assume that greater risk would result in more saving, but this may not always be true. If two households were to be exposed to the same risk of a possible debilitating illness, one might lower its original marginal rate of time preference to generate savings for this possibility while another household might raise it, preferring to enjoy life today while its members know they are still healthy.

Borrowing and raising household risk can increase the required return on investments, the extent of which also can vary by household. We can conclude by saying that borrowing may be used when its cost is below the risk-adjusted marginal rates of time preference and of investment return. Clearly, the higher the cost of debt, the less likely it is that it will be used.

Appendix II

Consumer Protection Laws

A variety of laws protect consumers in their purchases. You are entitled to fair disclosure of information that is relevant for purchase. You can sue if laws are violated. The government helps by reviewing the activities of such people as manufacturers, sellers, and lenders. The rights of the buyer in selected areas are provided below. They are all subchapters of the Consumer Credit Protection Act (CCPA), which is enforced by the Federal Trade Commission.

---

[29] Those for household production currently versus those for traditionally liquidative investments such as stocks and bonds.

TRUTH IN LENDING ACT

When you are provided with credit under the Truth in Lending Act, the lender is obligated to disclose such things as the cost of credit using the objective APR (annual percentage rate), annual and late payment fees, the actual amount being provided, and so on. Damages are measured by the difference between actual charges and those indicated.

FAIR CREDIT BILLING ACT

If there is a dispute about the amount owed, the Fair Credit Billing Act allows you to write the creditor explaining the difficulty, whether due to errors in calculating amount due, orders never received, returns never credited back, and so on. The comments must be received within 60 days of the bill. You can withhold the amount in dispute. The lender must resolve the claim within 90 days of receipt of the letter. Your credit isn't affected during this period.

If your credit cards are stolen or permanently lost, you are liable for a maximum of $50. If you report the loss before there are unauthorized transactions on your credit card or if the loss involves your credit card number but not the card itself, you have no liability for any unauthorized charges.

FAIR CREDIT REPORTING ACT

When applying for credit, the credit reporting agency must check the information, estimate the borrower's ability to handle the credit, and investigate the applicant's credit history. Adverse information more than seven years old is supposed to be deleted except for information about bankruptcy, which is available to lenders for 10 years.

The credit reporting agency is obligated to keep this information current and accurate. The information generated may only be used for narrowly selected reasons such as for credit or for employment.

EQUAL CREDIT OPPORTUNITY ACT

Under this act, no one can be discriminated against on the basis of race, sex, marital status, or national origin.

FAIR DEBT COLLECTION PRACTICES ACT

The Fair Debt Collection Act limits debt collection procedures to those that are fair. The debtor must be notified of background information on the debt and given 30 days to indicate disputes.

ADDITIONAL LAWS

Other selected laws are briefly summarized below.

Canceling a Purchased Item

If you change your mind about a purchase, a federal cooling-off period allows you to cancel a purchase for such things as a home improvement loan or sales for more than $25 if the sale hasn't taken place at the proprietor's place of business. States have different cooling-off periods. Exceptions are made for custom purchases.

Warranties

Federal law passed in 1975 refers to many types of warranties. Warranties are also known as guarantees by the product provider to you. Under implied warranties that are not stated by the provider, the law implies a product must perform as indicated and fit its purpose.

Consumer Leasing Act

The Consumer Leasing Act applies to leases of four months or more for a variety of consumer goods. You must receive information that permits comparison with other competing leases and with purchase of an item. You must be given information such as the amount due on signing, total amount of payments, any other expenses, warranties on the good, fees for default or late payment, information on normal wear and tear, and the terms of any purchase option at the end of the lease. Advertising of a lease must disclose some of this information.

Student Loan Defaults

When in default, the U.S. Department of Education will notify credit bureaus, tax refunds may be withheld, collection costs may be assessed, your wages may be attached, and you may be sued. Where there are special circumstances for nonpayment, extensions may be given and, less often, partial or full elimination of the loan may occur.

Appendix III

Privacy

Privacy is the ability to keep information about yourself free from unsanctioned examination. Privacy has become a more significant problem because of unauthorized tapping into information on computer hard drives and through communication via the Internet. One outcome of carelessness about safeguards can be identity theft, which is discussed in Appendix IV.

The Financial Modernization Act of 1999, known as the Gramm Leach Bliley Act (GLB Act), helps protect people who have information that resides at financial institutions. The GLB Act applies to all financial institutions that gather and release financial information, not just those that hold information for their own customers. Financial institutions must design, implement, and shield customer information. The act protects people against those who would acquire this information falsely, called "pretexting." The law requires financial institutions to notify and inform customers of their practices; customers have the right to restrict some institutional dissemination of their information.

To protect yourself follow many of the rules discussed under identity theft in Appendix IV. Don't provide personal information unless you are sure of the legitimacy of the company and the representative's position with it. Ask companies about their safeguards. If statements don't arrive on time or are erroneous, take immediate action. Safeguard personal information and tear up or shred old valuable financial information including checks, credit card information, etc. Add passwords to financial information and keep information private by using uncommon password numbers. Check your credit rating from each credit rating agency every year. If pretexting has occurred, follow the guidelines under identity theft.

Financial advisors should have a written plan to safeguard client information. The plan should be appropriate to its size and the sensitivity of the information it holds. The plan should include the following:

1. At least one person should be in charge of the effort overall or by area.
2. The risks to the customer should be assessed.
3. A safeguard system should be established and monitored with outsiders consulted when appropriate.
4. The program should be reviewed and updated as needed.

Included in the program are:

1. Checking references for new hires.
2. Training employees in basic safeguards.

   a. Lock rooms.
   b. They should become familiar with and sign a confidentiality agreement that includes abiding by established security standards.
   c. Establish passwords on computers and change them periodically.
   d. Do not give out information unless confident that the request for it is authorized.
   e. Implement a "need to know" policy for internal employees.
   f. Impose disciplinary proceedings against violators.

3. For information systems:

   a. Store information in secure area.
   b. Protect information against fire, flooding, and other hazards.
   c. Keep information away from machines having an Internet connection.
   d. Keep information transmission secure.
   e. Erase all data containing customer information that is no longer needed.
   f. Back up all data.

In line with the GLB Act, the SEC requires that advisory companies notify clients about their policies and implement safeguard policies including nondisclosure of nonpublic personal information to outsiders until clients have an opportunity to refuse its dissemination.

Appendix IV

Identity Theft

Identity theft occurs when a person or group steals your personal information and represents themselves as you, generally for purposes of financial gain. They can illegally assume your name, and use your Social Security number, address, credit card number, date of birth, or other information. They can do so by going through trash, stealing wallets and purses, accessing credit card numbers, posing as legitimate service companies, etc. Their tampering can result in one-time expenditures or outlays until being identified or systematic assumptions of all of your characteristics after completing a change of address form.

Some actions to protect yourself include:

1. Check your credit overall and charges on individual credit cards. As discussed, you can receive one credit report per year from each credit bureau at no charge. Consider purchasing a credit monitoring service that has a record of broad-based purchase information.
2. Notify your vendors and other creditors if expected bills have not arrived.
3. Follow up if you are denied credit.

If you have identified illegal activity:

1. Notify credit card companies or other relevant parties immediately of lost or stolen cards. As mentioned earlier in the chapter your losses may be restricted to a maximum of $50.
2. If checks are stolen or counterfeited, stop payment and change your bank account and notify bank information check system (1-800-428-9623) or other check verification service that your individual bank does business with.

3. Place an alert on your credit card reports with any one of the credit reporting companies listed in this chapter.

4. Refuse to give personal information such as Social Security numbers over the phone or online. To check if it is a legitimate vendor, say your bank, call the general number, and confirm the authenticity of the representative.

5. Tear up or shred sensitive material before throwing it out.

6. Don't carry your Social Security number around.

7. Take precautions to protect your computer-related files and communications.

8. Change bank accounts, credit cards, etc. Avoid new passwords related to your telephone or Social Security number, mother's maiden name, or date of birth.

9. File a complaint with the Federal Trade Commission, which is the federal clearinghouse for identity theft.

10. File a report with the local police in the precinct where the theft occurred.

Advisors' safety factors include:

1. Avoid receiving or sending sensitive client information via email.

2. Update virus protection software regularly to protect against intrusions.

3. Lock up sensitive hard copies of client information.

4. Shred all discarded client information.

5. Close down computers at the end of the day and use uncommon passwords to access.[30]

---

[30] For other computer-related protection information such as a firewall program, secure browser, strong password, etc., see Federal Trade Commission: Your National Resource About ID Theft— http://www.consumer.gov/idtheft.

Portfolio Management

This section deals with portfolio management, the household's overall investment function. The household is typically thought of as having two choices in employing its cash flows. The first choice is to spend the money on current living needs and desires. The second is to save and invest the money, keeping it in reserve for future deployment.

Actually, there is a third choice: to spend it on capital items. Capital expenditures are outlays that both are used today and benefit future periods. An example is the purchase of a new car, which will last for many years. We can call these outlays, which make the household operate more efficiently or provide extended pleasure for its members, nonfinancial investments. They are the subject of Chapter 8.

Those cash flows that are not spent currently but are reserved for future use are typically placed in financial vehicles such as stocks, bonds, and mutual funds. They are called financial investments and are discussed in Chapter 9.

Investments cannot be discussed solely in terms of returns. The household is subject to a variety of risks both for financial and nonfinancial assets. The general principles of investment risk and risk-return principles are explained in Chapters 9 and 10. Chapter 10 also focuses on insurance, perhaps the best-known risk management tool. Life insurance alternatives are presented in detail in that chapter.

These chapters should enable you to come away with an understanding of financial investments, as well as to appreciate the broader scope of investments the household makes and the approach to protecting them. Total portfolio management, a method of resolving household decision-making problems that integrates both financial and nonfinancial investments and incorporates risk, is discussed here and elaborated on in Part Seven.

Chapter **Eight**

Nonfinancial Investments

Chapter Goals

This chapter will enable you to:

- Make better choices by recognizing that household assets and investment planning are broader than believed.
- Differentiate a typical household cost from a capital expenditure.
- Become more effective in decision making by employing TPM, the household's all-asset approach.
- Benefit from linking household outlays on durable goods with business capital expenditures.
- Apply the methods of calculating returns on capital expenditures.
- Establish the advantages of owning a home.
- Determine whether to buy or lease a home or car.
- Utilize the knowledge that your salary is often your largest household asset.

Laura said, "Congratulate us; I'm pregnant." I thought to myself, This may only be one additional child, but it was a whole new ballgame as far as near-term planning was concerned. The four areas we would have to work on were a home, a new car, when to go back to work, and whether to enroll in a master's curriculum. This household investment program could bankrupt them if it wasn't drawn up carefully.

Real Life Planning

At a periodic meeting, Ken asked the advisor if he could help him become better informed in financial matters. Ken was a former radio announcer who made his living doing voice-overs on television and radio commercials. He had at least 10 different "voices" and could accommodate well to the needs of the particular situation. His most popular voice was used by major national sponsors who provided him with a payment every time it was repeated. Ken went to many auditions and ended up getting selected on one out of every five jobs for which he applied.

Like many creative people, Ken had little interest in financial matters. He was, however, very curious and intelligent and didn't mind being argumentative. Something he read in a financial magazine had piqued his interest. It was a statement that appliances were household assets. He had always regarded them as expenses. He wanted to know what the advisor thought was the proper answer. The advisor knew that the answer would have to be simple and practical; otherwise, Ken's eyes would move from side to side, signaling that his interest had been lost.

The advisor told him that by one measure, he was technically correct. The calculation of the country's output, gross domestic product (GDP), did not include appliances or any other individual purchase as a household asset aside from the house itself. The same item purchased for a business (for example, a car or a television set) would be treated as an asset. However, the advisor indicated his strong belief in separating assets, items that had usefulness over extended periods of time, from other outlays.

The advisor explained to Ken the idea and the benefits of treating the household as a form of business. He mentioned that a large part of a household's operations, the part not pertaining to pleasurable activities, closely resembled a business. The appliances purchased could be used to save money or time. Time could be used to earn money. Ken would have more time for auditions, which would likely raise his income. Ken nodded but asked about a television. How isn't that an indulgence, an expense?

The answer provided was that the television might not boost the cash flow of the household, but it could add to the enjoyment of its members. Even a household work-related appliance not used for earning income could benefit the household by adding to leisure time. Besides, the television was an asset that had an identifiable fair market value. The advisor mentioned that return on investment techniques can be used to decide whether to purchase work-related assets, but more subjective measures might have to be used for those related to pleasure.

The advisor said the key for outlays that aid household activities for a longer period than the current one was to treat them as investments. They should be segregated on current cash flow statements and in thinking about when future outlays will become necessary again. In that way, as does business, they are treated separately. We could call these expenditures with multiyear benefits capital expenditures. Ken flashed a wicked smile and asked for a financial rule of thumb in deciding whether to make or reject a work-related outlay for an appliance. The advisor responded with a rough rule for appliances that had around a five-year life: If the benefits exceeded the outlays within three years and were expected to continue significantly beyond that period, make it.

Ken, employing what sounded like his 11th voice, which was eerily similar to that of former President Reagan, said, "Thanks, I understand what you are saying."

OVERVIEW

Nonfinancial investments are the assets the household possesses that are often overlooked or that have less time devoted to them than to more glamorous stocks and bonds. This is ironic since the average household's assets in this area often exceed those for marketable financial securities. Consequently, efforts to improve decision making in this area can be highly productive for people. Said differently, capital expenditures and capital budgeting as related to investments are as important to a household as they are to a business.

In this chapter, you will learn how to identify and value nonfinancial investments in order to plan properly for their purchase and use. We will do so by separating the chapter into four parts: defining and detailing nonfinancial investments, examining the decision process, analyzing major capital expenditures, and evaluating the leasing alternative. There are a number of significant appendixes that extend the material, but the body of the chapter is no longer than many others.

DEFINING AND DETAILING NONFINANCIAL ASSETS

The investments the household makes can be separated into two major categories: financial and nonfinancial assets. **Financial assets** are those in which ownership is represented and traded solely through pieces of paper. Often financial assets are fully marketable. **Fully marketable assets** are those that can be sold currently in a public forum for fair value at low transaction costs. Examples of fully marketable financial assets are stocks and bonds. They are also known as marketable securities. They are what we typically put our savings into. We will discuss them in the next chapter.

Nonfinancial assets are all the other assets the household possesses. They can be segregated into real assets, human-related assets, and other assets. **Real assets** are items that you can see or touch that have market value. Included are your home and the possessions in it such as the furniture, household appliances, and the car parked outside. Sometimes these real assets are called tangible assets, physical assets, or hard assets. The term **durable goods** is more specific. For our purposes, it applies to household possessions. We will use it frequently in this chapter. Real assets, a broader term, can be separated into real estate, commonly the home, and durable goods.

Aside from their physical features, real assets differ from financial ones in that real assets generally decline in value over time. That deterioration may be due to changes in physical, technological, or fashion appeal over extended periods. A partial exception is the home, which, if maintained properly, can appreciate, at least for a relatively long time. Financial assets often maintain or increase in value over time, particularly when the cash they generate is reinvested. Finally, real assets are generally used in the household currently, while financial assets may be reserved for future use.

The second category of nonfinancial assets is **human-related assets.** Human-related assets are items that derive their value from particular people. In personal finance, we are principally concerned with assets in this category that generate income. For example, strength and beauty can be considered assets, but they don't qualify unless they produce cash flows. People most commonly generate income directly through their work efforts. We can call this income-earning ability a human asset. Closely allied are corporate pensions and government pensions such as Social Security, which are often based on work

TABLE 8.1   **Characteristics of Household Assets[1]**

Factor	Financial	Real Estate	Durable Goods	Human[2]	Human-Related
Practical example	Stocks, bonds	Home, residence	Auto, furniture	Job	Pension
Marketability	Fully marketable	Fairly marketable	Fairly marketable	Nonmarketable	Nonmarketable
Valuation over time	Increases in value[3]	Increases in value; cost for upkeep	Declines in value	Generally declines in value	Increases then declines in value[4]
Use	For future use	For current use	For current use	For current use	Varies
Associated costs	Little or none	Upkeep	Upkeep	Food, clothing, shelter, etc.	Varies
Example of capital expenditure	None directly	Renovation and expansion	Is itself a capital expenditure	Education and training	Varies
Direct cash inflows	Dividends and interest	None	None	Salary	Pension income, etc.
Indirect cash inflows	Appreciation	Appreciation	None	Employee benefits	Varies

[1] Excludes other assets, which are difficult to generalize about.
[2] Generally included under human-related assets in the book.
[3] Stable for bonds.
[4] It increases as the date that payoff begins draws closer, then declines after payoff begins.

FIGURE 8.1 **Common Household Assets**

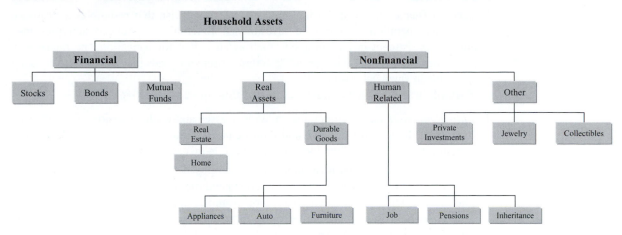

efforts.[1] Anticipated gifts and bequests represent another area that we include since they are most often received because of human relationships either through family relationships or friendship.

Human-related assets are sometimes called intangible assets because many—such as a Social Security right, a projected inheritance, or human education—cannot be touched. Another reason that they are termed intangible is that they are often nonmarketable—they cannot be sold to others, and, in any event, placing a fixed value on them may be subject to a greater measure of judgment. We will discuss human assets here and deal with pension assets and gifts and bequests in the retirement and estate planning chapters, respectively.

The third category, other assets, is a catchall. It comprises any other assets of worth. Some examples are jewelry, collectibles such as art or stamps, interest in a private business or other private investments, and prizes.

A summary of characteristics for household assets is given in Table 8.1. Note that it uses a new category of marketability: fairly marketable. Items in this category can be sold, but with one or more problems, which we can call inefficiencies. Inefficiencies can occur in such areas as transaction cost, time to find a buyer and close the sale, or time needed for the seller to substitute another asset for household use. Each can expose a person to higher cost or increased risk. Given this new category, the efficient marketable asset has been termed a fully marketable asset. In contrast to this more precise definition, in other uses throughout the book, the term *marketable* will stand for fully marketable.

A summary of household assets is given in Figure 8.1.

EXAMINING THE DECISION PROCESS

Decisions about which nonfinancial assets to select do not come out of thin air. Instead we form conclusions based on the values presented by investment alternatives. Our evaluation process for nonfinancial investments begins by looking at the three ways household decisions are made and how total portfolio management relates to them. It then describes capital expenditures and provides a step-by-step accounting for how decisions for many household assets should be arrived at. The final section describes the capital budgeting tools you need to measure attractiveness of proposed investments.

---

[1] Pension assets then are those that provide streams of income over time. Pensions that allow you to withdraw monies in lump sums are considered financial assets.

Household Finance and Total Portfolio Management

Household finance looks at the household as one enterprise that resembles a business. Each of its operations can require investments. External work-related activities may require an investment in human assets such as an outlay for education, the house may require a new roof or a new boiler, while future retirement needs may necessitate constant investments in financial assets.

Each of these investments can be evaluated from three perspectives:

1. *Individual-asset basis.* Under the individual asset approach, decisions are made by looking at the investment's risk and return characteristics on a stand-alone basis. The question to answer is, When looked at by itself, is this asset attractive?

2. *Within-activity basis.* An investment can be proposed in any household activity. The question asked is: How does this proposed expenditure compare with current or future alternatives within the same activity? For example, under human assets the question asked may be: Is it more attractive to pay for education to improve skills in the current job or to pursue an MBA? Sometimes the household thinks of investments in financial and nonfinancial assets as separate activities, comparing all alternatives within one of these two categories at the same time. For example, in financial investments, the question frequently asked is whether to sell selected bonds and buy additional stocks.

3. *Fully integrated basis.* Decisions are made not on a per-asset or per-activity basis but on an overall household basis. Each activity has assets that benefit the household. These assets can be grouped into financial and nonfinancial categories, as discussed. Together they form a portfolio of assets, the household portfolio. We can call the process of developing and maintaining an efficient combination of assets total portfolio management (TPM).

The nature of the household lends itself to centralized decision making. There are generally few adult members, thus permitting quick integrated decisions. The assets themselves are best assessed on a combined basis because resources are limited. Therefore, important goals are prioritized on an integrated household level. Moreover, tolerances for risk are set on an aggregate basis by household members.

TPM looks at the household as a portfolio of assets.[2] It presents solutions as to which assets should be placed in the household portfolio and how to weight them. Its approach incorporates both risk and return. In more sophisticated versions, it incorporates correlations—that is, the degree to which individual assets are subject to the same risks. Generally, the lower the correlations, the lower the risk. By providing the right blend of assets, TPM assists the household in operating efficiently.

The household may engage in all three decision-making approaches. The purest approach is evaluation through total portfolio management. Even traditional portfolio management, which will be discussed in the next chapter, can be considered as handled on a less comprehensive within-activity basis since it typically looks at financial assets alone.

Example 8.1

Sal and Diane, ages 31 and 30, are married and live in a rural town. The town was once a thriving mining and manufacturing center but now has a disproportionate number of elderly. When children grew up, they moved elsewhere and few new people moved in. Consequently, the population declines modestly each year. Sal leased and runs a lucrative mini-supermarket business that he inherited from his father. Diane is a clothing store manager in town who wants to become a lawyer.

---

[2] Liabilities are incorporated as negative assets here—terminology that has been used before. In other chapters, assets and liabilities will usually be treated separately.

The couple have a number of investments they are considering. Each investment had passed an initial screening and was thought to be attractive on a stand-alone basis.

1. Purchasing a vacation home in the mountains nearby.
2. Adding a bedroom to their existing home for anticipated children to come.
3. Beginning to put away money in stocks and bonds for retirement.
4. Diane applying to a law school located one hour away.
5. Sal attending an expensive cooking school one weekend a month. The store could then offer fresh-baked goods.

They did some preliminary calculations and decided that they didn't have enough resources for all these investments. Borrowing money would only provide limited help because they believed anything more than $150,000 in loans would exceed their household tolerance for risk. One of the five proposals would have to go.

The couple grouped their investment proposals into categories: real assets, financial assets, and human-related assets. They decided that both real-asset proposals were important. The addition to the home was needed because they expected to have children soon. The vacation home was required to offset the long hours at the store and because it could be purchased at a below-market price. The investment in financial assets for retirement had to begin. They were already behind where they wanted to be for an early retirement.

That left the two investments in human-related assets. On a within-activity basis, these two proposed assets were believed to have the lowest returns of all the alternatives. Between the two, Diane's attending law school would be more attractive than Sal's cooking school excursion. It would provide a higher return on human assets.

They had conducted their final evaluation on a total portfolio management basis, looking at all proposals at the same time. They thought they had completed their deliberations. However, when looking at the results on an overall household portfolio basis, they recognized a weakness. Household risk, even with the limitation on debt, would exceed their overall risk tolerance. Virtually all their real human-related assets and other assets where the supermarket was located were subject to the risk attached to (correlated with) a community suffering a population decline. Sal's business, Diane's job, and their home would all be negatively affected by a further drop in the town's population. If the decline accelerated, all their nonfinancial assets could be seriously affected.

They decided to substitute an equally attractive vacation home located near a large growing community. They would have to drive two hours to reach it, but it would materially reduce their dependence on their current community and therefore on overall TPM risk. Decision making was finally completed.

The balance of the chapter provides the method of selecting common nonfinancial investments—those having to do with real assets and human-related assets. It will enable you to decide if you should accept or reject proposed expenditures, whether they be for a house, a car, or a master's degree. It will detail whether to buy or lease a house or a car and how to decide on the amount you can spend for a home.

Making Capital Expenditure Decisions

Capital expenditures are outlays that provide benefits over an extended period of time. These outlays improve household operations as soon as they become available. Capital expenditures is the term used for outlays for real or human-related assets, but not for financial ones. The capital outlays can be used for purchasing new assets or improving existing ones. For a discussion of the theory for making capital expenditures, called *capital budgeting theory,* see Appendix I.

The benefits of capital expenditure may be greater revenues, lower cash cost, or less time to produce a desired result. Alternatively, the benefit may just involve an immediate increase in satisfaction. We are often faced with a variety of capital expenditure alternatives. We must decide which to fund from household cash flows and household assets and which merit borrowing money. We should do so by using the established business capital budgeting techniques: net present value (NPV) and internal rate of return (IRR).[3] Before we describe these techniques, let's go over the capital budgeting process.

The Capital Expenditure Process

The process of selecting capital expenditures is ideally the one that is presented below. In reality, adherence to this schedule depends in part on the type and cost of capital outlays. When the returns are measurable and the cost is great, it is more likely to be followed. For example, in considering the purchase of a fuel-efficient boiler, the process and quantitative measurement of returns are more likely to be followed than in the purchase of a new HDTV set where the satisfaction levels are hard to measure. But even when measurement is difficult, alternatives generally can be ranked in order of attractiveness. Here are the steps.

Review Goals

Households not only have desires; they have needs. We can loosely categorize them as discretionary and nondiscretionary outlays. For example, while retirement without assets in theory is an option, in reality we have a need to save sometime before retirement or we risk working forever or sustaining a sharp drop in our standard of living during retirement. Our goals of future priorities can result in our having limited resources for spending today, even capital spending. Thus it is important to place our nonfinancial investments in the context of our overall goals.

Establish Required Rate of Return

Our capital outlays must reach a required rate of return for all projects. We must decide on that return based on market figures for savings and investing in financial assets, and our priorities. For example, if market returns on stocks with comparable risk to our capital project are 10 percent, we will use that percentage as our required rate of return.

Identify Potential Projects

Households generally don't have to look for projects. They are usually apparent. They should just be set aside and brought up together at the time evaluation is to begin.

Evaluate Projects

Normally, we view the costs and returns for each project. When feasible, we calculate returns using IRR or NPV, to be discussed next.

Rank All Projects

Here we rank all projects using stand-alone calculations—first on a within-activity basis, then within the category, and finally on a total portfolio basis. Their risk and blending (correlations) with other assets will be taken into account, particularly on the total portfolio basis.

Establish Overall Capital Availability

Perhaps more so than for businesses, capital is limited for the household. Debt financing is available to some degree, but of course it raises risk. Taking into account all factors, the amount of capital to be made available is established.

---

[3]As Copeland and Weston say, "The decision criterion for investment decisions which is to maximize the present value of lifetime consumption can be applied to any sector of the economy." See Thomas Copeland and J. Fred Weston, *Financial Theory and Corporate Policy,* 3rd ed. (Reading, MA: Addison-Wesley, 1992), p. 17.

Select and Invest in Final Projects

Based on returns, capital availabilities, and risk and risk tolerance, the household decides on the assets it wants to fund. Some drop out forever; others are brought up at a future time when relative attractiveness and financial resources change.

Capital Budgeting Techniques

The two most prominent capital budgeting techniques are NPV and IRR. Let's discuss them separately.

Net Present Value (NPV)

In Chapter 2 you learned about the time value of money. Both NPV and IRR are time value of money concepts applied to capital budgeting. The **net present value (NPV)** can be defined as the present value of all projected future cash inflows and outflows. It provides the amount of benefit for a capital expenditure as compared with investing the money in marketable investments.

We receive the present value by discounting all cash flows back to the present at an appropriate **discount rate.**[4] This discount rate is generally equal to the investment return—what could be earned on marketable securities with similar risk characteristics. The market rate is used because it is the minimum rate that must be earned on the capital expenditure. If we can't earn that rate on capital expenditures, we probably should invest the money in marketable securities such as stocks and bonds.

We can call this discount rate based on market factors the **required rate of return.**[5] The NPV tells us whether we have earned the required rate of return. If NPV is 0 or higher, we have earned it, and the capital expenditure is accepted. In other words, when NPV is positive, the capital expenditure is preferable to a marketable investment. If NPV is negative, we have not earned the required return and the proposed expenditure is rejected. NPV is given by the following formula:

$$NPV = \sum_{t=1}^{n} \frac{CF_t}{(1+k)^t} - CF_0$$

where

CF = Cash flow generated

CF_0 = Amount invested (often a cash outflow) at time zero, the beginning of the period

k = Discount rate

t = Time period involved

n = Number of years

$\sum_{t=1}^{n}$ = Sum of the present values of cash flows from time 1 to time n

In sum,

$$NPV = \frac{\text{Sum of future cash inflows}}{\text{Discount rate}} - \text{Cash outflow in current period}$$

$$= \text{Present value of future cash inflows} - \text{Cash outflow in current period}$$

---

[4] Its definition, then, is the rate that we use to bring future cash flows to the present generally to establish their current value.

[5] It can be defined as the return that is needed to be earned to make an investment attractive. Market factors including the investment risk should be incorporated.

When the present value of future cash inflows exceeds the initial outflow, consider accepting the capital expenditure. When the present value of future cash inflows is less than the initial cash outflow, reject the capital expenditure.

Example 8.2

A capital expenditure with a $1,000 initial cost and present value of inflows of $1,500 would have a $500 NPV and be accepted. If the initial cost was the same $1,000, but the inflows were only $900, the NPV would be negative $100 and the project would be rejected. In the $100 case, you can do better by investing in marketable securities.

Calculator Solution

Step	HP12C	TI BA II Plus
Clear the register	Press f FIN	Press CF 2nd CLR Work
Enter initial outflow	Enter cash flow in CF$_0$ register as CHS g CF$_0$	Enter cash flow in CF$_0$ register as −/+ Enter ↓
Enter succeeding outflows or inflows	Enter cash flows in CF$_j$ register successively as g CF$_j$	Enter cash flows in C register successively as Enter ↓
Enter number of years for repeating cash flows	Enter number of years in N$_j$ register as g N$_j$	Enter number of years in F register as Enter ↓
Enter the discount rate	Enter number in i register	Enter number by pressing NPV key in the number Enter ↓
Solution	Press f NPV	Press CPT

Example 8.3

June was thinking of purchasing a new air conditioner for her den. She had a home office there, and the air conditioner would be on 16 hours a day for 9 months of the year. The existing air conditioner worked well but was not energy-efficient. The new air conditioner would save about $15 a month in energy costs. The new machine was of lower overall quality, and in fact was expected to last only five years, about the useful life of the existing machine. June wondered whether the new machine's energy efficiency would extend throughout its life span. Given the greater risk of this machine June decided to assign a higher discount rate. This required rate of return would be 12 percent, about equal to marketable securities/common stocks with the same risk profile. The machine would cost $650. Using annual figures, calculate whether June should purchase the machine.

$$\text{Initial cash payment} = \$650$$
$$\text{Yearly cash inflows} = \$15 \times 12 \text{ months}$$
$$= \$180 \text{ per year}$$
$$\text{Number of years of inflows} = 5$$
$$\text{Required rate of return} = 12\%$$

Calculator Solution

General Calculator Approach	Specific HP12C	Specific TI BA II Plus
Clear the register	f FIN	CF 2nd CLR Work
Enter initial cash outflow	650 CHS g CF$_0$	650 +/− ENTER ↓
Enter cash inflows Years 1 − 5	180 g CF$_j$	180 ENTER ↓
Enter number of years	5 g N$_j$	5 ENTER ↓
Enter the discount rate	12 i	NPV 12 ENTER ↓
Calculate the net present value	f NPV −1.14	CPT −1.14

The NPV is negative. The proposed capital expenditure should be rejected. June could do better by investing in marketable securities.

If we had access to unlimited funds, we would accept all capital expenditures that would have a positive NPV. However, often our source of capital is limited. In that instance, we have to select those investments that provide the highest returns.[6] Unfortunately, NPV alone doesn't provide that figure when comparing investments that differ in amounts invested.

To rank investments in terms of attractiveness, we can use the **profitability index (PI).** It relates the amount of the NPV to the size of the original investment. The higher the value of the profitability index, the more attractive the investment.

$$\text{Profitability index} = \frac{\text{NPV}}{\text{Original cost}}$$

Any savings in the opportunity cost of time should be included in calculating the additional cost or benefits for household expenditures. That is because this time used potentially could be employed in developing additional cash flows. As discussed in Chapter 4, we assign a cash flow figure to the cost of time based on the hourly wage rate that could be received if the time was spent working.

Example 8.4

Jason is considering the purchase of a new vacuum cleaner. There are two electric models. Both models would save him a quarter of an hour of time a week. The lower-quality vacuum would last three years and would cost $300; the higher-quality model would last eight years and cost $400. The purchase of either model would be funded from existing savings. Jason earns $15 an hour after tax in his job. His required rate of return based on what he could earn in the market is 6 percent after tax. Should he make the investment? If so, which one should he buy? Express all figures on an annual basis.

Lower-Quality Machine

$$\text{Initial outflow} = -\$300$$

$$\text{Weekly inflows} = \text{Savings in time} \times \text{Hourly wage}$$

$$= 1/4 \text{ hour} \times \$15$$

$$= \$3.75$$

$$\text{Yearly inflows} = \$3.75 \times 52 \text{ weeks}$$

$$= \$195$$

Calculator Solution

General Calculator Approach	Specific HP12C	Specific TI BA II Plus
		CF
Clear the register	f FIN	2nd CLR Work
Enter initial cash outflow	300 CHS g CF₀	300 +/− ENTER ↓
Enter cash inflows Years 1–3	195 g CFⱼ	195 ENTER ↓
Enter number of years	3 g Nⱼ	3 ENTER ↓
Enter the discount rate	6 i	NPV
		6 ENTER ↓
Calculate the net present value	f NPV	CPT
	221.24	221.24

Higher-Quality Machine

$$\text{Initial outflows} = -\$400$$

$$\text{Yearly inflows} = \$195, \text{ as above}$$

[6]Actually, the selection process under restricted borrowing would have to be made incorporating decision making over a multiyear basis. See Neil Seitz and Mitch Ellison, *Capital Budgeting and Long-Term Financing Decisions,* 3rd ed. (Fort Worth, TX: Dryden Press, 1999), pp. 722–25.

Calculator Solution

General Calculator Approach	Specific HP12C	Specific TI BA II Plus
		CF
Clear the register	f FIN	2nd CRL Work
Enter initial cash outflow	400 CHS g CF₀	400 +/− ENTER ↓
Enter cash inflows Years 1–8	195 g CFⱼ	195 ENTER ↓
Enter number of years	8 g Nⱼ	8 ENTER ↓
Enter the discount rate	6 i	NPV
		6 ENTER ↓
Calculate the net present value	f NPV	CPT
	810.91	810.91

Profitability Index

$$\text{Lower-quality machine} = \frac{221.24}{300}$$

$$= 0.74$$

$$\text{Higher-quality machine} = \frac{810.91}{400}$$

$$= 2.03$$

While both investments have positive NPVs, the higher-quality machine has a higher profitability index and is therefore the more attractive investment.

Internal Rate of Return (IRR)

The **internal rate of return (IRR),** which we discussed briefly in Chapter 2, provides a percentage return on investment. It can be defined as the rate of return that makes the present value of cash inflows equal to that of cash outflows.

The IRR is therefore the discount rate that makes NPV equal to 0. The IRR approach is very similar to obtaining an NPV with cash inflows and cash outflows calculated. However, instead of inputting a market-based discount rate, we solve for the IRR. We compare the IRR with our required rate of return, the return we could get on marketable securities with the same risk. If the IRR is greater than the required rate of return, we accept it. If it isn't, we reject the proposed capital outlay.

Calculator Solution

Step	HP12C	TI BA II Plus
Clear the register	Press f FIN	Press CF 2nd CLR Work
Enter initial outflow	Enter cash flow in **CF₀** register as CHS g CF₀	Enter cash flow in **CF₀** register as −/+ Enter ↓
Enter succeeding outflows or inflows	Enter cash flows in **CFⱼ** register successively as g CFⱼ	Enter cash flows in **C** register successively as Enter ↓
Enter number of years for repeating cash flows	Enter number of years in **Nⱼ** register as g Nⱼ	Enter number of years in **F** register as Enter ↓
Solution	Press f IRR	Press IRR CPT

Example 8.5

Brandt is considering purchasing a new personal computer and related software that would cost $4,500. He has a part-time job editing books at home. He receives a flat fee per book that averages about $25 an hour after tax for 15 hours per week, 50 weeks a year. He expects to maintain this job for three years until his regular career pays enough money, at which point he would stop the editing work. He believes the new setup would increase his output by 10 percent. Assuming his after-tax required rate of return is 11 percent, using annual savings calculations, should he purchase the computer?

$$\text{Initial payment} = \$4,500$$

$$\text{Weekly inflows} = \text{Existing hourly wage} \times \text{Hours per week}$$

$$= \$25 \times 15 \text{ hours}$$

$$= \$375$$

$$\text{Yearly inflows existing} = \$375 \times 50$$

$$= \$18,750$$

$$\text{Increase in yearly inflows} = 10\%$$

$$\text{Yearly inflows proposed} = 18,750 \times 1.10$$

$$= 20,625$$

$$\text{Yearly benefit} = 20,625 - 18,750$$

$$= 1,875$$

$$\text{Years benefit applicable for} = 3$$

Calculator Solution

General Calculator Approach	HP12C	TI BA II Plus
		CF
Clear the register	f FIN	2nd CLR Work
Enter initial cash outflow	4,500 CHS g CF₀	4,500 +/− ENTER ↓
Enter cash inflows Years 1–3	1,875 g CFⱼ	1,875 ENTER ↓
Enter number of years	3 g Nⱼ	3 ENTER ↓
Calculate the internal rate of return	f IRR	IRR CPT
	12%	12%

The IRR of 12 percent exceeds the required 11 percent. Therefore, the capital expenditure should be made.

Comparison of IRR and NPV Methods

In evaluating the two approaches, NPV is the purer, more accurate method. However, since IRR is expressed in percentage return terms, it can be easier to understand and relate to. Moreover, an IRR can compare returns for expenditures of different amounts and time frames. A major difference in approach is that NPV assumes that cash flows from projects are invested at the required rate of return while IRR assumes they are reinvested at the rate of return of that particular project. The weakness in the IRR approach is shown in Example 8.6. IRR also gives multiple answers under some circumstances.

Example 8.6

Suppose you were able to set up your first hamburger fast-food restaurant next to the sports center in your town with an inexpensive long-term lease. Other restaurants in the chain that were to be built had an expected rate of return of 15 percent. You would probably have a very high IRR, say 90 percent a year, due to your location. Clearly, cash flows from that hamburger capital expenditure used to build other restaurants would probably not earn the same rate of return as your original investment. Thus, the NPV method, which employs the required rate of return of 15 percent for reinvestment, is more accurate than the IRR, whose approach would assume a 90 percent return on the cash flows generated for the new restaurants.

There are ways to adjust for the reinvestment effect and other weaknesses of IRR. In most cases, both methods will provide the same ranking of alternative expenditures.

ANALYZING MAJOR CAPITAL EXPENDITURES

We know that households engage in production activities just as businesses do. They produce goods and services for internal household use and for external market-related activities. Capital expenditures make each more productive. Consequently, there are many types of capital expenditures the household makes. Selected ones were presented as examples illustrating NPV and IRR techniques.

In this section, we will concentrate on decision making for what is often the three largest capital expenditures a household has: the car, the person, and the home. All three are thought of as investments in contrast to other outflows, which are expenses. That is because they provide benefits that extend beyond the current period. We look at them separately below beginning with durable goods and the car.

Durable Goods

Consumer durable goods are capital expenditures that can benefit many types of household operations. Whether for a job, a nondiscretionary activity, or a discretionary activity, they provide returns to the household over an extended period of time. Among the reasons that you would purchase a durable good are

1. To take advantage of a technological improvement with the potential to make household maintenance more time-efficient. For example, a new dishwasher can free up time to be used to generate additional work-related income or to further leisure pursuits.

2. To replace an existing durable that has reached the end of its useful life due to physical wear and tear.

3. To reflect a change in circumstances—for example, a rise in the price of oil can substantially change the cost and therefore the economics of a "gas-guzzling" automobile. The result may be the purchase of a fuel-efficient car.

4. To provide more pleasure—for example, purchasing a home theater surround-sound system.[7]

5. To attempt to raise returns on assets—for example, buying an investment software package with the hope of increasing investment performance.

The Automobile

Since the car is generally the most expensive, pure consumer durable the household purchases, let's use it as a practical example. Like most other durables, a car declines in value over time.

This capital expenditure can assist in transportation to work, make household necessities easier to obtain, and provide pleasure in itself or through its ability to take you to other pleasurable activities. Most multiperson households have at least one car. Depending on operating patterns, they may exchange cars as often as once a year or as infrequently as once in, say, 10 years when, for practical purposes, the car may no longer be considered useful. The car may be purchased for cash or debt, or it may be leased. A lease-versus-purchase example is given in Appendix IV.

Some of the major factors in deciding to change automobiles, whether for a new or used car, are

Factor	Explanation
State of current car	The higher the repair bills, the lower the car's attractiveness, and the more likely a trade-in will be contemplated.

---

[7] To understand how capital expenditures on leisure products may be valued, see Appendix II, Assumed Rents.

Factor	Explanation
Existing finances	The greater the cash on hand, the more favorable the job and economic outlook, the more likely the trade-in.
Current car promotions	At certain times in the economic cycle, the purchase of a new or used car may be particularly attractive. This means that prices, leases, and financing terms may cause households to exchange cars prior to their intended date.
Attractiveness of new car	New cars may have style, safety, or mileage features that motivate people to buy them.

The factors that enter into a decision to purchase one car over another one include its cost, the quality leading to lower repair bills, its fuel efficiency, safety features, its ride and cabin comfort, its projected trade-in value, and its style and image.

Example 8.7

Nicole has a suburban home within walking distance of the railroad. She commutes to work in the city at a cost of $180 a month. She also rents a car every weekend, which costs $600 a month including insurance and fuel. She is considering purchasing a new car for cash to replace commuting and rental costs. It would cost $20,000, provide 28 miles per gallon, and be sold for $10,000 in five years. She would have maintenance and repairs of $2,000 per year, insurance of $1,500 per year, and fuel costs of $1.50 per gallon and would drive 15,000 miles per year. Assume all costs occur at the end of the year and that she sells the car at the end of the fifth year. If Nicole's discount rate is 7 percent after tax, should she purchase the car?

Annual Operating Cost of Car

Yearly Maintenance Cost

$$\text{Fuel consumption}\left(\frac{15{,}000 \text{ miles}}{28 \text{ mpg}}\right) = 535 \text{ gallons per year}$$

$$\text{Fuel cost } (535 \text{ gallons} \times \$1.50) = \$803$$
$$\text{Annual repairs and maintenance} = 2{,}000$$
$$\text{Annual insurance} = \underline{1{,}500}$$
$$\text{Total projected yearly cost} = \$4{,}303$$

Current Annual Cost

$$\text{Commute } (\$180 \times 12) = \$2{,}160$$
$$\text{Car rental } (\$600 \times 12) = \underline{7{,}200}$$
$$\text{Total current annual cost} = \$9{,}360$$
$$\text{Annual savings } (\$9{,}360 - \$4{,}303) = \mathbf{\$5{,}057}$$
$$\text{Cost to purchase car} = \$20{,}000$$
$$\text{Selling price Year 5} = \$10{,}000$$

Calculator Solution

General Calculator Approach	HP12C	TI BA II Plus
		[CF]
Clear the register	[f] [FIN]	[2nd] [CLR Work]
Enter initial cash outflow	20,000 [CHS][g][CF₀]	20,000 [+/−] [ENTER][↓]
Enter cash inflows Years 1–4	5,057 [g][CFⱼ]	5,057 [ENTER][↓]
Enter number of years	4 [g][Nⱼ]	4 [ENTER][↓]
Enter cash inflow Year 5	15,057 [g][CFⱼ]	15,057 [ENTER][↓][↓]
Calculate the internal rate of return	[f] [IRR]	[IRR] [CPT]
	18%	18%

The return for this capital expenditure is 18 percent. It significantly exceeds the required 7 percent rate. The car should be purchased.

Practical Comment   The Importance of Human Assets

In presentations of household assets, human assets are generally overlooked. For example, the household's balance sheet normally does not contain a calculation of human assets. That is true despite the fact that human capital is often the largest asset by far that a household has.

The lack of attention given to human assets extends to capital expenditures. The recognition of money spent for multiyear benefit is often restricted to durable goods. We can see or touch new durable goods. They are the household's equivalent of business equipment. Perhaps this overlooking of capital outlays on humans occurs because human beings can be seen but the capital expenditures on such qualities as knowledge are so intangible—such assets cannot be seen or touched. Nonetheless, most people would agree that education can add to long-

term income-earning capacity and therefore qualifies as a capital expenditure. For example, most people wouldn't be spending the money and time pursuing business-oriented education—including the study of this textbook—if it weren't for the potential impact on their income.

Personal financial planners are aware of how important human assets are in the work they do for clients. Although they do not normally place human assets on the balance sheet, they incorporate them in capital budgeting decisions and, of course, include them in projections of salaries in the cash flow statement. They recognize the relevance of capital expenditures on education and the capacity to earn additional income. In other words, planners recognize that capital expenditures can incorporate human assets as well as durable goods.

Human Assets

Our human assets are the human capital we have that we and others value: knowledge, skills, intellectual capacity, strength, beauty, compassion, ethical behavior, creativity, drive, health, and so on. From a financial standpoint, we often limit ourselves to those factors that directly enter into a person's income-earning ability. Often, these are simplified to two basic traits: knowledge and skills, with general health used as support for them.

We can now define **human assets** as the resource that reflects the current value of all our future earnings. It is a nonmarketable asset—that is, it cannot be sold. Instead, it is often rented to an employer for a period of time at an hourly fee or a salary. Without knowledge and skills, human capital can be viewed as a basic commodity with the ability to earn just the minimum wage. Capital expenditures in this area include time and money spent on formal education and other ways of developing knowledge, many through practical experience.

In effect, education, training, and proper health habits can provide us with a higher return on our life cycle human assets. Empirical evidence points to often-attractive returns of 14 to 16 percent on human assets,[8] although returns on human capital may vary among segments of society as well as between men and women.[9]

Capital expenditures to raise human assets are not restricted to job-related activities. They can be made in all relevant areas of the household. You may take a course to make you a better investor. You may read *Consumer Reports* each month to develop some expertise in purchasing useful household appliances and receive help in deciding which brand to buy. You may purchase a book on how to cook quickly but effectively. Finally, retired people may attend seminars on how to better enjoy retirement life.

[8] Gary Becker, *Human Capital: A Theoretical and Empirical Analysis with Special Reference to Education*, 3rd ed. (Chicago: University of Chicago Press, 1993).

[9] See, for example, F. Blau, M. Ferber, and A. Winkler, *The Economics of Women, Men and Work*, 4th ed. (Upper Saddle River, NJ: Prentice Hall, 2001).

Calculating Human Assets

The value of your human assets varies over your life cycle. If you are a skilled employee, your asset value may actually go up for a time.[10] However, as you age, the decline in the number of your earning years generally results in a drop in your human assets over your life cycle. In effect, like many other assets, human assets depreciate over time.

Capital expenditures on human assets are treated similarly to those for other assets with benefits compared with costs. Consider Example 8.8.

Example 8.8

Astrid, age 30, is a married architect with one child. Her salary had reached a plateau at $75,000 a year. She believed that if she pursued an MBA degree full-time, she would move into a managerial position and her salary would rise by $45,000 a year. Astrid wants to maintain her current lifestyle, which already generates substantial yearly cash savings, and accumulate the capital to leave to her son. Her MBA would take two years and cost $48,000 a year. Since she planned to pay for the MBA out of existing savings and was spending the money to qualify for a new position, she would not be eligible for any tax benefits.

Assume that she pays one-third of her salary in taxes and her tax bracket will remain unchanged after the raise; that she can earn 6 percent after taxes on investments with a similar risk to her job; and that she plans to retire at age 65. Furthermore, assume that all salary and schooling payments are made in a lump sum at the beginning of each year. What is her rate of return on this investment? Should she pursue an MBA? If so, what will her human capital be valued at, assuming a calculation that incorporates salary forgone and her MBA payments upon graduation.

Her after-tax increase in salary per year is

$$\text{After-tax gain} = \text{Pretax gain} \times (1 - t)$$
$$= \$45,000 \times (1 - 0.3333)$$
$$= \$30,000 \text{ per year}$$
$$\text{Numbers of years of gain} = \text{Retirement age} - (\text{Current age} + \text{Full time MBA study})$$
$$= 65 - (30 + 2)$$
$$= 33 \text{ years}$$

The cost of attending school is

$$\text{Schooling cost} = \$48,000 \text{ a year for 2 years}$$
$$\text{Opportunity cost of time} = 2 \text{ years of salary forgone}$$
$$= \$75,000 \times (1 - t)$$
$$= \$75,000 \times (1 - 0.33)$$
$$= \$50,000 \text{ a year for 2 years}$$
$$\text{Combined yearly cost} = \text{Schooling cost} + \text{Opportunity cost}$$
$$= \$48,000 + \$50,000$$
$$= \$98,000 \text{ a year for 2 years}$$

Calculator Solution

General Calculator Approach	HP12C	TI BA II Plus
		CF
Clear the register	f FIN	2nd CLR Work
Enter cash outflow Year 1	98,000 CHS g CF₀	98,000 +/− ENTER ↓
Enter cash outflow Year 2	98,000 CHS g CFⱼ	98,000 +/− ENTER ↓ ↓

(continues)

[10] That is due to the greater present value of higher-earning years as you draw closer to them. For a time, it can more than offset the effect of fewer work years.

(concluded)

General Calculator Approach	HP12C	TI BA II Plus
Enter cash inflows	30,000 $\boxed{g}\boxed{CF_j}$	30,000 $\boxed{ENTER}\boxed{\downarrow}$
Enter number of years	33 $\boxed{g}\boxed{N_j}$	33 $\boxed{ENTER}\boxed{\downarrow}$
Calculate the internal rate of return	$\boxed{f}\boxed{IRR}$	$\boxed{IRR}\boxed{CPT}$
	14.1%	14.1%

Internal rate of return = 14.1 percent

Since that rate exceeds Astrid's rate of return on marketable investments of 6 percent, she should pursue the MBA. The value of her human capital would be

$$\text{New salary} = \$75,000 + \$45,000$$

$$= \$120,000$$

$$\text{After-tax income} = \$120,000 \times (1 - 0.3333)$$

$$= \$80,000$$

Calculator Solution

General Calculator Approach	HP12C	TI BA II Plus
		$\boxed{CF}$
Clear the register	$\boxed{f}\boxed{FIN}$	$\boxed{2nd}\boxed{CLR\ Work}$
Enter cash outflow Year 1	98,000 $\boxed{CHS}\boxed{g}\boxed{CF_0}$	98,000 $\boxed{+/-}\boxed{ENTER}\boxed{\downarrow}$
Enter cash outflow Year 2	98,000 $\boxed{CHS}\boxed{g}\boxed{CF_j}$	98,000 $\boxed{+/-}\boxed{ENTER}\boxed{\downarrow}\boxed{\downarrow}$
Enter cash inflows	80,000 $\boxed{g}\boxed{CF_j}$	80,000 $\boxed{ENTER}\boxed{\downarrow}$
Enter number of years	33 $\boxed{g}\boxed{N_j}$	33 $\boxed{ENTER}\boxed{\downarrow}$
Enter the discount rate	6 $\boxed{i}$	$\boxed{NPV}$
		6 $\boxed{ENTER}\boxed{\downarrow}$
Calculate the net present value	$\boxed{f}\boxed{NPV}$	$\boxed{CPT}$
	883,527	883,527

Value of human capital = $883,527

The Home

The home is a structure whose traditional function is to shelter its occupants. However, ownership of a home, whether it be an apartment, a townhouse, or a full-fledged house, often carries significant symbolism. Some of the associations and feelings it can convey are achievement, stability, privacy, and comfort. Whether bought or rented, an apartment or house generally signifies a single financial structure for all its inhabitants. This unified structure allows us to utilize a household framework for financial planning purposes.

Housing Features

The house has a number of features that distinguish it from most durable goods.

1. *Unique physical characteristics.* No two houses are exactly the same and most can readily be distinguished from one another.
2. *Long-lasting.* Houses tend to have extended useful lives. Although the components of a house depreciate, through maintenance and renovation, the property's overall asset value often can be prevented from declining for many years.
3. *Tax benefits.* One government goal is affordable suitable housing for all Americans. The government provides tax benefits to owners, makes it easier for people to get mortgage financing, and subsidizes low-income housing.

Practical Comment   Use of Capital Budgeting Techniques

The degree to which households use financial analysis in making decisions on capital expenditures varies. When the expenditure is substantial and the benefits can easily be measured, stronger efforts are often made to include a cost-benefit analysis. For example, a household considering putting in a new, more efficient boiler to save fuel costs may compare the cost of the boiler with the projected annual fuel savings. They also may take into account the anticipated useful life of the new boiler and the remaining life of the old one. The financial analysis may be done by them exclusively or be based on information supplied by the manufacturer of the boiler or others.

The decision to buy a new pair of skis may be made more intuitively. The household members will anticipate the extra pleasure they will get from the equipment and compare it with the cost. To improve the process, the financial aspects of the transaction should be emphasized. Whenever possible, the costs and benefits should be drawn up. When the item is purchased for its increase in leisure satisfaction and is difficult to quantify, a ranking system of proposed uses for the money can help identify its contribution. In such cases, the effect of the outlay on the desired level of savings should be incorporated in the decision-making process.

BEHAVIORAL REALITIES

In general, the structure laid out for capital budgeting decisions in this chapter represents an ideal framework. In reality, many such decisions are made using mental shortcuts. The portfolio approach to capital expenditures in a one-person household can just be mental consideration of how this proposed asset affects cash flow, overall assets, and debt. In a two-person household with specialization of tasks, some less significant decisions are made on an individual-asset stand-alone basis. However, important decisions for all households are generally made or approved on an overall portfolio basis.

And last, as mentioned in Chapter 5, household members and financial advisors alike sometimes forget to place significant capital expenditures into cash flow forecasts. Thus, they may omit such items as household remodeling and replacement of automobiles. In either case, average amounts should be placed in yearly or lump-sum amounts assumed over appropriate time periods, adjusted for inflation. Without anticipating such items, savings needs can be materially understated.

4. *Appreciation potential.* Many properties that are taken care of tend to rise in value over time.
5. *A fixed location.* Generally, houses remain in one place. As a result, a house's location takes on significance in its maintenance and investment functions.
6. *Land.* The house sits on land that, in most instances, is owned. Land may fluctuate in value, but over a long period of time, value tends to rise when the house and land are looked at as a single asset. Unlike other durable goods, even over extended periods, they don't lose their entire value.

Housing Uses

Home ownership is normally the individual's largest single cash expenditure. Multiperson occupancies, as, for example, in marriages, carry significant efficiencies since costs of shelter can be shared. The home is also one of the clearest examples of multiple uses. Its first use is its classic role of providing shelter. In it the home has ongoing cash maintenance costs for such items as utilities and repairs and necessitates that worktime be expended for upkeep of the house. Moreover, the home requires periodic capital expenditures to sustain it such as putting on a new roof or buying a new boiler.[11]

Its second use is as a long-term investment. A well-maintained house can appreciate substantially over time. Its third use is in providing pleasure to its occupants. Among its

---

[11] Most people do not refer to a house as a durable good. Instead, they refer to it as real estate or property. We distinguish it here from other types of household assets and will treat it separately throughout the book.

TABLE 8.2

Home Ownership Rates by Household and Type of Structure

Source: U.S. Census Bureau, Historical Census of Housing Tables, http://www.census.gov/hhes/www/housing/census/historic/ownrate.html.

	Total	One-Family Detached House	Apartments with Five or More Units	Mobile Homes	One-Person Households
1950	**55.0%**	73.0%	4.1%	79.4%	42.1%
1960	**61.9%**	78.3%	4.6%	88.3%	40.8%
1970	**62.9%**	81.6%	5.2%	84.5%	42.4%
1980	**64.4%**	85.6%	10.2%	79.8%	43.5%
1990	**64.2%**	85.5%	9.6%	79.8%	48.7%
2000	**66.2%**	N/A	N/A	N/A	N/A
2004	**69.0%**	N/A	N/A	N/A	N/A

benefits are relief from daily stresses and the ability of household members to express themselves in putting the entire house together according to their taste and then maintaining it as an attractive place to live.

Because of its benefits and increases in household discretionary income in this country, the rate of home ownership has risen over the past 50 years, as we see in Table 8.2.

Tax Benefits for a Home

The government recognizes that owning a home is a principal goal of many people. Home ownership presents significant tax benefits because interest on a home mortgage is tax-deductible, as are property taxes. In addition, along with investment assets, appreciation in its value is not taxed until the home is sold. Upon sale, the first $250,000 of gain per person or $500,000 per couple is tax-free, with amounts over that taxed at capital gains rates. Capital expenditures on home improvements are added to the purchase price in calculating your basis in the property, which reduces the ultimate gain. This $250,000 or $500,000 benefit is allowed once every two years for those people who have had their home as their primary residence for any two of the past five years.

Since tax benefits can be highly significant, care must be taken to explicitly include them in decision making. They are incorporated in the market price of individual homes. A comparison of traditional durables with the home is shown in Table 8.3.

One way to obtain the benefits of a home is to include the cost of renting the home in the calculation of return. In effect, when you purchase your home, you can be considered to have rented the home to yourself (see Appendix II on assumed rents for more information). The outcome is that you save the cost of renting the home.

Annual returns would then be

$$\text{Return on house for period} = \frac{\text{Increase in house value during period} + \text{Rent not paid} - \text{Cost of upkeep}}{\text{Market value of house, beginning of period}}$$

Example 8.9

Sal owned a home that was worth $100,000 at the beginning of the year and $114,000 at year's end. The same house could be rented for $16,000 per year. It cost Sal $2,000 for upkeep for the year. What is his return for the year?

$$\text{Return on house} = \frac{(114,000 - 100,000) + 16,000 - 2,000}{100,000}$$

$$= \frac{28,000}{100,000}$$

$$= 28\%$$

Individual home values will be influenced by such factors as the status of the neighborhood, the style of the home, how well the home is kept up, and its proximity to the business area. Since constructing a home is very labor-intensive and factory mass-production

TABLE 8.3
Summary Table of Traditional Durables versus House

Factor for Comparison	Traditional Consumer Durables	House
Market value	Depreciates	Appreciates if well maintained
Characteristics	Uniform looking	Individually finished
Life	Limited	Long-lasting
Tax benefits	Generally none	Substantial

techniques are not generally used,[12] there are few technological developments that provide efficiencies in building new homes or remodeling older ones. Nor, given its long useful life, is there a stigma in purchasing a previously occupied home as there might be among purchasers of second-hand durables such as "used cars."

Therefore, existing home prices are strongly influenced by new home prices. New home prices in turn reflect changes in wage rates for construction workers and increases in raw material costs needed to build the home.[13] Since the consumer can generally select from new and existing homes, both may rise along with the inflation rate.

Home Affordability

Whether the purchase of a home is realistic and, if so, how expensive it can be depends on several factors:

- *Current income.* Obviously, the more you earn, the larger the home outlay you should be able to afford.

- *Tax bracket.* Ironically, the higher your tax bracket, the greater the "government subsidy" for tax-deductible real estate taxes and interest expense, the more expensive the home you can buy.

- *Liquid assets and debt accumulated.* The larger the down payment, the larger the home you can afford since ongoing demands on household cash flow will be lessened. On the other hand, the greater the amount of nonmortgage debt outstanding, the lower the overhead costs that can be undertaken through home purchase.

- *Value system.* The more important the home, the greater the sacrifice you are willing to make in other areas, and thus the higher-priced home you can afford.

- *The local realities.* Homes vary in price in different markets. A home in San Francisco can cost five times the same home in rural Ohio. The reality is that many people who live close to a major city in the Northeast or on the West Coast will probably violate the affordability rule we will explain below.

- *Outlook.* The more optimistic you are about your future income situation and about the price appreciation of real estate, the greater the outlay you will be willing to assume.

- *Risk tolerance.* The higher your risk tolerance, the greater the mortgage payment you will be willing to assume relative to your available cash flow.

Clearly, there is no quick and easy answer to how much home you can afford. The most common guide, the one used by banks in many situations, is to add up real estate taxes, insurance, and interest and principal payments on a mortgage. The total figure should not exceed 28 percent of your total income, with your total debt no greater than 36 percent of income. In expensive areas, that figure will be exceeded, however. In addition, banks have

---

[12] Lower-quality mobile homes are an exception.

[13] In addition, increases in discretionary income can result in more expensive homes being built. For example, homes have generally gotten larger in recent years, reflecting changes in taste that are probably occasioned by greater disposable income.

become more lenient about minimum down payments and may be more liberal about affordability issues if the buyer is willing to pay an extra fee that purchases insurance protecting the bank against default.

Example 8.10

Hanna was very interested in finding out whether she could afford the house she was considering. The mortgage payments were $1,000 a month; the taxes and insurance on the home were $3,600 per year. Hanna earned $60,000 per year before taxes and had no other debt. Could she qualify for the bank loan and afford the home?

	Calculations	Explanation
Gross income before taxes	$60,000	
Allowable percent of income	28%	
Allowable housing costs	$16,800	0.28 × 60,000
Actual annual mortgage costs	$12,000	12 × 1,000
Taxes and insurance	$3,600	
Total yearly cost	$15,600	

Hanna's actual costs are below the allowable level. She qualifies for purchase of this home.

EVALUATING THE LEASING ALTERNATIVE

Leasing often represents the alternative to making an investment in a nonfinancial asset. In many cases when the asset is essential such as with a car or home, we can perform a buy versus lease analysis to determine which approach to take. In this section, we examine leasing's strengths and weaknesses and evaluate its uses for the car or home. We conclude with an appraisal of the home as an investment using the lease as a benchmark.

An Introduction to Leasing

As stated many times, the investment values for capital expenditures such as durable goods usually decline in value over time. We tend to purchase them for their benefits for household activities today and for periods in the immediate future. Consequently, our principal purpose is to reap the benefits from the items directly since owning them does not provide appreciation in those assets as, say, owning stocks would. Therefore, we are often open to considering leasing assets.

A **lease** is a way to acquire the use of an asset without purchasing it. The lease allows you to receive the asset's operating benefits, generally for a stated period of time, in return for an obligation to make a series of payments over the term of the lease. The maintenance and overhead costs may be paid by the lessor, the company providing the equipment. For example, in an auto lease, with the exception of fuel or other items of "wear and tear," the lessor pays most costs in what can be termed a gross lease. On the other hand, these costs may be fully undertaken by the person using the equipment, called the lessee, in a transaction known as a net lease.[14,15]

[14] In theory, given a riskless environment with perfect capital markets, there should be no difference between buying an asset and leasing it. The cost of the leasing payment would include a return to the lessor for purchasing it. The depreciation in its value over time and maintenance expenses, if there are any, would be borne by the lessor. The lessee's cost would be equal to the lessor's costs and would include the costs for maintaining it over the term of the lease. A charge equal to the opportunity cost of capital also would be included since the capital not used to purchase the equipment could be invested elsewhere.

[15] There are two basic types of leases: closed-end and open-end leases. In a closed-end lease, the lessee does not have an obligation to purchase the leased asset at the end of the agreement. On the other hand, with an open-end lease, also called a finance lease, the lessee has the obligation to purchase the leased asset upon lease expiration.

Reasons for Leasing

There are economic reasons for leasing. The lessor may absorb the risk of technological or fashion obsolescence or large unforeseen expenditures on the asset. You might want to lease an expensive computer if you thought a better one might be introduced soon. Moreover, the lessor is sometimes able to develop efficiencies in specializing in that asset. For example, the purchase price of the asset and its repairs may be less costly to the lessor who buys, say, furniture in volume. Finally, the business owner may receive tax benefits that the lessor will not.[16]

Nonetheless, the cost of leasing generally is greater than the cost of purchasing, including the cost of borrowing money to do so. And perhaps, most important, it is greater because another cost structure is included: the lessor's administrative cost including the need for profit. It can, however, be the most profitable way to obtain use of an asset when it is needed for only part of the period. For example, it may be less costly to lease a car or house for a month in the summer than it is to own and maintain it all year.

Probably the most common reason for leasing an asset is that households are short of capital. Leases may be offered with no down payment. For example, we've mentioned that, for people in significant marginal tax brackets, buying a house carries substantial built-in tax benefits, and long-term renting may be due solely to the absence of sufficient funds to purchase your own house. Finally, leasing is generally not presented as a liability on the household's balance sheet, as it often is on the business statement. Therefore, when the household is short of funds and has limited ability to borrow, leasing may not show up in qualifying for a new loan.

Automobile Leasing

Today one out of four cars is leased. Consumers are attracted to the ability to buy with little or no down payment. Moreover, the cost of leasing has become more competitive with purchase; automobile companies have placed more emphasis on it and sometimes offer disguised subsidies to lessees in order to sell more cars. Whether it is preferable to lease or purchase a car is dependent on such factors as

- *How long the car is to be held.* Depreciation in prices of a car moderates after the first few years, which strongly favors purchase of the car if you plan to hold it for more than three or four years.
- *The age of the car.* New cars offer fewer problems and are covered by warranty. Leasing an older used car, where available, can subject you to significant extra costs.
- *The cost of time.* Selling a car that you own involves time and can expose you to price risk at the end of your designated ownership period. A lease can be drawn up quickly that only involves dropping off the car at the end of its term.
- *Inspection standards.* Lessees must comply with inspection standards in returning the car or face the consequences. What might be an almost unobservable scratch to you or the person that purchases a car from you can sometimes require an expensive repair to bring the vehicle up to inspection standards.
- *Mileage charges.* Leases contain maximum mileage charges. If you exceed the limit, you can pay expensive extra charges. If you are well under the limit, you receive no benefit. You are, in effect, being charged for mileage that you didn't use.
- *Lease obligation.* A lease is made for a fixed period of time and may be difficult or expensive to break or to get someone else to assume in the event of a change in your

---

[16] The lessor also takes the risk of higher interest rates by often providing flat lease payments, while purchase of an asset financed in part through adjustable-rate debt exposes the buyer to higher costs should market rates rise.

Practical Comment   Proper Analysis of Rent versus Own

Financial planners and accountants are frequently asked by their clients to decide whether it is better to rent or own, given their particular circumstances. The decision is generally made by comparing after-tax costs of purchase with those of renting in the first year only. No consideration is given to the opportunity cost for the down payment—the amount that could have been earned if it had not been used as a cash deposit on the home. Frequently, the potential yearly appreciation in the home is not included either. Moreover, the amount of the mortgage payment that is applicable to repayment of debt is treated as an expense. This simplistic way of looking at the rent-or-buy decision can lead to the wrong decision.

The correct method is not that much more difficult. It incorporates all the factors above using the proper marginal tax bracket for combined federal, state, and local taxes. Instead of a one-year analysis, it uses a multiyear framework. One reason this is preferable is that benefits of buying rather than leasing increase over time; that is true because the mortgage payment stays the same while the interest expense actually goes down, whereas rental costs increase in subsequent years. When the time frame for holding the home cannot be estimated with some realism, a seven-year period that often approximates the holding period for the average homeowner can be used.[17]

Perhaps most important, a true capital budgeting perspective should be used with the IRR (or NPV) employed to determine a projected rate of return. These techniques apply to one of the most important investment decisions—whether to buy or rent a house or, alternatively, which house offers a greater return. It is a prime example of the benefits of the IRR-NPV calculation and the overall rational financial approach for household capital expenditures set out in this chapter.

circumstances. Assumption of the lease by a third party also could expose you to liability in the event the sublessee defaults in payments. However, owners can readily sell their cars at a time of their own choosing.

- *Ability to fund monthly payments.* For those who have cash flow concerns, monthly payments for leasing will be lower than loan payments. On the other hand, once your loan payments have been completed, you own the car.

On balance, in the absence of manufacturer subsidies, leasing an automobile will generally cost more than purchasing it outright. However, the extra cost for leasing may be acceptable to many, particularly for new cars to be held for around three years. The disparity in cost can be smaller in that period and more than offset by the absence of effort in changing cars and the benefit of having a risk-free sale of the old car.

Appendix III offers a description of the factors that enter into a lease. It also provides the computation of an actual lease payment.

Buy versus Lease—Home

The buy-versus-lease decision for housing is somewhat sophisticated but can be handled without too much difficulty. Unlike the car lease-versus-buy issue, the details for a home are in the purchase decision; the cost to rent is given with no opportunity to find an identical home at a lower lease price as you can for a car. The weakness in taking a less sophisticated approach to decisions about housing is seen below.[18]

A buy-versus-lease example is shown in Appendix V.

[17] Recently that holding period has declined somewhat, but it may just be cyclical interest in investing in more expensive homes.

[18] In a purely competitive market with no transaction costs, no difference between borrowing and lending costs, and no taxes, the costs to own including an appropriate return on owner's capital invested in the property would equal the cost to rent. However, in reality, the government's subsidization of housing costs and its allowance of the sheltering of capital gains on sale alter the balance toward home ownership. Other considerations further alter the balance.

Practical Comment   When to Include a Home as an Investment

Including the house as an investment can be more involved than it looks. You cannot receive its full cash value without selling it. Selling it involves moving out and perhaps renting another residence. A partial solution can be to take out a reverse mortgage, which will give you cash proceeds up to a certain limit while you live in the house.

If you are not willing to move or to borrow against a home later in life, as many people aren't, incorporating it in your investment portfolio should be thought through carefully. On the one hand, in the event of extreme financial circumstances, it can and will be sold and could be borrowed against. On the other hand, people will often cut back on their standard of living to remain in their house. In that case, your house becomes an asset for your heirs.

If a client is unwilling to move or to borrow money against a house, advisors may include it as an asset on the balance sheet, but exclude it in assessing capital available for retirement needs. Alternatively, and perhaps preferably, an advisor may project using it for its potential cash proceeds only in the event that its occupants live an extra long life—for example, into their 90s. At that time, many people would be compelled to move into an assisted-living facility anyway.

Overall Appraisal of the Home as an Investment

As is shown by the buy-versus-lease example in Appendix V, the return on investment on purchase of a home can be highly attractive. This should not be surprising since the government provides tax benefits for interest and property tax deductions. There is no tax on the gain from the sale of this property—another advantage. Assuming reasonable maintenance costs, the two key factors in making the purchase of a home a generally attractive investment are tax benefits, when the person is in a substantial tax bracket,[19] and continued growth of the house at around the inflation rate—and in some cases significantly beyond that rate. Thus, the house provides a hedge against inflation and a return on the investment.

Other factors that people who purchase homes instead of renting them find appealing are pride of ownership and the forced-savings feature of homes. Mandatory repayment of debt as provided for in the mortgage contract is a savings and investment feature that many people overlook. Rental advantages include flexibility in changing your dwelling site and the lack of necessity for a capital commitment.

An unanticipated acceleration in the level of inflation makes purchase of a home even more attractive. It would raise the rate of return because, as mentioned, the house would likely rise in value along with the newer higher cost of building new homes. Thus, the home deserves its reputation as a good hedge against inflation.

The disadvantages of home ownership include (1) its lack of short-term liquidity should immediate sale become necessary; (2) the responsibility for maintaining the home and grounds; and (3) the cyclical nature of home prices over shorter periods of time that can result in a loss when, for example, you purchase a home and then a change in where you work results in an unexpected sale.

On balance, for expected holding periods of, say, three years or more, owning a home has historically been a highly rewarding investment.[20]

A summary of types of capital expenditures is shown in Table 8.4.

---

[19] The criterion should be the marginal tax bracket. *Marginal* means the tax on the next dollar earned. Substantial might be a marginal bracket of 20 percent or more. See Chapter 14 for a further explanation of marginal taxation.

[20] The recent sharp increases in home prices in many parts of the country could temporarily alter this conclusion.

TABLE 8.4   Analysis of Capital Expenditures

Type of Capital Expenditure	Category	Summary of Capital Expenditures	Specific Cost or Activity	Examples of Activity or Specific Capital Expenditure
Durable Goods	Nondiscretionary	Household overhead	Mortgage interest, rent, fuel, electricity	Boiler, furniture
	Nondiscretionary	Household work	Cooking, cleaning, child care, shopping	Dishwasher, oven
	Nondiscretionary	Biological maintenance	Food, clothing, sleep	Bed
	Discretionary	Active	Sports, traveling	Skis, golf clubs
	Discretionary	Passive	Watching television	Television, stereo
	Revenue related	Human revenues	Work	Automobile as transportation
	Revenue related	Marketable assets	Investing	Computer
Human Assets: Education	Nondiscretionary	All	Any	Books and seminars on improving productivity
	Discretionary	All	Any	Books and seminars on increasing pleasure
	Revenue related	Human revenues	Work	College, graduate school, conferences
	Revenue related	Marketable assets	Investing	Conferences
Real Estate: Home	Nondiscretionary	Household overhead	See Durable Goods above	See Durable Goods above
	Discretionary	Active or passive	Exercising, watching television	Construction of a den-exercise room
	Revenue related	Real assets	Investing	Purchase of a home

Back to Dan and Laura
NONFINANCIAL ASSETS—CAPITAL EXPENDITURES

When Dan and Laura sat down, I knew something was up. Laura had a smile on her face and Dan a frown. Laura said, "Congratulate us; I'm pregnant." After I did and Dan managed a quick smile, he indicated his concern. Basically, he wondered if he could afford to have two children. He said that they would have to move almost immediately since their apartment was too small for two children. He wondered if they would be better off renting. They expected to live in a house for seven years and then sell if they owned it or end the rental lease and move to a home closer to Laura's job, which would also cost about what the original house had. Both agreed that the cost of a home would be about $250,000 to buy and $15,000 a year to rent.

Dan indicated he was prepared to work additional hours during the week but wanted to keep some hours free for the children when he got home from work and his weekends free. He had thought about how to earn more money at a rate of $50 per hour without cutting into his nonwork time and decided he could reduce his commute by a half hour each way to and from work if he drove instead of taking a train. He felt he had to have a "status car." That car would cost him $30,000 net of the trade-in value of his old car that he drove to the station. His insurance would go up by $800 a year, his fuel by $750 per year, and his maintenance cost by about $1,000 per year. However, he would save train costs of $1,000 per year and would be able to use the car for seven years, at which time he believed it would have to be scrapped. He wanted to know whether this was a worthwhile investment. Dan planned to buy the car at the end of the year in December.

Laura was concerned about her family and her career. Many of her friends had gone back to work almost immediately after giving birth. She liked her work and believed that, as an elementary school teacher, she had a significant positive impact on the lives of many children. Moreover, she couldn't see herself being content by staying home all the time. On the other hand, she thought it might be best for the children if she raised them in their early formative years. She said she might enjoy that period herself. I sensed that she was conflicted and asked her if my thought was correct. She nodded yes. I also had the feeling that, all other things being equal, she wanted to stay home and raise her children until they began school. When I asked her that question, she agreed but wanted to know the financial implications of doing so.

Laura mentioned she had thought of pursuing a master's degree in teaching methodology with a specialty in reading. She believed that all the course work would help improve her performance in the classroom. She would begin in about a year, take the courses gradually while raising her children and have it completed in about five years. The cost would be $80,000 in current dollars spread equally over the four-year period with education costs rising by 6 percent a year. Upon completion of her degree, she would be entitled to an $18,000 annual increase in salary. She asked me if I thought doing that made sense financially.

I thought to myself, This may only be one additional child, but it was a whole new ballgame as far as near-term planning was concerned. The four areas we would have to work on were a home, a new car, when to go back to work, and whether to enroll in a master's curriculum. This capital expenditure program could bankrupt them if it wasn't drawn up carefully.

I have discussed purchase of a home (real estate assets), an outlay on a new car (durable goods assets), when to go back to work, and whether to enroll in a master's program (human-related assets); all lend themselves to financial analysis. Let's go over the home first.

There is no choice as to whether to move when a family situation dictates that one must take place. Given Laura's pregnancy, it must happen fairly soon. You have asked whether it would be better to buy or rent. Based on the figures supplied to us, $250,000 to buy or $15,000 to rent annually, I have calculated an after-tax rate of return. I have assumed that the house would increase in value by the projected rate of inflation, 3 percent a year.

We have included the cost of renting an apartment as an offset to higher household costs. Even though it is not a cash outlay of owning the home, it would be a cash payment if you didn't.

I recommend the purchase of a home and not the rental. The tax benefits available through deductibility of interest and real estate taxes plus the ability to sell your home without paying any tax (for a married couple the first $500,000 of gain is tax-free) can make it a highly profitable investment. Our projected return is 19 percent after tax.

Buy versus Rent

Inputs

Rental expense	$15,000
Cost of house	$250,000
Down payment	$12,500
Mortgage	$237,500
Interest rate	7.25%
Mortgage term (years)	30
Marginal federal tax rate	25.0%
Marginal local tax rate[1]	3.8%
Federal/state marginal tax rate	28.8%
Inflation rate	3.0%
Property taxes	$2,500
Upkeep and insurance	$3,000
Private Mortgage Insurance	$1,200

(continued)

(concluded)

	2007	2008	2009	2010	2011	2012	2013
Down payment	$12,500						
Beginning principal	$237,500	$235,393	$233,134	$230,711	$228,113	$225,325	$222,336
Mortgage payment	19,325	19,325	19,325	19,325	19,325	19,325	19,325
Interest paid	17,219	17,066	16,902	16,727	16,538	16,336	16,119
Principal paid	2,107	2,259	2,423	2,599	2,787	2,989	3,206
Mortgage outstanding	$235,393	$233,134	$230,711	$228,113	$225,325	$222,336	$219,130
Cash Flow							
Outflows							
Down payment	($12,500)	$0	$0	$0	$0	$0	$0
Mortgage payment	(19,325)	(19,325)	(19,325)	(19,325)	(19,325)	(19,325)	(19,325)
Interest payment	(17,219)	(17,066)	(16,902)	(16,727)	(16,538)	(16,336)	(16,119)
Principal payment	(2,107)	(2,259)	(2,423)	(2,599)	(2,787)	(2,989)	(3,206)
Property taxes	(2,250)	(2,575)	(2,652)	(2,732)	(2,814)	(2,898)	(2,985)
Upkeep and insurance	(3,000)	(3,090)	(3,183)	(3,278)	(3,377)	(3,478)	(3,582)
PMI	1,200	1,200	1,200	1,200	1,200	1,200	1,200
Balloon payment							(219,130)
Total	**($36,125)**	**($23,790)**	**($23,960)**	**($24,135)**	**($24,316)**	**($24,501)**	**($243,823)**
Inflows							
Tax deductions	$5,669	$5,625	$5,578	$5,528	$5,473	$5,415	$5,353
Proceeds from sale of home							$283,587
Total	**$5,669**	**$5,625**	**$5,578**	**$5,528**	**$5,473**	**$5,415**	**$288,940**
Net Cash Flow	**($30,456)**	**($18,165)**	**($18,382)**	**($18,608)**	**($18,842)**	**($19,086)**	**$45,118**
Rent not paid[2]	$15,000	$15,450	$15,914	$16,391	$16,883	$17,389	$17,911
Effective bottom line	($15,456)	($2,715)	($2,469)	($2,217)	($1,959)	($1,697)	$63,028
IRR	**19%**						

[1] Based on 5% state rate deductible on federal return.
[2] Not actual cash flow but assumed cost that would have been paid to rent a similar home.

The purchase of the car is simple. You would have a one-time cost of $30,000 net of trade-in plus extra yearly expenses of $1,550. The benefit at the $50-per-hour rate for your time assumed conservatively not to rise each year would be $50 per day, $250 per week, $12,500 per year before taxes and $8,906 after taxes. Unfortunately, this automobile expense is not tax-deductible. Your net inflows, therefore, are $7,356 per year. The return on this investment is very high at 19 percent. You should buy the car and start working extra hours as soon as it is feasible.

New Car

Inputs

Cost of new car	$30,000
Additional expenses	$15,550
Additional work hours/week	5
Hourly rate	$50
Marginal tax rate	28.8%
After-tax hourly rate	$35,63
Sale price	$8,000

	2006	2007	2008	2009	2010	2011	2012	2013
Cash Flow								
Inflows		$8,906	$8,906	$8,906	$8,906	$8,906	$8,906	$16,906
Outflows	($30,000)	$1,550	$1,550	$1,550	$1,550	$1,550	$1,550	($1,550)
Net Cash Flow	($30,000)	$7,356	$7,356	$7,356	$7,356	$7,356	$7,356	$15,356
IRR	**19%**							

Laura, you would be making $50,000 a year if you were working today. At an assumed marginal tax bracket of 28.8 percent when you work, plus Social Security payments of 7.65 percent, that would leave you with about $33,000 per year after tax. You mentioned that a full-time housekeeper would cost $25,000 a year and transportation, clothing, and eating out another $2,000 a year. The difference of $6,000 per year is not very meaningful, particularly given your wish to raise your children yourself.

The master's program provides the potential to earn an $18,000 raise after completion of $80,000 in costs over four years. Assuming that your marginal tax bracket is 28.8 percent, federal and state, when you return to work, your benefit is a raise of about $12,800 per year in today's after-tax dollars for 16 years to your intended retirement at 55.

Master's Program

Inputs

Cost of program	$80,000
Inflation (college)	6.0%
Pay raise upon completion	$18,000
Marginal tax rate	28.8%
After-tax pay raise	$12,825
Years of employment	16
General inflation	3.0%

	Inflows	Outflows	Net Cash Flow
2006	0	0	0
2007	0	($22,472)	($22,472)
2008	0	(23,820)	(23,820)
2009	0	(25,250)	(25,250)
2010	0	(26,765)	(26,765)
2011	$15,314	0	15,314
2012	15,773	0	15,773
2013	16,246	0	16,246
2014	16,734	0	16,734
2015	17,236	0	17,236
2016	17,753	0	17,753
2017	18,285	0	18,285
2018	18,834	0	18,834
2019	19,399	0	19,399
2020	19,981	0	19,981
2021	20,580	0	20,580
2022	21,198	0	21,198
2023	21,834	0	21,934
2024	22,489	0	22,489
2025	23,163	0	23,163
IRR	**13%**		

As you can see, on your worksheet, the return on the graduate degree is high at 13 percent, even without the additional pension benefits you would receive and the potential to receive an even higher return should you decide to retire later. Because it better fits your personal goals and provides an excellent return on investment, we believe it to be a highly attractive investment.

In sum, all of the proposed capital expenditures, with the exception of going back to work immediately, are considerably higher than those for investments in the marketplace with comparable risk, and therefore we recommend that you make them.

Personally, I commend you for being so quick to bring up these questions after finding out about the pregnancy. Although it may not seem so now, it will make my job as well as yours easier.

Summary

The household can be separated into financial and nonfinancial investments. Nonfinancial investments are the real and human-related assets that contribute importantly to your household portfolio. They are the ones covered in this chapter.

- Our objective is to select the best mix of household assets overall. Investment returns can be measured on an individual-asset basis, within a household activity, or on a total portfolio management basis. In this chapter, an individual-asset basis was used principally.

- Capital expenditures can be evaluated using either an NPV or an IRR approach. In each case, returns on projected outlays are compared with similar market-based investment returns. NPV uses market returns to develop current values and accepts all investments that have a positive present value. IRR provides a return that is compared directly with the market-based return that is used to accept or reject a proposed outlay.

- Real assets are often durable goods such as a car or an appliance. Human-related assets consist of job-related income discounted to the present plus those related to human work and other rights and relationships such as Social Security, corporate pension income, and anticipated gifts and bequests. Both use projected costs and benefits in determining whether to make proposed outlays.

- Home ownership is an asset with unique characteristics. It often presents advantages over renting because of its tax benefits.

- Leasing is an alternative way to obtain use of an asset. It is generally more costly than purchase but is attractive for people who are short of capital or who desire more flexibility with their monies.

Key Terms

capital expenditures, *183*	human assets, *192*	net present value (NPV), *185*
discount rate, *185*	human-related assets, *180*	nonfinancial assets, *180*
durable goods, *180*	internal rate of return	profitability index (PI), *187*
financial assets, *180*	(IRR), *188*	real assets, *180*
fully marketable assets, *180*	lease, *198*	required rate of return, *185*

Web Sites

http://www.studyfinance.com/lessons/capbudget
Capital Budgeting
This link presents several sections whose topics include capital budgeting, capital expenditures, cash flow analysis, and valuation techniques such as net present value and internal rate of return.

http://www.busadm.mu.edu/mandell/hcb.html
Household Capital Budgeting
Easy-to-navigate examples on household capital budgeting, annuities due, present and time value of money, amortization schedules, duration, and uneven cash flows are offered.

http://www.leaseguide.com
Lease vs. Buy Decisions
Extensive information including up-front fees, interest costs, maintenance fees, and so on, in lease-versus-buy capital expenditure decisions is offered. A kit that allows users to calculate the obligations in leasing or buying decisions is also featured.

http://www.ginniemae.gov
Ginnie Mae
This site provides a brief and useful comparison of buying a home versus renting one. It also provides a home ownership guide and various calculators that include a buy-versus-rent calculator, affordability calculator, and loan estimator calculator.

http://www.freddiemac.com
Freddie Mac
Two programs—one designed to provide adults with comprehensive homebuyer education; the other focused on savings and credit matters—are offered.

http://www.fanniemae.com
Fannie Mae
This Web site promotes home ownership and provides information on financial products and services that helps families buy homes of their own.

http://www.nahb.org
National Association of Home Builders (NAHB)
Instructive information about home building and new-house pricing is contained here. It serves as a guide for the home builders and people looking for newly built houses.

Questions

1. Describe the three approaches to decision making for capital expenditures.
2. Briefly explain total portfolio management.
3. Compare capital expenditures with marketable securities as an investment.
4. Why should capital expenditures be treated separately on a cash flow statement?
5. What are the strengths and weaknesses of the NPV and IRR methods?
6. Why calculate a profitability index?
7. Why are durable goods capital expenditures?
8. Why is education a capital expenditure?
9. Contrast life cycle human-asset valuations for skilled and unskilled workers.
10. Compare capital budgeting practices as outlined in this chapter with those used on a day-to-day basis.
11. What changes in day-to-day capital expenditure selections do you recommend?
12. Name three factors involved in the purchase of a car.
13. What factors should you consider when you are not sure whether to buy or lease a car?
14. What factors separate a home from most durable goods?
15. Why do people purchase a home?
16. Is the home likely to be a good investment? Explain.
17. Why is a home often a better investment than renting? Under what circumstances would renting be preferred?
18. Why is a home a good inflation hedge?
19. Should a home be included as an asset if its occupants aren't sure they would sell it? Explain.
20. What are the advantages of leasing over purchasing in general?

21. Why are more people leasing?

22. Is leasing less costly than purchasing? Explain.

23. Discuss the advantages and disadvantages of leasing a car.

Problems **8.1** Laurence was presented with a capital expenditure for a boiler that would cost $12,000 today and would generate the following savings.

Year	Amount
1	$2,000
2	$3,000
3	$2,000
4	$4,000
5	$5,000
6	$7,500
7	$5,000
8	$2,500

If the appropriate discount rate is 8 percent, what are the NPV and the IRR for this outlay?

8.2 Helen, a sociologist, is considering buying a new power lawn mower. It would save her 30 minutes of work a week, which she would use to see another client. Her fee is $16 per hour and she works 50 weeks a year. The lawn mower would cost $1,400. What would her IRR be if the mower was expected to last eight years? Express your figures on an annual basis and assume that her required rate of return is 9 percent.

8.3 Marcia had a choice of two washing machines of equal performance. One cost $400 and had a PV of $230 in savings over having clothes done through an outside service. The second cost $600 and had a PV of $450. Which one should she select?

8.4 Billy is considering enrolling in an MBA program. It would cost him $22,000 a year for two years. He believes it would raise his salary, which is now $50,000 a year, by the following amounts:

Year	Amount
1–5	$15,000
6–10	20,000
11–15	25,000

Currently, Billy pays 28 percent of his salary in taxes; his tax bracket will change to 30 percent after the raise. Assuming the required rate of return is 8 percent after taxes, should he make the investment? Use (a) the NPV method and (b) the IRR method.

8.5 Stan and Tracy don't know whether to rent or buy a home. Renting would be $1,000 a month while the home would cost $125,000. They would place $25,000 down and finance the balance through a 7.5 percent mortgage. Assume all costs for the two alternatives would be the same except for the following annual additional expenditures for a home:

Annual maintenance	$2,000
Property taxes	$3,000
Insurance	$1,000

Assume the mortgage is interest only (no principal payments are necessary) and that the couple is in the 30 percent marginal tax bracket. Their required rate of return is 6 percent after tax. Further assume that the value of the home and all expenditures rise at 4 percent a year. Finally, assume they sell the home themselves at the end of year 6. Indicate the IRR on the home and whether they should buy or rent.

8.6 John is considering buying a new car for $15,000 if purchased today. He also could wait to purchase the vehicle three years from now for $18,000. If John can invest in the capital markets and earn a 10 percent return, should he purchase the vehicle today or three years from now? John himself is indifferent about whether he buys the car today or in three years.

8.7 As the owner of a business, you are faced with an investment decision. The investment will expand your company's production plant at a cost of $1 million. The expansion will generate income of $150,000 per year for 10 years; the required rate of return on the investment is 9 percent. What is the net present value of the investment, and should you proceed with the expansion?

8.8 Item A has an NPV of $300 and an original cost of $500. Item B has an NPV of $350 and an original cost of $700. What is the profitability index (PI) of items A and B, and which is a more attractive investment.

8.9 Joan has a choice of purchasing a car for $20,000 with 9.7 percent interest cost to borrow and a three-year repayment period for leasing the vehicle. Leasing the auto would cost $300 a month for a three-year term. The sales tax is 6 percent. The car is expected to have a value of $14,000 at the end of the leasing period. Joan can obtain 7 percent after tax on similar marketable investments. Should she lease or buy the car?

CFP® Certification Examination Questions and Problems

8.1 Investment A costs $10,000,000 and offers a single cash inflow of $13,000,000 after one year. Investment B costs $1,000,000 and will be worth $2,000,000 at the end of the year. The appropriate discount rate or required rate of return is 10 percent compounded annually. Match the investment(s) listed below with the corresponding financial information in the items that follow.

A. Investment A

B. Investment B

C. Both A and B

D. Neither A nor B

1. ___ The net present value (NPV) is $818,182 and the internal rate of return is 30 percent.

2. ___ The NPV is $818,182 and the internal rate of return is 100 percent.

3. ___ The NPV is $1,818,182 and the internal rate of return is 30 percent.

8.2 Smith invests in a limited partnership that requires an outlay of $9,200 today. At the end of years 1 through 5, he will receive the after-tax cash flows shown below. The partnership will be liquidated at the end of the fifth year. Smith is in the 28 percent tax bracket.

Years	Cash Flows	
0	($9,200)	CF0
1	$600	CF1
2	$2,300	CF2
3	$2,200	CF3
4	$6,800	CF4
5	$9,500	CF5

A. The after-tax IRR of this investment is

1. 17.41 percent

2. 19.20 percent

3. 24.18 percent

4. 28.00 percent

5. 33.58 percent

B. Which of the following is/are correct?

1. The IRR is the discount rate that equates the present value of an investment's expected costs with the present value of the expected cash inflows.

2. The IRR is 24.18 percent and the present value of the investment's expected cash flow is $9,200.

3. The IRR is 24.18 percent. For Smith to actually realize this rate of return, the investment's cash flows will have to be reinvested at the IRR.

4. If the cost of capital for this investment is 9 percent, the investment should be rejected because its net present value will be negative.

   a. (2) and (4) only
   b. (2) and (3) only
   c. (1) only
   d. (1), (2) and (3) only
   e. (1) and (4) only

Case Application

NONFINANCIAL ASSETS—CAPITAL EXPENDITURES

Unlike Richard, Monica remained very concerned about their financial future. Specifically, she was fearful that the couple would not have enough money to retire comfortably as they had expected. She asked whether she should postpone or eliminate one improvement on her house. She estimated that a new boiler with a useful life of eight years would cost $20,000 and would save $4,000 a year in heating bills. Monica wanted to know whether they should sell their home now and invest the proceeds. She estimated that marketable securities would provide a return of 5 percent after taxes. They thought the value of the house, now worth $300,000, would increase by 6 percent a year. A rental in a comparable apartment would cost $2,200 a month. Assume for purposes of this section only that Richard and Monica's marginal tax bracket is 30 percent and other statistics include:

Annual maintenance	$3,000
Property taxes	$5,000
Insurance	$1,500

Case Application Questions

1. Do we know yet whether Monica's fears about retirement are justified? Do you have any preliminary opinion about this?
2. Do you think she should consider a new boiler now?
3. Complete the boiler problem and give your response.
4. Calculate the projected return on the house for the next year and give your recommendation.
5. Finish the nonfinancial investments section of the plan.

Appendix I

Capital Budgeting Theory

In this appendix, we will discuss capital budgeting theory first using the marginal rate of time preference and then considering consumption and capital expenditure decisions.

MARGINAL RATE OF TIME PREFERENCE

Under the theory of choice, to help us decide how much to invest and how much to allocate to current spending, we need to take into account our *personal rate of time preference*. The personal rate of time preference is the rate of return that makes us indifferent (exactly neutral) about the choice between spending today on a good or saving that money and spending it in the future. That rate varies with the individual. If you have a high rate of time preference, you would consume more today and save less. Those who have low incomes and not enough money to cover their basic needs[21] and others who "live for today" may have higher-than-average rates of time preference.

---

[21] Emily C. Lawrance, "Poverty and the Rate of Time Preference: Evidence from Panel Data," *Journal of Political Economy* 99, no. 1 (February 1991), pp, 54–77.

In making spending decisions, we use marginal rates because the same person may have different rates of time preference at different levels of income and spending. For example, lower-income people would usually have a higher rate of time preference in postponing spending on the first and only leisure time activity they could afford than they would if they had a higher cash flow and were considering forgoing their fourth leisure activity. We will focus on the marginal personal rate of time preference, which we'll simply call the *marginal rate of time preference.*

The marginal rate of time preference is compared with rates of return on investments to help determine whether to save or to consume. If you had a marginal rate of time preference of 3 percent in considering an investment and could receive a 5 percent return on that investment, you would be likely to save the money. Savings decisions are also influenced by other factors such as the need to accumulate assets for spending in retirement and, in a world that includes risk, the need for precautionary savings to provide for future uncertainties.

Often the personal rate of time preference is not stated but implied by our actions. We can compute the marginal rate of time preference by comparing cash outflows today with cash outflows in the future using the following formula.

$$FV = PV(1 + s)^n$$

where

s = Marginal rate of time preference.

n = Number of years

Example 8.A1.1 Brittany was contemplating taking a vacation at a seaside resort, which would cost $800. She could not decide between taking the vacation today and taking a vacation and a weekend trip costing $882 two years from now. Assuming that her preferred lifestyle expenditures include these two alternatives, what is her marginal rate of time preference? If a 7 percent return is possible by investing in the capital markets, what should she do?

$$882 = 800(1 + s)^2$$

Calculator Solution

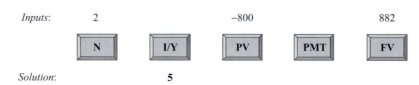

Inputs: 2   −800   882

| N | I/Y | PV | PMT | FV |

Solution: 5

Press i = 5%

Based on her indifference as to whether to take the vacation today or two trips two years from now, Brittany has a personal rate of time preference of 5 percent. Since the current market rate of return of 7 percent exceeds the 5 percent rate, she should save the money and use it to make two trips in two years. The 7 percent rate will actually provide her with more than the cost of the trip in two years. She can use the extra money to purchase other goods and services.

CONSUMPTION AND CAPITAL EXPENDITURE DECISIONS

Let us begin our capital expenditure discussions in a simple world that has perfect capital markets and no risk. In that world, outcomes are known with certainty; there are no inflation, no taxes, no transaction costs; and all assets are fully marketable. And, very important, there is no difference between borrowing and investing rates.

In theory, under perfect capital markets, consumption decisions are separate from capital spending decisions. The consumption decision is determined by our personal rate of time preference. As mentioned, we save when market returns exceed the personal rate of time preference. We borrow when we have a desire for more consumption today and our borrowing rate is below our personal rate of time preference.

Capital expenditure decisions in a world with perfect capital markets and no risk are based solely on market returns. We accept all capital expenditures whose returns equal or exceed the return on marketable investments. The reason is simple. We would have no incentive to make a capital expenditure if we could get a higher return by purchasing a marketable investment.

Keep in mind that in this world without risk there are no defaults, there is no limit on the amount we can borrow, and the cost to borrow monies and the returns on investments are assumed to be the same. When we run short of cash flow to place in capital expenditures, we borrow enough money to fund the capital projects whose returns exceed the borrowing/investing rate. Since there is no distinction between the rates to borrow and to invest and an unlimited amount of capital is available to borrow for either consumption or capital expenditures, the two decisions on whether to consume or to invest can be treated separately.

We will assume that we have a positive cash flow available to fund our investments. Let us trace how equilibrium for investment occurs in this ideal state. Capital projects, the rates of return on internal investments, meanwhile, are arrayed from highest to lowest returns. These projects are displayed in stepwise fashion because each capital expenditure has a different cash amount that is needed for investment. For example, you cannot buy one-half of a new boiler. Either you pay the full purchase price or you forgo the outlay.

The rates of return on marketable securities, on the other hand, are level and can be selected in any size needed. As mentioned, equilibrium for capital expenditures alone occurs where its rate of return meets that for marketable securities.

Clearly, marketable securities only come into play when there is cash flow available for external investment. If, instead of having money to invest, additional cash flows are needed, they would be supplied by borrowing along the borrowing/investing line again where the marginal rate of time preference intersects the line. (See Figure 8.A1.1.)

Example 8.A1.2   Greg has a rising marginal rate of time preference as savings increase, and it amounts to 8 percent where it meets the borrowing/investing line. At that point, cash flows from household operations amount to $6,000. His choices for savings include four capital expenditures, for (1) $2,000, (2) $500, (3) $2,500, and (4) $1,000 returning 12 percent, 11 percent, 10 percent, and 6 percent, respectively. Assuming an 8 percent rate for borrowing or investing in an equilibrium market environment, how should Greg invest?

Greg will consider the following:

	Amount	Rate of Return
Capital expenditure 1	$2,000	12%
Capital expenditure 2	$500	11%
Capital expenditure 3	$2,500	10%
Capital expenditure 4	$1,000	6%
Total	$6,000	

Capital expenditures 1–3, totaling $5,000, exceed the market rate of return and are therefore funded. Since the fourth capital expenditure at its 6 percent rate is lower than the 8 percent market rate of return, it is not used. The remaining $1,000 of Greg's cash flow is placed in marketable investments.

The equilibrium process is given in Figure 8.A1.1. Notice that point C in the figure delineates the point at which there is no borrowing or saving. Everything to the left of

FIGURE 8.A1.1 **Capital Expenditure Line**

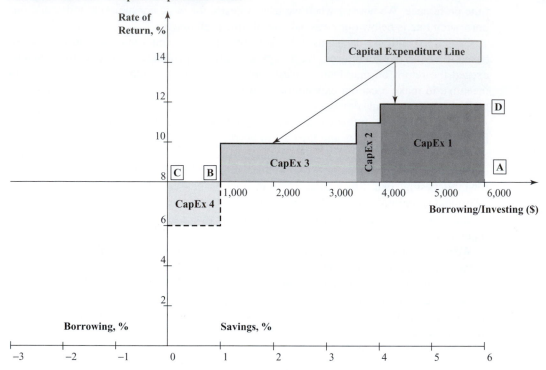

point C indicates borrowing; everything to the right, saving. The return on capital expenditures intersects the market line to the right, indicating cash flow is available. Equilibrium for investing occurs at point A where it meets the borrowing/investing line. Point A indicates the amount of operating cash flow available for internal and external investing.

Observe that the capital expenditure line starts directly above point A at the point of its maximum rate of return, point D, for capital expenditure project 1 (CapEx 1). The capital expenditure line then declines as succeeding capital projects—CapEx 2, then CapEx 3—offer lower and lower returns, until the line meets the borrowing/investing line at point B, its equilibrium point. The horizontal distance between points A and B delineates the amount of capital expenditures used and between B and C the amount of marketable investments used. Proposed capital expenditures below the return on marketable securities that are rejected are shown as a dotted line.

If the borrowing/investing line were changed from the 8 percent return figure shown to 11 percent, capital expenditures would decline as external investments proved more attractive relative to capital outlays. If the investment return on marketable securities were to be lowered instead of raised, the opposite effects would occur.

PRACTICAL ADJUSTMENTS

Once we use more practical assumptions, the situation changes somewhat. Transaction costs for buying and selling securities and taxes on income are now part of the process. Moreover, in real life there is usually risk present in making decisions—we cannot be sure of any outcome. As a result, there is a difference in the borrowing and the investing rates, as anyone who has both credit card debt and a position in a stock knows. We must accept fluctuations in performance whether that means the possibility of purchasing a car that is a "lemon" or investing in a stock that provides losses instead of gains.

In this more realistic environment that includes risk, we cannot be sure how much money we will need to save for future consumption. We will allocate extra money for precautionary savings to make more likely our ability to fund day-to-day and long-term retirement needs in the face of uncertainties. We will no longer be able to borrow unlimited amounts of funds at the low risk-free rate. Instead, the borrowing will include an extra cost for risk, which will increase as the amount of money borrowed increases. Decisions on the amount to consume and the amount to invest will be made together.

We discussed borrowing and its effect on consumption and investment in Chapter 7.

Appendix II

Assumed Rents

Assumed rents are hypothetical costs for assets owned. They are hypothetical costs because they are not paid to anyone. Since no cash is transacted, these rents are not normally considered financial outlays and are not tax-deductible. Nonetheless, that can be a useful tool in analyzing capital expenditures such as durable goods. Economists call these costs *implicit costs*. They are rents that would have to be paid to obtain use of an asset if we had not purchased it outright. When we buy something, we can be considered both owners of an asset, for which we would want to be compensated, and renters of the asset, only we rent the asset from ourselves.

Looking at an asset in this way can aid in establishing costs and its fair market value. For example, if you bought a television, its implicit cost would be how much it would cost you to rent that set. The value of that television could be considered the net present value of all of its yearly implicit costs while in use.

Analyzing implicit costs can shed some light on durable goods—for example, a house. When you buy a house you live in, you are both an owner who has invested in a home and the user of that home. If you divide the transaction into two parts, you can better understand the cost and the investment portion. The housing buy-versus-rent example in Appendix V includes the implicit rental cost in obtaining the investment return on owning it. Thus, your total cost of operating a home could be considered not only the costs of electricity, heat, gardening, and so on, which are not generally covered in a rental, but also the implicit rental cost, which is equivalent to how much you would pay to rent a similar property.

Appendix III

Understanding the Lease Payment

A lease payment has three parts. The first is the *finance cost,* the sum you pay to cover the borrowing cost and profit for the company that purchased the car and leased it to you. The second is the *depreciation cost,* the amount the market value of the car is expected to decline over the lease's life. The third is *applicable taxes* on purchase of the lease. Let's take each separately in calculating the lease payment.

FINANCE COST

The finance cost is expressed as a money factor. The money factor is the interest rate by custom divided by 2,400. The interest rate charged over the life of the lease is called the *base interest rate.*

Factor	Explanation
Finance Factors	
Money factor	The interest rate charged over the life of the lease, which is called the base interest rate. By custom, this rate is expressed as a decimal obtained by dividing the base rate by 2,400.
Selling price	The actual cost of purchasing the car. Sometimes called the *capitalized cost*.
MSRP	The list price of the car.
Depreciation Factors	
Residual value	The assumed value of the car at the end of the lease period. It may be expressed either as an amount or as a percentage of the list price. This value is the price you will pay should you want to purchase the car after expiration of the lease.
Calculation	Depreciation expressed as an amount is divided by the number of months in the lease. Depreciation is the negotiated sale price less the residual value.
Tax Factors	
State and local taxes	The taxes based on leasing the car. Often these taxes are lower than those for purchase since lease payments are not made on the full value of the car.
Calculation	Total taxes divided by the number of months in the lease to obtain the monthly tax.

CALCULATING LEASE PAYMENTS

$$\text{Monthly leasing price} = \text{Depreciation factor} + \text{Finance factor} + \text{Tax factor}$$

$$\text{Monthly leasing price}\,(K) = G + 1 + T$$

$$\text{Depreciation factor}\,(G) = \frac{A - (B \times D)}{C}$$

$$\text{Finance factor}\,(I) = (A + (B \times D)) \times E$$

$$\text{Tax factor}\,(T) = (G + I) \times F$$

where

A = Actual sales price

B = MSRP

C = Number of months

D = Residual value as percent of MSRP

E = Money factor (interest rate divided by 2,400)

F = Actual tax rate

G = Depreciation factor

I = Finance factor

T = Tax factor

Example 8.A3.1 Brad wanted to calculate the monthly payment for leasing a car. The negotiated price for the car for lease payment purposes was $30,647, down from the list price (MSRP) of $32,455. There was no down payment. The interest rate was 3 percent and the residual for a 39-month lease was 56 percent. What is the monthly payment assuming a 9 percent sales tax?

$$\text{Money factor} = \frac{3\%}{2,400} = 0.00125$$

$$\text{Monthly leasing price} = \text{Depreciation factor} + \text{Finance factor} + \text{Tax Factor}$$

$$\text{Depreciation factor } (G) = \frac{A - (B \times D)}{C}$$

$$= \frac{30,647 - (32,455 \times 0.56)}{39}$$

$$= \frac{12,472}{39}$$

$$= 319.80$$

$$\text{Finance factor } (I) = (A + (B \times D)) \times E$$

$$= (30,647 + (32,455 \times 0.56)) \times 0.00125$$

$$= 61.03$$

$$\text{Tax factor } (T) = (G + I) \times F$$

$$= (319.80 + 61.03) \times 0.09$$

$$= 34.27$$

$$\text{Monthly leasing price} = 319.80 + 61.03 + 34.27$$

$$= 415.10$$

Appendix IV

Buy versus Lease—Car

In the example we look at how to arrive at a financial decision about whether to buy or lease a car when lease payments are known.

Example 8.A4.1

Diane was interested in the Del Phillipo, an Italian sports car that came in one color—red. For that type of car, it was relatively inexpensive at $45,000. Diane was not sure whether she would keep the car for three years or six years. Consequently, she received lease quotations for both periods. The dealership indicated it would cost $650 a month for leasing for either period claiming that although the market value of the car was cheaper after three years, the car's value would drop more precipitously after that time. On her own, Diane made estimates of a market value of $30,000 after three years and $15,000 after six years.

The normal automobile warranty would cover special car problems and Diane would have to pay for normal wear and tear such as changing tires and brakes whether she leased or purchased the car. Therefore, Diane did not include such costs in her analysis. However, she did include a special $2,000 charge for a repair in the fifth year when she figured that her warranty, based on mileage, would run out.

Assume no down payment, a 6 percent borrowing rate for a car loan on purchase to be repaid over six years, and a sales tax of 5 percent. Assume there are no considerations other than return and that Diane's required rate of return is 6 percent. Use both a three-year and a six-year period. Calculate monthly mortgage payments, but use yearly figures for calculating IRR for both purchase and lease. Should she buy or lease?

Car Buy versus Lease

Inputs		Auto Loan Repayment (3-year period)	
Purchase price	$45,000	Monthly payment	$1,369
Market value in three years	$30,000	Annual payment	$16,428
Market value in six years	$15,000		
Repair cost in Year 5	$2,000		

(continued)

(concluded)

		Auto Loan Repayment (6-year period)	
Monthly lease payment	$650	Monthly payment	$746
Annual lease payment	$7,800	Annual payment	$8,949
		Tax Cost on Purchase	
Annual interest rate	6%	Tax cost (5% on purchase price)	$2,250
Monthly interest rate	0.5%		
Sales tax	5%		
Required rate of return	7%		

Year	1	2	3	4	5	6
Buy						
Yearly payment (3-year period)	$16,428	$16,428	$16,428			
Yearly payment (6-year period)	$8,949	$8,949	$8,949	$8,949	$8,949	$8,949
Tax and extra repair costs	$2,250				$2,000	
Lease						
Yearly payment	$7,800	$7,800	$7,800	$7,800	$7,800	$7,800
Ownership operating advantage (3-year period)	$10,878	$8,628	$8,628			
Ownership operating advantage (6-year period)	$3,399	$1,149	$1,149	$1,149	$3,149	$1,149
Market value of the car			$30,000			$15,000
Balance debt (3-year period)	($10,878)	($8,628)	$21,372			
Balance debt (6-year period)	($3,399)	($1,149)	($1,149)	($1,149)	($3,149)	$13,851

Three-year return = 6.0%

Six-year return = 10.7%

Ownership operating advantage = Buy cost − Lease cost

In year 1 we have $2,250 tax cost and in year 5 we add $2,000 extra repair cost to the annual loan payment. Balance debt for the three-year period equals the ownership operating advantage for each year except for year 3, when you have to subtract the ownership operating advantage from the market value of the car in year 3. The same approach is used in calculation of the balance debt for the six-year period.

	Calculation	Explanation
Auto Loan Repayment (six-year period)		
72n (6 years × 12 months), 0.50i (6% ÷ 12 months), 45000 PV		
Press PMT	= 746	Monthly loan payment
Annual loan payment	= 746 × 12	
	= 8,949	Yearly loan payment
Auto Loan Repayment (three-year period)		
36n (3 years × 12 months), 0.50i (6% ÷ 12 months), 45000 PV		
Press PMT	= 1369	Monthly loan payment
Annual loan payment	= 1369 × 12	
	= 16428	Yearly loan payment
Annual lease payment	= 650 × 12	
	= 7800	

Three-Year Return

General Calculator Approach	HP12C	TI BA II Plus
		CF
Clear the register	f FIN	2nd CLR Work
Enter cash outflow Year 1	10,878 CHS g CF₀	10,878 +/− ENTER ↓
Enter cash outflow Year 2	8,628 CHS g CFⱼ	8,628 +/− ENTER ↓ ↓
Enter cash inflow Year 3	21,372 g CFⱼ	21,372 ENTER ↓ ↓
Calculate the internal rate of return	f IRR	IRR CPT
	6.0%	6.0%

Six-Year Return

General Calculator Approach	HP12C	TI BA II Plus
		CF
Clear the register	f FIN	2nd CLR Work
Enter cash outflow Year 1	3,399 CHS g CF₀	3,399 +/− ENTER ↓
Enter cash outflow Years 2–4	1,149 CHS g CFⱼ	1,149 +/− ENTER ↓
Enter number of years	3 g Nⱼ	3 ENTER ↓
Enter cash outflow Year 5	3,149 CHS g CFⱼ	3,149 +/− ENTER ↓ ↓
Enter cash inflow Year 6	13,851 g CFⱼ	13,851 ENTER ↓ ↓
Calculate the internal rate of return	f IRR	IRR CPT
	10.7%	10.7%

The return for purchasing for three years (6 percent) does not meet the 7 percent required rate. However, the six-year rate substantially exceeds it. Therefore, it pays to lease a car for three years but to buy for the six-year period. Over the longer period of time, the ability to own and sell an asset more than offsets the extra monthly cost for the purchase.

Appendix V

Buy versus Lease—Home

The example of buying versus leasing that follows makes use of the Practical Comment on the topic given in the chapter.

Example 8.A5.1

Frederick and Dorothy, who have two children, are interested in moving from an apartment to a house. They don't know whether to buy the house or to rent it. They came across a house they liked that would require a $200,000 expenditure including closing costs. There was a house for rent on the same block that was almost identical to the one they are considering and had a rental cost of $2,000 per month. The rental contract stated that the renter would pay all normal maintenance costs inside and outside the house, but the owner would pay for repairs, maintenance, and improvements designed to maintain the value of the property in real terms, estimated to be worth $3,000 per year; property taxes totaling $4,000 per year; and insurance on the house at $1,000 per year. Aside from these items, the costs for renting and buying are assumed to be the same and therefore need not be included in a comparison.

To simplify the problem, assume that there is an interest-only loan; therefore, no payments of debt are required until the mortgage falls due. Further assume that it is a 10-year fixed-rate mortgage for 80 percent of the value of the property at a 7 percent interest rate. Assume Frederick and Dorothy are in the 35 percent marginal tax bracket and have a 5 percent risk-adjusted after-tax rate of return on alternative investments.

In addition, assume the house's value increases at the projected inflation rate of 3 percent per year, that all costs other than interest rise at 3 percent per year as well, and that costs are paid all at once at the end of each period with the exception of the down payment. Finally, assume that if they buy the house, they will sell it themselves at its market value seven years later. Should they buy or rent?

$$\text{Return on house} = \text{Proceeds from sale} + \text{Ownership operating advantage}$$
$$\text{Mortgage} = 80\% \text{ of purchase price}$$
$$= 0.8 \times 200.000$$
$$= \$160,000$$
$$\text{Down payment} = \$200,000 - \$160,000$$
$$= \$40,000$$
$$\text{Yearly rental cost} = 12 \times 2,000$$
$$= \$24,000$$

Home Buy versus Lease

Inputs		Explanation
Purchase price	$200,00	
Mortgage	$160,000	80% of purchase price
Down payment	$40,000	Purchase price − Down payment
Monthly rental cost	$2,000	
Yearly rental cost	$24,000	2,000 × 12 months
Mortgage interest rate	7%	
Required rate of return	5%	
Inflation rate	3%	
Marginal tax bracket	35%	
Holding period (in years)	7	

Value of House in 7 Years

Selling price	$245,975	
Capital gain from the sale	$45,975	Selling price − Purchase price

Yearly Costs	Pretax	Ownership Costs After Tax with- out Interest	After Tax with Interest	Rental Costs	Ownership Operating Advantage	Explanation
Interest	$11,200		$7,280			Pretax = 160,000 × 7% After tax = Pretax × (1 − 0.35)
Opportunity cost		$2,000				Opportunity cost = Down payment × Investment return = 40,000 × 0.05
Real estate taxes	$4,000	$2,600				After tax = 4,000 × (1 − 0.35)
Insurance	$1,000	$1,000				
Repairs and maintenance	$3,000	$3,000				
Total yearly costs	**$19,200**	**$8,600**	**$15,880**			Yearly after-tax costs = After-tax interest + Total after-tax costs

Year	Down Payment					
1	$40,000	$8,600	$15,880	$24,000	($31,880)[1]	Rental costs − Ownership costs (includes down payment cost)
2		$8,858	$16,138	$24,720	$8,582	
3		$9,124	$16,404	$25,462	$9,058	
4		$9,397	$16,677	$26,225	$9,958	After-tax costs excluding interest grow 3% a year
5		$9,679	$16,959	$27,012	$10,053	
6		$9,970	$17,250	$27,823	$10,573	
7		$10,269	$17,549	$28,657	$57,083	Plus capital gain from the sale

[1] Assumes for simplification purposes that all interest and rent payments occur at the same time as the down payment. The actual payment would on average be made at about the middle of the year, which would modestly reduce the IRR.

$$\text{Rate of return} = 33\%$$

At the end of year 7, close out the loan and resell the house.

Calculator Solution

Value of home in seven years:

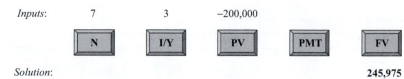

Inputs: 7   3   −200,000

| N | I/Y | PV | PMT | FV |

Solution: 245,975

Press FV = $245,975
Less purchase price of $200,000 yields pretax gain:

$$\$245,975 - \$200,000 = \$45,975$$

According to 2004 tax laws, up to $500,000 of the couple's gain could be excluded if they sold or exchanged their main home and they have owned it for more than two years. So there is no tax on the capital gain of $45,975.

Determine the IRR of cash flows from ownership operating advantage in years 1 to 7 plus the gain on sale of the home in year 7 or (11,108 + 45,975) in year 7.

General Calculator Approach	HP12C	TI BA II Plus
		CF
Clear the register	f FIN	2nd CLR Work
Enter cash initial outflow	31,880 CHS g CF₀	31,880 +/− ENTER ↓
Enter cash inflow Year 2	8,582 g CFⱼ	8,582 ENTER ↓ ↓
Enter cash inflow Year 3	9,058 g CFⱼ	9,058 ENTER ↓ ↓
Enter cash inflow Year 4	9,548 g CFⱼ	9,548 ENTER ↓ ↓
Enter cash inflow Year 5	10,053 g CFⱼ	10,053 ENTER ↓ ↓
Enter cash inflow Year 6	10,573 g CFⱼ	10,573 ENTER ↓ ↓
Enter cash inflow Year 7	57,083 g CFⱼ	57,083 ENTER ↓ ↓
Calculate the internal rate of return	f IRR	IRR CPT
	33%	33%

Since 33 percent substantially exceeds the comparable after-tax rate of return available for other investment alternatives (5 percent), the home should be purchased.

Appendix VI

Excel Examples for NPV and IRR*

This appendix demonstrates how you can solve problems involving NPV and IRR methods by using Excel.

NET PRESENT VALUE

Often we are faced with investment decisions involving capital outflows and cash inflows in different periods. Most investments don't have even cash flows in each period. We cannot use Excel's PV and FV functions for uneven cash flows because they assume equal payments or a lump sum. If we want to solve for the present value of uneven cash flows, we need to use the net present value. We will use two methods for solving NPV problems: using a time line and using the Excel NPV function.

* Adair, Troy A., *Excel Applications for Corporate Finance*, Burr Ridge: McGraw-Hill/Irwin, 2005, and Craig Holden, *Excel Modeling in Investments*, New Jersey: Prentice Hall.

FIGURE 8.A6.1 **Excel Model for Net Present Value**

	A	B	C	D	E	F	G
1	Net Present Value						
2							
3	Inputs						
4	Discount rate	8%					
5	Period	0	1	2	3	4	5
6	Cash outflows	($5,000)					
7	Cash inflows		$1,200	$1,500	$1,800	$1,300	$1,100
8							
9	Net Present Value Using the Time Line						
10	Period	0	1	2	3	4	5
11	Cash flows	($5,000)	$1,200	$1,500	$1,800	$1,300	$1,100
12	Present value of cash flows	($5,000)	$1,111	$1,286	$1,429	$956	$749
13	Net present value	$530		=C11/((1+$B$4)^C5)			
14							
15	Net Present Value Using the Excel NPV function						
16	Net present value	$530					
17			=B6+NPV(B4,C7:G7)				

Example 8.A6.1   Capital expenditure requires a current investment of $5,000 and yields future expected cash flows of $1,200, $1,500, $1,800, $1,300, and $1,100 for the next five years. The required rate of return on the investment is 8 percent. What is the net present value of the investment, and should you undertake it (see Figure 8.A6.1)?

Building This Excel Model

1. **Inputs.** Enter the required rate of return as Discount Rate in cell B4. Build a table entering cash outflows (or current investment) in cell B6 and cash inflows (or future expected cash flows) in cells **C7:G7.**

2. **Net present value using a time line**. We have a period 0 when current investment occurs and five consecutive future periods with the expected cash flows (see Figure 8.A6.2). Create a time line from period 0 to period 5 by entering 0, 1, . . ., 5 in the range **B10:G10.** Enter the corresponding cash flows in periods 0 through 5 in the range **B11:G11.** For your convenience, just copy the values from the Inputs table. Next calculate the present value of each cash flow using the formula for present value:

$$\text{Present value} = (\text{Cash flow})/((1 + \text{Discount rate})^{\wedge}\text{Period})$$

Enter =C11/((1+$B$4)^C5) in cell **C12** and copy it across to cell **G12.** The $ signs in $B$4 lock the column and row when copying. Put the same value in cell **B12** as you do in cell **B11** because this cash flow occurs in the current period, and you don't need to discount it.

Net present value is the sum of the present values of all cash flows. Enter **=SUM (B12:G12)** in cell **B13.**

3. **Net present value using the Excel NPV function.** The NPV function calculates the net present value of a stream of cash flows. It has the following format:

$$\text{NPV} (\textit{rate,range of values})$$

FIGURE 8.A6.2
Finding PV of Future Cash Flows

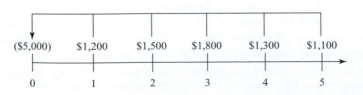

FIGURE 8.A6.3   Excel Model for Internal Rate of Return

	A	B	C	D	E	F	G	H
1	**Internal Rate of Return**							
2								
3	**Inputs**							
4	Required rate of return	9%						
5	Period	0	1	2	3	4	5	6
6	Cash outflows	($10,000)						
7	Cash inflows		$1,800	$2,000	$2,200	$2,500	$1,900	$1,700
8								
9	**Internal Rate of Return Using the Excel IRR function**							
10	Period	0	1	2	3	4	5	6
11	Cash flows	($10,000)	$1,800	$2,000	$2,200	$2,500	$1,900	$1,700
12			=IRR(B11:H11)						
13	Internal rate of return	6%						

The important thing that we should note here is that the NPV function discounts cash flows starting in period 1. Therefore, we must add the present value of the period 0 cash flow to the net present value of the period 1–5 cash flows. Enter =**B6+NPV(B4,C7:G7)** in cell **B16.**

The net present value of this investment is $530, which is a positive number. Therefore, you should accept the capital expenditure.

INTERNAL RATE OF RETURN

Often we need to determine the yield of an investment given its cost and cash flows. The internal rate of return approach helps us to solve for the yield of an investment. In the following example, we demonstrate the use of the Excel IRR function.

Example 8.A6.2   A project requires an initial investment of $10,000 and yields future expected cash flows of $1,800, $2,000, $2,200, $2,500, $1,900, $1,700 in the next six years. If the required rate of return of the investment is 9 percent, what is the internal rate of return and should we undertake this project (see Figure 8.A6.3)?

Building This Excel Model

1. **Inputs.** Enter the required rate of return in cell **B4**. You don't need it in your calculations, but it is convenient to have it there when evaluating your project. Build a table entering cash outflows (or initial investment) in cell **B6** and cash inflows (or future expected cash flows) in cells **C7:H7**.

2. **Internal Rate of Return Using the Excel IRR function.** The IRR function calculates the internal rate of return of a stream of cash flows. It has the following format:

$$\text{IRR } (range\ of\ values, guess)$$

Range of values is a range of cash flows including the investment cost, and *guess* is the optional first guess at the correct rate of return. Generally, it can be omitted. Create a table with the periods form 0 to 6 and corresponding cash flows. Enter =**IRR(B11:H11)** in cell **B13**.

The project's internal rate of return (6 percent) is less than the required rate of return (9 percent). Therefore, you should reject this project.

Note that in the original example, there is only one sign change in the cash flow stream (from negative in period 0 to positive in period 1 and thereafter). Generally, there will be one IRR solution to the problem for each sign change. If there is more than one sign change, you should use the second parameter of the IRR function, *guess*, to find all the solutions to the problem. By adjusting the *guess* you can identify all the IRRs.

Chapter Nine

Financial Investments

Chapter Goals

This chapter will enable you to:

- Apply risk and return principles to investments.
- Develop an overall asset allocation.
- Evaluate the factors that enter into investing in financial assets.
- Relate financial investing to overall household operations.
- Recognize how portfolio management differs from individual-asset selection.
- Distinguish among investment alternatives.
- Utilize leading ways of measuring investment risk.

Dan and Laura had a special interest in smaller companies, biotechnology, and investing in China. The trouble was their investment tolerances for risk were far apart with Laura more interested in stocks and having a much higher tolerance for risk. Constructing an investment portfolio for them looked as though it was going to be difficult.

Real Life Planning

One of the themes underlying this chapter is the principle of risk and return. That is, risk and return are related and, generally, the greater the return you expect to receive on an investment over time, the greater the risk you undertake. This principle can be overlooked by people who may measure performance by only one of those variables, return. When you consider buying a risky investment, you should anticipate purchasing an asset with a larger projected gain to compensate you for the possibility of loss. Many people say they don't understand why so much time is spent on measuring risk. The example below may help.

There was a mutual fund manager who developed a reputation for above-average performance using U.S. government bonds. Bonds are considered more conservative and more straight-laced than stocks. There are no bonds more "plain vanilla" than U.S. government since they are perceived as having no risk of nonpayment. Some people would say the only way to outperform using them is to be able to predict interest rates consistently. If there is anyone with that predictive ability over extended periods of time, he or she hasn't publicly demonstrated it.

Thus, it was all the more surprising that this manager of mutual funds pretty consistently did better than market returns by a substantial margin. When asked whether he was taking risk in his active management approach, he said he wasn't. His first priority was the safety of his investors' principal and using primarily U.S. government bonds helped him achieve it. He developed a growing following among individual investors, financial planners, and investment managers alike, who were all attracted to his returns and his firm answers to questions.

One day Federal Reserve actions raised interest rates sharply, which surprised virtually all investors in the bond market. It had a major effect on those bond managers who were using derivatives, a financial instrument sometimes employed to enhance returns. These derivatives were particularly hard hit at this time. While most bond funds were down, this manager's funds declined more than 25 percent, which, in the world of high-quality bond funds, happens less often than losing more than three-quarters of your money in stock funds. A fundamental analysis of his style would have uncovered his heavy use of derivatives.

However, there was a much more simple way to identify the greater risk he undertook. His standard deviation, the measure of risk represented by fluctuations in his returns over time, was much greater than that for any other fund in his category. It suggested that under certain negative circumstances, he could have problems. This information was available in an easy-to-understand format accessible in many public libraries. In other words, analysis of risk and return could have prevented the loss that many investors experienced.

OVERVIEW

Why do you make investments? Typically you don't save money because you like to perform investing as a leisure activity. Instead, investments are the result of a decision to spend less today so that you will have enough for your future spending needs. For example, one major reason for saving and investing is to have enough money to live comfortably in retirement when you no longer have active work-related income.

How much you set aside for investments depends on your goals, which are strongly influenced by the pleasure you get from spending today versus the satisfaction you get from saving monies so that you can live the good life in the future.

In the last chapter you learned that your investments can be separated into financial and nonfinancial ones. Frequently, nonfinancial investments such as your home and its possessions, your career, and other human-related benefits are connected to household functions today. Many fall under the umbrella of capital expenditures.

On the other hand, financial investments such as stocks, bonds, and mutual funds tend to be reserved for future household use.[1] Ownership of these assets is evidenced by pieces of paper instead of real assets you can touch. In contrast to many nonfinancial assets, they have little or no real cost of upkeep and often provide income and maintain or increase their value over time. For example, a financial asset such as a quality stock often provides dividend income and growth in price over time. In contrast, a nonfinancial real asset such as a washing machine or car has no cash income directly, requires upkeep, and tends to decline in value over time.[2]

Traditionally, investment theory and, to a large extent, investment practice tend to focus on financial assets, which are generally assumed to have readily available market prices. In this chapter, which concentrates on financial assets, we will assume that all assets discussed are marketable and are called marketable securities. Analyses of these marketable investments have some key advantages. Their values are objectively determined, competitively established, and easily measured.

---

[1] However, during retirement they are employed to fund current household functions and, in some cases, the investments or, more frequently, the income from those investments is used currently.

[2] A house is a partial exception. If well maintained, it may rise in price for many years before it begins to decline.

Given the focus on financial assets, when we discuss risk, we will concentrate on invest-ment risk. **Investment risk** is the risk principally associated with savings placed in finan-cial assets. The risk is of a decline in asset value, typically measured by its market price. This risk is in contrast to insurance risk. **Insurance risk** is the risk primarily associated with nonfinancial assets that can be reduced or eliminated by transferring it to an insurance com-pany. The risk is of deterioration in usability or valuation of a household's real or human assets. The analysis of household operations must, of course, incorporate both risks.

In this chapter we view investments and asset allocation from a financial planning perspec-tive. We describe the entire asset allocation process as an advisor would, beginning with goals and ending with portfolio management implementation. With this knowledge, you should be able to establish an overall asset allocation, one that can improve your investment performance.

Asset allocation for financial investments refers to the amount and type of securities we place our monies into. The financial instruments used are typically stocks and bonds or mutual funds. The exact breakdown by category and further separation into subcategory can vary depending on the person. For example, one person may have 100 percent all in large company stocks while another may have 60 percent in stocks and 40 percent in bonds with stocks of all sizes and investment styles and bonds of many types.

The planning system for asset allocation has eight components, which are given in Figure 9.1. We will examine each of them.

FIGURE 9.1
The Planning System for Asset Allocation

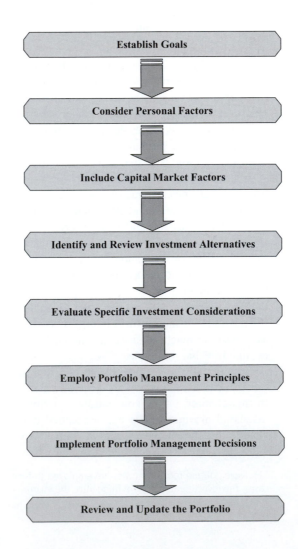

ESTABLISH GOALS

Goals are at the head of the financial planning process. They were discussed in detail in Chapter 3. Goals are, of course, determined by our needs and the things and activities that we enjoy. Common goals are becoming financially independent, saving for a major capital outlay such as a car, and putting away money for a child's college education. Once we have established our goals, we are in position to identify the role savings and investments play in the process. Investments can be viewed as a delivery mechanism: they help create sufficient assets to fund our goals. Our financial planning procedures can establish the amount of money needed for each goal. More narrowly, our investment focus is on the appropriate asset allocation to help meet our goals.

CONSIDER PERSONAL FACTORS

An asset allocation in practice is not a rigid representation of market factors alone. It is also influenced by personal characteristics. The factors listed below are some of the personal considerations that enter into the asset allocation process.

Time Horizon for Investments

We have many goals. They tend to vary in their horizon—that is, the time frame we have set to achieve our goals. Time frames are important because most investments fluctuate in value. It would be improper to place volatile stocks in an investment account due to be liquidated in three months; the risk of loss should the market decline would be too high. Similarly, for most people, it would be a mistake to place the entire sum in a money market account when the monies will not be needed for 20 years; the after-tax returns could trail the cost of living and instead of an increase in investable sums, the amount accumulated could decline on an inflation-adjusted basis.

We can group goals for investment purposes into five time horizons (see Table 9.1).

Liquidity Needs

Liquidity in an investment framework is the need or desire to be able to convert assets into cash. The need can come from a planned expenditure to be made at a fixed future period. In that case, it is covered under the time horizon just discussed. Alternatively, liquidity can be a need for current income to fund living expenses. It also can be a function of risk preference, employed for emergency use to reduce risk in general since typically the more liquid the financial instrument, the lower the risk of investment loss.

TABLE 9.1
Time Horizons

Horizon	Time Frame (years)	Examples of Goals	Investment Policy
Immediate	0	Emergency fund and other possible uses within days or weeks	Money market funds
Short-term	0–2	Vacation, new car	U.S. government bonds, certificates of deposit, short-term bond funds
Intermediate-term	2–4	Down payment for home, renovation of home	Conservative stocks, mutual funds, and bonds
Long-term	4–10	Education for a child	Normal long-term asset allocation
Very long-term	Over 10	Retirement	Normal long-term asset allocation

Investments vary in their degree of liquidity. For example, well-known large-sized issues like U.S. government bonds are generally more liquid than small local hospital obligations and publicly traded securities tend to be more liquid than private partnerships.

Current Available Resources

The investments you select are influenced by the amount that you have accumulated in financial assets. In addition, other assets such as real estate and human assets affect your asset allocation. This thinking is, of course, part of TPM. Simply put, under TPM your asset allocation is affected by the amount and risk characteristics of all your assets.

Projected Future Cash Flows

Projected future cash flows are obtained by subtracting outlays from revenue streams. We have called the difference *net cash flow,* the amount that we are free to employ in any way we wish. The greater our projected net cash flows and the lower their risk of a disappointing outcome for it, the more able we are to handle a risky investment. That is because we will have future monies to invest that will offset disappointing results for our current assets.

Taxes

People's tax brackets vary. Investment decisions should be made based on their after-tax returns. Therefore, our asset allocations can vary depending on our marginal tax bracket. For example, people in low tax brackets use taxable bonds while those in high ones often own tax-free municipal bonds. When changes in assets in portfolios are contemplated, the impact of gains or losses on sale must be included. For example, there is little purpose in selling a well-regarded stock to take advantage of a potential extra 10 percent price gain on another security purchased with the proceeds from sale of the well-regarded issue when the sale will result in a 20 percent federal and state tax payment due to the gain on liquidation of the original stock bought at a very low price.

Restrictions

Restrictions in formulating an asset allocation are limitations on freedom of choice in investment alternatives or investment practices. Many restrictions are included under the other items discussed—for example, not using municipal bonds for people in low

TABLE 9.2   Risk Profile Quiz

Source: Lewis Altfest and Karen Altfest, *Lew Altfest Answers Almost All Your Questions about Money* (New York: McGraw-Hill, 1992), p. 64.

Answer the following questions using ratings from 1 (strongly agree) to 5 (strongly disagree).

1. Short-term fluctuations in the value of my assets do not bother me.
2. I tend to buy and sell securities at the right time.
3. Having high current investment income is not important to me.
4. If an investment could not be sold quickly without a substantial financial penalty, it would not disturb me, provided the longer-term returns on the investment were favorable.
5. It would not bother me at all if I couldn't sell my new investment for many years if there was the potential for unusually good performance.
6. Investing in common stocks and common-stock mutual funds does not make me jittery.
7. I am willing to endure a significant decline in my principal over a few years if it will result in higher longer-term returns.
8. I am willing to take on greater risk so that I can obtain a hedge against inflation.
9. I don't need a guaranteed return of my principal if forgoing that will greatly increase the potential longer-term growth rate of my investments.
10. If the prevailing economic and investment sentiment seemed gloomy, I would not switch to safer securities.

	Score
Risk taker	Below 20
Middle of the road	20–40
Conservative	40 or higher

Practical Comment

There are a number of other factors concerning human characteristics that should be considered.

RISK

When a self-evaluation approach is used, care must be taken to relate the assessment of risk to types of investments. What one person thinks is conservative, another may think is aggressive. For example, some people, perhaps influenced by their personal experience of long-term appreciation of their home, regard both public and private real estate as less risky, like bonds, while others recognize that real estate risk is more closely aligned with equity investments.

Also keep in mind that self-assessment of risk tolerance and many other assessment techniques can reflect cyclical variations in tolerance for risk. Put simply, people's tolerance for risk often tends to rise when prior overall market performance has been good and when the outlook for investment returns appears very favorable. The opposite is true when past results and the outlook are poor. Unfortunately,

that can be the wrong time to change asset allocations. Financial planners should discourage changes for these reasons, pointing out that poor performance has often been the outcome. For example, when suspecting a rise in risk tolerance because of strong recent market performance, clients should be told to visualize how they would feel about changes if the market were in the midst of a decline. In general, it is advisable to stress a steady tolerance for risk over a long-term time frame.

PAST EXPERIENCES

Asset allocations overall can be influenced by past personal experiences that may not be entirely logical. A client may not want to purchase a particular type of security—say, a mutual fund offering small-sized companies—because she got "burned" in that type of security in the past. The planner can stress the benefits of investing in that asset class, but if the client is adamant, another type of security with many of the same characteristics can be substituted.

tax brackets. In addition, you may restrict the use of debt to finance purchase of investments or preclude the use of higher-risk options or commodities. Finally, individuals may have specific preferences; for example, there are those who prefer socially responsible funds.

Risk Tolerance

Risk tolerance is the amount of risk you are willing to undertake. Some people think of it solely as a function of one's personality. However, it can be influenced by many variables in addition to personality including upbringing, current circumstances, and the amount and type of current assets and future cash flows for the household.

A person's risk tolerance can be determined in many different ways. People can be asked to describe themselves and their tolerance for risk. For example, the question may be framed as "In investment matters, do you consider yourself conservative, moderate, or aggressive?" Alternatively, their prior actions can be observed. For example, looking at a breakdown of their current portfolio can help determine the appropriate asset allocation for them. Another approach is to give them a variety of oral or written questions that can be scored to help determine their risk tolerance. One such questionnaire is given in Table 9.2.

INCLUDE CAPITAL MARKET FACTORS

We have established the goals and the distinguishing features of individuals. At the same time, we need to examine the characteristics of the overall financial markets and of the various types of securities likely to be considered for the asset allocation. We begin by discussing two of the most basic characteristics of finance: risk and return.

Risk and Return

One of the most logical thoughts in investing is that risk and return should be related. If you select an investment that has a greater degree of risk, you expect to earn a higher return. Why else would you expose yourself to an above-average chance of loss? Generally, in finance it is assumed that risk and return are proportionately related. It is a basic assumption of modern investment theory.[3] For example, if you choose an investment with 20 percent greater risk, you should get a 20 percent higher return.[4] Let's look at the two factors, return and risk, separately.

Return

Return is the total of income and growth of monies invested over a period of time. We can establish the cumulative return using the following formula.

$$\text{Holding period return (HPR)} = \frac{\text{Sum of dividends or interest paid} + \text{Gain in principal invested}}{\text{Original cost}}$$

We are often interested in calculating time-weighted returns. These returns give effect to how long you have owned a security and the timing of income payments during that period. The internal rate of return (IRR) is often used to obtain this return, typically by providing a compound annual return.[5] An example of HPR and IRR for a bond is provided in Example 9.1. The example details IRR for both a stock and a bond; the bond is expected to be held until it matures. In that case, the IRR is also known as the yield to maturity (YTM).

Example 9.1

Betsy bought a stock three years ago for $20 per share and placed it in a tax-sheltered pension plan. In years 1 to 3, she received cash dividends of $0.30, $0.60, and $1.00, respectively. She sold the stock for $28 per share the day she received the $1.00 dividend. She also purchased a bond in the pension plan for $960 on January 1, paying $50 once a year, which is due to be repaid at $1,000 in eight years. Calculate the actual HPR and IRR for her stock and the projected IRR/YTM for the bond.

Stock

Year 3: $(28 + 1) = \$29$

Calculator Solution

General Calculator Approach	Specific HP12C	Specific TI BA II Plus
		CF
Clear the register	f FIN	2nd CLR Work
Enter initial cash outflow	20 CHS g CF₀	20 +/− ENTER ↓
Enter cash inflow Year 1	0.30 g CFⱼ	0.30 ENTER ↓ ↓
Enter cash inflow Year 2	0.60 g CFⱼ	0.60 ENTER ↓ ↓
Enter cash inflow Year 3	29 g CFⱼ	29 ENTER ↓ ↓
Calculate the internal rate of return	f IRR	IRR CPT
	14.6%	14.6%

[3] Three prominent parts of this theory—modern portfolio theory, capital asset pricing model, and efficient market theory—are discussed in this chapter and in Web Appendix A: Modern Investment Theory.

[4] After the risk-free rate, to be described, is taken into account.

[5] We can calculate average annual returns when provided with annual or cumulative statistics. Average annual arithmetic mean returns are given as

$$\text{Arithmetic mean returns} = \frac{\text{Sum of annual returns}}{\text{Number of periods}} \text{ or } \frac{1}{N}\sum_{1}^{N} r_N \text{ and}$$

$$\text{Geometric mean returns} = \sqrt[\text{Number of Periods}]{\text{Product of annual returns}} - 1 \text{ or } \sqrt[N]{\prod_{1}^{N}(1 + r_N)} - 1.$$

Bond

Year 8: $(1,000 + 50) = \$1,050$

Calculator Solution

General Calculator Approach	Specific HP12C	Specific TI BA II Plus
		CF
Clear the register	f FIN	2nd CLR Work
Enter initial cash outflow	960 CHS g CF₀	960 +/− ENTER ↓
Enter cash inflows Years 1–7	50 g CFⱼ	50 ENTER ↓
Enter number of years	7 g Nⱼ	7 ENTER ↓
Enter cash inflow Year 8	1,050 g CFⱼ	1,050 ENTER ↓↓
Calculate the internal rate of return	f IRR	IRR CPT
	5.6%	5.6%

The stock had a 14.6 percent annual return while the bond has a projected yield to maturity of 5.6 percent.

Risk

Risk, as most people view it, is the chance of loss on an investment. As you can see in Table 9.3, there are many types of risk for financial assets.

According to modern investment theory, the total risk of a security—one that includes all the fundamental risks shown in Table 9.2—can be represented by one measurement: its price action. The wider the fluctuations around its average price, the greater the stock's risk. The most common measurement of price fluctuation is the standard deviation.[6]

The idea of standard deviation and risk is shown in Figure 9.2. Notice that company A and company B both have the same return (they start and end up at the same price), but company B has greater total risk because its price has fluctuated more widely.

Since the standard deviation measures price change, it includes fluctuations that result in gains as well as those that result in losses. Therefore, this method contrasts with investors' measurement of loss only. The semi-variance, a less-used methodology, measures fluctuations resulting in losses.[7]

---

[6] The standard deviation is the square root of the sum of the squared deviations around the average return.

[7] Harry Markowitz, "Foundations of Portfolio Theory," *Journal of Finance* 46, no. 2 (June 1991), pp. 469–77.

TABLE 9.3
Fundamental Risks for Financial Assets

Risks	Explanation
Market	The risk of a decline in the overall stock or bond market
Liquidity	The risk of receiving a lower-than-market price upon sale of your holding
Economic	The risk of unfavorable business conditions caused by weakness in the overall economy
Inflation	The risk of an unexpected rise in prices that reduces purchasing power
Political	The risk of a change in government or governmental policy adversely affecting operations
Regulatory	The risk of a shift in regulatory policy impacting activities
Currency	The extra risk in international activities arising from currency fluctuations
Technological	The risk of obsolescence of a product line or inputs in producing it
Preference	The risk of a shift in consumer taste
Other industry	The risks other than the ones given above that affect companies in an industry
Company	The operating and financial risks that apply to a particular firm

FIGURE 9.2
**Companies with
Same Mean Returns
but Different Risks**

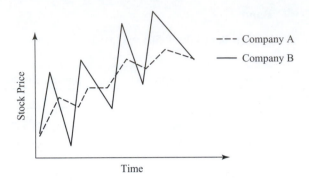

The capital asset pricing model (CAPM) is a specialized modern investment theory model that is based on risk-return principles. It, too, measures risk based on price changes. However, its risk is received by measuring price change of a security relative to a benchmark's price performance.

The benchmark for large company stocks is usually the S&P 500, the Standard and Poor's index of the 500 largest companies in the United States. The risk measurement is called the *beta coefficient* and the greater the price fluctuation of a security relative to the benchmark's movements, the greater the security's beta coefficient.

The benchmark is automatically given a beta of 1 and stocks or mutual funds of stocks having a beta coefficient greater than 1 are deemed to have more risk than the market, while those having a beta less than 1 have below-average risk.

Unlike the standard deviation, the beta coefficient doesn't claim to measure total risk, just systematic risk. **Systematic risk** is the risk of overall market factors such as the economy, inflation, interest rates, and the stock market. In contrast, **unsystematic risk** is risk related to an individual company such as a decline in market share, the loss of a key patent, and so on. CAPM says individual company risk can be diversified away when you hold a large portfolio of securities. Therefore, CAPM says that all you need to know is systematic risk as measured by the beta coefficient.

The standard deviation and the beta coefficient have a strong advantage. Unlike fundamental measures of risk, they both can be measured objectively. For each measure, the higher the figure, the greater the risk. In most instances, beta coefficients and standard deviations are developed by independent investment services such as Morningstar and Value Line, and their newsletters are available in many libraries.

As a practical matter, all you need to remember is that a beta greater than 1 equals above-average risk; a beta below 1 equals below-average risk.[8] Also keep in mind that both the beta and the standard deviation are best used when comparing securities that are similar to each other. For a more detailed explanation of beta coefficients, see Web Appendix A: Modern Investment Theory.

Example 9.2

Dana was down to one of two choices of investments in her pension plan at work. She wanted growth of assets, was fairly aggressive in her investment tolerance for risk, and, therefore, chose from stock, not bond, mutual funds.

She went to the library and found results for her pension plan's two stock alternatives. The first fund, the Oaktimber Fund, had a beta coefficient of 0.75 and a standard deviation of 15.8. The second, the Advanced Horizon Fund, had a beta of 1.54 and a standard deviation of 31.2. Both mutual funds invested in large companies. She looked up an S&P 500 index fund that had

---

[8] Relative to its benchmark.

FIGURE 9.3
Security Market Line

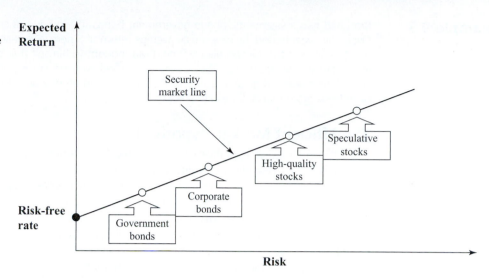

statistics very close to those of the actual index and found its beta to be 1.0, as she thought. She knew that the S&P was the benchmark of large company performance and 1.0 meant average. She also found out that the S&P 500 had a standard deviation of 21.0 for the past period being measured.

Dana instantly recognized that the beta coefficient of 1.54 for Advanced Horizon was well above the market, signifying higher-than-average risk. The standard deviation also was substantially above the market's 21.0. She also noticed that Advanced Horizon's three-year return of 13 percent a year was well above Oaktimber's 9 percent a year. She thought to herself, the higher the risk, the higher the return. She picked Advanced Horizon, which best fit her high risk tolerance.

Expected Rate of Return

Under modern investment theory, the expected rate of return combines risk-return principles to arrive at a projected future return. As the equation below indicates, the expected rate of return is equal to the risk-free rate plus a risk premium. Therefore, the **risk premium** is the extra return that compensates you for the additional amount of risk you are taking with a particular security over a completely safe one.

$$\text{Expected rate of return} = \text{Risk-free rate} + \text{Risk premium}$$

The risk-free rate, the completely safe one, is the rate of return you require even if there is no risk. The yield on 30-day U.S. government Treasury Bills is generally used to gauge this rate.[9]

The risk premium depends on the degree of risk undertaken. For example, a nearly bankrupt airline will have a much greater risk premium than a leading high-quality food company.[10]

The risk-return characteristics of various securities are demonstrated in Figure 9.3. Notice that the risk-free rate appears right on the expected return line. That is because it is viewed as having no risk. The diagram shows that the more risky the security, the greater the risk premium and the greater the expected or required rate of return.[11]

---

[9] Some would say 90-day or 10-year government issues are more appropriate depending on the time horizon for the investment.

[10] The investor may use either the standard deviation, the beta coefficient, or more judgmental factors as inputs in establishing the risk premium.

[11] For our purposes, expected and required rates of return are synonymous.

Example 9.3

Brad had two investments: one in government bonds, the other in a speculative stock fund. Over a five-year period, he received an average return of 5 percent a year in government bonds and 5.5 percent for the speculative fund. Brad thought to himself that he made more money in the stock than the bond. Yet he was dissatisfied with his stock performance. He felt he should have received greater return for the risk taken. In other words, his risk premium should have been more than 0.5 percent a year.

The Efficient Market Hypothesis

The efficient market hypothesis is one of the basic assumptions of a pure risk-return approach. When risk and return are exactly correlated, all investments sell at the prices they are expected to. As you can gather, the **efficient market hypothesis (EMH)** deals with investment information and valuation of individual securities. It says that the best valuation for an individual security is its current market price. This price reflects all information known about the security. It is the fair price for the asset. When new information is issued, it is quickly incorporated in the price of the shares.

A major conclusion of the EMH is that it will not be profitable to attempt to outperform the market. Even if there were people who were not fully informed or capable of appraising shares, and their actions could create particularly appealing prices, other investors would quickly step in to take advantage. By doing so, these investors would eliminate any above-average profit opportunities.

Example 9.4

Suppose a market analyst disclosed that, according to his tests, the length of women's skirts was an indicator of the future direction of the market. Actually, there reputedly was such a theory some 75 years ago. Suppose that buying stocks when skirt lengths rose and selling them when they dropped resulted in a doubling in investment returns. This information would spread quickly. The next step would be market analysts, portfolio managers, and television commentators positioned at the fashion openings of prominent designers to observe leading-edge fashion lengths.

As soon as the new skirt lengths were known, the investors would communicate orders via cell phone directly to the floor of the stock exchange and via television to all viewers. This information, now known by all who would try to act on it, would be instantaneously incorporated in stock prices. Knowledge of skirt lengths would no longer have investment use. The price of all shares would be efficient in that it would reflect all available information including the length of women's skirts.

There are three forms of the EMH: the weak form, the semi-strong form, and the strong form.

- *The weak form.* The weak form deals only with price and volume for a security. It says that looking at current and past information on stock price patterns and the number of shares traded will not be useful.
- *The semi-strong form.* The semi-strong form states that all publicly available information is incorporated in a stock's price. Therefore, not only information on price and volume but also fundamental analysis such as analysis of annual reports, brokerage firm recommendations, discussions with industry and company representatives, and so on, will not lead to better-than-average performance.
- *The strong form.* The strong form states that the share prices fully reflect not only public but also private information. Therefore, knowledge of information on a company's outlook that has not yet been released to the public or other insider information is not useful.

In effect, the weak form says that technical analysis has no use. That is because technical analysts use just price changes and volume to make predictions about future performance. If the weak form of EMH is true, then technical analysts are wasting their time. Some tests of this hypothesis have turned up anomalies—exceptions to efficient market beliefs and opportunities to use technical analysis for extra profit.[12] The strong form has not been tested as often,[13] perhaps because intuitively it does not seem logical that knowledge of what is going on inside a company before others know it would not be profitable.

Most tests of the EMH have focused on the semi-strong form and public information. It not only includes the weak form's technical analysis; it extends efficiency to include all public information. It isn't as broad as the strong form because it doesn't include private information. Contrary to efficient market theory, a relatively broad array of opportunities for profitable investing has been found including purchasing depressed stocks early in January,[14] small cap stocks,[15] those with low price to book,[16] and those with low p/e multiples;[17] eliminating or shorting those with high p/e multiples;[17] purchasing those that have been neglected;[18] and so on.

Mean Reversion and Efficient Markets

Mean reversion,[19] as it relates to groups of individual securities or overall markets, says that returns for securities tend to move toward average performance when the returns are examined over longer time frames. Therefore, if securities underperform for a period, they may be more likely to outperform later on. When their results are highly favorable for a period of time, they can be vulnerable to poor returns in the period beyond. Thus, in contrast to efficient market beliefs, future stock price movements may be somewhat predictable.[20]

Example 9.5

Phil was interested in stocks in two industries: beverage companies and manufacturers of branded foods. They had the same beta coefficients. Over the past year, beverage companies had performed extremely well, rising more than the overall market, while food companies had actually declined in price. There was no fundamental news to account for the discrepancy in performance. Each industry's earnings were in line with expectations.

---

[12] David P. Brown and Robert H. Jennings, "On Technical Analysis," *Review of Financial Studies* 2, no. 4 (October 1989).

[13] See Jeffrey F. Jaffe, "Special Information and Insider Trading," *Journal of Business* (July 1974), pp. 410–28; Nejat H. Seyhun, "Insiders' Profits, Costs of Trading and Market Efficiency," *Journal of Financial Economics* 16 (1986), pp. 189–212; and Lisa K. Meulbroek, "An Empirical Analysis of Illegal Insider Trading," *Journal of Finance* 47, no. 5 (December 1992), pp. 1661–99.

[14] See Michael S. Rozeff and William R. Kinney Jr., "Capital Market Seasonality: The Case of Stock Returns," *Journal of Financial Economics* 3, no. 4 (October 1976), pp. 379–402; and Marc R. Reinganum, "The Anatomy of a Stock Market Winner," *Financial Analysts Journal* 44, no. 2 (March–April 1988), pp. 272–84.

[15] Rolf Banz, "The Relationship between Return and Market Value of Common Stocks," *Journal of Financial Economics* 9 (March 1981), pp. 3–18; Marc R. Reinganum, "A Revival of the Small-Firm Effect," *Journal of Portfolio Management* 18, no. 3 (Spring 1992), pp. 55–62.

[16] Barr Rosenberg, Kenneth Reid, and Ronald Lanstein, "Persuasive Evidence of Market Inefficiency," *Journal of Portfolio Management* 11, no. 3 (Spring 1985), pp. 9–17; Eugene F. Fama and Kenneth R. French, "The Cross Section of Expected Stock Returns," *Journal of Finance* 47, no. 2 (June 1992), pp. 427–65.

[17] Sanjoy Basu, "The Investment Performance of Common Stocks in Relation to Their Price-Earnings Ratios: A Test of the Efficient Market Hypothesis," *Journal of Finance* 32, no. 3 (June 1977), pp. 663–82.

[18] Avner Arbel and Paul Strebel, "Pay Attention to Neglected Firms!" *Journal of Portfolio Management* 9, no. 2 (Winter 1983), pp. 37–42.

[19] See Werner DeBondt and Richard Thaler, "Does the Stock Market Overreact?" *Journal of Finance* 40 (1985), pp. 793–805; James Poterba and Lawrence Summers, "Mean Reversion in Stock Prices: Evidence and Implications," *Journal of Financial Economics* 22 (1988), pp. 27–59; Eugene Fama and Kenneth French, "Business Conditions and Expected Returns on Stocks and Bonds," *Journal of Financial Economics* 25 (November 1989), pp. 23–49.

[20] Nicholas Barberis, "Investing for the Long Run When Returns Are Predictable," *Journal of Finance* 55 (February 2000), pp. 225–64; John Campbell and Robert Shiller, "Stock Prices, Earnings and Expected Dividends," *Journal of Finance* 43 (July 1988), pp. 661–76.

Practical Comment Why Mean Reversion May Work

The reason for mean reversion may be human weaknesses such as overemphasis on near-term developments and lack of vision of longer-term events, or insufficient weighting given to the random nature of unexpected occurrences. Unexpected occurrences, both good and bad, can affect highly and poorly regarded companies equally.

Mean reversion can be viewed as a modified form of efficient markets. It can be interpreted as indicating that markets and individual securities may not be fairly priced over shorter periods but move toward efficiency over the longer term. That is, they reflect appropriate returns after adjustment for risk over extended periods. In shorter time frames, securities may be over- or underpriced, which presents potential opportunities for abnormal returns through fundamental analysis.

Phil believed that stocks and industries "come back" in price over time (reversion to mean performance) and chose to invest in the consumer food sector. Over the following year, he was rewarded with strong gains when their shares moved back to normal valuations, while the beverage companies underperformed the market. Over the combined two-year period before and after Phil's analysis, both industries had the same average performance of 11 percent per year. Mean reversion had brought both industries back into parity.

IDENTIFY AND REVIEW INVESTMENT ALTERNATIVES

We have inputted goals and other personal factors and examined capital market factors. Before proceeding, we need to identify and review the investment alternatives that are appropriate for the asset allocation. We will review those most used by households—bonds, stocks, and mutual funds, which, of course, are generally made up of bonds or stocks. In this way, you can become familiar with their investment characteristics such as their risk-return profiles and better understand how to employ them in the asset allocation process.

Bonds

Bonds are contracts in which an investor lends money to a borrower. As compensation for receiving the money, the borrower agrees to pay interest, often twice a year and generally of a fixed amount. The borrower also agrees to repay a stated sum at the end of a fixed period. The date that the loan is to be repaid is called the **maturity date.**[21]

Bonds of high-quality companies are considered safer than most other types of investments for the following reasons:

1. The annual income to be received is generally fixed in advance.
2. The contracted-for loan principal is likely to be repaid in full at the stated date.[22] In the event of financial difficulties, the borrower will have to comply with the terms of the contract. Interest and principal will be repaid on time or the company will be faced with bankruptcy. Should bankruptcy occur, bondholders have priority in receiving the proceeds from liquidation of business assets and are therefore repaid before stockholders receive any material proceeds.

[21] *Bonds* is the most popular term used for this type of investment, but a broader and perhaps more accurate term, *fixed obligations*, is sometimes employed. A fixed obligation is any investment in which the terms, including the returns, are known at the beginning of the period or depend on clearly defined factors such as the inflation rate. Fixed obligations consist not only of bonds but of other investments such as mortgages and bank certificates of deposits. Unless otherwise stated, we will use the terms *bonds* and *fixed obligations* synonymously. Fixed obligations as they pertain to future household outflows described in Chapter 6, as opposed to future financial investment inflows as indicated here, have a different meaning.

[22] Unless repaid earlier, generally at the option of the corporation under terms stated in the contract.

Common Stocks

Common stocks are very different from bonds. As a common stockholder, you are an owner, not a creditor, of a company. You are entitled to participate in the current profits and anticipated future growth of the enterprise. Of course, if there are no profits, your investment can end up having no value. As you can gather, stocks typically have higher risk premiums than bonds. In sum, stocks present potentially higher returns than bonds, but the shareholder must be prepared to take greater risk.

Individual common stocks, also called *equities*, can be placed in various categories. Professional investors often use these equity categories to concentrate in. Sometimes they use them to ensure that they are never too far away from overall market performance or that of the segment of the stock market they operate in. Some of the methods of categorizing stocks are given below.

Relative Growth Rates

Companies that grow more rapidly in sales and earnings than the overall economy and are less affected by cyclical business conditions are called **growth stocks.** Examples would be fast-growing technology leaders. Those that generally grow at average or below-average rates but are also less affected by business conditions are called **defensive stocks.** Companies in the consumer basics and utility sectors are examples of defensive companies. Firms whose growth rates are at or below those for the overall economy but whose operations are highly sensitive to aggregate business conditions are called **cyclical stocks.**

Sector and Industry

Sectors are the parts of the overall economy. The economic sectors that pertain to the stock market are sometimes divided into basic materials, capital goods, consumer cyclicals, consumer noncyclicals, energy, financial, health care, services, technology, transportation, and utilities.

Each sector, in turn, is divided into a number of industries. For example, consumer cyclicals would include, among others, autos, consumer appliances, and retail chains. Since sectors tend to share some similar characteristics, some active managers use these categories and industries to decide which areas to over- or underemphasize.

Geographic Area

Geographic area indicates which areas of the country or of the world you concentrate in. For example, the northeast area of the United States is the most populated but slowest-growing region. You may be interested in investing in faster-growing sections of the United States or in parts of the world that present potentially more rapid growth rates than the United States.

Company Size

Companies come in all sizes. As a generalization, larger companies are more secure, often having entrenched positions in major markets. Smaller companies can be more flexible since they may have more entrepreneurial management. On the other hand, they also may have more risk if the outlook changes dramatically. Medium-sized companies are a blend of the previous two.

Quality

Quality in stocks is a measure of how confident we are that the anticipated prospects for a company are going to be fulfilled. Those companies of high quality are more likely to be large and have a strong position in their markets. Often they have good returns on investment and are less likely to have large noneconomic-related disappointments in earnings. They are sometimes called **blue chips** and generally have risk that is below overall market averages.

TABLE 9.4
Total Industry Net Assets

Source: Investment Company Institute, *Mutual Fund Fact Book*, 45th ed, 2005. Available online at http://www.ici.org/pdf/2005_factbook.pdf

	Industry Net Assets (billions of dollars)			
Year	Stock Funds	Bond Funds	Total[1]	Total Number of Funds
1970	45.1	2.5	47.6	361
1975	37.5	4.7	45.9	426
1980	44.4	14.0	134.8	564
1985	111.3	122.7	495.4	1,528
1990	239.5	291.3	1,065.2	3,079
1995	1,249.1	598.9	2,811.3	5,725
2000	3,961.9	811.2	6,964.7	8,155
2004	4,384.1	1,290.3	8,106.9	8,044

[1] Hybrid and money market funds are also included in total.

At the opposite end of the quality spectrum are companies whose operations are less predictable, their profitability more precarious with current or potential losses possible. Sometimes these companies have a large amount of debt in relation to the value of their equity. They can be highly risky and, if so, are called **speculative investments**.

Mutual Funds

Mutual funds combine stock or bond assets[23] for investors, who receive centralized administration and investment management. In effect, people pay an investment company a yearly fee for handling their investment needs. Their investment is evidenced by shares of the mutual fund owned. Monies transferred to the investment company are pooled together with those of other shareholders for efficient management. This form of asset management has grown rapidly in recent decades, as shown in Table 9.4.

Below you see some selected mutual fund characteristics have been separated into strengths and weaknesses.

[23] Other types of assets also are used such as money market funds.

Characteristics	Explanation
Strengths	
Expertise	Fund companies are typically run professionally, and the portfolio managers in charge of investment activities are generally qualified.
Low cost	Mutual fund activities are provided at relatively low cost.
Diversification	Diversification generally into 50 or more stocks is possible with a modest sum of money.
Low minimum investment	The minimum investment to purchase many funds is as low as $500 to $1,000.
Professional recordkeeping	Records are kept by the fund management, who can provide you with information about performance or for tax purposes.
General information	Published information and telephone assistance from the fund management companies are generally available to help select mutual funds and monitor them. The information is either obtained yourself or through a broker or financial planner.
Safety	Mutual funds are supervised by the Securities and Exchange Commission and the fund's board of directors. Actual assets often are not directly under the manager's supervision but are placed with a third party, with the manager just making buy and sell decisions.
Daily pricing	The firm's price and performance statistics are available daily in some newspapers; in *Barron's*, which is issued weekly; through Internet sites; or from the funds directly.
Reinvestment and payout	Mutual funds can provide automatic reinvestment of their distributions and can accommodate the need for withdrawals of a stated amount per period.
Weaknesses	
Cost	The overhead costs are higher than they would be if you were to manage the money yourself.
Performance	The majority of mutual funds underperform their relevant markets.
Tax	Holders of mutual funds are subject to tax inefficiencies such as being taxed on realized capital gains from individual stocks or bonds liquidated by the fund manager even though the fund itself hasn't been sold by the investor.
Liquidity	Purchases and sales for most funds can be effected only once a day.

Mutual Fund Classification System

Mutual funds cover virtually all types of stocks and bonds. At over 8,000 in number, there are more mutual funds than stocks on the New York Stock Exchange. Historically, funds were categorized by risk. Thus, general stock funds ranged from most conservative, income-only, to aggressive growth. More recently, they have generally been listed by size and by investment style.

Size   Most stock mutual funds can be divided into small, medium, and large size categories for their investments. The basis for this separation is overall stock market worth of the companies that the mutual fund invests in. Smaller capitalization companies provide greater potential returns as they may have the potential for faster growth and have more managerial flexibility. However, they also have greater risk since they may not be as diversified as larger companies. Larger capitalization companies have more consistency of performance and lower company fundamental and stock market risk.[24] Medium capitalization companies provide a blend of the other two categories.

Investment Style   There are many styles of active investment. However, they are commonly separated into three categories: growth, value, and blend.

- *Growth.* A **growth style of investing** involves selecting companies that are expected to have rapid growth in revenues and earnings per share. These companies are more likely to be favorably thought of by investors and have higher-than-average valuations such as high price/earnings multiples.

- *Value.* A value investor employing a **value style of investing** places more emphasis on price in making purchase decisions. The manager looks for companies that are out of favor or otherwise mispriced in relation to their outlook for earnings growth. Their valuations of such ratios as their market price in relation to their earnings (p/e ratio) or market price in relation to their asset value as recorded on their books are likely to be below average. Their universe of stocks is broader, often with more emphasis on companies whose earnings growth or return on investment is temporarily or permanently below that for the average stock.

- *Blend.* The blend category is essentially all else. It may entail a manager who moves from value to growth style or buys a mix of the two. It also may involve a style of investing that cannot be defined in value or growth terms as, for example, a manager who largely uses technical analysis.

Example 9.6

Helen had a choice of three styles of larger company mutual funds for her pension. The first picked the fastest-growing companies in industries with favorable outlooks like those in the technology sector. The second selected individual companies that had some blemishes in outlook but were soundly positioned and financed and were cheaply priced. The third was a mixture of the other two styles. Helen quickly identified them as growth, value, and blend styles. She decided to select the value style, which suited her belief in making purchases for her household that were "bargains" and therefore represented value investments.

A sample grid employing these principles for stocks is shown in Figure 9.4.

EVALUATE SPECIFIC INVESTMENT CONSIDERATIONS

Individual preferences create issues and choices in the way investments are managed. Two of them—active versus passive investing and use of individual securities versus mutual funds—are dealt with below.

---

[24] Of course, many believers in risk-return theory and efficient markets regard the two as synonymous.

FIGURE 9.4
Morningstar
Investment Style Box

Source: Morningstar, Inc., 2005,
http://www.morningstar.com.

Morningstar Style Box™

Value · Blend · Growth
---------Style--------

An Active versus Passive Approach

Risk-return and efficient market theory say that attempting to outperform the market will not be fruitful. If you manage to do so, you are just lucky, not skilled. This thinking leads to a **passive approach** to investing. With a passive approach, no attempt is made to receive greater-than-market returns. Its proponents believe efforts can better be used to diversify in order to reduce risk and keep costs low. Passive investors tend to purchase index mutual funds of all types. An **index fund** attempts to duplicate market performance and keeps costs low by using computerized programs to purchase holdings and not employing high-priced investment managers and analysts.[25]

With the alternative, the **active approach** to investing, changes are made in holdings over time to take advantage of new opportunities. There are many different ways of performing active investing. However, they all have as their basis the belief that it is possible to outperform the market. Otherwise, it would be silly to make the effort.

One prominent active approach is fundamental investing. Under fundamental investing, analysis is made of overall market, industry, and company data to identify opportunities. Often the basis of this approach is the belief in mean reversion in investments with purchases made at below "true value" levels and sales made when they return to or attain correct valuations.

Individual Securities versus Mutual Funds

In establishing an investment portfolio, a decision should be made about whether to use individual securities or mutual funds.[26] Individual securities purchased by the household involve no fund-overhead expenses and offer a greater ability to buy and sell for tax planning purposes instead of typical annual taxable capital gains for mutual funds. With individual securities, there also can be the emotional "high" of watching a stock in your portfolio do well.

Mutual funds offer professional advice at reasonable cost, the ability to delegate the investment management and recordkeeping function, and simple diversification with low investment minimums by specialists in a wide variety of types of securities, geographic areas, and styles of investing. Although there are notable exceptions, the majority of mutual funds underperform the market.

Given the lack of expertise in many households, the lack of desire to monitor their investments, a sometimes emotional response to buy and sell decisions, and a desire for lower volatility, the majority of financial planners recommend implementing through mutual funds.

---

[25] It is generally included under the blend style of investing.

[26] Actually, mutual funds are just one of a number of investment alternatives including separate accounts and investment managers selected directly, tax-deferred annuities, hedge funds, exchange-traded funds, unit investment trusts, and so on. However, in this introductory text, we have limited ourselves to this most popular alternative.

EMPLOY PORTFOLIO MANAGEMENT PRINCIPLES

Portfolio management is the overall supervision of our investments program. It guides the decisions on asset allocation and individual investments. Each household does or should engage in portfolio management, which helps answer such questions as "Are my investments too concentrated in one area?" and "What returns am I likely to receive longer term." In this section, we discuss the principles that help establish portfolio management policies.

We have already described the characteristics of individual stocks and bonds and how risk and household needs both enter into decision making. Our approach was to look at each asset separately and decide whether it was attractive enough to purchase. There is a major weakness in using this approach.[27] It assumes that a portfolio is just the sum of all its individual securities.

Adding up all individual securities is roughly equivalent to saying that a house is only the sum of all the bricks and other materials that went into building it,[28] with no weight given to the safety and attractiveness of the building taken as a whole. Similarly, a portfolio is more than the sum of its parts because the individual assets are often related to each other. The interrelationships among the securities can create an attractive or unattractive portfolio just as the way the bricks are put together can create a beautiful or ugly house.

A **portfolio** can be defined as a grouping of assets held by an individual or a business. A portfolio that holds a diversified grouping of assets can be said to be attractively balanced and not easily influenced by events other than those that affect overall markets.

We also learned that individual securities are valued not only by the returns they offer but also by the risk they present in receiving their return. The two-parameter risk-return approach, here termed the mean-variance model,[29] serves as the basis for portfolio theory and its approach to constructing a portfolio.[30] Under portfolio theory, we strive to achieve the highest return we can, given the risk we are willing to undertake. Let's look at portfolio risk and return separately.

Portfolio return is fairly simple. It is just the sum of the returns for each security multiplied by the weighting it has in the portfolio. You might think, then, that portfolio risk is the weighted average sum of the risk for the individual securities. That isn't the case. The reason has to do with the correlation coefficient.

The **correlation coefficient** measures the degree to which investment in a portfolio is related to other investments in that portfolio. As a practical matter, for financial investments, it generally ranges from 0 to $+1$.[31] Often in portfolio management, we measure correlation through movements in prices. That is because price changes often largely determine performance, the reason for investing. Think of correlations as showing relationships. You are not going to get much portfolio diversification benefit from investing in Coca-Cola, Pepsi, and Cadbury Schweppes (Seven Up). They tend to be very similar and

---

[27] Of course, as we will see later in this chapter, there is a second possible weakness. If you are a believer in efficient markets, the effort to find attractive stocks will be fruitless.

[28] Just as we look at a house overall and decide whether it is attractive or unattractive, we can look at a portfolio overall and decide whether by placing the right investments in the right proportion we have a grouping of assets that appropriately answers our risk-return needs. Just as one building material may look attractive by itself but not fit the overall house effect, individual securities relate to one another and one that is attractive may not fit in with an individual's point of view.

[29] The variance measure of risk is just the standard deviation squared.

[30] Harry Markowitz, "Portfolio Selection," *Journal of Finance* 7, no. 1 (March 1952), pp. 77–91; Harry Markowitz, "The Early History of Portfolio Theory: 1600–1960," *Financial Analysts Journal* 55 (1999), p. 5.

[31] In theory its range is wider, from $+1$ to -1. Investments can be negatively correlated, which means that when one rises the other goes down. As a practical matter, negatively correlated investments are difficult to find.

therefore have high correlations. Combining a beverage company with a smaller technology company and a low-valuation automobile company would reduce the correlations. By reducing correlations, we lessen price fluctuations and overall risk in the portfolio.

Under Markowitz, forecasts of return, risk, and correlation[32] are combined to form what is called the mean-variance model. Its principles are key inputs into what is termed modern portfolio theory (MPT). The model computes the mix of portfolio assets that best meets the household's return-risk profile. The Markowitz model and its simplified off-shoot, the capital asset pricing model (CAPM), are provided in Web Appendix A: Modern Investment Theory.

We can conclude by saying that the most important concern to the investor is the risk of the overall portfolio, not the risk of individual securities. The portfolio risk will reflect the separate risks of each of its holdings and the degree to which the securities are correlated.

Total Portfolio Management (TPM)

The Markowitz portfolio approach is, at heart, a theory of how overall capital markets work using individual securities. The capital asset pricing model has similar intentions. In contrast, total portfolio management (TPM), presented by the author of this book, is a model of the individual household. It proposes that a household make investment decisions based not only on marketable financial securities but on all assets that it possesses. Although we have referred to portfolio analysis as employing securities, its approach can embrace all assets. In fact, Markowitz has made reference to doing so.[33] The concepts we have explained thus far in the chapter apply to TPM as well.

Under TPM, all household assets interact and their correlations are taken into account. Investment decisions that are made incorporate individual asset returns, risks, and the degree to which they are correlated. The traditional view is to treat financial assets such as stocks and bonds separately from other household assets. While this solely financial asset approach can be considered too narrowly focused, it is established thinking, and we have followed it in this chapter. The other components of TPM—real assets, human and human-related assets, and liabilities—have or will be discussed in other chapters. We will deal with total portfolio management with its full integration of all assets in Chapter 18.

IMPLEMENT PORTFOLIO MANAGEMENT DECISIONS

We have now examined all the major factors that enter into the asset allocation process. The next part of operations, portfolio management actions, can be viewed as the decision-making-implementation arm of the asset allocation process. We will assume that goals and evaluation of personal characteristics, including such factors as time horizon and risk tolerance, have been established. The remaining steps are listed below and then described separately.

1. Establish an active or passive management style.
2. Construct a strategic asset allocation.

---

[32] Actually, correlation is part of portfolio risk and risk in this sentence refers to individual asset risk. It is segregated in this manner to differentiate it from the capital asset pricing model, which simplifies correlation to individual asset relative to the overall market, thereby bypassing individual-asset correlations with other portfolio assets.

[33] Markowitz called them exogenous assets. For further details, see Harry Markowitz and Peter Todd, *Mean-Variance Analysis in Portfolio Choice and Capital Markets* (New Hope, PA: Frank J. Fabozzi Associates, 2000).

Practical Comment Use of Modern Investment Approach

Risk-return analysis, MPT, CAPM, and the efficient market hypothesis are very controversial among academics and practitioners alike. Many claim that the theories don't work in day-to-day analysis and cite academic tests that bear this out.[34] On the other hand, some advisors employ MPT and CAPM procedures, more often as an input to decision making than as the sole decision tool. Even if it doesn't fully work,[35] it is hard to disagree with the thought that risk and return are related.

[34] See Eugene Fama and Kenneth French, "The CAPM Is Wanted, Dead or Alive," *Journal of Finance* 51, no. 5 (December 1996), pp. 1947–58.

[35] One reason could be the lack of inclusion of all household asset categories within TPM.

The majority of financial planners and other investment advisors engage in portfolio management and attempt to diversify portfolios. Most do not use Markowitz portfolio theory techniques that imply that you can find the single best portfolio for a household. Instead, planners often separate clients by risk tolerance—for example, into conservative, moderate, and aggressive categories—and often make even greater distinctions. Typically, they then provide mixes of stocks and bonds to implement portfolios. As you will see in the next section, specific asset allocations are usually based on that stock-bond mix.

3. Develop a tactical asset allocation.
4. Select individual assets.
5. Finalize and implement the portfolio.
6. Review and update the portfolio.

Establish an Active or Passive Management Style

At this point in the process, since passive management may provide fewer investment choices, it is important to decide whether the portfolio is to be actively or passively managed. Underlying the active approach is the belief that changes can add to portfolio performance. With passive management, no attempt is made to anticipate future events. Changes under passive management are made to maintain a constant asset allocation and risk profile, not to improve returns, and costs are kept very low. As mentioned, index-type assets such as index funds are often used in implementing a passive management approach.

Construct a Strategic Asset Allocation

Asset allocation is the percentage makeup of the portfolio by asset type. Strategic asset allocation is the normal portfolio makeup over the longer term. The strategic allocation process begins by establishing allowable asset categories. This might include small, mid, and large cap stocks; international equities; bonds; and so on, or their mutual fund counterparts. Other categories may be eliminated, such as tax-free municipal bonds if the household's marginal tax bracket is modest, or private partnerships if the amount of assets or tolerance for risk is low. The strategic asset allocation stresses diversification.

The strategic allocation should be strongly influenced by the household goals and risk profile. For example, if the goals can easily be achieved, a conservative asset allocation may be used even though the household can tolerate a more aggressive one. A shorter-term goal also will dictate a more conservative allocation. The overall risk tolerance, as discussed, can incorporate many factors. As a rule, the younger we are, the more aggressive the allocation. An example of strategic allocations by age and presumed tolerance for risk is given in Table 9.5.

Practical Comment Active versus Passive Investing

The relative performance of active and passive management can vary over an investment cycle. Therefore, the popularity of one over the other can change at any point in time. However, as mentioned, the disagreement concerning approach is unlikely to end soon. The proponents of an active approach point to past opportunities and investment managers who they believe have systematically outperformed the overall market. They say that passive management results in mediocre and even below-average performance after the deduction of expenses. The passive managers either think it is not possible to outperform after deductions of expenses or don't feel they can or want to expend the time to do so and don't want to delegate the job to active managers.

Develop a Tactical Asset Allocation

A tactical asset allocation modifies the breakdown of the portfolio to attempt to profit from current circumstances. When constructing a tactical asset allocation for the current economic environment, the outlook for asset categories and prevailing asset valuations will be included. Often, maximum allowable deviations of the tactical asset allocation from the strategic one will be set. As conditions change, allocations are altered. Where a passive approach is taken, a tactical asset allocation is not performed. Some people and advisors skip the tactical asset allocation as well, preferring a fixed strategic allocation at all times.

Select Individual Assets

Once the strategic and tactical asset allocations are established, individual assets[36] are selected for each category. Clearly, the goal is to select the assets that provide the highest returns for the overall risk taken.

Finalize and Implement the Portfolio

At this point, the entire portfolio is checked overall. The following questions may be asked: Is the portfolio consistent with the overall tolerance for risk? Can risk be reduced with little sacrifice in return? Simply put, am I properly diversified and will my portfolio produce

[36] As one entity, a mutual fund is also considered an individual asset.

TABLE 9.5
Strategic Asset Allocation

Asset Category	Young/ Fairly Aggressive	Middle-Aged/ Moderate Risk	Retired/ Lower Risk
Stocks			
Small cap	15%	10%	5%
Mid cap	10%	5%	2%
Large cap	25%	30%	20%
International	20%	15%	5%
REIT	5%	5%	3%
Total Stock	**75%**	**65%**	**35%**
Bonds			
Short-term	5%	5%	10%
Intermediate	5%	10%	25%
Long-term	0%	5%	10%
High-yield	10%	5%	5%
Total Bond	**20%**	**25%**	**50%**
Money market	**5%**	**10%**	**15%**
Total	**100%**	**100%**	**100%**

attractive returns? Further changes may be made to accomplish these objectives. When finished, the portfolio is implemented.

An example of the diversification process by financial asset category is given below.

Example 9.7

Steve, who is 45, has set up his own strategic asset allocation based on his tolerance for risk. He believes that inflation will be higher than what investors expect and observes that small cap funds have valuations well below their historical level relative to mid and large company stocks. He further believes that large cap stock valuations are high relative to historical levels. He does not think bond-fund managers can predict interest rates but believes they can take advantage of relative valuations among sectors of the bond market. He has two short-term bond funds he is looking at: one has had the highest absolute return, the other the highest risk-adjusted return. He also has two small cap funds that are almost identical in most respects. An exception is that one has a correlation with the S&P 500 of .90 and the other a .30 correlation.

Steve's strategic and tactical asset allocations are shown below along with an explanation of the difference.

Asset Category	Strategic Asset Allocation	Tactical Asset Allocation	Explanation
Stocks			
Small cap	10%	20%	Attractive relative valuation
Mid cap	5%	5%	
Large cap	20%	10%	Unattractive relative valuation
International	15%	15%	
REIT	5%	5%	
Total Stock	**55%**	**55%**	
Bonds			
Short-term	5%	10%	Not as affected by higher inflation
Intermediate	15%	5%	Higher-than-expected inflation is anticipated to result in weak performance
Long-term	5%	0%	Same as intermediate, only even weaker results
Inflation-indexed	0%	10%	Benefits from higher inflation
High-yield	10%	5%	Can be negatively affected by higher interest rates
Total Bond	**35%**	**30%**	
Money market	**10%**	**15%**	Will easily reflect expected increases in current interest rates
Total	**100%**	**100%**	

Even though it had a lower absolute return, Steve selected the short-term bond fund with the highest risk-adjusted performance knowing that there typically is no "free lunch" for returns as far as investment performance is concerned. He also selected the small cap fund with the lower correlation coefficient, which he figured would reduce his portfolio risk while adding to the asset category he preferred.

REVIEW AND UPDATE THE PORTFOLIO

As time moves on, the economic outlook and relative valuations change, as do household circumstances. Both passive and active investors must take into account current actual allocations relative to strategic ones and consider making changes. Active investors may want to purchase newly attractive securities and sell old ones that no longer fit performance requirements.

Practical Comment Understanding the Portfolio Concept

People often have difficulty fully understanding the overall portfolio concept.[37] They can appreciate the idea of diversifying to reduce risk. However, the idea of correlations affecting portfolio risk and purchase decisions that are significantly influenced by the goal of achieving lower correlations among holdings can be hard to convey. People often think one asset at a time. They ask, "Why shouldn't I select the best-performing assets I can?" They will point to an individual security that lags behind other portfolio holding performances in a strong economic and stock market environment and say, "Shouldn't I get

rid of that dog?" The answer may be no because that asset will reduce overall portfolio fluctuations and could outperform in other economic and stock market environments.

It can help to introduce the idea of portfolio blending. Performance is expressed not in return alone but in risk-return terms. An investment is purchased not because of its appeal by itself but due to its effect on overall portfolio performance. A number of examples in daily life, while not exactly parallel, help explain this point.

Type	Explanation
Basketball	A team with four high-scoring, high-ego players may benefit from adding a player who cannot shoot a ball himself but knows how to pass well and can keep the others happy and productive.
Dressing style	Individual items of clothing may be attractive in themselves, but care must be taken that they don't clash when putting together a daily "dressing portfolio"—for example, wearing a plaid shirt, tie, and jacket all at one time.
Salad	Vinegar might be an unpleasant taste by itself but can produce a pleasing taste in a salad of fresh vegetables.

The financial point of placing less-correlated assets into a portfolio to reduce portfolio risk, even when understood by clients, is often forgotten and therefore should be revisited frequently.

[37] The work by Friend and Blume shows that individuals who are not well diversified would support this contention. See Marshall E. Blume and Irwin Friend, "The Asset Structure of Individual Portfolios and Some Implications for Utility Functions," *Journal of Finance* 30, no. 2 (May 1975), pp. 585–603.

A performance evaluation reviews past results. It should be done for an existing portfolio with the goal of answering the following questions: "How did I do?" "What were the reasons for the under- or overperformance?" "What can I do to improve future performance?" The evaluation also should be done when examining a potential future holding, as, for example, a mutual fund. The questions to be answered in both cases are somewhat similar: "How did the investment do?" "What were the reasons for the under- or overperformance?" "What does it suggest for future performance?" "How does or will that fund and its performance fit into my portfolio?"

Back to Dan and Laura
FINANCIAL INVESTMENTS

Dan and Laura came prepared for our discussion on financial investments. They had thought about the investments they were attracted to and mentioned to me that they believed that smaller companies were to their liking in general and that they considered them particularly attractive at that point in time. They also believed that biotechnology had great potential, as did China, and wanted my opinion about investing in all these areas. They were concerned that inflation was going to increase over time.

Our discussion on tolerance for risk was a little more difficult. Dan was fairly conservative, saying they didn't have enough money and couldn't afford to lose it. He was concerned over the fluctuations in the current prices of stocks, preferring a mix of 40 percent stock, 60 percent bond. Laura, on the other hand, said that investing represented a terrific opportunity for those willing to take it. If they lost money, they had plenty of time to make it up. She wanted 80 percent in stocks and 20 percent in bonds. She said Dan was always concerned over the current price of a stock. He replied that she was always optimistic. After discussion among the three of us—I had the feeling that we all knew what the outcome would be at the beginning of the conversation—we decided on a 60 percent stock, 40 percent bond mix.

They had their own economic scenario with normal economic growth but believed that higher inflation than generally expected would arrive fairly soon. They knew that I was a financial planner who provided ongoing investment management services and asked for some information on how I would manage their money. However, they wanted to maintain control of their assets until the financial plan was completed before deciding on investment management services. In the meantime, they would implement the recommendations I gave to them.

We are up to the investments portion of the financial plan. I am going to incorporate in it most of the basics of an investment policy statement for both of you as part of the presentation. The investment policy statement serves as a guide for the management of your portfolio. This statement, which I will present informally, includes many of the steps in my asset allocation process for you. It ensures that we are "on the same page" as to your personal requirements and our investment approach for you going forward.

Before we do that, however, I want to review some overall capital market variables. The first is that the outlook for stocks and bonds is strongly influenced by risk and return. In general, the higher the risk, the higher the return. For some, it indicates that most securities at any point in time are efficient; their current prices fairly reflect the outlook. For example, if it looks to you as though a bond had a very attractive yield and therefore high cash return, chances are it is because it has a higher risk attached to it.

On the other hand, other people believe in mean reversion. Those people, many of whom have a value-oriented style of investing, buy out-of-favor stocks that are "bargains." They have the conviction that a disciplined person can take advantage of the temporary mispricing of securities. Mean reversion implies that stocks that are temporarily selling for a lower price than they should will return to their fair value over time.

There are, of course, other styles of investing that attempt to take advantage of what are thought to be opportunities in individual securities or even the overall market at certain points in time. One, purchasing the fastest-growing companies available, is called the growth style of investing.

There is a significant difference between efficient markets and mean reversion and between value and growth investing. Efficient market people believe you cannot consistently outperform the market; they prefer a passive approach to investing. They emphasize keeping expenses low and concentrating on proper diversification to reduce risk. Efficient market people generally use index funds to implement. People who employ mean reversion, one form of value investing, generally believe that strong research and control over emotional reactions can lead to better-than-average returns.

This brings us to your asset allocation and my investment policy statement for you. You have several goals that we deal with in other parts of the plan, but you're overriding one for our purposes today is your desire to retire in 20 years. Thus, your time frame is longer term. Liquidity is not as large an issue for you, as we have stated, but not for the retirement monies already accumulated and to be invested in the future. We will be setting aside an emergency fund over time. In the interim, as you have indicated to me earlier, you can borrow from Laura's parents for any emergency.

You seek above-average returns and your risk tolerance, while somewhat different for each of you, is nonetheless consistent with that objective. In other words, your risk-return objectives are in line.

We will be thinking of tax consequences as part of our investment policy. For example, given their higher after-tax returns, tax-free municipal bonds of your state are likely to be used.

Some people have restrictions on types of stocks, such as not allowing tobacco stocks, but you have not indicated any such requirement.

For the time being, we will limit purchases to mutual funds. Mutual funds, in my opinion, provide the best balance of capable management and relatively low cost. They allow anyone to diversify widely to reduce risk and to take advantage of fund manager expertise in specific sectors of the bond and stock markets.

We will employ an active approach to portfolio management. By portfolio management, we mean looking at your financial assets overall, making sure that they fit your return and risk requirements as represented by your asset allocation. Our approach of diversifying widely can handle the sometimes overlooked part of supervision—correlation.

Correlation indicates the relationship between assets, the degree to which they react similarly to the same variables. All other things being equal, the lower the correlation, the lower the portfolio risks. For example, investments in Japanese stocks are going to be less correlated with U.S. ones than one large-sized economically sensitive U.S. industry is with another—say, retail stores and appliance stocks.

I employ a diversified style of investing, but with a value tilt. I base the portfolio on a longer-term investment horizon. An asset allocation provides the average weighting of securities by category in the portfolio over time. The average percentage weightings over the longer term are called a strategic asset allocation. I do not try to time the market. I do attempt to take advantage of disparities in valuations at the present time.

In other words, I try to moderately overweight those areas that appear to be attractive at the present time. For example, I overweighted international stocks because they seem to be fairly priced and provide attractive returns. On the other hand, I underweighted REITs, which, in my opinion, are overvalued at the moment. Unlike timing the market, which implies turnover for short-term profit, this approach expects that over the intermediate or longer term, our overemphasis of certain areas will lead to higher returns. I call the portfolio breakdown established our tactical asset allocation.

Based on those principles and an overall economic scenario, I have constructed your strategic and tactical asset allocations. They are shown in the accompanying table. Notice the wide diversity of asset classes in both stocks and bonds. In bonds they range in risk from short-term bonds, being the safest, to high-yield bonds, the most risky.

Similarly, for stocks they extend from larger capitalization companies, which have the least risk and lowest return, to small capitalization companies, with the greatest risk and highest potential return. Notice also that I have included an allocation in international securities. Part of that allocation includes an investment in a China fund; I believe the securities in this fund to be reasonably priced currently relative to prospects. International securities have the potential to lower your portfolio's overall volatility, even if they themselves are more volatile.

Based on our discussions, I have provided a breakdown of a diversified portfolio of 60 percent stocks, 40 percent bonds and money market funds. It stands in contrast to your current portfolio, which has 75 percent concentrated in large cap stocks and the rest in cash. The long-term bond area has not been given an allocation since, historically, intermediate-term bonds over longer periods have provided about the same returns but with lower risk.

In view of your concern about inflation, I have placed more money in the short-term area and underweighted intermediate-term bonds in the tactical allocation. This allocation is more oriented to the current outlook. Shorter-term bonds will be affected less than intermediate ones in any rise in inflation.

My recommendations will come in the form of mutual funds. I believe that funds offer an attractive alternative of expert management and ability to diversify widely.

In sum, I have provided a diversified portfolio of investment that should assist you in achieving sufficient funds to meet your life cycle needs.

Asset Category	Current Allocation	Strategic Allocation	Tactical Allocation	Standard Deviation 10-Year[1]
Stocks				
Small cap	–	10%	14%	21.0
Mid cap	–	8%	10%	20.7
Large cap	75%	20%	18%	17.8
International	–	17%	20%	17.8
REIT	–	5%	3%	14.1
Total Stock	**75%**	**60%**	**65%**	**18.4**
Bonds				
Short-term	–	10%	15%	2.1
Intermediate	–	15%	8%	4.1
Long-term	–	5%	0%	5.7
High-yield	–	5%	7%	7.9
Total Bond	**0%**	**35%**	**30%**	**4.6**
Money market	**25%**	**5%**	**5%**	**0.4**
Total	**100%**	**100%**	**100%**	**12.7**

[1] 10-year data from Morningstar® Principia® for the period February 28, 1993, through February 28, 2003.

Summary

Financial investments are generally the instruments for building assets for your future use. Without them, you would have difficulty funding those things you care about.

- Financial assets consist primarily of stocks, bonds, and mutual funds.
- Having an appropriate asset allocation is the goal of most investors.
- Important personal factors in asset allocations include time horizon, liquidity needs, available current resources, projected future resources, taxes, restrictions, and risk tolerance.
- Risk and return are basic finance concepts. In theory, the two factors move in proportion.
- A security's expected rate of return includes the risk-free rate plus a risk premium.
- The efficient market hypothesis indicates that efforts to systematically outperform the market will be unsuccessful.
- Mean reversion indicates that there may be patterns in stocks that can lead to outperformance.
- Portfolio management looks at all financial investments overall in making decisions, and the Markowitz approach includes correlations among them.
- Total portfolio management incorporates all assets and liabilities and includes correlations in its risk-return framework.
- A strategic asset allocation looks at investment policy over the long term, while a tactical one makes cyclical changes based on opportunities at the time.

Key Terms

active approach to investing, *240*
asset allocation, *226*
blue chips, *236*
bonds, *236*
correlation coefficient, *241*
cyclical stocks, *237*
defensive stocks, *237*
efficient market hypothesis (EMH), *234*
growth stocks, *237*

growth style of investing, *239*
index fund, *240*
insurance risk, *226*
investment risk, *226*
maturity date, *236*
mean reversion, *235*
mutual fund, *238*
passive approach to investing, *240*

portfolio, *241*
risk premium, *233*
risk tolerance, *229*
speculative investments, *238*
systematic risk, *232*
unsystematic risk, *232*
value style of investing, *239*

Web Sites

http://finance.yahoo.com
Yahoo's Finance Portal
This site provides a wide array of financial information for students and beginning investors. It presents key statistics, financial statements, analyst opinions, news and charts for the majority of U.S. and world market stocks, mutual funds, ETF, indices, and options. It also contains links to a number of topics in investing and personal finance.

http://www.naip.com
National Association of Investment Professionals
This organization provides information geared to the interests and needs of individuals working in the financial services industry. The site has links to resources of securities laws, rules, and regulation information. It covers topical information for investment professionals.

http://www.investopedia.com
Investing Glossary
Information for students and beginners in the finance field. The site contains a rich dictionary with finance term definitions, explanatory tutorials, useful articles, finance exam information, and tools such as financial calculators and free trading kits.

http://www.investorguide.com
Investor Information
While the previous Web site is more educational, this site offers current market information, quotes and charts, news and comments, and research company information. It also has a glossary of finance terms.

Web sites of U.S. and world stock exchanges include

http://www.nyse.com
New York Stock Exchange

http://www.nasdaq.com
NASDAQ

http://www.amex.com
American Stock Exchange

http://www.tse.or.jp/english/index.shtml
Tokyo Stock Exchange

http://www.londonstockexchange.com
London Stock Exchange

Questions

1. Explain why under CAPM company risk can be diversified away?
2. Under the EMH, can you outperform the market?
3. Under the weak form of the EMH, if you are given the following recent day price performance:

Day	2 Days Ago	The Day before Yesterday	Yesterday	Today
Price	6	7	8	9

   is the likely future performance greater than nine? Why?
4. Under the semi-strong form of the EMH, should you read an annual report? Why?
5. Investing abroad has substantial individual asset risk. Why invest in it then?
6. Why can real estate be an attractive portfolio holding?
7. What are the strengths of mutual funds?
8. What are the weaknesses of mutual funds?
9. What types of investments are most appropriate for short-term needs?
10. What kinds of investments are best suited to saving for the down payment on a house to be made in three years?
11. What types of investments are suited to retirement planning at age 67 assuming the person is 55 and has an average risk tolerance?
12. What are the advantages of a passive approach to investing?
13. How has mutual fund performance compared with overall indexes? Why do you think that is the case?
14. How are income taxes determined for mutual funds?
15. Stock A and stock B have no correlation. Does that mean we don't have to include correlation in calculating portfolio return? Explain.
16. Stocks C and D move in opposite directions. Does that mean they have no correlation? Explain.

Problems

9.1 Gennaro purchased a stock for $24 that paid $2.00 at the end of each year in dividends (dividends remained level over time). He sold it four years later for $28 at the time of the last dividend payment. What was his IRR?

9.2 A stock has an expected rate of return of 9 percent and the risk-free rate is 3 percent. What is the risk premium?

CFP® Certification Examination Questions and Problems

9.1 "Stock prices adjust rapidly to the release of all new public information." This statement is an expression of which one of the following ideas?

    a. Random walk hypothesis.

    b. Arbitrage pricing theory

    c. Semi-strong form of the EMH

    d. Technical analysis

9.2 If the client needs to accumulate wealth but is risk-averse, which of the following is the most crucial action the planner must take to have the client achieve the goal of wealth accumulation? Advise investing the client's current assets

    a. In the products that will bring the highest return to the client regardless of risk.

    b. In products that produce high income for the client because fixed-income products are generally safe.

    c. In diversified mutual funds because of the protection that diversity provides.

    d. After determining the client's risk tolerance.

    e. In 100 percent cash equivalents in the portfolio because most software programs recommend this safe approach.

9.3 If the market risk premium were to increase, the value of common stock (everything else being equal) would

    a. *Not* change because this does *not* affect stock values.

    b. Increase in order to compensate the investor for increased risk.

    c. Increase due to higher risk-free rates.

    d. Decrease in order to compensate the investor for increased risk.

    e. Decrease due to lower risk-free rates.

9.4 Which of the following are nondiversifiable risks?

    1. business risk

    2. management risk

    3. company or industry risk

    4. market risk

    5. interest rate risk

    6. purchasing power risk

        a. 1 and 3 only

        b. 1 and 4 only

        c. 2 and 4 only

        d. 4 only

        e. 1, 2, and 4 only

9.5 Modern "asset allocation" is based upon the model developed by Harry Markowitz. Which of the following statements is/are correctly identified with this model?

    1. The risk, return, and covariance of assets are important input variables in creating portfolios.

    2. Negatively correlated assets are necessary to reduce the risk of portfolios.

    3. In creating a portfolio, diversifying *across* asset type (e.g., stocks and bonds) is less effective than diversifying *within* an asset type.

    4. The efficient frontier is relatively insensitive to the input variable.

        a. 1 and 2 only

        b. 1, 2, and 3 only

        c. 1 only

        d. 2 and 4 only

        e. 1, 2, and 4 only

Case Application

FINANCIAL INVESTMENTS

When it came to investments, Richard and Monica could agree on only one thing—that they would have a tough time reaching a decision on asset allocations and individual investments. Previously, Monica had deferred to Richard on investment matters. Given Richard's large recent investment loss, however, Monica was much more forceful in expressing her feelings. She thought that a 40 percent stock, 60 percent bond allocation fit, particularly given the lower level of accumulated wealth they now had. Richard, on the other hand, wanted 100 percent of the funds placed in stocks. He asked if it wasn't true that stocks always did better than bonds over the longer term. He said that to reach their goals, they needed some aggressive investments. Monica interrupted, saying it was just that "stocks-had-no-long-term-risk" mentality Richard had that led to their investment losses. Richard then volunteered that there was an oil stock, "Energy Gulch," a friend of his recommended that "couldn't lose." He wanted to place 20 percent of his money in it.

Case Application Questions

1. What do you think of the Richard and Monica argument?
2. Using the asset allocation alternatives listed in this chapter as a guide, what should their asset allocation be? Why?
3. What do you think of the Energy Gulch idea? Why?
4. Select one mutual fund you find attractive and give the reasons why you chose it.
5. Complete the investments section of the financial plan.

Chapter Ten

Risk Management

Chapter Goals

This chapter will enable you to:

- Evaluate risk management as an overall household approach.
- Distinguish the types of risk that people are exposed to.
- Demonstrate how risk modification leads to improved financial management.
- Analyze the central role insurance plays in reducing risk.
- Establish the common types of insurance available.
- Compare whole life and term insurance.

Dan and Laura indicated they were uncomfortable with their current overall risk profile. They felt they didn't have enough insurance. They asked that all their assets be reviewed to make sure they weren't exposed to potential losses. Dan said, "We want all of our assets protected against loss. Please examine our assets and tell us what changes need to be made."

Real Life Planning

The topic of risk management as we know it today did not exist 50 years ago. At that time, people and businesses were more concerned primarily with limiting their risks through the use of insurance. As businesses grew larger, their owners recognized that they were subject to a wide array of risks.

Businesses not only had the risk of fire or stolen property to concern them. In addition, there was risk that raw materials' prices would skyrocket or that their product line would meet more competition. There was risk of a sharp drop in the stock market. If they didn't treat their employees well, there was risk of a strike or that sharp employees would leave.

The more that businesses looked at it, the more they saw that they had to assess their risk overall. In effect, they had a portfolio of risks. It called for a central focus on the problem. Many of the more dynamic companies hired a risk manager. Instead of focusing principally on negotiating contracts with insurance carriers, this person, or, in larger firms, this department, concentrated on risks in many aspects of the company's businesses. Risk managers' responsibilities included safety practices and educational procedures for employees, and sometimes they were even given a voice in operating matters like limiting investing in buildings in less developed countries. Their goal was to bring down losses in the company at a tolerable cost.

At about the same time, the field of finance began to broaden considerably. The advent of computers enabled companies to better measure their risk financially. New financial instruments like options and swaps and more futures-market alternatives added to the choices companies had to limit their risk.

The field of risk management had come into its own. The professional society for risk managers changed its name from the American Society of Insurance Management to the Risk and Insurance Management Society, Inc., in 1975. Occasionally, you may still hear people talk of risk management as the equivalent of insurance. However, an increasing number of people recognize that it is a far broader topic. Risk management can now be looked at overall as well as risk by risk.

This risk management approach is also relevant to individuals and households. Obviously, it isn't done in as sophisticated a way as it is in a large business, but the household still needs to look at all types of risks and to use the tools that are available to deal with them. Our objective is to reduce the risk that negative events could result in the household not meeting its goals.

OVERVIEW

The financial planning objective in risk management is to identify exposures that can create roadblocks to goal achievement or otherwise can be handled more effectively. People are often understandably nervous about the risks they encounter in daily life. Their concerns may mount as they age, if only because they have fewer opportunities to recover from what may be a major financial loss. Proper risk management practices should start at a young age.

These desirable practices are described in this chapter. We begin with a discussion of risk management in theory as well as in practical terms. The balance of the risk management portion of the chapter is presented as a flow process. It shows you step by step how to establish and implement a risk management program.

Information on overall types of insurance and their use is then provided. Finally, life insurance is discussed in some detail. After reading this portion of the chapter, you should be able to determine life insurance suitability and evaluate the alternatives. In Chapter 11 you will read about other kinds of insurance.

We can conclude by saying that risk management is a very broad topic affecting most of the things that you do. To refer to it simply as insurance does not do justice to the topic.

RISK MANAGEMENT

Risk Management Theory

Risk management in theory can be viewed as the study of methods for controlling portfolio risk. As discussed in the last two chapters, the portfolio for individuals consists of all their household assets. A variety of risk management tools are available to modify household risk. The ones you select will depend on such factors as the makeup of all of your household assets and your risk profile. The goal is to have the highest quality of life possible, given your tolerance for risk.

There is no grouping of assets or other techniques that can fully eliminate risk in your portfolio. Perhaps the biggest difficulty in doing so is the lack of a full hedge for the lifetime work-related income streams we call human assets. We cannot fully diversify human assets.[1] There are usually only one or two wage earners who make up human assets possible per household. Products with negative correlation with human assets, such as unemployment insurance to cover the possibility of layoff and health insurance

---

[1] For an explanation of the theory of hedging human asset risk, see Ney Brito, "Portfolio Selection in an Economy with Marketability and Short Sales Restrictions," *Journal of Finance* 33, no. 2 (May 1978), pp. 589–601.

for sickness, are available but do not control all the risks an individual worker is subject to. In addition, we cannot hedge away overall market risk—for example, the risk of a plague or an economic or stock market collapse.

There is usually a significant cost to purchasing these negatively correlated assets. This cost tends to reduce your household income, which we can call returns on your household assets. You purchase these assets because they also reduce portfolio risk. For example, purchase of automobile insurance reduces the amount of money available for spending on those items that give you pleasure. On the other hand, it eliminates the possibility of non-reimbursement if your car is stolen or, worse yet, having to fund a personal injury lawsuit in connection with an auto accident.

In sum, risk management techniques are methods of modifying a household's portfolio risk. They take into account all the assets of the portfolio and the risks attached to them. Importantly, an overall portfolio risk is established. Household members compare current portfolio risk with their preferences for risk. They then select the most efficient risk management technique to alter their portfolio and bring it in line with their own tolerance for risk. In revising their portfolio, they establish a risk-return strategy that attempts to optimize their portfolio income and brings about the highest standard of living possible for them. This approach, particularly when it is done in a structured way, is a part of the foundation for total portfolio management.

Risk Management in Practical Terms

We have said that, in theory, risk is the probability of an outcome different from the one expected. Outcomes above and below expectations are considered risky. In practice, we have a different definition. In practice, we are only concerned with outcomes that are below expectations; these are the outcomes that produce losses. Therefore, we can view risk in practice as the probability of a loss or an outcome that is below expectations.

People are exposed to risk in every aspect of their lives. **Risk management in practical terms** can be defined as the process by which we identify risks and control them so that we are able to achieve individual goals. Notice we use the word *control*. As we've said, we cannot hope to eliminate risk entirely; we can only attempt to keep risk within acceptable ranges of impact on our lives.

As you know, financial planning develops a path for achieving household goals and risk creates obstacles in that path. When engaged in financial planning, you must first identify risks, knowing that losses in any one area can jeopardize overall household goals. Given significant risks in one area of the portfolio, household members may make adjustments elsewhere. For example, if one wage earner has a very lucrative but risky job, the household may set aside extra money in household savings to compensate for the possibility of a layoff. Then the ways of dealing with the risks should be considered and the most efficient method selected. As you will see, sometimes it is best to just reduce or even assume the risk by doing nothing.

The Risk Management Process

Risk management is an organized process that looks at practices in broad terms and works its way to the most specific details. A household's members may be in charge of specific procedures such as obtaining needed insurance policies, but all people practice risk management sometimes, even when they don't realize it.

The six steps of this process are outlined in Figure 10.1 and then discussed individually.

Develop Objectives

Objectives determine the scope of the risk management process. Do you want to select one area or examine all household risks?

FIGURE 10.1
**Risk Management
Process**

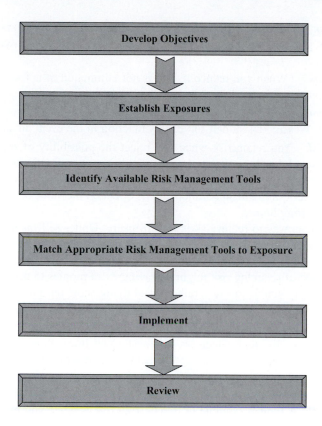

Establish Exposures

Each area of household assets has its own risks. We can separate them into financial and nonfinancial assets. Nonfinancial assets may, in turn, be segregated into human-related assets and real assets. For risk management purposes, we can call human-related and real asset exposures personal and property risks, respectively. As we will discuss, our liabilities also contain risk. A risk that we are concerned about for planning purposes is one that can significantly affect assets or cash flows.[2] The risk of your wallet or handbag being stolen is often present but, though frustrating should it happen, is not of the consequence of your car being stolen.

Identify Available Risk Management Tools

There are many techniques available to you in managing the overall risk of the household. Some of them have little or no cost. For example, being careful to lock the door to your apartment before going out involves no cash outlay and minuscule cost of time. If you lock the door, you may avoid loss and the cost of higher apartment owner's insurance.

Common risk management approaches are discussed below.[3]

---

[2] The TPM approach generally capitalizes cash flows as assets.

[3] These methods assume that the goal is to reduce risk. That approach is generally valid for assets designed for household usage but may not be so for investments intended for growth purposes, in other words, for real and human-related but not financial assets. For financial assets, risk-return principles hold, and we may actually want to increase risk. We can control financial risk by diversifying, as discussed here, or by borrowing money or adding to the bond or money market portion or through more sophisticated financial instruments. We will proceed with the risk-reduction assumption for the balance of the chapter.

Avoid Risk   Under the avoid risk method, you seek to eliminate exposure to risk. If there is risk that you will be injured if you cross the street on a red light, you may wait until the light is green.

Reduce Risk   When you reduce risk, it is not eliminated; it is lessened. When you exercise and eat the right foods, you reduce the risk of becoming ill.

Reduce Potential Loss   When you reduce potential loss, you lessen the damage should a loss occur. Wearing a seat belt serves this function in the event an accident takes place.

Retain Risk   You retain risk when you reject the possibility of reducing or eliminating risk but instead decide to absorb the potential loss yourself. Of course, in some cases, you are forced to retain risk because it is uninsurable. For example, there is no direct insurance against a deteriorating neighborhood and its effect on the value of your house. You have to consider shifting homes.

A desirable way to retain risk is to self-insure. Under self-insurance, you can actively set aside money to fund any losses should that occur.[4] The money may be part of a pool of capital to fund losses that are both insurable and uninsurable, called *precautionary savings*. One instance of retaining risk might be saving extra monies to use in case physically you are temporarily unable to work, rather than buying short-term disability insurance.

Diversify   With this method, assets are diversified so that the impact of an unfavorable outcome for any one asset is reduced. You diversify when you allocate your marketable assets to many different categories—domestic and international stocks including small, medium, and larger-sized companies. When you get married and both you and your spouse work, you are diversifying assets.

Transfer Risk   When you take the possibility of loss and give it to someone else, you transfer risk. A typical example of transferring risk is when you purchase a homeowner's policy that insures against the loss of your home being destroyed by a fire. You have transferred your risk to the insurance company.

Sharing Risk   When you share risk, the transfer of risk is not always a full one. Some risk may be retained, thereby limiting, though not eliminating, a risk. For example, when you coinsure medical policies, sometimes 20 percent of the risk is retained. When you transfer some risk and retain a part of it, we call that sharing risk. Sharing risk may have the advantage of making you more careful about your actions, thereby reducing the insurance company's exposure to loss. Therefore, the company is able to offer lower rates than it would without risk sharing.

Other Methods of Handling Risk   There are a host of other methods to aid in altering risk. Many are utilized principally for marketable securities and in businesses. They include options, futures, and swaps. These instruments can raise, lower, or eliminate risk. When you hedge risk, you transfer business risk to a third party. An example of hedging is a farmer who uses the futures market to sell a crop of corn today that won't be brought to market for many months. In doing so he eliminates the risk of a drop in corn prices from the date of futures sale until the date the corn is delivered.

Match Appropriate Risk Management Tools to Exposure

Different exposures call for separate risk management tools. You would not literally buy insurance against the risk of job obsolescence. Instead, you might go for additional training. Each major area of the household portfolio—human-related assets, real assets, and financial assets—has its own grouping of methods for managing them.

In determining the appropriate overall risk management tool, a number of factors should be taken into account. Among them are the cost of alternative risk management

---

[4] Often the term *self-insurance* is used more broadly to encompass all types of risk retention, not just instances in which money is physically set aside.

techniques, the amount and likelihood of loss, any convenience factors, and the risk tolerance of the person.

Example 10.1

Carol inherited an expensive diamond-studded necklace when her grandmother passed away. She indicated she had a moderate tolerance for risk.[5] She received an estimate on an insurance policy to cover her against theft; the cost was very high. On the other hand, there had been a number of recent break-ins in her neighborhood. She considered the alternative, keeping the necklace in a safe deposit box. It wasn't very convenient to go to the vault to take it out when needed. Then again, she wasn't likely to wear the piece more than once every two years at a wedding or other formal occasion. She was willing to absorb the risk of having it taken from her at that function, which, if she was careful, she believed would be relatively low. She decided that saving the insurance cost was preferable for her. She placed the necklace in the safe deposit box.

Let's look at the exposures by category and describe the risk management tools that apply.

Human-Related Assets   Human-related assets are generally the most significant portion of a household's portfolio for a large portion of its life cycle. The portfolio incorporates human assets, pension assets including Social Security, and gifts and bequests. Your human asset alone, which financially is derived from the income you earn but more broadly includes a variety of risks you are personally exposed to, can be listed separately. The risks include the following:

• *Longevity—premature death.* **Longevity** is the number of years you will live. Obviously, people generally cannot forecast this figure accurately. The insurance industry and the U.S. government do publish tables on average mortality and life expectancy. One is given in Table 10.1. However, as we know, there is great variation around the averages.

Longevity risk is the possibility of living beyond normal expectations or dying prematurely. If a person dies prematurely, the other members of the household may undergo a decline in, or elimination of, income. Life insurance provides payments to surviving household members to compensate for this loss. Taking company pensions out over both spouses' lives so that income continues at the death of the retired worker is another tool. Health measures discussed below can help as well.

• *Longevity—extended life.* The result of a good longevity program may be living an extra-long life. An extra-long life can result in a decline in your standard of living or running out of private funds. Establishing extra funds for the possibility of an extended life, a

[5] Many people indicate they have a moderate tolerance for risk. When someone says this, often more probing is needed. For this example, it is assumed that the self-description of moderate allowed assumption of the risk is associated with this situation.

TABLE 10.1
Number of Deaths, Death Rates, and Life Expectancy by Years[1]

Source: *National Vital Statistics System,* http://www.cdc.gov/nchs/nvss.htm.nvsr.htm.

Year	All Deaths	Death Rate	Life Expectancy
2003	2,448,288	832.7	77.5
2002	2,447,864	846.8	77.4
2001	2,416,425	854.5	77.2
2000	2,403,351	872.0	77.0
1990	2,148,463	938.7	75.4
1980	1,989,841	1,039.1	73.7
1970	1,921,031	1,222.6	70.8
1960	1,711,982	1,339.2	69.7
1950	1,452,454	1,446.0	68.2
1940	1,417,269	1,785.0	62.9

[1] Death rates are age-adjusted rates per 100,000 U.S. standard population; estimated life expectancy at birth in years.

form of precautionary savings, will help. Pension income provided by the U.S. government with Social Security benefits or by private businesses generates cash flow for the qualified worker throughout that person's life. In addition to Social Security, Medicare provides reimbursement for medical costs, which generally rise as one ages.

Medigap insurance pays for the portion of medical expenses not covered by the government, and long-term care insurance reimburses for assistance at home and payments to a nursing home if needed. Privately purchased annuities also reduce risk since payments are based on average life span but provide continuing income for extra-long lives, although they are generally not adjusted for inflation.

• *Health and disability.* Health and disability are expenses for sickness and inability to perform at your job. This, of course, can reduce your income and therefore human-asset value. Diet, exercise, and stress management can help here, as can safety measures to prevent illness and becoming disabled. Medical insurance can reimburse you for doctor and hospital expenses. Government-supplied and privately purchased disability insurance can partially reimburse you for income you have missed, whether due to poor health or accident-related occurrences.

• *Macro- and microeconomic risks.* **Macroeconomic risk** is the risk inherent in the general economy and **microeconomic risk** is the risk associated with the individual industry or company. Each can cause you to suffer from inflation, thereby causing declines in your real income. General economic, industry-, or company-related risks such as sluggish growth, overcapacity, technological obsolescence, or inefficient operations can result in layoffs or terminations.

Precautionary savings for such an event, government-supplied unemployment insurance, and diversification through an increase in the number of household members who work all can reduce economic risks related to your job.

In addition to your job income, there are human assets that are derived from your rights and relationships. Pensions both from governments and from the private sector are rights. Risks such as those from reduction in benefits or termination from a job can be reduced through diversification of savings, while inflation risk from flat business pension payments can be reduced through inflation-indexed bonds. Family relationships often result in gifts and bequests at the death of a loved one. While it may not be our focus, maintaining close relationships enhances the potential for ultimate sums.

Real Assets **Real assets** are tangible assets that the household owns. The most important one for nonrenters is the house they live in. Other items are automobiles, furnishings, and jewelry. Among other risks, the house is subject to fire, flood, termites, and accidents to people. The other household assets may be subject to accident and theft, while jewelry is subject to theft. Safety measures to prevent or reduce perils also help. Many houses carry homeowners' insurance, which includes protection for general possessions such as furniture, and most states require auto insurance. Other valuable assets such as jewelry may be insured separately or are self-insured.

Financial Assets **Financial assets** involve the ownership of assets that are typified by pieces of paper and are often marketable. Examples are stocks and bonds. Risk such as industry or company risk in investing can be covered by diversification strategies. Examples of risks that are difficult to diversify away are weakness in the economy or stock market and boosts in interest rates and inflation. Some examples of risk reduction techniques for financial assets include the use of assets less affected by overall economic factors such as food stocks, assets that are less correlated with the stock market such as real estate or gold, and others less influenced by inflation and interest rates such as inflation-indexed bonds or money market funds.

Liabilities   **Financial liabilities** are monies owed to others, as, for example, debt. Having significant debt increases household risk. When negative events reduce cash flows—for example, when job income declines or the cost of borrowing increases because of higher interest rates—individuals can become vulnerable. Reducing debt, placing caps on rates borrowed when they are available, and accumulating precautionary savings can serve to reduce this risk.

Intangible liabilities are less quantifiable current liabilities such as potential liabilities to third parties. For example, suppose someone slips on your sidewalk and sues you. A homeowner's policy protects against that type of occurrence. Care of personal property, such as shoveling your sidewalk after a snowstorm, and safety precautions also can be employed. Umbrella insurance can cover myriad types of lawsuits, and professional liability insurance can help protect you in our increasingly litigious society. In addition, education about individual exposures to third-party risk and what to do to avoid them can reduce your risk.

Although they don't carry the legal responsibilities to pay debt, nondiscretionary expenses also can be thought of as obligations and intangible liabilities. Overhead costs of your entire household can be subject to serious difficulties if, for example, you cannot support the cost of operating your house. Similarly, future goals that necessitate periodic funding such as sending children to college can be viewed as intangible liabilities. Without funding these additional expenditures, such as those for retirement, we cannot fulfill your standard-of-living requirements.[6] Long-term contracts and inflation-indexed bonds can help guard against inflation risk. You can buy insurance to protect tangible assets and establish precautionary savings to alleviate shortfalls from household operations.

Implement

Implementation is taking the action step. Sometimes people have difficulty implementing a risk management strategy. They procrastinate in beginning new personal practices or purchasing an insurance policy. Setting an implementation plan with specific dates to accomplish tasks can help.

Review

Risk management exposures can change. For example, a policy for household possessions may become insufficient over time because of inflation and new acquisitions. It is a good idea to review exposures at least once a year.

INSURANCE

We have discussed the role insurance plays and the various types of insurance as part of overall risk management. While we will maintain the risk management approaches, in this section we discuss insurance more extensively.

What It Is

Insurance is a method of transferring risk. Risk is shifted from the person exposed to it to the insurance company that assumes the risk for a fee. The process by which an insurance company agrees to assume the risk in return for a projected profit is called **insurance underwriting.** The insurance company can spread the risk among many policyholders. By using scientific methods, the company can estimate its exposure to loss and charge enough to make a profit. Our government also provides insurance in certain areas in the public interest.

---

[6] See Janet Bamford, "A New View," *Bloomberg Wealth Manager* (April 2004), pp. 72–82.

Insurance Theory and Practice

Insurance is one of the principal tools used to modify portfolio risk.[7] A good deal of academic research in risk management has been devoted to the efficiencies of insurance products. If insurance products were fully efficient, as they would be under theoretical assumptions—for example, assuming no transaction costs—the amount you paid for insurance would be exactly equal to the expected value of the loss. In other words, there would be no extra cost for the insurance company's overhead including its profits. Under that assumption, every risk-avoiding person would select insurance. Why? Because the insurance would provide a hedge against risk at no extra cost. However, as we discussed in looking at portfolio theory, as a practical matter, insurance policies involve extra expenditures. They provide lower risk at a cost. Let's look at some reasons why insurance products are not fully efficient in a financial sense.

Overhead Costs

Insurance companies have overhead costs to maintain and grow their businesses, pay out claims, and earn a profit. These costs are built into the price of insurance policies.

Incomplete Information

In a fully efficient market, all parties to a transaction share the same information. As a practical matter, insurance companies have incomplete information; in other words, they may have less knowledge about future claims than the applicant for an insurance policy. Specifically, less healthy applicants may pass insurance company screens. If the insurance company knew of their health problems, it would reject them.

A healthy purchaser of an insurance policy will bear part of the operating cost of any less healthy people in their pool of policyholders. They are negatively affected by a moral hazard. **Moral hazard** is the increased chance of loss due to policyholder extra risk arising from such things as undisclosed illness or faking injury after the policy is taken out.[8] Moreover, the insurance pool may reflect adverse selection over time. **Adverse selection** refers to people who have greater chance of loss, purchasing more insurance than they would normally do because of knowledge of their health that the insurance company does not possess. For example, under adverse selection, people who are healthy are more likely to discontinue insurance than those who are not. As with a moral hazard, healthy people who remain with the insurer suffer higher ongoing cost for the insurance policy since they are part of a less healthy population pool.

Example 10.2

Mary, age 45, was in good health at the time she purchased a term life insurance policy and remained so throughout the 20-year period she held it. Jim (age 45) had a family history of heart disease, and both his brothers died at age 49. The insurance company approved Jim's application for the same term policy without knowing about the vulnerability. He died at age 49 as well. Within the following 10 years, many other policyholders voluntarily dropped out, leaving a significant percentage of those remaining uninsurable due to ill health. Mary remained in good health.

Her cost may be significantly higher than people having her good health might suggest. In Mary's case, costs were higher because of the moral hazard arising from Jim's nondisclosure of his family history and subsequent premature death; Mary's premiums were also higher because

---

[7] For a study of insurance in a portfolio context, see David Mayers and Clifford Smith Jr., "The Interdependence of Individual Portfolio Decisions and the Demand for Insurance," *Journal of Political Economy* 91, no. 2 (April 1983), pp. 304–11; and Neil Doherty, "Portfolio Efficient Insurance Buying Strategies," *Journal of Risk and Insurance* 51, no. 2 (June 1984), pp. 205–24.

[8] For a finer definition of moral hazard and its distinction from morale hazard, see Chapter 11.

increasingly over time she was in a pool of policyholders with above-average mortality risk, an adverse selection problem.

Search Costs

These are costs that the person desiring to be insured undertakes to find out which policy is best. Most of the costs involve hours spent in selecting and processing the policy. According to economic theory, this search cost would be billed at the cost of time. In finance, this is called an opportunity cost. Self-insuring eliminates this cost and could allow the person to select either higher income through additional work or extra leisure time as an alternative.

Behavioral Factors

Some academic evidence suggests that humans may not always act efficiently in risk management activities. For example, one study has shown that people are underinsured for flood risk despite large government subsidies for that insurance. There is evidence that people prefer to have low deductibles instead of taking high deductibles, even when they are given economic incentive to do so. They may prefer to insure against small losses that have high probabilities of occurring and not larger losses with low probabilities of occurring. They tend to overestimate low probability losses and underestimate high probability losses. The way the risks are presented to people seems to matter.

These extra costs reduce somewhat the efficiency of insurance and result in some people substituting other risk management techniques such as self-insurance. However, as we know, people still find insurance attractive, particularly those who wish to protect themselves against catastrophic losses to the household. Purchasing insurance is an example of the trade-off between risk and return. Even with these extra costs, insurance may be the preferable alternative to reduce portfolio risk. However, it also reduces household returns. The degree to which insurance is used will depend on the household's tolerance for risk as it selects the risk-return mix that is preferable.

Types of Insurance Policies

As we discussed, insurance is used to shift part or all of the risk for certain exposures. The three major types of policies are private personal, private property, and government insurance. Personal policies have to do principally with insuring people and families. Property policies primarily involve insuring real assets that the household owns. Government can help both, but often that help only ensures a minimum standard of living for all Americans. The three types are shown in Table 10.2.

Insurance Providers

There are three major types of providers of insurance to individuals: the government, private insurance companies through group policies offered institutionally, and private insurance companies through individual policies offered by independent agents. Government policies tend to concentrate in items with widespread exposures by cross-sections or individual strata of society. The cost of these policies tends to be low or they are provided free of charge as social insurance that is part of the "safety net." Social Security may be an exception to low cost because it has income redistribution motives.

Group policies offered by private insurance companies to independent businesses for their employees, but also provided by insurance companies for fraternal or other organizations, often present the cheapest form of nongovernment contracts. Independent businesses can take advantage of low marketing costs, benefit from mass-volume efficiency, and may assist with screening and administrative costs, thereby further reducing premiums. There

TABLE 10.2
Types of Insurance

Insurance Categories	Coverage
Personal	
Life	Provides monies to others at the death of the insured.
Disability	Makes payments to replace income of the insured once the person is incapacitated.
Long-term care	Payment provided generally to the elderly, which assists those unable to care for themselves due to physical or mental conditions.
Health	Reimburses health-related expenditures.
Property	
Property and casualty	Pays for losses to home and possessions, and coverage for exposures to third-party losses.
Personal liability	Extends coverage for liabilities of many types of a personal nature.
Government	
Unemployment	Supplies income for a specified period upon job termination.
Social Security	Provides income, disability, and medical reimbursement after retirement. And, in the event of premature death, will provide payments to spouses, children, and parents being supported.
Other	
Welfare, food stamps, and medical preretirement	Allows support for lower-income Americans
Long-term care and nursing home assistance	Issued principally for support for disabled Americans, generally with few assets.

may be tax advantages to group policies when a company offers a policy[9] as well as company subsidization benefits.[10]

Individual policies bought directly from independent agents of insurance companies are often the most expensive but also the most flexible. Buyers can select the individual company and policy with the terms they prefer, which often will not be available in a group policy. Individual policies are portable, which allows the policyholder to maintain the policy at the same cost when leaving an employer. When a group policy is provided, the policy may end at employee separation or the person may be offered continuing coverage at a high rate. Changes in a person's health or in policy costs at that time may make new policies less attractive or even unavailable.

Analyzing an Insurance Company

An important factor in selecting among insurance policies is the quality of the company that offers the policy. The criteria to consider are

- *Financial strength.* How secure is the insurer's financial condition? Best, Standard and Poor's, Moody's, and other agencies evaluate and rate an insurer's finances. The ratings range from AAA to C with commensurate declines in your confidence in the insurance company's promise to reimburse you for losses you may have in the future.

- *Good operating sense.* Good operating sense contributes to financial strength. It measures how wise the company is in selecting risks it is willing to underwrite and how efficient it is in running its business and processing its claims. A more efficient company often has more competitive prices.

- *Service.* Important questions to ask are "How good is the company's service?" and "Does it pay out promptly and fairly on claims submitted?"

[9] Through tax-advantaged cafeteria plans, and others.

[10] In some instances, such as for disability insurance, when the company pays or subsidizes a policy, there may be a tax disadvantage at the time of payout for a claim.

Practical Comment Incorrect Insurance Coverage

A large number of people are either over- or under-insured. The amount will depend on such factors as the potential loss, cost, and the household's risk profile. The people who are overinsured throw large amounts of insurance at a problem that doesn't require it and hence have inefficient operations. For example, jewelry may be insured for more money than its replacement value. On the other hand, many people are underinsured. Their insurance for overall household possessions may have been set years ago before they bought many new, expensive items. In both cases, sitting down and estimating values and getting realistic appraisals can help.

POLICIES SHOULD BE READ

A great number of people sign insurance policies without reading them. This can lead to incorrect assumptions about what the policy covers. Most professionals recommend that the policies be read by the insured. It can prevent problems such as those of the surgeon who became disabled but could work in another field. Half of his policies had an own-occupation definition of disability that paid him substantial monies as long as he was unable to perform his existing occupation, while the other half lacked the definition and didn't pay anything. If he had read

the policies and consulted a qualified insurance professional or financial planner for the technical portions, all his policies would have had the desired own-occupation definition.

Where items in the contract are vague, sometimes the insurance company will supply elaborative language, which can be helpful at the time of a claim. If you consult an insurance agent, be aware that many knowledgeable insurance professionals have a CLU designation (Chartered Life Underwriter) and deal in life insurance and related fields; others have a CPCU (Chartered Property and Casualty Underwriter) and specialize in property and casualty fields.

CONSIDER THE COST OF REPORTING A CLAIM BEFORE DOING SO

When you have a claim against an insurance company, consider whether it is worth reporting it. Sometimes a claim, no matter how small, can trigger a potential rate increase or even a cancellation of the policy. Therefore, in deciding whether to report a claim, compare the cost of not reporting the claim with the extra cost of future coverage hikes. This line of thinking tends to favor purchasing policies with high deductibles and paying for frequent relatively small losses yourself.

- *Price.* As in other forms of merchandise offered to the consumer, price often varies by company policy. Price should be compared with quality to obtain the best value. When using price as a criterion, pay particular attention to financial strength.[11]
- *Other considerations.* Factors such as the size of the company, how long it has been in business, specialization, and so on, may enter into consideration. In addition, there is the question of location. Some states provide unofficial help for companies in financial difficulty in merging with stronger companies so that they don't default on their policies.

Insurance as an Asset

Insurance is commonly regarded as an expense, an appropriate designation. For certain uses, it can be viewed as an asset. This designation comes about because owning insurance can actually lead to higher net revenues.

As we know, decisions are often made on an overall portfolio basis based on risk-return principles and household risk tolerance. If insurance reduces risk in one area, it can allow greater risk-taking in another area. For example, a business that is able to hedge currency risk at an acceptable cost may go forward in a highly profitable overseas investment whereas it wouldn't do so otherwise.

[11] For certain types of insurance policies such as whole life insurance, it can be difficult to compare policies based on price.

Similarly, someone who is adventurous may be able to purchase life and disability insurance and then undertake a somewhat risky but lucrative overseas job assignment, whereas without the ability to provide funds for the household in case of an accident, he or she would decline the opportunity. Viewing the job as part of an overall household portfolio, insurance added value by increasing net profits as compared with a domestic position and therefore was an asset that built household equity.

SUMMARY OF RISK MANAGEMENT AND INSURANCE

We have described how important insurance can be in controlling risk. However, before we move into a fuller treatment of life insurance, remember again that it is only one tool in the risk management arsenal. The wide scope of risk management activities, as they pertain to individual exposures, is seen in Table 10.3.

TABLE 10.3 **Summary of Selected Risk Management Activities**

Asset Type	Example	Identify Risk	Selected Risk Management Tools
Human		Health	Diet, exercise, stress management, safety measures
		Illness or disability	Medical insurance, public and private disability insurance
		Longevity—early death	Life insurance, diet, exercise, safety measures
		Longevity—extra-long life	Precautionary savings, Social Security, government Medicare and private Medigap insurance, long-term-care insurance, annuities
		Lower income and layoff	Precautionary savings, government unemployment insurance, additional household wage earners
Human-Related		Integrity of pension assets[1]	Diversification of retirement savings, inflation-protected securities
		Anticipated gifts	Maintaining close relationship with asset owner
Real	House[2]	Fire, flood, accident	Safety measures, homeowners' insurance
	Car	Accident, theft	Safety measures, auto insurance
Other	Jewelry, collectibles	Theft	Safety measures, self-insure, individual possessions policy
Financial	Stocks, bonds	Macroeconomic inflation	Less cyclical equity assets, inflation-indexed bonds
		Interest rate and market fluctuation	Less correlated assets
		Industry	Diversification
		Company	Diversification
Liability	Financial	Financial leverage	Reduce debt
		Interest rate	Caps on rates charged, fixed-rate debt, precautionary savings
	Intangible	Third-party lawsuit	Umbrella insurance, professional liability insurance, education, maintenance of property, safety measures
		Maintenance	Inflation-indexed bonds, longer-term contracts, precautionary savings, insurance as given under tangible assets

[1] Fixed company pensions based on income and tenure, not 401(k) and other retirement after-tax savings established by individuals. Integrity expressed in inflation-adjusted terms. Social Security risk can include such factors as increased taxation for higher-income groups, outright emphasis on providing for those at the subsistence level, and increase in the age required for qualifying.
[2] And its possessions.

LIFE INSURANCE

Life Insurance Goals

In the balance of this chapter, we will explain life insurance, one of the country's most popular risk reduction techniques. You will learn about the various types of life insurance, how they work, the financial issues connected with them—including when they should be used—and how to determine the correct amount to have.

Life insurance is traditionally used to provide money that compensates for the death of a household wage earner. It is part of the case employed by those academicians who believe that the household is an economic and financial organization worth analyzing. Efforts focused exclusively on individual motivations, which indicate that people are concerned only about themselves, must explain why people carry life insurance. Its payments most frequently are made to other current or former members of the household after the death of the insured, who paid for the policy. If there are no other members of the household, there may be no need for life insurance.

As we mentioned, human-asset risk cannot be eliminated. Life insurance is one of the financial instruments that is negatively correlated with human assets, specifically, with the risk of premature death.[12] In terms of severity, mortality risk is one of the most serious risks a household may face. The current value of future job-related income from its principal benefit is often the most important asset by far in the household portfolio.[13]

The total amount of life insurance in force is given in Table 10.4.

In recent decades, life insurance has received more competition from other financial vehicles such as pension plans and mutual funds. Perhaps as a result, certain industry representatives have placed more emphasis on the investment aspects of whole life insurance. The monies you accumulate in a policy can be withdrawn or borrowed. Other sales representatives stress the pure risk management role of insurance as exemplified by a term policy.

Life insurance, together with disability insurance, unemployment insurance, and other human-asset risk management techniques, helps to significantly reduce human-asset risk. We can conclude this discussion by simply saying that life insurance helps diversify the portfolio of a household with two or more members and helps align it with the household's tolerance for risk.

Parts of an Insurance Policy

Every life insurance policy is made up of several parts, which determine the price you pay for the policy. They include mortality charge, investment return, and overhead expense.

[12] Life insurance pays out when death brings future job-related income and, therefore, human assets to zero.

[13] For a theoretical study of life insurance in a portfolio context, see Scott Richard, "Optimal Consumption, Portfolio and Life Insurance Rules for an Uncertain Lived Individual in a Continuous Time Model," *Journal of Financial Economics* 2, no. 2 (June 1975), pp. 187–203.

TABLE 10.4
Amount of Life Insurance in Force by Type of Insurance (1998)

Source: American Council of Life Insurers, *Life Insurers Fact Book, 2003.*

Type of Life Insurance	Face Amount	
	In Billions	As a Percentage of Total
Term insurance	$7,828	55%
Whole life	$2,535	17%
Universal life	$2,582	18%
Variable life	$1,282	9%
Other	$13	1%
Total	**$14,240**	**100%**

Mortality Charge

Mortality risk can be defined as the probability of dying. In any one year across the United States, the probability of dying for any one individual is relatively low. Of course, as you age, the probability rises, more steeply at age 60 and above. Life insurance has proven to be an attractive product because it compensates individuals for a generally unlikely event in any one year but one with potentially severe consequences.

At the same time, the insurance company diversifies its risk of any one person or group dying through having great numbers of policyholders. Insurance companies calculate the probability of death for any group of insurance holders scientifically and place that as one cost in the policy. They also engage in a screening process for insurance applicants, generally with the goal of keeping their annual mortality costs for a given segment of society below industry averages.

Investment Return

In the early years of a typical whole life policy, the annual premiums far exceed the mortality cost, providing the policy with extra cash to be invested. The return on this investment helps pay the mortality costs in later years, when these costs can far surpass the annual premiums.

Overhead Expense

These are the overhead costs that are added to the policy cost. They include such items as the costs to market the product and maintain the policy, and company profits. Low overhead cost per dollar of insurance revenues can be a measure of individual insurance company efficiency. This expense item is generally not separately reported but included in investment return figures.

Amount of Insurance

Life insurance is taken out to cover a need, the death of an income earner. It is a costly item because the possibility of loss of a sole or a principal income-earning asset through an untimely death can often place remaining household members in a serious financial bind.[14] We can view the amount needed using three different approaches: income replacement, life insurance needs, and partial replacement.

Income Replacement

If the amount of insurance is intended to cover the loss of income in full, it is called **income replacement.** The income replacement amount is equal to the present value of the lost income over a person's remaining life expectancy on an after-tax basis, plus any funeral expenses. The proceeds of any current insurance plus any investment assets already accumulated are subtracted from those figures. With this approach, generally the older you are, the lower the insurance requirement since the amount of your future income declines over time.

Life Insurance Needs

A second approach to how much insurance to purchase is to perform a life insurance needs analysis and calculate the requirements of the other members of the household in the event of the death of a wage earner. Adjustments to the needs analysis are made for

1. A decline in overall living costs caused by the reduction in household members.
2. Future education costs for children.
3. Repayment of the mortgage to reduce overhead costs and insurance needs resulting from (1).

---

[14] Life insurance is used for other purposes as well, such as for estate planning.

Practical Comment Changes in Insurance Needs

Whichever approach you use to determine how much insurance is to be held, take care to include projected changes in needs over time. Needs change because of changes in one's circumstances. Two important causes of those changes are inflation and asset accumulation. Inflation tends to raise the amount of insurance required over time. For example, if inflation rises at a 4 percent rate and the need remains the same, in 17 years a $100,000 policy will be worth $50,000 in purchasing-power terms. On the other hand, needs often tend to decline over time due to the accumulation of investable assets and the decline in the number of years that have to be covered when an income earner dies.

In other words, life insurance needs are a moving target. With the exception of changes in circumstances such as having more children, needs are likely to decline over time. This fact is often overlooked in making decisions on the correct amount of insurance to be held.

The calculation of the appropriate amount of insurance under an insurance needs analysis projects income expense and shortfalls by period. It is done using present and future value principles. A life insurance needs analysis is provided in the appendix to Chapter 18.

Partial Replacement

Insurance is costly, and funding can reduce cash flow availability for other purposes such as current cost of living. Therefore, a third approach may be employed that funds partially for needs or makes broader assumptions about future requirements. The household may only fund for a more modest lifestyle, or provide enough cash to educate a spouse so that he or she can generate higher wages, or just provide resources for a period of time until another marriage is assumed to have taken place.

Types and Uses of Life Insurance

There are five major types of life insurance: term, whole life, universal life, variable life, and variable universal life.[15] Many or all can provide benefits to other household members—life insurance's traditional role—or handle funding to compensate for the death of a divorced spouse or a business partner, and so forth. In addition, life insurance may be used to provide liquidity for estate taxes or to transfer assets upon death in a tax-efficient manner.

Term Insurance

Term insurance is the simplest and cheapest form of life insurance. Its premiums are based principally on mortality cost and life insurance company overhead. Its costs are relatively inexpensive when people are young and mortality rates are lower, but rise steadily, becoming relatively high for people in their 60s. Therefore, **term insurance** can be defined as life insurance providing fixed coverage for a stated period of time with policyholder premiums that vary based on the possibility of death of the insured during that time frame.

Term insurance has little asset value other than that for the probability of death at any given age multiplied by the amount of insurance for the period of coverage remaining. At the end of the year covered, if the insured is still alive, the payments made during the year are expensed. If the policy isn't renewed, it expires and is worthless. In renewable term life, the ability to continue coverage could be considered an asset, as we will explain.

---

[15] Whole life insurance is commonly thought of as all life insurance other than term. In actuality, permanent insurance is a more accurate characterization, with whole and universal life, etc., as subgroups of permanent insurance. In this book we will refer to whole life insurance in the broader phraseology.

During the term of the policy, the health of some insured people may have deteriorated. That risk could raise their rates or result in the insurance company choosing to cancel their policies, creating additional risk. To protect them against that risk, many term policies have a renewable feature. **Renewable term** guarantees that the policy will continue in force, regardless of the health of the insured, for a stated period of time—for example, to age 65.

The price for term insurance often increases each year as the possibility of death rises. Under **level term,** the price may be flat for 5, 10, or 20 years. In effect, like whole life, prices for term insurance in earlier years subsidize those in later years. Therefore, the term policy in the 17th year of a 20-year level-premium term will, in effect, have an asset value.[16,17]

Another feature of some term policies is a conversion provision. **Convertible term** allows the insured to swap a term policy in the future for a whole life policy, generally offered by the same company. This change can occur regardless of the insured's health at the time. This option can have some appeal for people who wish to switch when their finances permit substantially higher payments. Since term can be viewed by the insurance company simply as payout or no payout for annual payment, policies are to some extent indistinguishable commodities and very price competitive. The ability to convert into a whole life policy can be viewed as attractive and may make a particular term policy more appealing to a prospective buyer.

Another term variation is reentry. **Reentry** is the requirement that you pass health tests at stated times to qualify for the annual rates given in the policy. Nonqualification can result in significantly higher rates, but not cancellation of the policy. Policies also vary in terms of how long current prices hold; for example, some typical time frames for rate increases are annually, every 5 years, or every 10 years.

Finally, some policies pay dividends, as do certain whole life policies. They should be viewed as reductions in annual payments since payments are generally made at the beginning of the period, while dividends are often received at the end of the period. For time value of money purposes, they can be credited against the following year's payments.

Term policies pay out death claims much less often than most other forms of life insurance. The combination of term being used for limited periods of time over the life cycle and usually expiring by age 70 is the reason.

A quotation for an ordinary term policy for a man age 35 is given in Table 10.5.

Whole Life Insurance

Whole life is more complex than term. In contrast to term's ever-increasing cost, payments for whole life insurance are level over the life of the policy. Level payments are possible despite higher mortality costs over time because payments in early years are higher than policy needs. In other words, more money is paid into a policy in the early years than is needed to cover insurance company overhead and mortality payments. Therefore, **whole life** can be defined as life insurance providing fixed coverage for the life cycle of the insured. Level policyholder premiums are made possible by higher than pure mortality and insurance company overhead payments in early years, which bring about a cash value savings component

---

[16] The cost for a year late in the 20-year term policy if separately priced would be greater than the cost actually paid. That is because the price paid for the policy incorporates average morbidity for the 20 years, while actual morbidity rises over time. The asset value will be the NPV of the difference between the current premium and the premium on an assumed one-year policy for years 17 through 20. Therefore, if the insured's health has deteriorated and the person is no longer able to purchase new insurance, the asset value of a renewable noncancelable policy would rise significantly.

[17] Most term policies have a current premium and a guaranteed maximum premium. This gives the insurance company some discretion to raise rates if expense assumptions have been too low. A boost in premiums can only be done by class of policies, not selectively by individual.

TABLE 10.5
Term Insurance—
Man Age 35,
$100,000 Policy

Year	Policy Premiums (in dollars)
1	$156
2	$160
3	$164
4	$169
5	$174
6	$181
7	$188
8	$196
9	$205
10	$215
11	$227
12	$241
13	$256
14	$272
15	$291
16	$312
17	$337
18	$365
19	$394
20	$424

for the policy. The cost of a whole life policy for a man age 35 is represented in Table 10.6. Notice how much greater the cost in early years is for whole life as compared with term— more than seven times as much.

However, in later years, the cost comparison reverses. The relative costs over a full adult life cycle are provided in Figure 10.2.

TABLE 10.6
Whole Life Policy—
Man Age 35,
$100,000 Policy
(in dollars)

Year	Guaranteed Contract Premium	Guaranteed Death Benefit	Projected Dividend	Projected Cash Value[1]
1	$1,189	$100,000	0	0
2	$1,189	$100,000	$5	$105
3	$1,189	$100,000	$6	$711
4	$1,189	$100,000	$46	$1,858
5	$1,189	$100,000	$122	$3,182
6	$1,189	$100,000	$202	$4,490
7	$1,189	$100,000	$283	$5,986
8	$1,189	$100,000	$371	$7,678
9	$1,189	$100,000	$415	$9,328
10	$1,189	$100,000	$462	$11,238
11	$1,189	$100,000	$512	$13,114
12	$1,189	$100,000	$563	$15,158
13	$1,189	$100,000	$617	$17,275
14	$1,189	$100,000	$674	$19,570
15	$1,189	$100,000	$736	$21,949
16	$1,189	$100,000	$798	$24,515
17	$1,189	$100,000	$905	$27,215
18	$1,189	$100,000	$1,019	$30,058
19	$1,189	$100,000	$1,143	$33,058
20	$1,189	$100,000	$1,277	$36,327

[1] Includes accumulated dividends.

FIGURE 10.2

The Cost of Term versus Whole Life Insurance

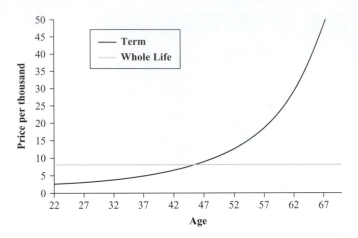

Annual payments in excess of mortality and overhead costs are placed in a cash value account. The cash value can be withdrawn less some redemption charge or borrowed against. You receive a return based on the insurance company's investment performance and competitive factors. As the cash value account amount increases, it provides higher income. In later years, assuming coverage remains level, premium payments are able to remain level despite the sharply higher mortality costs because of this return on the cash value account. In Figure 10.3, the cash flow process for life insurance is given.

Example 10.3

John, age 25, bought a $200,000 level-premium life policy for an annual payment of $500. The mortality charge was only about 25 percent of the total payment. The balance after expense charges was placed in a cash value account. At the end of 10 years, the cash value was about $4,500. At age 65, John's annual payment was still $500, but the mortality charge was approximately $2,000. The shortfall in cash flow for the insurance company was met from interest income and a decline in cash value in John's account.

Limited pay policies, sometimes illustrated as vanishing premium policies, are a variation on ordinary life insurance that has level payment throughout the insured's life. With this approach, yearly payments are even higher than with level pay.[18] This creates an even higher cash value with greater yearly income. After a period of time, say, 10 years, or at age 65, payments are scheduled to stop. At the time policies are thought to be fully paid up, the income and principal paydown on the cash value account is intended to cover all future life insurance needs, with no further payments anticipated. Similarly, a single-premium policy that necessitates only one lump sum at the beginning can be constructed so that if the assumptions built into the quote are correct, no additional contributions will be necessary.

[18] Limited pay policies also have level payment, but, as mentioned, they have a greater annual outlay.

FIGURE 10.3

Whole Life Insurance—The Cash Flow Process

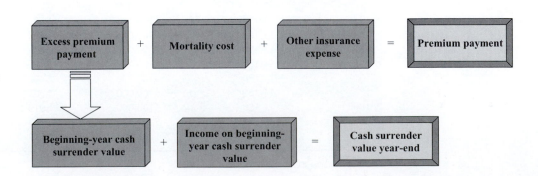

Universal Life Insurance

Universal life is more flexible than whole life insurance. It often has a significant cash value account, but yearly payments by the policyholder may vary. In essence, it combines term and whole life since it has both termlike charges and a side fund that receives an investment return intended to pay term insurance premiums. If payments and existing cash value are not sufficient to meet current insurance company needs, insurance coverage can be reduced. In contrast to whole or term life, insufficient payment does not automatically result in cancellation of the policy. Universal life policies can be cheaper than whole life policies, but, if policy projections are not met, the extra cost may be shifted to the policyholder through additional insurance payments; in contrast, whole life provides a guaranteed payout for a fixed stated annual premium.

Variable Life Insurance

Variable life is similar to whole life except that it transfers the investment function from the insurance firm to the individual. Individuals may select the proportion of stocks or bonds they would like and the types of funds within each category. The choices can be limited to monies managed by each insurance company or may include an outside money manager. There exists the potential for greater return than what an insurance company would offer in a whole life policy. Variable life might result in lower future premium payments or higher cash values, but there is also greater risk. If the funds have poor performance, greater premium payments may be needed or coverage could be jeopardized.

Variable Universal Life Insurance

Variable universal life combines the payment flexibility of universal life with the investment flexibility of variable life. It offers the choice of both time and amount of premium payments, as well as the opportunity to select bond or stock funds, frequently with a choice within category. On the other hand, it can be difficult to determine what an adequate level of funding is.

Term as Compared with Whole Life Policies

As we have seen, there are basically two types of insurance: term and whole life. Term is pure protection against premature death. Whole life adds an investment component. The individual characteristics among whole life–type policies may differ: whole life provides level payment, universal allows more flexibility in premium payment, and variable gives more flexibility in investment options, but they all offer an investment feature.

Consider this comparison of the two principal types of life insurance:

Term
Strengths

1. Pure insurance—risk management is the prime intent.
2. Unlimited flexibility in investment options is associated with buying term and investing the difference in costs between term and whole life.
3. There is highly competitive pricing.
4. It is relatively easy to compare policies against one another.
5. There is flexibility in reducing or eliminating coverage efficiently over time.

Weaknesses

1. Rates rise over time until they are prohibitively expensive.
2. There is the potential for underinsurance if individuals do not invest the savings in outlays between term and whole life, spending the money instead.

3. Some policyholders are uncomfortable with what can be significant payments without continuing values.

4. Policy may be more susceptible to moral hazard and adverse selection than other types of insurance, particularly if there is no reentry provision.

Whole Life
Strengths

1. The premiums remain level over time and thus aren't unaffordable in later years.

2. Higher payments than needed to cover mortality risk are an effective "forced savings" component for those who need it.

3. The amount in the cash value account that is built over time is tax-sheltered. No taxes are paid unless the policy is surrendered.[19]

4. Cash values accumulated can be borrowed against to help finance retirement.

5. Monies spent in premiums can provide a tangible cash benefit over time, not a pure expense as in term.

6. The policy is designed to commonly pay a cash benefit to the beneficiary in contrast to term's less frequent payout as temporary insurance.

Weaknesses

1. The costs for full coverage for young people on limited incomes can be very high.

2. The investment element of whole life, the cash value accumulated, is only available while the person is alive. The amount paid out at death is just the insurance amount, not the insurance amount plus the cash value.

3. Policies are difficult for the average person to compare.

4. Non-tax-deductible interest[20] is charged on amounts borrowed on cash value.

5. Termination of the policy in early years generally provides little or no cash value, making it an inefficient investment for many years. (Approximately 20 percent of the policies are canceled in the first two years.)

On balance, given the same coverage for both types of policies, decisions should be made based on

1. How long the policy is to be held. Term, which has no cash value, may be most competitive for periods of 10 years or less; whole life should be held for at least 10 years.

2. Whether in fact the "difference" is saved, not spent, when buying term and investing the difference.

3. The buyer's risk tolerance for investments. Those with low risk tolerance are more likely to find whole life returns attractive than are those with a high tolerance for risk.

4. The actual difference in return between a whole life policy and the investment alternatives available to the policyholder.

Example 10.4   Henry and Helen, two friends who had separate households, decided to investigate insurance policies together. They are both disciplined savers who could afford either term or whole life premiums. They each thought they would need the insurance for 20 years. Based on the current returns, they calculated that the return on a whole life policy was 6 percent. In other words, the return on a whole life policy after taking into account its higher payments in early

---

[19] When it is surrendered, taxes are only paid on the difference between cash value and total premiums paid, even though premiums covered the possibility of premature death since the policy was taken out.

[20] Unless the sum is used to finance a tax-recognized project such as an investment in a business venture.

Practical Comment Comparing Life Insurance Policies

People often don't understand how to differentiate properly between whole life insurance offerings.[21] They have greater success with term insurance where, once a few basic differences are explained, they select properly. Whole life insurance is much more complex with significant differences by company in mortality costs, overhead costs, and investment returns. Moreover, even if a company had above-average investment returns in the past, there is no assurance that this was not due to chance or to a portfolio manager who had left, and consequently

[21] This is corroborated in Albert Auxier, "A Test of the Usefulness of Policy Information in Ranking Life Insurance Alternatives," *Journal of Risk and Insurance* 43, no. 1 (March 1976), pp. 87–98.

past returns may not be a reliable indicator of future performance.

One alternative approach in comparing life insurance companies is to eliminate investment returns as a consideration and concentrate principally on mortality and overhead costs. With this approach, all companies providing policy illustrations would be asked to employ the same rate of return, say 6 percent. Then we could calculate their return on life insurance for all policies of the same type using the return method shown in this chapter. The policy with the highest return among those companies with well-established, high-quality operations would be selected. Interestingly, companies can come out with materially different relative rankings of return at different policyholder ages.

years as compared with term was 6 percent on a time-weighted basis. Henry, who had a low tolerance for risk, calculated that he would put any money saved by buying term into money market funds yielding 4 percent; he took the whole life policy. Helen, who had a higher risk profile, felt that she could invest the money at a rate of return in excess of 6 percent. She purchased the term policy.

If you seek insight on past returns, *Best's Review (Life-Health Edition)* could be used to compare past actual versus projected dividends. Also, where the life insurance company is willing to supply the information, Joseph Belth's method of calculating actual rates of return for policies already in existence for the current and past two years could be used as a representation of recent returns.[22] The Belth formula is provided in Appendix II. The most common quantitative comparisons of policies are given in Appendix I.

Back to Dan and Laura
RISK MANAGEMENT AND LIFE INSURANCE

Our meeting was set for late afternoon. Dan was able to get off from work early, and Brian was sleeping quietly in the carriage. Judging by previous discussions, I decided that Dan and Laura were too focused on insurance to the exclusion of other risk management techniques. I thought it would be helpful to provide some initial education. I mentioned that they needed to take an overall risk management approach. I indicated that risk management involves all of their assets and their personal practices. I told them that they should think of their assets, both marketable and nonmarketable, as part of a portfolio to supervise for overall return and risk maintenance.

Dan understood the approach right away and Laura picked it up after a brief example. Dan said, "I suppose I should tell you that I am a hot-rod racer. I have been ever since I was 16 and my uncle, who was a mechanic, taught me how much fun it was to enter and compete at a race track." A quick glance over at Laura indicated she didn't share his joy.

[22] Joseph Belth, *Life Insurance: A Consumer's Handbook,* 2nd ed. (Bloomington, IN: Indiana University Press, 1985).

She said, "Dan didn't tell you about the time he broke his collarbone in an accident and the other time they pulled him out of a burning car."

Their other personal practices seemed okay. They paid attention to their diet and exercised; Laura now jogged with her baby carriage in front and their dog following. Despite disagreements, Dan and Laura seemed to have a good relationship, with each deferring to the other's wishes. They did yoga exercises together to eliminate the day's stresses. Neither had any serious illnesses.

Dan and Laura had different points of view concerning the type of life insurance they should have. She was the more aggressive investor and preferred term insurance. She believed that gains of 20 percent a year were possible in stocks, providing you were in the "right investments." She wanted to have the maximum amount of cash available to invest. Dan was not sure that he wanted to place all household money in investments under their control. I had the feeling that Dan preferred whole life insurance and was attracted to the steady returns of a cash value insurance policy. They both indicated they preferred the structure of a fixed-payment whole life policy to a more flexible universal life policy. Neither one was attracted to variable life insurance. Both were confident that their recent inability to save money would end and be replaced by substantial yearly net cash inflows.

As the meeting wound down, they gave me insurance proposals with actual quotes on two whole life insurance and two term insurance policies. They asked me to review them and make some preliminary recommendations. They understood that I would not be able to tell them how much insurance they should have until later in the process. However, they wanted my preliminary opinion as to whether it should be whole life or term. We decided to end the conversation there. I told them I would send them a preliminary draft of overall risk management procedures and the life insurance section for their comments. At a future meeting, we would go over the other types of insurance.

Risk management is the method by which we control the risks for each household. It is much broader than just gauging insurance needs. It involves examining household assets overall and one by one.

You have asked me to look over all your exposures. To facilitate this process, assets are separated into three principal categories. The first category is human-related assets, which includes human assets. Human assets are derived from your salaries. Your exposures hence involve your personal health, safety practices, and insurance needs. They also include pensions and gifts derived from your work and relationships. Exposures involve inflation and relationship risk, respectively. The second category is financial assets, which involve your investment and financing practices. As you are aware, financial assets have a chance for loss particularly if they are not selected properly. The third category is the real assets comprising your house, furniture, car, and so on. Fire, theft, and depreciation in value are three exposures here. In addition, we will consider your intangible assets including household goodwill and liability exposure to others.

As we discussed, these assets should be thought of as being part of a special portfolio. It is special because it is yours. It comprises not only marketable assets but nonfinancial ones such as your careers. Our goal is to control individual assets and your overall portfolio risk to enable you to have confidence that you will reach your goals.

From a personal perspective we are pleased to affirm that you have good personal safety practices. You both are practicing good eating habits including balanced meals. Laura is to be commended for her quick loss of the 35 pounds she gained during her pregnancy with Brian. Both of you exercise regularly. Based on our discussions, you seem safety-conscious in your activities. At the present time, each of you is in good health. Your efforts to reduce stress through daily yoga exercises are a plus. However, Laura's side of the family's seeming genetic exposure to early mortality due to heart ailments bears watching. It could suggest the advisability of more savings today and perhaps more insurance coverage, since the household would be materially affected financially by any loss of her income and an inability later to qualify for insurance.

The only change of practice I could see would be to review Dan's participation in drag car racing. Dan, I recognize that you have enjoyed racing your 1953 hot rod Chevrolet for many years. I question, however, whether this hobby is appropriate given your responsibilities to Laura and Brian. Any personal injury could have a material effect on them. Moreover, it seems inconsistent with your generally conservative nature. Perhaps you could explore an alternative hobby that you might find satisfying.

I am pleased that you will have two sources of income once Laura goes back to work. Given her tenure as a schoolteacher, her position balances the higher levels of risk and higher returns that Dan has in his career. You have both indicated that your personal relationship is excellent and that having a child had not resulted in any friction between you.

Your exposures in property, health, disability, and miscellaneous areas will be handled later. Moreover, investments and debt risk, both of which are meaningful to you, have been covered in separate sessions. I will limit myself to life insurance at the present time.

Life insurance is a method of protecting family assets so that many goals can be reached in the event of the untimely death of an income earner. Thinking of life insurance is important to the household since both incomes will be needed long term to meet retirement goals. Your material current debt and your desire to fund a private college education for two children make it particularly relevant. The absence of a replacement source of income could place an inordinately large burden on the surviving spouse.

As mentioned before, I do not have enough data yet to recommend a specific amount of insurance. However, I will make a preliminary statement of the adequacy of your current coverage. You have separately indicated that in the event of the loss of one of you, the other should be funded comfortably for life. After careful thought, you have defined that as a 10 percent decline from current living costs now and in retirement; that figure reflects the absence of one household member and a modest reduction in leisure time expenditures. Based on that assumption, it is clear that both of you are currently underinsured.

You asked whether you should have term or whole life insurance. Actually, I am going to recommend a combination of both. Here is a brief description of both types and the reasons why I am making that recommendation.

Term life represents pure insurance today. Its advantage is low current cost and full freedom to place your savings from the lower cost of your policy in investments that you select. Based on our discussions, it is clear that Laura would like as much yearly cash flow as possible to invest herself. Furthermore, it is likely that much more expensive whole life could put a crimp in your current living style if it is used to fund your entire insurance need. Perhaps most important, based on a savings pattern that I will propose, you are likely to be financially independent at some point. At that time, you won't need any life insurance. Since the need is temporary and the return on alternative investments is likely to exceed life insurance rates, I will be recommending some term insurance.

On the other hand, I am recommending some whole life insurance as well. I am concerned about your ability to save. Your future goals of saving a material sum are reasonable, but, at the present time, judging by your current debt outstanding, you have not yet shown the discipline to save. The excess cash value that you accumulate can be made available to you at the time you cash in your policy. This could be done at the point you reach financial independence. In addition, I believe that Laura's projection of 20 percent a year growth in investments is too optimistic. This life insurance can be considered a conservative investment in your portfolio to help diversify and balance your aggressive aspirations.

As for the comparison between the two term policies (see Appendix I), it is clear that policy A is cheaper in the early years. On the other hand, policy B becomes less expensive after year 8 and the disparity grows in subsequent years. Both insurance companies are of high quality. The policies are guaranteed renewable and convertible into whole life. If I thought your need was only for eight years, I would recommend A. You could always purchase A and in eight years attempt to go through the process again. I say "attempt" because there is no assurance that you would qualify if some unforeseen decline in health occurred. I believe you will need life insurance for an extended time and I would prefer not running the risk of your becoming uninsurable. Plan B's 20-year net present value is materially below plan A's. Consequently, I prefer B.

As I mentioned, these preliminary recommendations are intended to move our conversations forward. They are subject to insurance amounts that I will give in a later section of your plan and an overall integration of your goals and resources.

Summary

Risk management is an underappreciated part of PFP. It too often is equated with insurance alone.

- Risk management is an overall household approach that identifies and controls uncertainty. It eliminates obstructions to goal achievement.
- Common risk management approaches are to avoid risk, reduce risk, reduce potential loss, transfer risk, and share risk.
- Common human-asset risks are shorter and longer life spans, health and disability, and macro- and microeconomic risks.
- Insurance transfers specific asset risk and, in doing so, modifies overall household portfolio risk.
- Insurance can be separated into personal, property, and government categories.
- When analyzing an insurance company, the following factors are important: financial strength, good operating sense, price, and service.
- There are five main types of life insurance: whole life, term, universal life, variable life, and variable universal life.
- Term insurance is pure mortality insurance.
- Some advantages of term are it is highly competitive, is easy to compare, and provides flexibility in reducing coverage.
- Whole life combines mortality with a savings feature through prepayments.
- Whole life advantages are level premiums over time, forced savings for those who need it, and cash values accumulated that can be borrowed against.
- Choosing term versus whole life depends on such factors as how long the policy is being held, need for forced savings, and effectiveness of investing on your own.

Key Terms

adverse selection, *262*
convertible term, *270*
financial assets, *260*
financial liabilities, *261*
income replacement, *268*
insurance, *261*
insurance
underwriting, *261*
intangible liabilities, *261*
level term, *270*

life insurance, *267*
longevity, *259*
longevity risk, *259*
macroeconomic risk, *260*
microeconomic risk, *260*
moral hazard, *262*
mortality risk, *268*
real assets, *260*
reentry, *270*
renewable term, *270*

risk management in
practical terms, *256*
risk management
in theory, *255*
term insurance, *269*
universal life, *273*
variable life, *273*
variable universal
life, *273*
whole life, *270*

Web Sites

http://www.acli.com
American Council of Life Insurers
This site offers educational information on life insurance; annuities; disability income and long-term care insurance; pensions; 401(k), 403(b), and 457 plans; and IRAs. The site provides insurance industry facts in the annual "Life Insurers Fact Book."

http://www.rmahq.org
Risk Management Association
Web seminars on interesting risk management topics and useful advice on handling risk management problems are presented.

http://www.irmi.com
International Risk Management Institute
The site offers practical strategies and tactics to help understand insurance and risk management information.

Questions

1. Define risk management.
2. How does portfolio management enter into the risk management process?
3. Why is diversification important in risk management?
4. What are the functions of a risk manager?
5. Contrast business and personal risk and separate the household's risk exposure into one or the other.
6. Which type of insurance might be more susceptible to moral hazard: term or whole life? Why?
7. A person who trades in his 15-year-old automobile and purchases a new car with disk brakes is practicing which method of managing risk?
8. How would you decide whether to transfer risk or share risk?
9. Indicate what type of life insurance you would recommend for someone who is scheduled to be financially independent in eight years. Why?
10. How can insurance modify portfolio risk?
11. What are the significant factors in selecting an insurance company?
12. List the types of risks to human assets and briefly explain how to reduce them.
13. How is whole life insurance able to maintain a flat payment?
14. Describe the insurance needs approach.
15. Assuming continuing payments, will the cash value of whole life always go up over a life cycle? Why?
16. Why can term insurance be deducted from whole life to determine the return on the whole life policy?
17. Contrast variable and universal life insurance.
18. Julian was considering whole life and term insurance for his 20-year need. Which one should he select?
19. Name three strengths and weaknesses of whole life and term insurance.

Problems

These problems are based on information provided in Appendix I.

10.1   Randy had two term policies to compare, with costs as shown below. Calculate the NPV at a 6 percent after-tax discount rate and the IRR. Which one should she select and why?

Years	A	B
1	$225	$300
2	$275	$310
3	$350	$320
4	$400	$330
5	$500	$340

10.2   Given the following information:

Guaranteed Contract Premium	Guaranteed Death Benefit	Projected Dividend	Projected Cash Value	Term Premium
$2,300	$200,000	0	0	$325
$2,300		0	0	$330
$2,300		0	0	$335
$2,300		0	$3,500	$340
$2,300		$250	$6,000	$355
$2,300		$400	$9,000	$370
$2,300		$600	$12,000	$390
$2,300		$750	$15,000	$400
$2,300		$900	$18,000	$410
$2,300		$1,000	$24,000	$430

Find the return on the whole life insurance policy when the cost of term is included. Which would you select if you can invest the difference between the term and whole life policies' premiums at a 9 percent rate? Explain your reasoning.

**CFP®
Certification
Examination
Questions
and Problems**

10.1   Regarding the characteristics of insurance, which of the following is/are fundamental?

1. probability (possibility and predictability of a loss)
2. law of large numbers
3. transfer of risk from individual to group
4. insurance is a form of speculation

   a. (1) and (2) only
   b. (1), (2), and (4) only
   c. (2) and (4) only
   d. (4) only
   e. (1), (2), (3), and (4)

10.2   What is the main responsibility of the underwriting department of a life insurance company?

   a. to guard against adverse selection
   b. to set a limit on the amount of insurance issued
   c. to set adequate insurance rates
   d. to avoid exposures that could result in loss

10.3   Veronica recently purchased a car for $1,500 for her 16-year-old child. Which of the following risk management techniques would be most appropriate for handling the collision exposure of this automobile?

   a. Subrogation
   b. Insurance

    c. Retention

    d. Avoidance

10.4 Which of the following best describes the difference between a variable life policy and a universal life policy?

    a. Variable life has a variable death benefit and universal life has a fixed death benefit.

    b. Variable life subaccounts do not guarantee market returns, while the universal life contracts contain a guaranteed rate.

    c. Universal life has guaranteed mortality charges, while variable life has nonguaranteed mortality charges.

    d. Variable life contracts do not guarantee market returns, while the market interest rates in universal life contracts are guaranteed.

Case Application

RISK MANAGEMENT AND LIFE INSURANCE

In our meeting, it became apparent that Richard's investment loss was not a solitary act. Richard was very indulgent and paid little attention to his health. He went out on shopping sprees that he and Monica couldn't afford. He was overweight. He used alcohol excessively and smoked. His doctor had warned him of his unhealthy habits including a high cholesterol level, which placed him at risk of a major illness. His work output was excellent, but he often got into verbal arguments with superiors. The result was a reputation as a brilliant but unsteady worker who shifted from job to job often.

Monica, on the other hand, was as steady as Richard was fickle. She was a vegetarian who exercised regularly. Her doctor told her she had the physical condition of a woman 10 years younger. Given Richard's erratic behavior, one would think Monica would be under great stress. When I posed that question to her, she said that she had learned to cope with Richard's behavior.

The couple had no life insurance except for a policy providing one times Richard's salary at work. Monica had often asked Richard to get some additional insurance. His reply was that they did not have enough money. Monica specifically requested that I look at term and whole life insurance and tell her the type and amount of insurance that was appropriate.

As we completed the topic, Richard said he was sorry for his behavior and would "turn over a new leaf." Monica replied that she was not sure Richard could do it.

Case Application Questions

1. What do you think of this couple's overall risk profile?
2. What recommendations would you make to improve it?
3. Do you believe these recommendations will be followed?
4. Assuming there is some uncertainty that the advice will be followed, what other recommendation might you make?
5. Do you believe they should have more insurance?
6. Which type would you recommend: whole life or term insurance?
7. Prepare the overall risk management and life insurance parts of the financial plan.

Appendix I

Quantitative Comparison of Policies

Insurance policies can be compared within each category—for example, one term policy with another. In addition, one category's policies can be compared with those from another area—for example, term versus whole life. The return on investment method, an interest-adjusted method, and the net payment cost index are two common insurance industry methods. They appear on many policy quotations and are used to compare like kinds of investments. The lower the figures presented, the more attractive the policy.

However, the purchase decision for insurance policies can be looked at as just another household capital budgeting problem. The cash outflows and inflows can be developed and compared both within each category and across categories using normal NPV and IRR methods. Collectively, we can call these approaches the return on investment methods to differentiate them from common insurance industry methods.

The NPV method just employs a discount rate to solve for the term policy with the lowest current cost. The IRR method can be used to compare alternative types of policies—say, a whole life with a term policy. It does so by taking the difference in costs between the two types of policies to see if the higher outlay for whole life in early years is justified on a return basis. It is sometimes called buy term and invest the difference. Term is preferable when the person will actually save and invest the sums at a rate that exceeds the return built into the whole life policy. The NPV method also can provide a solution under this method. The IRR calculation, which we can call the return on investment method, is further described later in the appendix.

Example 10.A1.1 Lisa wanted term insurance coverage for 10 years and had two finalists. One policy, policy A, was advertised as remarkably cheaper in the first year than the other. Which should she select, assuming the discount rate is 7 percent after taxes? (See Table 10.A1.1.)

TABLE 10.A1.1

Year	Policy A Premium	Policy B Premium
1	$105	$156
2	140	160
3	180	164
4	190	169
5	200	174
6	210	181
7	220	188
8	225	196
9	235	205
10	240	215

Excel Solution

	A	B	C	D	E
1	**Year**	**Policy A Premium**	**Policy B Premium**		
2	1	($105)	($156)		
3	2	($140)	($160)		
4	3	($180)	($164)		
5	4	($190)	($169)		
6	5	($200)	($174)		
7	6	($210)	($181)		
8	7	($220)	($188)		
9	8	($225)	($196)		
10	9	($235)	($205)		
11	10	($240)	($215)		
12					
13					
14	Discount Rate	7%			
15					
16					
17	**Net Present Value**				
18			= B2+NPV(B14, B3:B11)		
19	Policy A	($1,404.49)			
20					
21			= C2+NPV(B14, C3:C11)		
22	Policy B	($1,332.11)			
23					

Practical Comment   Use of Cost as a Selection Criterion

Some people do not look at the cost of an insurance policy over time. Instead, they throw up their hands concerning the relative cost and features of alternative whole life policies and depend almost solely on the opinion of the insurance broker and possibly the reputation of the insurance company. For term insurance, they may place heavy weighting on the first year's cost. Any method that compels them to look at costs over an appropriate time frame can be highly useful. Selecting the correct time frame for a term policy based on the period the policy is expected to be in force is very important. Consider Example 10.A1.1 using the capital budgeting technique to reach a decision.

Calculator Solution

Policy A

General Calculator Approach	Specific HP12C	Specific TI BA II Plus
		$\boxed{CF}$
Clear the register	$\boxed{f}$ $\boxed{FIN}$	$\boxed{2nd}$ $\boxed{CLR\ Work}$
Enter cash outflow Year 1	105 $\boxed{CHS}$ $\boxed{g}$ $\boxed{CF_0}$	105 $\boxed{+/-}$ $\boxed{ENTER}$ $\boxed{\downarrow}$
Enter cash outflow Year 2	140 $\boxed{CHS}$ $\boxed{g}$ $\boxed{CF_j}$	140 $\boxed{+/-}$ $\boxed{ENTER}$ $\boxed{\downarrow}$ $\boxed{\downarrow}$
Enter cash outflow Year 3	180 $\boxed{CHS}$ $\boxed{g}$ $\boxed{CF_j}$	180 $\boxed{+/-}$ $\boxed{ENTER}$ $\boxed{\downarrow}$ $\boxed{\downarrow}$
Enter cash outflow Year 4	190 $\boxed{CHS}$ $\boxed{g}$ $\boxed{CF_j}$	190 $\boxed{+/-}$ $\boxed{ENTER}$ $\boxed{\downarrow}$ $\boxed{\downarrow}$
Enter cash outflow Year 5	200 $\boxed{CHS}$ $\boxed{g}$ $\boxed{CF_j}$	200 $\boxed{+/-}$ $\boxed{ENTER}$ $\boxed{\downarrow}$ $\boxed{\downarrow}$
Enter cash outflow Year 6	210 $\boxed{CHS}$ $\boxed{g}$ $\boxed{CF_j}$	210 $\boxed{+/-}$ $\boxed{ENTER}$ $\boxed{\downarrow}$ $\boxed{\downarrow}$
Enter cash outflow Year 7	220 $\boxed{CHS}$ $\boxed{g}$ $\boxed{CF_j}$	220 $\boxed{+/-}$ $\boxed{ENTER}$ $\boxed{\downarrow}$ $\boxed{\downarrow}$
Enter cash outflow Year 8	225 $\boxed{CHS}$ $\boxed{g}$ $\boxed{CF_j}$	225 $\boxed{+/-}$ $\boxed{ENTER}$ $\boxed{\downarrow}$ $\boxed{\downarrow}$
Enter cash outflow Year 9	235 $\boxed{CHS}$ $\boxed{g}$ $\boxed{CF_j}$	235 $\boxed{+/-}$ $\boxed{ENTER}$ $\boxed{\downarrow}$ $\boxed{\downarrow}$
Enter cash outflow Year 10	240 $\boxed{CHS}$ $\boxed{g}$ $\boxed{CF_j}$	240 $\boxed{+/-}$ $\boxed{ENTER}$ $\boxed{\downarrow}$ $\boxed{\downarrow}$
Enter the discount rate		$\boxed{NPV}$
	7 $\boxed{i}$	7 $\boxed{ENTER}$ $\boxed{\downarrow}$
Calculate the net present value	$\boxed{f}$ $\boxed{NPV}$	$\boxed{CPT}$
	−1,404.49	−1,404.49

Net present value = −$1,404.49

Policy B

General Calculator Approach	Specific HP12C	Specific TI BA II Plus
		$\boxed{CF}$
Clear the register	$\boxed{f}$ $\boxed{FIN}$	$\boxed{2nd}$ $\boxed{CLR\ Work}$
Enter cash outflow Year 1	156 $\boxed{CHS}$ $\boxed{g}$ $\boxed{CF_0}$	156 $\boxed{+/-}$ $\boxed{ENTER}$ $\boxed{\downarrow}$
Enter cash outflow Year 2	160 $\boxed{CHS}$ $\boxed{g}$ $\boxed{CF_j}$	160 $\boxed{+/-}$ $\boxed{ENTER}$ $\boxed{\downarrow}$ $\boxed{\downarrow}$
Enter cash outflow Year 3	164 $\boxed{CHS}$ $\boxed{g}$ $\boxed{CF_j}$	164 $\boxed{+/-}$ $\boxed{ENTER}$ $\boxed{\downarrow}$ $\boxed{\downarrow}$
Enter cash outflow Year 4	169 $\boxed{CHS}$ $\boxed{g}$ $\boxed{CF_j}$	169 $\boxed{+/-}$ $\boxed{ENTER}$ $\boxed{\downarrow}$ $\boxed{\downarrow}$
Enter cash outflow Year 5	174 $\boxed{CHS}$ $\boxed{g}$ $\boxed{CF_j}$	174 $\boxed{+/-}$ $\boxed{ENTER}$ $\boxed{\downarrow}$ $\boxed{\downarrow}$
Enter cash outflow Year 6	181 $\boxed{CHS}$ $\boxed{g}$ $\boxed{CF_j}$	181 $\boxed{+/-}$ $\boxed{ENTER}$ $\boxed{\downarrow}$ $\boxed{\downarrow}$
Enter cash outflow Year 7	188 $\boxed{CHS}$ $\boxed{g}$ $\boxed{CF_j}$	188 $\boxed{+/-}$ $\boxed{ENTER}$ $\boxed{\downarrow}$ $\boxed{\downarrow}$
Enter cash outflow Year 8	196 $\boxed{CHS}$ $\boxed{g}$ $\boxed{CF_j}$	196 $\boxed{+/-}$ $\boxed{ENTER}$ $\boxed{\downarrow}$ $\boxed{\downarrow}$
Enter cash outflow Year 9	205 $\boxed{CHS}$ $\boxed{g}$ $\boxed{CF_j}$	205 $\boxed{+/-}$ $\boxed{ENTER}$ $\boxed{\downarrow}$ $\boxed{\downarrow}$
Enter cash outflow Year 10	215 $\boxed{CHS}$ $\boxed{g}$ $\boxed{CF_j}$	215 $\boxed{+/-}$ $\boxed{ENTER}$ $\boxed{\downarrow}$ $\boxed{\downarrow}$
Enter the discount rate		$\boxed{NPV}$
	7 $\boxed{i}$	7 $\boxed{ENTER}$ $\boxed{\downarrow}$
Calculate the net present value	$\boxed{f}$ $\boxed{NPV}$	$\boxed{CPT}$
	−1,332.11	−1,332.11

Net present value = −$1,332.11

Although policy A is much cheaper in the first year, it more than makes up for it with rapidly increasing premiums in subsequent years. Its net present value is higher than policy B's, which means it costs more to buy on a time-weighted basis.[23] Thus, the answer is that Lisa should select policy B.

Once the decision is made to purchase life insurance, the question is which policy. The two insurance methods discussed below, the interest-adjusted method and the return on investment method, can help the purchaser make that decision. These approaches are the established insurance company alternative to the return on investment method we have discussed in this chapter.

INTEREST-ADJUSTED METHOD

The interest-adjusted method is used to compare like kinds of investments. Using this approach, all cash outflows for insurance premium payments and all cash inflows from policy dividends are brought forward to a specified future date, often 20 years. The discount rate used to adjust for the timing of cash flows is the investor's assumed after-tax return on alternative use of the money in the market. In the following calculations, a 5 percent after-tax return was assumed. The future value of the net cash flows (outflows less inflows) is divided by the cash surrender value of the policy. With the cash surrender value approach, the lower the ratio of the future value of cash outflows to cash surrender value, the more attractive the policy.

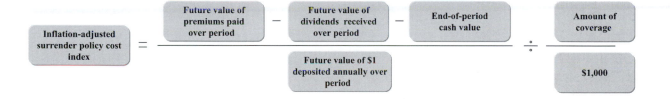

The net payment cost index is similar, except that the cash surrender value is excluded in the calculation.

Table 10.A1.2 compares two term policies using a net payment cost index. Neither has dividends. Since term policies have no accumulated cash value, the cash surrender index and the net payment index produce the same result. Note that policy A produces a better 10-year cost and policy B a more advantageous 20-year figure. The reason is evident when we compare the differences in cost by year, as shown in the last column.

RETURN ON INVESTMENT METHOD

The second method, which is called the return on investment method, allows comparison between whole life contracts and term as well as among whole life contracts that are being considered. It estimates the rate of return on the cash value of whole life contracts. Our construct below can be viewed as a modified insurance industry approach.[24] In it the premium from a competitive independent term policy is used as a proxy for the mortality and overhead costs of the life insurance policy being considered. This amount

---

[23] Note that in contrast to capital expenditures the calculation provides a negative sum. That is because it represents an expense, not an inflow (asset). Consequently, the alternative selected is the one that provides the lowest amount possible.

[24] Called the Linton yield approach.

TABLE 10.A1.2
Comparison of Two Term Policies—Man Age 35, $100,000 Policy

Year	Policy A Premium	Policy B Premium	Difference (A – B)
1	$110	$156	($46)
2	$110	$160	($50)
3	$110	$164	($54)
4	$110	$169	($59)
5	$110	$174	($64)
6	$174	$181	($7)
7	$191	$188	$3
8	$207	$196	$11
9	$224	$205	$19
10	$240	$215	$25
11	$374	$227	$147
12	$398	$241	$157
13	$424	$256	$168
14	$452	$272	$180
15	$484	$291	$193
16	$517	$312	$205
17	$557	$337	$220
18	$602	$365	$237
19	$654	$394	$260
20	$713	$424	$289
Current Cost Index			
10 Years	1.52	1.78	
20 Years	2.85	2.26	
Net Payment Index			
10 Years	1.52	1.78	
20 Years	2.85	2.26	

is subtracted from the whole life payment, as is the projected dividend. The result is a "pure" extra payment by the holder for which an investment return is expected. The annual extra payment for investment is the sum that could alternatively be used each year for investment.

The extra payments are compared with the inflow from the cash surrender value, assuming the policy is cashed at a given point in time. An NPV at an assumed discount rate based on the rate of return for alternative investment or a time-weighted return on the cash value (IRR) is calculated. Taxes are taken out of the cash surrender value at the policyholder's marginal tax rate and should be compared with the after-tax returns available on alternative investments. The outcome can indicate whether it is more favorable to purchase whole life or to buy term and invest the difference in alternative investments. With the return on investment method, the rates of return between two whole life insurance policies can also be compared.

Example 10.A1.2 Michael didn't know whether to purchase a whole life or a term policy. He narrowed his search to two policies—one life, one term. He wasn't sure he needed the insurance for more than 20 years and wanted the comparison to be done purely on both a 10-year and a 20-year financial basis. He had no concern that he wouldn't save the difference between the term and whole life policies and believed that if he bought the term policies, he could invest the monies on a 10 percent pretax basis. Assume that Michael was not subject to taxes. Which policy should he select? (See Table 10.A1.3).

TABLE 10.A1.3
Whole Life versus
Term Policy—Man
Age 35, $100,000
Policy

Year	Guaranteed Contract Premium	Guaranteed Death Benefit	Projected Dividend	Projected Cash Value	Term Premium	Life Premium Minus Term Premium and Dividend
1	$1,189	$100,000	$0	$0	156	$1,033
2	1,189	100,000	5	105	160	1,024
3	1,189	100,000	6	711	164	1,019
4	1,189	100,000	46	1,858	169	974
5	1,189	100,000	122	3,182	174	893
6	1,189	100,000	202	4,490	181	806
7	1,189	100,000	283	5,986	188	718
8	1,189	100,000	371	7,678	196	622
9	1,189	100,000	415	9,328	205	569
10	1,189	100,000	462	11,238	215	512
11	1,189	100,000	512	13,114	227	450
12	1,189	100,000	563	15,158	241	385
13	1,189	100,000	617	17,275	256	316
14	1,189	100,000	674	19,570	272	243
15	1,189	100,000	736	21,949	291	162
16	1,189	100,000	798	24,515	312	79
17	1,189	100,000	905	27,215	337	(53)
18	1,189	100,000	1,019	30,058	365	(195)
19	1,189	100,000	1,143	33,058	394	(348)
20	1,189	100,000	1,277	36,327	424	(512)

Projected Internal Rate of Return on Whole Life Policy

Calculator Solution

10 Year

General Calculator Approach	Specific HP12C	Specific TI BA II Plus
		[CF]
Clear the register	[f] [FIN]	[2nd] [CLR Work]
Enter cash outflow Year 1	1,033 [CHS] [g] [CF$_0$]	1,033 [+/−] [ENTER] [↓]
Enter cash outflow Year 2	1,024 [CHS] [g] [CF$_j$]	1,024 [+/−] [ENTER] [↓] [↓]
Enter cash outflow Year 3	1,019 [CHS] [g] [CF$_j$]	1,019 [+/−] [ENTER] [↓] [↓]
Enter cash outflow Year 4	974 [CHS] [g] [CF$_j$]	974 [+/−] [ENTER] [↓] [↓]
Enter cash outflow Year 5	893 [CHS] [g] [CF$_j$]	893 [+/−] [ENTER] [↓] [↓]
Enter cash outflow Year 6	806 [CHS] [g] [CF$_j$]	806 [+/−] [ENTER] [↓] [↓]
Enter cash outflow Year 7	718 [CHS] [g] [CF$_j$]	718 [+/−] [ENTER] [↓] [↓]
Enter cash outflow Year 8	622 [CHS] [g] [CF$_j$]	622 [+/−] [ENTER] [↓] [↓]
Enter cash outflow Year 9	569 [CHS] [g] [CF$_j$]	569 [+/−] [ENTER] [↓] [↓]
Enter cash inflow Year 10	10,726 [g] [CF$_j$]	10,726 [ENTER] [↓] [↓]
Calculate the internal rate of return 10-year	[f] [IRR]	[IRR] [CPT]
	6.11%	6.11%

In year 10, subtract $512 from $11,238 (projected cash value for year 10) to get the net inflow of $10,726.

Internal rate of return = 6.11%

20 Year

General Calculator Approach		Specific HP12C				Specific TI BA II Plus			
							CF		
Clear the register		f	FIN			2nd	CLR Work		
Enter cash outflow Year 1	1,033	CHS	g	CF₀	1,033	+−	ENTER	↓	
Enter cash outflow Year 2	1,024	CHS	g	CFⱼ	1,024	+−	ENTER	↓	↓
Enter cash outflow Year 3	1,019	CHS	g	CFⱼ	1,019	+−	ENTER	↓	↓
Enter cash outflow Year 4	974	CHS	g	CFⱼ	974	+−	ENTER	↓	↓
Enter cash outflow Year 5	893	CHS	g	CFⱼ	893	+−	ENTER	↓	↓
Enter cash outflow Year 6	806	CHS	g	CFⱼ	806	+−	ENTER	↓	↓
Enter cash outflow Year 7	718	CHS	g	CFⱼ	718	+−	ENTER	↓	↓
Enter cash outflow Year 8	622	CHS	g	CFⱼ	622	+−	ENTER	↓	↓
Enter cash outflow Year 9	569	CHS	g	CFⱼ	569	+−	ENTER	↓	↓
Enter cash outflow Year 10	512	CHS	g	CFⱼ	512	+−	ENTER	↓	↓
Enter cash outflow Year 11	450	CHS	g	CFⱼ	450	+−	ENTER	↓	↓
Enter cash outflow Year 12	385	CHS	g	CFⱼ	385	+−	ENTER	↓	↓
Enter cash outflow Year 13	316	CHS	g	CFⱼ	316	+−	ENTER	↓	↓
Enter cash outflow Year 14	243	CHS	g	CFⱼ	243	+−	ENTER	↓	↓
Enter cash outflow Year 15	162	CHS	g	CFⱼ	162	+−	ENTER	↓	↓
Enter cash outflow Year 16	79	CHS	g	CFⱼ	79	+−	ENTER	↓	↓
Enter cash inflow Year 17	53		g	CFⱼ	53		ENTER	↓	↓
Enter cash inflow Year 18	195		g	CFⱼ	195		ENTER	↓	↓
Enter cash inflow Year 19	348		g	CFⱼ	348		ENTER	↓	↓
Enter cash inflow Year 20	36,839		g	CFⱼ	36,839		ENTER	↓	↓
Calculate the internal rate		f	IRR			IRR	CPT		
		9.70%				9.70%			

In year 20, add $36,327 (projected cash value for year 20) to $512 to get net inflow of $36,839.

Internal rate of return = 9.70%

Michael selected the term policy. Since the whole life insurance policy provided a return of 6.11 percent pretax for 10 years and 9.70 percent for 20 years, he believed he would do better by buying term and investing the difference at his 10 percent rate than by purchasing whole life insurance. If his rate of return on investments had been 5 percent, he would have come to the opposite conclusion.

ANALYSIS OF EVALUATION METHODS

Each of the two methods of comparing policies has advantages. The interest-adjusted method places emphasis on costs for life insurance policies. Individual policies are compared with one another to find the lowest cost. Normally, capital budgeting problems of this type in finance solve for present value using the net present value technique, as was shown in this chapter, but the custom in insurance is to calculate the value of cash value to life insurance outlays at a future point in time. Since the reason for purchasing life insurance is most often to protect, and protection involves expenses, a cost-based system of analysis has the advantage of being consistent with that intent.

The second method is a return-based system. It takes into account the investment component of life insurance policies and calculates the net return on the investment. The lower

Excel Solution TABLE 10.A1.4 Whole Life versus Term Policy—Excel Solution

	A	B	C	D	E	F	G	H	I
1									
2									
3	Year	Guaranteed Contract Premium	Guaranteed Death Benefit	Projected Dividend	Projected Cash Value	Term Premium	Life Premium Minus Term Premium and Dividend	10-Year Cash Flows	20-Year Cash Flows
4	1	$1,189	$100,000	0	0	$156	$1,033	($1,033)	($1,033)
5	2	$1,189	$100,000	$5	$105	$160	$1,024	($1,024)	($1,024)
6	3	$1,189	$100,000	$6	$711	$164	$1,019	($1,019)	($1,019)
7	4	$1,189	$100,000	$46	$1,858	$169	$974	($974)	($974)
8	5	$1,189	$100,000	$122	$3,182	$174	$893	($893)	($893)
9	6	$1,189	$100,000	$202	$4,490	$181	$806	($806)	($806)
10	7	$1,189	$100,000	$283	$5,986	$188	$718	($718)	($718)
11	8	$1,189	$100,000	$371	$7,678	$196	$622	($622)	($622)
12	9	$1,189	$100,000	$415	$9,328	$205	$569	($569)	($569)
13	10	$1,189	$100,000	$462	$11,238	$215	$512	$10,726	($512)
14	11	$1,189	$100,000	$512	$13,114	$227	$450		($450)
15	12	$1,189	$100,000	$563	$15,158	$241	$385		($385)
16	13	$1,189	$100,000	$617	$17,275	$256	$316		($316)
17	14	$1,189	$100,000	$674	$19,570	$272	$243		($243)
18	15	$1,189	$100,000	$736	$21,949	$291	$162		($162)
19	16	$1,189	$100,000	$798	$24,515	$312	$79		($79)
20	17	$1,189	$100,000	$905	$27,215	$337	($53)		$53
21	18	$1,189	$100,000	$1,019	$30,058	$365	($195)		$195
22	19	$1,189	$100,000	$1,143	$33,058	$394	($348)		$348
23	20	$1,189	$100,000	$1,277	$36,327	$424	($512)		$36,839
24									
25									
26	IRR								
27				= IRR(H4:H13)					
28	10-year		6.11%						
29				= IRR(I4:I23)					
30	20-year		9.70%						

the cost of the term policy used in the example, the lower the return on the investment will be. One advantage of the return-based system is that the average buyer can relate better to a given return. That number can easily be compared with estimates for alternative investment uses for the money as well as with individual whole life policies.

Appendix II

Belth Method

Joseph Belth has presented a method for calculating the yearly rate of return on the savings component of a life insurance policy. It is given in the following formula:

$$R = \frac{(CV + D) + (YPT) \times (DB - CV) \times (.001)}{(P + CVP)} - 1$$

where

$$R = \text{Yearly rate of return on savings component of policy, expressed as a decimal}$$

$$CV = \text{Current cash value at end of year}$$

$$D = \text{Annual dividend}$$

$$YPT = \text{Yearly price per \$1,000 of protection}$$

$$DB = \text{Death benefit}$$

$$P = \text{Annual premium}$$

$$CVP = \text{Cash value at end of preceding year}$$

Part Four

Specialized Planning

Specialized planning involves areas of PFP that require particular knowledge and frequently uses focused analytical tools. Insurance has a broad scope. In the previous risk management chapter, we discussed insurance overall and life insurance in particular. In Chapter 11, which deals with other insurance, we explain additional insurance essentials and present the other major types of insurance such as disability, homeowners, and automobile insurance.

Chapter 12 discusses retirement planning, often the most compelling reason for saving money—particularly for people who are middle-aged or older. Fortunately, there is a method for establishing the amount needed; it is outlined here and described in the final section of the book.

Educational planning, as given in Chapter 13, is a second major household outlay, often for children of adult household members, and presents an approach to establishing adequate resources for college. We have included financial literacy in this chapter as well because a lack of financial knowledge is so common among some groups. Several educational methods for attaining financial literacy are suggested.

Chapter **Eleven**

Other Insurance

Chapter Goals

This chapter will enable you to:

- Determine when insurance should be used.
- Describe the role property and liability insurance has in managing potential losses in real property and legal liability.
- Indicate how personal insurance can reduce losses in human exposures.
- Explain how significant the federal and state governments are in limiting risks.

Our meeting was brief. Dan and Laura dropped a satchel full of individual insurance policies on my desk and said, "Please examine them."

Real Life Planning

Our country has come a long way over the past half century. An average family then might have had a life insurance policy, a modest amount of bank savings, and a union or company pension to carry them through retirement. Life insurance was particularly important because there was typically only one wage earner in a family and if something happened to that person, usually the husband, the family could be in dire straits. Over the 50 years since, things have changed significantly: two-wage-earner households have grown in popularity, life expectancies have risen, and disposable incomes have increased. The insurance industry has had to compete more intensely with other financial institutions and products offering returns for the consumer dollar. For example, believe it or not, 60 years ago many considered stocks too risky to be placed in company pension funds or the average household's portfolio, nor were mutual funds widely used.

Insurance companies responded to the heightened competition with equity-related products such as variable life and variable annuities. Many grew larger by offering products in several different areas of the insurance industry. Moreover, the lines of distinction between an insurance company, a bank, a stock-brokerage firm, and an investment company began to blur, with some companies taking on several of these functions. Consequently, insurance companies developed a significant position in return-related products.

Meanwhile, from a risk standpoint, the increase in the average household's wealth allowed people to focus on additional risk management tools. Disability policies for working-age people and long-term care, which, in essence, is a disability policy after retirement, grew in popularity. So did cost-of-living adjustments in policies to protect against the impact of inflation. The government's role in risk management increased. Programs such as workers' compensation for disabilities developed on the job, and Social Security, Medicare for medical attention for the elderly, and Medicaid for the poor were either developed or expanded.

In some cases costs for existing insurance coverage grew as well. The desire for high-quality medical attention and the increased expense for sophisticated medical devices and drugs made medical coverage perhaps the single most expensive insurance coverage. Accident and settlement claims cost in automobile, medical, and other areas rose sharply in an increasingly litigious society.

The safety net around individuals and families as established by government and private insurance has grown significantly, which has created an environment conducive to spending with little fear and investing more aggressively than in previous periods. As future incomes and technological capabilities increase the range of risk management, offerings for households are likely to continue to expand.

OVERVIEW

In the previous chapter, you learned about the important role that risk management has in household planning. Often people's attention is focused on investments and improving financial and nonfinancial asset returns. However, by balancing risk and return and helping protect valuable assets, risk management in general and insurance in particular contribute significantly to achieving household efficiency and well-being.

In this chapter, we will continue the analysis of insurance begun in the previous one with life insurance. You will learn about specific risk management tools provided by insurance companies and the government, for each of the major household assets.

We will start by explaining when insurance is suitable and discuss common risk management terms. We will then elaborate on difficulties that insurance companies have in determining risks and the ways they have developed to reduce their expenses. It is helpful to understand why insurance companies institute the procedures they do.[1] Following that, we will describe the private policies that protect household tangible and human assets. Finally, we will discuss governmental policies that provide coverage.

WHEN IS INSURANCE SUITABLE?

From a practical standpoint, insurance should be used when you want to alter your exposure to risk and can do this efficiently. Insurance can be attractive when infrequent but severe losses that can cause hardship to you are present. The insurance company can diversify away its risk. Hardship means the losses can have a material impact on the household's overall financial condition or current cash resources. Insurance agents call this hardship **severity.** Insuring against all losses is extremely costly and therefore inefficient. Although it may seem surprising to some, when losses are material and there is a strong likelihood that they will occur, insurance may not be the appropriate choice. When losses happen very often, referred to as high **frequency,** insurance companies end up adding on their overhead costs to the losses; you end up paying more with insurance than without it.

Try to develop a rough idea of the cost of the loss and its probability and compare it with the premiums. If the costs are too high, and the impact is manageable, consider self-insuring. For example, many years ago when disability insurance first was offered, many insurance brokers said the cost was too high relative to the benefit. Once the insurance companies had more claims experience and competition increased, disability coverage became a more efficient risk-reduction mechanism.

---

[1] It can foster a more positive attitude toward their goals, which, with the possible exception of personal claims, may not be that dissimilar from policyholder objectives. It also can result in a more efficient search for low-cost policies. For example, given the knowledge that life payouts are based on policyholder life spans, it may be useful to be aware that certain professionals live longer than average, thereby making policies for professionals potentially more cost-effective.

TABLE 11.1
Loss Frequency
and Severity

	High Severity	**Low Severity**
High Frequency	Retention	Retention
Low Frequency	Purchase insurance	Retention

Table 11.1 summarizes an appropriate insurance strategy for pure risks. Notice that it only calls for purchasing insurance under high-severity, low-frequency circumstances. In other cases, retaining risk by self-insurance is the appropriate strategy. Retaining risk highlights the need to practice other risk management approaches such as risk avoidance and diversification.

Insurance often also can be made more cost-efficient by considering high deductibles in coverage. Processing a claim can be relatively expensive for an insurance company. Often you can receive a higher potential return on your insurance payment by selecting a copayment up to a high but still manageable amount.

Example 11.1

John, young and in good health, bought a medical insurance policy with a $2,000 annual deductible that cost him $1,000 less than the normal $200 deductible. John's medical payments had not exceeded $200 annually over the past several years.

Therefore, since in the past John had not had a high frequency or severity, he decided to assume some initial risk by self-insuring by selecting a large deductible, and saving on the costs of a higher premium.

RISK MANAGEMENT AND INSURANCE TERMS

There are a variety of terms commonly used in connection with risk management overall and insurance in particular. In many cases, there are two terms in each category that can be contrasted with one another. Occasionally they are used incorrectly—for example, peril and hazard are sometimes confused, as are risk and uncertainty. We have listed some terms below.

There are two types of risk we should differentiate, business risk and pure risk:

A **business risk** is a risk taken for potential reward. An example of business risk might be expanding your business into a new area. If you succeed, say your overall profits might increase 20 percent; if you don't succeed, your entire investment becomes an unrecovered cash outflow or, in other words, a loss.

Pure risk is a risk that carries no financial reward. An example might be skydiving. This is a hobby that might cause an insurance company not to issue a life insurance policy to you. Most exposures are pure risks since the loss of income or assets carries no reward.[2] This leads to efforts to reduce pure risk.

We should be able to distinguish risk from uncertainty. Uncertainty involves no knowledge of outcomes. With risk, the exact outcome is not known, but the probabilities for alternative outcomes are. For example, if someone asked you what the weather was going to be tomorrow and you hadn't listened to the weather report, you would say you were uncertain. If you had heard the forecast, you might have said there was an 80 percent probability of rain and could add that the person would be taking a risk by not carrying an umbrella. In common parlance, the two terms are often used interchangeably.

We also should understand the following commonly used terms in connection with risk:

Perils are exposures to the risk of loss. Examples are floods or fires.

---

[2] Taking a high-paying job that carries a health risk is an exception.

Hazards increase the probability of a peril. For example, having a home near a river that overflows every 10 years or so increases the likelihood of a flood. There are three types of hazards:

- A **physical hazard** is a deficiency in physical property that increases the possibility of loss. Leaving your car door unlocked when leaving it on a busy city street would be one example.

- A **moral hazard** arises from actions taken by the insured person that increase the possibility of loss. A dishonest person purchasing a disability insurance policy from a company with the intention of aggravating a nagging back injury because he or she plans to collect on the policy is an example of a moral hazard. Another is taking out a life insurance policy because you know something the insurance company doesn't—that heart disease at an early age is common in your family background.

- In a **morale hazard,** the risk comes not from dishonesty but from a person behaving negligently because he or she has insurance coverage. An example would be getting into an accident because a person was driving while intoxicated, knowing that any damage to the car would be paid by the insurance company.

If insurance companies had perfect information, they could place clients in risk classes based on probabilities of losses at the beginning of the business relationship and provide less expensive policies for the average client. But as you know, there is asymmetric information in connection with insurance. That means insurance applicants know more about themselves and their probability of future actions than their company does.

Under adverse selection, the customer base drawn to an insurance product may differ and be less attractive than that of the population as a whole. For example, people with family histories of Alzheimer's disease may purchase long-term care insurance and the greater payments to that group of individuals could drive up the cost of buying long-term insurance for people who have a normal chance of an insurance policy payout.

The industry's competitive drive to identify these problems and minimize them to lower costs has resulted in the following practices:

Insurable interest simply says you generally can only insure against loss of items that you yourself would suffer a loss on, should they be damaged or eliminated entirely. For example, if you took out an insurance policy on a building you were scheduled to buy in three days, but the building was destroyed the next day, you would not be able to collect. You did not suffer a loss. By restricting most insurance to those adversely affected by the loss, insurance companies hope to limit the use of policies to earn a profit instead of to hedge potential losses.

Under **indemnity,** your maximum reimbursement in the event of loss of an asset you own is the value of the item. As with insurable interest, there is an economic reason for indemnity. If you could gain personally by triggering a loss, you might be tempted to do so. Not only would rates rise for other people insured, but the economy would operate less efficiently. For example, if you were earning $100,000 a year but had insurance coverage when disabled for $200,000, more people might attempt disability leave, thereby reducing the productivity of the overall economy. Indemnity therefore reduces potential moral and morale hazards of dishonest and careless behaviors that lead to greater insurance claims.

The industry has further reacted by several means.[3]

---

[3] See David Mayers and Clifford W. Smith Jr., "Contractual Provisions, Organizational Structure, and Conflict Control in Insurance Markets," *Journal of Business* 54, no. 3 (July 1981), pp. 407–34.

Screening and Segregation of Applicants

Screening and segregation of insurance applicants involves separating people based on their risk categories. Two examples are rejecting people with serious illnesses from life insurance coverage and placing smokers in a higher-risk, higher-premium class.

Institution of Deductibles

Under deductibles, the insurance company reimburses individuals' claims only for the amount above an established minimum. The process of coinsuring can reduce moral and morale hazards as well as processing costs.

Use of Coinsurance

With **coinsurance,** the policyholder pays a certain percentage of the outlay along with the insurance company; often this is subject to an overall cap on payments by the holder. Coinsurance makes the insured more careful in practice and also reduces the need for insurance companies to monitor payments on claims. Coinsurance can take the following forms:

1. *Instituting exclusions and waiting periods.* Exclusions involve eliminating certain conditions from insurance company payout when a new contract is drawn up. For example, the contract may exclude coverage of prior health conditions on a new health policy often for a fixed amount of time. It serves to screen against adverse selection. Having periods before reimbursements are allowed can serve the same function, as can reducing moral and morale hazards.

2. *Prespecified limits.* Prespecified limits establish the amount the insurance company is willing to pay contractually. They can limit the amount of litigation and absolute exposure for the company. Examples would be $1 million for medical expenses in total or four visits per year to a psychologist.

3. *Experience-based alteration in policy costs.* Charging rates to policyholders based on their loss experience after they have become clients reduces the problems of moral and morale hazards and makes insurance more competitive and attractive for those people with low claims experience.

4. *Use of group policies.* Group policies can offer a number of advantages over individual policies for both the company and the policyholder. If the groups are not established for insurance purposes alone, and the insurance covers all the participants such as all corporate employees, insurance companies are not subject to adverse selection. Monitoring costs for moral and morale hazards are covered, at least in part, by the business itself. For example, the corporation may itself investigate the validity of an illness for an employee who is not working and is receiving disability payments.

   In some cases, employees may be more straightforward about their actions in group insurance claims because they know that not doing so might inhibit their progress within the company. Finally, taking out a group policy can reduce processing and marketing costs. Consequently, group policies may cost significantly less for coverage, although in some cases they also may provide less flexibility in tailoring terms to individual needs.

Coinsurance is most commonly associated with major medical insurance where the insurer and the insured share costs up to a certain point, say 80 percent for insurer and 20 percent for the insured, up to a certain amount per year. Beyond that amount, the insurer pays all. It is also commonly used for property insurance when, as will be explained later in the chapter, replacement cost comes into play.

Mutual Companies versus Stockholder-Owned Companies

There are two major forms of legal structures for private insurers: mutual and stockholder-owned companies. Mutual companies in insurance are those that are owned by the policyholders. Stockholder-owned insurance companies are run for the benefit of the stockholders.

Practical Comment   Claims Practices

The feeling exists among some policyholders that insurance companies attempt to find ways to not pay out claims. A more favorable and perhaps more accurate view would be that competition forces the companies to make their policies more efficient and less expensive for their current and potential customers. Items such as deductibles and the exclusions discussed can help achieve that goal. From an economic standpoint, insurance companies may be driven by market forces to pare down their costs, while those that move too far in rejecting claims can develop a less favorable reputation. Each individual will naturally try to maximize reimbursement for a claim from the insurance company and should examine the terms of each insurance policy. Nonetheless, at least in theory, more stringent restrictions in insurance company payouts can be viewed as in the policyholder's interest.

Stockholder-owned company actions in attempting to maximize profits for their owners may conflict with the interests of policyholders. In recent times, several large insurance companies have switched from mutual to stockholder status.

NEEDS ANALYSIS

The question of how much insurance is needed arises in all areas of insurance coverage. The calculation of need can simply be the net present value of potential losses in income or assets. The methodology for doing so will be presented in Chapter 18, Appendix I. However, deciding on the amount and types of insurance to pay for varies by household. One household may seek protection against all losses, another partially insure, and still another not insure at all. Here we discuss some of the many factors that enter into household decision making.

General Characteristics

In this instance, the term *need* has to do with whether the household believes purchasing the insurance is essential. Households may be more apt to purchase insurance against a loss that is more likely to occur or one that would have more impact on their lifestyle. They are attracted to policies whose costs they consider affordable.

Tolerance for Risk

The expected value of payments for losses will be lower than the amount policyholders contribute to purchase the policy. Therefore, insurance is a cost that can limit a household's current and prospective future funds available for leisure expenditures. Consequently, households will clearly differ on the amount and type of insurance purchased based on their willingness to assume risks, thereby trading off income for safety. In short, households with low tolerances for risk will be more attracted to insurance.

Personal Likelihood of Occurrence

Insurance will be a "better buy" the less it costs relative to the probability of risk. When a person believes he or she is at more risk for a negative occurrence than the population at large, and the insurance cost has not been raised for that increased occurrence, he or she is more likely to take out insurance. It is this greater willingness that ensures adverse selection difficulties for insurance companies and other holders.

FIGURE 11.1
Major Types of
Insurance

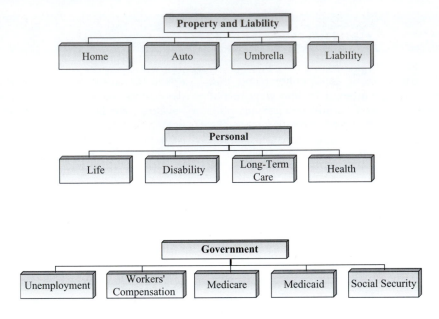

TYPES OF INSURANCE COVERAGE

Insurance coverage can be separated into three areas. The first, property and liability, generally is concerned with coverage arising from losses in real property and in connection with legal liability. It includes homeowners insurance, automotive insurance, umbrella insurance, and liability to others. The second is personal insurance, which is concerned with losses in human assets. Personal insurance includes life insurance, which we discussed in Chapter 10, as well as disability insurance, long-term care, and health insurance. The third type of coverage, the many forms of insurance provided by the federal and state governments, can be called social insurance. It includes Social Security, unemployment insurance, Medicare and Medicaid, and workers' compensation.

The types of coverage are given in Figure 11.1.

PROPERTY AND LIABILITY INSURANCE

Property and liability insurance is concerned with protection of the assets used in household production and any personal liabilities that arise because of them. The major areas we will discuss are property insurance for the home, automobile, liability, and umbrella insurance.

Property Insurance

Homeowners insurance is concerned with losses, fire, theft, flood, termite damage, hurricanes, and so on. Both real property and personal property related to the home are covered. **Real property** includes dwellings and other structures that are affixed to land. Land itself is not covered by insurance, perhaps because it generally cannot be destroyed. **Personal property** comprises assets that are not affixed to the land and therefore are usually portable. Originally, the individual risks involved with the home were separately insured; now they are usually combined in a single policy. The risks covered may be listed separately. Often 16 separately stated risks are used. These may be similarly stated among policies or may include all relevant risks except the ones separately stated.

TABLE 11.2
Types of Homeowners
Policies

Name	Type of Dwelling	Type of Coverage	Comments
HO-1	Homeowner	Basic coverage	Less comprehensive, less popular, and not always available.
HO-2	Homeowner	Broad coverage	It has separately stated risk coverages.
HO-3	Homeowner	Special coverage	It covers more risks than HO-1 and HO-2 and is the most popular policy of the three.
HO-4	Tenant	Contents broad form	Since house or apartment is not owned by a tenant, the policy principally covers risks to personal property.
HO-5	Homeowner	Comprehensive coverage	The standard HO-5 policy offers broader coverage than an HO-3 policy. While the HO-3 policy provides named-perils coverage, the standard HO-5 provides open-perils or all-risks coverage on personal property.
HO-6	Condominium and cooperative	Unit owner's form	For people who share ownership in a building such as an apartment or a townhouse.
HO-8	Homeowner	Modified coverage	For houses that have replacement cost greater than their fair market value. For example, a historic or period house.

Types of Policies

There are various types of homeowners policies, as listed in Table 11.2.

Contract Terms

Property insurance contracts generally have structured terms. We will use HO-3 as an example. It specifies which assets are covered and for what types of losses. Perils that are excluded are stated. It also lists the conditions under which the policy will pay out benefits.

The assets that are included are separated in Table 11.3.

Liability to others as covered under coverages E and F have different standards depending on whether the person injured was a trespasser or was invited into the house. The dwelling and personal property exclusions often differ somewhat. Major overall exclusions include war, earthquake, flood, intentional loss, neglect, nuclear hazard, defects in title for property bought, and so on.

Amount of Coverage

Assets are valued for loss purposes either on an actual cash value at the time of the loss or on a replacement cost basis. The actual cash value approach uses replacement cost but takes into account depreciation, the physical wear and tear on the asset. For example, your roofing may have cost $6,000 and lasted for eight years. Its replacement cost could be $10,000 due to rapid inflation. Assuming a complete loss after four years, under actual cash value your maximum reimbursement subject to policy limits would be 50 percent of $10,000, or $5,000. That is because you had use of the asset for half of its useful life, four of its eight years.

TABLE 11.3
Types of Property
Coverages

Coverage Type	Explanation
A	The dwelling and other property attached to it such as a garage.
B	Structures not attached to the dwelling.
C	Personal property.
D	Outlays for expenses when damage does not allow occupation.
E	Personal liability, which includes the cost of litigation and the proceeds of the suit.
F	Medical payments to injured parties.

With the replacement cost method, depreciation is not deducted. You would receive the full $10,000 in the example above. Your actual reimbursement with either method would depend on deductibles and coinsurance clauses. Deductibles limit small claims, which are costly to the insurer and would reduce major losses by a relatively modest amount. Company insurance in which you coinsure part of the cost in the event of loss is more involved. The policy states what percentage of replacement cost you are required to maintain to receive full payment from the insurer. Often it is 80 percent or 90 percent of the needed outlay. If you are below that figure, you will absorb part of the loss according to the following formula:

$$\text{Insurance reimbursement} = \frac{\text{Amount of insurance in force}}{\text{Amount of insurance required}} \times \text{Amount of loss}$$

where

$$\text{Amount of insurance required} = \text{Coinsurance percentage} \times \text{Replacement cost}$$

Example 11.2

Martin had a fire resulting in a $110,000 loss on his home. The cost to replace the home was $300,000. Martin had a policy requiring that, for full payment, he maintain insurance coverage of 90 percent of replacement cost. At the time of the loss, he had $250,000 of insurance outstanding with no deductibles. How much will he collect?

$$\begin{aligned}
\text{Insurance reimbursement} &= \frac{\$250,000}{90\% \times \$300,000} \times \$110,000 \\
&= \frac{\$250,000}{\$270,000} \times \$110,00 \\
&= \$101,852
\end{aligned}$$

Martin would receive $101,852 from the insurance company and would, in effect, coinsure for the remainder of the loss, which is $8,148.

Note that in the event of full loss, unless insurance coverage taken out equaled 100 percent of the loss, the amount reimbursed would be less than the full value of your loss. To prevent this from happening, in addition to the policy, an inflation guard that would increase coverage each year can be put into effect. Alternatively, you can take out guaranteed replacement cost coverage, which will ensure your receiving full replacement cost for loss even if it exceeds the face value of your policy.

The replacement cost method is often viewed as an exception to indemnity because you can be better off after a loss than before.[4] For example, you could have paid $200,000 for a house, but, if it is completely demolished in a fire, you may receive $350,000, the current replacement cost for the home. Because of that, insurers may require that you rebuild to collect on a replacement cost policy. If you choose not to rebuild, you may receive only an amount equal to the actual cash outlay.

There are exceptions to coverage. Earthquake insurance may be available through a rider to the policy. Flood insurance is supervised and underwritten by the Federal Emergency Management Agency (FEMA). There are requirements to qualify for the insurance. Title insurance reimburses you for loss in the event the title you received is defective in whole or in part. It is available through a separate policy that requires a single payment at inception.

---

[4] Another point of view is that to indemnify means to make secure against loss and that is what replacement cost coverage provides. However, by providing you with the funds to purchase a brand new property, you are generally in a more advantageous position than with a partially worn one.

Practical Comment   Property Coverage

Many people are unaware that insurance covers property losses for example, a house, and not the land on which the property is sited. Land by itself is seldom permanently affected by a catastrophic event. The lack of knowledge extends to property and people are often underinsured on real property and its possessions. Property prices tend to be correlated with inflation and can be volatile. In a strong economic period for houses, prices can increase at a rate well in excess of inflation. A family's possessions can become more valuable through additional purchases over a number of years. Consequently, it is a good idea to review property coverage periodically and consider replacement cost coverage.

Second, it is important not to lose sight of personal practices that can reduce the possibility of losses. Keeping doors closed with secure locks, turning off water pipes when leaving homes for winter vacations, installing smoke detectors and a burglar alarm system are a few such safety precautions. In some cases, insurance rates can be reduced by such precautions—for example, installing an alarm system and smoke detectors.

Thus, it is not part of a homeowners policy. Each time you refinance your mortgage, generally a new policy is written.[5]

Personal property is always included under a homeowners policy but with significant limits on coverage available.[6] Personal articles can be handled through a floater. A **floater** covers the named items wherever they may be located. Examples of items that a floater might cover are jewelry, fine art, and silver above the limits in the policy for these items.

Taxation

Payments as reimbursement for property losses are not taxable. Property losses themselves, whether the result of theft, an act of nature, an accident, or some other cause, are tax-deductible to the extent they exceed $100 per occurrence and 10 percent of your adjusted gross income for the year.[7]

Automobile Insurance

Automobile insurance is the most widely used form of property and liability insurance. Most households own a car and accidents occur. Further efforts are being made to build safer cars, have less injury-prone highways, and require that seatbelts be used on a regular basis. The emphasis for automobile insurance has been broadened over the past 50 years from protecting yourself and your property to paying for suits from third parties. In fact, having personal auto insurance in prestated amounts, which is mandatory in some states, is done in part to protect third parties. In addition to injury to others, coverage includes you and your family members and other persons using your car.

The automobile policy is separated into six sections:[8] bodily injury liability, medical payments, property damage, collision, uninsured motorist coverage, and the comprehensive section. Each part is separately priced. Bodily injury liability covers injury to others caused by you and injury to you and members of your family when driving someone else's automobile.

Medical payments reimburse you for injuries to the driver and passengers within your car. Property damage covers damage you or a designated driver in your car makes to someone

---

[5] Actually there are two policies: lender's title policy that indemnifies the lender up to the amount of the mortgage and owner's title policy that indemnifies the borrower (owner) for the full value of the house.

[6] Usually a percentage of the insurance value of the homeowners policy.

[7] Or to the extent that they are not reimbursed by insurance and meet the other limits, such as deductibles or coinsurance costs.

[8] See "Auto Insurance Information" seciton on the Web site of the Insurance Information Institute, http://www.iii.org/individuals/auto.

else's property. Most frequently it involves your damage to another's automobile, but it also covers damage to other property such as buildings or lamp posts. Collision covers damage to your car whether through impacting another automobile or by the vehicle turning over. If the accident wasn't your fault, your insurance company will seek to recover from the other driver's insurance company.

Uninsured motorist coverage reimburses you for uninsured, underinsured, and hit-and-run drivers who cause losses to you. Comprehensive insurance covers auto-related losses that arise from theft or damage to your property, but not those that come from another automobile.

The price of automobile coverage depends on such factors as the type of the car, the age of drivers, and their previous accident and driving violations record. Your rate can be changed to reflect your incidence of accidents during the time you are covered by the company.

Many states have instituted modified no-fault automobile insurance claims. No-fault does not seek to assign blame for an accident. With no-fault automobile insurance, each person is paid for damages by his or her own insurance carrier. Unlike the traditional system, there is no need for an injured party to sue in order to collect damages. Damages under no-fault may exclude pain and suffering. Modified no-fault may use no-fault for cases that are not as involved and revert to the traditional tort system for serious injuries or death. (A tort is an act of wrongdoing and serves as the basis for the lawsuit to be compensated for the loss.) The no-fault approach is intended to reduce litigation expenses and help protect third parties.

Liability Insurance

Liability insurance protects you personally against having to pay for a variety of potential losses to others. Consequently, it is called **third-party coverage.** Third-party liabilities occur through personal injuries and property damage to others caused by you. Such liabilities extend to your home and you and other family members and to personal operations as they pertain to exposures to others. Third-party coverage stands in contrast to losses to you or to your property directly, which is sometimes called **first-party coverage.**

An individual's exposure to others has expanded considerably since the early 1970s.[9] Historically, in order to collect money from others, you had to prove negligence, which involved establishing that the party who caused the injury had been careless. Establishing negligence and the amount of loss was left up to the jury to decide.

In the 1970s, according to Priest, judges began to award much larger sums as damages when the judges found defendants at fault. They were influenced by what they thought would be a deterrent to accidents in the future.[10] In addition, there was a shift from the doctrine of strictly causing a loss to contributory negligence by each party to a loss, and greater sums were provided for poor victims. In the 1980s and 1990s, there was some shift back, with caps set on damages and limits on reimbursement for pain and suffering.[11] But all in all, individuals become more vulnerable to significant damages in third-party suits.

Basically, a personal automobile policy covers auto-related bodily injury and property damage to others. An umbrella policy, discussed below, may be purchased to augment coverage.

Umbrella Insurance

Umbrella insurance is a broadly diversified grouping of property and liability coverages in addition to liability coverage under existing home owners and automobile insurance policies. It is also known as excess liability insurance. This means that, generally, it does

---

[9] See George L. Priest, "The Modern Expansion of Tort Liability: Its Sources, Its Effects, and Its Reform," *Journal of Economic Perspectives* 5, no. 3 (Summer 1991), pp. 31–50.

[10] Ibid.

[11] Patricia H. Born and W. Kip Viscusi, "The Distribution of the Insurance Market Effects of Tort Liability Returns," *Brookings Papers on Economic Activity* (1998), pp. 55–100.

not pay until the limits of coverage in the primary insurance policy are reached. In today's litigious society with large awards being made, umbrella insurance can reduce your exposure to catastrophic losses.

Umbrella insurance generally has a minimum coverage of $1 million and rises in increments of $1 million. Since the prospect of insurance company payout is relatively low, coverage is often inexpensive. Contract provisions are nonstandard, which means you must read each policy carefully to see what is or is not covered.

The scope of umbrella coverage is often greater than that of comprehensive personal liability insurance. For example, it may include personal liabilities other than bodily injury such as slander and defamation of character. Property that you own or rent is often excluded, as are your business activities. Umbrella insurance may be offered by your auto insurer or your homeowner insurer, giving you broader coverage and higher limits than in the normal automobile policy or homeowner policy. Normally, an umbrella policy requires certain basic coverage to qualify for its usage.

PERSONAL INSURANCE

Whether they are expressed in strict economic money terms or in broader lifestyle terms, human assets usually represent our most important holding over our life cycle. Personal insurance protects our human assets against losses for our own and other household members' benefit. Life insurance, which protects our heirs against the wage earner's untimely death, was discussed in Chapter 10. In this chapter, we consider Social Security benefits to spouse and other dependents after the wage earner dies.

In addition, we will discuss many other types of insurance, whether they are funded by the people covered, the corporation that employs them, or the federal or state government. Health insurance provides funds to defray the costs of sickness through individual and group health insurance policies and government Medicare and Medicaid plans. Disability insurance provides cash flows to partially or fully replace your salary, as does workers' compensation when your injuries are job-related. Long-term care through personal and government policies defrays the cost of being disabled after you retire. Unemployment insurance protects against loss of income due to termination of your job.

Health Insurance

Background

Health insurance provides direct payment or reimburses you for medical expenses in connection with illness or accident. Health care is one of the country's most expensive costs, and, as shown in Table 11.4, this cost has risen over the past 40 years.

The majority of individuals and their families receive their medical coverage through the workplace or the government. A breakdown of sources of coverage is shown in Table 11.5.

TABLE 11.4
Health Care Costs

Source: U.S. Department of Health and Human Services, Centers for Medicare and Medicaid Services, "National Health Expenditures Data 1960–2004."

Year	National Health Care Expenditures		
	Amount (in billions)	Percentage of GDP	Per Capita Amount (in dollars)
1960	$28	5.2%	$148
1970	75	7.2	357
1980	255	9.1	1,106
1990	717	12.4	2,821
2000	1,359	13.8	4,729
2004	1,878	16.0	6,280

TABLE 11.5
Health Insurance Coverage

Source: U.S. Census Bureau, "Income, Poverty, and Health Insurance Coverage in the United States: 2004."

	Coverage as a Percentage of the Population	
Type of Health Insurance	**2004**	**2003**
Private insurance	68.1%	68.6%
Employment-based	59.8	60.4
Direct purchase	9.3	9.2
Government insurance	27.2	26.6
Medicare	13.7	13.7
Medicaid	12.9	12.4
Military health care	3.7	3.5
Insured	**84.3%**	**84.4%**
Uninsured	**15.7**	**15.6**

Group policies through business are an efficient method of receiving coverage. As mentioned earlier, businesses assume a portion of the administrative costs, and, particularly when they pay for the cost of the policy for all workers, they protect against adverse selection. The economies of scale in group policies are indicated by the fact that overhead expenses account for 51.6 percent of premium income for individual policies but only 9.5 percent of group policies.[12]

The structure of the health care industry has changed significantly in recent decades. As a major funder of medical costs, large corporations and others sought ways of reducing their expenses as their cost of coverage rose. The outcome was a change from the individual doctor to the group practice, the rise of health maintenance organizations (HMOs) and other health care management systems, and more emphasis on decision making by the insurance company.

Your goal is to identify the health need and then to find the type of provider that best meets that need. For example, if you are a healthy individual earning a modest income, you might select an HMO, while an older person, having some physical problems might use a point of service (POS) or preferred provider organization (PPO). Of course, some businesses do not offer alternatives. Clearly, cost and the choice of doctors are key determinants.

Types of Providers

Blue Cross–Blue Shield   Blue Cross–Blue Shield is a traditional provider that has been given nonprofit status by individual states. Different regions or states will have different approaches. With rates regulated by the states and their charter often restricting their ability to limit their clientele, many local Blue Cross–Blue Shield providers have had financial difficulties. Some have reorganized and moved to profit status.

Health Maintenance Organizations   Health maintenance organizations, or HMOs, provide a full range of medical services for a flat fee. Often there is a physician as primary care provider who may control the level of specialized medical services. The HMO may support regularly scheduled checkups and healthful practices. The doctors can work for the insurer, as an independent group, or as individual practitioners, in which case they may be paid based on the volume and complexity of services rendered. Such an approach is called a fee-for-service basis. Alternatively, doctors may be paid a total amount per patient under management, regardless of the amount of service rendered. This approach is called being compensated on a capitation basis.

---

[12] See Kenneth Arrow, "Uncertainty and the Welfare Economics of Medical Care," *American Economic Review* 53, no. 5 (December 1963), pp. 941–73.

Point of Service Systems   With point of service systems (POSs), patients can choose either POS doctors or non-POS providers of health care. The patient receives a greater choice of doctors but must finance a significant coinsurance payment for each visit.

Preferred Provider Organizations   Preferred provider organizations (PPOs) are fairly similar to point of service providers. One difference is that while PPOs use primary care physicians, they are not used as gatekeepers whose approval is needed in order to be reimbursed for additional services. The providers are often independent individual or group practices that offer a discount for a volume of patients.[13]

Individual Contracts   Individual contracts may separately cover hospitalization, surgery, and ongoing medical expenditure or cover all in the form of a major medical policy. The policies may be noncancelable, in which case your coverage cannot be dropped in the event of illness, and renewable so that your annual fee is not raised unless all members of your group are given a similar price increase. To discourage frequent use, many policies have deductibles and a copayment, with individual payments per illness or per year limited in amount. There is also a stated maximum amount over a life span that the insurance company will have to pay.

In sum, most types of medical coverage include a basic medical expense policy for doctors; nonsurgical costs whether in or out of the hospital; a basic hospital policy for hospital costs such as room, board, and ancillary services (testing costs, etc.); and a basic surgical policy to pay for the surgeon's costs, whether in or out of the hospital. Major medical policies can provide broad coverage and are used for expensive care. They usually have deductible and participation requirements. They generally have high maximum payments allowed. They may be the sole coverage a person has or, in some cases, may provide additional coverage when another policy providing basic coverage has reached its limits. In all cases, the insured generally doesn't receive a benefit in excess of the cost no matter how much coverage exists.

Policy Differentiation

The majority of people are given policies at their workplace. Their choice may be limited to HMOs versus a broader variety of doctors at a higher cost. For those who select individual policies or who are given a choice, some features in which policies differ include

1. Deductible copayment and coinsurance clauses.
2. Ease with which you can be approved for services you desire or wish to have.
3. Inclusion of such things as prescription drug costs.
4. Exclusions—for example, initial lack of coverage for current illnesses or preexisting conditions.
5. Stated lifetime limits, which in some contracts and cases can actually exceed those limits.
6. Benchmarks for reimbursement levels, which can result in your not being reimbursed fully for the insurer's share of the coinsurance payment. There may be less than full reimbursement because of internal dollar limits on any one procedural cost, hospital room cost, or nursing cost, often based on reasonable and customary averages for the procedure in your geographical area.

---

[13] Some POS providers are now offering direct access to specialists as well, thereby diminishing the differences between them.

7. Ability to interact with a skilled employee representative and receive an appropriate response to questions about coverage and disputed reimbursement allowances.

Under the Consolidated Omnibus Budget Reconciliation Act of 1986, or COBRA, the federal government requires that people who leave positions be allowed to maintain their medical coverage for a maximum of 18 months regardless of their medical condition at the time.[14] The former employee must pay for the policy. The law requires that employers who have more than 20 employees and maintain a group medical plan follow COBRA's continuation provisions.[15]

Disability Insurance

Disability insurance provides cash flows to compensate you when you are unable to work due to an accident or illness. Long-term disability is a very costly problem. In effect, you can be compelled to retire temporarily or permanently with insufficient income to support yourself and members of your family. Yet disability insurance is not nearly as popular as life insurance. Apparently, 22 percent of those in the working population have long-term disability policies, while over 80 percent of all families have some form of life insurance.[16] This disparity exists even though it costs a family more to sustain itself when the disabled family member is living than when that person dies and the cost is eliminated.

There are many types of disability insurance including those from Social Security, state workers' compensation, and corporate and personal policies. We will discuss private plans first, which encompass those offered through business, often either partially or fully subsidized as an employee benefit, or directly through employee purchases.

Private Disability Insurance

Private insurance can be divided into two parts, short-term and long-term disability in one policy or separate policies. Short-term disability policies provide income for illnesses for up to a few years, while long-term disability covers longer periods, most commonly ranging from 10 years and usually up to ages 65 or 70. Short-term illnesses can be covered through sick days, continuing compensation by a business that may self-insure for this expense, or short-term disability policies. Approximately 60 percent of the workforce is covered by short-term disability policies. For long-term disability, 15 percent of the workforce is covered under group policies and 7 percent under private policies.[17]

Here we look at some of the important features that differentiate private long-term disability policies.

Definition of Disability   The definition of disability describes the terms under which the insurance company will pay money out. The strongest definition of disability is **own occupation.** Under this definition, payments are made when you are unable to work in your existing occupation. A broader definition would have payment begin when you are

---

[14] May be extended to 36 months under some circumstances.

[15] In some cases, widows and students may have longer than 18 months. Also, many states have continuation coverage copying the federal law.

[16] Larry A. Cox, "Disability Income Insurance and the Individual," *Financial Services Review* 1, no. 1 (1991), pp. 61–78.

[17] Ibid.

unable to work at any occupation that you are qualified for based on your education experience and training. The more restrictive the definition the better because it can allow payments to begin even though you can work in another occupation.

Example 11.3   John was a gynecologist. He developed an inner ear problem and was unable to deliver babies anymore. He took a position as business manager for a medical practice. Only one of his two disability policies had an own occupation definition in it. It paid the face amount of monthly income despite the fact that he earned a comfortable salary in a related field. The other policy did not provide any support.

Elimination Period   The elimination period is the time before disability payments begin, which is often three to six months.

Residual Benefit   Residual benefit is a partial payment when you have returned to your job but with a shorter work week and reduced income. In effect, at that point, you are partially disabled. Payments are based on the difference between your former and current salaries.

Preexisting Condition   A preexisting condition clause in a policy may state that it will not pay out benefits for illnesses or injury that occurred within a period of time before the policy was taken out, or the policy may state that such conditions are permanently excluded from reimbursement.

Rehabilitation Benefit   Some policies will reimburse you for outlays that help to rehabilitate you and may serve to bring you back into the workforce more quickly. Insurance carriers generally offer these programs that assist in going back to work so as to reduce the amount of payments to the insured that would have been necessary with a slower return to work.

Cost-of-Living Rider   The cost-of-living rider can adjust the amount of the initial payment and/or the ongoing payment once disabled for the effects of inflation. The increase may be based on the consumer price index or rise by a stated amount per year, and it can be subject to an overall cap.

Due to insurance company concerns about potential worker incentives to profit from illnesses, most coverage of disability policies is limited to 60 to 70 percent of income. Disability income is taxable if the policy was paid for by the company and is tax-free if the policy was paid for by the policyholder with after-tax money.[18]

Social Security Disability

The Social Security system pays disability income to people who, because of illness or accident, are unable to work for at least two years, or whose illness will result in death. There are eligibility requirements including a time frame for previous contributions to the Social Security system, a history of working prior to disability, and a period of six months before payments begin. Eligibility has become more stringently enforced and is defined as the inability to be gainfully employed in any position in the workforce. Amounts paid are

[18] When paid with pretax dollars—for example, when part of a tax-deductible cafeteria plan—the insurance payment would be taxable to the policyholder.

Practical Comment Difficulty in Understanding Policies

Disability policies are often very difficult for the average person to understand. The language of policies is not standard, and seemingly subtle differences in wording can have important effects on payout. In contrast to the usual circumstance in this part of the process, the insurance company often has more knowledge of potential payout than the individual.[19]

LOW COVERAGE

The low incidence of long-term disability coverage relative to life insurance coverage is somewhat puzzling. As Cox, Gustavson, and Stam point out, the incidence of disability at any age is considerably greater than that of death.[20] As mentioned, the

[19] Larry A. Cox and Sandra G. Gustavson, "The Market Pricing of Disability Income Insurance for Individuals," *Financial Services Review* 4, no. 2 (1995), pp. 109–22, support this observation: "Finally, our findings provide a preliminary indication that disability definitions, preexisting conditions clauses, and insurer solvency may not be fully impounded in DII (disability) prices."

[20] Larry A. Cox, Sandra Gustavson, and Antonie Stam, "Disability and Life Insurance in the Individual Insurance Portfolio," *Journal of Risk and Insurance* 58, no. 1 (March 1991), pp. 128–37.

cost to replace the income of a disabled wage earner is also greater for households than the death of that wage earner. Then why do fewer than one-quarter of families have personal disability policies while over three-quarters have life insurance? Possible answers might include (1) the lack of an "investment component" or cumulative cash value in disability policies in contrast to many life insurance policies; (2) finding the policy too expensive and overemphasizing the more prevalent short-term disability policies; (3) difficulty in understanding and finding an efficient policy; (4) reliance on Social Security disability or on other immediate or extended family members; (5) from a behavioral standpoint, death may be more "salient"—easier to visualize happening—than a long-term disability; and (6) lack of disability offerings for the full population—many disability insurance companies only market to certain people such as business owners, executives, and professionals.

comparable to what you would have received if you were retired. As of 2006, you are able to earn up to $860 a month without losing disability payments.[21]

Long-Term Care Insurance

Long-term care insurance reimburses you for expenses incurred when you are unable to perform certain activities of daily living on your own. It often pays a fixed benefit according to a level of purchased coverage. Long-term care covers expenses when in a nursing home and often covers home health care expenses as well. The importance and value of long-term care coverage will increase as our population continues to age. The number of seniors over age 60 will double by about 2020 and the number over age 80 who most need care will quadruple.

The long-term care approach is similar to disability insurance with a principal difference being an ability to independently take care of yourself as opposed to the disabled person's inability to work as a trigger for receiving benefits. Approximately one in three people over age 65 will spend some time in a nursing home facility, with an average stay of three years. However, only 9 percent of the people over 65 stay in a nursing home for over five years.[22] The length of stay is important because the cost of a nursing home can be very expensive, ranging from $30,000 to well over $100,000 a year in high-cost locations.

[21] If total income exceeds base amounts, 50 to 80 percent of the benefits may be taxable.

[22] National Association of Insurance Commissioners, "NAIC Shopper's Guide" [Draft], August 7, 1998.

Practical Comment Whom Policies Are Best Suited For

Unlike many other types of insurance, the majority of long-term care needs occur at a fixed time frame within the life cycle. With the exception of those who have Alzheimer's disease, long-term care is more often required for people over 80. Although payments are the same, it is women who more frequently receive long-term care. More married women tend to take care of their spouses because women are more likely to live well into their 80s and men may not survive long enough to take care of their wives.

People are showing more interest in long-term care policies, but only a modest fraction of the elderly has them. Possible reasons include significant costs; no expected near-term benefit since need doesn't generally arise until one's 80s, when it can be too late to buy a policy; and a desire to have spouses or children assist instead of being placed in a nursing home. Generally, people prefer remaining in their own home. The trend toward greater coverage of home health care with payments of the same amount for qualified home and nursing home care may make these policies more appealing.

The policies may not be as well suited for people who have few assets or who are affluent. Those who have few assets often qualify for Medicaid payments when their money runs out. Those who are affluent may be able to cover these expenses with their own assets. For them, long-term care insurance would only be attractive as a method of helping ensure that their estate is left intact to their heirs. (Many are attracted to the policies for that reason.) Middle-income people may have the greatest need for the policies since these payments may support custodial care in their home and keep them out of a nursing home. The policies, particularly those that combine private and governmental sources of reimbursement may keep their spouses from drawing down their assets.

As with many other types of insurance, policies may be less expensive when bought through a business or association. If purchased through a business, the lower cost must be weighed against a frequent practical lack of portability if you should you leave the firm, as well as less flexibility in tailoring a policy to your needs.

With people living longer and a growing percentage of the population in the elderly bracket, long-term care expenditures may be a growing concern for the entire country, not just the elderly.

You qualify for long-term care payments when you are unable to perform a number of the activities of daily living (or ADLs) such as eating, dressing, showering, transferring from bed, and toileting. An alternative way of qualifying is through cognitive impairment such as Alzheimer's or other severe cognitive diseases. The policies cover costs ranging from skilled nursing to custodial care and also may include medical and therapeutic expenditures. As with disability coverage, the length of the policy period, cost-of-living rider, the elimination period, and preexisting conditions are all relevant factors.

Policies generally have caps on the total amount that will be paid in any period as well as overall limits. The policies may offer a flat daily amount when you meet the definition of disability or may reimburse you for actual expenditures made. Unlike many disability policies, the yearly cost may be raised after the contract is in effect but the policy is normally guaranteed renewable.

Common policy coverage periods can range from three to six years to a lifetime. In a growing number of states, there are special partnership policies that integrate private and governmental aid. You pay for the first three years of coverage and then the government pays the excess of care cost over the income you generate. Your assets are protected for your spouse or your heirs, but not your income.

A portion of the premium paid may be tax-deductible. However, it is subject to the normal 7.5 percent floor on medical outlays before tax deductibility is allowed. The insurance company payments for care are tax-free to the extent of reimbursement for actual expenses. Payment beyond expenses may be taxable. Additional factors related to long-term care policies are discussed in Table 11.6.

TABLE 11.6
Long-Term Care—
Other Variable
Factors

Factor	Explanation
Age	The younger the age, the lower the yearly cost, but generally the longer the period of pay in until potential reimbursement begins.
Maximum benefit	Generally depends on reimbursement amount, with sum needed contingent in part on insured location.
Average usage	Forty percent of seniors receive long-term care usage and use it for about 2.5 years.[1]
Years covered	Often 3, 5, 6, or lifetime.
Inflation adjustment	Costly; can be CPI or as much as 5 percent a year. Inflation in long-term care is expected to exceed CPI.
Premium price	Not capped as it is in disability policy. Likely to increase, as, say, needed costs have risen, although not necessarily at same pace.
Waiting period	Benefits may not start for say 0, 30, or 100 days. Cost and client financial position are decision factors.
Underwriting	Client health a factor in quotation.
Reimbursement and selection policy	Ability to select caregiver can save middleman agency costs.

[1] Based on long-term care data in nursing homes.

GOVERNMENT INSURANCE

Social insurance is insurance provided by governments. It can be distinguished from public assistance because employers and employees fund social insurance payments directly, generally through mandatory payroll withholding. The justification for these programs includes absence of adverse selection, and income redistribution, which helps establish a minimum quality of life for all citizens.

The principal government insurance programs are Social Security, workers' compensation, disability payments, and unemployment insurance. These will be discussed here except for Social Security "old age" pension payments, which we look at in Chapter 12.

Workers' Compensation

Workers' compensation provides income to people who are disabled because of work-related activities and payments to their families in the event of death. The system is regulated by individual states, which impose their own requirements. The majority of the policies are offered by private companies, with the states and company self-insurance providing the rest. Individual businesses are required to participate. Medical care and rehabilitation costs also are covered. Workers' compensation is no-fault; you don't have to prove negligence and sue the company to collect. Payments can be made for the life of the disability; therefore, depending on the circumstance, it will be either short or long term. Amounts payable relative to predisability earnings may be lower for long-term as opposed to short-term disability.

Medicare

Medicare coverage is provided for all people and their family members age 65 or over who are covered by Social Security. Medicare is divided into Parts A and B. Part A is given to all and includes hospital care for the first 60 days for a deductible of $912.[23] There is a maximum coinsurance charge of $228 a day for days 61–90 and $456 a day for days 91–150. Home health care services are paid in full subject to the recommendation of a doctor for such things as part-time nursing, physiotherapy, social worker services, and medical

[23] All the figures provided are as of 2005.

supplies. The first 20 days of an approved stay in a facility providing qualified nursing is free, with a copayment of $114 thereafter.[24]

Part B is a supplement that covers doctor's charges and related expenses. To qualify for the benefit, a monthly premium is charged. Only certain expenses are covered and sometimes in limited fashion. Consequently, Medigap insurance is available to cover those items not fully covered by Medicare. The scope of coverage under Medigap is coded by letters from A to J, with J providing the most comprehensive coverage and requiring the highest premium.

Effective January 1, 2006, Medicare under Part D has been expanded to offer prescription drug coverage. Those who select this option pay a monthly premium and full or copayments ranging from 5 to 100 percent of annual drug costs, with only 5 percent paid once a yearly out-of-pocket cost of $3,600 is reached. Coverage varies by state.

Medicaid

Medicaid is run by individual states and is supported by a combination of federal and individual state funds. It is intended to cover those people who cannot afford coverage themselves. Even with Medicaid, approximately 15 percent of people have no insurance at all, as you can see in Table 11.5. Medicaid covers not only those traditionally thought of as disadvantaged but also many younger people or those who otherwise don't qualify for Medicare.

Unemployment Insurance

Unemployment insurance provides payments when you have been terminated from your previous job. It is a benefit organized by the federal government but largely run by the individual states. It is funded by individual businesses. The benefits amount varies by state and may be a fixed sum or a percentage of your income up to a sum. It generally lasts for 26 weeks but may be extended in times of high unemployment. Thus, unemployment insurance provides short-term benefits giving people time to find another position.

You must have had a history of working prior to the application, be interested in obtaining a new job, and not turn down a position that is appropriate for you. You will not qualify if you were fired for misconduct or left because of a labor dispute.

Social Security Survivor's Benefits

Survivor's benefits are benefits given to family members when a qualified wage earner dies. The children each receive 75 percent of what a wage earner would receive at age 65. Payments to children end at age 18.[25] Elderly parents (over 62) who were supported by the wage earner also each receive the 75 percent payment. If there is only one dependent, he or she receives 82.5 percent. The widower's benefit is 100 percent of the age 65 payment if the spouse was 65 or over. A surviving spouse under age 65 or caring for a child under age 16 receives between 71.5 and 83 percent.

Back to Dan and Laura
OTHER INSURANCE

The meeting for all insurance other than life took place at the same time as the overall risk management session. Dan and Laura's discussion was very brief. They dropped a satchel full of insurance policies on my desk and said, "Please examine them."

I reviewed all of your insurance excluding life insurance, which has already been discussed. My impression is that you generally have done a good job of protecting yourself. My specific recommendations follow.

[24] Payment for skilled nursing care in nursing homes stops after 100 days.

[25] Age 19 if the child is still in high school.

In your auto insurance policy, you currently have $100,000 for bodily injury and property damage and $300,000 per accident, which is the state minimum. I recommend that you increase that coverage to $250,000 and $500,000, respectively. Coverage in today's litigious society, in which costs for claims have climbed steeply, suggests that this is a more appropriate figure. The cost increase isn't that great. You should save money on my next recommendation, which is to eliminate collision coverage on Laura's car. The car is 10 years old and the current cost you are paying for collision is too high relative to the benefit. You should self-insure for that risk.

Your rental coverage on your apartment is adequate for now. As you accumulate more expensive furniture, appliances, and other items, you will need higher amounts. I believe we will be revisiting this question should you purchase your home. Although we can discuss homeowners insurance in more detail at the appropriate time, I believe a broad form HO-5 policy is best and prefer one that has guaranteed replacement cost so that you are fully protected as the market value of your home increases. You should review your apartment or homeowners coverage every two years or so to make sure that the coverage reflects the then-current value of your possessions.

The entire family is currently covered under a comprehensive medical plan. In recent years, you have not had any medical expenditures other than for delivery and follow-up for your son. You mentioned that your experience with the HMO doctor was only fair. I recommend that you consider a point of service policy that your company offers and that you would have to contribute to. This policy is partially subsidized by the employer and will allow you to select a physician of your choice. Be prepared to pay coinsurance for many medical occurrences. I believe the cost-to-benefit ratio is worth it, if only for your ability to select a doctor of your choice in the unlikely event of a major illness.

Dan has a disability policy at work that is paid for by his employer and pays 60 percent of his total compensation in the event of a disability. Unfortunately, the coverage is limited to one year for any type of disability. Thereafter, the policy will pay only if he is unable to perform a position he is suitable for. I would prefer an own occupation definition that would pay if he could no longer perform in the career he has now. Moreover, the policy isn't portable. If Dan were to have some mishap that rendered him uninsurable and then for any reason he left his job, he would be vulnerable. Since there is a viable policy in force, the question is whether you want to fund a more desirable policy. If you do, please let me know within the next week so that I can include its cost in our projection (they subsequently declined).

Long-term care insurance is, in my opinion, a worthwhile product to consider. It can provide funds for extraordinarily high-cost nursing home care that might otherwise impoverish the still healthy spouse and provide more assurance of leaving funds for your children. Its home health payments to aides also can actually allow people who might otherwise have to move to a facility to remain in their own home. However, I believe it is too early to consider this type of policy. The costs would be relatively inexpensive, but they are not locked in and can be increased based on insurance company experience. Interim investing may provide a better rate of return. At a later date, say, in your 50s when you hope to retire, your financial circumstances may be better known. Of course, you would have to assume the risk of an illness in the meantime that rendered you uninsurable.

Finally, I recommend a $1 million umbrella insurance policy. As the term indicates, an umbrella covers you for a variety of losses. It will support you against a very large automobile suit (the cost to obtain it is reduced by the extra auto coverage I am recommending on your existing policy). It also will provide coverage for miscellaneous losses such as slander and defamation of character.

Summary

This chapter largely provides the facts on individual types of insurance based on the risk management and insurance principles established in Chapter 10. That chapter also detailed life insurance.

- Insurance is most suitable when frequency of loss is low, but its severity is high.
- Insurance can be separated into property and liability, life and health, and government social insurance.
- Property and liability insurance is involved with protection of real and personal property while liability protects you against losses to others.
- Property insurance includes home, home's possessions, auto, liability, and umbrella insurance.
- Life and health protects human assets of household members against loss.
- Personal insurance includes life, disability, health, and long-term care.
- Government insurance includes workers' compensation, Medicare, Medicaid, unemployment, and Social Security.

Key Terms

business risk, *294*
coinsurance, *296*
disability insurance, *306*
floater, *301*
frequency, *293*
hazard, *295*
health insurance, *303*
indemnity, *295*
insurable interest, *295*

liability insurance
(first-party coverage), *302*
liability insurance (third-party coverage), *302*
long-term care insurance, *308*
moral hazard, *295*
morale hazard, *295*
own occupation (definition of disability), *306*

peril, *294*
personal property, *298*
physical hazard, *295*
pure risk, *294*
real property, *298*
severity, *293*
social insurance, *310*
umbrella insurance, *302*

Web Sites

http://www.iii.org
Insurance Information Institute
An online guide for all types of insurance and insurance industry facts and statistics. It also has a search tool for finding insurance companies in your state.

http://www.healthinsurance.org
Health Insurance Resource Center
This Web site provides free information and links to additional information about health care and health insurance. The site also has a small glossary of health insurance terms.

http://www.naic.org
National Association of Insurance Commissioners (NAIC)
The NAIC's home page gives insights into the insurance industry regulations.

The links below provide information about Medicare and Medicaid services:

http://www.medicare.gov
The Official U.S. government Web site for Medicare Services

http://www.cms.hhs.gov
Center for Medicare and Medicaid Services

Questions

1. Define adverse selection and give an example of it.
2. Why are insurable interest and indemnity basic insurance beliefs?

3. Gerald wanted to purchase a medical policy with 100 percent coverage. The best he could get was $200 deductible and 80 percent coinsurance. Why wouldn't companies provide fuller coverage?

4. Why are group policies often cheaper than individual ones?

5. Distinguish between an HO-3 and an HO-4 property policy.

6. Marisa has a policy with replacement cost coverage and has a loss of $100,000 on a house. Total policy coverage is $300,000 and replacement cost is $400,000. Since the loss is less than the coverage, she expects to get the full amount of the claim paid by the insurance company. Is she correct? Why?

7. Erin purchases disability insurance from her employer. Will any payments she receives be taxable?

8. Contrast the traditional tort system and no-fault auto insurance.

9. Why should a family have umbrella insurance?

10. Contrast an HMO and a PPO.

11. John was young and Lisa elderly. Discuss potential provider preferences.

12. Why is an own occupation definition for disability so valuable?

13. Explain why life insurance is so much more popular than disability insurance.

14. For what type of retired individuals is long-term care insurance particularly appropriate?

15. Identify and briefly explain the principal types of social insurance.

Problems

11.1 Jeremy lost a wing on his house, which resulted in an outlay of $250,000 to replace it. The replacement cost on the house was $900,000, and he had $500,000 of insurance. His policy had an 80 percent coinsurance clause. How much will the insurance company reimburse him for?

11.2 Paulette, a trial attorney for a corporation, was forced to leave the field due to an injury to her vocal chords. She switched careers and became a lower-paying author. Fortunately, she had three disability policies. Policy A had an own occupation definition that was paid for by her employer and was for $20,000 per year. Policy B, which she paid for, had an own occupation definition and was for $30,000 of coverage per year. Policy C, which also was purchased by her, had no own occupation definition and was for $60,000 in coverage per year. Paulette's marginal tax rate was 33 percent. How many after-tax dollars did she receive per year?

CFP® Certification Examination Questions and Problems

11.1 Bob, age 47, has worked for XYZ Company the past 12 years. XYZ Company has lost a major contract and must begin downsizing immediately. Bob was laid off yesterday. What should Bob do first?

a. File for unemployment benefits.

b. Roll over his company 401(k) plan.

c. Convert disability coverage under COBRA provisions.

d. Notify the bank holding the mortgage on his house.

11.2 Conditions that increase either the frequency or severity of loss are called

a. subrogation

b. risks

c. hazards

d. perils

e. extenuating circumstances

11.3   A client recently purchased a new home from a builder for $150,000, including the lot valued at $40,000. How much insurance would you recommend that your client purchase to cover full replacement of the house in the event of a loss?

   a. $88,000
   b. $110,000
   c. $120,000
   d. $150,000

11.4   A successful architect wants to purchase disability income insurance. She is concerned about becoming totally disabled, but also about a reduction in income if she is obliged to reduce her workload because of a less-than-total disability. To satisfy these concerns, which of the following should be included in her disability income coverage?

   a. Residual disability benefits
   b. A change-of-occupation provision
   c. Dismemberment benefits
   d. A relation of earnings-to-insurance provision

11.5   Terry Underwood purchased a 15-year-old compact car with 10,000 miles for his teenage son who recently received his license. Which of the following auto insurance coverages should be included in the policy for this auto?

   1. Part A—liability coverage
   2. Part B—medical payments coverage
   3. Part C—uninsured motorist coverage
   4. Part D—damage to insured's auto
      a. (1), (2), and (3) only
      b. (1), (2), and (4) only
      c. (1), (3), and (4) only
      d. (2), (3), and (4) only

11.6   Typically, when group long-term disability income insurance premiums are paid by a C corporation, all disability benefit amounts received by an employee are

   a. *not* includable in the income of the employee for federal tax purposes without regard to any other sources of income.
   b. includable in the income of the employee for federal tax purposes without regard to any other sources of income.
   c. *not* includable in the income of the employee for federal tax purposes if any portion of the benefit is reduced/offset by other income.
   d. includable in the income of the employee for federal tax purposes if any portion of the benefit is reduced/offset by other income.
   e. includable in the income of the employee for federal tax purposes unless he or she is over age 65.

11.7   Under the Consolidated Omnibus Budget Reconciliation Act (COBRA) of 1985, an employer is required to extend medical plan coverage to eligible members of the employee's family if the employee

   1. dies.
   2. retires.
   3. divorces.

4. terminates employment (prior to retirement).

   a. (1), (2), and (3) only

   b. (1) and (3) only

   c. (2) and (4) only

   d. (4) only

   e. (1), (2), (3), and (4)

11.8 Ginny is a sole proprietor. She wants to provide 60 percent of salary disability coverage to Joanna, her employee who is in a 35 percent combined tax bracket. Joanna's W-2 wages are $40,000 and Ginny's annual contribution to her qualified profit-sharing account on Joanna's behalf is $4,000.

1. Ignoring cost-of-living adjustments or any possible Social Security benefits, calculate Joanna's net-of-tax monthly disability payment if *Ginny* pays the disability premium and Joanna's tax bracket during disability remains at 35 percent.

   a. $1,300

   b. $1,430

   c. $2,000

   d. $2,200

2. Ignoring cost-of-living adjustments or any possible Social Security benefits, calculate Joanna's net-of-tax monthly disability benefit if *Joanna* pays the disability premium and Joanna's tax bracket during disability remains at 35 percent.

   a. $1,300

   b. $1,430

   c. $2,000

   d. $2,200

11.9 An HO-3 policy (Special form—"All risks of physical loss" except those specifically excluded) with *no* endorsements excludes which one of the following perils?

   a. flood

   b. fire

   c. collapse

   d. weight of ice

   e. volcanic eruption

Case Application

OTHER INSURANCE

When I examined Richard and Monica's insurance policies, I found the following:

a. Medical coverage was adequate.

b. Auto insurance was at the minimum level for the state of $50,000 to $100,000 per accident.

c. Homeowners insurance was at a level of 50 percent of replacement cost for the house. They had a 90 percent coinsurance clause.

d. Richard had no disability coverage.

e. A note saying that Richard didn't want long-term care insurance, but Monica was interested in looking at it.

Case Application Questions

1. What is your recommendation for auto insurance?
2. What is your homeowners insurance recommendation?
3. Give the advantages for Richard obtaining disability insurance.
4. Do you believe Richard and/or Monica should have long-term care insurance? Why?
5. Complete the other insurance part of the financial plan.

Appendix I

Monetary Windfalls

A *monetary windfall* is generally the creation of new liquid assets currently or over time due to the resolution of an event, dispute, family occurrence, or other matter. It is a windfall because it is not recurring and it takes place outside the normal cash flow generation of the household. Examples are insurance proceeds, lottery winnings, legal settlements including structured ones, and inheritances. Aside from tax and timing of payment considerations, they all have many similarities. Essentially, people receive cash currently or distributions over time. Monetary windfalls are in this chapter because insurance is often related to the payment or the investment vehicle, which, for settlement purposes, may have a special tax-advantaged feature.

The range of people receiving significant assets is often broader than just middle- or upper-income people. Moreover, the impact on a household's standard of living can be greater for lower-income people. Many people are unprepared for the sudden inflow of assets. They often lack financial knowledge. Their spending pattern may appear short-term-oriented, taking the form of a splurge in outlays. Purveyors of investments both from questionable external sources and sometimes from friends and relatives can create risk of loss.

What is often needed is a financial plan. The plan should be highly specific in detailing spending plans and simple and direct in presenting the operating parts of the document. Just as important, it should be monitored closely because failing to maintain structure and not adhering to the plan are common shortcomings. When there is an inability to convert the lump-sum payments to a lifetime income stream, using an insurance company's annuity can be appealing.

TAXABILITY

Disability payments received are not taxable if the person paid for them directly but are taxable if an employer paid. If the employee paid through a cafeteria or other plan that made such payments for the policy tax-deductible, then payments from the policy upon disability are taxable.[26] Compensation for physical injury or illness other than through disability policies is not taxable. Therefore, payments received from suits or settlements for these types of illnesses are not taxed. Payments received from an accident and health policy for permanent loss of a bodily function or permanent disfigurement are also not taxable. That is true whether you or your employer paid for the policy. Disability income from Social Security is not taxable for lower-income people, but it is for people who have significant other income.

On the other hand, punitive damages awarded from suits for physical injury or physical illness are taxable. Emotional distress is not considered a physical illness. Therefore, payments received for emotional distress are taxable. An exception is made for payments for medical care for emotional distress, which are nontaxable.

Payments received from lottery winnings or other monetary windfalls are generally taxable. Life insurance payments are not subject to income taxes if they are paid upon death or in a viatical settlement, meaning advance payments for those with a terminal illness. Distributions from life insurance based on cash surrender value are taxable to the extent they exceed prior payments into the policy.

STRUCTURED SETTLEMENTS

Structured settlements are payments made of a fixed nature, in lump sum or over time, or a combination of the two, to resolve claims generally related to personal injuries. Typically, at least part of the claim is in annuity form. When such settlements are for physical injury or physical illness, the payments are not taxable. The income, received from the payments after lump-sum payments are received, is taxable. Therefore, lump-sum payments will generate greater taxable income than equivalent periodic payments. Consequently, from a tax standpoint, it can be beneficial to take annuity payments for living costs for part or all of the settlement. Annuity payments also ensure that the person receives a material sum annually, often over his or her life span, although inflation generally reduces the purchasing power of that annual sum over time.

On the other hand, the annuity payment is highly inflexible. As with other annuities, once agreed to, it cannot be altered because the recipient needs cash or wishes to invest the proceeds personally. Often a combination of a lump-sum amount and annuity payments is selected by the recipient.

The amounts and terms of a structured settlement can be very involved. At least to some extent, there is often an adversarial relationship between the parties to the settlement. Financial advisors are needed by the payer to establish costs and can be helpful in finding efficient products to fund the costs of a settlement. A separate financial advisor can be used by the recipient to assist in calculating the true amount of benefits and the terms to fit the need. Therefore, the benefits of a lump sum versus a series of payments, competitive policies, and approaches, including whether payments should incorporate inflation adjustments, all must be calculated.

---

[26] Disability benefits under a no-fault car insurance policy, whether you paid for the policy or not, are not taxable.

Chapter Twelve

Retirement Planning

Chapter Goals

This chapter will enable you to:

- Recognize the importance of planning for retirement.
- Evaluate retirement savings structures.
- Weigh the advantages and disadvantages of pensions as compared with personal savings vehicles.
- Summarize the retirement planning process.
- Identify and describe the risks that can affect retirement planning.
- Contrast pre- and postretirement alternatives when shortfalls in capital needs become apparent.

Dan and Laura were surprisingly detailed about their retirement goals. Both wanted to retire when Dan became 55 so that they could share a life of almost total leisure, with virtually the only work being to split the household chores. They added that they would like to travel more both in the United States and in Asia.

Real Life Planning

Many financial planners observe that the desire and ability to save money varies by person and by stage in life. Some people want to save money, expect to do so, but end the year without anything in their savings account. Others, particularly at earlier stages in their adult life, prefer living for today. Tomorrow, they say, will take care of itself.

So, the advisor was somewhat surprised by the actions of the 29-year-old man, Tom, who came to see him. Tom was married and said that his wife was one of those who felt no need to plan for tomorrow. He, on the other hand, had a very structured list of things to accomplish. As an industrial psychologist with a reputation in a desirable specialty, he said he could work as hard as necessary in his consulting practice to earn the money to achieve his goals.

Tom wanted a gradually increasing standard of living including a more expensive car. He said that he preferred that his older child, his son, become a doctor and his daughter be a lawyer. He would pay for their entire education through medical school and law school, respectively. His retirement planning goals were particularly important to him. He wanted to retire at age 55, take frequent trips, and have a second home in the country near a golf course. He said his father never had a chance to enjoy life, having had to work until he died.

The advisor thought to himself that these were lofty goals and that Tom was pretty young to be thinking of retirement. He was heartened by the fact that Tom was very disciplined about strong savings. He wasn't living high on the hog. Tom told him to provide exactly how much money would have to be put aside conservatively each year for each goal and it would be done. The advisor looked into Tom's eyes and saw a sincerity and fierceness that said that he would deliver on his promise.

The advisor designed a financial plan for Tom with particular emphasis on retirement planning. He took into account Tom's growing consulting revenues and an expense structure that would climb over the years. He provided for an additional home at retirement and living costs that would increase although from a fairly modest base. He took into account existing investments and found out what additional savings were needed annually. The savings figure was not that much larger than what Tom had been saving to date. Tom thanked him and made plans for a yearly update.

Some 20 years and updates later, Tom is around 50 and heading into the home stretch. He is actually ahead of schedule and is likely to be able to retire at around 55. The advisor thought about the reasons for his success. The first was an ability to anticipate future developments. His investment portfolio benefited from some high-risk medical technology and drug stocks that he bought at their infancy. But the positions were too modest to account for his progress by themselves.

The principal reasons for his retirement asset growth were that Tom started to save earlier in his adult life and his machinelike method continued it each year.

The advisor wondered whether there was a way to bottle that ability to plan so carefully. He decided it ran contrary to most people's nature. He chuckled when he remembered finding out that their planning together including setting aside money for Tom's two children had occurred before they were born. And as a further sign of his uncanny predictive ability, Tom did have a boy and a girl. Now his son was old enough to think about a career and he wanted to become a doctor.

OVERVIEW

Retirement planning is the single biggest long-term issue for many households. For younger people, this planning is frequently expressed positively, as an opportunity to achieve financial independence. Many think of financial independence as the ability to move on to other active pursuits without the further need to consider money issues.

For many people who are middle-aged or older, retirement generates a different thought. They are concerned that they will not be able to retire when they want to or to maintain their current standard of living in retirement. Alternatively, they fear that they could run out of retirement funds, particularly if they live to a ripe old age.

The answer for both groups is to have an organized approach to the topic, to plan with an objective in mind. Planning for retirement has as its objective providing sufficient assets to enable you to live comfortably in retirement. Too little accumulated carries a risk of prematurely running out of money, while saving too much means that you could be enjoying a higher standard of living. PFP helps identify the goals, ascertain their cost, and calculate the savings needed to accomplish them by using the most attractive savings structures available.

In this chapter, we will look at retirement planning as a process. Once that process has been implemented correctly, all groups can be optimistic about achieving retirement goals. The nine steps in the retirement planning process are given in Figure 12.1.

FAMILIARIZE YOURSELF WITH RETIREMENT ISSUES

It is useful in planning to familiarize yourself with some overall background retirement facts and issues. The concerns of retired people are assigned a relatively high priority by the working population and the government. Per capita spending by the government on the elderly substantially exceeds that for the rest of the population.

FIGURE 12.1
Retirement Planning Process

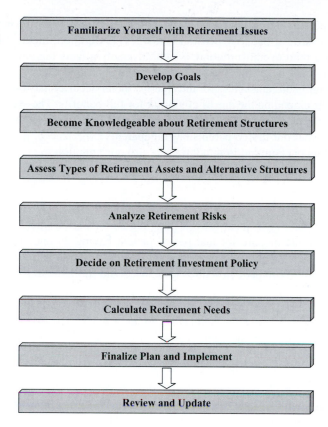

Familiarize Yourself with Retirement Issues

Develop Goals

Become Knowledgeable about Retirement Structures

Assess Types of Retirement Assets and Alternative Structures

Analyze Retirement Risks

Decide on Retirement Investment Policy

Calculate Retirement Needs

Finalize Plan and Implement

Review and Update

People have been retiring earlier. Although there has been a modest upturn since 1985, the average age of retirement has declined from 67 in 1950 to 62 in 2000.[1] The array of labor force participation rates is shown in Table 12.1. Note that the participation rate for men aged 60–64 is down from 78 percent to 55 percent whereas growth in the participation rate for women is likely due to their greater numbers in the workforce.

The outlook for the elderly creates some important issues. In the past 50 years, the quality of life of the elderly has risen absolutely and probably relative to the average worker. Now the percentage of the elderly population is expected to rise from 15 percent in 2000

[1] Murray Gendell, "Retirement Age Declines Again in 1990s," *Monthly Labor Review* 124, no. 10 (October 2001), pp. 12–21, available at http://www.bls.gov/opub/mlr/2001/10/art2full.pdf.

TABLE 12.1
Labor Force Participation Rates

Source: Richard Johnson, "Why the 'Average Age of Retirement' Is a Misleading Measure of Labor Supply," *Monthly Labor Review* 124, no. 12 (December 2001), pp. 38–40, available at http://www.bls.gov/opub/mlr/2001/12/comntry.pdf.

| | Labor Force Participation Rate (percent) | | | |
| | Men | | Women | |
Age	1960	2000	1960	2000
40–44	95.4	92.1	45.3	78.7
45–49	94.5	90.1	47.4	79.1
50–54	92.0	86.8	45.9	74.1
55–59	87.7	77.1	49.7	61.2
60–64	77.8	54.8	29.4	40.1
65 and older	30.6	17.5	10.4	9.4
Labor participation rate of population 16 years and older	80.4	74.7	35.7	60.2

to 20 percent in 2030.[2] This greater concentration of retired people is projected to create a shortfall in Social Security pension resources. In addition, medical costs are rising at a faster pace than overall inflation, which adversely affects the elderly on fixed-cost pensions and government funding to assist in medical cost reimbursement. The outcome may be challenging circumstances for the elderly. Social Security may be cut back by, for example, further extending the age of eligibility for full benefits. The average age of retirement may move back up significantly. Planning for retirement may require more effort and savings than what our retired parents or grandparents experienced.

With this background in mind, we can turn our attention to goals.

DEVELOP GOALS

Retirement planning is just life cycle planning for the period when working 9 a.m. to 5 p.m. stops. You must prepare for that period or risk having an uncomfortable outcome. That means an assessment of your assets, projected cash flows and costs, and savings patterns as well as the retirement structures to be used and the individual investment assets to be placed in them.

At the head of this planning process are your goals. What do you want retirement to look like? Will your overall living costs go up or down? For example, will it involve more high-cost travel or perhaps more leisure activities in a less expensive part of the country? When do you want it to happen? For the majority of Americans, it is the sooner the better. However, a significant number view retirement differently, as something you do when you are unable to continue working. Clearly, the retirement sum you need to accumulate if you delay your retirement date will be lower. An increasing number of people may choose a combination of the two: retiring and working part-time for financial, personal interest, or mental health reasons.

In planning, many people select an early retirement or financial independence date.[3] That can provide them with the option of retirement at that time and also better accommodate a forced retirement due to health or company layoffs. In any event, many financial planners discourage the use of a figure beyond age 70, even if clients indicate that they never want to retire. Beyond this age, health reasons or a change in interests or job circumstances raise risks considerably.

BECOME KNOWLEDGEABLE ABOUT RETIREMENT STRUCTURES

Retirement structures are financial frameworks such as pensions, annuities, and Social Security that are established specifically for retirement. Many can make it easier to save money for retirement and to provide tax benefits by doing so. In other words, where you put your money can influence how much money you end up with. Each structure is described below.

Pensions

Introduction

Pensions are the savings structures into which money is deposited to generate income for retirees. In private pensions, they may be funded by the retiree, by the employer, or through

---

[2] Catherine Montalto, Yoonkyung Yuh, and Sherman Hanna, "Determinants of Planned Retirement Age," *Financial Services Review* 9, no. 1 (2000), pp. 1–15.

[3] For financial purposes, the two are equal. However, financial independence suggests an earlier retirement date, say, prior to 60, and a more active period thereafter including the possibility of a full-time occupation without worry about compensation.

a combination of the two. Virtually all those who work help fund the U.S. government's public Social Security system, and if they spend at least 10 years working, they receive pension income from it at retirement. The monies deposited in private pensions grow through investment returns, which are often tax-advantaged and are generally paid out over a person's retired lifetime. Some private pensions start at a certain designated age, such as 65, while the public Social Security system's payout at full rates depends on your year of birth.

Private pensions used to be largely limited to fixed monthly retirement sums set by companies.[4] They were sometimes heavily weighted toward highly compensated workers and those who had worked for a company for many years. It was not uncommon for eligibility for private pensions to begin after 15 years of service. Therefore, **vesting,** the point at which an employee is entitled to a stated amount of nonrevocable benefits from an employer, escaped most workers who moved from job to job.

In recent decades, the U.S. government, concerned that the average worker was being slighted, has mandated that plans be nondiscriminatory by being open to all workers. Maximum periods before full vesting were reduced sharply and generally are no more than six years. The government passed the Employee Retirement Income Security Act (ERISA), which required that employers act as fiduciaries managing investment assets in the employee's best interests. The government later established the Pension Benefit Guarantee Corporation (PBGC), which was funded by corporate pension plans and guarantees pension assets or income when companies go bankrupt.[5]

Qualified Plans

Pension plans provide significant tax benefits. **Qualified plans** are those pension structures that comply with established government regulations. They allow you to place pretax (untaxed) dollars into the plan. Having pretax dollar deposits means that you can place a greater sum in the plan, which results in higher earnings. All dividends and capital gains generated while in the pension plan are tax-deferred as well. It is not until monies are withdrawn that taxation begins. Since your deposits have not been taxed previously, all amounts you withdraw are treated as taxable income and are taxed at ordinary income rates.

Regular withdrawals from pensions can start at age 59½ and must start at age 70½. Withdrawals that you make before 59½ are generally penalized with an extra 10 percent tax. At death, the entire sum left in a qualified plan is subject to income taxes at ordinary income rates.[6] Contributions to qualified plans are usually limited to a maximum of $42,000 annually.[7] The qualified pension's combination of pretax dollars deposited and tax-free compounding is what makes it such an appealing way of saving. Its benefits are shown in Example 12.1.

Example 12.1	Alex and Stewart, both age 25, had identical salaries and each saved $12,000 annually over their working lives. Alex saved his money in personal accounts; Stewart placed his savings in a pension account. Both worked until age 65 and died at age 85.
	Assume that investment returns in each case were 7.5 percent pretax and that both were in the 33 percent marginal tax bracket throughout their lives. Assume that Alex turned over his portfolio every year and the combination of ordinary income on dividends and interest and capital gains on sale of stock came to a 25 percent tax rate on investment returns. What is

---

[4] Or, in some cases, set by unions with amounts directly or indirectly funded by the retiree.

[5] The guarantee is subject to a maximum amount.

[6] There is a method for avoiding this—by a tax-free rollover of the lump sum to an IRA account.

[7] As of 2005, and this figure is inflated every year by $1,000.

the difference in amounts saved, assuming that Stewart withdrew the entire amount from his pension at age 65?

	Alex	Stewart
Savings		
Pretax dollars saved	$12,000	$12,000
Tax at 33% rate	(3,960)	—
After-tax dollars saved	$8,040	$12,000
Investment Return		
Pretax return	7.5%	7.5%
Tax at 25% rate	−1.9%	—
After-tax return	5.6%	7.5%
Number of years	40	40
Gross assets at age 65	$1,125,905	$2,727,078
Tax on withdrawals at 33%	—	($899,936)
Net assets at age 65	**$1,125,905**	**$1,827,142**

Calculator Solution

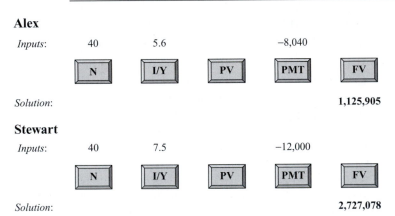

Alex

Inputs: 40   5.6   −8,040

[N]   [I/Y]   [PV]   [PMT]   [FV]

Solution: **1,125,905**

Stewart

Inputs: 40   7.5   −12,000

[N]   [I/Y]   [PV]   [PMT]   [FV]

Solution: **2,727,078**

Although Alex and Stewart took the same amount from their salaries for savings and earned the same pretax return, Stewart actually saved about $700,000 more, or almost 40 percent more money. The differential would not be as dramatic if Alex had chosen to hold his stocks for a longer period of time before selling them. On the other hand, if Stewart had chosen to keep the money in the pension longer, making withdrawals only when needed, the differential would be even greater.

There are two principal types of qualified plans: defined contribution and defined benefit. **Defined contribution plans** place an amount of money in the pension regularly. The amount available in retirement depends on the sum contributed and the returns on that money. Defined contribution plans are often portable when you change jobs or retire. Examples are company profit-sharing plans, 401(k) plans, 403(b) plans, and IRAs.

Defined benefit plans provide a stated stream of income, often a level amount, throughout retirement. The amount of income received generally depends on the time you spent with the corporation or other organization and on your salary in the period around retirement. Defined benefit plans may just be thought of by an employee as annual income for retirement. The normal pension by a company or a union offering yearly income is a defined benefit plan. Social Security can be considered one as well.

It is the emphasis on end-of-working-period time and/or salary for calculating benefits in contrast to beginning-of-working-period contributions that distinguishes defined benefit from defined contribution plans. Defined benefit and defined contribution plans are described more fully in Appendix I.

Practical Comment   Attractiveness of Pension Savings

For the majority of Americans, pensions may be the most efficient way to save large sums and invest monies, with the possible exception of another tax-favored investment—the house. The principal advantage the pension has over most other forms of investment is the ability to place pretax dollars into it. The benefit becomes clearer to people when you tell them that when they earn $50,000 and place $10,000 in a pension plan, $40,000 appears as income on their tax return and $10,000 is put away, growing tax-free. They will only pay taxes years later, when they make withdrawals. Those looking for a tax shelter need go no further.

The pension's disadvantage is the lack of liquidity on withdrawals before 59½ unless one pays a tax penalty. However, after an extended period, it can pay to save in a pension, even when early withdrawals have to be made. Moreover, the perceived absence of liquidity has a positive aspect; people are more reluctant to withdraw money placed into a pension. Another possible advantage is that deposits sometimes are augmented by contributions from the employer. Where motivation is needed for saving, a pension can be called a "government gift" with the implication that a very strong reason must be present to turn it down.

Nonqualified Plans

Nonqualified plans are those that may be used for retirement but whose deposits are generally not eligible to receive a tax deduction. Therefore, less desirable after-tax dollars are placed into the plan. While deposits are in the plan, investment income and capital gains are not taxed. Withdrawals are taxed only on appreciation in asset values. The original amounts placed in the plan are not assessed by governmental authorities since they were taxed prior to their deposit. The taxable portion of withdrawals is subject to ordinary income rates. Two common examples of nonqualified plans are tax-deferred compensation and tax-deferred annuities.

Tax-Deferred Compensation   **Tax-deferred compensation** refers to monies that employees have earned that is not paid out by their employers until some future time. Selected employers offer this option as a company benefit. In the interim, the sums grow tax-deferred. The amounts may be paid out at a stated date, at retirement, or over a period of years. Since tax-deferred compensation is an exception to the nonqualified pensions' after-tax rule (perhaps because the money has not yet been physically received by the employee), a requirement of these plans is that the employee be subject to risk; if the employer goes bankrupt, the employee becomes a general creditor of the company.

Tax-Deferred Annuities[8]   **Tax-deferred annuities** are savings vehicles that allow for retirement or other purposes; after-tax deposits grow tax-free until monies are withdrawn.[9] Since after-tax dollars are placed into accounts, withdrawals are taxed only to the extent of income and gains on original deposits. You are not required to make withdrawals. If not withdrawn at the time of your death, all gains over original cost are subject to tax at ordinary income rates.

Tax-deferred annuities can be separated into fixed and variable types.[10] **Fixed annuities** provide an interest rate that is established by the issuer and often changes annually. Frequently, there is a guaranteed minimum rate that the issuer must provide. Rates for fixed annuities paid by the issuer are influenced by market interest rates, the investment

---

[8] Excludes 403(b) plan annuities for nonprofit organizations.

[9] Members of nonprofit organizations can place pretax dollars in 403(b) plan annuities.

[10] There are also variations on these two types of annuities that combine a fixed payout with a variable one. The holder combines a lower upfront payout with a market-based extra return. One such product is called an equity-indexed annuity.

performance of the issuer, and competitive factors among annuity companies. Their returns are often compared with bank certificates of deposit, investment-quality taxable bonds funds, and municipal bonds.

Variable annuities offer a range of investment choices to be selected by the purchaser, often in stock and bond mutual funds. Thus, the returns are established by market factors as opposed to rates that are decided by the insurance companies on fixed annuities. Variable annuities can be compared with mutual funds of the same type. In fact, some individual mutual funds available to the general public are also included in variable annuity choices, called subaccounts, or similar formats.

Most annuities also have a redemption charge for liquidation or transfer prior to a fixed period of 5 to 10 years with a declining rate as the period the annuity is held increases. Withdrawals of a fixed percentage annually, sometimes 10 percent, are not subject to this redemption charge. Because liquidations are subject to ordinary income taxation and redemption charges, they often are viewed as more restrictive than individual securities and funds. They can, however, be transferred to another annuity without generating taxable income.

An important feature of annuities is the ability of holders to annuitize if they wish. **Annuitization** refers to converting a lump-sum asset accumulated into the payment of a fixed flow of income per year based on life expectancy.

Annuities have significant advantages and disadvantages over competing financial instruments. For example, annuities have the benefit of tax deferral. On the other hand, their returns are taxed at ordinary income rates in contrast to favorable capital gains, dividend rates for equity mutual funds, and municipal bonds, which are not taxed. A comparison of fixed and variable annuities with selected alternative investment structures is given in Table 12.2.

TABLE 12.2
Comparison of Annuity with Other Investments

	Advantages of Annuity	Advantages of Competing Instrument	Explanation or Additional Information
Fixed Annuity versus			
CD	Tax deferral	Safety of U.S. government agency guarantee	Comparison of returns varies
Taxable bond	Tax deferral Lack of fluctuation in principal	Flexibility in shifting Annuity has redemption charge for a number of years	Comparison of returns varies
Municipal bond	Higher pretax return	Tax-free return[1]	Highest return often depends on length of holding period; very long periods often favor annuities
Variable Annuities versus			
Mutual funds	Tax deferral Guaranteed death benefit	Favorable capital gains rates on equity fund, appreciation, and dividends Higher total expense ratios and a redemption charge for annuities Limitation on investment choice for annuities	Death benefit is guarantee of return of original principal or, in some cases, a higher interim amount Most variable annuities have total charges of 0.75 to 2.0 percent

[1] If you buy muni in the state you reside in.

Social Security

Introduction

Social Security principally provides monies to retirees and their spouses to live on. It also extends benefits to surviving spouses and the family's minor children when a wage earner dies before retirement. It also gives benefits to those who are permanently disabled. The stream of income that the U.S. government provides to retirees resembles a private company's defined benefit plan.

When the Social Security system was passed in 1935, it was a more modest system in which life spans were lower and many didn't survive until the age 65 payout. Over the succeeding period, benefits were broadened. These include benefits to survivors and dependents, making more people eligible to receive benefits; the addition of disability and Medicare coverage; and adjusted payments for inflation.

The Social Security system is a blend of two goals. The first is to provide retirement payments to individuals based on their contributions. The second is to redistribute income so that all workers may retire at a minimum standard of living. Those who favor the current system point to its advantages, which include its efficiencies[11] with overhead costs at less than 1 percent of payouts and its form of forced savings. Others say it discourages savings[12] and work and provides a low rate of return on investment. Since the system was established, poverty has declined and the poverty rate may now be lower for retirees than for the population as a whole.

How It Operates

Social Security is a mandatory system that is funded by a payroll tax on both employers and employees. Each paid a tax of 6.2 percent on a maximum of $84,900 in 2002 and a Medicare tax of 1.45 percent with no maximum. In order to be eligible to receive full retirement benefits, you must have completed 40 quarters, equivalent to 10 years of work. The retirement age for full benefits, once age 65, rises to age 67 for those born in years 1938 to 1959 and is maintained at 67 thereafter. Early payments can begin at age 62 at a reduced level, with those retiring after their eligibility for full benefits receiving a greater sum.

Benefits are linked to the amount of contributions.[13] Spouses receive the greater of their own work contribution or 50 percent of that of the sole or other wage earner. If the wage earner passes away first, the surviving spouse payout is raised to 100 percent.

Your date of birth determines the percentage you receive for early retirement at age 62. It ranges from 70 percent to 80 percent, depending on the date you were born. That percentage rises proportionately the longer you wait until retiring. If you wait until after your normal retirement age to start taking payments, they will rise by 4.5 percent to 8 percent a year until you are age 70. There is no incentive to delay payments beyond age 70. In addition, no further payroll taxes are taken out of wages at age 70 and beyond. Your normal retirement date based on your date of birth is shown in Table 12.3.

Finally, those who choose to work beyond their full entitlement date (age 65 and 4 months or older) are entitled to full Social Security benefits regardless of the amounts they earn. Those who are eligible for payments but are younger than age 65 and 4 months were allowed to earn $11,640 in 2004 with a phaseout of benefits of $1 for every $2 earned above this amount. Social Security payments for people earning more than certain threshold levels of income are subject to taxation on 50 percent or 85 percent of the cash received.

---

[11] Joseph Stiglitz, *Economics of the Public Sector,* 3rd ed. (New York: W.W. Norton & Company, 2000).

[12] Martin Feldstein, "Social Security, Induced Retirement and Aggregate Capital Accumulation," *Journal of Political Economy* 82, no. 5 (September–October 1974), pp. 905–26.

[13] The average person will receive a benefit of 41 percent of preretirement earnings, and those contributing the maximum will receive 25 percent of the maximum contribution amount and a lower percent of their total compensation. The maximum monthly amount paid in 2004 at retirement age of 65 was $1,784.

TABLE 12.3
Normal Retirement Age Based on Date of Birth

Source: Adapted from Tax Partners and Professionals of Ernst & Young LLP, *The Ernst & Young Tax Guide* (Hoboken, NJ: John Wiley & Sons, 2004). Reprinted with permission of John Wiley & Sons, Inc.

Birth Year	Year Worker Attains Age 62	Normal Retirement Age
1938	2000	65 + 2 months
1939	2001	65 + 4 months
1940	2002	65 + 6 months
1941	2003	65 + 8 months
1942	2004	65 + 10 months
1943–1954	2005–2016	66
1955	2017	66 + 2 months
1956	2018	66 + 4 months
1957	2019	66 + 6 months
1958	2020	66 + 8 months
1959	2021	66 + 10 months
1960	2022	67
1961 and thereafter	2023 and thereafter	67

The analytical questions asked concerning Social Security benefits are often: "When should I start taking Social Security benefits?" "Should I begin at a permanently lower payout at age 62, or full payout at my normal retirement age?" Of course, the longer you wait to retire, the greater your ability to fund your retirement lifestyle. From a financial standpoint, the answer to whether you should take reduced early Social Security payments, assuming your payment date is independent of your actual retirement date, will depend in part on the factors listed in Table 12.4.

TABLE 12.4
Factors in Decision on Social Security Payout Age

Factor	Reasoning
Risk tolerance—investments	The lower the person's risk tolerance, the lower the investment return on the money taken at an earlier age. A low investment return favors a full payout date.
Longevity	People in good health from families with longevity may want a full date while others with weak health and life-span factors might favor early Social Security. Payouts are not differentiated by sex. Women statistically live longer than men. Therefore, all other things being equal, women should be more likely to take a later payout than men.
Desire for current funds	Those retirees having a preference for spending as much as possible today will favor an early retirement payout. Those with modest assets and a desire to retire early also will favor early payout.
Tax bracket	People currently in high marginal tax brackets, which are likely to decline over time, favor later Social Security payouts.

Example 12.2

Elyssa is about to turn age 62. She retired at age 60 and has sufficient funds to support her retirement. She wants to know whether it would be best to take Social Security at age 62 or wait until age 65. She will receive $19,920 in current after-tax dollars at full retirement age and would receive 77.5 percent of that amount if she decides to take Social Security currently. Assuming that she will earn 5 percent after tax on the money received, has a life expectancy of 82 (that is, she will live 20 more years), and will have a constant marginal tax bracket over time, what should her decision be? Express all amounts in current dollars.

Step	Statistic	Explanation
Benefit starts today at age 62	$15,438	$19,920 × 77.5%
Period for benefits	20 years	

Practical Comment   Social Security Practices

People generally favor early retirement payouts. In fact, they often use payment of Social Security income as a key factor in determining their retirement date. Since the government is viewed as providing equal time-weighted payments over a life span whichever payout alternative is selected, there is no general difficulty with choosing early retirement. However, if the household is too short-term-oriented and has not covered its living costs for an appropriate retirement time frame, it may be best to use a later retirement payout. In that case, the later date is being used as a forced savings procedure.

Calculator Solution

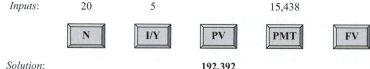

Inputs: 20   5   15,438

| N | I/Y | PV | PMT | FV |

Solution: **192,392**

Step	Statistic	Explanation
Benefit starts at age 65	$19,920	
Period for benefits	17 years	Benefits start three years from now and end at age 82

Calculator Solution

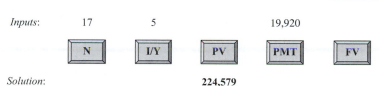

Inputs: 17   5   19,920

| N | I/Y | PV | PMT | FV |

Solution: **224,579**

This is the present value at age 65. We now have to bring that amount back to age 62 so that it can be compared with the benefit that starts at that age.

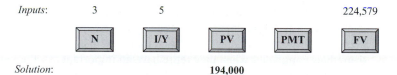

Inputs: 3   5   224,579

| N | I/Y | PV | PMT | FV |

Solution: **194,000**

This is the present value at age 62, today. Since it is higher than the benefit that starts at age 62, it is the preferred alternative.

You can ignore the negative sign obtained in the results. Taking retirement payments at full retirement age has a higher PV at age 62 and therefore is the preferred choice.

ASSESS TYPES OF RETIREMENT ASSETS AND ALTERNATIVE STRUCTURES

The assets that are important for retirement use are diverse. Each can provide cash flows to fund retirement living. We can separate the principal resources into financial assets, human-related assets, and real assets.[14]

[14] Retirement assets are sometimes categorized by the cash flows they generate. The cash flows often have been portrayed as coming from a "three-legged stool." The stool consists of Social Security, personal savings, and company pensions. With the shift to employee-funded pensions and the frequently offered choice of lump-sum payouts at retirement instead of streams of income, this model gets more complex. We have chosen an alternative approach that, of course, produces the same total cash flows.

Financial Assets

Financial assets are often considered the backbone of retirement planning. They can be divided into pension and personal assets. Savings through qualified pension structures—principally, defined contribution plans—offer the benefit of pretax contributions and tax deferral. Savings in personal accounts are more liquid in case of need. When withdrawn through asset sales, personal account savings are taxed at favorable capital gains and dividend income rates as opposed to ordinary income rates on pension withdrawals. Annuities, which can be used as nonqualified pensions, offer tax deferral and annuitization features and, like qualified plans, have withdrawals at ordinary income rates. Annuities that are converted into fixed annual payments most resemble company pensions. We will discuss company pensions under human-related assets.

Human-Related Assets

Human-related assets can be defined as assets whose worth is typically derived from streams of income related to a person's life span. Social Security and company pension payments from defined benefit plans are two such assets related to retirement.

You have less control over these human-related assets. In the case of Social Security, the money is automatically taken from your paycheck. For company pensions, money need not be taken from you, but the company may have an obligation to pay you a fixed sum based on your salary and years employed. You are paid in yearly income streams that you cannot sell, nor can you otherwise control the payout. These income streams are discounted back to the present using an appropriate market-established discount rate. An important feature of human-related retirement assets is that they are typically nonmarketable; they cannot be sold to others.

The human-asset portion, your salary, is generally worth more than that for Social Security or pension assets for working people not close to retirement. That is easy to figure out as salaries typically exceed these other income streams, and they go on for a longer period of time. However, as you approach retirement, your human-asset values decline sharply; and because Social Security and pension payments draw nearer, their discounted values become larger. Social Security and pensions, of course, start to decline in their discounted asset values once retirement payments begin.

It is important to take into account human-related asset values for retirement planning purposes. Presently, their values are not placed on balance sheets, yet few would argue that these are not significant assets. For example, people who receive a large yearly pension from their companies when they retire have an important asset, a big advantage over those who have no private pensions. Financial planners take into account these flows in their recommendations and the total portfolio management approach uses the asset values and their relationship to other assets in helping make investment decisions.

Company pension and Social Security retirement income streams have significant benefits over income generated from financial investments. Company pensions generally provide a predictable level annual payment not subject to market fluctuations.[15] Social Security's payout is even more attractive because it is adjusted for inflation and is at least partially tax-exempt, with full exemption for those in lower income brackets. The disadvantages of company pensions and Social Security payments are the absence of an option to draw down the money earlier than the scheduled date of payment and the inability to transfer this asset to others at death.[16]

---

[15] For a discussion of pension payments as a bond, see William Reichenstein, "Rethinking the Family's Asset Allocation," *Journal of Financial Planning* 14, no. 5 (May 2001), pp. 102–09.

[16] Company pensions often can be set up to continue partial or full payments to the spouse after the death of a worker, and Social Security provides surviving spouses with the full payment made to workers after their death.

A simple calculation of the value of these pension streams is provided in Example 12.3.

Example 12.3

Tony was about to retire and wanted to establish the current value of two of his three assets. He already had the value for his 401(k) pension plan, which was worth $102,000. The first was a corporate pension paying $30,000 and the second was Social Security, which would offer $19,000 a year. Regular U.S. government bonds were currently yielding 6 percent while U.S. government inflation-indexed bonds provided a current return of 5.5 percent. If his remaining life span is 18 years, what are his pensions worth?

Calculator Solution— Company Pension

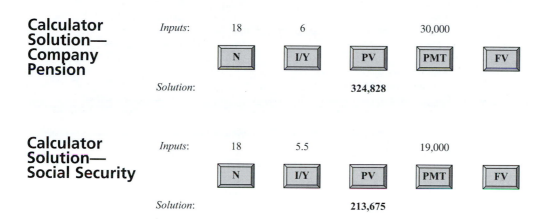

Calculator Solution— Social Security

You can ignore the negative sign obtained in the results.

Combined Worth of Tony's Assets

401(k) Pension Plan	$102,000
Company Pension	324,828
Social Security	213,675
PV of Tony's Assets	**$640,503**

By placing the present value of these two pension flows into asset form, we obtain a value of $324,828 for the company pension and $213,675 for Social Security, which together with the 401(k)'s $102,000 provides a combined worth of $640,503.

As you can see, there are significant differences in retirement savings structures. A detailed comparison of the advantages and disadvantages of saving through alternative retirement structures is given in Table 12.5. It is followed by a comparison of the treatment of payout for alternative retirement structures in Table 12.6.

The Home

Unlike most other retirement assets, the home serves many functions. It is a maintenance expense that provides shelter, it is a leisure refuge, and it can be a sound retirement investment. For those who own a home, thinking of it as a retirement savings structure, an investment for retirement, is complicated. We know it has certain cost advantages including a tax deduction for mortgage interest and property taxes, and no taxation at sale on the first $250,000 of gains per person or $500,000 per couple, with any remainder taxed at favorable capital gains rates. In addition, homes are a good inflation hedge and can be financed largely through debt.

TABLE 12.5   **Comparison of Saving through Alternative Retirement Structures**

	Advantages	Disadvantages
Qualified pension plans	✔ Pretax dollar contributions ✔ Tax deferral ✔ Modest administrative charges or none ✔ Often the most attractive retirement savings vehicle	✔ Money generally cannot be withdrawn without penalty until age 59½ ✔ Withdrawals taxed at ordinary rates ✔ Overall limits on annual contribution ✔ Mandatory withdrawals must start at age 70½
Annuities	✔ Tax deferral ✔ No price fluctuation and guaranteed rate for fixed annuities ✔ The option to annuitize ✔ No limits on annual contributions ✔ No mandatory withdrawals	✔ Withdrawals taxed at ordinary rates ✔ Material overhead charges ✔ After-tax dollar contributions
Personal savings using mutual funds	✔ Capital gains and dividends taxed at favorable rates[1] ✔ Broad flexibility in shifting investment positions ✔ Ability to select from the universe of choices ✔ No limits on annual contributions ✔ No mandatory withdrawals	✔ No overall tax shelter ✔ After-tax dollar contributions

[1] Mutual funds offer a form of tax deferral because gains are not taxed until shares are sold either by the fund manager (net of losses or other holdings sold) or by the fund holder. When accounts are individually managed instead of managed in mutual fund format, holdings can be deferred indefinitely as it is the holder who decides exactly when to sell each asset.

TABLE 12.6   **Comparison of Retirement Payouts by Type of Retirement Structure**

Factor	Defined Contribution	Defined Benefit	Annuity[1]	Personal Savings	Social Security
Tax treatment of initial deposit	Pretax dollars	Pretax dollars	After-tax dollars	After-tax dollars	N/A
Tax deferral on income and capital gains	Yes	Yes	Yes	No	N/A
Taxation of pension payout of original deposit	Yes	Yes	No	No	N/A[2]
Taxation of pension payout of gains on original investment	Yes	Yes	Yes	N/A	N/A
Type of taxation on gains	Ordinary income	Ordinary income	Ordinary income	Capital gains[3]	N/A
Government-backed guarantee	No	Yes	No	No	Yes
Typically indexed for inflation	No	No	No	No	Yes
Is sum liquid?[4]	No[5]	No[6]	No[6]	Yes	No
Total portfolio asset category	Financial	Human-related	Financial	Financial	Human-related

[1] That is annuitized.
[2] Taxation, if any, based on overall household income.
[3] For sales at a profit. Dividends taxed at favorable capital gains rates and interest at ordinary income rates.
[4] Assuming person currently works for a company.
[5] In some cases, money can be borrowed for a limited time.
[6] Yes, if not annuitized.

Practical Comment Calculation of Resources on Sale of Home

Sometimes, in calculating resources needed for retirement, financial planners exclude the value of a home, unless directed not to do so by their clients. House liquidation can be viewed as a safety alternative to be used if a financial shortfall occurs. When valuing the home for retirement need purposes, the home should not be assessed at its fair market price alone; the net present value of future rental payments should be deducted from the price (as well as any applicable taxes). Note that this net value will differ depending on the age of the retirees and the rental costs of the dwelling they are moving into. The older the retirees and the lower the rental costs, the greater the asset value that represents the proceeds if the house is sold.

However, treating the home as an investment can be involved. In order for something to be considered an investment, cash flow should be received or there should be an expectation of selling it at a profit at some future time. The home doesn't provide cash flow unless part or all of it is rented out.[17] It can usually be sold as long as an alternative dwelling can be found. But many retired people prefer living in the same home for the rest of their lives. That is true despite the fact that housing for an individual or a couple may be economically inefficient; the residence can be too big or otherwise inappropriate from an economic standpoint.

The household could borrow money based on the house's asset value even when there is no visible means of paying it back. The vehicle is called a **reverse mortgage**.[18] A reverse mortgage provides borrowed funds based on the market value of the house and the age of the borrower. There is often no need to pay back the money. Instead, the amount of debt grows due to interest charged on the amount outstanding. The debt is repaid from the proceeds of the home upon voluntary sale or upon the death of the borrower.

This money from the reverse mortgage can generate cash flow for living needs from the house as an investment. Yet the reverse mortgage has not proven to be popular. Since the home is not intended to be sold, aside from any planned benefit for heirs, should it be considered an asset?

Even when the intention is to remain in it forever, the home generally contains what is called an embedded option—meaning the alternative of selling, provided there is some preparation for moving. The option may be exercised under certain conditions—for example, when you live an extra-long life and need additional capital; when you become ill and prefer more help—the kind you would receive in an assisted-living facility or nursing home; or simply when you change your mind about living in your home. Obviously, the greater the home's value, the greater the option's value.

ANALYZE RETIREMENT RISKS

Risk management as it concerns retirement covers many risk factors. Its objective is to control risks so that retirees can fund the standard of living they plan for. It can be divided into investment risk, inflation risk, longevity risk, and health risk.

Investment Risk

Investment risk for retirement purposes can be thought of as the potential for below-average returns. While large companies have averaged 10 to 12 percent per year over the past 75 years, they have declined almost one-third of the time. Declines are of particular relevance to retirees because of withdrawal risk.

---

[17] Of course, the absence of rental expense could be considered as cash flow.

[18] A person generally has to be advanced in age to be eligible for this alternative.

Withdrawal risk is the uncertainty created by taking monies out to fund retirement when asset prices are depressed. Withdrawals made at that time have a great effect on accumulated savings since generally the same amount is withdrawn whether the market is up or down. In other words, a fixed amount taken out when the market is down will result in an extra percentage of the portfolio being withdrawn. When the market is down, the extra percentage taken is lost forever: There can be no price recovery on that extra percentage of withdrawal since that money has already been spent. Consequently, there is less money left to generate investment income. When declines in assets happen at the beginning of retirement, they have a much greater effect than they might at the end of the retirement period.

Withdrawal risk for retirees contrasts with the experience of working people. For those who are still working, the timing of negative investment returns makes little difference. Unless assets are withdrawn, the average compounded return over a period of years is the only item that matters. Consider the difference in impact of market declines occurring at the beginning and end of retirement in Example 12.4.

Example 12.4

Let's look at the effect of a decline in the stock market at the beginning of the investment period versus one at the end of the period. We will do so by taking two people whose beginning assets and withdrawal rates were identical. By doing so we can make clear the important impact of these alternatives on ending dollars.

Michael and Helen each started with $80,000. They retired, and both took out $12,000 of their money at the end of each year and spent it. Michael had a 40 percent decline in his assets in year 1 whereas Helen's occurred in year 4. They both had a 10 percent increase per year in their assets in the remaining years. Assuming no tax impact, what sums did each have at the end of the period?

Year	Michael	Explanation[1]	Helen	Explanation[1]
	Year 1 Price Decline Balance		Year 4 Price Decline Balance	
0	$80,000		$80,000	
1	36,000	80,000 × (1 − 0.4) − 12,000	76,000	80,000 × (1 + 0.1) − 12,000
2	27,600	36,000 × (1 + 0.1) − 12,000	71,600	76,000 × (1 + 0.1) − 12,000
3	18,360	27,600 × (1 + 0.1) − 12,000	66,760	71,600 × (1 + 0.1) − 12,000
4	8,196	18,360 × (1 + 0.1) − 12,000	28,056	66,760 × (1 − 0.4) − 12,000

[1]Annual withdrawals = $12,000.

Notice that Helen has more than three times as much money left at the end of year 4 as Michael, even though they differed only in the timing of their one-year 40 percent decline.

That is because the permanent drop in Michael's asset value left less for investing earlier than for Helen. In sum, we see that the timing of price declines, whether they come in year 1 or year 4, matters, with greater impact for the one occurring earlier.

Withdrawal risk can be reduced by taking money from the bond portion of portfolios, which tends to be less volatile. You could keep one year's worth of income in money market funds, to be used instead of liquidating stocks when there are sharp declines in the stock market.[19] Adjustment for overall investment uncertainties can come in part through diversification, a higher bond allocation, and more conservative projections of future returns, or through the risk-adjusted projections discussed in Chapter 9.

[19] Fred Ogborne, Paul Hoffman, and Walt Woerheide, "Sustainable Withdrawal Rates from Retirement Portfolios: The Impact of a Buffer Portfolio," Working Paper, presented at the 2001 MFA Annual Meeting and the 2001 AFS Annual Meeting.

FIGURE 12.2 **Annual Inflation 1914–2004**

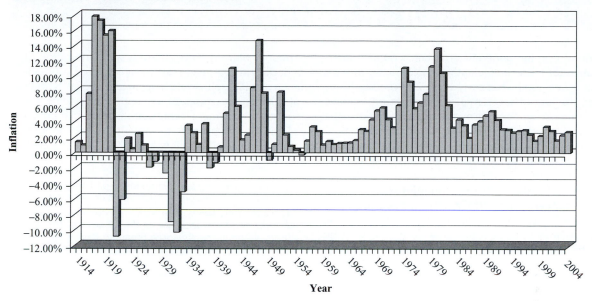

Inflation Risk

Inflation risk is a particular problem for retired people. That is because salaries are often adjusted to take into account inflation, but the retired don't have that job-related revenue buffer to offset increases in living costs. Instead, many retirees have flat-payout company pensions and own fixed-payout bonds, which result in difficulties when their living costs rise sharply. In addition, extra withdrawals due to higher costs leave fewer dollars to generate investment income. This situation can lead to a downward spiral in savings with little opportunity for retired people to make it up.

Inflation rates vary considerably over time. In the post–World War II period, the consumer price index peaked at 13.6 percent in 1980 and was as low as 1.6 percent in 2002. The change in the consumer price index over time is shown in Figure 12.2.

In plain terms, it means that your standard of living goes down because your income fails to keep pace with the spiraling cost of supporting yourself.

Recourses for retired people include inflation-indexed bonds, whose principal value is indexed for inflation and should not decline when inflation moves up, and significant equity positions that adjust for inflation after a lag. Consideration should be given to indexing insurance policies such as those for housing through replacement-cost coverage and long-term care through a cost-of-living rider. Making inflation assumptions that are at the high end of the range, having substantive concentrations in stocks, and owning a home that one is willing to liquidate also can help.

Longevity Risk

Longevity risk[20] is the possibility of death occurring well before or after it is expected. Dying considerably before anticipated can pose a risk for other household members when they are counting on the deceased's labor income. In retirement, the financial risk is of living longer than the average person your age does. If you are healthy, doing so can provide you with many more years of pleasure in retirement. At the same time, living longer requires greater retirement resources. Since usually you cannot know when you will die,

---

[20] A dictionary definition of longevity indicates that it refers exclusively to a human life of long duration. The definition here for longevity risk expands this definition to include premature death.

Practical Comment   The Popularity of Annuities

Annuitizing has generally not been a popular alternative for most people, although consumer interest has grown somewhat early in the 21st century. Many cite the lack of substantially higher returns relative to purchasing long-term bonds. In addition, the annuities lack flexibility and inflation protection. Finally, resources to heirs are cut off. Insurance company overhead and problems with who selects them limit payouts.

Nonetheless, in theory, annuities retain significant appeal in a portfolio setting since they substantially reduce both longevity and market risk. What may be needed is a way to provide both higher returns and an inflation-protection option.[21] More recently, there is some indication of a decline in overhead costs for annuities.[22] A broadened appeal itself would help by creating economies of scale, more competition, and, under some circumstances, a more representative population. In any event, the payouts for annuities vary considerably and thus individual policies should be shopped.

[21] There have been some offerings in the past and perhaps today, but the vast majority of companies do not offer it.
[22] Olivia Mitchell, James Poterba, Mark Warshawsky, and Jeffrey Brown, "New Evidence on the Money's Worth of Individual Annuities," *American Economic Review* 89, no. 5 (December 1999), pp. 1299–318.

most people provide resources for a longer-than-usual life. The average male and female who retire at age 65 have 16 years and 19 years of projected retirement, respectively; 14 percent of males and 27 percent of females have a 25-year retirement; and 10 percent of males and females have 27 years and 30 years of retirement, respectively. Social Security extends until death as company defined benefit pension plans typically do.

Annuities and Longevity Risk[23]

Earlier in this chapter, we described tax-sheltered annuities as retirement savings vehicles. Here we concentrate on annuity payouts through annuitization. **Annuitization** provides level payments or, less typically, payments indexed for inflation that may last as long as you are alive. It is often set up by exchanging a fixed amount of cash, sometimes called a lump sum, for a stream of income payments. Social Security and private yearly income from company pension flows are, in effect, annuities but with their cash contributions coming over an extended period of time.

Traditional annuities are typically offered by insurance companies or other companies that usually contract with insurance firms to provide these policies to the public. Here are their strengths and weaknesses:

Strengths

1. By paying out monies over your lifetime, they can significantly reduce longevity risk. You cannot outlive your annuity payments.
2. Annuities allow you to receive a fixed sum of money each year regardless of market fluctuation. Therefore, they are particularly appealing to people with low risk tolerances.

Weaknesses

1. Annuity payments are usually not inflation-adjusted. The flat payments tend to decline in purchasing-power terms over time.
2. Sometimes liberal assumptions favorable to them are used by companies on the length of life. In addition, the people attracted to annuities may be expected to live longer lives

[23] See Moshe Arye Milevsky, "Optimal Asset Allocation towards the End of the Life Cycle: To Annuitize or Not to Annuitize?" *Journal of Risk and Insurance* 65, no. 3 (1998), pp. 401–26.

(the sick don't apply). The outcome can be lower-than-optimal payouts for the person having an average life span.

3. There is a lack of liquidity once you annuitize, with no way to recover your lump sum or to speed up payment. Similarly, there is no sum to liquidate at death and leave for your heirs since payments stop upon your death.

4. The payout guarantee is from a company that itself is subject to bankruptcy risk. Thus, you must investigate the quality of the company offering the annuity.

Health Risk

Health risk as it pertains to financial matters is the possibility of large unreimbursable costs. All people are subject to health risk. However, as one ages, health risk increases materially. A great number of elderly people find that their medical costs more than double in retirement, even without a catastrophic illness. Many medically related costs for the elderly are paid for under Medicare. If the elderly are required to take expensive medications not approved for payment or they need human assistance during illness not covered by the government, these costs may force them to live at a lower standard of living. Medigap insurance, which can pay part or for some people all of the drug costs as well as certain supplemental medical payments, is a way of meeting this risk.

Another cost, which can be very high, is long-term care. As retired people age, particularly into their 80s, their ability to take care of themselves may diminish. Since more women reach this age than men, they are at greater risk. The elderly may need partial or full assistance from another person either in a facility or in their own home at costs that can be sizeable. Government assistance in this area tends to be limited in what is covered and the time period for coverage.

Those daunting costs sometimes compel people to enter a nursing home. For most, nursing homes are not perceived as a desirable personal option. In addition, the cost of a nursing home, which in certain parts of the country amounts to over $100,000 per year, can cut into or eliminate the funds available for a spouse. Home health care designed to allow you to stay in your home when you have difficulty operating independently also can be very costly, particularly when care is needed 24 hours a day.

Long-term care insurance, discussed in Chapter 11, can meet part or all of this cost. Inflation riders on the policy can further reduce the risk in this area. Another way of meeting these costs is by having significant cash reserves. This precautionary savings is one reason that people have cash remaining at death.

DECIDE ON RETIREMENT INVESTMENT POLICY

The retirement investment policy comprises types of assets and, in many cases, which investment structures they go into. We have already reviewed types of relevant assets—typically, stocks, bonds, and mutual funds—in Chapter 9 on financial investments and houses in Chapter 8 on nonfinancial investments. Retirement investing is just investing for these assets with a longer-term outlook. Therefore, in many cases, the allocation for these assets will be similar to the overall longer-term asset allocation.

To sum up, typically the most attractive place to save for retirement is a qualified pension. The principal exception can be the purchase of a home. A home not only provides tax deferral for increases in its worth and partial or no taxation on gains upon sale of the home but also financial and nonfinancial benefits in living in one. However, in order to realize the financial benefits of homeownership for retirement planning, the home must be sold or borrowed against.

Once the investment policy has been established, we can project the returns on investments and begin our retirement needs analysis.

Practical Comment   Asset Allocation and Safe Withdrawal Rates

The approach of placing 100 percent of retirement money in either bonds or stocks may be short-sighted. Retirements extend for approximately 20 years on average and a substantial number for 30 years. For that period of time when withdrawal rates are sizeable, having a majority of financial assets in stocks but also owning bonds may provide the greatest certainty of success. Using an acceptable probability of success of around 80 percent, a 100 percent bond portfolio will not generate a high enough return to support an initial withdrawal rate of anything above 3 percent when the payout grows by inflation and extends for 30 years.

In the majority of cases, under similar circumstances, an asset allocation of at least 50 percent in stocks will fund an inflation-adjusted withdrawal rate of 4 percent with a relatively high degree of certainty. The probabilities of having sufficient funds for retirement by withdrawal rate and asset allocation are shown below.

Portfolio Success Rates[24] for 30-Year Period

Source: Adapted from Philip Cooley, Carl Hubbard, and Daniel Walz, "A Comparative Analysis of Retirement Portfolio Success Rates: Simulation versus Overlapping Periods," *Financial Services Review* 12, no. 2 (2003), pp. 115–28. Reprinted with permission from Academy of Financial Services.

Asset Allocation	Withdrawal Rate as Percent of Initial Portfolio Value							
	3%	4%	5%	6%	7%	8%	9%	10%
100% stocks	97	88	75	59	42	28	19	11
75% stocks/25% bonds	96	84	67	48	30	17	9	4
50% stocks/50% bonds	98	81	53	30	12	5	2	0
25% stocks/75% bonds	94	66	29	93	3	1	0	0
100% bonds	79	35	10	2	0	0	0	0

[24] Portfolio success rates with inflation-adjusted monthly withdrawals are derived by Monte Carlo simulation. For a discussion of this technique, see Chapter 18.

ASSET ALLOCATION AND HUMAN BEHAVIOR

For many people, asset allocations, whether before or after retirement, tend to shift with recent performance figures. For example, people often increase their allocation to stocks after unusually good performance. There is no indication that these timing shifts are successful, and to the extent that sharp increases in stocks connote movement away from fundamental value, the moves may be detrimental. Thus, it may be advisable to stay with a more constant asset allocation approach, one that takes into account a more gradual decline in the equity portion in the period beyond age 65.

CALCULATE RETIREMENT NEEDS

Capital needs analysis is a way of establishing how much money we have to save to meet our goals. Under the household approach, then, internal funds generated, specifically savings and often higher future income (in effect, money retained in the household business), are used as the principal approach to support future capital needs. Although we make important decisions on an overall organizational basis, as a business does, we fund each objective separately, using a capital needs approach. We often restrict our use of a formal capital needs analysis to items of great significance to our goals. Four of them are the purchase of a house, life insurance needs, disability needs, and retirement needs. The actual method of calculating a capital needs analysis and the final two steps in the retirement process are covered in Chapter 18.

RETIRED HOUSEHOLDS

Retirement planning can be viewed as not ending at retirement. Instead, planning goes on for the remainder of retirement. Retirement planning must be reviewed periodically for goals as well as current and projected assets change. The outcome can be an alteration in savings, cost-of-living, or other retirement strategies. One of the greatest changes may occur in the postretirement period. We will deal with it in some detail.

Postretirement planning is in many ways similar to preretirement analysis. In fact, they would likely be the same if all the factors that we thought would come to fruition did. As we know, however, this generally is not the case. That is why financial planning incorporates risk into its analysis.

Some common risk factors are

- Health difficulties force retirement at an earlier age than expected.
- Your company forces you to take early retirement or you are terminated and at an advanced age cannot find a replacement job.
- Medical bills are higher than expected, and later in life costly human care assistance is needed at home or at a facility.
- The investment returns proved lower than expected.
- Planning for retirement was not done in a logical, structured way; often it was not done at all. (This is true of many Americans.)

A major difference between pre- and postplanning is that choices are more limited in retirement. Basically, the opportunity to enhance cash inflows is limited or nonexistent. The full-time job at a large salary is typically a thing of the past. Therefore, the changes in household operations are likely to be largely focused on costs.

Common alternatives are

1. *Cutting back in cost of living.* Cutbacks can include any number of things such as eating out, gifts, and vacations; unless active, retirement as one ages may help reduce expenses without the need for sacrifice should medical costs not rise too much.
2. *Moving to a lower-cost region.* For those in a higher-cost metropolitan region, moving to a lower-cost area can reduce expenses by as much as 25 percent.
3. *Receiving help from others.* Typically, financial aid can come from children. When possible, the amounts advanced may be paid back from the proceeds of the estate at death.
4. *Taking a part-time job.* This is an exception to the cost-only emphasis. When available, a part-time job can bring in additional monies and also may be looked at as a pursuit that keeps you physically and mentally healthy.

Not all planning surprises result in cutbacks. A large number of the retired generate funds that are in excess of their needs, even given conservative assumptions for investment returns, long lives, and high reserves for extraordinary expenses. As these people age, it becomes clear to them that they have choices.

When there is free cash flow generated net of potentially higher medical expenses, they can spend and raise their standard of living. Many times comfort with their established way of doing things can limit these expenditures. Another alternative may be to gift children and grandchildren and receive pleasure from the effects it has on their quality of life.

In any event, as people age, more time is spent on estate planning for other household members, elder care matters in case of physical or mental impairment (see Chapter A on the Web site), and gifting and bequests. Strategies not only may be legal or insurance-related but also can include moving closer to children.

Back to Dan and Laura
RETIREMENT PLANNING

Dan and Laura were surprisingly detailed about their retirement goals. Often people their age in their circumstances are more concerned about moving their careers forward and raising their children. Both wanted to retire at age 55. They particularly wanted to retire at the same time so that they could share a life of almost total leisure, with virtually the only work being to split the household chores. Laura mentioned that many elementary school teachers tended to retire early and that with generous retirement packages, some teachers felt there was little incentive to stay on past their mid-50s. She indicated that if she retired at 55, she would receive a pension worth $40,000 per year in today's dollars, beginning at age 65. If she were to work until age 60, it would be worth $45,000 and at age 65, $50,000. Unfortunately, Laura had no voluntary pension savings vehicle such as a 403(b) plan available to her.

I asked them how important the age 55 goal was, and they replied that they would like to retire then but would be satisfied if they could retire at age 60. Both wanted to move in retirement to an area about 150 miles away that had three attributes. First, it had a large university within it, and they liked the cultural activities and ability to interact with younger people when they were older. Second, there was a long-established retired population there. Finally, the costs were about 15 percent cheaper than where they lived.

I asked them about other costs that might change in retirement. They said they would like to travel more both in the United States and in Asia and estimated that would add $10,000 per year to living costs. Medical costs would not be a problem. Laura's generous school retirement package would cover them both. They couldn't think of any other major changes except taxes. They said they simply wanted to maintain their current standard of living into retirement, which they thought could be done at lower cost in the retirement community.

Dan mentioned his concern that he was not saving enough money for retirement. He didn't believe he would be receiving a pension from his present company or from any other company he might work for in the future. His private pension would have to come from the 401(k) plan entirely funded by him. He asked whether I thought he should continue contributing to the 401(k) in light of his planned capital expenditures and debt problems.

I asked them if there were any inheritances in their future. Dan laughed and said far from it. His parents, currently age 60, had enough savings to last until age 80. He and his brothers would have to contribute part of their living cost thereafter. Laura said her parents, age 66 and 65, were expecting to leave some money to her and her siblings. I asked her to provide conservative projections of the amount. She thought that she might receive $100,000 in today's dollars but insisted strongly that it not be included in retirement planning.

Dan believed that his compensation would grow 10 percent a year for the next 10 years and then level off, with raises growing at the rate of inflation. Laura indicated her compensation would increase at the rate of inflation after the step-up due to her projected completion of a master's degree. Both thought their standard of living after purchase of the house was what they would like to maintain throughout their lives. They wanted to fund their children's undergraduate education at a good state university in their area, which would cost approximately $20,000 per year per child. In addition, Dan asked me what I thought of long-term care insurance for them at this time.

Finally, I mentioned that our plans generally provide for funding to ages 95 for females and 91 for males based on about a 10 percent probability of their exceeding that age. They looked at each other and laughed and said they wanted funding for both to age 95.

Retirement planning is considered by many to be the focal point of financial planning. For those people being able to enjoy a comfortable retirement, it is their uppermost concern and goal. To be able to do so with confidence, it is important that long-term planning for retirement start at an early date. Your insightful comments on what retirement might look like have made it easier for me to calculate the financial steps that should be taken to ensure that you can reach your retirement objectives.

The process of establishing your current situation includes ascertaining your required savings as compared with your current savings. It reflects your retirement goals and all resources to be established before and after retirement. First, I will answer the questions you have asked for they bear on the questions of resources generated. Then I will state the assumptions made in calculating retirement needs. I will then calculate your retirement needs. Using the retirement needs and the educational funding you intend to provide, I will calculate your life insurance needs. Placing your entire life cycle inflows and outflows together with your resources, I will indicate whether your current savings pattern appears adequate to meet your goals.

Dan asked whether he should continue funding his 401(k) plan in view of spending pressures on the two of you. The 401(k) plan is not an ordinary savings vehicle. It is one that includes special tax benefits. Pretax dollars are placed into it, which means that the deposits are not taxed at that time. For tax purposes, then, it is as if you didn't earn that money despite the fact that it will be a strong source of investment and retirement dollars. Income and capital gains are also not taxed currently. It is only when you start withdrawals that the money is taxed. By then you should have generated a substantial nest egg.

I refer to qualified plans such as the 401(k) as a "government gift" to make my clients aware of the benefit in participating in it and the concurrent loss if they choose not to fund the payments. I believe that thinking applies to you as well. You should make the payments once Laura returns to work and even earlier if possible.

Finally, I will comment that your goals and resources appear to be out of balance. Specifically, your resources are likely to fall short of your goals. This is not unusual, particularly for people your age. I will leave the discussion until after the capital needs analysis is completed (Chapter 18). At that time, we will have a better handle on what is doable.

Summary

Having sufficient capital to retire comfortably is the number one financial concern for many people. As such, it has particular importance in PFP.

- Of the two types of pension plans, qualified and nonqualified, generally only qualified plans allow for a tax deduction for plan deposits.
- Tax-deferred annuities are nonqualified retirement plans in which after-tax dollars are contributed.
- Generally, only Social Security is indexed for inflation.
- A home may be considered a retirement asset if the owner intends to sell it at some time in the future. Even without that statement, a home may be sold in a financial emergency.
- Four particularly important types of risks in retirement planning are inflation, investment including withdrawal risk, longevity risk, and health risk.
- Annuities deal with longevity risk. You can get a fixed sum regardless of market fluctuations.
- An inflation-adjusted withdrawal rate of 4 percent annually as a percentage of original capital appear possible for 30-year retirement periods.

Key Terms

annuitization, *336*

defined benefit plans, *324*

defined contribution plans, *324*

fixed annuities, *325*

health risk, *337*

longevity risk, *335*

nonqualified plans, *325*

pension, *322*

qualified plans, *323*

reverse mortgage, *333*

tax-deferred annuities, *325*

tax-deferred compensation, *325*

variable annuities, *326*

vesting, *323*

withdrawal risk, *334*

Web Sites

http://www.ssa.gov
Social Security Administration (SSA)
This is the home page of the Social Security Administration. It offers complete information about regulations on Social Security benefits, statistical data, and helpful topics discussing the most important issues regarding Social Security.

http://www.pbgc.gov
Pension Benefit Guarantee Corporation (PBGC)
Comprehensive information about defined benefit pension plans and how PBGC guarantees timely and uninterrupted payments of pension benefits is featured.

http://www.dol.gov/ebsa
Employee Benefits Security Administration (EBSA)
Assistance and educational information on pension, health, and other employee benefit plans for both employers and employees are presented.

http://www.dol.gov/dol/topic/health-plans/erisa.htm
ERISA
This link provides complete information about the Employee Retirement Income Security Act (ERISA), which deals with voluntarily established pension and health plans.

http://www.irs.gov/retirement
Internal Revenue Service (IRS)
This link offers useful tax information for retirement plans.

http://www.navanet.org
National Association for Variable Annuities
This site provides comprehensive learning material, statistical data, and publications on both fixed and variable annuities.

http://www.401k.org
401(k) Plans
This site has valuable information about 401(k) retirement plans, tax legislation regarding these plans, and answers to frequent questions about these plans. A 401(k) calculator also is provided.

http://www.aarp.org
American Association of Retired People
The home page of American Association of Retired People provides people age 50 and over with useful information in various areas they are concerned about. The topics include health and wellness, community service, learning and technology, travel and leisure, and so on.

http://www.tiaa-cref.com
TIAA-CREF
This is the home page of TIAA-CREF, a group of companies that includes Teachers Insurance and Annuity Association and College Retirement Equities Fund and is the

nation's largest pension fund manager with over $300 billion in assets under management. The site features various retirement plans, individual investing, insurance planning, practical tips in the savings and retirement area, and calculators and planning tools.

Questions

1. Why is retirement perceived as so important to people?
2. List the principal concerns of people in planning retirement.
3. Explain the relationship of life cycle theory to retirement planning.
4. Explain the difference between a defined benefit and a defined contribution plan.
5. Which plan is more likely to be attractive to a younger person, a defined benefit or a defined contribution plan?
6. Why do people save through qualified pension plans?
7. What is the principal benefit of nonqualified plans over other forms of savings?
8. When would a mutual fund be more attractive than an annuity?
9. What does capital needs analysis provide?
10. What is longevity risk?
11. What are the similarities and differences between retirement needs and insurance?
12. How does investing for retirement differ from investing after retirement? Why?
13. Why is it advisable to have a significant amount of a retirement portfolio invested in equity?
14. Explain withdrawal risk.
15. Name three strengths and weaknesses of annuities.
16. Identify the factors that will help make the decision as to whether to take Social Security early.

Problems

12.1 Marisa and Jennifer both attempted to put away $10,000 a year toward savings. Marisa used a 401(k) pension plan while Jennifer tried to do the same but was forced to pay taxes on that $10,000 in savings each year. Assuming that the process was the same each year for 40 years, how much will Marisa and Jennifer have at the end of the period, assuming identical investments providing pretax returns of 10 percent annually? The marginal tax brackets for both are 35 percent overall and for Jennifer's investments 27 percent due to blending income with favorable capital gains rates. (*Note:* Be sure to use after-tax figures for Jennifer's deposits and investment returns.)

12.2 Dawn and Mildred had the same starting sum of $120,000. Each made withdrawals of $24,000 a year. In years 2, 3, and 4, each had returns of 9 percent a year. Dawn had a 50 percent drop in year 1 and a 50 percent gain in year 5, while Mildred had a 50 percent gain in year 1 and a 50 percent drop in year 5.

   a. Calculate the remaining sum for each woman at the end of year 5.

   b. Explain why there is such a big difference in the remaining amounts.

12.3 Kenneth was considering whether to place $10,000 in a tax-deferred annuity or a tax-free municipal bond. Assume the municipal returned 5 percent a year and the tax-deferred annuity 6 percent. Calculate approximately how long he would have to hold the annuity so that, if he withdrew the money and paid taxes on it, he would come out ahead. His marginal tax rate is 35 percent.

12.4 Elizabeth, age 62, wanted to consider the benefits of age 62 Social Security at a reduced 80 percent payout versus full payments at age 65. She could invest the monies at 5.5 percent after tax and expects to live until age 88. She will receive $15,000 a year after tax at age 65. Which alternative should she select? Show all calculations.

CFP® Certification Examination Questions and Problems

12.1 The investment portfolio for a defined benefit retirement plan has declined in value during a year in which most financial market investments have incurred losses. Which one of the following entities would be impacted most by this decline in portfolio value?

    a. individual participants in the plan

    b. company sponsoring the plan

    c. investment banker handling the plan

    d. plan underwriters

12.2 Which one of the following statements is *not* true for a defined benefit plan?

    a. favors older participants

    b. arbitrary annual contribution

    c. requires an actuary

    d. maximum retirement benefit of the lesser of $90,000 (indexed) or 100 percent of pay per year

    e. requires Pension Benefit Guarantee Corporation (PBGC) premiums

12.3 Your client, the chief financial officer of a new company, wishes to install a retirement plan in the company in which the pension benefits to employees are guaranteed by the Pension Benefit Guarantee Corporation (PBGC). Identify the plan(s) below that must meet this requirement.

1. profit-sharing plan
2. money purchase plan
3. target benefit plan
4. defined benefit plan

    a. (1) and (2) only

    b. (2) and (3) only

    c. (1) only

    d. (3) and (4) only

    e. (4) only

12.4 Which of the following is/are true concerning nonqualified deferred-compensation plans?

1. They can provide for deferral of taxation until the benefit is received.
2. They can provide for fully secured benefit promises.
3. They can give an employer an immediate tax deduction and an employee a deferral of tax.

    a. (1) only

    b. (2) only

    c. (3) only

    d. (1) and (3) only

    e. (2) and (3) only

12.5 Which of the following are common actuarial assumptions used in determining the plan contributions needed to fund the benefits of a defined benefit plan?

1. investment performance
2. employee turnover rate
3. salary scale

   4. ratio of single to married participants

    a. (1), (2), and (3) only

    b. (1) and (3) only

    c. (2) and (4) only

    d. (4) only

    e. (1), (2), (3), and (4)

12.6 Marcus has a salary of $150,000. He contributes the maximum to his 401(k) and wishes to make the highest possible level of additional tax-deferred savings for retirement. Which of the following are feasible options for Marcus?

1. Invest in a flexible premium, deferred annuity.
2. Make annual contributions to an IRA on a pretax basis.
3. Make annual contributions to an IRA on an after-tax basis.

    a. (1) only

    b. (3) only

    c. (1) and (2) only

    d. (1) and (3) only

Case Application
RETIREMENT PLANNING
Part 1

At the retirement planning meeting held recently, Richard and Monica were in agreement that they were well short of the money they needed for retirement at Richard's age 65. Monica said she was thingking of handling investments herself. Richard said he wanted to do it and thought that savings outside the pension given current lower tax rates for capital gains and dividends made sense.

Case Application Questions

1. What do you think of Monica's idea of taking control of retirement investing?
2. What is your opinion of Richard's contention that saving outside the pension was best?
3. What are their alternatives in covering the shortfall in annual retirement savings?
4. What are you recommendations?
5. Construct the retirement planning portion of the financial plan.

Part 2

Brad and Barbara also attended the meeting. They said they were too young to start saving for retirement. Retirement seemed "hundreds of years" away and they wanted to have fun today. They would have plenty of time to save for retirement when they were in their 50s.

Case Application Questions

1. How do you feel about their beliefs?
2. Describe the disadvantages of their approach.
3. Suppose they wanted to have $1 million accumulated in 40 years. Indicate how much money would have to be saved each year if they started now. Assume that the money would be accumulated in personal accounts and earn 6 percent a year after taxes.

Appendix I

Pension Plans

This appendix provides additional information on pension plans. Unless otherwise indicated, the statistics on income eligibility and maximum contributions are as of 2005.

DEFINED CONTRIBUTION PLANS

Defined contribution plans are pensions that specify the amount of money that can be placed into them. They limit the amount or percentage of salary that may be deposited. They make no restrictions on the amount accumulated or yearly income that can be withdrawn from the pension other than the 59½ age limitation before payout. Defined contribution plans take many forms. As compared with defined benefit plans, they have grown in favor over recent decades in part because of a trend toward employee-funded pensions. Some types of these plans are discussed below.

IRA Plans

IRAs are open to all people who earned taxable income. If you are not eligible for any other pension plan, you can place pretax dollars into an IRA if your adjusted gross income is below $50,000 and you are single or $70,000 if you are married and filing jointly. Otherwise, after-tax dollars will be used. Limits are $4,000 for an individual and $8,000 for a married couple.[25]

Rollover IRAs

Rollover IRAs are structures for which qualified pension plans of all types may be transferred without triggering a current tax. Generally, the transfers occur when you retire or move to another job. You may combine amounts in other qualified plans in one rollover, although it is generally considered advisable to segregate sums in a separate rollover in which after-tax pension dollars were originally deposited. That segregation is advisable because no income is assessed on withdrawals of after-tax deposits, only on the income they generated.

Roth IRAs

Roth IRAs are pensions into which after-tax dollars are placed, and no further income tax is paid on the sums accumulated. Roth IRAs can receive rollovers from other IRAs, providing that current taxes are paid on the rollover sums. Taxation is made on the amount rolled over, which is included in ordinary income in the year transferred. It can place you in a higher marginal tax bracket for that year. Rollovers are allowed only for those who have an adjustable gross income of $100,000 or less. General contributions are limited to those who have earned income and have AGIs of $110,000 or less per individual or $160,000 or less jointly. Maximum ordinary Roth IRA contributions are $4,000 per year.[26]

Profit-Sharing Plans

Profit-sharing plans are qualified pensions whose funding varies based on the profits of the firm. The maximum contribution allowed is the lesser of $42,000 or 25 percent of each employee's salary.

Target Benefit Plans

Target benefit plans are qualified pensions in which a fixed percentage of profits is contributed to an employee's pension each year. The maximum contribution allowed is the lesser of $42,000 or 25 percent of each employee's salary.

SEP IRAs

A Simplified Employee Pension (SEP) is a qualified pension plan that is simpler to set up and to run. It is normally limited to small businesses. The maximum that can be contributed is the lesser of $42,000 or 25 percent of each employee's salary.

Keogh Plans

Keoghs are another form of simplified defined contribution plan or a defined benefit plan that is used by people who are self-employed or in a partnership.

---

[25] Plus $500 extra per year for a person over 50.

[26] $4,500 if you are 50 or older by the end of applicable year.

401(k) Plans

The 401(k) is the most popular defined contribution plan in the United States today. These plans are generally funded largely by employees, although employers may contribute as well. Because of government requirements to make the plans broad-based among employees, employers have an incentive beyond concern for their workers to make voluntary contributions if the employees also contribute so that they attract more employee participation. The contributions by employees and employers are generally based on a percentage of salary, with employee contributions limited to $14,000 per year[27] and the limits increase each year with inflation. Contributions vest immediately, and departing employees generally transfer these plans to their new employers or to rollover IRAs.

Typically, employees are given a number of investment choices in their 401(k). They are required to provide at least three choices, which may include a money market fund, a bond fund, and a stock fund. However, the trend is for employers to present a widening array of selections, particularly in the equity area. The choices may extend beyond mutual funds to individual asset managers and less often to other types of structures such as hedge funds. The employer is required to monitor the performance of those choices on behalf of the employees and provide up-to-date figures on overall performance for the alternatives and results for each employee's account.

The 401(k) plan perhaps best symbolizes the growing shift from fixed pension sums to those that are funded and run by employers. Today the most popular pension is one largely employee-financed, with investment risk and employer choices self-selected and entirely portable upon leaving.

Effective January 1, 2006, businesses have the ability to offer their workers a Roth 401(k) plan. Unlike a traditional 401(k), under the Roth option employees place after-tax dollars into the plan. Employees can deposit the same amount as allowable for traditional 401(k)s. As we have mentioned in the chapter, the traditional 401(k)'s pretax dollar contribution is an important benefit. However, assuming they hold the money in the Roth 401(k) plan for at least five years and they do not withdraw it before age $59\frac{1}{2}$, they pay no income taxes on the money at all forever. Among people who may find the Roth 401(k) particularly appealing are any of the following: (1) are younger and have many year of tax-free compounding ahead of them, those who (2) are affluent and don't need to make withdrawals to live on, (3) want to leave money to their children—as the children will not pay income taxes on future withdrawals either, (4) can afford to pay for the income taxes due up front and still put the maximum allowable cash contribution into the plan, (5) expect to be in a higher tax bracket in retirement. For those in a higher tax bracket when retired, Roth 401(1) plans can provide an especially important advantage over traditional 401(k) plans.

403(b) Plans

The 403(b) plan was established for nonprofit institutions. It is in many respects like a 401(k) plan. The limitations on contributions are $14,000 per year with the amounts raised periodically. Unlike 401(k) plans, 403(b)s are annuity plans. They may be annuitized, which means that, generally, fixed payments may be received over the life of the retiree or a husband and wife.

DEFINED BENEFIT PLANS

Defined benefit plans are the second major type of qualified pension plan. They fund for a predetermined amount or percentage of salary, generally to be paid out upon retirement. Thus, unlike a defined contribution plan, the contribution at the beginning of each period

---

[27] Plus $4,000 for people over 50.

is not set but the payout at the end of the period—the beginning of retirement—is established. The defined benefit plan used to be the most common plan in the United States. Typically, a person receives a pension sum based on years of service and ending salary for the year or years immediately preceding retirement. When the employer wants to encourage early retirement, the company will often offer incentives in the form of reducing the years of service or make additional annual contributions to make an early retirement package more attractive.

The defined benefit plan is also used by smaller businesses, which may employ a Keogh format. In the case where the principal or principals are close to retirement, relatively large sums can be contributed to fund large retirement payouts. Defined benefits can be an exception to the $42,000-per-year maximum on pension contribution, with yearly amounts deposited potentially exceeding $100,000 per year for people in their late 50s or early 60s. Retirement payouts are based in part on business income and can be as high as $170,000 per year, adjusted for inflation.

In comparison with the defined contribution plan, the defined benefit plan has distinct advantages for mature individuals who may have more money placed into a plan by their corporation or, in the case of ownership in a small business, as a tax shelter for themselves. Where the principals are older and the other employees are younger, the principals can receive a disproportionate share of the overall contributions. As a fixed sum, a defined benefit corporate payout that is guaranteed by the PBGC[28] can be considered a very-low-risk policy.[29]

The defined contribution may be more favorable to younger employees. Their monies contributed can grow to large sums over their working years. For smaller businesses, the plans are simpler to supervise since they don't require actuarial computations of allowable contributions as defined benefit plans do. For businesses, defined contribution plans financed by business are easier to control since they can be partially or fully funded based on profitability. They therefore can be cut back when profits decline. Employee-funded plans like the 401(k) can reduce or eliminate employer cost.

Defined contribution plans also pass market risk onto the employee. Disappointing results lead to a lower sum available to employees at retirement. Any reduction in the market value of investments set aside for future pensions would have to be absorbed by the corporation under a defined benefit plan since its obligation to provide a fixed pension at employee retirement would remain the same regardless of the return on investment.

[28] The maximum annual amount of pension guaranteed by the PBGC varies by the year the plan terminated and the retiree's age.

[29] See Zvi Bodie, "Pensions as Retirement Income Insurance," *Journal of Economic Literature* 28, no. 1 (March 1990), pp. 28–49. He calls it an insurance policy.

Chapter Thirteen

Educational Planning

Chapter Goals

This chapter will enable you to:

- Create an educational planning policy.
- Calculate the amount of educational savings needed annually.
- Establish the relevance of educational planning to overall needs.
- Select the proper educational structure for savings.
- Differentiate the educational investment policy from others.
- Identify the financial literacy problem and what can be done about it.

I could see Dan and Laura regarded educational planning as a headache. In their current situation, there were other obligations that had a higher priority. I knew that as part of the financial plan, I would have to figure out how much money it would cost them.

Real Life Planning

Hector was a city kid. He grew up on the affluent Upper East Side of New York. His parents emigrated from Mexico and his father was a superintendent in a high-rise luxury building. The family had an apartment provided at no charge so that Hector's father would always be on call for building emergencies.

Hector went to a public high school attended by students whose parents had much more money than his did. He developed many of the same aspirations but believed that his parents didn't have the means to fulfill them. Hector wanted to become a lawyer and thought his best path to it was a particular out-of-town private college. He felt uncomfortable around the other students who had little concern about being able to afford the college of their choice.

Hector did not know that his parents had been saving money for his college education since he was born. They had gone to a financial planner at that point for a one-time consultation. She told them that they would probably be eligible for substantial aid and therefore to keep any college savings in their name, not his. The planner told them how much of the total cost of a four-year education in a private college they would be able to pay for.

The planner indicated the amount they would have to save each year to make college enrollment happen. She told them in what structure to place the savings and discussed the investment policy that was appropriate given their tolerance for risk. Both the mother and father took part-time jobs to help finance the savings for Hector and his sister.

When the time came close, Hector was told that the money was available for him to go to virtually any college he wanted. His parents were familiar with the fact that many schools supply financial aid based on need and that in some cases the parental contribution may not be altered much even though the total cost of four-year college educations (before any aid allowances) can vary significantly. Hector would have to work while at college but would not be saddled with undergraduate school debt.

The money that Hector made working while living at home would be applied to law school. His parents pledged to help as much as they could for this advanced education. Hector's educational debt at the time he graduated from law school at the university he wanted to attend would be manageable. For the first time, Hector began to relax and relate better to the other students in the school.

OVERVIEW

Education can enhance a person's quality of life. Consequently, many people believe improving themselves educationally—particularly, through a higher education—is an extremely desirable goal. It is something we often drive ourselves and our children to achieve. Education has many benefits, but often none exceeds the opportunities it provides financially. From a PFP standpoint, it is a key to higher lifetime income. If you think of it in the terms discussed in the nonfinancial investments chapter, your education is a capital expenditure that yields a return on your human asset.

We can define **educational planning** as the programming of direct financial and time resources that enables household members to improve their capabilities, typically through enrolling at a college or university. Our outlays on education are generally made for household members. When they are for adult members, they produce higher household income and a high return on investment.[1] Such outlays made for children can be viewed as discretionary items or obligations to help ensure that they become well-rounded adults qualified for attractive careers.

Education can be a highly costly matter that for some will be exceeded only by their outlays for retirement and for the purchase of a home. It typically requires significant planning. We can estimate educational cost and savings needed to fund education well before the actual event. The process can perhaps best be reflected in what we can call an educational policy statement.

The **educational policy statement** is a financial plan that sets out the goals, costs, and best method for achieving the educational objectives desired. The process provided in Figure 13.1 establishes the steps including the final one, which shows you how to calculate your educational need. The process serves as an outline of the major portion of this chapter.

There are two other related areas that you will learn about in this chapter. The first is financial literacy. Many lack the ability to be knowledgeable in financial matters. In fact, it is a general problem in the United States. It is relevant for a PFP book because financial education often must be undertaken for a spouse, parent, or client.

The second area, to be discussed in Appendix II, concerns job change and job loss. If formal education provides a good background for career success, educational planning in how to select a new position, whether voluntarily as a career move or involuntarily, also can add to returns on your human assets.

EDUCATIONAL POLICY STATEMENT

The following process should be adhered to in developing an educational policy statement.

Establish Educational Goal

The overall goal of educational planning is to provide a quality education that enables the recipient to receive a high return on investment. Deciding on educational needs for adult

---

[1] Miguel Palacios Lleras, *Investing in Human Capital: A Capital Markets Approach to Student Funding* (Cambridge, UK: Cambridge University Press, 2004).

FIGURE 13.1
Educational Policy
Statement Process

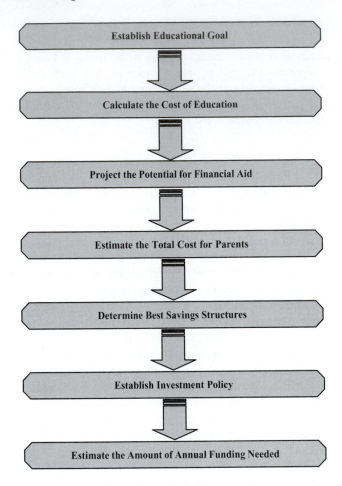

Establish Educational Goal

Calculate the Cost of Education

Project the Potential for Financial Aid

Estimate the Total Cost for Parents

Determine Best Savings Structures

Establish Investment Policy

Estimate the Amount of Annual Funding Needed

household members can be fairly simple. The cost of the education in hard dollars and opportunity cost of time is compared with the payoff in higher salary earned. A discussion and example on this topic were presented in Chapter 8. For the balance of the policy statement, we will assume that the educational planning is for a child. Planning for another household member is often similar but perhaps less elaborate.

Educational planning for children can be involved. There is generally no direct financial benefit for this outlay.[2] The selection of the type of schooling, whether the student will live at home or the new school, and whether the school will be a public or private university are functions of many variables. Among them are household resources, parental values, and the child's wishes and particular talents and needs.

Some parents cannot afford or do not feel the obligation to pay anything for their children's higher education. Others pay for undergraduate and graduate education in full. Many provide a partial payment with the student left with some debt after graduation.

Household goals and, as an outgrowth, funding obligations should be set out well before the actual event. From a PFP standpoint, the earlier the savings begin after birth, the easier it will be to achieve the goals established.

---

[2] Sometimes there is the thought that the child can provide some income, typically later in life—during retirement if needed. However, this practice is more prevalent in other cultures than it is in the United States.

Calculate the Cost of Education

The cost of a four-year education will vary depending on the type of school, region of the country, and whether the student lives at home or at school. It is also important to recognize that tuition and books are not the only costs. Other expenses include rent, food, entertainment, and transportation both at college and, if it is out of town, to and from home. The total cost for a student attending private school and living away from home could exceed $50,000 a year. The cost of attending a public university away from home would be considerably lower. And of course, living at home while attending a public university would cost even less.

In projecting college costs, a figure in excess of the overall inflation rate is generally called for. Over the period from 1990 to 2004, college inflation rose 5.7 percent a year, as compared to 2.9 percent for overall inflation. The increase in college costs may have some relationship to discretionary incomes, with increases in discretionary cash flow leading to a boost in demand for costly high-quality education. The statistics on college costs are shown in Table 13.1.

Project the Potential for Financial Aid

Aid, whether it be in the form of outright grants, work-study programs, or loans, can help accomplish the educational goals.

All government aid is applied for through Free Application for Federal Student Aid (FAFSA), which is offered by the U.S. Department of Education. Early application for those eligible for aid increases the chance of receiving aid.

TABLE 13.1

Average Annual Undergraduate Costs[1] for 4-Year College and Annual Increase of the Costs

Source: U.S. Department of Education, National Center for Education Statistics, http://nces.ed.gov/.

Academic Year	All Institutions		Public Institutions		Private Institutions	
	Total Cost	Increase	Total Cost	Increase	Total Cost	Increase
1977–78	$2,725	5.7%	$2,038	5.3%	$4,240	6.6%
1978–79	2,917	7.1	2,145	5.3	4,609	8.7
1979–80	3,167	8.6	2,327	8.5	5,013	8.7
1980–81	3,499	10.5	2,550	9.6	5,594	11.6
1981–82	3,951	12.9	2,871	12.6	6,330	13.2
1982–83	4,406	11.5	3,196	11.3	7,126	12.6
1983–84	4,747	7.7	3,433	7.4	7,759	8.9
1984–85	5,160	8.7	3,682	7.2	8,451	8.9
1985–86	5,504	6.7	3,859	4.8	9,228	9.2
1986–87	5,964	8.4	4,138	7.2	10,039	8.8
1987–88	6,272	5.2	4,403	6.4	10,659	6.2
1988–89	6,725	7.2	4,678	6.2	11,474	7.6
1989–90	7,212	7.2	4,975	6.3	12,284	7.1
1990–91	7,602	5.4	5,243	5.4	13,237	7.8
1991–92	8,238	8.4	5,693	8.6	14,258	7.7
1992–93	8,758	6.3	6,020	5.7	15,009	5.3
1993–94	9,296	6.2	6,365	5.7	15,904	6.0
1994–95	9,728	4.6	6,670	4.8	16,602	4.4
1995–96	10,330	6.2	7,014	5.2	17,612	6.1
1996–97	10,841	4.9	7,334	4.6	18,442	4.7
1997–98	11,277	4.0	7,673	4.6	19,070	3.4
1998–99	11,888	5.4	8,027	4.6	19,929	4.5
1999–2000	12,352	3.9	8,275	3.1	20,706	3.9
2000–01	12,922	4.6	8,653	4.6	21,856	5.6
2001–02	13,639	5.5	9,196	6.3	22,86	4.8
2002–03	14,504	6.3	9,828	6.9	23,940	4.6
2003–04	15,539	7.6	10,720	9.5	25,204	6.0
1977–1980	2,936	7.1	2,170	6.4	4,621	8.0
1980–1990	5,344	8.6	3,778	7.9	8,894	9.4
1990–2000	10,031	5.5	6,831	5.2	17,077	5.4
2000–2004	14,135	5.9	9,589	6.7	23,436	5.0

[1] Costs include tuition, fees, and room and board rates.

Practical Comment   Titling of Accounts

How a bank account is titled can have a significant effect on the amount of financial aid offered to a student. Placing money in a child's name in regular accounts or in Coverdell accounts will help reduce taxes but may not be advisable if financial aid is being sought.

Money saved in a child's name will reduce financial aid by up to 35 percent of the amount accumulated. The same amount of money placed in a parent's account will be subject to a maximum reduction of 5.6 percent. The 29.4 percent difference between the two can have a substantial impact on the aid package.

OTHER FINANCIAL AID STRATEGIES

Apportioning monies to certain asset and liability accounts can have an impact on financial aid. For example, paying off credit card debt with a home equity loan can reduce the amount of net real estate assets, which in turn can increase the amount of eligible aid. Saving more money in retirement accounts as opposed to regular accounts also can be helpful in increasing aid, although more colleges are including retirement assets in their assessment of parental assets whereas they were previously excluded.

Grants

Grants are outright monies given. They are based on need and the cost of the college you are enrolled at. Government aid includes Pell grants for undergraduates for a maximum of $4,050 for 2004–2005. These grants are currently being scaled back by the federal government. Federal Supplementary Education Opportunity Grants (FSEOGs) are for undergraduates with particularly low family income. Federal work-study programs for graduates or undergraduates provide jobs for income generally at either the college or a private nonprofit organization. In addition, colleges, states, corporations, or other institutions may provide aid.

Work-Study Programs

Student aid takes the form of an obligation to work a certain number of hours for the school during the year. The program may be set up by the federal government as part of a grant or by the college itself.

Loans

Often there are insufficient funds available to finance college costs. Amounts must be borrowed that will be repaid either by the parents or by the child who is attending college.

Stafford loans are the most popular form of borrowing established by the federal government. These loans are sometimes subsidized by the government. The interest rate on a Stafford loan is a maximum of 8.3 percent regardless of market rates and for 2004–2005 the rate charged was 3.4 percent. It is the student's responsibility to repay them loan. There are also parent Federal PLUS loans. That loan rate was 4.2 percent for 2004–2005. The liability to repay is the parents'. Federal Perkins loans are low-interest loans for graduate and undergraduate students who have exceptional need. Their borrowing rate is 5 percent.

Home equity loans may be used as well. In the absence of a major subsidization of interest cost, these loans generally have the lowest costs. Interest payments on student loans were tax-deductible up to $2,500 as of 2005. Full deduction is allowed when modified adjusted income is $100,000 for married couples filing jointly or $50,000 for single people.

Estimate the Total Cost for Parents

Once the full education cost is known and the amount of any financial aid package has been estimated, it is possible to estimate the parental cost. As mentioned, the cost will vary depending on how much or what fraction of it parents are willing and able to assume.

Determine Best Savings Structures

There are a variety of ways to save and invest for educational purposes. Some of them include special structures set up for college or private school purposes. We will consider these alternatives below.[3]

Coverdell Education Savings Accounts

Coverdells are special savings accounts set up with after-tax dollars for educational purposes. A maximum of $2,000 can be contributed for each child each year with annual income limitations of $95,000–$110,000 for individuals and $190,000–$220,000 for people filing jointly. Income earned while in the account is not subject to federal taxation and is tax-advantaged for many states as well when amounts are used for any educational expenses. The tax benefit in 2005 was phased out for annual incomes between $95,000 and $110,000 for individuals and between $190,000 and $220,000 for people filing jointly. Educational expenses can include room and board, transportation, and tutoring, as well as tuition, fees, textbooks, and many other items. Private school payments for the period before college are also eligible for Coverdells, but no contributions can be made after a person reaches age 18. The money must be spent by the time the family member reaches age 30 but can be rolled over to another family member who is less than 30 for educational purposes.[4]

Qualified Tuition Plans—Section 529 Plans

Qualified tuition plans, also known as Section 529 plans, are perhaps the most commonly used special savings plans for college. There are two types: prepaid plans and private savings plans.

Prepaid plans provide advance payment of monies to the state. If required minimums are met, the student may attend a state college at no further charge. These amounts also may be used at a private college within the state or at any out-of-state college. When used for out-of-state colleges, there is no guarantee that costs will be fully paid.

The second type, private savings plans, employ after-tax dollars as deposits. There is no further federal taxation, provided the funds are used for a broad variety of college expenses. The tax-free distribution program is in effect through 2010. Many states provide tax benefits for deposits and withdrawals from this account as well. There are no income qualifications for this program, which is run by the individual states. Many states allow cumulative deposits of $200,000 or more. Five years of gifts may be contributed at once without triggering gift tax consequences. That means that given the $11,000 yearly gift tax exclusion, as much as $55,000 per person or $110,000 per couple can be contributed in one year without gift tax consequences.

Monies for these programs are deposited with a state-designated investment advisory firm, which establishes the investment program. Some states have choices of conservative (all-bond), moderate (stock-bond), and aggressive (all-stock) formulations based on parental preferences and, in some cases, proximity to the date of entering college.

Funds in 529 plans must be used for qualified withdrawals; otherwise a 10 percent penalty will be incurred. Qualified withdrawals include tuition, fees, books, and supplies required by the college. Reasonable costs for room and board for students attending college at least half time are also qualified withdrawals.

Funds in the account can be used by the beneficiary to attend any postsecondary educational institution that can participate in the Department of Education's student aid program. This also can include foreign schools that can participate in the student aid program.

---

[3] Consideration will be given by some to the ethics of changes.

[4] An exception is made for people with special needs.

Practical Comment   Gifts from Grandparents

Those grandparents with material accumulated savings and conservative spending structures often have funds available for gifts for items they consider meritorious. Aside from significant needs of their offspring due to illness, financial setbacks, and perhaps a down payment on a home, few things are generally as motivating to many grandparents as a gift to contribute to educational savings.

If the family is eligible for financial aid, any proposed gift might be deferred until after the awarding of the aid package. If aid is not going to be forthcoming when the child is to enter school many years in the future, the grandparents may themselves contribute to a 529 plan or a Coverdell savings account. Make sure only one set of grandparents contributes $2,000 to the Coverdell for that year or in any other format chosen since that is the maximum yearly contribution. If a payment is made directly to the educational institution for a grandchild, there is an unlimited gift tax exclusion.

The 10 percent penalty does not apply if the withdrawal from the account is due to the death or disability of the designated beneficiary. Other exceptions to the penalty include withdrawals of excess funds due to receipt of a scholarship (up to the amount of the scholarship) and noncollege-expense withdrawals arising from attendance at a U.S. military academy. Monies taken out for noneducational purposes are considered nonqualified withdrawals and are subject to normal income taxes and the 10 percent penalty tax.

Contributions to 529 plans must be in cash. Funds from existing custodial accounts can be transferred into a 529 plan, but they retain the character of a custodial account. That is, the minor retains ownership of the account assets. Prior to the transfer, funds in the custodial accounts must be liquidated. Therefore, there may be income tax implications of transferring the money from these accounts.

Leftover funds can be rolled over to relatives for their use. Qualified rollovers include a father, mother, brother, sister, and a first cousin of the beneficiary. The 529 plan is treated as a parental asset for educational aid purposes.

Regular Investment Accounts

Regular investment accounts are those ordinary savings accounts with no special educational benefits. They have become more competitive with special educational accounts under the Jobs and Growth Tax Relief Reconciliation Act of 2003. That is because qualified dividends and capital gains on stocks and stock mutual funds are now taxed at a maximum of 15 percent on a federal basis. Monies placed in that state's municipal bonds or bond funds remain tax-free.

If assets are placed in the child's name, the first $800 annually is not taxed at all and the next $800 is taxed at the child's rate. If the child is 14 or over, the balance will be taxed at the child's low tax rate.

Regular investment accounts allow ultimate flexibility. You can place the money in any form of investment you wish and make withdrawals for any purpose without penalty.

Other

Regular IRAs and Roth IRAs may be used to fund educational programs. Amounts deposited grow tax-free and withdrawals for educational purposes from regular IRAs are not subject to the 10 percent early distribution tax. Roth IRAs are open to all people with income limitations of $95,000 and $150,000 for single people and married couples, respectively, and are phased out for those with incomes of $110,000 and $160,000, respectively. Withdrawals from Roth IRAs are tax-free provided they have been established for at least five years and are made for a qualified reason. Contributions except from conversion or earnings may be withdrawn at any time without tax or penalty.

Practical Comment Educational Planning and Debt

Two subjects not directly dealt with are actual educational planning and student educational debt.

ACTUAL EDUCATIONAL PLANNING

Our discussion on educational planning suggests that educational savings should start early to ease the parental burden of this large outlay. However, many people are unwilling or unable to set aside sums until college draws much closer. For some, college saving never occurs. Where financial aid does not cover the shortfall, the choices then include a lower-cost college education, perhaps including living at home, or a large debt burden on the parent or student.

In some cases, the cash requirement is covered by a home equity loan that modestly lowers spendable income and perhaps results in less money for heirs. The recognition of potential restrictions on future living standards can, when faced, result in more incentive for parents to save prior to the start of college. In any event, care should be taken to ensure that parental retirement planning is not jeopardized by this debt.

STUDENT EDUCATIONAL DEBT

As a result of a college education, many students are faced with a continuing debt burden. The pretax interest rate on that debt can be lower than on other obligations with tax deductibility for those eligible for it. This benefit can encourage postponing repayments beyond those required to comply with the borrowing term. However, given the sheer size of the debt for some, it is best to pay it off as soon as possible. Doing so will enable the person to qualify for a larger loan for such purposes as the purchase of a home. No payment at all can result in a growing amount of debt, and potential attachment of a portion of salary, which would not be eliminated by bankruptcy.

Roth IRA deposits are made with after-tax dollars, while regular IRAs can be made with pretax dollars subject to income limitations and nonavailability of a company pension plan.[5] Each form of IRA has significant flexibility as to which investment vehicle is to be used. Many financial planners recommend retaining IRA monies for retirement needs exclusively due to concern that there won't be enough accumulated to meet those needs.

The Uniform Gifts to Minors Act (UGMA) and Uniform Trust for Minors Act (UTMA) can be used to fund college monies. Each can take advantage of low child-tax rates, beginning at age 14.[6] UGMAs are restricted to financial assets as investment vehicles, while UTMAs can use real estate, limited partnerships, and other investment vehicles as well as financial assets. Control over UGMAs can be exercised by beneficiaries at ages 18 to 21 depending on the state, which means they are available at that time for noncollege use. The UTMA is a more costly document to set up but, in some states, allows restrictions on use to age 21 instead of UGMA's age of 18.

Establish Investment Policy

Investment policy, as we have learned, is based on two parameters: risk and return. The risk of a disappointing outcome grows as the period to college payment date draws nearer and nearer. At this point, the timetable to raise additional cash or to reverse a decline in securities prices is limited. A drop in the markets, of course, could lead to insufficient funding for impending payments.

Therefore, the allocation to bonds and money market assets should probably increase as the time to age 18 or another starting date draws closer. For aggressive investors, an allocation for education at a child's birth may be 100 percent stocks, while that same household a few years away from enrollment may have a material shift to bonds or money market accounts. At this point, then, the asset allocation in the educational account is likely to be very different than the one for, say, retirement planning, but both will incorporate the household's tolerance for risk.

[5] See Chapter 12, Appendix I, for a fuller explanation.
[6] See Chapter 14 for limited benefits for children under 14 as well.

TABLE 13.2 Summary of Educational Savings Alternatives

	Series EE	Coverdell Education Savings	IRA	529 Plans	Traditional Savings
Deposit					
Taxation	After-tax dollars	After-tax dollars	Pre- or after-tax dollars	After-tax dollars	After-tax dollars
Limitation	None	$2,000 yearly	$4,000 yearly	$55,000 single[1] $110,000 joint	Unlimited
Taxation of qualified withdrawals	None	None	None	None	None
Qualifying expenses	Tuition and fees	Related expenses[2]	Tuition and fees[3]	Most college-related expenses	N/A
Financial aid effect	Reduces aid	Reduces aid	Reduces aid	May reduce aid[4]	Reduces aid
Income eligibility[5]			Roth IRA		
Single	$61,200–$76,200	$95,000–$110,000	$95,000–$110,000	None	None
Joint	$91,850–$121,850	$190,000–$220,000	$150,000–$160,000		
Control	Parents	Parents[6]	Parents	Parents	Parents[7]
Penalty for unused money	0	10%	0	10%	0
Age limitation for use	None	30	None	None	None
Transferability	N/A	Yes	N/A	Yes	N/A
Investment flexibility	Limited to EE bonds	Financial assets principally	Financial assets principally	Little choice, supervised by state	Any assets
Advantages for educational savings	Easy and safe No taxation	No taxation Broad choice of investments	No taxation Broad choice of investments	No taxation Large savings allowed	Full flexibility
Disadvantage for educational savings	Little investment flexibility Income limitation	Small amount of deposit allowed Income limitation	Should be retained for retirement Small amount of deposit allowed	No control over investing Penalty for noneducational withdrawals	Some taxation

[1] Without triggering gift tax consequences.
[2] Primary and secondary school ones as well.
[3] For Roth IRA, any withdrawal.
[4] If the money in a 529 plan is in the child's name, it might have a substantial impact on financial aid.

[5] For 2005.
[6] Parents have partial control. Trustee or custodian administers the account for the benefit of the child.
[7] Depends on how account is titled.

Estimate the Amount of Annual Funding Needed

At this point, all the quantitative inputs that are required have been established. The approach to describe and compute educational needs is shown in Appendix I. It contains an actual problem and the specific solution to it. Its form is very similar to the one used for the retirement needs calculation that is given in Chapter 18, which provides a fuller presentation of needs analysis in general.

A summary of educational savings alternatives is provided in Table 13.2.

PLANNING FOR FINANCIAL LITERACY

Educational planning has a role that extends beyond setting aside money for a formal education. It has to do with **financial literacy,** which refers to the degree to which a person is educated in financial matters. In practical terms, it means being able to make financial decisions capably. Many finance and economics theories assume that people have perfect knowledge of financial issues. Obviously, this is not the case. For example, many people do not know what a bond is or how it operates.

This issue is relevant for readers of this textbook because they may be called upon to help educate a spouse, a parent, a child, or a friend. One of the duties of financial planners is to educate their clients. For example, the CFP Board® of Standards indicates that financial planners should hold frequent meetings with their clients to educate them about the financial planning process and their own financial situation. It also encourages that CFP registered programs discuss the clients' level of knowledge, experience, and expertise. Thus, giving clients proper recommendations is not a CFP practitioner's only responsibility. The planner should make sure the client understands the advice. The hope is that the client will then be more capable in that area when future decisions have to be made.

The absence of financial literacy has important financial consequences. For many households, the outcome is a lower accumulation of wealth and therefore a reduced standard of living. In some more extreme cases, it leads to financial ruin. From an economic standpoint, it results in a misallocation of resources that affects society's productivity and therefore adversely affects all households.

There are many reasons why individuals are not adept in financial matters. These include a lack of exposure to financial issues as a child, a belief that financial issues cannot be handled capably, poor mathematical skills, or a lack of interest in the subject. It also may include gender-related issues—a belief, which was prevalent among some in earlier generations, that money is a man's not a woman's responsibility. People may have highly developed verbal and written skills, even possess advanced degrees, yet be financially illiterate.

Clearly, fostering greater financial awareness could be beneficial to many households. Developing this awareness may be particularly important at the present time when people are being asked to make more of their own savings and investment decisions regarding retirement in 401(k) and other pension plans, when investment alternatives are growing in number, and when some people are calling for do-it-yourself Social Security investing.

TABLE 13.3   **Financial Planning for Literacy: Basic Principles**

Concept	Explanation
Simplicity	Financial issues are daunting to many people. At least initially, the topics should be simple to explain and understand.
Easy to relate to Practical examples	The items described should be easy to relate to and emphasize everyday situations. It is not enough to demonstrate how financial items relate to people's lives. Practical examples with worked-out solutions should be established to ensure an understanding and ability to implement them.
Use a process approach	A detailed step-by-step approach will help people understand why something is being done and provide a systematic approach. Under some circumstances, this approach will work even when the financial reasoning is not fully understood.
Accommodate different learning styles	People have different learning styles. Some learn best from lectures and discussions; others from reading; others from illustrations, numbers, and tables; and so forth. A combination of approaches often works well. Explanations using familiar experiences and emphasizing the right learning style for that person can be particularly effective.
Provide the benefits	Since financial issues can be difficult to understand, people need benefits for doing so. The more tangible and meaningful the benefits, the greater can be their motivation[1] and therefore the greater their success rate in obtaining the requisite knowledge.
Other principles	When an outside person is providing the knowledge, an interesting style, reassuring manner, and dialogue with solicitation of questions can be helpful. Using a game approach such as a stock market game also may be useful.[2]

[1] See John Conlisk, "Why Bounded Rationality?" *Journal of Economic Literature* 34, no. 2 (June 1996), pp. 669–700.
[2] See Lewis Mandell, "Financial Literacy, Financial Failure and the Failure of Financial Education," University at Buffalo, research paper (September 5, 2004), presented at the Academy of Financial Services Annual Meeting, New Orleans, October 2004; and Lewis Mandell, *Our Vulnerable Youth: The Financial Literacy of American 12th Graders* (Washington, DC: Jump$tart Coalition for Personal Financial Literacy, July 1998).

Planning for financial literacy can occur at any age and ranges from presenting simple financial tasks to children at home or in classroom settings to concentrated education when a surviving member assumes the household financial responsibilities previously handled by a now-deceased spouse.

Awareness can come from a number of sources, including radio, television, books, newspapers, magazines, newsletters, audio or video tapes and discs, friends, relatives, advisors, and so on. There are several basic principles that should be followed in financial planning for literacy. Some of them are identified in Table 13.3.

Financial literacy encompasses all parts of the financial planning process. Often the two major issues are establishing an appropriate savings pattern and investing effectively. Some of the important topics to be discussed in helping people become financially literate are presented in Table 13.4 by areas of the financial plan. It should not be

TABLE 13.4 **Financial Planning for Literacy: Important Topics**

Area	Topic
Goals	• How to establish goals. • How to use goals as a motivational tool.
Cash flow	• Establishing a formal or informal family budget. • Planning for future household outlays.
Saving	• Why saving is important for you. • How to control unneeded spending. • Establishing a saving pattern. • How much saving is enough? • How to deal with savings setbacks.
Debt	• The appropriate use of borrowed funds. • How to get out of debt. • What is the best source of credit?
Taxes	• Gaining a basic understanding of the tax code. • Developing knowledge of deductible items and planning to maximize them.
Investments	• Understanding risk and return. • Developing skepticism about seemingly high-return investments. • Understanding prominent investment vehicles such as bonds, stocks, and mutual funds. • Appreciating diversification and the benefits of long-term investing. • Understanding the advantage of index funds for low-maintenance supervision. • How to deal with impulsive investment behavior. • Explaining the most attractive way to purchase investment selections.
Risk management	• Obtaining proper insurance coverage personally and for possessions. • Developing healthy risk management practices. • Placing emphasis on potential losses that could be injurious to the household's financial future, regardless of their probability of occurrence.
Retirement planning	• Knowledge of 401(k) and other pension plans. • Awareness of the benefits of saving through a pension plan. • Knowing how much to save for retirement. • Starting retirement planning at an early age.
Estate planning	• Knowledge of the benefits of making out a will. • Planning for the family, particularly at an advanced age.
Educational planning	• Planning to send children to college.
Overall	• Taking control of your financial life. • Dealing with adversity. • Allocating money when there are alternative demands for it. • Engaging in long-term thinking. • Learning not to worry about financial matters. • Finding advisors. • Working successfully with advisors. • Communicating with other household members about financial issues.

Practical Comment Lack of Financial Literacy

Lack of financial literacy is a major problem for many households. As indicated, modern investment theory emphasizes ideal behavior, including making correct investment choices. In reality, many households fall far short of that behavior. It is not at all uncommon for households to suffer major losses or to see their assets completely eliminated through high fees and illogical schemes of unscrupulous promoters and "advisors." For such households, it is more accurate to say that the higher the risk, the lower the return. Moreover, the word *money* evokes a different response depending on one's knowledge. For an informed business major, it often connotes opportunity and a means to validate future success. For a great many Americans, it evokes a feeling of insecurity and even stress and pain if they feel inadequate to handle their own financial situations.

The answer for the poorly informed is, of course, greater knowledge. Many corporations have made some strides in reducing the difficulty for their workers and the mass media also have made efforts to educate the public. Yet the problem persists. In many cases, it is advantageous to start as early as possible in teaching financial facts and good habits.[7] Often people assimilate basic financial information easily when they are young. In addition to improving the way they handle financial matters, they can use the information developed to better understand business matters in college and in the workplace.

Organizations such as the National Endowment for Financial Education (NEFE), which is a non-profit foundation associated with the CFP Board, and JumpStart are involved with helping present financial information to high school students. The 2002 study by Lewis Mandell for JumpStart[8] showed a decline in financial literacy among high

school students and a high failure rate on basic knowledge. The lower the educational level and income of the parents, the worse students did. Achieving financial literacy is a worthwhile endeavor from the standpoint of the individual household as well as society in general.

A laissez-faire approach may not be as effective as one that provides financial education at a young age. Parents can help by giving their children an allowance and encouraging them to save part of it. Where feasible, modest amounts of money can be gifted to children for investment purposes with the provision that they think about and justify their proposed actions.

For more formal education, along with liberal arts subjects, math, and so on, a high school course in personal finance followed by a more advanced course in college would appear beneficial. Perhaps a requirement that all high school graduates not only be literate in reading and writing but also be financially literate is in the best interests not only of the individuals but society.[9]

Basic literacy need not involve a highly sophisticated approach to financial affairs. A good savings program and index funds for stocks and bonds can go a long way. For those who need or want a more advanced approach, financial planners and other advisors often can be helpful. Professionals can assist with financial literacy, reducing personal responsibility for individuals in making selections and loosely monitoring individuals' actions.

[7] In teaching a fifth-grade class about finance, the author used an annual report for Marvel Entertainment, a comic book publisher, as the example. The students showed genuine interest in the subject and the questions they asked suggested that the exercise was productive.

[8] Lewis Mandell, *Financial Literacy: A Growing Problem* (Washington, DC: Jump$tart Coalition for Personal Financial Literacy, 2002).

[9] According to the National Council on Economic Education (NCEE), as of April 2004, only four states mandate that a student complete a course covering personal finance before graduation from high school. To underline and elaborate on the discussion above, parents can help by giving children an allowance for which they are accountable, perhaps giving them cash for household duties or later on encouraging them to take a part-time job. When children become teenagers, they can be given a modest sum of money to invest in a stock or mutual fund that they themselves research and decide on. See Willard Stawski, *Kids, Parents and Money: Teaching Personal Finance from Piggy Bank to Prom* (New York: John Wiley & Sons, 2000).

surprising that many are the same as those presented in this book. The difference is often in the depth of presentation, which under many circumstances should be highly elementary to make it easy to follow—in some cases because the principal needs may be very basic.

Practical Comment   College Funding Discussion

It is often a good idea for parents to discuss with their child the role they will play in funding a college or graduate school education. Although the discussion can be uncomfortable for some, it can set out the guidelines and establish proper expectations.

This approach can affect important decisions on the child's part such as attitude about taking on debt, realistic preference about type of college, and part-time work to accumulate savings.

Back to Dan and Laura
EDUCATIONAL PLANNING

Dan and Laura came in to discuss educational planning needs. I could see they regarded the topic as a headache. In their current situation, there were other obligations that had a higher priority. I knew that as part of the financial plan, I would have to assess how much money it would cost them. But it was obvious to me that beginning funding for the obligation would have to be postponed.

I discussed with them the key parts of the educational plan that would have to be decided upon before being able to calculate the obligation.

Their overall goals, both short and long term, were clear. That their children go as far as they wanted educationally was one of them. They decided they would pay for the cost of undergraduate school in full for a public college or half of the total for a private college. The children would be able to go out of town to the private college of choice.

We estimated that the full cost of college would come to $40,000 for a private college or half that for a public university per year in today's dollars. Assuming scholarship based on need seemed out of the question given the sizeable incomes for both of them. Thus, the total cost of college Dan and Laura would pay would be $20,000 a year for each child in today's dollars. I quickly decided that Section 529 educational plans were the best vehicle to place educational savings into given their tax benefits.

We decided on an 80-20 stock-bond mix with stocks reduced by 20 percentage points each year beginning four years before the payout was scheduled to begin at age 18. The monies liquidated would be put in money market funds and short-term bonds. The average relevant rates were 5.7 percent before tax for investments (conservatively estimated) and 6 percent for educational cost increases.

Just as we were about to end the meeting, Laura interjected. She said she was uncomfortable with the fact that many of the money issues in connection with the plan were over her head. Her father had taught her male cousin he was close to all about financial matters. She was not expected to be concerned with them. She said she felt financially illiterate and wanted to know what she could do about it.

Educational planning is something for the entire family. However, we have already discussed Laura's graduate school costs under nonfinancial investments. Therefore, we will limit our discussion to children's educational costs.

Let me address educational planning first. Proper educational planning for your children is one of the highest priorities you have. We have already gone over many of the relevant factors. Let me discuss in what structure the money should be placed.

Holding money in a parent's name has certain advantages and disadvantages. It allows maximum flexibility so that if you change your mind about funding or want to borrow education funds for a time you can. In addition, keeping it in your name will ensure that it cannot be used for noneducational purposes by your children at 18 as could be done if you gifted monies to them.

For financial aid purposes, you are more likely to qualify for aid when the money is in the parent's name. Finally, the tax advantages for holding money in special education accounts have diminished now that tax rates on capital gains and dividends on common stocks have dropped.

On the other hand, placing monies in special education accounts has distinct tax and other benefits. In your circumstance, given your income tax bracket, 529 plans may be best. You can deposit up to $110,000 in after-tax dollars over a five-year period. The money will compound tax-free and not be subject to taxes, providing it is used for defined educational purposes. If you don't use all of the monies on education, it will be subject to income taxation and an extra 10 percent penalty on withdrawals. The lack of flexibility can be a plus since it will prevent you from withdrawing sums for less important purposes. Moreover, in your state, the deposits into the 529 account will allow specific state tax benefits.

These 529 accounts have little flexibility as to investment decisions. You must delegate investment responsibility to a state-designated investment firm with little choice on asset allocation. If you were to invest the money yourself, of course, you would have much greater freedom to decide on investments. Think about the options and we will speak further about them in the implementation stage of the plan.

I am recommending that you postpone educational funding for five years. At that point, you will be in a better position to make the required savings. I have calculated that at 6 percent inflation, the $20,000 payout today for each child will be approximately $54,000 for Brian and $60,000 for your unborn child. At the time of starting the savings, Brian will be six and your yet unborn will be four but will enter school at 18.

My calculations are shown in the attached schedule. Your goals for each offspring are similar. I have illustrated both. The cumulative figures for the second funding will be approximately the same with a greater period for accumulating the money. For Brian, you would need a lump sum today of about $89,000; for your new baby, the figure would be about $90,500. However, our projections indicate that you will not be able to start contributing to the college accounts until 2011, when Laura returns to work. At that time, you will need to save $12,990 per year for 12 years to fund Brian's education. For the new baby, we project that you will need to save $11,836 per year for 14 years.

The second subject is financial literacy. I want to congratulate you, Laura, on becoming interested in this area. It would have been much simpler to just let Dan handle it. Incidentally, you are not alone. The rate of financial literacy in our country is much lower than it should be and I suspect may be more prevalent among women.

The ways to become literate can start with reading the parts of the financial plan and asking me questions about it. As a financial planner, one of my functions is to educate my clients so that they understand as well as follow my recommendations. You may want to read a basic financial planning book and I will supply you with a name on request. Relevant television, radio, magazines, and newsletters can help as well. However, starting with the plan has a great advantage. You have considerable interest in the topic from the very beginning. Let me know how I can further help you.

Education Needs Analysis

Brian

Age	1
Years to college	17

Child 2

Age	0
Years to college	19

(continued)

(concluded)

General

Annual cost today	$20,000
General inflation	3.0%
College inflation	6.0%
Investment return	5.7%
Tax rate[1]	10.0%
After-tax investment return	5.1%
Years to college age, Brian	17
Years to college age, Child 2	19
Brian Costs Inflated	**$26,928**
Lump sum needed at beginning of period[2]	$208,326
Needed now	$89,000
Lump sum needed in year 6	$114,294
Annual payment needed beginning in year 6	$12,990
Child 2 Costs Inflated	**$30,256**
Lump sum needed at beginning of period	$234,075
Needed now	$90,479
Lump sum needed in year 6	$116,194
Annual payment needed beginning in year 6	$11,836
Total needed now	$179,479
Total needed in year 6	$230,488

[1] This is an estimated average tax rate based on the assumption that many but not all of the college funds would be invested in 529 accounts.

[2] This is a net present value calculation, which uses for its discount rate the after-tax return.

Summary

Educational planning involves investing in obtaining information that enhances the knowledge base of household members. It most often deals with placing money aside for a formal college education for children, but it can extend beyond it. For example, becoming financially literate is another facet of the area. The steps in an education plan include

Steps	Explanation
Establish goals	Decide on educational goals and the intended household funding role.
Calculate the cost of education	Determine tuition, books, living money, transportation, and so on, for each year of college.
Project the potential for financial aid	Establish whether aid is likely and for how much.
Estimate total cost for parents	Compute total education cost minus potential for financial aid.
Determine savings structure	Look at advantages and disadvantages of alternative savings structures and select one.
Establish investment policy	The asset allocation is likely to differ from that for other purposes due to differing times to payout. It also should vary because asset allocations should generally become more conservative the closer they are to the payout period.
Estimate amount of annual funding needed	The annual funding can be calculated once such factors as cost per year, length of payout period, current savings accumulated, and the current and projected payout dates are known.

Financial literacy

- Is a major problem in some households that leads to inefficient decision making and a lower standard of living.
- Can be rectified through a variety of methods ranging from attending lectures, watching media presentations, seeking the advice of more experienced people, and so forth.
- Is a financial planning function and planners should educate their clients so that they can make choices based on knowledge.

Key Terms

Coverdells, *355*

educational planning, *351*

educational policy
statement, *351*

financial literacy, *358*

grants, *354*

Web Sites

http://www.collegesavings.org
College Savings Plans Network

This site features, generally, Section 529 state college savings programs and provides a network intended to make higher education more attainable and to improve college savings plans. The site also contains useful links to other college savings–related Web sites, publications and articles, and general information for these plans divided into sections for parents, grandparents, and employers.

http://www.independent529plan.org
Independent 529 Plans

The site mainly deals with independent 529 college savings plans, emphasizing their advantages and latest news. It also has a small glossary with related terms.

http://www.teri.org
The Education Resource Institute

The institute's home page presents information about private education loan programs, the financial aid process and resources, and research studies related to college planning and financing.

www.jumpstartcoalition.org
Jump$tart Coalition for Personal Financial Literacy

This site features comprehensive education programs teaching children pre-K–12 life skills and money management techniques. It includes a section with informative surveys about the financial literacy of the American youth population.

http://www.students.gov
Student Resource

This comprehensive information portal provides answers to questions on education, career, and government-related issues. A collection of links to a variety of government resources geared toward students is presented.

www.savingforcollege.com
Savingforcollege.com LLC

This site offers information about 529 plans, Coverdells, and other ways to save and plan for college.

http://www.ed.gov
U.S. Department of Education

This home page includes thorough information on federal student aid, grants, education statistics, policy, and regulations.

www.federalreserveeducation.org
Federal Reserve Education

This site has a section with a number of links on personal financial education. Among them are consumer banking, interest rates, loans and credit, home and mortgages, and general information on financial literacy. The site also includes links to non-Fed Web sites.

http://www.salliemae.com
Sallie Mae
This is the home page of Sallie Mae, the leading provider of educational funding. It provides information about higher education including planning for college, financial resources available, managing loans, and finding a job.

http://www.finaid.org
Student Guide to Financial Aid
A general guide to student scholarships, education loans, savings plans, and other types of financial aid. It also includes a section on calculator tools for calculating college costs, loan payments, savings, and the expected family contribution (EFC).

www.collegeboard.com
College Board
The home page of College Board, the SAT test provider, offers college search, college application tips, and college funding information. It has separate sections for students, parents, and educators.

http://www.asec.org
American Savings Education Council
This site features savings tools and resources such as worksheets, calculators, and savings brochures intended to improve the financial literacy among the American people. It also provides links to educational programs and research and statistics in the savings area.

http://www.irs.gov/publications/p970/index.html
Internal Revenue Service (IRS)
This link is also on the IRS Web site. It offers a publication on tax benefits for education.

http://www.nefe.org
National Endowment for Financial Education (NEFE)
The Web site offers an online high school program in financial planning which has great interactive tools designed for students. It also provides valuable personal finance information and resources for the general public under the multimedia access section. There is also available NEFE's newsletter featuring interesting personal finance articles.

Questions

1. Why is education planning important?
2. Why are educational costs expected to continue to rise at a rate in excess of inflation?
3. What is an educational policy statement?
4. Why are overall goals relevant in educational planning?
5. Do you believe parents should discuss with a teenager the role the parents are willing to take in funding education?
6. What factors should go into determining the cost of attending college?
7. What is financial aid based on?
8. Does it matter who saves money for college: parents or child? Explain.
9. Discuss the advantages and disadvantages of three educational savings structures.
10. What are the common sources of loans to finance education?
11. Compare the features of a Coverdell savings account with a Section 529 plan.
12. Why are Section 529 plans attractive and what are their weaknesses?

13. A person should have one pool of money for all savings needs. True or false? Explain.

14. Why should a person select a regular investment account over a tax-advantaged educational savings account?

15. Explain why the asset allocation for saving for education differs from that for retirement.

16. Explain why the asset allocation for education funding can change as the payout date draws nearer.

17. Why are there many people who are not financially literate?

18. What are the consequences of lack of financial literacy?

19. List some of the key features connected with educating for financial literacy.

Problems

13.1 Sam and Sue wanted to provide full funding for their son, age 4, to go to college at age 18. The cost to them was $35,000 per year. Calculate the amount of savings they would need per year to fund college, assuming that the education inflation rate was 3 percent and the investment return was 5 percent after tax. (See Appendix I).

13.2 Jason, age 14, was given a choice of $150,000 to be deposited in his account today or his parents would fund 50 percent of college costs, expected to amount to exactly $30,000 a year (and for four years) in future dollars. Which should he take given a 6 percent after-tax investment return in both cases and four years until he starts college? Show your calculations.

13.3 Warner and Aileen asked you to calculate how much money it would take to save annually for their son's college education. The cost of college today was $30,000 and their son would enter in eight years. The inflation rate for college was 5 percent and investment returns were 7 percent after tax. (See Appendix I).

CFP® Certification Examination Questions and Problems

13.1 Mr. and Mrs. Smith come to you for advice on the financing of their son's college education at their state university. Even though their annual family income exceeds $70,000, they have *not* saved enough for his college expenses. You advise that their best opportunity to acquire education funds would be through

    a. Pell Grants.

    b. Subsidized Stafford student loans.

    c. Supplemental education opportunity grants.

    d. Parent loans for undergraduate students (PLUS).

13.2 John Hendrick wants to pay one-half of the college costs for his daughter, Ruth. She will be attending a private college with annual costs of $20,000 today. Ruth is 10 years old and will be starting college in eight years. If these costs are expected to increase annually by 8 percent, how much will Mr. Hendrick need to provide for her first year of college?

    a. $18,509

    b $23,409

    c. $27,371

    d. $37,019

    e. $74,037

Case Application
EDUCATIONAL PLANNING

Brad and Barbara asked to come in. There were two items on the agenda. The first was a disagreement between the two concerning educational planning. Brad believed that education was a cost that could be financed from current savings when the kids entered college. Barbara said they should begin right now even though no children were planned for at least three years.

The second subject had to do with Brad's mother Monica. They thought that Brad's father's behavior in financial considerations was a little risky and that his mother was at a disadvantage because she knew little about finance matters. What would I recommend in terms of a "crash course" in becoming more knowledgeable financially? She had approved their asking me for my help.

Case Application Questions

1. What information would you need to answer the Brad and Barbara dispute?
2. Who is likely to be right? Why?
3. What would happen if proper funding were not to take place?
4. Provide an estimated yearly college savings needed assuming that the two wanted to fund for a four-year private school education. Assume a 3 percent college inflation and a 5 percent investment return with annual savings beginning currently and their child being born in three years with college starting at age 18.
5. What recommendations do you have to make Monica more financially literate?

Appendix I

Educational Needs Calculation

This appendix provides a description of how to calculate educational needs in Table 13.A1.1, followed by a problem and actual calculation in Table 13.A1.2. A greater description of needs analysis is given in Chapter 18.

Example 13.A1.1 Steven and Dawn wanted to know how much it would cost to send their daughter Linda to a private college. They have saved $20,000 to date. Linda is six years old and will be enrolling in a four-year college at age 18. Assume that the college inflation rate is 5 percent, investment returns are 6 percent after tax, and total college costs are $50,000 a year in today's dollars. Calculate the amount they would have to save each year to have full college costs funded by the beginning of college.

As the educational needs calculation in Table 13.A1.2 shows, Steve and Dawn would need to save $18,606 yearly to fund future college costs for their daughter.

Table 13.A1.1 Educational Needs Calculation—Described

Step	Item	Symbol	Explanation or Calculation
1	Investment rate	IR	The average rate of return for investment
1	Education inflation rate	ER	The rate of increase in expenses
1	Real rate	RR	The combination of the inflation and investment rates
			Formula: $RR = \left(\dfrac{1 + IR}{1 + ER} - 1 \right) \times 100$
1	Present time	t_0	Today
1	Future time	t_1	Beginning of payout period
1	Number of years for payout period	N_{t_p}	From beginning to end of payout period
1	Number of years to beginning of period	N_{t_1}	From today to start of payout period
1	Number of years to today	N_{t_0}	From beginning of payout period to today
2	Cash outflows	CO_{t_0}	Total college or other educational-related outlays for the year in current dollars
3	Cash outflows future	CO_{t_1}	Current yearly outflows brought forward to beginning of payout period. The educational inflation rate is used to calculate the estimated future cost of the present cash outflow.

Calculator Solution

Inputs:

N_{t_1}		ER	CO_{t_0}			
N		I/Y	PV		PMT	FV

Solution: Press for CO_{t_1}

3	Lump-sum outflow future	LS_{t_1}	Amount of full payout period yearly outflow discounted back to beginning of payout period. Since there is a series of payments occurring over a period of time, both investment and inflation rates are employed by using the real rate. Use BEGIN function for beginning of the year payments.

Calculator Solution

Inputs:

N_{t_p}		RR		CO_{t_1}	
N		I/Y	PV	PMT	FV

Solution: Press for LS_{t_1}

4	Assets accumulated today	AA_{t_0}	Assets available today to help fund educational need
4	Assets accumulated future	AA_{t_1}	Assets accumulated today brought forward to beginning of payout period. The investment rate is used to calculate the estimated future value of today's sum.

Calculator Solution

Inputs:

N_{t_1}		IR	AA_{t_0}			
N		I/Y	PV		PMT	FV

Solution: Press for AA_{t_1}

5	Additional assets required future	AR_{t_1}	Lump-sum outflow less estimated future assets accumulated $AR_{t_1} = LS_{t_1} - AA_{t_1}$
5	Required yearly savings	$RS_{t_0 \rightarrow t_1}$	The yearly saving required to produce the additional sum needed at the beginning of the payout period. The investment rate is used because investment return influences the amount required for the series of savings deposits.

Calculator Solution

Inputs:

N_{t_0}		IR				AR_{t_1}
N		I/Y	PV		PMT	FV

Solution: Press for $RS_{t_0 \rightarrow t_1}$

Table 13.A1.2   Educational Needs Calculation—Performed

Step	Item	Symbol	Explanation or Calculation
1	Investment rate	IR	6% given
1	Inflation rate	ER	5% given
1	Real rate	RR	$RR = \left(\dfrac{1 + 0.06}{1 + 0.05}\right) \times 100$ $= .9524$
1	Number of years for payout period	N_{t_p}	Age 18 to age 22 = 4
1	Number of years to beginning of period	N_{t_1}	Age 6 to age 18 = 12
1	Number of years to today	N_{t_0}	Age 18 to age 6 = 12
2	Cash outflows	CO_{t_0}	$50,000 given
3	Cash outflows future	CO_{t_1}	*Inputs:*

Step 3 — Cash outflows future:

12	5	50000		
N	I/Y	PV	PMT	FV

Solution: Press **$89,793** (FV)

Step 3 — Lump-sum outflow future (Use BEGIN function) — LS_{t_1} — *Inputs:*

4	0.9524		89793	
N	I/Y	PV	PMT	FV

Solution: Press **$354,121** (PV)

4	Assets accumulated today	AA_{t_0}	$20,000 given
4	Assets accumulated future	AA_{t_1}	*Inputs:*

12	6	20000		
N	I/Y	PV	PMT	FV

Solution: Press **$40,244** (FV)

5	Additional assets required future	AR_{t_1}	$AR_{t_1} = 354{,}121 - 40{,}244 = \$313{,}877$
5	Required yearly savings	$RS_{t_{0 \to 1}}$	*Inputs:*

12	6			313877
N	I/Y	PV	PMT	FV

Solution: Press **$18,606** (PMT)

Appendix II

Career Planning—Job Change and Job Loss

Your career is generally your most valuable household asset. Your education, interest, and efforts all help to make your work time more lucrative. They help produce attractive job raises and promotions. In your work life cycle, there are two events that may influence your normal internal work progression: voluntary consideration of a shift in jobs and involuntary shifts due to job loss. Proper education and planning can assist you in making the change more rewarding.

JOB CHANGE

People often consider a change in jobs because they find that their growth potential with their existing employer is limited or because there is a more attractive opportunity elsewhere. The number of job shifts has likely grown over the past 50 years, and the government has recognized this fact by making retirement plans such as 401(k)s portable through transfer to new employers and rollovers to IRAs.

When contemplating a job change, you should consider a number of financial variables.

Salary

The new salary is perhaps the lowest-risk portion of the new compensation package. As a motivating factor by itself, the salary may have to be 10 to 20 percent higher to attract people to leave.

Incentive Compensation

Incentive compensation is the reward for good performance. The bonus may be based on company, division, or departmental criteria. It often has a substantial component based on individual contribution. By industry or company custom, it can range from 5 to 15 percent to as much as 50 to 100 percent or even more of salary.

Stock Participation

Stock participation has been a growing feature of total compensation. Stock options, which are discussed in Chapter A on the Web site, have been perhaps the most popular form of stock compensation, although there are some recent signs that interest in using them may be declining. Shares also have been awarded to executives and loans made to assist key executives in purchasing shares.[10]

Pensions

Companies differ in the plans offered such as defined benefit pensions with fixed payouts or defined contribution plans such as profit-sharing and 401(k) plans. They also differ in the amount of money contributed.

Deferred Compensation

Deferred compensation is generally a way to postpone payout of funds and therefore taxation. In the interim, the money can grow tax-free.

Insurance

Because of its reduction in exposures, insurance can be an attractive part of a compensation package. For key executives, split-dollar life insurance can provide company assistance in funding life insurance with an outcome that accrues significant benefits to the family. Health insurance policies for individuals, their families, and coverage during retirement can be important considerations in a job change. A strong long-term disability policy, perhaps including an own occupation definition, also can be a motivating factor.[11]

Fringe Benefits

Aside from the benefits already mentioned, vacation policy, cafeteria plans, cars, internal dining and health facilities, tuition, and scholarships are other benefits that can enter into decision making.

Other Considerations

There are some less tangible considerations that influence decisions on whether to make a job change:

- *Fundamental outlook.* The outlook for the company itself will help determine the raises, bonuses, value of stock options, and opportunity for advancement.

---

[10] Recent criticism of stock options as an efficient compensation tool may alter their usage in the future.

[11] See Chapter 11 for a discussion.

Practical Comment   Changing Jobs

Where there is no clear-cut advantage in changing jobs, a decision to make a job move is often subjective. Salary is often given a strong weighting. In the last analysis, the appraisal of the entire package, including the atmosphere of the new company, can be the determining factor. Many Americans in skilled positions, particularly professionals and executives, in effect, blend work with leisure. For example, some people remain at their jobs even when they have sufficient monies to retire comfortably. And in some positions, people stay well beyond normal work hours for reasons other than possible advancement. Yet in some countries, a job is regarded purely as work and people might question employees who work after hours, wondering whether they lack the capability to finish their tasks within the normal workday.

- *Company style.* The entire company atmosphere, including regard for employees, is often a key factor in considering job offers. Analysis may be made as to how paternalistic the company is and the turnover rate of employees.
- *Diversification.* Portfolio assets for company employees, particularly for executives, are often highly concentrated in stock of the company in which they work. From the standpoint of risk management, this is a distinct weakness. A shift to a new company can have positive effects on diversification, particularly when the former employer's stock is being retained.

JOB LOSS

Job loss can be an unexpected firing or a drawn-out affair in which both parties negotiate a severance package with at least the semblance of a mutually beneficial outcome. People lose their jobs for many reasons, ranging from cyclical economic difficulties or long-term industry problems to personality conflicts and being in ill-suited positions. When the layoffs recur, it may be a sign to change types of positions or industries. For example, anyone involved with the printing industry is aware that technology has allowed more printing tasks to be performed in-house and Internet communication may add to industry concerns. For people working in industries with unfavorable outlooks, it may be time to consider whether it is in their best interest to shift to a new area.

Most corporations want to present a favorable image to the public and their workers. Moreover, many recognize their responsibilities to their workers who may have done nothing to merit termination. The result is that often a severance policy and negotiations are put into place. The higher the position and the longer the period of employment with the company, the more likely the negotiations. When available the severance package may include a number of items.

- *Salary.* The longer the period with the company, the greater the amount of cash provided. Some companies use two weeks for each year served.
- *Time on the payroll.* Some companies allow people to remain on the payroll for an extended period. The advantage is that the company continues the fringe benefit package, which can include contributions to the 401(k) plan. It also can provide a "cover" to allow a person to seek new employment without mentioning termination. In contrast, an immediate severance package can place a lump sum of capital for investment in hand, but it also can place a worker in a higher tax bracket.
- *Stock options.* Severed workers often have to exercise stock options within a short period after termination. A request for an extension of exercise time can be beneficial, particularly when the shares are depressed.

Practical Comment   Unemployment and Its Effects

A period of unemployment can be highly stressful. Often people who are career-oriented temporarily question their capabilities and feel ill at ease among those who are working. Former colleagues sometimes feel uncomfortable as well, as if the unemployed had a disease that might rub off on them. On the other hand, many attempt to help and are often successful in providing good leads.

It is important that unemployed workers feel positive about themselves since their self-confidence will help in finding a new position. Being active in the job search often helps confidence. While it is sometimes unavoidable, cutting back on leisure time outlays can have the opposite effect. Thus, there needs to be a careful balance between maintaining self-esteem and placing a household in financial difficulty. When there is not a substantial emergency fund, it can be helpful to negotiate a home equity loan prior to a possible layoff. The cash available in a bank account also can be reassuring. If debt is a problem, often the companies providing credit will be amenable to a temporary suspension of payments.

Finally, significant investment decisions such as changes in asset allocation should be thought over carefully and perhaps postponed until a new job is acquired. People's thinking during this period can become unduly pessimistic, which can translate into aversion to taking risk. While it is appropriate to incorporate job-related risk into household decisions, this human-asset risk is often short term and changes in investments can have significant consequences such as generating a current income tax payment from sale of investments at a profit.

- *Health benefits.* COBRA specifies that if your employer has 20 or more workers, you must be offered continuation of health services for 18 months. The worker must pay. Although the requirement may offer you peace of mind, the cost, which often is considerably higher than with the former group policy, can warrant looking for a new policy. The search is particularly useful when unemployment may be for more than a few months.

- *Unemployment benefits.* Each state oversees a federal program providing unemployment benefits for a period of six months or, in some cases, longer—for example, 52 weeks in Minnesota. This taxable money can be advantageous during this time and is a factor arguing against being kept on the payroll after the decision for ultimate termination has been made.

- *Other services.* Companies can provide offices, telephone-answering, and outplacement services.

Early Retirement

Companies find that early retirement can offer a graceful way out of an overstaffed situation. Offering early retirement can be a truly optimal or alternatively face-saving way of getting a less productive worker to leave. From the worker's standpoint, the incentive can be additional work years that count toward eligibility for a retirement pension. For example, a person age 59 with a long history with a company may be given three years of pension time in order to qualify for a full pension at age 62. Clearly, this can be a benefit worth negotiating for.

The severance strategy can include

- *Accumulating negotiating points.* Think of points that can improve your negotiating position. These may include specific contributions made, your present financial circumstances, the potential for instituting a lawsuit, and citation of more attractive packages given to others.

- *Maintaining a relationship.* As mentioned, severance often has relatively little to do with the individual. If you maintain a good relationship with the company, you could be rehired or given consulting work, or at least a good recommendation.
- *Consulting a lawyer.* When a severance package is offered in writing, you should consult a lawyer before signing it.
- *Announcing your availability.* Contacts through friends and acquaintances are often the best way to find a new job. It stands to reason that you should announce your availability and the kind of position you are looking for. Often, the earlier this is done, the better it is.

Part Five

Tax and Estate Planning

Tax planning and estate planning are two essential elements of a financial plan. They share a heavy orientation toward minimizing taxes and present a legal basis for much of the analysis. For financial planning majors, perhaps because of the detailed nature of the material presented, part or all of one or both of these topics is sometimes postponed to advanced courses.

Taxes, the subject of Chapter 14, enter into most parts of a financial plan. It is easy to grasp the importance of this topic. A dollar saved in taxes is another dollar of cash flow generated for household use. We will go over income tax planning strategies to schedule and reduce the tax burden.

Estate planning has a tax-planning element as well but extends beyond that to the welfare of others. Chapter 15 presents the major estate planning tools and strategies that can be used to take advantage of them. Appendixes in both chapters present the theories that underlie their disciplines.

Chapter Fourteen

Tax Planning

Chapter Goals

This chapter will enable you to:

- Discuss the widespread role of taxation in PFP.
- Develop a knowledge of key tax-planning strategies.
- Compare the tax benefits of major investment vehicles.
- Understand and complete a tax return.

Dan had decided to do his own tax returns. Dan and Laura's current return was being done by Laura's father. As Dan viewed it, "We are grown up and can take care of our own activities." It turned out that, like some of my other clients, he had become almost obsessed with the idea of finding another tax deduction. Laura said she didn't expect to see him from April 1 to April 15 when the tax return was to be mailed.

Real Life Planning

The elderly woman who came in had an air of elegance and entitlement. She was well dressed, lived in the expensive part of town, and spoke as if she had been sent to finishing school. She wasn't very friendly and wanted the advisor to restrict the analysis to tax matters only. In fact, the only time she showed any change from her smooth manner was when she said the word *taxes*. It was uttered with complete disgust.

The advisor explained that he didn't do tax returns but would be happy to see if there were ways to reduce her outlays through proper tax planning. They agreed on an hourly fee and the work began. The advisor attempted to put together some background information. She mentioned that her husband had taken care of financial matters but recently had died. The advisor looked at her current tax return and noticed that she had paid substantial taxes on the distribution of her husband's IRA monies.

The woman was very cost-conscious and had chosen not to hire any professional help. It was clear that a simple election to transfer (roll over) the funds to her would have increased her wealth. One of the most basic tax-planning techniques was to defer taxes as long as possible. The advisor thought about mentioning the words that Marlon Brando spoke in the movie *Godfather I*, "If you would have come to me before, I could have helped you," but decided there was no sense in upsetting her over something that could no longer be changed.

He developed her current and projected income and deductible expenses and exemptions. It became clear that she was in the very lowest tax bracket. There were few tax-planning strategies open to her. He told her that her donations of clothing to charity were deductible. He mentioned to her that he would not be recommending tax-free municipal bonds. Based on her tax bracket, taxable bonds provided a higher after-tax return. She quickly interrupted, saying, "Young man (the advisor was in his 50s), I want to pay the lowest tax I can." He elaborated simply on the calculation that showed that municipal bonds would provide her with less money to spend. She again responded angrily, saying, "You don't understand. I don't want to give the government one cent more than I have to." She signed a letter indicating that she knew taxable bonds were better for her but that she wanted tax-free bonds. The driving force for her was the goal that fewer of her dollars go to the government. The advisor gave her some recommendations on municipal bond funds and she thanked him for being sensitive to her needs.

The advisor thought to himself that the woman's feelings, while extreme in execution, were fairly common. To many, a dollar saved in tax matters is somehow worth more than one saved in, say, shopping more carefully. It was true despite the fact that more time may be expended on generating tax deductions than on careful shopping. The reasons varied. For some it was the belief that they were paying more than their fair share of the tax burden. For others it was the challenge of reducing their taxes to the minimum possible.

OVERVIEW

Taxes are another expense for our household enterprise. However, for many of us, tax takes on greater significance. It is often a large outlay, and we receive no pleasure in paying it. Often our objective is to minimize the payment and we employ planning techniques to help us do so.

There are many types of taxes. Some are income-based, like federal income taxes; some are consumption-based, like the sales tax; others are event- and asset-based, like the estate tax, which is triggered by the death of the estate owner. In this chapter, we will concentrate on income taxation and leave the discussion of estate taxes to Chapter 15 on estate planning. We will begin with some background information on taxes and the tax return. The tax return can be viewed as a type of income statement with qualifying expenses reducing the income for tax purposes. Following that, tax-planning strategies are presented using both stand-alone techniques and tax-advantaged investment vehicles. Tax theory is provided in Appendix I. Finally, a case study for completing an income tax return is provided in Appendix II along with step-by-step illustrations of the return. It should help anyone who needs to fill out a tax return.

INCOME TAXATION

Income taxes are a nondiscretionary cost in household operations, with the outlay dependent on both revenues and expenses. Decision making in most household activities is influenced by taxes. A brief example of the tax impact in each area of a financial plan is given below.

Category	Explanation
Cash flow planning	Taxes influence the timing of transactions and preparation for payment of sums due.
Investments	The calculation of returns is often done on an after-tax basis.
Financing	The calculation of the cost of borrowing is done on an after-tax basis.
Risk management	There is often a clear preference for tax-deductible employee health and life insurance.
Retirement planning	There is a substantial benefit when saving through qualified retirement-pension vehicles.
Estate planning	Tax minimization comprises a large part of estate planning activities.

TABLE 14.1
Principal Components of Tax Return[1]

Section	Explanation
Income	Sources of returns
Wages	
Dividends	
Capital gains	
Other income	
Adjustments	Special deductions from revenues
401(k), IRA contributions	
Student loan interest	
Deposits to other qualified plans	
Adjusted gross income	Adjusted revenues
Deductions	Allowable reductions based primarily on operating costs
Standard or itemized deduction	
Exemptions	Allowable reductions based primarily on number of household members
Taxable income	Income subject to tax
Tax	The gross amount to be paid
Credits	Dollar-for-dollar reductions in gross tax
Other taxes	Dollar-for-dollar additions to amount due
Total tax due	The amount to be paid
Total payments made	
Amount owed	

[1] Schedule A will be discussed in Appendix II.

INCOME TAX FORMAT

Income taxation is generally based on transactions typically involving cash inflows and outflows. Income earners are taxed on an individual basis except for married couples, whose income is generally combined for income tax purposes. The income tax return resembles a household cash flow statement in form. All cash receipts are recorded, adjustments are made for certain expenses, and the net is the adjusted income figure called **adjusted gross income (AGI).**

Deductions follow based on fairness,[1] popularity, and society's goals, and exemptions are allowed based on the number of people in the household and other factors. The result is the amount available to be taxed, called **taxable income.** The tax rate is established based on progressive rates, and the total tax calculated, less any credits, is due. The amount due for the year less payments already made is the sum to be enclosed with the return.

We summarize the individual income tax return, IRS Form 1040, in Table 14.1.

A summary breakdown of the components of the tax return is given in Example 14.1. A more detailed breakdown of the components including tax-deductible items is given in Appendix II. An extensive tax-planning statement is provided in the Dan and Laura case study.

Example 14.1

Beverly had taxable revenues of $60,000 last year and expects $68,000 in the current year. Her adjustments to revenues were $2,000 last year and are projected to be $3,000 this year. Her deductions and exemptions last year were $18,000; this year they are projected at $23,000.

[1] For example, someone would say it is fairer to recognize as deductions large casualty losses—which can be looked at as losses of important assets—after having taxed the income that led to these assets.

There is no state income tax where Beverly resides. Compute her federal tax under an assumed 20 percent average tax bracket for both years.

Abbreviated Tax Planning Worksheet

	Last Year	This Year
Revenues	$60,000	$68,000
Adjustments	2,000	3,000
Adjusted gross income	58,000	65,000
Deductions and exemptions	18,000	23,000
Taxable income	$40,000	$42,000
Tax	**$8,000**	**$8,400**

TAX PLANNING: A GENERAL ANALYSIS

Tax planning is the analysis and implementation of strategies to reduce tax expenditures. It also involves the scheduling of tax payments and the programming of tax-related cash outlays. Your overall goal is generally to minimize taxes, provided that doing so is consistent with efficient household operations. If you were sick and postponed going to the doctor for three months until the new year so that you qualified for a tax deduction, you would not necessarily be operating efficiently. Another way to define your goal for tax-planning purposes would be to maximize your after-tax returns on investments including your investment in human assets.

A tax-planning statement provides a projection of future tax expenses by year. Often the most recent year's actual tax return figures are used as a basis for them. Such a tax-planning worksheet is shown in Table 14.2.

Marginal Analysis

In making tax-planning decisions, you often must weigh the benefits of alternative approaches. For example, which should you purchase: a higher-yielding taxable bond or a lower-yielding municipal bond? The answer often depends on your marginal tax bracket. The **marginal tax bracket** is the sum you pay on the next dollar that you earn. It is expressed as

$$\text{Marginal tax bracket} = \frac{\text{Tax on next dollar earned}}{\text{Next dollar earned}}$$

It is to be distinguished from the **average tax bracket,** which is total tax dollars expended as compared with total earnings.

$$\text{Average tax bracket} = \frac{\text{Total income tax outlays}}{\text{Taxable income}}$$

Example 14.2

Edward and Mary had $90,000 of combined adjusted gross income. They had paid $30,000 in federal, state, and local taxes and $40 on the last $100 of income. What are their marginal and average tax brackets?

$$\text{Marginal tax bracket} = \frac{\$40}{\$100}$$

$$= 40\%$$

$$\text{Average tax bracket} = \frac{\$30,000}{\$90,000}$$

$$= 33\%$$

TABLE 14.2
Tax Planning Statement

	2006	2007	2008	2009	2010
Income					
Wages					
Dividends and interest					
Capital gains					
Other income					
Total income					
401(k), IRA contributions					
Student loan interest					
Deposits to qualified plans					
Total					
Adjusted gross income					
Personal exemptions					
Standard deduction					
Deductible medical and dental expenses					
Deductible taxes					
Deductible interest					
Deductible gifts to charity					
Allowable miscellaneous expenses					
Total itemized deductions					
Total deductions					
Total taxable income					
Tax					
Total credits					
Total other taxes					
Total federal tax					
Total state tax					
Total federal and state tax					
Social Security (FICA)					
Medicare tax					
Total tax					
Average tax rate					
Marginal tax rate					

We often use the marginal, not the average, tax bracket because many decisions need to be made based on the next dollar earned, not the average dollar.[2]

Example 14.3

Esther found an additional tax deduction of $6,000. She was in the 33 percent average tax bracket and the 40 percent marginal one. If she stays in the same tax brackets, how much will her tax bill be lowered?

$$\text{Lower tax} = (\text{Amount of deduction}) \times (\text{Marginal tax bracket})$$
$$= \$6{,}000 \times 40\%$$
$$= \$2{,}400$$

The correct figure is $2,400. If she used the average tax bracket, she would have misestimated her benefit as $2,000 from the new deduction.

To obtain a total marginal tax bracket, you add your federal state and local taxes and subtract the tax benefit arising from the ability to deduct state and local taxes on the federal return.[3]

---

[2] The calculation assumes that the person remains in the same marginal tax bracket after deduction or extra income is reflected. Where this assumption is not correct, a more elaborate calculation is required.

[3] Under the Jobs Creation Act of 2004, you can take either state and local taxes or sales tax as a deduction for 2004 and 2005. At the time this book was published, it had not been established whether this deduction will continue for future years.

The formula is

$$
\boxed{\text{Marginal tax bracket}} = \boxed{\text{Marginal federal bracket}} + \boxed{\text{Marginal state bracket}} + \boxed{\text{Marginal local bracket}} - \boxed{\text{Marginal federal bracket}} \times \left(\boxed{\text{Marginal state bracket}} + \boxed{\text{Marginal local bracket}} \right)
$$

Example 14.4   Albee was in the following marginal brackets: 33 percent federal, 7 percent state, and 2 percent local. What is his total marginal bracket on income earned?

$$
\begin{aligned}
\text{Marginal tax bracket} &= 33\% + 7\% + 2\% - 33\% \times (7\% + 2\%) \\
&= 42\% - 3\% \\
&= 39\%
\end{aligned}
$$

You can use the marginal tax bracket to compare alternative investments on an "apples to apples" basis. Doing so is necessary because market forces adjust prices for investments with tax benefits and reduce their pretax returns to investors. Two approaches can be used to compare investment alternatives: after-tax returns and pretax equivalents.

After-Tax Returns

This approach simply reduces returns on alternative investments to after-tax figures in order to compare their benefits. It is given by the following formula:

$$
\text{After-tax return} = \text{Pretax return} \times (1 - t)
$$

where

t = Marginal tax bracket, expressed as a decimal

Pretax Equivalent Returns

Pretax equivalent returns compute tax-advantaged returns on a before-tax basis. In effect, this approach takes the investments with tax benefits and grosses them up to the equivalent return on investments without tax benefits. If an investment has no tax benefits, no calculation for it is necessary.

$$
\text{Pretax equivalent return} = \frac{\text{After-tax return}}{1 - t}
$$

Example 14.5   Karen was offered two investments. One, a corporate bond, provided a 7 percent return with no tax benefits. The other was a tax-free municipal bond with a 5 percent return. Karen is in the 40 percent marginal tax bracket. Calculate comparable after-tax and pretax equivalent returns and indicate which is more favorable.

After-Tax Returns

$$
\begin{aligned}
\text{Corporate bond} &= 7\% \times (1 - 0.4) \\
&= 4.2\% \\
\text{Municipal bond} &= 5\% \times (1 - 0) \\
&= 5\%
\end{aligned}
$$

Pretax Equivalent Returns

$$
\begin{aligned}
\text{Corporate bond} &= 7\% \text{ (as stated)} \\
\text{Municipal bond} &= \frac{5\%}{1 - 0.4} \\
&= 8.3\%
\end{aligned}
$$

The muni bond provides a higher tax-adjusted return.

382 Part Five   *Tax and Estate Planning*

Both approaches should provide the same conclusion about which investment to select. The after-tax return method is more common whereas the pretax equivalent is often used by investment professionals; it more favorably highlights the benefits of a particular tax-advantaged investment because of its higher-yield figure.

TAX-PLANNING STRATEGIES

We can use a number of techniques to reduce our taxes. Many of these techniques involve planning well before the actual tax return needs to be filed. They include increasing deductible expenses, deferrals, conversions, transfers, eliminations, timing of income and expenses, and tax planning for investments.

Increasing Deductible Expenses and Credits

Tax law is involved, and with each new "tax simplification" act, it seems to get more complex. By carefully going through IRS publications or a good tax-planning manual,[4] you may be able to develop new deductions or credits. For example, you may not have been aware that a 10 percent tax credit is available for those who purchase an electric car.

Clustering can be a productive tax-planning tool. If you have medical or miscellaneous expenditures that fall below the 7.5 percent or 2 percent limitations, respectively, you may be able to pay and group two years' outlays together in one year to bring your deductible expenditures above their respective floors. This strategy is aided by the ability of individuals to deduct expenses on a when-paid rather than an accrual basis.

Example 14.6

John made $40,000 a year and had investment costs of $200 per year and fees to a tax preparer of $500 per year. Each year John's total deductions of $700 fell short of the miscellaneous expenditures floor of $800. He decided to cluster two years of his tax-planning expenditures by visiting his tax preparer in March for the past year and December for the current year. His deductible expense for each for the two years is now $200 and $1,200 instead of $700 and $700. John has developed a way to generate a new $400 deduction every two years.

$$\text{Miscellaneous expenditures floor} = \$40,000 \times 2\%$$
$$= \$800$$
$$\text{New deduction} = \text{Miscellaneous expense} - \text{Expenditures floor}$$
$$= \$1,200 - \$800$$
$$= \$400$$

Tax Deferral

Tax deferral refers to postponing taxes to be paid today to some time in the future so they can provide sizeable benefits due to your ability to use that money in the interim. The deferral may be for one year or for a considerably longer period.

Example 14.7

Susanna, a businesswoman, asked her client to bill her in early January instead of December. Therefore, her taxes were due one year later. Her billing was for $10,000.

Susanna was in the 40 percent marginal tax bracket and was able to earn 7 percent a year after tax on the money deferred, which was also the discount rate. She repeated this process

---

[4] See, for example, *The Ernst & Young Tax Guide* for the latest year.

each year for the 25 years she was an individual proprietor. Compute her yearly tax deferral, yearly tax benefit, and cumulative tax benefit at the end of 25 years.

$$\text{Yearly tax deferral} = \text{Yearly bonus} \times \text{Marginal tax bracket}$$
$$= \$10,000 \times 40\%$$
$$= \$4,000$$

$$\text{Yearly tax benefit} = \text{Yearly tax deferral} \times \text{After-tax return on investment}$$
$$= \$4,000 \times 7\%$$
$$= \$280 \text{ per year}$$

For as long as she performed this service, Susanna had a continuing tax benefit of $280 a year when a December payout was compared with a January one. You can find the cumulative benefit as follows:

Calculator Solution[5]

Inputs: 25   7   280

| N | I/Y | PV | PMT | FV |

Solution: **17,710**

$$\text{Cumulative tax benefit} = \$17,710$$

Tax deferral is the key to the benefits of a pension or deductible IRA. Taxes are deferred on the portion of salary placed in the pension or IRA as well as on the interest, dividends, and capital gains earned while it is in this tax shelter. Taxes are paid on withdrawals and, in many cases, for the remainder upon death. The older the person making the contribution, the less the benefit of tax-free compounding until withdrawals at retirement. However, in many instances where withdrawals will be spread over normal life expectancies, even people nearing retirement will find it beneficial to continue to make deposits into pensions or deductible IRAs.

Conversion

Conversion involves the change from one amount of tax due to a lower one. There are two ways that this can happen. The first involves shifting income; the second, transforming income.

Shifting Income

Shifting income involves transferring income from a person in a higher bracket to someone in a lower bracket. Most commonly, this is done by gifting money from a parent to a child.

Example 14.8

Paul and Marisa were in the 40 percent marginal tax bracket and decided to gift $5,000 a year to their daughter Melanie for her college education. They did so for 15 years from the time she was 3 to her 18th birthday. Melanie was in the 15 percent marginal income tax bracket throughout this time. Assume that the money would be placed in fully taxable investments earning 10 percent whether it were kept in the parents' or child's name. How much did they save per year?

$$\text{Taxable income per year} = \text{Amount invested} \times \text{Pretax return}$$
$$= \$5,000 \times 10\%$$
$$= \$500$$

---

[5] Ignore the negative sign obtained in the result in this and succeeding problems in the chapter.

$$\text{Tax due if in parents' name} = \text{Taxable income} \times \text{Tax rate}$$
$$= \$500 \times 40\%$$
$$= \$200$$
$$\text{Tax due if in child's name} = \$500 \times 15\%$$
$$= \$75$$
$$\text{Tax benefit of income shifting} = \$200 - \$75$$
$$= \$125$$

Note that as cumulative savings grew and compounded, the tax saving over time could be substantial.

Transforming Income

Transforming income means changing it from a high-tax to a lower-tax status. Typically, it involves changing from being taxed at ordinary income rates to being taxed at more favorable capital gains rates.

Example 14.9

Frances decided to purchase an apartment for $100,000 and then rent it to a third party. Her thought was that even if she wouldn't make money on the apartment rental, she would take advantage of losses[6] at ordinary tax rates and a sale at a capital gains rate. She depreciated the property on a straight-line basis (equal depreciation each year over 27.5 years). Things actually turned out that way with a breakeven yearly on an operating cash flow basis and a sale 10 years later at the $100,000 she paid for it. How much, if anything, did she earn? Assume Frances was in the 35 percent marginal tax bracket for ordinary income and 15 percent for capital gains income and earned 6 percent after tax on the cash flow generated.

$$\text{Yearly deductible depreciation} = \$100,000 \div 27.5 \text{ years}$$
$$= \$3,636$$
$$\text{Yearly tax benefit} = \$3,636 \times 35\%$$
$$= \$1,273$$

Cumulative Tax Benefit

Calculator Solution

Inputs:

10	6		1,273	
N	I/Y	PV	PMT	FV

Solution: **16,779**

Tax Paid on Sale

Cost of property	= $100,000
Cumulative depreciation	= $36,360 $3,636 per year × 10 years
Adjusted cost	= $63,640
Sale price	= $100,000
Gain on sale	= Sales price − Adjusted cost
	= $100,000 − $63,640
	= $36,360

---

[6] Fully available to people actively managing property who earn less than $100,000 a year and are not subject to the alternative minimum tax.

Tax on gain	$= \$36,360 \times 15\%$
	$= \$5,454$
Cash inflow from yearly tax benefits	$= \$16,779$
Cash outflow from sales	$= \$5,454$
Net cash earned	$= \$16,779 - \$5,454$
	$= \$11,325$

Note that this business transaction turned out to have no economic merit. There were no earnings from renting out the apartment, and there was no gain on the sale of it. The only benefit came from the difference between taking a deduction at the 35 percent marginal tax bracket for ordinary income and investing the proceeds over the years and a tax on sale at the 15 percent capital gains rate. In other words, these benefits came from the use of the tax-deductible money in the interim until sale (deferring) and the lower tax rate on capital gains (transforming).[7]

Elimination of Taxes

Tax elimination involves not paying taxes at all on a specific type of income being generated. Permanent elimination of taxes can be a particularly powerful tool. Some methods of eliminating taxation include gifts to charities, transfers to children, establishment of Roth IRAs, and structuring of employee benefits. Other methods, including purchase of tax-exempt securities and continual investment in residential real estate, will be discussed under tax shelters.

Gifts to Charities

A broad cross-section of taxpayers make tax-deductible gifts to charities. Many charitable donations are in the form of cash, check, or property. Those donations made in property form are based on fair market value, not cost. If you sell property that has appreciated since you purchased it, the property will be subject to taxation at capital gains rates. If, on the other hand, you donate an investment to a charity, the capital gains tax on any increase in the value of the investment, which, under normal circumstances, would have had to be paid by you when it was sold, is eliminated. Therefore, charitable gifts have two tax benefits: a tax deduction for the contribution and the elimination of any capital gains tax.

Example 14.10

John gave $12,000 to his church in cash each year. This year he had a $10,000 gain on a stock that he thought had limited prospects. John is in the 33 percent marginal tax bracket on ordinary income and 15 percent on capital gains income. (1) How should John handle the transaction? (2) How much of a cash benefit will John have from the contribution? (3) How much of a cash saving will he have from any tax strategy proposed?

John should donate the appreciated shares of stock to the charity instead of selling them. His sales of the shares would result in a $1,500 tax bill (15% rate × $10,000). His donation of those shares, therefore, saves $1,500. In addition, John receives a tax deduction for a charitable contribution worth $4,000 (33% rate × $12,000), whether his donations were in the form of cash or stock.

In sum, the use of appreciated stock instead of cash in making the charitable donation saved John $1,500, for a total benefit of $5,500 since it eliminated the capital gains tax that would have resulted had he donated cash and sold the stock separately.

Transfers to Children

The first $800 of investment income earned by a child under 14 is not subject to tax. For example, assume you transferred $10,000 worth of bonds with an income of 8 percent per year to your child who had no other income. The amount would be tax-free to your child, whereas retaining it in your name would result in your paying taxes on the income generated,

---

[7] The example above made tax advantages the sole source of return on investment. Normally, income-producing property provides positive pretax cash flow as well. The combination of pretax cash flows plus tax benefits often makes income-producing real estate an attractive form of investment.

based on your marginal tax bracket. For children under 14, amounts of investment income over $1,600 are taxed at the parent's rate; amounts between $800 and $1,600 are taxed at the minimum rate, currently 10 percent.

Establishment of Roth IRAs

Roth IRAs are IRAs that are never subject to income taxation once sums are placed into them. Deposits into Roth IRAs are made with **after-tax dollars**—dollars of income on which taxes have been paid. In contrast, regular IRAs under some circumstances can reduce taxable income. This is commonly referred to as deposits coming from **pretax dollars**—dollars of income on which no taxes have been paid. There are restrictions on the amount of money you can deposit in your Roth IRAs, generally $4,000 per person per year with a phaseout based on income. It is also possible to transfer money from a regular to a Roth IRA, after paying a tax on the money transferred.

Structuring of Employee Benefits

Certain benefits provided to employees are not taxable to them. One of those benefits is medical coverage. Dollar for dollar, it can be preferable for both employee and employer to contract for extra benefits rather than salary, with income taxes eliminated for employees and Social Security taxes eliminated for both the employee and employer.

Example 14.11   Samantha was negotiating with a small firm about coming to work for them. They offered her $33,000 per year with no medical benefits. These benefits cost Samantha $3,000 per year. Samantha said she would take the job if the company would give her $30,000 per year and pay for her medical policy. Samantha would save income and Social Security taxes on $3,000 of income, while her new employer would save the employer's portion of Social Security taxes on $3,000 of Samantha's salary.

Timing of Income and Expenses

The timing of income and expenses involves optional selection of the year in which to report transactions. The simplest use of timing methods is to maximize tax-deductible payments in the current year. By doing so, you can lower taxes in the current year and have use of that cash for an extra 12 months instead of waiting until the following year to take the deduction. Your marginal tax bracket may vary from year to year because of such factors as fluctuations in income earned, unusually high or low deductible expenses, or just a change in the country's taxation methods or tax brackets. In a year in which your marginal tax bracket is high, you may wish to postpone income to the next year but accelerate the reporting of deductible expenses to the current year. You would take exactly the opposite approach if your current marginal tax bracket was low. Cash-basis accounting for tax purposes makes it easier to shift income and expenses.

Example 14.12   Because she had a large gain on the sale of stock, Adriana did some tax planning. She calculated that she would be in the 44 percent marginal tax bracket in the current year as compared with her normal 28 percent. She decided to make her charitable contribution of $3,000 in December instead of her normal practice of doing it in February of the following year. She also shifted her overtime by one week so she would be paid her $2,000 in January instead of December. How much money would she save?

Adriana's After-Tax Return on Investments

	Without Tax Planning		With Tax Planning	
	Current Year	**Following Year**	**Current Year**	**Following Year**
Income from overtime	$2,000	–	–	$2,000
Charitable contribution	–	($3,000)	($3,000)	–

Total income	$2,000	($3,000)	($3,000)	$2,000
	×	×	×	×
Marginal tax bracket	44%	28%	44%	28%
	=	=	=	=
Tax payments	$880	($840)	($1,320)	$560
Two-year balance		$40	($760)	
Saving in taxes		($760) − $40 = ($800)		

Her saving in taxes is $800. Moreover, the timing of the payments (with a $1,320 current-year tax deduction versus an $880 current-year tax payment without tax planning) would add to the benefit.

Tax Planning for Investments

Tax planning for investments is generally weighted more heavily toward the timing of revenue transactions. The principal tax-planning tools for household operating activities, on the other hand, are often heavily weighted toward the timing of expenditures by year. The reason is that the receipt of income from job-related activities is often beyond the control of the taxpayer, whereas an investor often has a choice as to when to sell an investment and declare the gain.

There are four types of income from financial investment activities: ordinary income, dividend income, short-term capital gains and losses, and long-term capital gains and losses.[8]

Ordinary Income

Ordinary income is income taxed at normal rates based on your taxable income. It is appropriate for interest or other operating income from investments. It is taxed at the same rate as income from job-related activities.

Dividend Income

Dividends are received on payouts from corporations. Qualified dividends are eligible for special taxation. The maximum federal tax rate for years 2003–2008 will be 15 percent. The minimum rate is 5 percent for 2003–2007 and 0 percent for 2008. To receive the tax benefit, common stock dividends must have been taxed on a corporate level. Although most common stock dividends will qualify, only a fraction of preferred stocks will. To receive the benefit, the shares must be held for at least 60 days prior to the payment and cannot be paid to a tax-deferred account such as a pension. Those dividends that don't qualify such as the ones from a real estate investment trust (REIT) will be taxed at ordinary income rates.

Short-Term Capital Gains and Losses

Short-term transactions arise from gains and losses when sales prices for investments are compared with their costs. The tax code defines *short term* as sales that are made in one year or less from the date of purchase. In the absence of long-term transactions, short-term gains and losses are taxable at ordinary income rates. Net short-term losses are limited to $3,000 per year, but amounts in excess of $3,000 can be carried forward to future years indefinitely until the entire amount is utilized.

Long-Term Capital Gains and Losses

Long-term transactions for financial securities are those that are held for more than one year. Long-term capital gains on these securities are tax-favored, having a minimum

---

[8] In addition to financial investments, there are such things as passive and active investments in real estate and oil and gas and other natural resources that may have separate tax treatment and differentiation between passive and active participation in the activity.

federal rate of 5 percent and a maximum rate of 15 percent.[9] Long- and short-term investment transactions are netted against one another.[10] The following are some tax-planning strategies.

Take Capital Losses This strategy proposes that you take advantage of losses on current holdings by selling the shares. If they are sold within the current year, you realize the tax benefit from the loss earlier than if you postpone the sale. The benefit of this strategy is, of course, limited to $3,000 of capital losses net of capital gains for the year. In addition, the tax benefit from the losses must be measured against the potential investment gains in continuing to hold the shares. For example, there is some indication that stocks that have performed poorly during the year are subject to unusual declines at year-end due to people taking advantage of this strategy (called tax-loss selling), and that shares rebound sharply in January.[11] It can sometimes be beneficial to wait and sell in January as the gains in price can more than compensate for the deferral of the tax-loss-selling benefit by one year.

Take Capital Losses to Offset Capital Gains

This strategy is very close to the one above. However, its trigger is the desire to reduce or eliminate taxes on gains on already-sold securities. It is done by selling shares with losses to the extent of gains or for $3,000 more of losses than gains.

Postpone Capital Gains to the New Year

This strategy defers taxes by postponing gains until the new year. It is subject to the same provision that it must be measured against the risk of changes in stock prices—in this case, share declines in the interim while waiting to sell.

Postpone Sales until Investments Are Held More than One Year

As mentioned, investments that you have held for more than one year are subject to favorable long-term capital gains tax rates. Therefore, if you have a material gain, you may benefit from waiting until the investment has been held more than one year before selling.

A summary of the tax-planning strategies discussed is shown in Table 14.3.

TAX-ADVANTAGED INVESTMENTS

There are a variety of investments providing tax benefits that can be used in tax planning. They can be separated into investment structures and individual investments.

Tax-Advantaged Investment Structures

Tax-advantaged investment structures are entities that provide an umbrella of tax benefits for investments made within the entity. Some of the leading ones are discussed below.

Pension Plans and Regular IRAs

Qualified pension plans along with certain IRAs are among the few entities that allow pretax dollars to be invested. As you have learned, placing pretax dollars into a pension means

---

[9] The long-term capital gains rates for real estate and collectibles are 25 percent and 28 percent, respectively.

[10] Long-term capital losses after netting out capital gains, as with short-term capital losses, can only be taken for the first $3,000. The balance is carried forward until the losses are offset against gains or applied against ordinary income at the rate of $3,000 annually.

[11] Jay Ritter, "The Buying and Selling Behavior of Individual Investors at the Turn of the Year," *Journal of Finance* 43, no. 3 (July 1988), pp. 701–17.

TABLE 14.3 **Summary of Tax-Planning Strategies**

Strategy	Explanation	Example
Increase deductible expenses and credits	Finding new deductions and clustering existing ones	Bunching two years of medical visits and payments into one year to get over floor deductible
Tax deferral	Postponing taxes and investing the money	Placing money into a 401(k) pension plan
Conversion	Bringing about a lower tax rate by: a. shifting income from a higher- to a lower-income person	Gifting to child
	b. transforming income from one taxed at an ordinary income tax rate to taxation at a more favorable rate, normally a capital gains rate	Holding an investment asset that has appreciated for 12 months to receive long-term capital gains treatment
Timing of income and expenses	Selecting the year to declare a gain or loss to take tax advantage of a more favorable marginal tax bracket	Postponing the subscription to a deductible business magazine until the new year when you will be in a higher marginal tax bracket
Elimination of taxes	Pay no further income taxes on a sum after taking a certain action	Purchase of municipal bonds of the state you reside in
Take capital losses	Selling investments with losses to reduce current taxes	Sell stock with $3,000 loss before the end of December
Postpone capital gains to new year	Delay selling an investment that has risen in value until the new year	Waiting until January to sell a profitable investment you intended to liquidate in December
Postpone capital gains until held more than one year	Delay selling an investment that has appreciated in value until it qualifies for favorable long-term capital gains treatment	Retaining a profitable investment until owning it for at least 12 months

that no taxes are paid on the deposits currently. Taxation is deferred on initial deposits and on subsequent dividends, interest, and capital gains on deposits until monies are withdrawn. Pension plans come in many formats including 401(k) plans, profit-sharing plans, and so on. Their tax deferrals, including one for contributions with pretax dollars, make pensions a particularly attractive tax-advantaged investment.

Roth IRAs and Roth 401(k)s

Roth IRAs require that after-tax dollars be placed into them. In contrast to regular IRAs and pensions, which provide tax deferral, Roth IRAs are not subject to any further taxation. There is a current limit of $4,000 annually that can be placed in a Roth IRA and some overall limits, based on income, as to who can take advantage of a Roth. It is particularly beneficial for younger people who have opportunities for many years of tax-free compounding without an ultimate income tax. Roth 401(k) plans offered by selected employers have the same general characteristics as Roth IRAs but can allow larger yearly contributions. For a description of them, see Chapter 12, Appendix I.

Employer Nonqualified Plans

Certain employer plans offer both pretax-dollar deposits and tax deferral for nonqualified plans. We will be discussing them in the next section of this chapter.

Tax-Deferred Annuities

Tax-deferred annuities are investments in which after-tax dollars are placed into entities. The tax on all earnings on deposits is deferred until withdrawals are made. There are two types of annuities: fixed and variable. As we discussed in Chapter 12, fixed annuities have stable principal and earn a rate of return determined by the market, contract terms, and the discretionary factors of individual annuity companies. Variable annuities offer an investment alternative in which returns are generally determined by market factors. Both choices offer the option of paying out money accumulated, generally in level sums for the life of the holders, based on projected life expectancy.

Life Insurance

Sums deposited and accumulated in life insurance policies beyond policy costs, called cash value, earn income. That income grows tax-deferred in the same way annuities do. There are fixed and variable life insurance policies as well. The cash value can be withdrawn, at which point the portion of the withdrawal representing monies earned is taxed, or it can be borrowed without a taxable-income event occurring.[12] If the cash value is left in the policy without purchasing more insurance, it will not increase the payout at death, with the payout generally limited to the stated amount of the policy.[13]

Individual Tax-Advantaged Investments

Tax-advantaged individual investments are those in which the specific investment, not the overall investment structure, provides the tax benefit. Some of them are discussed below.

Home

Investment in an apartment or home you live in provides many tax advantages. Interest to finance the home is tax-deductible, as are real estate taxes. The first $250,000 of gain on sale of a home ($500,000 per couple) that is your primary residence is excluded from taxation. You must have lived in and owned a home for at least two of the previous five years[14] before being eligible for this exclusion of gain on sale. Taxation on gains beyond this exclusion is based on favorable long-term capital gains rates.

Real Estate Investment

Real estate that you don't reside in full time but is intended as an investment allows tax deductibility of interest, taxes, and other operating costs. It also allows you to take depreciation on the investment. This depreciation expense can be employed as a tax deduction despite the fact that well-located and -maintained properties appreciate in price. Depreciation is allowed to the extent of taxable profits on the property and other similar assets plus an additional maximum of $25,000, subject to overall taxpayer adjusted gross income limitations. Finally, business real estate that you own can be exchanged for other "like kind" property without triggering taxation on gains.

Municipal Bonds

Most municipal bond interest is free from federal taxation. When you purchase qualified municipal bonds of the state you live in, your interest is not subject to state and local taxes either.

Series EE Bonds

Series EE bonds are U.S. government bonds. Effective May 2005, new bonds purchased will earn a fixed rate of interest. For bonds purchased between May 1995 and April 2005, the interest rate floats with five-year U.S. government Treasury securities and pays 85 or 90 percent of that rate depending on the issue date of the bond. Interest is not paid out but

---

[12] Only when cumulative withdrawals begin to exceed cumulative payments do the withdrawals become taxable.

[13] Except for certain universal life contracts that, in effect, add cash values to the face amount at death and for dividend-paying life insurance policies which use the dividends to purchase paid-up additional insurance which increases the death benefit.

[14] With some exceptions.

Practical Comment Taxes and Investment Merit

Care should be taken to ensure that these investments have genuine investment merit. Sometimes people are lured into uneconomical investments by tax benefits. Having tax benefits may be more than offset by investments priced too high or otherwise lacking investment merit. Moreover, the IRS is likely to disallow deductions for any investment lacking in true investment merit and entered into solely for its tax benefits.

deferred until the bonds are cashed in. Cashing in the bonds isn't required for many years, and until they are cashed, taxes on the bonds' income can be deferred.

U.S. Government Bonds

Although subject to federal taxation, U.S. government bonds are free of state and local taxes. This tax benefit is only useful, of course, in states that assess income taxes.

Tax-Sheltered Investments

There are a variety of investments on which the federal government has elected to bestow tax benefits. Some of them include oil and gas, low-income housing, rehabilitation of classics, tax credits on certain investments, and so on.[15]

Example 14.13 Adam and Corina were in the 40 percent tax bracket and decided to compare investments in various tax-advantaged alternatives starting with $80,000 in each. Assume that all amounts were to be withdrawn and used in 20 years and had the pretax return listed below.[16] What are the after-tax sums available at that time?

	Qualified Pension	Nonqualified Pension	Tax-Deferred Fixed Annuity	Municipal Bond	Roth IRA	Equities	House
Pretax dollars	80,000	80,000	80,000	80,000	80,000	80,000	80,000
After-tax dollars	80,000	48,000	48,000	48,000	48,000	48,000	48,000
Pretax return	10%	10%	6%	5%	10%	10%	4%
After-tax return	10%	10%	6%	5%	10%	9.4%[1]	4%
Accumulated amount—20 years	538,200	322,920	153,943	127,358	322,920	289,459	105,174
Tax rate	40%	40%	40%	0%	0%	20%	0%
Tax on accumulated amount	215,280	109,968	42,377	0	0	96,584	0
Amount remaining	**$322,920**	**$212,952**	**$111,566**	**$127,358**	**$322,920**	**$192,875**	**$105,174[2]**

[1] Assume 3 percent dividends and 7 percent deferred appreciation.
[2] Excludes other nontax benefits, including inputted rent.

[15] See Andrew A. Samwick, "Tax Shelters and Passive Losses after the Tax Reform Act of 1986" (National Bureau of Economic Research working paper no. 5171), in *Empirical Foundations of Household Taxation,* ed. Martin M. Feldstein and James M. Poterba, pp. 192–233 (Chicago: University of Chicago Press, 1996).

[16] These figures are not intended to fully represent the relative attractions of these assets. Relative returns can differ between assets at a point in time and when compounded over time. They also differ depending on the household's marginal tax bracket and the specific investment used within the tax-advantaged structure. For example, a variable annuity generally provides a higher rate than a fixed annuity.

Back to Dan and Laura
TAX PLANNING

Dan came alone to the tax meeting as Laura said she was tied up on Brian matters. Dan now felt very strongly about taxes. He said, "Every dollar I save in taxes is one more dollar that I can spend on things that we enjoy." I reminded him that I was not a tax accountant or tax preparer but would point out the tax strategies that were available and how he and Laura related to them. He also asked about tax shelters. He said that one of his neighbors claimed to have a tax shelter that eliminated all the taxes he had to pay for the year. And he wanted to know how much money he should place in his company's flexible spending plan. His medical expenses above insurance-reimbursable amounts would be either $3,000 or $4,000, with $4,000 highly likely. He was concerned that under the flexible rules, he would either use or lose the $1,000 if he committed to $4,000 and his actual expenditures came to $3,000.

Laura later called and informed me that Dan was going to do their tax return. She said it turned out that Dan really liked learning how to do it. In fact, she said he had become like some of my other clients, almost obsessed with the idea of finding another tax deduction. He had mentioned to me previously that he was researching the idea of deducting the cost of his gym membership with the thought that it was needed to improve a two-year-old knee injury that had required arthroscopic surgery. He had gained access to tax court rulings throughout the country and had set up an appointment with the manager of the gym.

I thought of mentioning to Dan that his time might be more productively spent on his career pursuits. However, income tax work for him seemed to have a leisure component. He got pleasure from the challenge of finding allowable deductions. I raised the issue in speaking to Laura when she dropped off some information. She smiled and said jokingly that she didn't expect to see Dan from April 1 to April 15 when their tax return was to be mailed.

Tax planning is taking advantage of all established methods of reducing your outlays to the government. There are five established ways of doing so plus a separate category for investments, and I will explain them all and indicate whether there is any potential for you to use each method.

1. *Increasing deductible expenses.* Increasing deductible expenses means finding expenses that you did not know were deductible. In addition, you can develop them by grouping expenses of more than a year into one year or by some other method. You indicated that you and Laura contribute your used clothing to charity. You can deduct your contribution at the market value of those clothes.

2. *Deferrals.* By deferring taxes, you postpone them, which allows investing the amount deferred in the interim. You are doing this now by investing in a Keogh, which places pretax dollars in and isn't taxed until you start withdrawals.

3. *Conversion.* Conversion involves shifting income to reduce the tax rate. It can be done by gifting money directly to your child, who is in a lower tax bracket. I don't recommend this. As you will see in point 4, there is a better solution. The second method is to transform ordinary income into capital gains income. I will discuss this soon.

4. *Eliminations.* With this method, taxes are eliminated entirely. I have two recommendations. The first is to shift from taxable bonds to municipal bonds in your taxable accounts. Municipals from the state you live in provide tax-free income. The second is to consider saving education money in Section 529 plans. After-tax monies are placed in these plans; they compound tax-free and are not taxable when withdrawn and used for defined educational expenses. More about this later under educational planning.

5. *Timing of income and expenses.* Where appropriate, income and expenses can be timed to take advantage of changes in marginal tax rates. I don't believe there is any opportunity here for you.

6. *Tax planning for investments.* Tax planning for investments uses short- and long-term gains and losses from investments in strategies designed to reduce taxation. You mentioned to me that you had a significant loss on investment in Hypotronics stock, which you intended to sell within the next few months. I noticed you have a gain on Clioxin stock already sold. Unless there is some investment reason not to do so, you should consider selling the Hypotronics before the end of the year to partially offset the gain on Clioxin.

As you are probably aware, flexible spending accounts provide a tax deduction but operate under a "use it (by finding a qualified deduction) or lose it approach." I would take the $4,000 amount. I recognize that you may lose $1,000, but after deduction at your marginal tax rate of 29 percent, it would only come to $710. Your indication of a high likelihood of reaching $4,000 makes that the better opportunity. However, if the possibility of an overpayment is disturbing to you, you can skip the last $1,000. Your tax-planning worksheet with the above recommendations included follows.[17] Notice that after this year, your combined marginal tax rate of 29 percent stays constant throughout the next three years, but your average tax rate declines. This is due to the favorable tax effects of owning a home.

Finally, I am pleased that you are taking over preparation of your tax return. The draft work you have shown me up to now suggests that you are handling it in a competent way. It is likely to make you more knowledgeable in financial matters, which won't hurt personally or in business activities. If your tax work results in further organization of your records and thinking, it is likely to save me time and therefore you money in future follow-up work. Why not take a part of any tax savings and spend it together with Laura on a restaurant or a weekend away, depending on your success in chipping away the tax bill?

Tax-Planning Statement

	2006		2007	2008	2009	2010	2011	2012
	Before Plan	**After Plan**						
Income								
Wages	$100,000	$100,000	$110,000	$121,000	$133,100	$146,410	$239,882	$258,352
Dividends and interest	2,500	2,500	2,500	2,500	2,500	2,500	2,500	2,500
Capital gains	1,500	1,500	1,500	1,500	1,500	1,500	1,500	1,500
Retirement account distributions	0	0	0	0	0	0	0	0
Other income	0	0	0	0	0	0	0	0
Total income	**$104,000**	**$104,000**	**$114,000**	**$125,000**	**$137,100**	**$150,410**	**$243,882**	**$262,352**
401(k), IRA contributions	0	0	0	0	0	0	18,000	18,000
Student loan interest	2,500	2,500	2,452	2,226	1,985	1,729	1,458	1,170
Total	2,500	2,500	2,452	2,226	1,985	1,729	19,458	19,170
Adjusted gross income	**101,500**	**101,500**	**111,548**	**122,774**	**135,115**	**148,681**	**224,424**	**243,182**
Personal exemptions	9,600	9,600	9,888	10,185	10,490	10,805	11,129	11,463
Standard deduction	10,000	10,000	10,300	10,609	10,927	11,255	11,593	11,941
Medical and dental expenses	1,350	1,350	1,648	1,697	1,748	1,801	1,855	1,910
AGI times 7.5%	7,613	7,613	8,366	9,208	10,134	11,151	16,832	18,239
Deductible medical and dental expenses	0	0	0	0	0	0	0	0
State and local income taxes	4,575	4,575	4,566	5,132	5,753	6,436	10,229	11,172
Real estate taxes	0	0	2,500	2,575	2,652	2,732	2,814	2,898

(*continued*)

[17] The 1040 schedule is presented in Appendix II. We use 2004 income tax returns, the latest available on the IRS Web site at the time of publication.

(concluded)

Personal property taxes	0	0	0	0	0	0	0	0
Other taxes	0	0	0	0	0	0	0	0
Deductible taxes	4,575	4,575	7,066	7,707	8,405	9,168	13,042	14,071
Home mortgage interest and points	0	0	17,219	17,066	16,902	16,727	16,538	16,336
Investment interest	0	0	0	0	0	0	0	0
Deductible interest	0	0	17,219	17,066	16,902	16,727	16,538	16,336
Deductible gifts to charity	500	500	500	500	500	500	500	500
Unreimbursed employee expenses	0	500	515	546	597	672	779	930
Tax preparation fees	0	0	0	0	0	0	0	0
Other miscellaneous expenses	0	2,000	515	530	546	563	580	597
Total miscellaneous expenses	0	2,500	1,030	1,077	1,143	1,235	1,358	1,527
AGI times 2%	2,030	2,030	2,231	2,455	2,702	2,974	4,488	4,864
Allowable miscellaneous expenses	0	470	0	0	0	0	0	0
Total itemized deductions	5,575	5,545	24,785	25,273	25,808	26,394	30,081	30,907
Total deductions	10,000	10,000	24,785	25,273	25,808	26,394	30,081	30,907
Total taxable income	**81,900**	**81,900**	**76,875**	**87,317**	**98,818**	**111,481**	**183,214**	**200,812**
Tax	**$13,605**	**$13,605**	**$12,142**	**$14,541**	**$17,197**	**$22,263**	**$42,079**	**$46,730**
Total credits	0	0	0	0	0	0	0	0
Total other taxes	0	0	0	0	0	0	0	0
Total federal tax	**$13,605**	**$13,605**	**$12,142**	**$14,541**	**$17,197**	**$22,263**	**$42,079**	**$46,730**
Total state tax	**4,575**	**4,575**	**4,566**	**5,132**	**5,753**	**6,436**	**10,229**	**11,172**
Total federal and state tax	**$18,180**	**$18,180**	**$16,709**	**$19,672**	**$22,950**	**$28,699**	**$52,308**	**$57,903**
Social Security tax	$5,450	$5,450	$5,613	$5,782	$5,955	$6,134	$12,636	$13,015
Medicare tax	1,450	1,450	1,595	1,755	1,930	2,123	6,957	7,492
FICA tax	**$6,900**	**$6,900**	**$7,208**	**$7,536**	**$7,885**	**$8,257**	**$19,592**	**$20,507**
Total tax	**$25,080**	**$25,080**	**$23,917**	**$27,209**	**$30,835**	**$36,956**	**$71,900**	**$78,410**

Summary

Tax planning is a crucial factor in PFP because of the size of the outlay and the possibility of reduction with proper procedures.

- Taxes enter into virtually all major elements of financial planning.
- There are a variety of tax-planning strategies. These include increasing expenses and credits, deferring taxes, making a conversion, shifting income, transforming income, eliminating taxes, and timing income and expenses.
- Among the tax-advantaged investment structures are pension plans and regular IRAs, Roth IRAs, nonqualified plans, tax-deferred annuities, and life insurance.
- Individual tax-advantaged investments include the home, other real estate, municipal bonds, series EE bonds, U.S. government bonds, and other tax-sheltered investments.

Key Terms

adjusted gross income (AGI), *378*
after-tax dollars, *386*
average tax bracket, *379*
clustering, *382*

conversion, *383*
marginal tax bracket, *379*
ordinary income, *387*
pretax dollars, *386*
shifting income, *383*

tax deferral, *382*
tax elimination, *385*
tax planning, *379*
taxable income, *378*
transforming income, *384*

Web Sites

http://www.irs.gov
Internal Revenue Service (IRS)
This is the Internal Revenue Service's home page, which provides thorough information on taxation in all areas of economic life. The site lets the user download forms, instructions, and publications by the IRS. It also features a fill-in form service where users can directly fill in tax forms and print them out.

http://www.taxprophet.com
Taxation Issues
An extensive list of tax topics from taxation of employee stock options to estate taxation, information for foreign taxpayers, real estate taxation, and a column featuring published tax articles is provided.

http://www.taxsites.com/rates.html
Taxation Rates
Links to different tax and accounting topics are given. There is a link that could be of particular interest for taxpayers providing information on tax rates and tables ranging from alternative minimum tax rates, automobile rates, depreciation, and Section 179 rates to IRA, per diem rates, state taxes, and withholding tables.

http://www.cch.com
CCH Incorporated
This is the home page of CCH Inc., which is a leading provider of tax and business law information and software.

Questions

1. State how taxes are relevant in five major financial planning areas.
2. Why perform tax planning?
3. Contrast marginal and average tax brackets.
4. Which is the most appropriate tax bracket to use in making investment decisions: marginal or average tax bracket? Why?
5. A person's marginal tax bracket includes the sum of the relevant federal, state, and local income taxes. True or False? Explain.
6. John discovered a $400 tax deduction. In order to calculate its cash benefit, should he use his marginal or average tax bracket? Why?
7. What is the difference between shifting income and transforming income?
8. What is clustering of expenses? Give an example of it.
9. Why can tax deferral be so advantageous?
10. What is the difference between conversion and shifting income?
11. Give three examples of tax elimination.
12. Sarah had unrealized long-term capital gains and Marcy had unrealized long-term capital losses at year-end. When should each sell her shares: the current year or the next year?
13. Assuming that you didn't regard a stock that declined since you bought it particularly highly, why wouldn't you want to take a loss in the current year?
14. Why is a qualified pension plan such an attractive tax shelter?
15. Using the table in Example 14.13 on page 391 providing a comparison of tax-advantaged structures, explain why the qualified pension plan and the Roth IRA seem to be particularly attractive investments.
16. Compare a municipal bond with a tax-deferred annuity. When would one be more attractive than the other?

Problems   **14.1**   Melinda earned $50,000 and paid taxes of $12,500. She would have paid $35 on the next $100 she made. Compute her average and marginal tax brackets.

14.2   Murray was in the following marginal tax brackets: federal, 35 percent; state, 7 percent; local, 4 percent. What is his total marginal tax bracket?

14.3   Sally was able to negotiate a deferral in her $8,000 bonus from December to the beginning of January. Compute the benefit of receiving the bonus in January, assuming that she is in a 30 percent marginal tax bracket and could earn 6 percent after tax per year and that the bonus would remain for 30 years until retirement.

14.4   What is the annual benefit of parents gifting $300 each year to their child if the parents are in the 35 percent bracket and the child is in the 15 percent bracket?

14.5   Laurence bought a classic car for $40,000 as a business investment opportunity. He was allowed to depreciate it over 10 years and take the amount as a business tax deduction on his return. At the end of 10 years, the car was sold for $40,000. If Laurence was in the 38 percent marginal tax bracket and could earn 8 percent after tax on the cash flow generated, what was his cumulative cash benefit after sale on this transaction?

14.6   Frances donated $20,000 to a charity each year. This year she thought that, instead of cash, she would donate $25,000 of a stock that cost her $8,000. She was going to sell the shares anyway. If the combined federal and state capital gains tax for Frances is 20 percent, how much would she save in taxes by donating stock instead of selling the shares and then donating the proceeds?

14.7   Compare a pretax $10,000 sum placed in bonds yielding 6 percent in a qualified pension with an investment in a municipal bond yielding 5 percent. The municipal bond sum deposited was made with after-tax dollars on the same pretax $10,000. The marginal tax rate was 32 percent. Assume that the sums were accumulated for 25 years and the pension was liquidated at that time.

CFP®
Certification
Examination
Questions
and Problems

14.1   Your client's federal marginal tax rate is 36 percent, and the state marginal rate is 7 percent. The client does not itemize deductions on his federal return and is considering investing in a municipal bond issued in his state of residence that yields 5 percent. What is the adjusted taxable equivalent yield?

a. 3.2%

b. 4.65%

c. 5.38%

d. 7.81%

e. 8.40%

14.2   The tax bracket and holdings of your client are as follows:

Federal tax bracket = 33%

Investment*	Annual Income	June 30, Last Year Purchase Price	June 30, This Year Market Price
Money fund	$6,500	$100,000	$100,000
11% T bonds	$11,000	$100,000	$140,000
S&P index fund	$6,000	$100,000	$160,000
Computer stock fund	$3,000	$100,000	$85,000

*There have been *no* capital gains distributions.

During the 12 months from June 30 last year through June 30 this year, the portfolio earned, in annual yield and before-tax appreciation, respectively

a. 5.5% and 17.5%

b. 5.5% and 21.3%

    c. 6.6% and 17.5%

    d. 6.6% and 21.3%

14.3 A client purchased a mutual fund with a $10,000 lump-sum amount four years ago. During the four years, $4,000 of dividends were reinvested. Today the shares are valued at $20,000 (including any shares purchased with dividends). If the client sells shares equal to $13,000, which statement(s) is/are correct?

1. The taxable gain can be based on an average cost per share.

2. The client can choose which shares to sell, thereby controlling the taxable gain.

3. To minimize the taxable gain today, the client would sell shares with the higher cost basis.

4. The client will *not* have a gain as long as he/she sells less than what he/she invested.

    a. (1), (2), and (3) only

    b. (1) and (3) only

    c. (2) and (4) only

    d. (4) only

    e. (1), (2), (3), and (4)

14.4 Jorge is single and owns $30,000 of stock he originally purchased four years ago for $7,000. His adjusted gross income (AGI) is $40,000. If Jorge donates the stock to his church, which of the following is the maximum amount he can deduct as a charitable contribution for this gift on his federal income tax return this year?

    a. $12,000

    b. $15,000

    c. $20,000

    d. $30,000

Case Application

TAX PLANNING

Richard and Monica estimated they would have adjusted gross income of $108,000 in the current year and would have exemptions of $6,400 and deductions of $25,000. Their average combined federal and state tax bracket was 33 percent.

Case Application Questions

1. Compute their projected taxes for the year.
2. Richard wanted to know if he should take a $10,000 tax deduction this year or wait until next year to do so. He was inclined to do so now even though his average tax bracket would likely be 28 percent next year. What do you think he should do?
3. Monica wanted to know if they should place their savings into a qualified pension or save it personally. She said that Richard often had modest losses, not gains, each year. What is your recommendation?
4. Monica asked what tax-planning strategies you would recommend for them? Do so while completing the tax-planning section of the plan.

Appendix I

Tax Theory

Let's look at a theory of taxation from society's and your point of view. Taxation is, of course, the method by which governments raise the funds to carry out the activities for the people they serve. There are a variety of methods of developing the required government revenues and the question can arise concerning how much each of society's income groups should pay. The alternatives are as follows:

- *Proportional payment.* Individuals pay in the same ratio that they receive government services.
- *Progressive payment.* Individuals fund the services on the basis of their ability to pay, with higher-income people paying more.
- *Regressive payment.* Individuals in lower income groups pay a greater percentage.

A problem with proportional payments is the difficulty in assigning the amount of benefit to such services as clean air, external defense, and internal security.

One theoretical approach to determine how much each group should pay employs utility principles. Paying taxes provides negative utility. With this approach, payouts would be assessed so that all people's disutilities from the tax payments are the same.[18] This theory would likely be consistent with a progressive approach. People with greater incomes generally are better able to afford taxes. They therefore may have a higher threshold of "tax pain," which would allow them to take on above-average tax burdens. In taking an applied approach with the overall society's well-being in mind, we would have to include the impact of higher taxes on an individual's incentive to work. If an increase in taxes resulted in lower tax revenue to the government, the system would be counterproductive.

There are two main methods of taxation: consumption based and income based.

[18] Joseph Stiglitz, *Economics of the Public Sector,* 3rd ed. (New York: Norton, 2000), p. 476. Stiglitz takes issue with this approach, explaining its weaknesses.

THE CONSUMPTION-BASED METHOD

Under this method, people are taxed on the amount that they consume and the amount that they save. Importantly, savings are defined not as the sum you deposit in savings accounts but as the amount your total assets rise during the period.[19] Its proponents say it is fairer because, among other reasons, taxes are paid on amounts consumed that give the individual pleasure and withdraw needed resources from society.[20] An income tax, on the other hand, is uneven. For example, it discriminates against workaholics who benefit society by providing above-average labor productivity and by utilizing little of society's leisure resources. In addition, the consumption tax is nondiscriminatory; it takes gains on all types of wealth. A weakness is the difficulty in objectively assessing the amount that a certain asset has appreciated. Since a sales tax is dependent on purchases, it is an example of a tax based on the consumption method.

THE INCOME-BASED METHOD

This approach taxes your total income less certain allowable deductions. It uses a broad cash flow framework. In general, if money is received, it is taxed. Under the income method, the interest and dividend income, and the gain from sale of an investment, called a realized gain, would be included. The gain on assets not sold, on the other hand, called unrealized appreciation, would not be included since no transaction occurred. Its advantage is the ability of the government to determine gains objectively and to monitor compliance since transactions are often verifiable through third-party records. An example of an income approach is the federal income tax.

Some economists believe that a consumption approach is preferable because it is fairer.[21] There would be fewer loopholes or inconsistencies such as the income approach's taxation of gains on a stock sold but no taxation of the same stock purchased at the same time but not liquidated.

In deciding on which tax to assess and on whom, there are a number of factors that are considered.

- *Fairness.* Any system must take into account how fair it is for different strata of society. Fairness should mean that people with similar incomes and in similar situations in life pay the same amount in taxes. This is called *horizontal integration*. Society also may want people to be assessed based on their ability to pay, which is called *vertical integration*.

- *Administrative efficiency.* The costs to run the system should be low, with tax evaders kept to a minimum.

- *Transparency.* The system should be easy to understand by all individuals. In this manner, all can determine if it is fair to them and can lobby for change if a different system is thought better.

- *Minimum impact on economic choice.* Taxes are generally meant to raise revenues, not affect the normal operations of the economy. Therefore, the goal in most cases should be to minimize the impact on society's operations. A tax that is onerous enough to materially reduce the incentive to work or to channel resources into inefficient areas can lead to a less productive economy.

---

[19] Called the "Haig-Simons" accretion income. See David Wildasin, "R. M. Haig: Pioneer Advocate of Expenditure Taxation?" *Journal of Economic Literature* 28, no. 2 (June 1990), pp. 649–60.

[20] David F Bradford, *Taxation, Wealth, and Saving* (Cambridge, MA: MIT Press, 2000).

[21] For arguments in favor, see Stiglitz, *Economics of the Public Sector,* pp. 579–82; and Bradford, *Taxation, Wealth, and Saving,* pp. 3–40.

- *Societal benefits.* Governments use progressive taxation in part to redistribute wealth and benefits to individual groups thought to be deserving of aid, while other taxation policies may be meant to direct funds into activities deemed to be in society's best interests.

There are a number of taxes that governments use, including personal income taxes, corporate income taxes, import taxes, excise taxes, value-added taxes, Social Security taxes, and sales taxes. Our federal and state governments use a balance of consumption and income taxes. Relative to most other developed countries, we utilize income taxes more and consumption taxes less.

On balance, our system is progressive with higher incomes assessed at a greater rate. Whether the system is fair depends in part on individual beliefs and economic and political considerations. From an economic and finance standpoint, our focus should be on efficiency. Efficiency from the standpoint of an individual household involves minimization of taxes paid. Therefore, it targets income and estate taxation since efforts in both areas may have the most impact on the total amount of outlays for taxes.

Appendix II

Detailed Segments of an Income Tax Return

This appendix provides a detailed breakdown of the income tax return. Each income tax category occupies a separate section of a tax return. We will explain each category and then show the corresponding segment of a tax return after it has been filled out. We will then show the complete tax return at the end of the appendix.

Let's start at the top of the numbers portion of the tax statement with income. We will use Dan and Laura's case, although the education figures will differ from the final ones, due in part to timing. Some additional information on Dan and Laura follows. (Not all the examples in the case will be those of Dan and Laura.)

INCOME AND ADJUSTMENTS

Dan called to say he was in the neighborhood; he wanted to know if he could stop by for a few minutes. He provided some further details on his thinking. He asked if I could help him become more knowledgeable about taxes. He had decided to do his own tax returns. Their current returns were being done by Laura's father. Her father had no special background in taxes but didn't mind doing them for his children. Dan didn't know how well he was doing, and, though grateful, he was uncomfortable with the idea of his father-in-law preparing their return. As he viewed it, "We are grown up and can take care of our own activities." Besides, the do-it-yourself project seemed interesting to him.

As I did when he came in with Laura, I again mentioned to Dan that I was not a tax preparer myself but that tax planning was part of the financial work we were doing for him. I had to gather and input the relevant current tax information to generate the planning projections. I had developed some sheets explaining how to fill out a tax return and would fill them out using the projected figures for the year that would soon end. All he had to do was e-mail the projected amounts on income, expenses, and growth rates over the next two years using a sheet I had given him.

Shortly after that, I received the information, which is listed below. The sheets following represent the information and explanations that were sent back to Dan.

Tax Figures

	Amount	Growth Rate
Income		
Wages—before 401(k)	$100,000[1]	10%
Dividends and interest	2,500	0
Capital gains	1,500	0
Other	—	
Total	$104,000	
Adjustments		
Student loan interest	$2,500	
Standard deduction	10,000	
Personal exemptions	9,600	
Total taxable income	$81,900	
Total tax	$13,605	
Tax withheld	12,500	
Tax due	$1,105	

[1] Figures for wages and salaries are entered on the tax return after 401(k) and other qualified pension contributions by employees have been deducted. Therefore, they do not appear on the tax return.

Income

Included in income are all qualifying cash payments less cost figures or, in some instances, a basis other than cost.

Category	Explanation
Salaries, wages, tips	Based on cash received
Interest	Taxable interest on bonds, CDs, and so forth
Tax-exempt interest	Listed on return in memo column but not included in income
Dividends	Received from stocks, and so on
Alimony	Received from former spouse
Business income	Shown net of expenses with the details provided on a separate tax schedule
Capital gains	Profits on sale of assets with sales price less purchase price; other basis of taxation shown on a separate schedule
IRA and pension distributions	Taxable portion included
Unemployment compensation	A form of government salary that may be included
Social Security	A portion taxable to certain higher-income households
Other	Taxable refunds, other gains and losses, rental real estate income, royalties, farm income, and so forth
Total income	The sum

Income	7	Wages, salaries, tips, etc. Attach Form(s) W-2	7	100000	
	8a	Taxable interest. Attach Schedule B if required	8a	500	
Attach Form(s)	b	Tax-exempt interest. Do not include on line 8a	8b		
W-2 here. Also	9a	Ordinary dividends. Attach Schedule B if required	9a	2000	
attach Forms	b	Qualified dividends (see page 20)	9b		
W-2G and	10	Taxable refunds, credits, or offsets of state and local income taxes (see page 20). . . .	10		
1099-R if tax	11	Alimony received	11		
was withheld.	12	Business income or (loss). Attach Schedule C or C-EZ	12		
	13	Capital gain or (loss). Attach Schedule D if required. If not required, check here ▶ ☐	13	1500	
If you did not	14	Other gains or (losses). Attach Form 4797	14		
get a W-2,	15a	IRA distributions . . .	15a		b Taxable amount (see page 22)	15b		
see page 19.	16a	Pensions and annuities	16a		b Taxable amount (see page 22)	16b		
Enclose, but do	17	Rental real estate, royalties, partnerships, S corporations, trusts, etc. Attach Schedule E	17		
not attach, any	18	Farm income or (loss). Attach Schedule F	18		
payment. Also,	19	Unemployment compensation	19		
please use	20a	Social security benefits .	20a		b Taxable amount (see page 24)	20b		
Form 1040-V.	21	Other income. List type and amount (see page 24)	21		
	22	Add the amounts in the far right column for lines 7 through 21. This is your total income ▶	22	104000	

Adjustments

Adjustments, which reduce gross income, come from a variety of areas.

Category	Explanation
IRAs	Payments as qualifying deposits into these pension-type accounts for a maximum of $3,000 in 2002–2004; $4,000 in 2005–2007; $5000 in 2008[1]
Student loan interest	Qualified loan interest deductible up to $2,500 per year
Higher-education expenses	Deductible for as much as $3,000 in 2002–2003 and $4,000 thereafter, subject to income limitations
Medical savings accounts	Withdrawals from account for qualified medical expenditures
Moving expenses	To a new job using standard mileage rate of 15 cents a mile[2] plus other allowable costs
Pension plans	Payments into qualified retirement accounts
Alimony	Paid to former spouse
Other	One half of self-employment tax, self-employed health insurance, self-employed pension plans, penalty paid on early withdrawal of savings
Total adjustments	The sum
Adjusted gross income	Total income minus total adjustments

[1] For people over 50, $500 extra for years 2002–2005 and $1,000 extra for years 2006–2008.

[2] For miles driven from January 1 through August 31, 2005, and 22 cents a mile for miles driven from September 1 through December 31, 2005.

Adjusted Gross Income	23	Educator expenses (see page 26)	23			
	24	Certain business expenses of reservists, performing artists, and fee-basis government officials. Attach Form 2106 or 2106-EZ	24			
	25	IRA deduction (see page 26)	25			
	26	Student loan interest deduction (see page 28)	26	2500		
	27	Tuition and fees deduction (see page 29)	27			
	28	Health savings account deduction. Attach Form 8889	28			
	29	Moving expenses. Attach Form 3903	29			
	30	One-half of self-employment tax. Attach Schedule SE . . .	30			
	31	Self-employed health insurance deduction (see page 30)	31			
	32	Self-employed SEP, SIMPLE, and qualified plans	32			
	33	Penalty on early withdrawal of savings	33			
	34a	Alimony paid b Recipient's SSN ▶ _____ : :	34a			
	35	Add lines 23 through 34a		35	2500
	36	Subtract line 35 from line 22. This is your **adjusted gross income** . . . . ▶		36	101500

DEDUCTIONS

You may select a standard deduction whose amount varies depending on such factors as filing status—single, married joint return, and so forth—or itemize your deductions based on actual transactions. When itemized, deductions are placed on a separate tax schedule called Schedule A. Certain categories of expenditures are deductible to the extent they exceed a minimum amount called the *floor*. The floor is usually based on adjusted gross income (AGI). The formula is

$$\text{Deductible amount} = \text{Actual payments} - \text{AGI} \times \text{Floor percentage}$$

Example 14.A2.1 Harold had $100,000 of gross income and medical expenditures of $9,300 for the year. Since medical outlays are deductible to the extent they exceed 7.5 percent of adjusted gross income, Harold would be allowed to deduct $1,800.

$$\text{Deductible amount} = \$9,300 - \$100,000 \times 7.5\%$$

$$= \$9,300 - \$7,500$$

$$= \$1,800$$

On the other hand, certain deductions are phased out based on income. The phaseout for 2005 is AGI of over $142,700 ($71,350 if you are married filing separately). The expenses that qualify for this phaseout are taxes, charitable contributions, home mortgage interest, job expenses, and miscellaneous itemized deductions. The total of your itemized deductions falling in these categories is reduced by the smaller of 3 percent of the amounts of AGI over $142,700 or 80 percent of the itemized deductions subject to this limit. The AGI figures are adjusted annually for inflation. The phaseout of allowable deductions is itself scheduled to begin being phased out in 2006.

The major categories of deductions follow:

Category	Explanation
Medical and dental	Qualifying expenses subject to 7.5 percent floor
Taxes	State and local income taxes,[1] real estate and personal property taxes, excise taxes, and certain other taxes
Interest paid	Qualifying home mortgage interest and qualifying points, investment interest limited to total interest and dividends and other forms of income less noninterest investment expenses and the option of including income from capital gains received during the year
Charitable gifts	Gifts to qualified charities subject to maximum yearly deductions generally of 50 percent of AGI, but in some cases 20 percent or 30 percent
Casualty and theft losses	Subject to floor of 10 percent of AGI after deduction of $100 per occurrence
Miscellaneous	Subject to floor of 2 percent of AGI for total miscellaneous expenditures. Miscellaneous expenses include unreimbursed business expenses such as business-related travel and entertainment at 50 percent of amount paid, union dues, education to improve your performance in an existing position, and so on; in addition, tax preparation fees, safe deposit fees, and investment-related expenditures (excluding interest deducted in the interest section), such as newsletters, books, payments to advisors, and so on
Other miscellaneous	Other items to be deducted
Standard deduction	You can take a standard deduction if you do not care to itemize as above or if your deductions total less than the allowable standard deduction; the standard deduction is increased for people over 65 or those who are partially or completely blind

[1] Under new tax law, can take either state and local income taxes or sales tax as a deduction for 2004–2005. At the time of publication, periods beyond 2005 have not been established.

Possible economic reasons to justify a deduction for certain expenditures include

- *Medical and dental.* To protect and repair human capital, which can be viewed as an investment asset. Expenses supporting investment assets, including investments in businesses, are generally deductible.
- *Other income taxes.* Federal method of evening out variations in estate and local income taxes by area.
- *Interest paid.* Interest is deductible when made for investment purposes, with a residence also treated as an investment.
- *Charitable gifts.* To support nonprofit charitable operations, which are viewed as in society's interest.
- *Casualty and theft.* To reflect a decline in investment assets with capital items treated as an investment.
- *Other business expenses.* A necessary expense supporting business assets.

Form 1040—Schedule A

| SCHEDULES A&B (Form 1040) Department of the Treasury Internal Revenue Service (99) | Schedule A—Itemized Deductions (Schedule B is on back) ► Attach to Form 1040. ► See Instructions for Schedule A and B (Form 1040). | OMB No. 1545-0074 2004 Attachment Sequence No. 07 |

Name(s) shown on Form 1040   Your social security number

Medical and Dental Expenses		Caution. Do not include expenses reimbursed or paid by others.		
	1	Medical and dental expenses (see page A-2)	1	
	2	Enter amount from Form 1040, line 37	2	
	3	Multiply line 2 by 7.5% (.075)	3	
	4	Subtract line 3 from line 1. If line 3 is more than line 1, enter -0-.		4

Taxes You Paid (See page A-2.)	5	State and local (check only one box): a ☐ Income taxes, or b ☐ General sales taxes (see page A-2)	5	
	6	Real estate taxes (see page A-3)	6	
	7	Personal property taxes	7	
	8	Other taxes. List type and amount ►........................	8	
	9	Add lines 5 through 8		9

Interest You Paid (See page A-3.) Note. Personal interest is not deductible.	10	Home mortgage interest and points reported to you on Form 1098	10	
	11	Home mortgage interest not reported to you on Form 1098. If paid to the person from whom you bought the home, see page A-4 and show that person's name, identifying no., and address ►........................	11	
	12	Points not reported to you on Form 1098. See page A-4 for special rules	12	
	13	Investment interest. Attach Form 4952 if required. (See page A-4.)	13	
	14	Add lines 10 through 13		14

Gifts to Charity If you made a gift and got a benefit for it, see page A-4.	15	Gifts by cash or check. If you made any gift of $250 or more, see page A-4	15	
	16	Other than by cash or check. If any gift of $250 or more, see page A-4. You must attach Form 8283 if over $500	16	
	17	Carryover from prior year	17	
	18	Add lines 15 through 17		18

Casualty and Theft Losses	19	Casualty or theft loss(es). Attach Form 4684. (See page A-5.)		19

Job Expenses and Most Other Miscellaneous Deductions (See page A-5.)	20	Unreimbursed employee expenses—job travel, union dues, job education, etc. Attach Form 2106 or 2106-EZ if required. (See page A-6.) ►........................	20	
	21	Tax preparation fees	21	
	22	Other expenses—investment, safe deposit box, etc. List type and amount ►........................	22	
	23	Add lines 20 through 22	23	
	24	Enter amount from Form 1040, line 37	24	
	25	Multiply line 24 by 2% (.02)	25	
	26	Subtract line 25 from line 23. If line 25 is more than line 23, enter -0-		26

Other Miscellaneous Deductions	27	Other—from list on page A-6. List type and amount ►........................		27

Total Itemized Deductions	28	Is Form 1040, line 37, over $142,700 (over $71,350 if married filing separately)? ☐ No. Your deduction is not limited. Add the amounts in the far right column for lines 4 through 27. Also, enter this amount on Form 1040, line 39. ☐ Yes. Your deduction may be limited. See page A-6 for the amount to enter.	►	28

For Paperwork Reduction Act Notice, see Form 1040 instructions.   Cat. No. 11330X   Schedule A (Form 1040) 2004

37	Amount from line 36 (adjusted gross income)	37	101500
38a	Check If: ☐ **You** were born before January 2, 1940, ☐ Blind. ☐ **Spouse** was born before January 2, 1940, ☐ Blind. } Total boxes checked ▶ 38a ☐		
b	If your spouse itemizes on a separate return or you were a dual-status alien, see page 31 and check here ▶ 38b ☐		
39	**Itemized deductions** (from Schedule A) or your **standard deduction** (see left margin).	39	10000
40	Subtract line 39 from line 37	40	91500
41	If line 37 is $109,475 or less, multiply $3,200 by the total number of exemptions claimed on line 6d. If line 37 is over $109,475, see the worksheet on page 33	41	9600

EXEMPTIONS

Exemptions are based on the number of people who are supported by the household. People who qualify for that status, which provides a fixed reduction in taxable gross income per person, are called *dependents*. In order to qualify as a dependent, you must be a household member or a relative. To qualify for the exemption, the household must provide over 50 percent of the living costs for that person, who earns less than a stated amount of income, unless it is one of your children who is under age 19 or a full-time student under age 24. Children have no income limitation. As of 2005, your exemptions phased out at approximately $109,475–$218,950 depending on filing status—single, head of household, or married filing jointly. Exemption amounts are subject to the same phaseout rules based on income as deductions and, as with deductions, the phaseout rules themselves will begin to be phased out in 2006.

Exemptions

6a ☑ Yourself, If someone can claim you as a dependent, do not check box 6a . . . .
b ☑ Spouse . . . .
} Boxes checked on 6a and 6b: 2

c Dependents:

(1) First name Last name	(2) Dependent's social securiy number	(3) Dependent's relationship to you	(4) ✓ if qualifying child for child tax credit (see page 18)
Brian Jones	038 | 35 | 5213		☐
			☐
			☐
			☐

If more than four dependents, see page 18.

No. of children on 6c who:
• lived with you: 1
• did not live with you due to divorce or seperation (see page 16): ____
Dependents on 6c not entered above: ____

d Total number of exemptions claimed . . . . Add numbers on lines above ▶ 3

TAXABLE INCOME

Taxable income is the amount from which your tax liability is calculated. The federal rates progress from 10 percent to 35 percent depending on income.

TAX

This is the amount computed as due before other items below.

Example 14.A2.1 (Update) Mary and Henry are married and are filing a joint return. They have no children. Their taxable income was $87,000 in 2005. They elected the standard deduction. Compute their tax. Answer per Tax Table.

$$\text{Tax} = \$8{,}180 + 25\% \times (\$87{,}000 - \$59{,}400)$$
$$= \$15{,}080$$

42	**Taxable income**. Subtract line 41 from line 40. If line 41 is more than line 40, enter -0-	42	81900
43	**Tax** (see page 33). Check if any tax is from: a ☐ Form(s) 8814 b ☐ Form 4972	43	13605

ALTERNATIVE MINIMUM TAX

This is an alternative income tax that must be paid if it exceeds the regular tax. It adjusts for certain special categories such as installment sales, accelerated depreciation, and incentive stock options. It was intended to promote a fairer tax, particularly for those who paid little in tax. However, because it hasn't been indexed for inflation, more and more people are paying an extra amount of tax.

The alternative minimum tax (AMT) can result in a material shift in approach. For example, real estate and state and local income taxes are not deductible for AMT purposes. When a choice is possible, it can benefit those who are under AMT to locate in a state with little or no state income tax.

44	Alternative minimum tax (see page 35). Attach Form 6251	44	-
45	Add lines 43 and 44 . . . . ▶	45	13605

CREDITS

Credits are amounts that reduce taxes owed. They are more valuable than deductions or exemptions because they reduce taxes dollar for dollar. Deductions or exemptions reduce taxes by an amount equal to the marginal tax bracket you are in, multiplied by the amount to be deducted.

Example 14.A2.2 What is the difference in benefit between a tax credit and a tax deduction, assuming the amount is $3,000 and the person is in the 40 percent marginal tax bracket? The amount of taxes owed before giving effect to this benefit was $14,000.

The tax credit is a $3,000 cash benefit, which would result in a net amount owed of $11,000. The tax deduction is only a fraction of that $3,000 amount because the person is in the 40 percent bracket.

In this instance, the cash benefit is $1,200 and the net amount owed would be $12,800.

$$\text{Cash benefit} = \text{Deduction} \times t$$
$$= \$3,000 \times (.40)$$
$$= \$1,200$$

Some common tax credits follow:

Category	Explanation
Child and dependent care expense	Expenses outlaid for dependents to allow you to work; subject to limitations including a maximum amount of $1,000 for each qualifying child
Care of elderly or disabled	For low-income people with low Social Security benefits; subject to limitations with maximum credit of about $1,125
Adoption	Maximum of $10,390 for outlays to adopt a child as of 2004, subject to income limitations
Foreign	Taxes paid on income to a foreign country are credited against U.S. taxes, subject to limitation to the extent that the same income is taxed by the United States
Education	Lifetime learning credits of $2,000 per year each year of college or higher, with maximum of one per tax return, or Hope Scholarship credit of up to $1,500 per student for initial two years with phaseout based on income

46	Foreign tax credit. Attach Form 1116 if required	46	
47	Credit for child and dependent care expenses. Attach Form 2441	47	
48	Credit for the elderly or the disabled. Attach Schedule R . . .	48	
49	Education credits. Attach Form 8863	49	
50	Retirement savings contributions credit. Attach Form 8880 . .	50	
51	Child tax credit (see page 37)	51	
52	Adoption credit. Attach Form 8839	52	
53	Credits form: a ☐ Form 8396 b ☐ Form 8859	53	
54	Other credits. Check applicable box(es): a ☐ Form 3800		
	b ☐ Form 8801 c ☐ Specify _____ . . .	54	
55	Add lines 46 thorugh 54. These are your **total credits**	55	-
56	Subtract line 55 from line 45. If line 55 is more than line 45, enter -0- . . . . ▶	56	13605

OTHER TAXES

These are additions to taxes due for items such as the following:

Category	Explanation
Self-employment tax	Social Security and Medicare tax to be paid for people who have their own business
Alternative minimum tax	This additional tax is designed to make a greater percentage of people pay equitable income taxes; certain items are subject to it, including incentive stock options, installment sales, certain property transactions, and others
Domestic employee	Social Security and Medicare taxes (and federal and state unemployment taxes) must be paid on employees, including domestic workers

TOTAL TAX

The total tax is your calculated tax plus any "other taxes" due.

57	Self-employment tax. Attach Schedule SE	57	
58	Social security and Medicare tax on tip income not reported to employer. Attach Form 4137 . . .	58	
59	Additional tax on IRAs, other qualified retirement plans, etc. Attach Form 5329 if required . .	59	
60	Advance earned income credit payments from Form(s) W-2	60	
61	Household employment taxes. Attach Schedule H	61	
62	Add lines 56 through 61. This is your **total tax** . . . . ▶	62	13605

PAYMENTS

Payments are amounts already paid against taxes owed. They normally include amounts withheld by employers and estimated payments made by individuals filing the return. Also included in this portion of the tax return is an earned income tax credit for certain individuals having low income, including some who may not have to pay taxes but nonetheless may be eligible to receive some cash from the government.

Payments	63	Federal income tax withheld from Forms W-2 and 1099 . .	63	12500	
	64	2004 estimated tax payments and amount applied from 2003 return	64		
If you have a qualifying child, attach Schedule EIC.	65a	Earned income credit (EIC)	65a		
	b	Nontaxable combat pay election ▶	65b		
	66	Excess social security and tier 1 RRTA tax withheld (see page 54)	66		
	67	Additional child tax credit. Attach Form 8812	67		
	68	Amount paid with request for extension to file (see page 54)	68		
	69	Other payments from: a ☐ Form 2439 b ☐ Form 4136 c ☐ Form 8885 .	69		
	70	Add lines 63, 64, 65a, and 68 through 69. These are your total payments . . . . ▶	70	12500	

NET AMOUNT

The net amount is your total tax less your payments to date. It may require an additional payment or you may be entitled to a refund from the federal government.

Refund	71	If line 70 is more than line 62, subtract line 62 from line 70. This is the amount you **overpaid**	71		
Direct deposit?	72a	Amount of line 71 you want **refunded to you** . . . . ▶	72a		
See page 54 ▶ b	b	Routing number		▶ c Type: ☐ Checking ☐ Savings	
and fill in 72b, ▶ d	d	Account number			
72c, and 72d.	73	Amount of line 71 you want **applied to your 2005 estimated tax** ▶	73		
Amount You Owe	74	**Amount you owe.** Subtract line 70 from line 62. For details on how to pay, see page 55 ▶	74	1105	
	75	Estimated tax penalty (see page 55)	75		

Form 1040—Complete[1]

Department of the Treasury—Internal Revenue Service
U.S. Individual Income Tax Return 2004 (99) IRS Use Only—Do not write or staple in this space.

For the year Jan. 1-Dec. 31, 2004, or other tax year beginning , 2004, ending , 20   OMB No. 1545-0074

Label (See instructions on page 16.) **Use the IRS label.** Otherwise, please print or type.

L A B E L   H E R E

Your first name and initial: **Daniel C**   Last name: **Jones**   Your social security number: 042 : 31 : 5312

If a joint return, spouse's first name and initial: **Laura S**   Last name: **Jones**   Spouse's social security number: 039 : 29 : 4614

Home address (number and street). If you have a P.O. box, see page 16. **123 Canyon Drive**   Apt. no. **7B**

City, town or post office, state, and ZIP code. If you have a foreign address, see page 16. **Middletown, IL 62666**

▲ **Important!** ▲
You **must** enter your SSN(s) above.

Presidential Election Campaign (See page 16.) ▶

Note. Checking "Yes" will not change your tax or reduce your refund.
Do you, or your spouse if filing a joint return, want $3 to go to this fund? . . . . ▶

   You: ✔ Yes ☐ No   Spouse: ✔ Yes ☐ No

Filing Status

Check only one box.

1 ☐ Single
2 ✔ Married filing jointly (even if only one had income)
3 ☐ Married filing separately. Enter spouse's SSN above and full name here. ▶
4 ☐ Head of household (with qualifying person). (See page 17.) If the qualifying person is a child but not your dependent, enter this child's name here. ▶
5 ☐ Qualifying widow(er) with dependent child (see page 17)

Exemptions

If more than four dependents, see page 18.

6a ✔ **Yourself.** If someone can claim you as a dependent, **do not** check box 6a . . . . .
b ✔ **Spouse** . . . .
c Dependents:

(1) First name Last name	(2) Dependent's social security number	(3) Dependent's relationship to you	(4) ✔ if qualifying child for child tax credit (see page 18)
Brian Jones	038 : 35 : 5213		☐
			☐
			☐
			☐

Boxes checked on 6a and 6b: **2**
No. of children on 6c who:
• lived with you: **1**
• did not live with you due to divorce or separation (see page 18):
Dependents on 6c not entered above:
Add numbers on lines above ▶ **3**

d Total number of exemptions claimed . . . .

Income

Attach Form(s) W-2 here. Also attach Forms W-2G and 1099-R if tax was withheld.

If you did not get a W-2, see page 19.

Enclose, but do not attach, any payment. Also, please use **Form 1040-V.**

7	Wages, salaries, tips, etc. Attach Form(s) W-2	7	100000
8a	**Taxable** interest. Attach Schedule B if required	8a	500
b	**Tax-exempt** interest. **Do not** include on line 8a	8b	
9a	Ordinary dividends. Attach Schedule B if required	9a	2000
b	Qualified dividends (see page 20)	9b	
10	Taxable refunds, credits, or offsets of state and local income taxes (see page 20) . . .	10	
11	Alimony received	11	
12	Business income or (loss). Attach Schedule C or C-EZ	12	
13	Capital gain or (loss). Attach Schedule D if required. If not required, check here ▶ ☐	13	1500
14	Other gains or (losses). Attach Form 4797	14	
15a	IRA distributions . . 15a b Taxable amount (see page 22)	15b	
16a	Pensions and annuities 16a b Taxable amount (see page 22)	16b	
17	Rental real estate, royalties, partnerships, S corporations, trusts, etc. Attach Schedule E	17	
18	Farm income or (loss). Attach Schedule F	18	
19	Unemployment compensation	19	
20a	Social security benefits 20a b Taxable amount (see page 24)	20b	
21	Other income. List type and amount (see page 24)	21	
22	Add the amounts in the far right column for lines 7 through 21. This is your **total income** ▶	22	104000

Adjusted Gross Income

23	Educator expenses (see page 26)	23	
24	Certain business expenses of reservists, performing artists, and fee-basis government officials. Attach Form 2106 or 2106-EZ	24	
25	IRA deduction (see page 26)	25	
26	Student loan interest deduction (see page 28)	26	2500
27	Tuition and fees deduction (see page 29)	27	
28	Health savings account deduction. Attach Form 8889 . . .	28	
29	Moving expenses. Attach Form 3903	29	
30	One-half of self-employment tax. Attach Schedule SE .	30	
31	Self-employed health insurance deduction (see page 30)	31	
32	Self-employed SEP, SIMPLE, and qualified plans . . .	32	
33	Penalty on early withdrawal of savings	33	
34a	Alimony paid b Recipient's SSN ▶	34a	
35	Add lines 23 through 34a	35	2500
36	Subtract line 35 from line 22. This is your **adjusted gross income** . . . . . ▶	36	101500

For Disclosure, Privacy Act, and Paperwork Reduction Act Notice, see page 75.   Cat. No. 11320B   Form **1040** (2004)

[1] Note that 2005 figures were used on the 2004 tax return which was the latest one available at that time.

Form 1040 (2004)

Tax and Credits	37	Amount from line 36 (adjusted gross income)	37	101500

38a	Check if:	☐ **You** were born before January 2, 1940, ☐ Blind. ☐ **Spouse** was born before January 2, 1940, ☐ Blind. Total boxes checked ▶ 38a	
b	If your spouse itemizes on a separate return or you were a dual-status alien, see page 31 and check here ▶ 38b ☐	

Standard Deduction for—

- People who checked any box on line 38a or 38b or who can be claimed as a dependent, see page 31.
- All others:

Single or Married filing separately, $4,850

Married filing jointly or Qualifying widow(er), $9,700

Head of household, $7,150

39	**Itemized deductions** (from Schedule A) **or** your **standard deduction** (see left margin) . .	39	10000
40	Subtract line 39 from line 37	40	91500
41	If line 37 is $109,475 or less, multiply $3,200 by the total number of exemptions claimed on line 6d. If line 37 is over $109,475, see the worksheet on page 33	41	9600
42	**Taxable Income.** Subtract line 41 from line 40. If line 41 is more than line 40, enter -0-	42	81900
43	Tax (see page 33). Check if any tax is from: a ☐ Form(s) 8814 b ☐ Form 4972	43	13605
44	**Alternative minimum tax** (see page 35). Attach Form 6251	44	-
45	Add lines 43 and 44 . . . . ▶	45	13605

46	Foreign tax credit. Attach Form 1116 if required	46	
47	Credit for child and dependent care expenses. Attach Form 2441	47	
48	Credit for the elderly or the disabled. Attach Schedule R .	48	
49	Education credits. Attach Form 8863	49	
50	Retirement savings contributions credit. Attach Form 8880 .	50	
51	Child tax credit (see page 37).	51	
52	Adoption credit. Attach Form 8839	52	
53	Credits from: a ☐ Form 8396 b ☐ Form 8859 . . .	53	
54	Other credits. Check applicable box(es): a ☐ Form 3800 b ☐ Form 8801 c ☐ Specify _____	54	

55	Add lines 46 through 54. These are your **total credits**	55	-
56	Subtract line 55 from line 45. If line 55 is more than line 45, enter -0- . . . . ▶	56	13605

Other Taxes	57	Self-employment tax. Attach Schedule SE	57	
	58	Social security and Medicare tax on tip income not reported to employer. Attach Form 4137 .	58	
	59	Additional tax on IRAs, other qualified retirement plans, etc. Attach Form 5329 if required	59	
	60	Advance earned income credit payments from Form(s) W-2	60	
	61	Household employment taxes. Attach Schedule H	61	
	62	Add lines 56 through 61. This is your **total tax** . . . . ▶	62	13605

Payments	63	Federal income tax withheld from Form W-2 and 1099 . . .	63	12500
	64	2004 estimated tax payments and amount applied from 2003 return	64	

If you have a qualifying child, attach Schedule EIC.

65a	Earned income credit (EIC)	65a	
b	Nontaxable combat pay election ▶ 65b		
66	Excess social security and tier 1 RRTA tax withheld (see page 54)	66	
67	Additional child tax credit. Attach Form 8812	67	
68	Amount paid with request for extension to file (see page 54)	68	
69	Other payments from: a ☐ Form 2439 b ☐ Form 4136 c ☐ Form 8886 .	69	

70	Add lines 63, 64, 65a, and 66 through 69. These are your **total payments** . . . . . ▶	70	12500

Refund	71	If line 70 is more than line 62, subtract line 62 from line 70. This is the amount you **overpaid**	71	
Direct deposit? See page 54 and fill in 72b, 72c, and 72d.	72a	Amount of line 71 you want **refunded to you** . . . . ▶	72a	
▶ b	Routing number ☐☐☐☐☐☐☐☐☐ ▶ c Type: ☐ Checking ☐ Savings		
▶ d	Account number ☐☐☐☐☐☐☐☐☐☐☐		
	73	Amount of line 71 you want **applied to your 2005 estimated tax** ▶ 73		

Amount You Owe	74	**Amount you owe.** Subtract line 70 from line 62. For details on how to pay, see page 55 ▶	74	1105
	75	Estimated tax penalty (see page 55) 75		

Third Party Designee

Do you want to allow another person to discuss this return with the IRS (see page 56)? ☐ **Yes.** Complete the following ☐ **No**

Designee's name ▶   Phone no. ▶ ( )   Personal identification number (PIN) ▶ ☐☐☐☐☐

Sign Here

Joint return? See page 17.

Keep a copy for your records.

Under penalties of perjury, I declare that I have examined this return and accompanying schedules and statements, and to the best of my knowledge and belief, they are true, correct, and complete. Declaration of preparer (other than taxpayer) is based on all information of which preparer has any knowledge.

Your signature	Date	Your occupation **Engineer**	Daytime phone number **(361) 422-0899**
Spouse's signature. If a joint return, **both** must sign.	Date	Spouse's occupation **Housewife**	

Paid Preparer's Use Only

Preparer's signature ▶	Date	Check if self-employed ☐	Preparer's SSN or PTIN
Firm's name (or yours if self-employed), address, and ZIP code ▶		EIN	
		Phone no. ( )	

Form **1040** (2004)

Chapter Fifteen

Estate Planning

Chapter Goals

This chapter will enable you to:

- Determine what estate planning is and how to employ its key topics.
- Conclude that estate planning isn't only for the rich.
- Recognize the merits of having a will.
- Establish the steps in an overall estate plan.
- Develop several tax reduction strategies.
- Assess the advantages and disadvantages of many estate planning tools.

Dan and Laura did not have wills. They couldn't agree on who would be the guardian of their children or the executor should they die in a joint accident. Besides, Dan said, "We have time to get a will. We don't plan to leave anytime soon."

Real Life Planning

The advisor was familiar with the practices of many people concerning wills. Although most agreed that having a will was important, many didn't execute one. Often when he mentioned the absence of a will, the reply was, "I have to get around to doing it." It almost did not matter how old the person was. In the advisor's experience, even many estate attorneys who could draw up a comprehensive will for themselves in no time, for no money, did not have wills. Consider the very different life situations contained in the following two cases.

Ted and Louise

Ted and his girlfriend Louise lived together for nine years. For most of that time, they saw no reason to get married even though they were committed to each other. They said that their bond, though it was not legal, was much stronger. But their plans to have children changed that. In fact, they were going to be married in early October of 2001. But a tragedy, 9/11, intervened. Louise was killed when the second tower at the World Trade Center collapsed.

Consistent with their beliefs about legal documents, neither Ted nor Louise had a will. When Ted was asked, he said that both he and Louise were common people, had next to nothing in assets, and besides, "Who expects to die in their 20s?" While no one could bring Louise back, an executed will or marriage a few weeks earlier would have changed things financially. Louise's parents were the statutory designated beneficiaries, not Ted. The average payout for 9/11 victims was over $2 million.

Hillary

In contrast to Louise, Hillary was one of the heirs to a retailing fortune. She was brought up in style and never had to worry about money. Actually, she lived fairly modestly, but she maintained her parents' values of caring financially for her children and donating money to charity.

Hillary was a rebellious child who balked at her parents' supervision, which carried through to her present age, which was 60. She had no financial knowledge and no financial advisors, a potentially lethal combination. In fact, she had little more than a will. She was freely gifting money to her children and to charities, a few thousand dollars at a time. She said why not do so, given her eight-figure fortune. One child in particular seemed particularly needy. Hillary's reason for the visit with the advisor was to program an efficient way of stepping up her gifting.

The advisor evaluated her situation, projecting her income, expenses, assets, and gifting policy. He found that if her present program continued, she would be broke in less than 15 years. When he explained her vulnerability, she was shocked and asked that the figures be rechecked, which was done.

The advisor recommended several changes in strategy, including a change in gifting strategy to her daughter and in gifting to many members of her daughter's family and gifting stocks with built-in gains to charities instead of cash. Both changes were made to take advantage of tax benefits. He set up trusts. And perhaps most important, he persuaded Hillary to cut back on gifting during her lifetime in favor of leaving money at her death, a safer approach.

The advisor chuckled when he thought about her situation. While no one needed to cry over her circumstances, it was interesting that even very affluent people needed to have controls, estate planning limits to protect them from an untimely negative outcome.

OVERVIEW

Estate planning is what we do principally to protect and benefit others we care about after we die. According to pure economic and financial theory, we are supposed to be interested solely in our own well-being. Any consideration of others comes out of a contractual relationship to provide mutual services in our own interests. In practice, however, we are often concerned about household members and other people, which often gives rise to the focus on estate planning. For more on this issue, see Appendix I.

From a household enterprise standpoint, we are planning for a period when the wage earner is incapacitated or has died. The goal is to keep the household functioning efficiently. In some ways, it resembles the succession planning by key executives of a business for the period beyond their active management. The household is maintained until the last member reaches adulthood, remarries, or dies. The responsibility is there whether you believe the obligation arises from a businesslike contract or true concern.

We have several financial planning objectives. The first is to pay as little in taxes as possible. In that way we can distribute the maximum to our heirs. The second is to match amount and type of assets to be distributed to circumstances and our wishes. The next is to leave other heirs with little or no conflict wherever possible. A final objective is to protect ourselves while we are still alive.

This chapter will deal with the estate planning decision-making process as a series of steps that should be executed. Sometimes, particularly when planning is complex, the approach will be established with the assistance of an attorney who will draw up the final documents. However, the financial aspects, particularly the financial calculations such as projected resource availabilities, are generally beyond a lawyer's scope. The end result can be termed an estate plan. The steps of such planning are given in Figure 15.1.

FIGURE 15.1

Estate Planning Steps

ESTATE PLANNING

1) Understand what estate planning is
2) Identify objectives
3) Identify assets
4) Establish a will
5) Consider other estate planning tools to meet objectives
6) Evaluate obstacles and ways to overcome them
7) Become familiar with all types of relevant taxes
8) Determine available financial-planning strategies
9) Incorporate estate risks
10) Consider separately estate planning for minors
11) Assess anticipated resources
12) Finalize the estate plan
13) Implement the plan
14) Review periodically

UNDERSTAND WHAT ESTATE PLANNING IS

Estate planning is analyzing and deciding on how your assets are to be managed and apportioned to others in the event of your death or disability. The goal is to establish an estate structure that will maximize assets left to your beneficiaries and achieve your other wishes in an efficient way. That structure may just be a simple will. On the other hand, if needed, it could include an elaborate system of trusts and other mechanisms intended to minimize taxes and strengthen your ability to accomplish your objectives.

The estate planning process can extend from accumulating the assets to be left along with retirement planning sums to managing those assets properly, and ultimately to distributing them as intended. The process, while varying in the amount of supervision needed, can be the same whether it is for a large estate or just to ensure that some family heirlooms are protected and go to the appropriate party. As you can see, estate planning is not reserved just for the wealthy; it concerns virtually everyone.

IDENTIFY OBJECTIVES

Estate planning uses financial and legal inputs, among others, to accomplish personal objectives. Clearly, the objectives, which vary widely from person to person, need to be known at the beginning. The key question, then, is, What am I trying to accomplish? Am I trying to set aside monies for the people with the greatest need? Alternatively, do I want to provide for people I care most about? Do I want to gift at least in part now or wait until my death?

When we speak of maximization of assets as an objective, we have to decide on the priority that we give to others as compared with ourselves. To pick extremes, for some, estate planning is giving to others only what is left over after you die. On the other end, estate planning might mean assigning a higher priority to lifetime gifting and bequest procedure by specifically providing a stated sum for beneficiaries—for example, saying that your three children will receive $100,000 each means that $300,000 will not be available for your own use.

IDENTIFY ASSETS

All household assets currently available should be identified and their owner specified. Information should include whether assets are jointly or separately owned, the original cost, and current fair market value. The total amount, cost, and way that assets are titled are relevant to the outcome strategies that you will select.

ESTABLISH A WILL

A will is often the most important document in estate planning. A **will** is a legal instrument that specifies who is to receive a person's assets upon death[1] and that expresses other wishes. Everyone has a will whether he or she knows it or not. If you don't execute one, the state in effect provides one for you—but uses its standards and wishes, not yours.

To be legally recognized, a will must conform to certain requirements. For example, generally it must be in writing and be witnessed.[2] The will generally follows a structured format, including clauses for who gets what assets and for the powers of the **executor,** who is in charge of administering the estate,[3] complying with legal requirements, and liquidating its assets. There is also a clause designating a **guardian,** where appropriate, who is in charge of people unable to care for themselves—for example, any children.

General Evaluation

A will, even if legally recognized, should be evaluated for a number of factors, including the following:

1. Does the will reflect your wishes? Most people have their wills written by a lawyer. Lawyers can inform you about requirements and alternatives and make sure you comply with legal requirements. However, they cannot always reflect your wishes within one draft. You should examine the draft and, where necessary, have it modified to express your wishes.

2. Are your wishes unambiguously stated in the will? Make sure who gets what is clearly stated and generally that the terminology in the will is easy to understand.

3. Once written, is the will completely up to date? Personal circumstances change, and so does tax law. Your current will should be examined periodically to ensure that it complies with your needs at the time. Wills often can be modified by a simple "codicil."

4. Are there overlooked assets? Are there assets that you have strong feelings about? If so, they should be individually described and who they are meant for should be separately stated.

5. Can the will cause conflict? If the beneficiaries are likely to have negative feelings because of its contents, consider modifying the will to reduce or eliminate the problem.

6. Is the will stored in a safe place?[4] If the will can't be found, it is as if you don't have one.

7. Does the will comply with state law? State laws differ in many requirements. One is the number of witnesses needed at the time of signing. This item can be particularly important when you don't use a lawyer to draw up a will or when you move to another state.

[1] Except for assets that have designated beneficiaries, which are discussed later in the chapter.
[2] Some states recognize an oral will when there is an immediate possibility of death, and some states allow handwritten wills without witnesses.
[3] When a person dies without a will, the person in charge of supervising the estate is called an **administrator,** not an executor.
[4] Common places can be in a locked drawer with valuables in the home where it can be found by heirs and in the safe deposit box. The lawyer who drew it up usually has a copy as well. Since it is usually stored in a vault, it may be the least likely to be misplaced, and most easily accessible.

TABLE 15.1 **One Possible Division of Assets**

Personal Situation	Spouse	Children	Parents	Sisters and Brothers	Nieces, Nephews, and Other Closest Relatives
Married with 1 child	50%	50%			
Married with 2 or more children	33%	67% E			
Married—children dead	33%	67% among grandchildren			
Married—no children, parents alive	50%		50%		
Married—no children, parents dead	50%			50%E	
Married—no children, no parents, no brothers or sisters, nieces or nephews	100%				
Unmarried with children		100%E			
Unmarried—no children, no parents				100%E	
Unmarried—no children, no parents, no brothers or sisters					100%E
No relatives found					100% to state

Note: E = equally divided.

8. If there are assets in other states, make sure that the will complies with their laws as well.

Intestate

Many people do not have a will. Possible reasons include not recognizing its importance, believing you don't have assets worth giving away, feeling when young that you have time to set one up, having difficulty determining whom to name as heirs or as executors or guardians, and finding the subject too uncomfortable to think about. **Intestate** means dying without a will. The division of assets depends on the applicable state and sometimes on the size of your assets as well as how they are titled. Table 15.1 provides one possible breakdown. Keep in mind that moving to a neighboring state can result in a completely different division of assets.

As you can see, dying without a will can have significant consequences.

Selected Reasons for Having a Will

Some selected reasons for having a will are listed below.

1. You may want your spouse to receive all your assets. Instead, he or she may often receive only a fraction of them.
2. States may mandate that assets be given to elderly parents who may not need the money.[5] Giving your assets to them could cause an estate tax many years earlier as compared with leaving that money to someone younger who has a longer-expected life span.
3. In the event that there is no surviving spouse, the guardian of any children would be selected by the court, which might assign a person other than the one you would prefer.
4. Your particular wishes as to who gets items of sentimental worth would not be accommodated.

[5] The state statute.

5. When your intentions are not stated, conflict over the distribution of assets becomes more likely.

6. The assets would pass to the children at age 18 or 21 when they might not be mature enough to handle this responsibility.

7. Important friends are entitled to nothing. As discussed, if you were engaged to be married, that person would probably not receive anything.

8. As discussed, many items vary by state. For example, in some states, when the second marriage has no children and there is no will, money is given to estranged children of the first marriage even when the second spouse is in desperate need of funds.

9. The will can provide for tax-advantaged trusts.

The argument that you do not have material assets may be erroneous. For example, in the event of your death from an accident, your estate could receive the proceeds of a wrongful death lawsuit brought by your executor.

In sum, virtually anyone can benefit from having a will. Having a lawyer draw up a will is generally not that costly and will significantly reduce the risk of nonqualification or incorrect meaning or vague terms in do-it-yourself wills sold in stationery stores.

CONSIDER OTHER ESTATE PLANNING TOOLS TO MEET OBJECTIVES

We have already discussed a will, a basic document that all people should have. There are a variety of other instruments that can help in overall estate planning. They include trusts, gifts, titling, insurance, powers of attorney, and letters of instruction.

Trusts

Trusts are separate legal entities in which a third party manages property for the benefit of another person.[6] The person who manages the trust assets is called the **trustee.** The trustee is considered a fiduciary, meaning he or she must act in the best interests of the person the trust is established for. The person to whom the property is given or for whom the property is being managed is called the **beneficiary.** The person setting up the trust to comply with his or her own specifications is called the **grantor** or **trustor.** A trust is created by a written document. It can be highly flexible, accommodating many wishes of the grantor. It can be established by a will to take effect on death.

Some common reasons for setting up a trust are

- *To obtain professional management.* The person setting up the trust may believe that the beneficiary is unable, because of age, education, or personality, to handle his or her affairs. The trustee is charged with fiduciary responsibility to make decisions in the beneficiary's best interests. The duties can include transferring assets, managing those assets including obtaining an investment subadvisor where necessary, and distributing assets. For example, a trust may be set up for a minor and extend well into adulthood. In the meantime, the trustee may not only manage the assets but, if given the power in the trust document, decide whether interim payments of principal, such as one for starting a business or going to college, are worthwhile to fund.

- *For tax purposes.* Certain trusts can provide significant tax benefits. For example, bypass trusts, which will be discussed later, can save money in taxes.

- *For control purposes.* An outright gift is not reversible. A revocable trust can put the ultimate beneficiary in place to receive the gift or inheritance but maintain the grantor's influence over the beneficiary since the trust can be changed or abolished.

---

[6] In some states, grantors can be their own sole trustees.

- *To bypass probate.* Probate is the procedure after a person's death where the will is validated and the period during which the court supervises the administration of estate assets. It is viewed by some as bothersome and costly and exposes their assets to public scrutiny. Placing assets in trust bypasses the probate process and may allow a person's affairs to remain private.
- *To strengthen protection from creditors and dissatisfied relatives.* Since a trust is a separate legal entity, placing assets into it often can protect them from creditors and people who believe they did not get their rightful share of assets.
- *To consolidate management.* Trusts can provide consolidated management of property where there are several beneficiaries and centralized decision making is needed. The heirs may dispute items or be otherwise incapable of managing the property themselves or assigning someone to handle the task.
- *To provide for different people over time.* A trust can provide for one person during his or her lifetime and then give the remaining principal to another.

The disadvantages of setting up a trust are

- *Cost.* It can be costly to set up a trust. Moreover, as a separate entity, the trust has to file a tax return each year, which can involve an ongoing fee to a professional.
- *Deviation from the grantor's wishes.* Trustees are charged with the duty to act in the beneficiary's interest according to the terms of the trust. However, there is often considerable leeway in interpreting that mandate and trustees may perform in a way inconsistent with the wishes of the grantor. They also may clash with the beneficiaries in interpreting the trust or just do not get along well with them due to conflicts in personality.
- *Effort required to set up.* Certain trusts can require effort to set up—for example, changing the title to all trust assets.
- *Resentment.* The beneficiaries may resent the fact that the grantor did not leave the assets to them outright.

Clearly, the selection of the trustee is very important. As with an executor, the trustee can be someone you know, a bank, or a professional advisor. The advantages of a spouse, relative, or friend are familiarity with your circumstances, close individual attention, and, in many cases, lower cost. The advantage of a bank or advisor is experience in handling similar situations, an ability to closely interpret the mandate of the trust without fear of affecting personal relationships, and, in the case of a bank, perpetual existence of the trustee. Where the grantor believes it is best, two or three trustees may be named to act in concert. Figure 15.2 summarizes the advantages and disadvantages of setting up a trust.

Trusts can be separated by various characteristics. These include whether they are living or testamentary trusts and whether they are revocable or irrevocable. (You can read about many types of trusts in Appendix IV.)

Living Trust

A **living trust** is one set up during a grantor's life. Living trusts have become popular in certain regions as a method for the elderly to organize their assets and place them in position for professional management by an independent trustee in the event of disability or for disposition of assets at death. Until then the grantor can be the trustee.

Testamentary Trust

A **testamentary trust** is provided for in the will and comes about after death. Proponents of testamentary trusts believe that living trusts are sometimes unnecessary.

FIGURE 15.2   The Advantages and Disadvantages of Setting Up a Trust

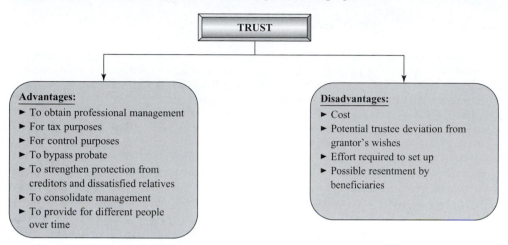

```
                          TRUST
```

Advantages:
► To obtain professional management
► For tax purposes
► For control purposes
► To bypass probate
► To strengthen protection from creditors and dissatisfied relatives
► To consolidate management
► To provide for different people over time

Disadvantages:
► Cost
► Potential trustee deviation from grantor's wishes
► Effort required to set up
► Possible resentment by beneficiaries

They say the net present value of the cost of setting up a living trust is high since the outlay for expenses can come many years earlier and bypassing probate in many states does not save much money. They recognize, however, that a living trust can be advantageous in other circumstances.

Revocable Trust

A **revocable trust** is one that can be revoked or changed by the grantor whenever desired. It allows the grantor to view the trust's workings and make alterations whenever circumstances change or even to terminate the trust with the assets returned. Generally, a revocable trust becomes irrevocable at the grantor's death. It usually has no impact on gift or estate taxes.

Irrevocable Trust

An **irrevocable trust** is one that cannot be altered. Its main advantage over other trusts is the ability to qualify for favorable estate tax treatment. In order to qualify, all incidents (characteristics) of ownership by the grantor must be given up. Its disadvantage is, of course, the finality of the decision. As with a gift, care must be taken that the grantor has enough capital to provide for the household and will not regret the trust decision later due to a shortage of funds. Irrevocable trusts usually have gift tax and/or estate tax consequences.

Gifts

Gifts, a major estate planning tool, are irrevocable transfers of property to others. They are called *intervivos* transfers because they happen while the giftor is alive. Gifts can be made for any number of reasons. From a theoretical standpoint, they are like **bequests,** which take place by will after the donor's death. Both often have concern for others as a reason for giving the sum. Gifts, as opposed to bequests, can provide funds when needed, thereby raising the satisfaction of the recipient and providing donors with the satisfaction of observing their gifts providing pleasure. Common reasons for gifting include giving funds for college education or for down payments on a home, items for newborns, and jewelry that others will use and enjoy and for reducing ultimate estate taxes.

In order for an item to be considered a gift, it must be given without any characteristics of control left with the giftor. That means the giftor cannot normally influence the gift after

Gifts are sometimes used as a method of helping particular children in need without having to deal with the conflict-producing approach of unequal bequests. The funds could be said to be available for any one of the offspring in need at that moment. In some cases, the other beneficiaries may never have to be made aware of it. Where the need is only short term, however, the gift could be deducted from that person's ultimate bequest share.

it has been given, as, for example, by taking it back. Nor can the item be exchanged for an agreement to provide a contra gift or service. It would then be a contract, and any gift portion would be represented by the excess of the value of the gift over the value of the services to be received.

Example 15.1

Ernesto told his son he was giving him $10,000, which his son could keep if he graduated from college. Is that a gift?

The answer is no because his son would have to give the money back if he didn't graduate. Ernesto retained a characteristic of control.

Gifts are combined with estate assets to establish the exemption from estate taxes. That means that the fair market value of any gift will be deducted from each person's lifetime exemption. The first $1 million of lifetime gifts will not be subject to federal taxes.[7] In other words, in the vast majority of cases in which, say, $1 million isn't gifted, in contrast to what some people believe, there is no current tax to be paid on gifts by either the giftor or the recipient. In smaller estates, no federal estate or gift tax will be due at all.

An exception is a gift of property. The recipient there takes the cost basis of the person providing the gift. When the property is sold, the recipient will pay an income tax at capital gains rates on the difference between the proceeds received and the cost basis.

Example 15.2

Flynn received a gift of his parent's home when they moved into a retirement community. The house had cost them $25,000 and was worth $240,000 at the time of the gift. He never lived in it and sold it five years later for $425,000. His basis for cost purposes was $25,000. He had to pay taxes on a gain of $400,000.

There are many types of gifts that don't count as a deduction from the lifetime exemption, an additional benefit. Here we discuss three.

Gifts between Married People

An unlimited number of gifts are allowed between husband and wife, regardless of their amount.[8]

Gifts of Under $11,000 per Year

Each person is allowed to make a gift of $11,000 per year per person without it affecting the $1 million lifetime gift tax exemption or the amount of the combined gift-estate tax exemption. Spouses can combine their deduction to gift $22,000 per year to each person. If they wished to, for their child's family of four they could gift $88,000 per year by gifting $22,000 to each member.

There is nothing to stop anyone who had the desire and the funds to do so from gifting $11,000 to an unlimited number of people without triggering a gift tax. Clearly, gifting where appropriate can reduce estate taxes. Gifts over the $11,000 level per person per year will reduce the uniform lifetime tax exemption by the amount the gift exceeds $11,000.

[7] Unless it happens in 2010, when no tax is due. Note that the estate tax exemption grows through 2009 while the gift tax exemption remains level.

[8] There are special rules for noncitizens.

Example 15.3 Helena gave her daughter jewelry worth $50,000. Will she pay a gift tax that year? By how much will her $1 million lifetime exemption be reduced?

As discussed, she will not pay a gift tax. Her lifetime gift tax exemption would be reduced from $1 million to $961,000. The first $11,000 of the $50,000 gift is excluded, and the remaining $39,000 is deducted from the $1 million exemption.

Charitable Gifts

Charitable gifts are also not subject to lifetime exemption. Although there are some limitations for allowable deductions for income tax purposes, an unlimited amount of money may be donated to charitable institutions for estate tax purposes. A charitable contribution is income tax–deductible based on its fair market value at the time of the gift. Gifts to charities may be made outright or with some benefits to be received through trusts set up for that purpose.

Two principal types of charitable trusts for gifting purposes are charitable remainder trusts and charitable lead trusts. Under a **charitable remainder trust,** the donor receives a stream of annual income for a fixed period or for life, and the remainder is given to the charity. The NPV of the remainder portion is deductible for income tax purposes.

Under the **charitable lead trust,** the charity receives the stream of income for a designated term, and the balance thereafter goes to an heir. The income tax deduction in this case comes from the NPV of the charity's income received.

Either trust's benefits increase when the gift is in the form of property that would have high taxable profits on sale that is donated instead of being sold on the open market. In that case, there is no income or estate taxation on the sale of an appreciated property. On the other hand, the government will not allow tax benefits for any charitable transaction that lacks charitable intent.

Titling and Transferring of Assets

Many people believe that a will is the final determinant of who will have legal ownership of a deceased's property. In reality, this is often not true.[9] It is very important to determine the way an asset is titled, not only for inheritance but for tax purposes as well. In this section, we look at property that is owned by two people.

Joint Property

Property owned jointly with someone else can be titled in one of three ways: joint tenancy with right of survivorship, tenancy by the entirety, and tenancy in common.

- **Joint tenancy with right of survivorship (JTWROS)** allows a person to automatically inherit the property upon the death of the other owner. The surviving co-owner's right to the property takes precedence over the provisions stated in a will and, as mentioned, bypasses probate. A common joint tenancy is a bank account. The account should clearly state that it is a joint tenancy and should recognize the right of the other to inherit the property upon the death of the co-owner.

- **Tenancy by the entirety,** the second form of joint ownership, is only allowed in some states. In many respects, it is like JTWROS. In the event of death, the surviving co-owner receives full ownership. However, it is only available to married persons and, unlike JTWROS, can only be undone by consent of both parties.

- In **tenancies in common** each co-owner owns a specified percentage of a property. That percentage may be different from the amount invested. There can be any number of co-owners. The sale of an interest is permitted and, in the event of death, the interest

[9] A will is often superseded. For example, beneficiaries of a life insurance policy or bank account will inherit the money even if the will stipulates that the same beneficiary will have no share of the decedent's assets. Also, a spouse generally can inherit a certain percentage of the assets whether provided for in the will or not. A possible exception is where there is a prenuptial agreement.

will pass to the individual's heirs, not the co-owners unless so specified. When there is no indication of type of tenancy, it will be assumed to be a tenancy in common. When one owner in a JTWROS sells his or her share of assets, the ownership form becomes tenancy in common.[10]

Trust Ownership of Property

Property owned by a trust is usually treated the same way as property owned by an independent entity. It is subject to similar tax treatment based on income generated and any tax-related benefits. The trustee is responsible for preserving trust assets and attempting to enhance their value over time.

Marital versus Separate Property

Marital property refers to rights in property gained through marriage. It may be in your spouse's property or in property deemed to have mutual marital rights. **Separate property** is an asset owned entirely by a person. Generally, assets owned before marriage and gifts and inheritances made specifically to a person are considered separate property—but only if they are kept in separate accounts.

Why do we care about distinguishing between marital and separate property? Because it can determine who is entitled to receive the assets at death or divorce. For example, if pre- and postmarriage gifts and property inherited are jointly titled, they may be deemed to be a tenancy in entirety. In such case, premarital property that if separately titled would have gone to the decedent's heirs but is intermingled could now be given to your spouse with the right to designate who receives it upon his or her death.

Surviving spouses have certain rights to property by law whether the decedent provided for them or not. Their rights will differ by state and may include ownership of a share of the decedent's assets, often one-third to one-half or a life estate. A **life estate** refers to rights to property while the spouse is alive but with no right to pass the rights on to heirs.

There are eight community property states in which the rules differ: Arizona, California, Idaho, Louisiana, Nevada, New Mexico, Texas, and Washington. Community property states make a clear distinction between marital and separate property and believe marriage forms a kind of business partnership in which assets accumulated during marriage are the equal property of both spouses, regardless of who earned the money. Equal rights to these assets in community property states stand in contrast to some of the other states in which who earned the money can help determine who is entitled to it.

Life Insurance

Life insurance has a number of potential roles in estate planning. These include liquidity, relative assurance of payment, and tax savings.

Liquidity

For people with considerable resources, estate taxation can be sizeable. There also may be other expenses such as funeral, burial, and business interruption. Decisions such as the sale of estate property could be compelled under less-than-optimal conditions. Buyers sometimes regard the term *estate sale* as a potential license to get a bargain. Life insurance can provide a ready source of cash flow, which can fund estate taxes and enable postponement of the sale of property and other business decisions to an optimal time.

Relative Assurance of Payment

Monies supposed to be set aside for beneficiaries may never be deposited, or they may be spent by the estate owner subsequent to their accumulation. Alternatively, the sums

---

[10] Unless a state statute provides otherwise.

invested may involve considerable investment risk. The insurance policy can provide the structure that enables a stated sum to be left to beneficiaries at death.

Escape from Probate and Spousal Election

Life insurance payable to others, whether from an ordinary policy or from a life insurance trust, escapes probate because it is not payable to the deceased or the estate. In addition, in some states, life insurance may not be subject to a requirement that husband or wife receive a certain minimum amount at death of their spouse.

Tax Savings

As a general rule, the proceeds from insurance arising from the death of a person are not subject to income taxation but are subject to estate taxation. There are generally a maximum of three parties to an insurance policy: the owner of the policy, the insured, and the beneficiary. When the owner is also the insured, the amount will be taxable for estate purposes. However, in most cases where the proceeds are payable to another beneficiary and all incidents of ownership are eliminated by the insured, no estate taxes will be assessed on the estate of the insured.

Therefore, life insurance can be a viable way of reducing estate taxes. Ownership of a policy can be transferred to another person, say a child,[11] or a new policy established. The ongoing contributions to pay for the policy would come from the parent. Amounts contributed in excess of $11,000 per person or $22,000 per couple would be considered a gift. Sometimes the cash value of a policy is borrowed before a transfer since its value at that time is also considered a gift.

Life Insurance Trust

As with other types of trusts, the life insurance trust must be irrevocable to qualify for estate tax savings. Sometimes this trust is "funded," which means there are enough other assets placed in the trust to cover the annual premium payment. Certain procedures must be followed in how gifts are made for insurance payment purposes so that they are not included as part of the deceased person's estate. A life insurance trust may be used when outright gift of the policy to the beneficiary is not desired. That could happen if the grantor was afraid the new owner would cash in the proceeds or change the beneficiary.

Life insurance and the life insurance trust can be viewed as an alternative to a gifting plan. Both insurance payments and cash gifts reduce the size of estates and can add to the assets of the beneficiary. The gift can be more efficient economically and more flexible, while the life insurance trust can better control the timing of payments and will be more productive in the event of a premature death.

Power of Attorney

A **power of attorney** is a legal document that lets someone act on your behalf. Powers of attorney will be discussed under incapacity.

Letter of Instruction

The final estate planning tool we will discuss is a letter of instruction. It is not a legal document. The **letter of instruction** is a supplement to a will that helps people understand your thinking and provides direction for matters to be accomplished. It can indicate where the will and other important papers are located as well as the telephone numbers of advisors and perhaps an evaluation of them. It can discuss sensitive family matters that an executor may find helpful such as conflicts, untrustworthy individuals, and so on. It can include burial wishes and provide a justification for certain life actions including those provided in the will.

---

[11] An exception is a policy transferred within three years of death, as discussed under tax savings.

EVALUATE OBSTACLES AND WAYS TO OVERCOME THEM

Obstacles are impediments to the estate planning process. They may be legal obstacles such as probate, but many stem from human variables such as lack of knowledge or discomfort in decision making. Finally, the obstacles can involve protecting minors as beneficiaries. Here we will discuss each of them separately.

Probate

Probate, as mentioned, is the process after a person's death when the court supervises the review procedures to facilitate fair assignment of estate assets. After all estate obligations have been taken care of, the court will approve termination of probate and the assets may be distributed.

Probate is sometimes viewed as a ponderous process, an obstacle particularly in certain states. This is because the procedures that must be followed result in expenditures and delay in distributing estate assets. Some lawyers recommend procedures to avoid probate, such as setting up a living trust and transferring all assets into it. Some other assets that bypass probate are (a) those that are titled joint with right of survivorship, (b) qualified pension plans such as IRA and 401(k) and nonqualified deferred compensation plans, and (c) proceeds from life insurance on the decedent's life payable to a named beneficiary other than the decedent or the estate of the decedent. Finally, probate opens up your private affairs to public scrutiny.

Probate has some significant advantages as well. The process places court-approved finality on the estate. Creditors are given an opportunity to present their claims in court, and, after probate is terminated, no further liabilities need be paid. Disputes between interested parties such as the heirs can be resolved by the court. Thus, after probate is over, beneficiaries know they have the assets free and clear of disputes.

Although there are costs in connection with probate in certain states, they may not be that significant, particularly after attorney's fees are deducted, which may, for the most part, be needed with or without probate. Therefore, establishing trusts that separately title assets to bypass probate in many situations may not be necessary.

Conflict

Conflict in estate planning matters can come about because of differences in opinion between spouses about who should be appointed for various estate administrative and supervisory tasks, concern over the receptivity of other interested parties to decisions made, or just internal conflict in making decisions when alternatives have strong strengths and weaknesses. Selected common conflicts are given below. Because of the personal nature of the decisions, overcoming these conflicts can be difficult. However, consultations with people who have made similar decisions, or with close friends, relatives, and, of course, spouses, can help. Often lawyers specializing in these issues also can provide insights.

Division of Assets

Perhaps the most difficult issue for many is how assets are to be divided, particularly for children. Should they be apportioned equally or based on another factor such as need or closeness of relationship? Equal apportionment has the advantage of objectivity. Need can be more subjective. Should need be related to the amount your beneficiaries make or to the amount of assets they have accumulated or should it be related to how happy they are in their current occupation, regardless of their income and assets?

The closeness of relationship may be characterized in many ways—for example, who visits most often and who performs the most services when you are elderly. On the other hand, should children be penalized because their jobs take them away from the area?

Practical Comment   Problems with Unequal Distributions

Many people are afraid to allocate on the basis of need, even though they find the approach attractive. They believe that if they do, money may be equated with personal regard for the child. They have heard stories about friends and relatives whose children felt slighted by receiving less than an equal share. They may not like the thought that a child could be angry with them, which they anticipate could happen if they used a need-based solution. In effect, they may be giving weight to their own discomfort in contemplating that outcome. Moreover, the children's relationship with siblings can be altered by the unequal distribution, which also may be included in the decision making. That may account for the fact that many opt for equality.[12] Where the division is to be unequal, the reasoning, however apparent, should generally be communicated to the child or children receiving the lower amount, either in person or in a letter attached to the will stressing that "money isn't equivalent to caring."

[12] See B. Douglas Bernheim and Sergei Severinov, " Bequests as Signals: An Explanation for the Equal Division Puzzle," *Journal of Political Economy* 111, no. 4 (August 2003), pp. 733–64.

Concern for others might suggest a need-based solution. A more businesslike rewarding for services rendered would indicate allocation on an unequal basis. However, the vast majority of people allocate equally among their children.[13]

Executors and Guardians

As mentioned, executors are assigned the task of administering the estate and carrying out the deceased's wishes. A good deal of the work is usually done by a lawyer, so many people select a person they are close to as executor. When the assets are not that substantial, the individual executor, who may not be paid, can be the most popular choice. The person selected should have the time, the concern, and a sense of fairness and practicality in going about the task of dividing up the estate. When assets are sizeable, sometimes professionals—particularly lawyers and bankers—are selected as executors.

Determining the guardian for your children in the event that both parents—you and your spouse—die can be a perplexing issue. Should it be the person who is concerned most about the child? Or is it more important to select someone who has done a good job of raising his or her own offspring? How important is it that the person share your values? How much weight should be given to his or her financial means? Sometimes the decision is clear, and at other times it can lead to uncertainty and conflict between husband and wife. Whoever is chosen should be informed and should assent to the selection. For a divorced couple, the guardianship may go to your former spouse no matter what your wishes may be.

The Age of Inheritance

Money left to minors will not be given to them until they become adults, which, depending on the state, will be defined as between 18 and 21 years of age. In the interim, it will be managed by a guardian you name, who need not be the same one who supervises your children. The question can be whether the child is mature enough to handle the money at the age he or she receives it. If not, at what age? Commonly, that age is thought to range from 18 to 35. In the absence of a trust, the monies will have to be distributed when the children reach adulthood. If a trust is set up, the trustee can be given discretion about

[13] See Mark O. Wilhelm, "Bequest Behavior and the Effect of Heirs' Earnings: Testing the Altruistic Model of Bequests," *American Economic Review* 86, no. 4 (September 1996), pp. 874–92. Research indicates that over two-thirds (68.6 percent) allocate evenly.

TABLE 15.2
Federal Estate
Taxation

Year	Estate Tax Exemption	Maximum Estate Tax	Step-Up in Basis Allowed
2006	$2,000,000	46%	Yes
2007	$2,000,000	45%	Yes
2008	$2,000,000	45%	Yes
2009	$3,500,000	45%	Yes
2010	Taxes repealed	0%	No[1]
2011	$1,000,000	55%	Yes

[1] Limited to $1.3 million for heirs and an additional $3 million for a spouse.

interim amounts for education or for other significant costs and a series of payments at whatever ages are specified.

BECOME FAMILIAR WITH ALL TYPES OF RELEVANT TAXES

Taxes are one of the most important factors in estate planning. There are three types of assessments in connection with planning in this area: estate, gift, and income taxation.

Estate Taxes

Estate taxes that are due after the death of the owner are based on assets owned at death. Only certain assets qualify. For example, those assets gifted or left to a spouse are not taxed until the surviving spouse's death. Estate taxes can be substantial since current rates can amount to almost 50 percent. Estate taxes should not be confused with income taxes, which also can add to the tax burden at death.

Estate tax law provides an exemption from taxation for initial asset accumulation. The exemption is in the form of a credit against taxes called a **unified credit.** In 2006, the tax on the first $2 million of assets owned per person will be credited.[14] The unified credit is the tax on the sum that is eliminated by the exemption.

Gift Taxes

Gifts used to be taxed separately, but lifetime transfers are now combined with estate assets to compile $1 million to $3.5 million total exemption (see Table 15.2). In other words, there is what is termed a unified gift and estate tax process in effect. As we've seen, certain gifts are not subject to taxation. Even though gift and estate taxes are combined for calculating any tax due, the exemption for lifetime gifts alone is limited to $1 million, with any amounts over $1 million subject to estate taxation.

Income Tax

Income taxes are assessments based on job-related and investment earnings. More relevant for estate matters, income taxes on gains on sale of assets are based on selling price minus original cost. In recognition of the sizeable estate and income taxes, Congress passed into law a bill providing that assets at death be given a fair-market-value basis for income tax purposes instead of the original cost. Basis can be viewed as the amount of an asset's value that isn't taxed. This new valuation for taxation purposes is called a **step-up in basis.** You have the option of selecting either the fair market value at the date of death or six months later for basis purposes, but your choice must be taken for the entire estate and not done separately by asset.[15]

The effect of the step-up in basis is to eliminate income taxation on unrealized capital gains at death for stocks, houses, and other assets that have appreciated during the period

[14] Those who are not U.S. citizens have separate requirements for estate and gift tax purposes.

[15] Fair market value may be established by published market prices, as in the case of stocks; by appraiser, as in the case of a home or a business; or through some other method.

since purchase. There is no benefit for unsold assets that have declined since original purchase. Their basis becomes the market value at death. Finally, assets in tax-sheltered accounts such as IRAs do not benefit from tax-favorable step-up in basis.[16]

Table 15.2 presents estate tax law as of the raising of the unified credit in 2000. Notice that as a quid pro quo for elimination of estate taxes for one year in 2010, the step-up in basis was eliminated. However, at the present time, the period after 2010 reverts to year 2001 rules, the $1 million exemption, and the step-up in basis. There are state estate taxes as well. They vary widely and may have greater impact on modest estates than on larger ones.

DETERMINE AVAILABLE FINANCIAL PLANNING STRATEGIES

A variety of financial planning strategies are available for estate consideration. Most of them, at least in part, have a numbers orientation, frequently with a potential for saving tax dollars. Those that are ultimately selected will depend, of course, on individual circumstances. Virtually any strategy considered for all but the very affluent will have to include the life cycle needs of the grantor. That means estate planning must incorporate retirement needs. Here are some basic strategies.

Consider a Bypass Trust

Taxes can be sizeable for estates having assets beyond the exempted amount. For those in that circumstance, about one-half of their assets will go for government taxation, resulting in lower sums accruing to heirs. People are entitled to their own unified credit. However, instead of using it and reducing ultimate total estate taxation, many people who are married individuals leave substantially all of their money to their spouses. In most circumstances, the spouse is the person they are principally concerned with. However, there is a trust alternative that, when suitable, can accomplish many of the family's goals yet save the heirs a substantial amount of money. The most common form of trust for doing this is called a bypass trust.

A **bypass trust**—also known as a **nonmarital, exemption-equivalent, type B,** or **credit shelter trust**—is a document that is set up while the grantor is alive or is provided for in the will. As mentioned, it must be irrevocable to qualify for tax savings. Under a bypass trust, funds are provided for two beneficiaries: the income beneficiary and the remainder person. The income beneficiary, normally the spouse, receives the income from the trust. The **remainder person** receives the principal remaining after the death of the income beneficiary.

Where the grantor doesn't exclude it, the surviving spouse may take not only income but five withdrawals of 5 percent of the principal each year or $5,000, whichever is larger. In fact, many lawyers permit the trustee other than the spouse to withdraw any amount necessary to cover spousal illness or just to maintain the spouse's ordinary and customary standard of living. For many surviving spouses, that may allow all the funding they require. Many lawyers also allow the surviving spouse to be a trustee (although not the sole trustee), in order to have some influence over how the trust is operated.

The principal benefit of the bypass trust, then, is the ability to use both the husband's and wife's unified credit to advantage while providing funds for the surviving spouse to live on. Potentially, this advantage can save hundreds of thousands of dollars in estate taxes, as you can see in Appendix II.

The amount placed in a bypass trust depends on the needs of the surviving spouse for principal. Clearly, only money in excess of projected living costs would be put there. The maximum that would make sense from a tax standpoint would be equal to the exclusion

---

[16] In a gift, as opposed to being a beneficiary, at death your basis is the owner's original cost or the market value at date of gift, whichever is lower.

Practical Comment Bypass Trusts and Control

There are many couples who care about their children and would like to save significant estate taxes yet will not set up a bypass trust. In some cases, this reluctance is attributable to the fear of a catastrophic illness, even though this can be addressed by careful will drafting. In other cases, it is due to the desire to maintain control over their money. Being accountable to someone else and potentially having to convince him or her that an outlay qualifies as ordinary and necessary or, more broadly, losing the option of using the entire estate assets, even if they will never do so, makes them uncomfortable. However, as estate assets rise well beyond the exclusion amount, when the couple has enough money in pension income to live on, their resistance often diminishes and many more people set one up.

amount. The balance of the money would be left outright to the spouse, assuming he or she is the primary beneficiary. Because of the unlimited marital deduction, the money left outright by the spouse would not be subject to estate taxation at that time.[17]

The primary disadvantage of a bypass trust is the inability of the beneficiary to have all the household funds available to spend.

In addition to the bypass trust, there are two other types of trusts that can qualify for the marital deduction and therefore will not be subject to taxation. They are the powers of appointment trust and the QTIP trust, both discussed in Appendix III.

Gifting versus Bequests

Giving money while you are still alive versus waiting until your death is often an active issue. As we saw, gifting provides resources when needed—say, for the down payment on a home—and allows you to observe the benefits of your gift. If the gifting is under the $11,000-per-person-per-year limit, it is a highly efficient tax-free transfer for those with significant assets that will be subject to estate tax.

Bequests, on the other hand, can be safer, allowing the grantor to maintain all assets for household use. They also can postpone providing assets to younger people when there is concern about negative influences of money on career choices and drive. Some people choose a combination of gifts and bequests.

Follow an Investment Policy for Estate Planning

Investment policy is generally the same for estate planning as it is for any long-term planning function such as retirement planning. Where the money has been set out exclusively for beneficiaries, however, the investment policy can take on the risk tolerance of the beneficiaries instead of the grantor.

Example 15.4

Mary Ann was perplexed. She wanted to provide as much money as possible to her heirs, her three children. On the other hand, she herself was very conservative and was afraid of losing her money. She asked the advisor for help.

The advisor performed a retirement plan analysis and found that, based on her lifestyle and investment in very-low-risk securities, she would need about half her current savings in retirement. He split her money 50 percent into U.S. government bonds for her use and 50 percent in a much more aggressive portfolio consistent with her children's risk preference. Mary Ann felt that the recommended asset allocation accommodated both her wishes.

---

[17] Here again, the regulations are different for those who are not U.S. citizens.

Where liquidity or estate taxation is an issue, life insurance can be considered as an investment asset in the asset allocation. For example, when the estate consists of a business that will be retained or is difficult to sell, insurance on the life of the grantor can provide the cash to pay off estate taxes.[18] Placing the insurance in a life insurance trust payable to the beneficiaries can take the proceeds out of the estate and bypass both estate and income taxes.

Consider Placing Monies in Joint Name in Smaller Estates

Where assets at death are not likely to reach federal unified credit limits and material state taxation levels, taxes may not be an issue. In that circumstance, placing money in joint accounts can ensure that the intended person receives the money quickly and free of probate expenditures.

On the other hand, be aware that you are providing another person with ownership rights in your estate while you're alive, which, under some circumstances, could result in significant financial losses. For example, either party may be allowed to withdraw the entire sum deposited. A dual signature required on withdrawals can help but may restrict your movement. Limiting joint accounts to people you absolutely trust or to monies that are needed for your support should be considered.

Where assets are or will be over the maximum estate exemption, you should take the opposite approach. Assets in joint name generally should be separated so that each qualifies for estate exemption purposes.

Integrate Estate and Income Tax Considerations in Planning

There are many occasions when possible actions involve a choice between an income tax and an estate tax. Often the alternative triggering an income tax comes first and the estate tax later at death. Before arriving at a decision, your goal should be to consider both by using a time value of money technique such as obtaining the NPV of both alternatives and selecting the one with the greatest sum made available net of taxes.

Gift Fast-Growing Assets

Assets that are expected to increase rapidly in value are often preferred gifting vehicles. They eliminate assets that can increase the estate's valuation and therefore estate taxes.

Pay Compensation to Executor on Large Estates

Large estates often have higher estate tax rates than income tax ones for beneficiaries. Consequently, paying an executor who is a beneficiary for his or her services can be advantageous.

Think about Designating Younger People as Heirs

Estate taxation repeats at each death of the owner. Therefore, the net present value of estate taxes is likely to be lower for each generation below yours that you provide for. Clearly, the least efficient way is to select another elderly person, say a father or mother, as a beneficiary. A second death that occurs after 10 years or more will result in a second full estate tax levied.[19] Generation-skipping trusts, provided you can do so for $2 million in total[20]

---

[18] Such insurance also might be especially useful to cover the estate tax on inherited IRAs and Roth IRAs. This will enable the beneficiary to utilize the tax deferral from the regular IRA and tax-free accumulation for the Roth IRA throughout much of his or her lifetime.

[19] Estate taxes for second death that occurs within 10 years are benefited by a credit that declines with time.

[20] For 2006–2008.

without triggering onerous extra taxation, can be attractive. Of course, consideration of the needs of the person who is your primary beneficiary and who may resent gifting to grand-children can take precedence.[21]

Give Consideration to the Step-Up in Basis

The step-up in basis can be a powerful antitax tool. The elimination of income taxes on assets with a low cost basis by retaining instead of selling should be considered by people who are elderly or seriously ill. When a spouse is seriously ill but expected to live for at least one year, the required minimum for this type of transaction to be effective, a gift of assets with low basis to that spouse may be an attractive alternative.

Example 15.5   Rod had a close relationship with his grandmother, now 93, and was one of her beneficiaries. She had a modest country home on the water in Cape Cod, Massachusetts. The home was bought for $15,000 when she was first married. Now it was worth $1 million. She was too old to use the house anymore and wanted to sell it. Rod explained to her that selling it would involve paying taxes of over $200,000. If they waited until her death, the estate would receive a step-up in basis and would not have to pay any income tax at all. They decided to wait and rent the house out in the meantime.

Pay Particular Attention to IRAs and Other Qualified Plans

Upon death, both estate and income taxes are due on qualified pension plans. Spouses have the option of electing a spousal rollover, which can defer current taxation. In a process somewhat similar to a rollover, nonmarital beneficiaries of an IRA can defer taxation upon death and take mandatory withdrawals based on their life expectancy. In order for this option to be available for the beneficiaries of the IRA, they must ensure the title of the account retains the name of the decedent. It should then state "for the benefit of the beneficiary."

INCORPORATE ESTATE RISKS

There are many risks to which estate plans are subject. The primary ones have been covered in risk management chapters. The two principal risks that are particularly relevant for estate planning are longevity and incapacity.

Longevity

The age at which death occurs has a significant effect on estate planning. Dying prematurely can alter all plans, including those of household members. Where there is a desire for a fixed or minimum amount to be given, whether to household members or others, it can be ensured using insurance on the estate owner's life, payable to the intended beneficiaries.

Ironically, dying in the period close to the retirement date can place greater resources in the hands of beneficiaries. That is because the retiree often has accumulated substantial sums for retirement. Unusually long lives (or large age-related medical or care benefits) can place retirement and therefore estate sums in jeopardy. An active gifting policy can increase the exposure.

A policy practiced by many people and proposed by some financial planners is to plan conservatively for retirement needs incorporating the possibility of living well past age 90, although it is likely that death will occur before that time. The remaining assets, possibly including a home, would then be made available to beneficiaries.

---

[21] A disadvantage is that the tax can be punitive if the limit is exceeded.

Incapacity

Incapacity, the inability to function on your own behalf because of sickness or some other reason, obviously can disrupt the normal functioning of the household. There are a number of legal documents that can help, including trusts, powers of attorney, and medical powers of attorney, which will now be discussed.

Health-Related Trusts

Trusts can be set up for almost any reason. In this case, a revocable living trust can provide the funding to administer a person's care under the supervision of a trustee when the person can no longer handle his or her own affairs. For example, for a person suffering from Alzheimer's and no longer considered mentally competent, an independent trustee could hire people to administer home care or to ensure that the person is well taken care of in a nursing home.

Durable Power of Attorney

A power of attorney is a legal document that lets someone act on your behalf. A **durable power of attorney** remains in effect over time with the amount of power and the circumstances under which it can be used stated in the document. A durable power of attorney survives incompetency. You might want to give someone a power of attorney when expertise is required and you are not equipped to handle the matter yourself, when you are out of the country and a business matter may come up, when you are ill, or in a host of other circumstances.

The power may be temporary or potentially permanent, specified to stay in effect until revoked. It may be limited to specific areas or it may be a general power. The form itself is intended to affirm that person's ability to act, which, in a durable general power, is not affected by any subsequent incapacity of the person giving it.

If a person becomes senile, a durable power generally eliminates the need for the court to appoint a guardian or a conservator. The durable power of attorney is less costly than a living trust. If the power of attorney is not worded as a durable one, it will terminate on the disability of the person, as it becomes legally invalid. The durable power terminates upon the death of the person.

A **springing power of attorney** does not take effect until a specific event stated in the document occurs, such as incompetency. For example, it could come into effect when the person is mentally or physically disabled. Its weakness is a potential problem in determining whether that event has occurred. This can make it difficult for the person possessing the power to be recognized by third parties as legally able to act.

Medical Power of Attorney

A **medical power of attorney,** also called a **health care power of attorney,**[22] allows someone else to make medical decisions when you are not capable of doing so yourself. It is used because a general durable power of attorney is not recognized in medical matters. This format is stronger than a living will, which also can indicate definitive beliefs about your right to refuse artificial treatment to prolong your life.

CONSIDER SEPARATELY ESTATE PLANNING FOR MINORS

Children are treated separately because they are deemed incapable of handling their own affairs. Gifts to them have a tax advantage. As we saw in Chapter 14, when children are under 14, the first $800 of income on investments owned is not taxable and the next $800

---

[22] Or a **health care proxy.**

Practical Comment Powers of Attorney

Powers of attorney can be a simple, cost-effective way of having someone represent your interests. However, the person giving it should be aware that it can be very powerful and, if placed in the wrong hands, can have substantial impact, financial and otherwise. Any powers given should be thought through first as to the trust and competence of the person being considered and, where a general power is not called for, should be carefully worked out as to the specific duties and limitations on those duties.

---

is taxed at the child's low tax rate. The rest of their investment income will be taxed at the parent's marginal rate. On the other hand, children or even young adults may be viewed as not capable of handling monies. For example, there may be concern that they would spend the money without thinking about the long-term effects.

Under the Uniform Gifts to Minors Act,[23] a donor can make a gift to a minor and have a guardian supervise that gift in a way similar to that of a guardian acting as a trustee. This right may be limited to financial assets; and if the donor acts as custodian and dies, the money will remain in the donor's estate for estate tax purposes. Moreover, it must be terminated when the minor reaches adulthood, which, depending on the state, is between the ages of 18 and 21.

A trust for minors called a 2503C trust can be set up. It provides more flexibility. Many kinds of assets, including property, can be placed into it. Any outlays of income from the trust must be spent on behalf of the child and the money distributed when the child becomes 21. Income spent is taxed to the recipient and that reinvested income is taxed at the trust's rate. If the grantor is not the trustee, it will not be includable in the grantor's estate.[24]

If you want to provide for extension beyond age 21 and the sums are considerable, a trust may be the best solution. It can allow the trustee the flexibility to vary the terms of payout, if you wish.

Bank accounts set up with the words "in trust for" or "trustee for" are not gifts nor are they, technically, a trust. The donor can withdraw the monies at any time. The income on the sum will be taxable to the donor, not the child, and the sum accumulated will be part of the donor's estate. At the donor's death, the sum will be transferred to the child and will not go through probate.

When the child or children have disabilities, special actions may be called for. A special needs trust may be set up that can be instituted when the beneficiary is a child or during adulthood. It can provide financial support or be considerably broader, providing for supervision of operating functions. When the disability is covered by government support, care must be taken to ensure that the trust does not disqualify that aid. See Chapter A on the Web site for more information on the special needs trust.

ASSESS ANTICIPATED RESOURCES

The amount of current assets accumulated was established earlier in the PFP process. Here we are projecting what resources will be available for estate planning. Since the date of death is not known, the figure will be an estimate. Where amounts are specifically set aside

---

[23] Called in some states Uniform Transfers to Minors Act.

[24] If the child is given the option of taking the money out at age 21 and refuses, the trust terms can provide for extension beyond that age. The grantor may suggest to the beneficiary separately that if the money is withdrawn, additional sums that are potentially in excess of those in the trust will not be forthcoming.

TABLE 15.3   **Summary of Estate Planning Tools**

Document	Characteristic	Material Tax Advantage	Principal Advantages	Principal Disadvantages
Will	Provides for division of untitled assets upon death	Possibly[1]	Legally recognized document of wishes	None
Gift	Transfers assets when alive	Yes	Flexible Giftor can observe benefit Reduces size of estate	Loss of control over asset
Trust	Separate entity with trustee managing property	Possibly	Expertise Protects against disputes Bypasses probate Flexibility	Costs Potential risk of inappropriate actions by trustee Effort to set it up
Durable power of attorney	Allows someone to act for you	No[2]	Inexpensive Flexible	Risk of financial loss through delegation of control
Medical power of attorney	Allows someone to act for you in medical affairs when you are incapacitated	No	Specific power to take or approve medical actions	Risk attached to having inappropriate actions taken
Joint account	Share in control	No	Bypasses probate Quick liquidity Targeted beneficiary	Risk of financial loss through delegation of control

[1] Where the will provides for tax-advantaged trusts.
[2] Except for making tax-exempt deathbed gifts.

for estate planning and not used for retirement planning purposes as well, the figure will be easier to ascertain.

The total amount projected as available will help determine the tools and strategies used. For example, if $400,000 is likely to be a peak sum, holding assets in joint name may be the strategy used, whereas a $4,000,000 ultimate sum could result in an extremely different approach.

FINALIZE THE ESTATE PLAN

This step integrates the original objectives, which are typically both financial and personal. In other words, it combines estate planning tools and strategies with personal wishes about who gets what. The strategies and tools will attempt to maximize assets; selecting those that achieve the purpose depends on circumstance.

Table 15.3 is a summary of estate planning tools available and the advantages and disadvantages of using them.

IMPLEMENT THE PLAN

Implementation involves drawing up the legal documents by the estate attorney and the actions that the grantor must take. For example, if a living trust is set up, the assets that are going to be part of it must be transferred in. If, on the other hand, the estate plan calls for more equal separation of spousal assets, then transfer from one spouse to the other must take place.

REVIEW PERIODICALLY

Estate planning is one of those financial areas that should be reviewed fairly frequently. Economic circumstances change and people's opinions on what they want to do with their monies and their other wishes can shift over time. Besides, tax and other estate planning laws are altered by the government and new tax strategies arise.

Practical Comment Implementation

Although the implementation part of the process may appear pro forma, particularly after the time and expense of engaging in estate planning, a surprisingly large number of people don't do it. Whether because of lingering uncertainty about decisions made, the effort needed to complete the procedures, ignorance, or some other reason, too many legal documents stand as empty shells.

An understanding of the behavior patterns of people, including the need for prodding by the financial planner or lawyer, can be helpful. For example, financial planners almost always recommend a will. When they do, if they also schedule an appointment with the lawyer while the client is present, the odds of successful completion increase considerably.

Back to Dan and Laura
ESTATE PLANNING

The meeting we had on estate planning did not take very long. Dan and Laura did not have wills. They agreed that the executor of the will should be Dan's older brother. They couldn't agree on who would be the guardians of their children should there be a joint accident. Dan wanted his older brother; he was well-established and could provide the monies to have the children live comfortably, and he shared the same values the couple had. Laura wanted her sister to take care of them. She said that although her sister's lifestyle was more "counterculture" and she and her husband lived modestly, she really cared for their children and had already formed a relationship with Brian. In the event one of them died, Dan and Laura agreed that they wanted 100 percent of their money to go to the surviving spouse. With a smile on his face, Dan added, "We have time to get a will. We don't plan to leave anytime soon."

As for bequests, Laura wanted each child to be guaranteed a substantial sum as her parents planned to do for her. She planned to leave each child $100,000. Dan said that their investment in their children in the form of college aid was enough. Besides, he said, both children were likely to receive a significant sum since the probability was that Dan and Laura wouldn't live until age 95 as funded for in the retirement planning section. Dan's opinion carried the day, but I had the feeling Laura would bring it up again later in their lives.

Estate planning is the method of providing for your heirs according to your wishes in a tax-efficient manner. You are at a relatively young age in your marital lives with limited assets now. Estate planning is relatively simple. I have assumed that there will be two children, as is your wish, as you are well on the way to fulfilling that intention.

My principal objective here is to get you to obtain a will. There are many people who say they should have a will but, for whatever reason, never actually do it. If you die intestate (without a will), the state will determine the division of your assets. For example, if Dan were to pass away in this state, the children would receive half of the assets. I know, Dan, that you want Laura to receive all of your assets. And you are correct, Dan, that the likelihood is you will both live long lives, but the will provides important protection in the event of a premature outcome.

The issue of who should be guardian is a contentious one and beyond the scope of the financial plan. I am confident that you will select the person who is best suited to raising your children.

Even giving the effect to the potential insurance proceeds, should either of you pass away while being covered by life insurance, you are both well under the federal estate and gift tax minimums. Anyway, with estate and gift tax laws likely to be revised as the pivotal year 2010 approaches, I am not going to focus on the tax savings and disadvantages inherent in setting up bypass trusts.

I believe that you should both establish durable and medical powers of attorney and living wills. The durable powers will allow each of you to act on behalf of the other at times of incapacity, in general situations for the durable power and in times of serious illness for the medical power. The living will can indicate your desires in connection with terminal illness. You also should have a document that details your personal wishes and where assets and personal papers are as well as the name, address, and telephone number of your advisors.

Keep in mind that estate planning should be reviewed periodically as your assets grow and the needs for your children change.

Finally, I want to underline my desire for you to obtain a will as soon as possible. If you like, I will supply some recommendations of attorneys to consider.

Summary

Estate planning is a PFP activity that increases in importance in later years in the human life cycle.

- Estate planning is analyzing and deciding how your assets are to be managed and apportioned to others in the event of your death or disability.
- The financial planning objectives are to minimize taxes and to provide assets to the ones we care for with as little conflict as possible.
- A will, which virtually everyone should have, is often the most important document in estate planning.
- Trusts are separate legal entities in which a third party usually manages property for the benefit of another person.
- Gifts are irrevocable transfers of property to others, and if the giftor maintains some ownership rights, they are not gifts.
- Life insurance roles in estate planning include providing liquidity, relative assurance of payment, and tax saving.
- Probate is the procedure after death during which the court validates the will and/or administers certain estate assets.
- The principal estate risks are longevity and incapacity.
- A power of attorney is a legal document that allows someone to act on your behalf.

Key Terms

administrator, *413*
beneficiary, *415*
bequest, *417*
bypass trust (nonmarital, exemption-equivalent, type B, or credit shelter trust), *425*
charitable lead trust, *419*
charitable remainder trust, *419*
durable power of attorney, *429*
estate planning, *412*
executor, *413*
gifts, *417*

grantor (trustor), *415*
guardian, *413*
intestate, *414*
irrevocable trust, *417*
joint tenancy with right of survivorship (JTWROS), *419*
letter of instruction, *421*
life estate, *420*
living trust, *416*
marital property, *420*
medical power of attorney (health care power of attorney or health care proxy), *429*

power of attorney, *421*
probate, *422*
remainder person, *425*
revocable trust, *417*
separate property, *420*
springing power of attorney, *429*
step-up in basis, *424*
tenancy by the entirety, *419*
tenancy in common, *419*
testamentary trust, *416*
trust, *415*
trustee, *415*
unified credit, *424*
will, *413*

Web Sites

http://www.nafep.com
National Association of Financial and Estate Planning (NAFEP)
The NAFEP's site contains information on estate planning, ranging from estate planning basics to articles discussing methods helpful in performing estate planning.

http://www.estateplancenter.com
Estate Planning Center
Trusts, probate, estate taxes, joint tenancy, Medicaid, and conservatorship are discussed. Detailed content on living trusts, how they work to avoid probate, and the costs associated with them.

http://www.nolo.com
Nolo
This is the home page of Nolo, the nation's leading provider of do-it-yourself legal solutions for consumers and small businesses. The site offers articles and information about wills, living trusts, power of attorney, and estate taxes.

http://www.gift-estate.com
Estate Planning and Gifting
This site offers a large number of links that stress the importance of gifting in estate planning. There is extensive coverage of charitable trusts.

http://www.niepe.org
National Institute for Excellence in Professional Education
This is the home page of the organization that administers the Certified Specialist in Estate Planning® (CSEP) designation. Relevant information regarding the designation is provided.

http://www.pueblo.gsa.gov/cic_text/money/will/makewill.htm
Wills
This link gives insights into why a will is important, how to prepare one, what to include, and how to keep it current.

Questions

1. Identify five reasons for having a will.
2. Explain the difference between an executor and a guardian.
3. What is a letter of instruction and why have it?
4. Detail the advantages and disadvantages of probate.
5. Identify the alternative ways of titling and transferring assets and indicate how they differ.
6. Shelly had just inherited money from her parents that she was considering placing in a joint account with her husband. She also was contemplating a legal separation from her husband. What advice would you give her? Why?
7. Howard said he wouldn't have to pay taxes on the money he inherited from his deceased father because it was under the $2 million threshold. He promptly withdrew the $900,000 that was in his father's IRA. Was his belief correct? Explain.
8. Why are basis and a step-up in basis important?
9. Sally gave $200,000 to her daughter and said, "It's yours as long as you agree to support me when I am older, if I should run out of my funds." Is that a gift? Explain.
10. Samantha was affluent and gave $5,000 to each of 1,000 needy individuals. Someone told her that under the uniform estate and gift tax, she would have to pay a tax on the amount over $1,000,000. Were they correct?
11. Why is it preferable to donate appreciated property to a charity rather than sell it and contribute the cash?

12. Detail the advantages and disadvantages of setting up a trust.

13. Why set up an irrevocable trust when you can establish a revocable one that provides you with more flexibility?

14. Shane didn't want to establish a bypass trust with her son as remainder beneficiary even though it would reduce the tax on her estate. She said her husband might need some of the money. Is that wise? Explain.

15. Morris didn't understand why he should set up a bypass trust. He said that without a trust, upon his death the $2,000,000 in assets in his name could go to his wife free of estate tax. Why should he put restrictions on his wife by transferring the money to the trust with his wife as income beneficiary and his son as remainder person? (His wife also had $2,000,000 in assets in her name) Did he have a full perspective? Explain. (See Appendix II for further elaboration)

16. Carl and his wife had a total estate of $400,000. What estate planning tool would you recommend? Why?

17. Why is life insurance potentially useful in estate planning matters?

18. What are the strengths and weaknesses of a durable power of attorney?

19. Name the three major ways of receiving non-work-related funds from acquaintances and indicate how they should be valued.

Problems **15.1** John inherited $1 million in an IRA, which comprised the entire estate from his father, who had recently died. He promptly withdrew the funds. The appropriate marginal tax rate was 28 percent. Was there any tax due? If so, how much? Assume it was $1 million in stocks held in a personal account. Would your answer be the same? Explain.

15.2 Sophia inherited 1,000 shares of IBM that her father's parents bought for her when she was a child. The father's cost was $2 per share at the time of purchase and $84 per share at the time of his death. Sophia sold them at $86 per share. Calculate the total amount of her capital gain.

15.3 Henry will be giving $50,000 to each of his five children. Indicate how much of his assumed $1 million gift tax exemption will remain.

15.4 Hilda wanted to know how much her children would be saving if she set up a bypass trust for $300,000 rather than giving it directly to her husband. She had an illness that made it likely that she would be the first to die. Assume she and her husband each had over $2 million in assets and no change in the amount over time, as well as an estate tax of 50 percent. What would her savings be? (See Appendix II for the method of solution.)

15.5 Maurice gave $20,000 to charity each year. He had $20,000 in stock that cost him $14,000 to buy. Assuming he is in the 23 percent marginal tax bracket for capital gains, how much will he save by donating the stock directly to charity?

CFP® Certification Examination Questions and Problems **15.1** Before her death, LaDonna Kiniston, age 74, gave her three grandchildren some money for their private school education. She paid $12,000 to the school for Jake's tuition and gave a like amount to Sarah and Nicole. What would be the adjusted taxable gifts calculated in her estate taxes?

    a. $0
    b. $2,000
    c. $6,000
    d. $16,000
    e. $36,000

15.2 What is an appropriate standard estate planning strategy for married couples to *minimize* taxes over two deaths?

    a. Bequeath the entire estate to a trust, giving the surviving spouse a general power of appointment.

    b. Bequeath the applicable exclusion amount to a qualified terminable interest property (QTIP) trust and the balance to the surviving spouse.

    c. Bequeath the application exclusion amount to a bypass trust to take advantage of the unified credit at the first death.

    d. Bequeath the applicable exclusion amount to the surviving spouse and the balance to the children.

15.3 Five years ago, Tom Mohy bought 10,000 shares of stock at $10 per share in a pharmaceutical company. Today, the stock is worth $200,000 and is paying a dividend of $8,000 per year. Tom feels that the stock will continue to appreciate at a rate of 12 percent per year, including the dividend. Tom wants to establish a college education fund for his two daughters, ages 15 and 9. Which of the following is/are true?

1. If Tom gives 2,500 shares of stock to his 15-year-old daughter, all dividends from the 2,500 shares will be taxed at her income tax bracket.

2. If Tom gives 2,500 shares of stock to his nine-year-old daughter, all dividends from the 2,500 shares will be taxed at her marginal rate.

3. Two years from now, if Tom's older daughter sells her 2,500 shares of stock at $30 per share, Tom will need to report the gain as a long-term capital gain on his personal income tax return.

4. All dividend income earned by his nine-year-old daughter that exceeds $1,400 in 1998 will be taxed at Tom's marginal tax rate.

    a. (2) only

    b. (1) and (2) only

    c. (1) and (3) only

    d. (1) and (4) only

    e. (3) and (4) only

15.4 If a client's primary goal in making lifetime gifts to his children is to lower his estate taxes, he should make gifts of property that

    a. are expected to depreciate significantly in the future.

    b. are expected to appreciate significantly in the future.

    c. have already depreciated significantly.

    d. have already appreciated significantly.

15.5 Doris Jenkins is a 71-year-old widow with a son and daughter ages 43 and 45, respectively, and six grandchildren. Doris has an estate currently worth $572,000, which includes her home valued at $250,000 and a life insurance policy on her life with a face value of $160,000. Her children are named as primary beneficiaries. Doris recently suffered a severe stroke that left her paralyzed on her right side. She is home from the hospital, but her health will continue to decline and she will need to go into a nursing home within one year. The only estate planning she has done to date is to write a will in 1989 that left all her assets to her children equally. Of the following estate planning considerations, which is/are appropriate for Doris at this time?

1. Transfer ownership of her home to her children so it will *not* be counted as a resource should she have to go into a nursing home and apply for Medicaid.

2. Execute a durable general power of attorney and a durable power of attorney for health care.

3. Place all assets in an irrevocable family trust with her children as beneficiaries.

4. Start a gifting program transferring assets up to the annual exclusion amount to each of her children and grandchildren.

a. (1), (2), (3), and (4)

b. (2) and (3) only

c. (1) and (4) only

d. (4) only

e. (2) only

15.6   Bruce, age 55, is the beneficiary of his mother's $200,000 life insurance policy. The insurer has requested that he select a settlement option for payment of the proceeds. What factors should he consider before making the election?

1. his current income needs

2. his asset management ability

3. his net worth

4. his estate planning goals

5. his tax liability on the $200,000

    a. (1), (2), (3), and (5) only

    b. (2) and (4) only

    c. (1) only

    d. (3), (4), and (5) only

    e. (1), (2), (3), and (4) only

15.7   Mr. and Mrs. Jones own 640 acres of farmland deeded as "joint tenants, *not* as tenants in common." Currently, the land is appraised at $3,000 per acre and continues to escalate annually in value. In addition, Mr. Jones holds a $250,000 CD in his name only, and Mrs. Jones holds a $250,000 CD in her name only. Mr. and Mrs. Jones have *no* debts. Mrs. Jones's last will and testament provides that "all of my assets at my death shall be divided in three equal portions among my children and my husband."

1. Mrs. Jones dies unexpectedly, leaving her husband and two children as her sole heirs. Which of the following statements is true?

    a. The children will inherit two-thirds of Mrs. Jones's interest in the CD and her 50 percent interest in the farm.

    b. The children will inherit two-thirds of Mrs. Jones's interest in the CD and *no* interest in the farm.

    c. The children will inherit two-thirds of Mrs. Jones's interest in the CD and two-thirds of her 50 percent interest in the farm.

    d. The children will inherit a statutory interest in the CD and the farm.

    e. The children's share of Mrs. Jones's CD and her 50 percent interest in the farm are subject to probate.

2. Two weeks after Mrs. Jones's death, Mr. Jones dies, and his will provides that, "I hereby give all my real property to my brother James, and I give all my personal property to my children, share and share alike." Which one of the following statements is true?

    a. The children will inherit Mr. Jones's CDs and his interest in the farm.

    b. The children will inherit Mr. Jones's CDs and *none* of his interest in the farm.

    c. The children will inherit *no* interest in either Mr. Jones's CDs or the farm.

    d. Mr. Jones's CDs are subject to probate, but Mr. Jones's farm interest is *not* subject to probate.

    e. Neither the CDs *nor* Mr. Jones's interest in the farm are subject to probate.

15.8 Which of the following circumstances would definitely cause the date-of-death value of the gifted property to be included in the donor's gross estate?

1. Donor retains a life estate in the gift property.
2. Donor retains the power to revoke or amend the gift.
3. Donor gives more than $10,000 to one donee in one year.
4. Donor dies within three years of the date of the gift.
    a. (1), (2), and (3) only
    b. (1) and (2) only
    c. (2) and (4) only
    d. (3) and (4) only
    e. (1), (2), (3), and (4)

15.9 While deciding whether to equalize the estates at the death of the first spouse or to defer estate taxes until the death of the surviving spouse, it is important to consider

1. the age and health of the surviving spouse.
2. whether the combined estates exceed two unified credit equivalents.
3. whether the surviving spouse wants to make gifts to the children.
4. whether the estates have substantial appreciation potential.
    a. (1), (2), and (3) only
    b. (3) only
    c. (2) and (4) only
    d. (1), (2), and (4) only
    e. (1), (2), (3), and (4)

15.10 An individual received a bequest of 100 shares of XYZ stock from a relative who died on March 1 of this year. The relative bought the stock at a total cost of $5,500. The value of the 100 shares of XYZ stock was $5,750 on March 1. Its value rose to $6,250 on July 1 of this year, on which day the individual sold it for $6,250, incurring expenses for the sale of $250. The taxable gain on the sale would be a

    a. $250 long-term capital gain
    b. $250 short-term capital gain
    c. $500 long-term capital gain
    d. $500 short-term capital gain

Case Application
ESTATE PLANNING

Richard and Monica maintained their contrasting views when it came to estate planning. Even though their assets were well under the $2 million threshold, he wanted to set up a bypass trust. Monica wanted the personal assets, now mostly in Richard's name, placed in joint name. I had the feeling that she would prefer to have as many of the assets in her name as possible as a control on Richard's investment policy. She wanted her daughter, who might be divorced fairly soon, to receive the majority of their estate. Richard said that fact did not persuade him and that their son (who had an average career potential) should not be penalized due to their daughter's situation. Somehow it did not surprise me that they didn't have wills currently.

Case Application Questions

1. Why should Richard and Monica have wills drawn up?
2. Discuss your opinion about equal versus unequal division of estate assets.
3. Do you believe they should establish bypass trusts?
4. What do you think of the advantage Monica would gain having all personal assets including Richard's placed in her name? Does she deserve this?
5. What other estate planning recommendations do you have?
6. Complete the estate planning section of the financial plan.

Appendix I

Altruism and Bequest Theory

Do we always act in our own interests or are we capable of feeling and acting unselfishly so that others benefit?[25] Two economists, Robert Barro and Gary Becker, popularized the term *altruism* for family relationships.[26] Altruism can be defined as unselfish concern for others. As it pertains to estate planning, it means providing some of our money to others when we are alive or after we pass away instead of spending it all on ourselves. These economists and many others maintain that altruism, while not present in everyone and certainly not practiced at all times, is fairly common. An example cited for altruism is charitable giving.

There are economists who argue that altruism doesn't exist or is overemphasized. They say that many of the things people do that appear altruistic are really exchanges of services. For example, you may help your elderly widowed mother get along in return for an unwritten understanding that you will receive a sizeable estate payment after her death. If

---

[25] Gary S. Becker, "Altruism in the Family and Selfishness in the Market Place," *Economica,* New Series 48, no. 189 (February 1981), pp. 1–15.

[26] Gary S. Becker and Robert J. Barro, "A Reformulation of the Economic Theory of Fertility," *Quarterly Journal of Economics* 103, no. 1 (February 1988), pp. 1–25; and Robert J. Barro and Gary S. Becker, "Fertility Choice in a Model of Economic Growth," *Econometrica* 57, no. 2 (March 1989), pp. 481–501.

altruistic intent is not present and the estate tax is increased, thereby reducing the potential financial reward, you may cut back on services to your mother. Alternatively, your mother may try to maintain the same ultimate payment to you by paring living expenses. Knowing how people think and act about estate planning matters can help us improve our own financial and other personal activities as children, parents, grandparents, spouses, and advisors.

The strict form of life cycle theory implies that people think only of their household with the goal of having no money left after the death of the last member-owner. Any money remaining is purely incidental, caused by the inability to determine when we will die. Of course, that would mean that estate planning is not important; it has no priority in people's financial actions.

Many people leave material bequests when they pass away. *Bequests* are gifts of assets intended to be transferred to others subsequent to the owner's death. There are a number of theories about why households have assets remaining at the time the last member-owner dies. Identifying the appropriate motivating factor is important because it can influence the choice of an estate planning strategy. Some of the predominant approaches are given below.

ACCIDENTAL BEQUESTS

Accidental bequests occur when assets are left to others as an incidental outcome of other planning. Most commonly, with this approach you are likely to have an estate at death because you cannot be sure how long you will live. You may want to provide for a bequest that has a reasonable possibility of occurring even though it isn't the most likely estimate. For example, you may establish funding through age 95 when the average mortality age is 80 because you could live longer than average. You also may want to provide a sum in case of catastrophic illness.

In either case, the resultant bequest is unintentional and thus is what is left over from normal life cycle planning. The capital needs analysis for retirement planning discussed in Chapter 18 would therefore not factor in any amount for bequests. Proponents of this approach point to research showing relatively little bequest behavior beyond that for the affluent.[27] For example, one study of bequest intent showed no difference in the degree to which people reduced their assets when retired between those who had children and those who did not.[28]

BEQUESTS AS COMPENSATION

Bequests can be used as a reward to garner attention by children or other relatives and friends. For example, there may be an understanding that care given by a child when a parent is elderly will result in a large bequest to that child upon the parent's death. This agreement may be explicitly stated or may just be understood.

In this case, the bequest can be viewed as a kind of liability, even though generally not a legal one. The liability can be established as a minimum amount in real terms that would be paid out to the beneficiary at death. In this approach, the capital needs analysis is run with that minimum fixed payout incorporated as a deduction in amounts available for consumption over the remaining life span.

---

[27] Franco Modigliani, "The Role of Intergenerational Transfers and Life Cycle Saving in the Accumulation of Wealth," *Journal of Economic Perspectives* 2, no. 2 (Spring 1988), pp. 15–40.

[28] Michael D. Hurd, "Savings of the Elderly and Desired Bequests," *American Economic Review* 77, no. 3 (June 1987), pp. 298–312.

Advocates of bequests as compensation point to the absence of both widespread annuitization and gifting as support for their position.[29] Annuitization would leave nothing for heirs, and gifting could be interpreted as more of an altruistic measure since the amount gifted ceases to be a potential future reward. They also point out that people who have more money to reward service providers receive more attention from their children than do lower-income people. Critics say analysis of estates shows that the majority of people divide their estates equally among their children. Therefore, this businesslike strategy of implied contracts to favor children providing more attention to needs cannot be too widespread.

ALTRUISTIC BEQUESTS

In financial terms, *altruism* is the sacrifice of your resources for the benefit of others. Bequests given without requiring offsetting services qualify because they reduce the amount you can spend over your life span. The altruistic bequest variable in a capital needs analysis could be handled in several different ways, depending on the wishes of the asset holder.

One approach would, in effect, result in risk sharing. An intended sum would be provided, assuming a normal life span and no abnormal medical expenses. The sum would be reduced to a minimum level or eliminated entirely if there were extended life cycles or major extraordinary expenses. If, on the other hand, life spans in retirement were shortened, payouts would be greater than expected.[30]

Proponents of this approach can point to the large amount of assets left at death, which may be well beyond the sums set aside for longevity risk and reasonable catastrophic illness risk. Like people who believe in bequests as compensation, proponents of risk sharing interpret the absence of annuitization as interest in bequests. Critics ask, If altruism exists, why don't more people leave money to heirs based on need instead of leaving them equal shares? Other researchers believe that altruism may exist but that it is not very common.[31]

OTHER APPROACHES

Any of the reasons for bequests given above can generally be incorporated under a broadened form of the life cycle hypothesis and personal financial planning. Each approach can be integrated into capital needs analysis. There are other motivations that are not necessarily consistent with a life cycle framework. One would be a desire to accumulate money to provide utility to the holder for status or other reasons. Another is related to satiation.[32] Here it is argued that people have enough money to spend additional amounts but choose not to because they have all they want, and additional spending will not provide any further pleasure.

[29] B. Douglas Bernheim, Andrei Shleifer, and Lawrence H. Summers, "The Strategic Bequest Motive," *Journal of Political Economy* 93, no. 6 (December 1985), pp. 1045–76.

[30] Laurence J. Kotlikoff and Avia Spivak, "The Family as an Incomplete Annuities Market," *Journal of Political Economy* 89, no. 2 (April 1981), pp. 372–91.

[31] Mark O. Wilhelm, "Bequest Behavior and the Effect of Heirs' Earnings: Testing the Altruistic Model of Bequests," *American Economic Review* 86, no. 4 (September 1996), pp. 874–92.

[32] Laurence J. Kotlikoff, "Intergenerational Transfers and Savings," *Journal of Economic Perspectives* 2, no. 2 (Spring 1988), pp. 41–58.

Practical Comment   Handling Bequests Overall

There are many different ways that people handle the bequest issue. They must decide whether to leave sums to others, and, if so, in what amount. In making that decision, they may be influenced by their upbringing, friends, and relatives, and perhaps by an innate sense of concern for others. In more practical terms, they take into account the beneficiaries' current needs, those of their children, and a sense of whether their children or others who they have strong feelings for will be able to enjoy a similar or better lifestyle than they now have. They can take into account how close they feel to the beneficiary and what that person has done for them, particularly in old age.

In other words, there is little doubt that altruism and an altruistically derived bequest motive exist among some people. It is more likely to exist among people who are wealthy than those who are poor. The sacrifice in consumption means much less to affluent people and the poor may feel that their children are likely to do at least as well as they have.[33] The bequest motive may be combined with other needs to satisfy joint goals. For example, placing extra money aside for longevity and catastrophic illness risk integrates well with altruistic bequests. In most instances, there will be assets left for others. In any event, we've seen that many people prefer to remain in their home and are uncomfortable with placing a reverse mortgage on it. Their heirs will receive the proceeds from its sale at the time of death.

GIFTING AND BEQUESTS

Many people decide to combine gifting while they are alive with bequests after they die. They may provide funds for their children for college education[34]

and for a down payment on a home. They view those outlays as a gift in the form of a capital expenditure for their children that will provide a higher return and more pleasure than a comparable cash sum upon their death. Moreover, giftors can have the pleasure of seeing the impact of their gifts while they are still alive.

There are those who believe that their bequest motive or even obligation as a parent is taken care of at the time of the gift. Some say, in effect, "I gave them a good start; the rest is up to them. My remaining funds are for me." If there is a child with disabilities or one whose career is likely to render him or her incapable of providing a satisfactory lifestyle, the plan may be adjusted.

ABSENCE OF BEQUEST MOTIVE

Other people have little gift or bequest intention at any time but still accumulate more money than they need. They are comfortable with their current situation and because of habit or satiation would not want to alter their lifestyle no matter how much extra money is available. The money they accumulate may not be for bequests or to provide for risks but just because they have no strong feelings about what to do with it.

Clearly, there are many motivations for gift or bequest behavior and therefore reasons for which assets are left at death. This multimotivational way of thinking is supported by an unusually detailed study made available concerning TIAA-CREF participants, a sampling that is heavily weighted toward educators.[35] Since there are many ways of viewing bequests, it is important that an individual's particular way of thinking be established as early as possible in the estate planning process.

[33] John Laitner, "Random Earnings Differences, Lifetime Liquidity Constraints, and Altruistic Intergenerational Transfers," *Journal of Economic Theory* 58, no. 2 (December 1992), pp. 135–70.

[34] On the other hand, some funds provided for a college education as a parental obligation are not a gift.

[35] John Laitner and F. Thomas Juster, "New Evidence on Altruism: A Study of TIAA-CREF Retirees," *American Economic Review* 86, no. 4 (September 1996), pp. 893–908.

Appendix II

BYPASS TRUST

The following is an extended example of the benefits of a bypass trust.[36]

[36] This example deals only with federal estate tax and ignores state estate tax, which may be substantial on the death of the first to die.

Example 15.A2.1

Frederick and Marion each had $2 million in their own name. Assume that the unified credit at the time was $2 million. Each was the beneficiary of the other's estate. They had one daughter, Elena, who was to be the ultimate beneficiary after they had both died. They wanted to know how much money they would save personally and how much Elena would save if both established bypass trusts. Assume that Frederick died first and then Marion and that the money that they had in each name stayed constant throughout the period. Compare the net proceeds under the two approaches.

Solution

When Frederick dies, no taxes are due under their current nontrust setup. Marion would receive Frederick's $2 million, due to the unlimited marital exemption for transfer of estate assets. Nor would there be a tax under the bypass trust since the $2 million in exempt assets would exactly meet the limit under the unified credit. However, under their current setup, when Marion died, her $2 million in exempt assets would be less than the $4 million in combined assets she owned and Elena would have to pay estate taxes on the second $2 million. This would amount to approximately $780,800 after the unified credit.

If a bypass trust was set up, Elena, not Marion, would receive Frederick's $2 million free of any estate tax since Frederick's unified credit is used. The $2 million Marion owned at her death would be covered by her unified credit, and no tax would be paid. In other words, by allowing both Frederick and Marion's unified credits to be utilized, their combined estates would pay no estate taxes and Elena receives $780,800 more in assets. The two different approaches are shown in Figure 15.A2.1.

FIGURE 15.A2.1   Benefits of a Bypass Trust

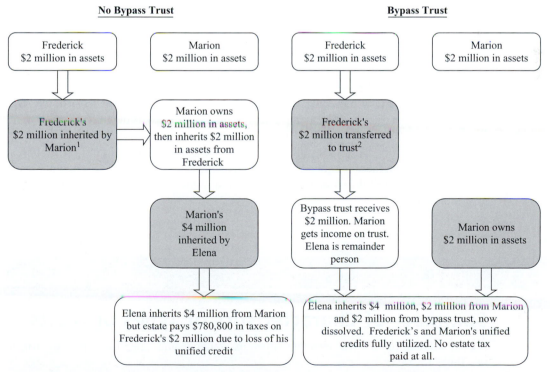

Note: Shaded boxes arise through death of individual.

[1] No estate tax owed at this point due to unlimited marital deduction, but unified credit is lost.

[2] No estate tax owed due to utilization of unified credit in transfer to the trust.

Appendix III

Power of Appointment and QTIP Trusts

There are two other types of trust that provide estate tax benefits: power of appointment and QTIP.

POWER OF APPOINTMENT

Power of appointment trusts[37] are set up either when the grantor is alive or by trust, and allow the recipient, called the *donee*, to decide who is to receive property or in what share he or she will receive it. It may be either a special or a general power. The *special power* limits the donee decision to an established group of individuals; the *general power* allows the donee to choose anyone. The power of appointment trust qualifies for a marital exemption if the spouse receives all the trust income at least annually and possesses a general power to select the ultimate beneficiary. The power of appointment trust will be included in the estate of the surviving spouse at death.

As with the previous approach, money left outright to the bypass trust is used for amounts up to the exemption equivalent in order to take advantage of the grantor's unified credit, with the power of appointment trust taking the balance of the property. The power of appointment trust can be used when the decedent wants further observation of the children or other heirs by the donee before a decision is made on the division of the property. The power of appointment is no longer required to qualify for the marital deduction.

QTIP

The *qualified terminal interest property* (QTIP) trust requires that all income be given to the surviving spouse at least annually and will be included in the surviving spouse's estate. However, unlike the power of appointment trust, the QTIP allows the decedent to name the ultimate or remainder beneficiary over all the assets in the trust. It also can be used in conjunction with the bypass trust to take advantage of the unified credit. The assets placed into the trust must be income-producing. The QTIP's principal attraction is the aforementioned ability for the decedent to control the disposition of the money— for example, when there is concern that the surviving spouse may remarry and not leave the money to their children or leave some of the money to his or her children from a prior marriage.

Appendix IV

Summary of Characteristics of Types of Trusts

For a summation of the characteristics of general and specific types of trusts, see Table 15.A4.1.

---

[37] Actually power of appointment is a clause in a trust or will rather than a separate trust in itself.

TABLE 15.A4.1 **Types of Trusts**

Document	Characteristic	Who For	Tax Advantage	Principal Advantages	Principal Disadvantages
General					
Living	Established when alive	Anyone	Yes, if irrevocable	Bypasses probate Expertise Trustee in place in event of incapacity	Cost to set up and operate
Testamentary	Takes effect by will after death	Anyone	May be	Similar to living trust but can have lower NPV cost and may not bypass probate[1]	Cost to operate may not bypass probate[1]
Revocable	Grantor can reverse	Anyone	None	Flexibility	Cost to set up and operate
Irrevocable	Grantor cannot alter	Anyone	Yes	Tax advantage	Cost to set up and operate
Specific					
Bypass	Two beneficiaries: income person and remainder person	Principally for married couples	Yes	Use of decedent's unified credit	Some loss of control for surviving spouse
Power of appointment[2]	Allows another person to make decision on division of assets	Anyone	Possibly	Qualifies for marital deduction Tax benefits if used with bypass trust	Possible loss of control by grantor
QTIP	Allows grantor to retain control over who receives estate principal	Married couples	Possibly	Qualifies for marital deduction	Assets placed in trust must be income-producing
Life insurance	Set up to accommodate life insurance	Anyone	Yes, when irrevocable	Can save estate taxes	Can provide lower return than gifting
Charitable remainder	For charitable intent	Anyone	Yes	Used when grantor is to receive income with remainder to charity	None
Charitable lead	For charitable intent	Anyone	Yes	Used when charity is to receive income with remainder to third party	None
Generation skipping	Monies left to someone at least two generations younger than grantor	Anyone	Yes	Saves one generation's estate taxation	May not go to true intended beneficiary
Trust for minors	Established for people not yet adults	Minor children	Yes	Flexibility in payout	Cost

[1] Probate may either be an advantage or a disadvantage depending on the state a person resides in and other individual factors.

[2] A clause in a trust or will; not a separate trust.

Planning Essentials

Personal financial planning requires knowledge of a great deal of descriptive material. We have covered some of it in previous chapters, but there is additional highly useful information that you can benefit from having knowledge of. Investments, insurance, economics, and law, in particular, are often the subject of a separate course or courses.

In Chapter 16 on stocks, bonds, and mutual funds, we elaborate on material presented in conceptual form in the financial investments chapter. Each of the three subtopics is described and methods of evaluating them are presented.

PFP requires knowledge of disciplines that are not directly part of the planning process. Three of them—economics, law, and organizational structures, with its roots in law and taxation—are presented in Chapter 17. For some, it will be a review of what they already know; for others, a very basic introduction to those fields.

Chapter Sixteen

Stocks, Bonds, and Mutual Funds

Chapter Goals

This chapter will enable you to:

- Illustrate the characteristics of bonds, stocks, and mutual funds more fully.
- Calculate the value of a bond and bond yields.
- Compute the value of a stock.
- Differentiate between fundamental and technical stock analysis.
- Develop a logical approach to selecting individual mutual funds.

I was surprised to find that Dan and Laura had not followed my advice completely. They had a sheepish look on their faces as they entered. The two confessed that when the market started to move up, they had changed my recommended asset allocation and placed more monies into the best-performing areas.

Real Life Planning

The advisor had two clients who managed their own monies and they could not have been more different. When thinking about them, he was reminded of the contrast in their personalities. The first, a management consultant, was very bright, but he used his emotions rather than his intellect in making decisions. He could cite logical reasons at any time why he wanted to be in or out of the market. But the truth was that he was an impulsive momentum investor.

Whenever stocks went up, he wanted to get in, and when they declined, he wanted to get out. One day he phoned in the morning to get into the market because of the last few weeks' positive performance. When the market declined by 100 basis points, or around 1 percent, during the day, he changed his mind, which resulted in both purchases and sales in the same day.

The advisor tried to counsel him to take a longer-term approach but met with only limited success. Needless to say, his account substantially underperformed the market.

The second investor was a fairly young woman. She had originally intended to become an actress and had begun the necessary training after attending undergraduate school. Then an unfortunate accident with a malfunctioning car left her critically injured. In fact, she was thought dead and had a near-death experience of her soul floating from her body. But thanks to some excellent medical care, she made a complete recovery.

The experience persuaded her to become a doctor so that she could help others. She chose as her specialty emergency room care. She said that when things were highly emotional in the emergency room, she became most relaxed in making life and death decisions. She attributed this ability to her having faced her own death.

Her investments were made with the same cool detachment. She could see beyond the temporary emergency that panicked other people to the fundamental merits of an individual security or sector of the market. She enjoyed investing and spent considerable time doing it. Her performance was extremely good as she picked securities that were temporarily out of favor and over an extended period of time returned to their historical valuation and performance.

The advisor asked himself how he could capture her logical unemotional take on alternative investment choices and use it for other clients. He decided that for most people, given their personality and lack of devotion to the task, it was impossible. He took what he believed was the next best alternative. His approach was to stress upper and lower limits in weightings for mutual funds in different major asset sectors determined by their relative values and emphasize that individual selections within those sectors should be made based on their longer-term performances.[1]

When that selection process could not be made properly, either alone or with the help of a financial planner or other investment advisor, the advisor took a passive approach. He recommended index funds—a diversified mix of mutual funds intended to reduce overhead expenses and duplicate market performance. There were alternative styles of investing that other people used successfully, but the advisor felt comfortable with the two above. The details of these two as well as other methods of investing are discussed in this chapter.

OVERVIEW

Our discussion of financial investments in Chapter 9 focused primarily on general principles such as risk-return and ways of establishing an overall financial allocation. In this chapter, we get to the details of stocks, bonds, and mutual funds and summarize other types of managed accounts. We will stress critical factors and ways of measuring returns and attractiveness for each type of financial asset and will place somewhat greater emphasis on mutual funds, which are often the desired implementation tool for individuals and financial planners.

We look first at bonds, then stocks, followed by mutual funds and other managed accounts. An easy "one-stop" way of selecting mutual funds, using the material presented in Chapter 9 and this chapter, also is provided. Finally, Web Appendix A presents a detailed analysis of modern investment theory.

In this chapter, our financial objective is to familiarize you with all the investment alternatives and allow you to begin to make logical rather than emotional investment choices. Such an approach is a key to success in financial investing.

BONDS

The many types of bonds can be broadly classified by two characteristics: maturity and quality. **Maturity** refers to the number of years until the amount borrowed is to be repaid. The longer the period until maturity, the greater the risk the bond has. That is because the longer the period, the greater the potential for a change in the ability of a company to repay

---

[1] Performance is viewed relative to other funds like it, as discussed in the chapter. The capability and investment style of the fund manager also are taken into account.

TABLE 16.1
Bond Classification

Category	Maturity Date (in years)	Risk for Given Change in Interest Rates
Money market	0–1	Extremely low
Short term	1–3	Low
Intermediate term	3–10	Medium
Long term	10–30	High

its debt. Also, a broad-based change in interest rates will have a greater effect on long-term bonds. Both factors are included in the term **maturity risk.** Consider Example 16.1.

Example 16.1

Sean bought two bonds: the first had a 2-year maturity, the second a 20-year maturity. Both bonds had provided 5 percent yields when purchased. The very next day, an announcement that inflation was unexpectedly high drove market interest rates up to 6 percent. Sean learned about the relationship between bonds and interest rates. He knew his bonds would decline in price because of the rate hike. Both of his bonds would decline by an amount that would offer 6 percent returns to new buyers. Sean knew that would happen because his 5 percent contracted-for rate couldn't compete with new 6 percent market rates unless the price of his bonds dropped to a level that allowed them to offer an identical 6 percent return in the marketplace.

The price of the 2-year bond dropped 2 percent while that of the 20-year bond declined 11.5 percent. Initially, Sean was surprised by the difference in market performance, but after thinking about the greater number of years a holder of the 20-year bond would receive the now-lower interest rate, it began to make sense. He calculated the yields to possible buyers based on the new market prices for the bonds and found that they were both 6 percent.

He noted that when market interest rates rose, bond prices dropped, and when market interest rates declined bond prices increased. He would tell this to his friends, some of whom believed a rise in interest rates was good for bondholders. From then on, he always remembered that the longer the time until being repaid, the greater the maturity risk.

Bonds are generally given their classification and risk profile by maturity date, as seen in Table 16.1.

Quality, the second classification of bonds, refers to the likelihood that the bond will fulfill its obligation to pay interest and repay the amount owed at maturity. There are bond rating agencies such as Standard & Poor's and Moody's that assign ratings indicating the relative quality of a bond. They range from AAA, the highest, to C, the lowest. BBB represents the lowest possible rating for which the rating agency believes the bond will fulfill all its obligations.

Anything below BBB is regarded as a high-yield bond or a junk bond with a chance of default (nonpayment), which typically results in bankruptcy. We can call this risk **default risk.** Naturally, the lower the rating, the greater the default risk. Of course, given our knowledge of risk-return principles, we would expect bonds with higher default risk to provide higher anticipated returns and they do.

Bonds can be classified into the categories given in Table 16.2.

When we want to calculate expected returns for a bond, we have to add one more factor to maturity and default risk: liquidity risk.

TABLE 16.2
Characteristics of Bond Ratings

Quality	Rating	Risk of Default	Expected Relative Yield
High	AAA, AA	Very low	Low
Medium	A, BBB	Low	A little higher than high-quality bonds
Low [1]	Below BBB	Considerably higher, with those rated C having a distinct possibility	Significantly higher to account for the possibility of bankruptcy

[1] Called high-yield or junk bonds.

Liquidity Risk

Liquidity is the ability to convert an asset into cash quickly and at a relatively low transaction cost. **Liquidity risk** is the possibility that you will not be able to find a buyer at the current market price for an asset. Assets vary in terms of liquidity. For example, a U.S. Treasury bond is more liquid than one from a small city. Even if the small city were to have the same assurance of payment of interest and repayment of principal at maturity, U.S. Treasury bonds are traded daily in large quantity. If you were to purchase the small-city bond, you would have to spend costly time investigating it. You would worry that, in selling it, you might have to accept a lower price than you would if you bought a comparable U.S. government issue. The outcome is that the small-city bond will have to offer an inducement in the form of a higher yield to attract investors, just because of its higher liquidity risk.[2]

We can express the expected return for bonds as

$$\text{Expected bond return} = \text{Risk-free rate} + \text{Risk premium}$$

where

$$\text{Risk premium} = \text{Liquidity risk} + \text{Maturity risk} + \text{Default risk}$$

Example 16.2

Anna noticed that a 10-year U.S. government bond was offering only a 5 percent yield while the newly issued bond of a small startup airline company, also due in 10 years, offered a 14 percent return. At the time, the anticipated inflation rate was 2.5 percent and U.S. Treasury bills were yielding 4 percent. She thought the airline's return of 14 percent a year for 10 years looked attractive and decided to investigate further. Her examination indicated that the airline had a speculative outlook. After looking at bonds offered in the marketplace, she was able to separate the U.S. government and airline bonds into the following components at the time:

	U.S. Government	Airline
Pure rate of return[1]	1.5%	1.5%
Inflation premium	2.5	2.5
Total risk-free rate	**4.0%**	**4.0%**
Liquidity risk	—	1.0%
Maturity risk	1.0%	1.0
Default risk	—	8.0
Total risk premium	**1.0%**	**10.0%**
Expected bond yield	**5.0%**	**14.0%**

[1] The risk-free rate minus the inflation rate. This is the real return after adjustment for inflation and other risks. In theory, the rate is supposed to be level at all times but as a practical matter it fluctuates.

After her investigation, she concluded that both bonds were fairly priced—that is, their required rates of return were consistent with the risks they represented.

Bond Characteristics

Interest payments on bonds are called **coupon payments.** The amount provided is stated in the bond instrument. It is important to note that bond coupons are fixed contractual payments that are not affected by changes in market rates over time.

Principal is the payment due at maturity. The amount due at maturity is called the **par value, face value,** or **maturity value.** The majority of bonds have a par value of $1,000—that is, one bond costs $1,000. However, the market price of a bond is quoted one decimal point lower. Therefore, a bond quoted at 100 has a market value of $1,000.

[2] There is another risk called **reinvestment risk,** the possibility that cash received through payments of interest and principal will not be reinvested at the original rate on the bond. The reinvestment rate can be more difficult to factor into the required interest rate for bonds.

Returns on bonds are called yields. There are a number of yields on bonds that are calculated. Three yields that will be discussed below are coupon yield, current yield, and yield to maturity.

The **coupon yield** is the return that is calculated based on the annual coupon and the face value of the bond. By knowing the coupon yield, you can calculate how much you will receive in cash payments per year.

$$\text{Coupon yield} = \frac{\text{Annual coupon}}{\text{Face value of bond}}$$

The **current yield** is the annual coupon divided by the market value of the bond. The current yield provides you with the current return on a bond should you purchase it at that time.

$$\text{Current yield} = \frac{\text{Annual coupon}}{\text{Market value of bond}}$$

The **yield to maturity** indicates the return you would receive if you purchased the bond today and held it until it was repaid. The return can be separated into two parts: the coupon yield and the appreciation or depreciation in the price of the bond. The yield to maturity is the appropriate benchmark to use in calculating financial return on investment. It can be approximated by the following formula:

$$\text{Yield to maturity} = \frac{\text{Annual coupon} + \dfrac{\text{Face value} - \text{Market price}}{\text{Number of years to maturity}}}{\dfrac{\text{Face value} + \text{Market price}}{2}}$$

A more accurate calculation for yield to maturity would be

$$PV = \frac{CF_1}{1 + y} + \frac{CF_2}{(1 + y)^2} + \cdots + \frac{CF_n}{(1 + y)^n}$$

where

PV = Current price of the bond

CF_n = Cash flow in year n

n = Maturity date

y = Yield to maturity

To find the yield to maturity, we solve the above equation for y.

Example 16.3

Elizabeth was offered a bond selling at $700 with annual coupon payments of $60. Calculate her coupon yield, current yield, and yield to maturity under the approximate and correct methods. Assume the bond is due in eight years and has a par value of $1,000.

$$\text{Coupon yield} = \frac{60}{1,000}$$
$$= 6.0\%$$

$$\text{Current yield} = \frac{60}{700}$$
$$= 8.6\%$$

$$\text{Approximate yield to maturity} = \frac{60 + \dfrac{1,000 - 700}{8}}{\dfrac{1,000 + 700}{2}}$$
$$= 11.5\%$$

Calculator Solution— Yield to Maturity

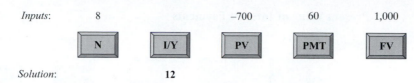

Inputs:

8		–700	60	1,000
N	**I/Y**	**PV**	**PMT**	**FV**

Solution: **12**

Press I/Y = 12.0%

When a bond sells for more than its par value, generally $1,000, it is said to sell at a premium and is known as a **premium bond.** When the coupon yield is lower than the current market yield, the bond will sell at less than $1,000 and be called a **discount bond.** A discount bond will have a greater fluctuation in price than a premium bond when market interest rates change.

Calculating the Value of a Bond

A bond's current price is equal to the present value of its future cash flows discounted to the present by the market interest rate. The market interest rate is equal to the investor's required rate of return for the bond reflecting its risk characteristics.

The value of a bond can be separated into its two components: the present value of its interest payments and the present value of the principal at maturity. We can express it as

Value of bond = Present value of interest payments + Present value of principal payment

The mathematical formula for a bond price is

$$PV = \sum_{t=1}^{n} \frac{PMT_t}{(1 + i)^t} + \frac{FV}{(1 + i)^n}$$

where

PMT = Annual coupon payment

  i = Market interest rate

 FV = Face value of the bond

  n = Numbers of years to maturity

Market interest rates fluctuate over time depending on such factors as changes in the expected rate of inflation, economic activity, Federal Reserve actions, prospects for the company issuing the bonds, and cyclical investor interest in bonds. This change in market rates will alter the market price of the bond.

Example 16.4

Yesterday Matthew bought a bond due in 12 years at $1,000 yielding 6 percent. Demonstrate that the combined present values of the principal and interest payments equal the market value of $1,000. Then, assuming rates rose to 7 percent today, calculate the new present value of the bond and compute the loss in bond value due to the rise in rates.

Annual Interest Payments

$$PMT = \$1,000 \times 6\% = \$60$$

$$PV = \sum_{t=1}^{12} \frac{60}{(1 + .06)^t} + \frac{1,000}{(1 + .06)^{12}} = \$1,000$$

| **Calculator Solution** | **Present Value of Interest Payments** | | | | |

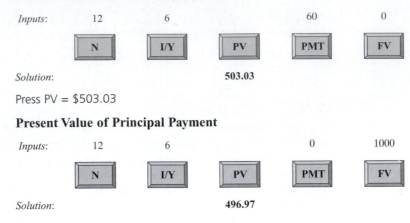

Inputs: 12   6   60   0

| N | I/Y | PV | PMT | FV |

Solution: **503.03**

Press PV = $503.03

Present Value of Principal Payment

Inputs: 12   6   0   1000

| N | I/Y | PV | PMT | FV |

Solution: **496.97**

Press PV = $496.97

Present Value of Interest and Principal Payments

Value of bond = Present value of interest payments + Present value of principal payment

                  = $503.03 + $496.97

                  = $1,000

Calculator Solution—Rise in Rate to 7%

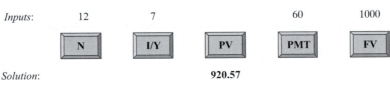

Inputs: 12   7   60   1000

| N | I/Y | PV | PMT | FV |

Solution: **920.57**

Press PV = $920.57

$$\text{Percentage change in price} = \frac{\text{New price}}{\text{Former price}} - 1$$

$$= \frac{920.57}{1,000} - 1$$

$$= -7.9\%$$

The loss is 7.9 percent.

Types of Fixed Obligations

The types of bonds and other fixed obligations[3] are given below.

Cash Equivalents

Cash equivalents include money market accounts, bank savings accounts, and U.S. Treasury bills. They can be liquidated at little or no charge because they are considered low-risk securities.

Certificates of Deposit

Certificates of deposit (CDs) are a form of bank debt with maturity dates often clustered from three months to five years. The repayment of interest and principal is guaranteed by a federal agency for amounts totaling under $100,000 per account.

---

[3] *Fixed obligations* is a broader and more accurate title than bonds. Some financial instruments that we consider bonds are not—for example, a mortgage or a certificate of deposit. However, they are often categorized as bonds and, for the sake of simplicity, we will do so as well.

U.S. Treasury Securities

U.S. Treasury securities are the highest-quality securities. All are rated AAA. They are separated by maturity date: Treasury bills (0–1 year), Treasury notes (2–10 years), and Treasury bonds (10 years or more). Many Treasury securities are not callable,[4] which guarantees the buyer that the rate contracted for will be paid until maturity. U.S. government bonds are subject to federal but not state taxes.

Corporate Bonds

Corporate bonds are issued by businesses. Their returns vary with the quality of the bonds as reflected by the issuer's bond rating. Standard & Poor's ratings of AAA to BBB are considered to be of investment quality. Most corporate bonds are callable, which means that the bond and its interest rate may be retired if interest rates rise sharply.[5]

High-Yield Bonds

High-yield bonds, often called *junk bonds,* are bonds rated below BBB, usually BB to C. These bonds are more speculative, and, in the past, a significant portion of them have gone bankrupt before maturity. The yields, which are materially higher than those for investment-quality bonds, usually incorporate an assumed potential for bankruptcy.

Inflation-Indexed Bonds

Inflation-indexed bonds are securities most often issued in the United States by the U.S. government. The interest rate paid for these bonds varies with the inflation rate.

Series EE Bonds

Series EE bonds are U.S. government bonds that pay both interest and principal when the bonds are redeemed. As we discussed in Chapter 14, bonds purchased after April 2005 will earn a fixed rate of return. The maturity date varies with the rate of interest, but the bonds can be held well beyond that date. The buyer has the option of deferring taxes on interest paid until the date they are cashed in.

Zero Coupon Bonds

Like Series EE bonds, zero coupons are bonds whose interest is paid at maturity. Because no cash payments are made until maturity, the bonds are more volatile than normal bonds, which pay interest semiannually. Despite the fact that no cash is received, the bonds are subject to income taxes on a current basis, which can make them most suitable for tax-deferred accounts.

Collateralized Mortgage Obligations

Collateralized mortgage obligations (CMOs) are fixed-income securities that are backed by pooled mortgages on real estate. Technically speaking, they are synthetic securities; however, in common parlance, they are considered bonds. The best known are mortgages guaranteed by the Government National Mortgage Association (GNMA), an institution backed by the federal government. These are mortgages taken out by Americans to purchase their homes; they are pooled by mortgage originators such as banks and sold in the

---

[4] This means that the issuer of the bonds will not be able to retire them before the indicated date at which they are due to be repaid. Generally, an issuer will not do so unless it will be rewarding to call a bond in when the current market interest rate is below the bond's contracted-for rate. By retiring the old bond and bringing out a new issue, the company can reduce its interest cost.

[5] Many bonds have a stated period from time of issuance in which they cannot be called.

marketplace. Investors, including individuals and mutual funds, receive on a current basis not only interest but principal repayments as well. A portion of the mortgages in the pool are repaid as people move or refinance their mortgage.

Municipal Bonds

Municipal bonds are tax-advantaged. They are issued by state and local municipalities and others with nonprofit or other public benefit in mind. They are generally not subject to federal taxes and are free of state taxes if you purchase them in the state you reside in. Reflecting their tax advantage, the bonds' yield is usually lower than that of taxable bonds, with yields influenced by the ratings of the state or local issuer.

International Bonds

International bonds are bonds of government and private organizations. Their rates will depend on local country economic conditions and their credit ratings. The international bonds have an additional amount of volatility due to currency fluctuations but also can provide diversification benefits since the amount paid is partially independent of U.S. market factors.

PREFERRED STOCKS

While preferred stocks sound like they are like common stocks, in many ways they resemble bonds. For example, holders of preferred stocks are not owners of a business but provide common stockholders with a source of capital in return for a fixed annual payment.

Preferred stocks have a lower priority on assets than bonds in the event of bankruptcy and lack the assurance of a bond's contracted-for return of principal. Consequently, preferred shares are generally considered more risky and typically have higher yields than bonds, and their prices can be more sensitive to a change in market interest rates.

Preferred stocks can be valued using the following formula:

$$P = \frac{D_0}{k_e}$$

where

P = Price of the preferred shares

D_0 = Current dividend

k_e = Required rate of return

The required rate of return is based on current market rates of interest for preferred shares having the same risk this company possesses.

Example 16.5

Alan wanted to know the price sensitivity of preferred shares to a 2-percentage-point increase in market interest rates. At the time, the required rate of return on preferred shares of a company he looked at was 7 percent and the dividend was $3.00. What did the preferred sell at originally, and how much would it decline if rates were to rise to 9 percent?

Price of the Preferred Stock before Increase in Market Interest Rates

$$P = \frac{3.00}{0.07}$$

$$= \$42.86$$

Price of the Preferred Stock after Increase in Market Interest Rates

$$P = \frac{3.00}{0.09}$$

$$= \$33.33$$

$$\text{Percentage change in price} = \frac{33.33}{42.86} - 1 = -22.2\%$$

STOCKS

The key to common stocks, as it is for most investments, is valuation. Under efficient market theory, the price of a stock at any time fairly presents its true value. Therefore, it is not possible to find undervalued stocks and to outperform the market. Anyone who has done so has merely been lucky and is as likely to underperform as to outperform in the future. Efficient market theory suggests that you should confine yourself to reducing risk by diversifying and save your money and effort rather than become involved in fruitless attempts to receive above-average results.

Two other approaches to be discussed here are fundamental and technical analysis. Proponents of each believe it is possible to outperform the market. Fundamental analysis is the principal alternative because it, too, is based on logical thinking

Fundamental Analysis

Fundamental analysis involves looking at economic industry and company data to help determine the fair value for a company. For example, a fundamental analyst would ask such questions as

1. What is the outlook for the economy, and how does it affect the company being looked at?
2. What stage of development is the industry in, and will it grow at a faster or slower rate than the overall economy?
3. Is the company growing faster or slower than the industry and how does its return on investment compare with that of other companies in the industry?

Fundamental analysis may involve looking at annual reports, testing the products offered, calculating ratios, and using overall valuation models.

Technical Analysis

In contrast to fundamental analysis, **technical analysis** focuses exclusively on price and volume. In effect, it says that everything you need to know is in the stock's past price action and the number of shares traded. There are many approaches to the interpretation of price action. One popular one is relative strength, sometimes called **momentum investing.** With this approach, stocks that have had large price movements relative to the market are purchased.[6] To the extent that it works, it may be due to people's behavior patterns in purchasing stocks that have performed well. Technical analysis contrasts with fundamental analysis, which says that the higher a stock rises without new positive developments, the less attractive it is. Of course, efficient market analysis, which maintains that the fair price for a security is the current one, would disagree with both technical and fundamental analysis.

Example 16.6 illustrates the differences among the three alternatives.

[6] Charles M. C. Lee and Bhaskaran Swaminathan, "Price Momentum and Trading Volume," *Journal of Finance* 55, no. 5 (October 2000), pp. 2017–69.

Example 16.6   Marie, a security analyst for a Wall Street brokerage firm, researched the retail company L Mart. A fundamental analyst, she believed that the stock was undervalued at its current price of $10 per share. She thought the stock had a fundamental worth of $16 and recommended it to her clients. Here is her reaction as well as the reactions of technical analysts and efficient market proponents as the stock rose.

Price	Fundamental Analysis	Technical Analysis	Efficient Market Hypothesis
$10	*Buy*—Stock is undervalued.	*Don't buy*—Stock has no momentum.	Stock is fairly priced.
$12	*Buy*—Stock is still undervalued.	*Buy*—Stock has relative strength.	Stock is fairly priced.
$16	*Hold*— Stock is fairly priced.	*Buy*—Stock has relative strength.	Stock is fairly priced.
$20	*Sell*—Stock is overpriced.	*Buy*—Stock has relative strength.	Stock is fairly priced.

Fundamental analysis forms the basis for the valuation models discussed in the next sections.

Valuation Methods

There are many methods of valuing securities. These include dividend models, earnings models, and other models that use the current market price in relation to individual factors in the company's financial statements such as cash flows. We will discuss two methods: the dividend discount model and an earnings model.

Dividend Discount Model

The **dividend discount model** assumes that a stock is equal to the sum of all its future dividends discounted to the present. It is given by the formula

$$P_0 = \frac{D_1}{k_e - g}$$

where

P_0 = Current value of the security

D_1 = Annual dividend payable next year

g = Projected growth rate in dividends

k_e = Company's required rate of return on its equity

Thus,

$$D_1 = D_0 \times (1 + g)$$

D_0 = Current annual dividend

The company's required rate of return is the return that an investor would require, given the company's growth prospects and risk profile. We can solve for it using a variety of methods. One is to estimate the risk premium using another company in the marketplace that is like it and add the risk-free rate to it. Another method is to use the formula above but transposing its terms. Note that in this form, the g represents the market's expectation of the growth rate as reflected in its current price.

$$k_e = \frac{D_1}{P_0} + g$$

Example 16.7   John thought the Hickary Food Manufacturing Company might be undervalued and decided to use the dividend discount model to find out if that was so. The company paid a $2.00 dividend, and he believed the dividends would grow 5 percent a year. Hickary was then selling at $20 per share, and companies with its return-risk profile had a required rate of return of 12 percent. Should he purchase the stock?

Solution

$$P_0 = \frac{D_1}{k_e - g} = \frac{2.00 \times (1 + 0.05)}{0.12 - 0.05}$$

$$= \frac{2.10}{0.07}$$

$$= \$30.00$$

The projected price of $30.00 is well above the current market price of $20.00. Consequently, John should purchase the shares.

Price-Earnings (P/E) Multiple

The **P/E multiple method** is based on earnings. It is literally the number of years of current earnings it takes for you to "pay off" (reach) the cost of purchasing the shares at the current price. It is given by the following formula:

$$\text{P/E multiple} = \frac{P}{E}$$

where

P = Price

E = Earnings

Generally, for stocks, the above figures are expressed on a per-share basis. The price expressed is usually the current price per share. Most commonly, the earnings per share (EPS) figure can be either the

1. Latest 12-month actual EPS
2. Projected EPS for the current year
3. Projected EPS for a future year

This future-year figure, called the normalized P/E, is often used when the current EPS is not representative either because the company is growing quickly or because profitability is depressed and a return to a more normal earnings figure is anticipated.

When earnings are not subject to unusual or cyclical factors, the higher the P/E ratio, the more highly regarded the company. Therefore, a fast-growing technology company would get a higher P/E than a slow-growing steel company. The P/E multiple for the typical large company has fluctuated widely over the past 50 years but has averaged 15 to 20 times earnings, as you can see in Table 16.3.

Example 16.8

Lucinda was interested in becoming the owner of a local drugstore that was for sale. The net profit for the store was $200,000 per year and was expected to remain at that level for the foreseeable future. She agreed to buy it for $800,000, thinking that she would recover her investment back fairly quickly and afterward would continue to receive $200,000 of profits per year. Calculate her P/E multiple to purchase the business.

$$\text{P/E multiple} = \frac{800,000}{200,000}$$

$$= 4$$

Example 16.9

Frank thought that United Motors, a major truck manufacturer, might be an interesting investment. At the time, the country was in recession, the company's earnings were off sharply, and the share price had dropped from $50 to $30. The last 12-month EPS was $0.50, and estimated current earnings per share for the year were $2.00. Frank figured that in two years, the company could return to its previous peak earnings per share of $5.00. The market's P/E multiple was 18 times for the latest 12-month earnings, and 17 times expected earnings for the year. Calculate the three P/E multiples and indicate which one is most appropriate to use.

TABLE 16.3
Historic P/E Multiples for S&P 500

Source: Standard & Poor's, "S&P500 Earnings and Estimate Report," 2005.

Year	Reported P/E	Year	Reported P/E
1967	28.1	1987	14.1
1968	28.6	1988	11.7
1969	25.9	1989	15.5
1970	18.0	1990	15.5
1971	17.9	1991	26.1
1972	18.4	1992	22.8
1973	12.0	1993	21.3
1974	7.7	1994	15.0
1975	11.3	1995	18.1
1976	10.9	1996	19.1
1977	8.7	1997	24.4
1978	7.8	1998	32.6
1979	7.3	1999	30.5
1980	9.2	2000	26.4
1981	8.0	2001	46.5
1982	11.1	2002	31.9
1983	11.8	2003	22.8
1984	10.0	2004	20.7
1985	14.5	2005	18.3*
1986	16.7		

* This figure is an estimate.

Solution

Latest 12 Months

$$P/E = 30/0.50$$
$$= 60$$

Expected Earnings for the Current Year

$$P/E = 30/\$2.00$$
$$= 15$$

Normalized Earnings in Two Years

$$P/E = 30/\$5.00$$
$$= 6$$

The normalized P/E appears most appropriate. Since the other P/Es are based on depressed earnings, they make the shares appear expensively priced, while the projected normalized figure of six times earnings indicates the shares are very reasonably valued compared to the market's P/E and may be attractive.

The dividend discount approach to valuation is theoretically purer, and changes in dividends tend to be more reliable than those for earnings. The P/E approach is simple to employ and is used more often by financial planning and investment practitioners as well as by the public.[7]

MUTUAL FUNDS

Mutual funds are often the choice of people with little time or inclination to manage individual monies themselves. Given the public's potential for inefficient selections and frequent unproductive changes in holdings, many financial planners would like to see even

[7] The price-earnings to growth ratio (PEG) relates the P/E multiple to the growth rate. It is given in the following formula: PEG Ratio = $\frac{P/E \text{ Ratio}}{\text{Annual EPS Growth}}$. Under this approach, the lower the ratio, the more attractive the company is since you are paying a lesser amount for future earnings progress.

greater use of mutual funds. The general mutual funds are typically extensions of the size and styles for stocks and maturities and qualities for bonds already discussed in this chapter and in Chapter 9.

Aside from these general funds, there are special-purpose stock funds, those with specific mandates. The categories below offer specialized funds that concentrate in publicly traded securities.

Type	Examples
Sector funds	Utility, technology, energy
Industry funds	Drug and REIT
Commodity	Gold, precious metals, oil and gas
Regional	Midwestern United States
International	Pacific Rim, European
Balanced	Blend of stock and bond
"Hedge"	Mergers and acquisition, market neutral
Other	High dividend yield, asset allocation

Bond Funds

Bond funds have their own categorizations. One criterion is maturity; the other is degree of risk. Maturity can be divided into short, intermediate, and long term while risk can be separated by gradations of quality: high, medium, low. Aside from general categories, more specialized funds include the following:

Type of Bond Fund	Explanation
Government securities	U.S. government bond funds invest in U.S. government bonds and also in mortgage-backed securities handled by a U.S. governmental agency called GNMA. The latter are often called GNMA funds.
Corporate	Generally searches for higher-than-government yields in investment-quality bonds.
High yield	Below investment quality, more risky. Generally invest in high-yield or so-called junk bonds.
Municipal	Bonds issued by local municipalities, regulatory authorities, and others that are tax-favored.
International	Investment-quality government and other bonds from abroad.
Emerging market	More speculative bonds from more speculative countries.
Floating rate	Adjusts to market rates, often through purchase of adjustable-rate mortgages or corporate debt.
Inflation indexed	Often U.S. government bonds whose rates and principal values vary with inflation.
Other	Zero-coupon bond funds, convertible securities funds, multisector bond funds, etc.

Open-End versus Closed-End Funds

Mutual funds can be further separated into open-end and closed-end funds.

Open-End Mutual Funds

An **open-end mutual fund** is generally open to new deposits by existing or new investors,[8] and redemptions by current holders. The price established for the purchase or sale transaction is **net asset value (NAV),** less commissions or redemption costs where applicable. The NAV is obtained by adding up the market values of all of the stocks in the portfolio and dividing by the total number of fund investor shares outstanding. The NAV is calculated at the end

---

[8] Unless it is closed temporarily or, less frequently, permanently, often due to larger inflows than the fund wishes to manage.

Practical Comment Closed-End Fund Discount

There are few good reasons why a closed-end fund should sell at a sizeable discount from NAV. After all, NAV is based on the market value of all the assets in the portfolio. It is somewhat analogous to offering your wallet with $500 in it and finding that bidders are willing to pay only $400 for it. Of course, you typically cannot sell off the parts of the stockholdings of the fund individually as you can the parts of the money contents of a wallet. Nonetheless, while items such as an unusually high expense ratio or poor management team might account for the disparity, frequently the discount or premium over NAV fluctuates sharply and a sizeable discount may present a potential opportunity for unusually large profits.[9]

[9] Greggory Brauer, "Closed-End Fund Shares' Abnormal Returns and the Information Content of Discounts and Premiums," *Journal of Finance* 43, no. 1 (March 1988), pp. 113–27.

of each day for purposes of determining the price of purchases and sales of shares for that day. The transactions are effected through the management company operating the mutual fund, although a brokerage firm may be an intermediary.

Example 16.10 Assume a new mutual fund held only three stocks. It had 500 shares of General Motors selling at $50, 1,000 shares of IBM selling at $100, and 800 shares of Microsoft offered at $60. Further assume that there were just four shareholders, each owning 10,000 shares. What is the mutual fund's NAV?

	Amount	Explanation
General Motors	$25,000	500 $\times$ $50
IBM	100,000	1,000 $\times$ $100
Microsoft	48,000	800 $\times$ $60
Total portfolio value	$173,000	
Total shares outstanding	40,000	10,000 $\times$ 4
NAV	$4.33	173,000 $\div$ 40,000

Closed-End Mutual Funds

The management company for a **closed-end mutual fund** does not engage in any regular purchase or sales transactions after the initial offering. Instead, the shares are typically traded through a stock exchange, often the New York Stock Exchange. Purchases or sales prices are not necessarily made at NAV but are established by supply and demand for the fund. Therefore, the shares may be offered on the exchange at a premium—a price higher than NAV when the fund has great appeal to investors—or at a discount, a price below NAV when it doesn't.

Load versus No-Load Funds

Mutual funds also can be segregated into load and no-load funds. A **load fund** is one that provides a sales commission to the individual or brokerage firm that markets the fund with the new fund holder paying the charge.[10] A **no-load fund** is one that does not offer sales commissions to the marketers of the funds. Load funds are offered by full-service brokerage funds and financial planners who are compensated by commissions. In effect, the commissions are a charge for the advice and convenience of having the transaction done for investors. No-load funds are offered directly by fund management companies and by discount brokerage firms representing them.

[10] A few management companies also charge a load that they retain.

TABLE 16.4
Characteristics of Load and No-Load Funds

Type Load	Front-End Charge	Annual Sales Charge	Redemption Charge	12b1 fee
A	Yes 4–6 percent	No	No	Possibly 0.25 percent
B	No	Yes 0.75–1.0 percent	Yes	Generally 1.0 percent
C	No	Yes 0.75–1.0 percent	No[1]	Generally 1.0 percent
No-load	No	No	No[2]	Possibly 0.25 percent or less

[1] There is a 1 percent charge if the shares are sold within the first year.
[2] The redemption charge when imposed varies in time frame and amount. A common range for inclusion of the charge is time frame 5 to 365 days and fee 1 to 2 percent.

Loads on funds can be divided into front-end and back-end loads. A front-end load is one that is charged when the shares are initially purchased. It is done by adding a commission to the transactions, often 4 percent for a bond fund and 5 percent for an equity fund. For example, a new investor in an equity fund with a $10.00 NAV that has a load attached might be charged $10.50.

A back-end loaded fund places the entire investor deposit in a fund and then charges an annual sales commission. Often that amount is 1 percent per year for stock funds and 0.75 percent a year for bond funds. The ongoing sales charge may go on for a fixed period or forever.[11] Type B funds may have a charge for redemptions prior to a stated number of years, often six to eight. The amount of the redemption charge generally declines as the number of years the fund is held increases. There is no charge if a transfer in assets is made within the same management company, called a fund family. Sometimes the sales charges are covered under marketing fees for the funds, which are called 12b-1 fees.[12]

A no-load fund is one that charges no sales commission to buy the fund. The investor generally executes transactions directly through the management company. As mentioned, no-load funds are often also available through discount brokerage firms. If purchased through a discount brokerage firm, the individual will be charged a transaction cost or the mutual fund will absorb the transaction cost and typically incorporate it in the 12b-1 fee passed along to all the shareholders. These transaction charges are generally less than 1 percent when bought in amounts over $5,000. Since the ongoing fee is often spread over all fund assets, not just those assets transacted by discount brokers, an overall charge can amount to less than 0.20 percent per year for no-load funds and is generally under 1 percent for load funds.

A summary of the relevant characteristics of various load and no-load funds is given in Table 16.4.

Mutual Fund Performance

The majority of all actively managed mutual funds underperform the averages. This record, which supports CAPM and the efficient market theorists, has led to the growth in popularity of index funds. Possible reasons for this underperformance are

1. Significant expenses to support analysts, portfolio managers, and other overhead costs as well as trading costs to shift investment holdings. These expenses, including trading costs, often reduce portfolio returns by 1 to 2 percent per year.

[11] Forever for type C shares and for a fixed period for type B shares.

[12] No-load funds also may have 12b-1 fees; these tend to be more modest. They are generally 0.25 percent or under of the fund's average annual net assets. The SEC allows certain funds that provide commissions to brokers and financial planners that have no redemption charges but have higher 12b-1 fees, many known as type C funds, to be called no-load.

2. Mutual funds frequently keep 5 percent or more in cash for such reasons as meeting unusually large redemptions. That money is invested at rates substantially lower than long-term equity returns. The fact that cash positions also reduce portfolio risk is often overlooked. Therefore, risk-adjusted performance can be a better comparison of individual fund versus index fund results than one based solely on returns.

3. The relative performance between categories—for example, large versus small capitalization funds—may differ substantially over extended periods of time. Many managers in one category may have holdings in another. For example, large capitalization fund managers may have holdings in mid and small capitalization funds. When mid and small capitalizations underperform, as they did, for example, for a large part of the 1990s, large capitalization managers underperform their indexes.

4. Fund overhead expenses, including direct management fees, can provide benefits other than performance. These include the cost in time saved in selecting and monitoring individual stocks and in recordkeeping as well as in assuming a task that many lack interest in or are unable to perform effectively. Consequently, the amount of underperformance may be reduced by the value of these other services.

Studies of whether individual funds are able to consistently outperform their peers or the market overall on a risk-adjusted basis have been mixed, with some indicating there is some evidence and others not.[13] To the extent that running larger sums of money reduces performance, having a favorable record that attracts many new investors may inhibit continuation of those results.

Taxation

Investment companies such as mutual funds are not taxed as an entity provided they pay out all dividends and capital gains income to investors yearly. Mutual fund dividends are taxed at ordinary income tax rates, whereas long-term capital gains distributions are subject to favorable tax rates. Capital gains taxes are paid by shareholders on net gains on fund sales of securities in their portfolio for the year based on fund costs to purchase those securities. Therefore, capital gains taxes may be paid yearly even though the shareholder has not sold any fund shares. Taxes are due on fund gains even if you personally had a loss in the shares you owned.

Example 16.11   Hedda purchased shares in a volatile emerging-markets fund on December 8 at $15.00 per share. The shares dropped sharply in the next two weeks and by December 22 were down to $12.00 per share. The fund made considerable changes in its portfolio during the year, selling at a large profit shares that it had purchased three years ago. It declared a capital gains dividend of $2.00 per share. Hedda has to pay $2.00 per share in capital gains taxes for the year. This is true despite the fact that she had an unrealized loss of $3.00 ($12 current price − $15 cost) and that the taxable gains in the portfolio occurred in the months before she owned the fund.

OTHER INVESTMENT MANAGEMENT STRUCTURES

There are many investment management structures aside from mutual funds that are relevant to households. Among them are separately managed accounts, exchange-traded funds, unit investment trusts, variable annuities, and pension plans.

---

[13] See, for example, Russ Wermers, "Mutual Fund Performance: An Empirical Decomposition into Stock-Picking Talent, Style, Transaction Costs, and Expenses," *Journal of Finance* 55, no. 4 (August 2000), pp. 1655–95.

Practical Comment   Mutual Fund Taxation

The often-yearly tax on mutual fund distributions is a significant disadvantage when compared with ownership of individual securities in a buy-and-hold strategy. However if you assume the individual securities will eventually be sold, it is not an extra tax but an earlier payment. Whether it is best for the shareholder depends on relative investment performance of a buy-and-hold versus a more active strategy and the extent to which the portfolio manager takes into account planning to minimize taxes in the portfolio changes. A growing number of mutual fund managers try to offset gains on shares sold because they no longer appear attractive by liquidating securities that they have losses in, thereby reducing the shareholders' tax burden for the year.

Separately Managed Accounts

Separately managed accounts, also called *separate accounts,* are segregated assets that are managed personally for each individual. They are managed much like mutual funds. However, while a mutual fund pools all investor funds in one account and each investor owns shares of that fund, in separate accounts investors own stocks and bonds that are placed in their name in a segregated account. In some instances, managers of mutual funds provide separate account management to other investors as well. Separate accounts have been growing rapidly in recent years.

One of the advantages of separate accounts is improved tax management. You may have more flexibility as to when to realize capital gains, and you don't have the problem of paying capital gains taxes on fund sales made prior to your date of entry, as you do with mutual funds.[14] Another advantage is your ability to exclude certain assets. Reasons for exclusion can range from too close a correlation with other household assets to your own negative opinion of certain securities. Brokerage firms offering a client a portfolio of separate accounts often include transaction costs to buy and sell securities and all management fees in one charge, called a *wrap account*, for a price that is often 1 to 3 percent annually, depending on size.

Disadvantages include more difficulty in diversifying properly since account minimums often range from $100,000 to $500,000 and can occupy a large percentage of total household assets. In addition, there are problems in switching managers quickly and without objections, as you can with mutual funds. The cost of a separate account ranges widely and can be considerably higher or moderately lower than that of an individual mutual fund. Larger-sized separate accounts may provide greater service to clients, while service for minimum-sized accounts run by a computer can be lower than that for a mutual fund and subject to similar yearly tax treatment.

Exchange-Traded Funds

Exchange-traded funds are portfolios of stocks and bonds that are traded on the major exchanges. They typically differ little from a mutual fund that is constructed as an index fund for the overall market or specific industries or sectors. Thus, there is no portfolio manager or strategy to outperform the market through individual stock selection. One difference with an index mutual fund is that an exchange-traded fund allows you to purchase and sell assets at a current market price throughout the day, whereas with mutual funds your transactions can be made only once a day, and the purchase price is established

---

[14] Many separate account managers discourage highly customized portfolios for tax and other reasons.

after you have purchased the shares. The price you receive for an exchange-traded fund may not be NAV, and you normally pay a transaction cost to purchase or sell the shares, which often can be avoided with mutual funds. There is no load with exchange-traded funds, just a trade commission. Exchange-traded funds have some tax advantages over index mutual funds.

Unit Investment Trusts

Unit investment trusts are portfolios that are set up at a point in time, as are mutual funds, but are generally unmanaged. They are sometimes employed in the bond area to provide clusters of securities, with the fund being liquidated at the maturity date of the bonds. They have no ongoing overhead costs and are sometimes difficult to sell at their NAV.

Variable Annuities

Variable annuities wrap mutual funds in a tax-sheltered framework for an extra ongoing charge. They are discussed in Chapter 9.

Pension Plans

Pension plans are run by a corporation or provide a range of investment vehicles for the employee to select from. Where the employees select the investments, the alternatives may be in the form of mutual funds or pooled pension account managers. Where the corporation invests the money, individual employees' assets typically are pooled together within it. This type of organization is discussed in Chapter 12.

MEASURING PERFORMANCE

Performance for an investment should be measured on a risk-adjusted basis. That means including not only return for a period of time but the risk you took to obtain that return. If you bought a five-year bond in a nearly bankrupt airline that eventually repaid the debt and returned 5.5 percent a year, did you really outperform a 5 percent a year return available in a U.S. government bond? The answer from a risk-adjusted standpoint is no. Ask yourself if you would invest in a new issue by the same airline for a 0.5 percent extra return.

Both the standard deviation and the beta coefficient measure risk—the standard deviation, total risk and the beta, market risk relative to a market index. The Sharpe ratio, which is just the return less the risk-free rate divided by the standard deviation, measures return per unit of risk. The higher the Sharpe ratio, the better the performance.

The alpha coefficient provides actual return minus expected return, given market performance and the individual security or mutual fund's beta coefficient. A positive alpha coefficient signifies market outperformance—the larger the alpha, the better the performance. A negative alpha coefficient signifies underperformance.

The formulas and examples using these two performance measures are given in Part III of Web Appendix A. Figures for alpha coefficients and Sharpe ratios for mutual funds are available through publicly available mutual fund services such as Morningstar.

Another method of measuring performance is comparing results for a fund with others like it. For example, a small cap value fund's results are compared with other small cap value funds or a benchmark of that size and style. Given the variation in performance by size and style, this approach is used instead of comparing results with one generally recognized benchmark of performance for the market such as the S&P 500 or the Dow Jones Industrial Average. Some advisors use this approach exclusively; they assume that risk is taken care of by grouping investments into the same size and style grid.

Practical Comment Behavioral Principles

A variety of theories and academic studies show that the reactions of investors to new circumstances are less than optimal. Among other things, investors can be overconfident,[15] overreact to new information,[16]

[15] Brad M. Barber and Terrance Odean, "Trading Is Hazardous to Your Health: The Common Stock Investment Performance of Individual Investors," *Journal of Finance* 55, no. 2 (April 2000), pp. 773–806; James Scott, Mark Stumpp, and Peter Xu, "Behavioral Bias, Valuation, and Active Management," *Financial Analyst Journal* 55, no. 4 (July–August 1999), pp. 49–57.

[16] Kent Daniel, David Hirshleifer, and Avanidhar Subrahmanyam, "Investor Psychology and Security Market Under- and Overreactions," *Journal of Finance* 53, no. 6 (December 1998), pp. 1839–85; and Werner F. M. De Bondt and Richard H. Thaler, "Further Evidence on Investor

be too short term in their thinking,[17] and follow what others are doing.[18] Such responses can result in underperformance. They argue in favor of maintaining investment positions and using mutual funds for people prone to this type of behavior. We will discuss behavioral financial planning in Chapter 19.

Overreaction and Stock Market Seasonality," *Journal of Finance* 42, no. 3 (July 1987), pp. 557–81.

[17] Terrance Odean, "Are Investors Reluctant to Realize Their Losses?" *Journal of Finance* 53, no. 5 (October 1998), pp. 1775–98.

[18] Roger G. Clarke and Meir Statman, "Bullish or Bearish?" *Financial Analysts Journal* 54, no. 3 (May–June 1998), pp. 63–72.

INDIVIDUAL FUND ANALYSIS

Asset allocation typically involves placing monies in a wide variety of areas. For the majority of individuals and financial planners, mutual funds are the appropriate and most popular form of managed account. Here we will focus on how to select an individual mutual fund. This approach can be useful for other asset types as well.

Individual fund ideas can come from such places as media recommendations, advisors, friends, or your own examination of a mutual fund database. With passive management, the prime screen may be availability of a diversified mixture of funds benchmarked to the categories stated in the asset allocation. The final choice for passive management might include exchange-traded funds as well as traditional funds, selected on the basis of their correlation with the benchmark, with those having the lowest expense ratios and the highest returns preferred.

Active fund selection is more involved. Some of the relevant steps and information for active fund selection of a proposed investment follow:

1. *Try to obtain relevant descriptive information on the fund.* Write-ups by the press, by the management company, and by industry sources can help.

2. *Identify the fund size and style.* The size of the companies it has in its portfolio and the style of investing are the appropriate beginning point for analysis.

3. *Compare fund returns.* Comparison should be with other funds with the same size and style. In theory, all markets move together. In reality, this isn't always true. For example, large cap growth funds were up an average of 30 percent a year for the five-year period of 1995–1999 while small cap value was up less than half that amount, an average of 14.9 percent a year for the same period. Comparing apples with apples—for example, large cap growth with large cap growth indexes—will give you the most insight.

4. *Look at the fund's risk.* Know the risk that you are taking relative to the category and to the overall market. The beta coefficients and the standard deviations can give you the information. A beta coefficient of 1 indicates average risk relative to the index it is compared to. A beta above 1 indicates above-average risk; below 1, below-average

risk. The higher the standard deviation, the higher the risk of the security. The S&P 500 for the three-year period ended in August 2004 had a standard deviation of 16.34. The higher the Sharpe ratio, the better the performance. Interpreting the alpha coefficient is even easier. A positive alpha coefficient indicates above-average performance; the higher the figure, the greater is the amount by which it exceeded the yearly market performance. Similarly, a negative alpha indicates negative performance. Obtain Sharpe ratios and alpha coefficients relative to other funds like it.

5. *Look at consistency of performance.* Performance should be measured over a minimum of three years and preferably five years or more. Fund performance that ranks in the top quartile for four out of five years may be preferable in anticipating future returns to an alternative that has higher cumulative returns but received all cumulative outperformance in only one out of five years.

6. *Look at the tenure of the current portfolio manager.* With some exceptions, the portfolio managers are the individuals most responsible for fund records. Once they leave, the records may be meaningless when attempting to forecast future performance.

7. *Look at the fund's correlation coefficient.* All other things being equal, from an overall portfolio standpoint, the lower the correlation (R-squared) with the overall market, the more attractive the fund is. Identical price movements of a fund and the overall market index would result in an R-squared of 100.

8. *Observe the fund's size.* Many equity portfolio managers will admit it is easier to manage $50 million than $500 million, $500 million than $5 billion, and so on. Bond fund managers in broad-based high-quality funds may not have that difficulty.

9. *Weigh the growth of assets in recent periods.* Many times when a fund has outstanding performance, it receives media attention and a large inflow of cash. The greater cash can force it to purchase larger securities or less-attractive ones than those that produced the record. The result can be a regression toward mean performance and, in some cases, underperformance.

10. *Look at tax efficiency.* Observe whether a fund manager is concerned with taxes.

11. *Incorporate the fund's expense ratio.* Fund average expense ratios for domestic stocks may be 1.46 percent[19] and for bonds 0.98 percent.[20] Deviations well above or below that level can have an impact, particularly for bond funds. Expenses include whether funds are load or no-load.[21,22]

The factors listed in the steps given above can all be found in a good statistical source such as Morningstar. You can see how to do so by examining the Morningstar page provided in Figure 16.1, which is keyed to the step numbers above. For example, for step 3 Vanguard Windsor II, a large value fund, is compared with the Russell 1000 Value Index, demonstrating the amount by which the fund generally outperformed this index.

Finally, a significant number of financial planners use modern investment theory risk-return concepts such as overall portfolio analysis and examination of beta, alpha, standard deviation, and correlations. Although some planners use a passive approach including index funds, the majority use these figures to support rather than provide automatic approval for an investment in the decision-making process. In other words, modern investment theory statistics are one ingredient to help an advisor make a judgment as to when to make changes in a portfolio.

[19] Domestic large, mid, and small cap stock funds, per Morningstar data.

[20] Domestic long-term, intermediate-term, and short-term bond funds excluding municipal bonds, per Morningstar data.

[21] Those stock and bond funds in the same categories identified by Morningstar as being no-load had expense ratios of 1.11 percent and 0.75 percent, respectively.

[22] Except for type A loads, whose additional expenses are not included.

FIGURE 16.1   Morningstar Mutual Fund Page with References

Source: Morningstar© Mutual Funds™, downloaded from Morningstar® Principia® in September 2004.

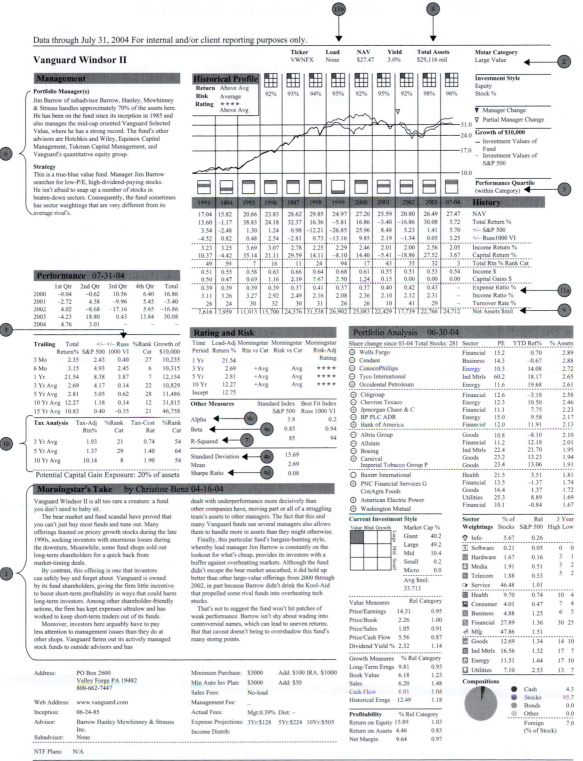

Note: Where there are more than one reference per "step" they are numbered as a,b, etc.

Back to Dan and Laura
STOCKS, BONDS, AND MUTUAL FUNDS

It was now some time since I made my original investment recommendations for Dan and Laura. In the meantime, the stock market had some change in price with small and mid cap funds performing extremely well, large cap up less sharply, and international securities actually declining. During this period, the performance of bond funds was about normal. However, the threat of inflation seemed to have receded.

I was surprised to find that Dan and Laura had not followed my advice completely. That became apparent when they asked for a meeting. They had a sheepish look on their faces as they entered. The two mentioned that they had implemented their asset allocation as agreed upon. However, when the market started to move up, they had taken some money out of bonds and international and large cap stocks and placed it into the best-performing areas, small and mid cap stocks. They had come in to see if they should place even more money into these areas.

Finally, they had one large capitalization fund with a value style of investing they were very interested in. They wanted an in-depth report of that fund's performance and my opinion of it.

First, let me congratulate you on your call on overweighting the small cap area. That call plus higher valuations for stocks overall should make our job a little simpler for achieving your shorter-term goals. However, I am concerned about your shifts in asset allocation. They suggest a style of investing called relative strength or momentum investing. In essence, people who practice this approach believe that whatever has moved up strongly will continue to do so. This approach is one of many proponents of technical analysis use.

I believe that financial investments should be looked at as being similar to any other purchase. The higher the price without a supporting reason, the less attractive the item to be purchased is. This type of thinking is more in line with an approach known as fundamental investing in which decisions are made based on logical thought. Small cap and mid cap have moved; they are currently less attractive from a fundamental standpoint.

You are considering having me manage your investments and will decide, in part, based on your satisfaction with the quality of the financial plan and your comfort with our relationship. However, there is no absolute need for you to have me perform this service. You can do it yourself. You can follow the instructions on the handout I had given you earlier how to select mutual funds with accompanying indexed Morningstar page (see pp. 467–469).

As far as the asset allocation is concerned, I have supplied it in the following table. Notice that I have recommended a return to the original asset allocation. Given your attraction to making short-term movements based on market performance, I have decided that you are better off maintaining a consistent asset allocation. When there are movements between securities, this system will be purchasing those that are more reasonably valued. The approach is demonstrated in the accompanying table.

Asset Category	Recent Annual Performance	Strategic Asset Allocation	Current Asset Allocation	Alterations	Proposed Asset Allocation
Stocks					
Small cap	22%	10%	25%	−15%	10%
Mid cap	18%	8%	20%	−12%	8%
Large cap	7%	20%	15%	+5%	20%
International	−2%	17%	15%	+2%	17%
REIT	10%	5%	5%	0%	5%
Total Stock		**60%**	**80%**	**−20%**	**60%**

Asset Category	Recent Annual Performance	Strategic Asset Allocation	Current Asset Allocation	Alterations	Proposed Asset Allocation
Bonds					
Short term	3%	10%	4%	+6%	10%
Intermediate	5%	15%	3%	+12%	15%
Long term	6%	5%	0%	+5%	5%
High yield	7%	5%	8%	−3%	5%
Total Bond		**35%**	**15%**	**+20%**	**35%**
Money Market	3%	**5%**	**5%**	**0%**	**5%**
Total		**100%**	**100%**		**100%**

There are three mutual funds that I will provide opinions on. The first is at your request, the next two are recommendations.

I have examined your Highrise mutual fund. Highrise has had a strong performance relative to other large cap value funds over the past 5- and 10-year periods. The portfolio manager is known for his style of purchasing value-oriented companies in industries that are out of favor. The fund has performed particularly well in periods of sharp market decline. It has a beta coefficient that is 25 percent below that for the average company, which provides the funds with a significant positive alpha coefficient. It has a consistent record of placing in the top half of all funds.

While it currently has $5 billion under management, the manager has demonstrated he knows how to supervise large sums. I believe Highrise is an attractive fund that should be maintained. In view of diversification needs, however, you should reduce your holding from 75 percent to 5 to 10 percent of your total assets.

I am recommending that we add Surveyor International Small Cap Fund. While moderately volatile, the fund has had an excellent longer-term record. During all but one year, it has been in the top half of all international small cap growth funds. Its manager has a knack for selecting smaller companies that have proprietary products and good management teams and are on their way to becoming larger companies. While the beta coefficient is 1.35, the standard deviation is 26 percent, and the risk-adjusted performance, the alpha, is a positive 2 percent a year. I particularly like that the fund has slipped under the radar because it has never had a "top ten" performance and hasn't had an inrush of money. Should that happen, we might have to sell the fund.

Straight Arrow Bond Fund has had a consistent record of favorable performance. It has usually been in the top quartile of all intermediate-term bond funds and has a leading Sharpe ratio for its category. The fund has two distinct advantages. The first is a relatively low expense ratio, which I believe is more important for bond than stock funds. The second is an ability to select sectors of the bond market that are undervalued. It shows no ability to predict interest rates, but I have not found any fund that is able to do this. Although the fund has a large amount of money under management for a diversified bond fund, this is not as important as it can be for stock funds.

The monies in the categories to be reduced can be taken from each holding proportionately.

To sum up, I have provided a diversified portfolio of investment that should assist you in achieving sufficient funds to meet your life cycle needs.

Summary

This chapter provided the practical facts and financial tools to implement the principles established in Chapter 9.

- The expected bond return is made up of the risk-free rate and the risk premium. The risk premium consists of liquidity risk, maturity risk, and default risk.
- Technical analysis focuses on price and volume.

- Fundamental analysis looks at basic competitive factors, among others, to arrive at a fair value for a company that may be at variance with its current price.
- The dividend discount and P/E multiple are two of the principal methods of valuing a company. One approach uses dividends, the other earnings, to arrive at decisions.
- To attempt to select attractive mutual funds, among other things you should look at their risk-adjusted performance relative to other funds in the same category.

Key Terms

bond quality, *450*
closed-end mutual fund, *462*
coupon payments, *451*
coupon yield, *452*
current yield, *452*
default risk, *450*
discount bond, *453*
dividend discount model, *458*
exchange-traded funds, *465*
fundamental analysis, *457*
liquidity, *451*

liquidity risk, *451*
load mutual fund, *462*
maturity, *449*
maturity risk, *450*
momentum investing, *457*
net asset value
(NAV), *461*
no-load mutual fund, *462*
open-end mutual fund, *461*
preferred stock, *456*
premium bond, *453*

price-earnings (P/E)
multiple method, *459*
principal (par, maturity, or
face value), *451*
reinvestment risk, *451*
separately managed
accounts, *465*
technical analysis, *457*
unit investment trusts, *466*
yield to maturity, *452*

Web Sites

http://bonds.yahoo.com
Bond Center
The bond center on Yahoo's finance portal provides bond rates; commentary and analysis about the bond market; search tools for corporate, municipal, zero coupon, and Treasury bonds; bond calculators; education sections; and glossary.

http://finance.yahoo.com/etf
Exchange-Traded Funds (ETFs)
This is a special section on Yahoo's finance portal that contains extensive information about exchange-traded funds. The site features ETF overview and coverage, search tool, education material, annual reports, news, and small glossary.

http://www.aaii.com
American Association for Individual Investors
This Web site is generally geared toward providing investment education to individual investors. There is also a research section that contains quotes, risk grades, S&P reports, commentaries, and analyses.

http://www.ici.org
Investment Company Institute (ICI)
The ICI's home page is an excellent source for the latest developments in the securities industry, investor education, mutual fund statistics, and research materials. The site offers guides for mutual funds, closed-end funds, and unit investment trusts. The ICI publishes annually the *Mutual Fund Fact Book,* which is a valuable source for information and statistics.

http://www.mfea.com
Mutual Funds Investor's Center™
This site serves as a resource for investors who want to use mutual funds to reach their financial goals. The Web site offers a large collection of mutual fund companies, Web site links, fund listings, and exclusive planning, tracking, and monitoring tools available on the Internet.

http://www.schwab.com
Charles Schwab
The home page of Charles Schwab, discount brokerage firm, offers information and access to online brokerage services.

http://www.nyssa.org
New York Society of Security Analysts (NYSSA)
Awareness and understanding of securities analysis, investing, and the operation of the securities markets is the NYSSA's objective. The site presents information of particular interest to investment professionals including conferences, seminars, professional courses, and the taking of the CFA exam. There are also job search tools and career development programs.

http://www.cfainstitute.org
CFA Institute
The Web site of the CFA Institute, the administrator of the CFA exam, features preliminary information, brochures, online registration services, and readings for the CFA exam. CFA candidates have the option to order online the books needed for the exam.

http://www.valueline.com
ValueLine
ValueLine's home page is a comprehensive source of information and advice on approximately 1,700 stocks, mutual funds, special situations, options, and convertibles. The site also offers information on investor education.

http://www.morningstar.com
Morningstar
This is the home page of Morningstar, a leading authority on information on stocks, mutual funds, variable annuities, closed-end funds, exchange-traded funds, separate accounts, and 529 college savings plans.

www.equis.com
Stock Analysis
Equis, a subsidiary owned by Reuters, develops and markets the MetaStock range of products for charting and technical analysis.

http://www.fool.com
Motley Fool
This site features stock and portfolio analysis. There is available information for ETFs, index funds, and mutual funds.

http://www.bloomberg.com
Bloomberg
Bloomberg is one of the leading Web sites for financial news and stock performance information.

http://pages.stern.nyu.edu/~adamodar/
Aswath Damodaran
The Web site of the well-known NYU professor Aswath Damodaran offers rich content from his books on corporate finance, investments, and valuation. It also contains downloadable data sets and various Excel models.

Below are the Web sites of the world's leading companies in credit ratings, stock and bond research, and risk analysis:

http://standardandpoors.com
Standard & Poor's site

http://www.moodys.com
Moody's site

Here are the Web sites of newspapers providing financial information:

http://www.wsj.com
The Wall Street Journal

http://www.barrons.com
Barron's newspaper

http://www.ft.com
Financial Times

Questions

1. List the maturity dates for classification purposes for bonds.
2. Why are bond maturity dates important?
3. What is the significance of bond ratings?
4. List and give examples of the three types of bond risks.
5. Distinguish between a bond's coupon yield and a current yield.
6. Compare preferred shares with common shares and with debt.
7. Distinguish between technical analysis and fundamental analysis.
8. Distinguish between a dividend discount model and a price-earnings model.
9. How do an open-end and a closed-end mutual fund differ?
10. What is the difference between a load and a no-load fund?
11. Explain the separate characteristics of three prominent types of load funds.
12. How does a separate account differ from a mutual fund?
13. What is an exchange-traded fund?
14. What are the Sharpe ratio and the alpha coefficient used for? Contrast them.
15. Fred compared smaller-company fund returns against the Dow Jones Industrial Average. Is that advisable? Explain.
16. List and explain four key steps in selecting a mutual fund.

Problems

16.1 Tricontinental's bond had a liquidity risk of 1 percent, a maturity risk of 2 percent, a pure rate of return of 1.5 percent, and an inflation premium of 4.0 percent. If the expected bond yield was 17 percent, what was the default risk? What does your answer indicate about this bond?

16.2 Multicolor Corp. had an annual coupon of $60.00, a face value of $1,000, and a market value of $840. Calculate the coupon yield and the current yield.

16.3 Beth bought a bond at $800 with annual coupon payments of $40. If the bond is due in nine years and has a par value of $1,000, what is her yield to maturity under both the approximate method and the more exact method.

16.4 If a bond has annual interest payments of $50 and a par value of $1,000, with six years to maturity, what is its current market value if bonds like it are currently offering a 7 percent yield?

16.5 Pamela bought a bond for $926 with a face value of $1,000 and an annual coupon of $50. If the bond matures in 18 years, what is her yield to maturity?

16.6 If a preferred stock has annual payments of $6.00 and a required rate of return of 8 percent, what is its current price?

16.7 Y Co. has a projected dividend of $2.00, has a required rate of return of 8 percent, and is expected to grow 6 percent a year. Solve for its anticipated stock price.

16.8 X Co. has the latest 12 months' earnings per share (EPS) of $2.50, expected EPS in the current year of $3.00, and normalized EPS of $4.00. If its current stock price is $20, solve for its three P/E multiples based on the separate time frames given.

CFP® Certification Examination Questions and Problems	

16.1 Which combination of the following statements about investment risk is correct?

1. Beta is a measure of systematic, nondiversifiable risk.
2. Rational investors will form portfolios and eliminate systematic risk.
3. Rational investors will form portfolios and eliminate unsystematic risk.
4. Systematic risk is the relevant risk for a well-diversified portfolio.
5. Beta captures all the risk inherent in an individual security.

    a. 1, 2, and 5 only

    b. 1, 3, and 4 only

    c. 2 and 5 only

    d. 2, 3, and 4 only

    e. 2 and 5 only

(See Web Appendix A)

16.2 Given the following diversified mutual fund performance data, which fund had the best risk-adjusted performance if the risk-free rate of return is 5.7 percent?

Fund	Average Annual Return	Standard Deviation of Annual Return	Beta
A	.0782	.0760	0.950
B	.1287	.1575	1.250
C	.1034	.1874	0.857
D	.0750	.0810	0.300

    a. Fund B because the annual return is highest

    b. Fund A because the standard deviation is lowest

    c. Fund C because the Sharpe ratio is lowest

    d. Fund D because the Treynor ratio is highest

    e. Fund A because the Treynor ratio is lowest

(See Web Appendix A)

16.3 The standard deviation of the returns of a portfolio of securities will be_____ the weighted average of the standard deviation of returns of the individual component securities.

    a. equal to

    b. less than

c. greater than

d. less than or equal to (depending upon the correlation between securities)

e. less than, equal to, or greater than (depending upon the correlation between securities)

(See Web Appendix A)

16.4   Match the investment characteristics listed below with the appropriate type of investment company in the items that follow.

    A. Passive management of the portfolios

    B. Shares of the fund are normally traded in major secondary markets

    C. Both A and B

    D. *Neither* A *nor* B

    1. ____ closed-end investment companies

    2. ____ open-end investment company

    3. ____ unit investment trust

16.5   The Performance Fund had returns of 19 percent over the evaluation period and the benchmark portfolio yielded a return of 17 percent over the same period. Over the evaluation period, the standard deviation of returns from the fund was 23 percent and the standard deviation of returns from the benchmark portfolio was 21 percent. Assuming a risk-free rate of return of 8 percent, which one of the following is the calculation of the Sharpe index for the fund over the evaluation period?

a. .3913

b. .4286

c. .4783

d. .5238

e. .5870

(See Web Appendix A)

16.6   Company ABC is currently trading at $35 and pays a dividend of $2.30. Analysts project a dividend growth rate of 4 percent. Your client, Tom, requires a rate of 9 percent to meet his stated goal. Tom wants to know if he should purchase stock in Company ABC.

a. Yes, the stock is undervalued.

b. No, the stock is overvalued.

c. No, the required rate is higher than the projected growth rate.

d. Yes, the required rate is higher than the expected rate.

e. No, the required rate is lower than the expected rate.

16.7   The current annual dividend of ABC Corporation is $2.00 per share. Five years ago, the dividend was $1.36 per share. The firm expects dividends to grow in the future at the same compound annual rate as they grew during the past five years. The required rate of return on the firm's common stock is 12 percent. The expected return on the market portfolio is 14 percent. What is the value of a share of common stock of ABC Corporation using the constant dividend growth model?

a. $11

b. $17

c. $25

d. $36

e. $54

16.8   According to fundamental analysis, which phrase best defines the intrinsic value of a share of common stock?

    a. the par of the common stock

    b. the book value of the common stock

    c. the liquidating value of the firm on a per-share basis

    d. the stock's current price in an inefficient market

    e. the discounted value of all future dividends

16.9   Which of the following is/are characteristics of a municipal bond unit investment trust?

    1. Additional securities are *not* added to the trust.

    2. Shares may be sold at a premium or discount to net asset value.

    3. Shares are normally traded on the open market (exchanges).

    4. The portfolio is self-liquidating.

        a. (1) only

        b. (1) and (4) only

        c. (2) and (3) only

        d. (2) and (4) only

        e. (1), (2), (3), and (4)

16.10   A $1,000 bond originally issued at par maturing in exactly 10 years bears a coupon rate of 8 percent compounded annually and a market price of 1,147.20. The indenture agreement provides that the bond may be called after five years at $1,050. Which of the following statements is/are true?

    1. The yield to maturity is 6 percent.

    2. The yield to call is 5.45 percent.

    3. The bond is currently selling at a premium, indicating that market interest rates have fallen since the issue date.

    4. The yield to maturity is less than the yield to call.

        a. (1), (2), and (3) only

        b. (1) and (3) only

        c. (2) and (3) only

        d. (4) only

        e. (1), (3), and (4) only

16.11   The Zeta Corporation's current dividend is $3.85. If future dividends are expected to grow at 4 percent forever, which of the following amounts should Zeta stock sell for if the required rate of return on the stock is 14 percent?

    a. $28.57

    b. $38.50

    c. $40.04

    d. $41.60

Chapter Seventeen

Background Topics

Chapter Goals

This chapter will enable you to:

- Better apply key economic concepts.
- Determine the contribution and regulation of major financial institutions.
- Assess the advantages and disadvantages of alternative forms of business entities.
- Recognize important concepts of business law.

OVERVIEW

This chapter provides information that is very helpful in performing financial planning activities. The subcategories are on the topic list for the CFP® Certification Exam.

The first, economics, provides insight into macroeconomics, the study of how our overall economic system operates. It includes such topics as demand and supply analysis, inflation, the business cycle, and fiscal and monetary policy. In the next segment of this chapter, we deal with financial institutions. The characteristics, function, and regulation of these financial services organizations are described here.

The section following pertains to business entities. Business organizations can have direct effects on business control and profitability. Finally, business law is one of the underpinnings of performing financial-planning operations. Basic concepts of contracts, torts, negligence, negotiable instruments, liability in general, and fiduciary liability, as well as arbitration and mediation, are all considered in the final section.

MACROECONOMIC TOPICS

Macroeconomics is the study of how our overall economy operates. Here we look at selected aspects of macroeconomics that are particularly helpful in approaching personal financial planning. These include a knowledge of how demand and supply establish prices and production, inflation, business cycle analysis, and economic indicators that reflect where we are in the business cycle. In addition, you will learn how governments influence the course of business cycles through monetary and fiscal policy. You also will learn about how interest rates and yield curves are established. We use this economic information to understand why things happen the way they do and to help you perform financial planning effectively.

Demand and Supply Analysis

The amount of output produced for any commodity is a function of the demand and supply for that item. In the simplest form, demand comes from the consumer. For example, let us look at demand for a particular type of personal computer, say, a lightweight and

FIGURE 17.1
Demand and Supply

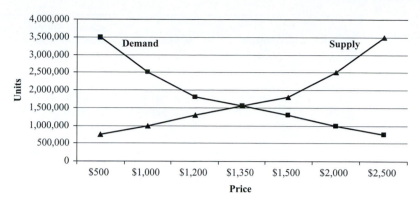

portable one. If you were to plot the demand for such a computer, you would see that demand varies with price: the lower the price, the greater the quantity demanded. At higher prices, consumers will substitute. Demand and supply curves are shown in Figure 17.1.

You can see that at a price of $2,500 per unit, about 750,000 units are demanded per year, while at a price of $500 per unit, 3,500,000 units are demanded.

Supply comes from businesses seeking to make the most money possible. The amount business will supply is a function of price; in this case, the greater the price, the greater the amount supplied. This is true because more profits are possible, at least up to the point at which costs per unit rise and ultimately exceed the benefits of higher prices. Table 17.1 indicates that at a price of $500 for the computer, 750,000 units would be supplied because the cost to produce is greater than that, whereas at a price of $2,500, 3,500,000 units are supplied. At a price of $2,500, there is an excess supply of 2,750,000 units. Equilibrium is set where quantity demanded is equal to quantity supplied. In this case, 1,550,000 units will be produced at a price of $1,350 each, as shown in Table 17.1.

Inflation

Inflation is the increase in price for a given good or service or the growth of overall costs in the economy over time. Inflation can be caused by any number of factors, some of which are:

1. Excess of demand for a good or goods as compared with the supply.
2. Increases in the cost of items needed to produce a good.
3. Lack of competition arising from few producers for that item and barriers to new companies entering the market.
4. An excess supply of money in the economy.

Inflation has been present in our economy from time to time since our country was first established. It has been omnipresent since World War II, as our government has placed more emphasis on limiting weak economic periods and maintaining high overall employment rates. However, the rate of inflation has varied, with high rates recorded in the 1950s at the time of the Korean War and the 1970s when oil prices moved up sharply.

Inflation, particularly when it is accelerating, is a problem for our economy and for many households. Among inflation's effects, it can

1. Redistribute wealth. Owners of large amounts of property such as real estate, whose value tends to rise with inflation, and borrowers on fixed-interest loans who can pay back in cheaper dollars are the beneficiaries. The losers are the people on fixed incomes—for example, retired people. They get paid in the same amount of dollars, which is worth less and less over time. When prices rise steadily, each dollar purchases fewer and fewer goods. It is as if the dollar shrank by being placed in a washing machine. You can see the impact of inflation at various rates on purchasing power in Table 17.4.

TABLE 17.1
Demand and Supply

Price	Demand	Supply	Excess of Supply over Demand	Excess of Demand over Supply
$500	3,500,00	750,000	—	2,750,000
1,000	2,500,000	1,000,000	—	1,500,000
1,200	1,800,000	1,300,000	—	500,000
1,350	1,550,000	1,550,000	0	0
1,500	1,300,000	1,800,000	500,000	—
2,000	1,000,000	2,500,000	1,500,000	—
2,500	750,000	3,500,000	2,750,000	—

2. Change economic behavior and bring about inefficient economic activity. When inflation is high, consumers may purchase goods today to avoid higher prices tomorrow. Businesses may raise prices in anticipation of higher costs. Both factors can lead to a ratcheting up of the rate of inflation.

3. Result in action by the Federal Reserve to stop the inflationary spiral. Often the resultant moves by the Fed can bring about a recession, which limits activity relative to the economy's potential and brings about higher unemployment.

4. Increased uncertainty about the future, which can reduce the amount of long-term investment and result in a preference for more short-term decision making.

The rate of inflation is measured by

$$\text{Rate of inflation} = \frac{\text{Current price} - \text{Price in previous period}}{\text{Price in previous period}} \times 100$$

Over the past 20 years, the rate of inflation in consumer prices has averaged 3 percent per year. Inflation figures by year and by decade are presented in Tables 17.2 and 17.3 for the period 1950–2004.

Real items are figures adjusted for inflation. They are important because sometimes people are influenced by money illusion—that is, they think they are growing richer as their incomes rise when, in fact, inflation has resulted in a decline in the purchasing power of income they receive. You can use the following formula to obtain figures that are adjusted for inflation.

$$\text{Real amount} = \frac{\text{Current amount}}{(1 + \text{Inflation rate})^n}$$

where

n = Number of periods

The impact of inflation on the purchasing power of the dollar is given in Table 17.4. Notice that the longer the time period, the more meaningful the impact of inflation. For example, at an inflation rate of 2 percent, after 20 years the purchasing power rate of $100,000 has been reduced to about $67,000; at a 10 percent inflation rate over the same time period, the value of $100,000 has declined to about $15,000.

Example 17.1   Helen received a raise from $25,000 to $26,000 a year. During that year, the rate of inflation was 8 percent. Did her real salary go up or down over time? By how much?

$$\text{Real salary} = \frac{\text{Current salary}}{(1 + \text{Inflation rate})^n}$$

$$= \frac{\$26,000}{(1.08)^1}$$

TABLE 17.2

Inflation over Time, 1950–2004 (Based on Consumer Price Index)

Source: U.S. Bureau of Labor Statistics, 2005.

Year	Average Annual Inflation	Year	Average Annual Inflation
1950	1.1%	1978	7.6%
1951	7.9	1979	11.2
1952	2.3	1980	13.6
1953	0.8	1981	10.4
1954	1.3	1982	6.2
1955	−0.3	1983	3.2
1956	1.5	1984	4.3
1957	3.3	1985	3.6
1958	2.7	1986	1.9
1959	1.0	1987	3.7
1960	1.5	1988	4.1
1961	1.1	1989	4.8
1962	1.2	1990	5.4
1963	1.2	1991	4.3
1964	1.3	1992	3.0
1965	1.6	1993	3.0
1966	3.0	1994	2.6
1967	2.8	1995	2.8
1968	4.3	1996	2.9
1969	5.5	1997	2.3
1970	5.8	1998	1.6
1971	4.3	1999	2.2
1972	3.3	2000	3.4
1973	6.2	2001	2.8
1974	11.0	2002	1.6
1975	9.2	2003	2.3
1976	5.8	2004	2.7
1977	6.5		

$$= \$24,074$$

$$\text{Change in salary} = \text{Current real salary} - \text{Original salary}$$

$$= \$24,074 - \$25,000$$

$$= -\$926$$

The answer is that while Helen's salary went up, the amount it could purchase declined by $926.

Disinflation refers to a period in which inflation is rising but at a rate of increase that is declining. For example, if inflation had been running 6 percent a year, but, in the past two years, it had dropped first to 5 percent and then to 4 percent, we could say that we were in a period of disinflation. Often a period of disinflation not accompanied by recession is positive for many sectors of the economy and for investments. The period from 1982 to 2002 was a disinflationary period overall and generally a favorable period for our economy and investments.

TABLE 17.3

Average Inflation by Decade, 1950–2004

Source: U.S. Bureau of Labor Statistics, 2005.

Period	Average Inflation
1950–1959	2.1%
1960–1969	2.3
1970–1979	7.1
1980–1989	5.6
1990–1999	3.0
2000–2004	2.5

TABLE 17.4
The Purchasing Power of $100,000 at Alternative Inflation Rates over Time

Inflation Rate	Years					
	0	1	2	5	10	20
2%	$100,000	$98,039	$96,117	$90,573	$82,035	$67,297
3	100,000	97,089	94,260	86,261	74,409	55,368
4	100,000	96,154	92,456	82,193	67,556	45,639
6	100,000	94,340	89,000	74,726	55,839	31,180
8	100,000	92,593	85,734	68,058	46,319	21,455
10	100,000	90,909	82,645	62,092	38,554	14,864

Deflation is a period in which the absolute level of prices declines. In many areas of the economy, its effects are the opposite of inflation's impact. People owing large amounts of debt have difficulty, while those who live on fixed incomes do well because the value of the dollar increases over time. For example, during the Great Depression of the 1930s, many people suffered, but retired people who received their income from ownership of high-quality bonds actually prospered. A problem with deflation for our economy can be the reluctance of consumers to spend money currently since they expect products to become cheaper in the future.

The Business Cycle

The **business cycle** refers to the periodic ups and downs in total economic activity over time. There are many triggers to a change in business conditions, and many patterns of business cycles. We will describe one traditional pattern and start from a period of normal growth.

An acceleration in consumer demand or other factors results in production that begins to reach capacity as insufficient new plant and equipment has been put into place. Given strong demand and tight supply, producers strain to put on new units of production and do so at an ever-increasing cost. The increase in the cost of labor results in a boost in income for households and higher spending by them. The economy enters into **expansion,** which is an increase in real overall economic output of a country over a period of two quarters or longer. Prices are raised to reflect the robust demand and higher costs. At some point, producers' profits begin to decline as the marginal cost to produce an extra unit accelerates and exceeds the marginal revenues from the next unit sold. Thereafter, producers have no incentive to bring on more capacity from existing plants.

The outcome is higher and higher prices for goods, resulting in a boost in the rate of inflation. Higher inflation brings about a moderation in demand as the purchasing power of consumers is squeezed. The outcome is a **peak** in economic activity followed by a decline as the weakness in consumer demand for goods begins to spread.

As the economy turns sluggish, business capital expenditures, which are relatively volatile and influential for economic growth, turn down. At the same time, businesses lay off workers, and real household incomes drop, leading to a further cutback in demand. The economy enters a **recession,** which is defined as a two-quarter or longer decline in real overall output for the nation.

The government, aware of the economic difficulties, attempts to influence the economy. Government outlays may be raised directly, or more money may be placed into people's hands through tax cuts. Meanwhile, businesses benefit from a decline in interest rates as weak business conditions result in a decline in demand for funds and Federal Reserve actions increase the supply.

The economy reaches bottom, called a **trough,** and begins to turn up. Outlays by businesses and consumers, spurred by government actions, enable the economy to pick up its pace. The economy continues to progress and establishes normal growth until the

FIGURE 17.2
Business Cycle

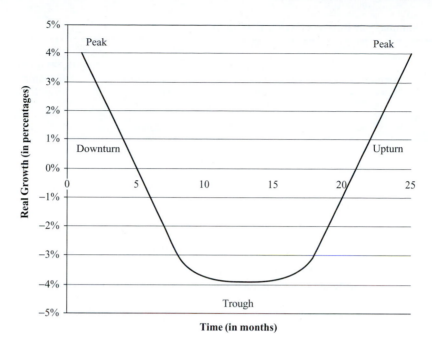

next shock to the system. The business cycle has been completed. This cycle is shown in Figure 17.2.

As mentioned, when production is significantly below full capacity, as occurs in the down part of the business cycle, the outcome is a missed opportunity to operate the country at full efficiency and to provide as much employment as possible. Fortunately, as demonstrated in Tables 17.5 and 17.6, the frequency and magnitude of economic cycles appear to be lessening. The impact of cutbacks in business inventories and capital expenditures appears to be diminishing as the country becomes more concentrated in the production of services instead of goods, and as computers and communications allow quicker and more flexible decision making. Moreover, the government and the Federal Reserve have attempted to further reduce the downtime by acting more quickly when inflation starts to gain momentum.

Economic Indicators

Economic indicators are those statistics that represent where our economy, or parts of it, has been, is going, or is expected to be headed. The broadest indicators are gross national product and gross domestic product. **Gross national product (GNP)** is the measure of overall

TABLE 17.5
Business Cycles, 1945–2001

Source: National Bureau of Economic Research (NBER).

Recessions		Expansions	
Reference Dates	Duration (months)	Reference Dates	Duration (months)
February 1945–October 1945	8	October 1945–November 1948	37
November 1948–October 1949	11	October 1949–July 1953	45
July 1953–May 1954	10	May 1954–August 1957	39
August 1957–April 1958	8	April 1958–April 1960	24
April 1960–February 1961	10	February 1961–December 1969	106
December 1969–November 1970	11	November 1970–November 1973	36
November 1973–March 1975	16	March 1975–January 1980	58
January 1980–July 1980	6	July 1980–July 1981	12
July 1981–November 1982	16	November 1982–July 1990	92
July 1990–March 1991	8	March 1991–March 2001	120
March 2001–November 2001	8		

TABLE 17.6 Summary of Business Cycles, 1945–2001

Period	Number of Recessions	Average Duration of Recessions (months)	Number of Expansions	Average Duration of Expansions (months)	Ratio of Expansionary to Recessionary Months
1945–1975	7	11	6	48	4.5
1975–2001	4	9.5	4	70.5	7.4

U.S. economic activity produced by U.S. businesses. GNP records activity of our country's business, whether produced in the United States or abroad. **Gross domestic product (GDP)** is a measure of all activity by U.S. or foreign businesses produced solely in the United States. These goods and services produced may be expressed in total revenues (nominal dollars) or inflation-adjusted dollars (real dollars). They are most commonly expressed in real dollars, which is a measure of output in units. In Table 17.7, percent GDP growth is presented by year. Notice that although many people considered the 1990s a great decade for economic progress and stock market prices, aggregate economic growth of 3.1 percent annually was only about average, as you can see in Table 17.8.

TABLE 17.7 Real GDP by Year, 1950–2004

Source: U.S. Bureau of Economic Analysis, 2005.

Year	Real GDP — GDP Amount (in billions)	Real GDP — GDP Growth (in %)	Year	Real GDP — GDP Amount (in billions)	Real GDP — GDP Growth (in %)
1950	$1,777	8.7	1978	$5,015	5.6
1951	1,915	7.7	1979	5,173	3.2
1952	1,988	3.8	1980	5,162	−0.2
1953	2,080	4.6	1981	5,292	2.5
1954	2,065	−0.7	1982	5,189	−1.9
1955	2,213	7.1	1983	5,424	4.5
1956	2,256	1.9	1984	5,814	7.2
1957	2,301	2.0	1985	6,054	4.1
1958	2,279	−1.0	1986	6,264	3.5
1959	2,441	7.1	1987	6,475	3.4
1960	2,502	2.5	1988	6,743	4.1
1961	2,560	2.3	1989	6,981	3.5
1962	2,715	6.1	1990	7,112	1.9
1963	2,834	4.4	1991	7,101	−0.2
1964	2,999	5.8	1992	7,337	3.3
1965	3,191	6.4	1993	7,533	2.7
1966	3,399	6.5	1994	7,836	4.0
1967	3,485	2.5	1995	8,032	2.5
1968	3,653	4.8	1996	8,329	3.7
1969	3,765	3.1	1997	8,704	4.5
1970	3,772	0.2	1998	9,067	4.2
1971	3,899	3.4	1999	9,470	4.5
1972	4,105	5.3	2000	9,817	3.7
1973	4,341	5.8	2001	9,891	0.8
1974	4,320	−0.5	2002	10,049	1.6
1975	4,311	−0.2	2003	10,321	2.7
1976	4,541	5.3	2004	10,756	4.2
1977	4,751	4.6			

TABLE 17.8
Average Real GDP by Decade, 1950–2004

Source: U.S. Bureau of Economic Analysis, 2005.

Period	Real GDP	
	GDP Amount (in billions)	**GDP Growth (in %)**
1950–1959	$2,132	4.1
1960–1969	3,110	4.4
1970–1979	4,423	3.3
1980–1989	5,940	3.1
1990–1999	8,053	3.1
2000–2004	10,17	2.6

One common use of indicators is to attempt to forecast where our economy is headed. We often look at the Index of Leading Indicators, which measures 11 factors that help us to project its direction. Here we look at six important leading indicators:

1. *Stock prices.* Stock prices are a highly sensitive index that anticipates all recessions by declining materially but sometimes drops without a recession occurring.

2. *Consumer expectations.* Waves of consumer optimism or pessimism about the economy can result in changes in actual consumption expenditures. Consumer expectations are obtained through surveys. Surveys of overall consumer confidence are closely aligned and can be highly influential.

3. *Manufacturers' new orders.* New orders are a sign of business intent to produce new goods, and changes in their production have a significant effect on the overall economy.

4. *Money supply.* Changes in relative growth of the money supply can affect the economy currently and can indicate Federal Reserve intent, which will influence interest rates and the economy in the future.

5. *Changes in selected prices of materials.* These materials provide a measure of costs entering into the production of goods and hence of future inflation.

6. *Initial unemployment claims.* Unemployment claims represent a measure of current economic activity. A rise in unemployment, which generally comes at a time of weaker economic activity, can affect future purchases both by the unemployed and by the employed, who may be fearful of being laid off or earning lower incomes.

These indicators don't generally all act in unison, but the Index measures net progress each month. Net progress is announced publicly and can influence business and consumer economic decisions. The Index itself is not always accurate. It can give false readings and the lead time to actual changes in the economy also can vary.

Fiscal Policy

Fiscal policy is the role played by government in attempting to favorably influence the course of economic activity through changes in government receipts and disbursements. The goal is to lessen economic fluctuations and have the economy grow close to full employment. The two major tools that the government has are increased spending and tax cuts.

Increased Spending

In a recession or a sluggish growth period, the government may choose to raise its expenditures to counteract the weak spending by businesses and households. Among its choices are

1. Public works spending on such projects as roads and transportation vehicles.
2. Spending to improve our educational system.
3. Increases in military programs to improve preparedness.
4. Programs to benefit certain age and income brackets.

An advantage of increased spending is that the government is relatively assured that the money will result in a change in economic output. On the other hand, implementation is often delayed, which can reduce effectiveness in overcoming a current economic problem.

Tax Cuts

The government can institute temporary or permanent declines in tax rates. The tax cut has the effect of placing more money in the hands of the public fairly quickly. The expectation is that households will spend it. One advantage is the relatively brief time it takes to implement the cut, but the disadvantage can be uncertainty as to whether the households will actually spend the money returned to them. If the households are pessimistic about the future, they may save the money instead. The tax cut would then have little influence on economic weakness at that time.

Monetary Policy

Monetary policy refers to government actions intended to influence the amount of money in circulation in the economy. Although the U.S. Treasury prints new money, it is the Federal Reserve that places the money into circulation and is therefore the primary institution in charge of monetary policy. The Federal Reserve is a quasi-independent agency, with members nominated by the executive branch and funding provided by Congress. Not being fully accountable to any one branch of government has created an environment for the Federal Reserve to act independently of political influence.

The member banks of the Federal Reserve are allowed to issue loans to the public up to a fixed multiple of their reserves. The greater their reserves, the more money can be loaned to the public and the greater the potential money in circulation.

The Federal Reserve's movements to change the money supply influence the economy. When the Fed wants to enhance growth, it "loosens" the money supply, which is known as pursuing an easy monetary policy. The more money that can be loaned by member banks, the easier it is for businesses and consumers to borrow. Importantly, additional borrowing by banks, which increases the amount of money in circulation, often lowers interest rates as well. The greater borrowing capacity and lower cost of borrowing generally lead to higher spending and increased economic output.

When the Fed wants the economy to slow down, it attempts to take money out of circulation, which is known as "tightening." Businesses find it harder to borrow and interest rates tend to rise, which tends to discourage new investments.

There are four actions that the Federal Reserve can take to influence economic activity: open market operations, changes in the discount rate, changes in the reserve ratio, and moral suasion.

Open Market Operations

The Federal Reserve engages in open market operations in one of two ways. It can purchase government bonds from member banks and pay them cash, which increases the banks' reserves and the potential money in circulation. This is known as "loosening monetary policy." Alternatively, it can issue government bonds, with the Fed receiving cash from the member banks, which shrinks the banks' reserves and the potential money supply, thereby tightening monetary policy.

The Federal Reserve often sets a target Federal Funds rate. The **Federal Funds rate** is the rate at which banks borrow reserves from each other, which helps establish overall market interest rates. The Federal Funds rate is set by market forces, but it is highly influenced by Federal Reserve actions. The most influential Federal Reserve action is its open market operations.

Changes in the Discount Rate

The **discount rate** is the interest rate that member banks pay the Federal Reserve for borrowing from it. When the discount rate is increased, the banks have less desire to borrow from the Fed and lend money in the public market. The net result is a decline in the money supply in circulation. The opposite is true when the Fed lowers the discount rate.

In addition, a change in the discount rate is usually a well-publicized event that signals Federal Reserve intent. Banks, businesses, and many consumers take heed of Federal Reserve intent either because of its direct impact on the economy or because of its frequent influence on stock market prices.

Changes in the Reserve Ratio

The **reserve ratio** is the amount of money the banks have to keep in reserve for each dollar they lend. If the Fed lowers the reserve ratio, the banks will lend more and increase the amount of money in circulation; if, on the other hand, the reserve ratio is raised, the amount of money in circulation will drop. This tool is used less frequently by the Fed than changes in the discount rate.

Moral Suasion

Moral suasion is the effort by the Fed to influence the economy without actually doing anything. Members of the Federal Reserve Open Markets Committee and executives of regional Federal Reserve branches can signal their feelings in testimony before Congress, speeches in front of economic groups, and well-timed interviews, sometimes not for attribution, in such influential media as *The Wall Street Journal* and *The New York Times*. The Fed's chairman and the entire committee have significantly influenced the economy in the past. Consequently, there is an established expression, "Don't fight the Fed" (and its intent), in decision making. Any indication that the Fed is even considering a change in its policy can affect bank lending and overall economic activity.

Yield Curves

In order to become familiar with bond rates at a given time, you should understand what a yield curve is. A **yield curve** is the connection of individual points on a graph representing separate returns for one type of bond over all its maturity dates. It is important to remember two things:

1. Each yield curve represents only one type of bond.
2. The curve presents all yields based on all maturity dates for that type of bond on the same day.[1]

You can see six-day data on yields to maturity for U.S. Treasury bonds in Table 17.9. Based on the data, a graph of a yield curve for these U.S. government instruments is displayed

[1] Or other time frame such as an hour or a minute.

TABLE 17.9 Yield to Maturity for U.S. Treasury Bonds, October 2004 (in percent)

Source: *Selected Interest Rates,* Federal Reserve Statistical Release, October 2004, http://www.federalreserve.gov/releases/h15/update/.

Date	1 Month	2 Months	6 Months	1 Year	2 Years	3 Years	5 Years	7 Years	10 Years	20 Years
October 1	1.52	1.71	2	2.21	2.63	2.92	3.44	3.85	4.21	4.95
October 4	1.54	1.71	2.04	2.25	2.65	2.93	3.44	3.84	4.19	4.93
October 5	1.57	1.71	2.03	2.23	2.65	2.93	3.44	3.83	4.18	4.93
October 6	1.56	1.71	2.04	2.26	2.7	2.99	3.51	3.88	4.23	4.97
October 7	1.56	1.7	2.03	2.26	2.72	3.01	3.53	3.92	4.26	5
October 8	1.56	1.71	2.01	2.21	2.61	2.88	3.39	3.8	4.15	4.91

FIGURE 17.3
Yield Curve for U.S.
Treasury Bonds,
October 2004

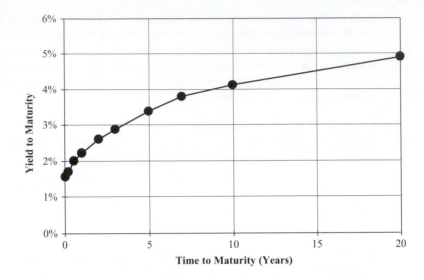

in Figure 17.3. Note that the yield is 1.5 percent for those with 0 maturity—just coming due—and 4.0 percent for those with 10 years before maturity. The yield curve that is traced out is a snapshot as of the same time frame, often the current day. As you will soon see, its shape can vary.

Interest rates can be thought of as another commodity, with yields established by the interaction of demand by borrowers of money and supply by lenders of capital. The Federal Reserve, of course, has significant influence on their interaction by tightening or easing the supply of money.

FINANCIAL INSTITUTIONS

Financial institutions typically serve as middlemen between those providing funds and individuals and institutions seeking to obtain funds to use for their own purposes. In other words, financial institutions bring together borrowers and lenders.

There are two main types of middlemen. Some serve as intermediary without use of their own capital. An example is a broker. Others use their own monies in their intermediary function, thereby placing their own capital at risk. An example is a bank.

The personal objective of financial institutions is to make as much money as possible. However, their role in society is often to create an efficient market in funds so that borrowers and lenders both benefit from relatively stable fair prices with narrow transaction costs. Given the importance of this function, mishaps within the industry can easily affect the overall economy; financial intermediaries are highly visible and highly regulated.

Over recent decades, the distinctions between various types of financial institutions have become blurred as individual firms have expanded and offer more than one service. Citicorp is currently or has been involved with commercial banking, brokerage, investment banking, and life insurance—traditionally, distinct businesses with separate functions. Let's examine the characteristics of leading financial institutions.

Commercial Banks

Commercial banks are the largest depository institutions in the country. A depository institution takes cash from clients as deposits. In addition to accepting deposits, commercial banks make loans to businesses and individuals. The majority of their loans are personal loans, commercial loans, or real estate loans.

Banks generally make their money through the difference, called the spread, between the money they charge for loans and their cost to borrow funds. Although you may not think of it in this way, the monies you place on deposit in commercial banks for money markets or certificates of deposit (CDs) make you a creditor of the bank and the cash return paid to you is a cost of borrowed funds to the bank.

Banks are the intermediary through which the Federal Reserve carries out its monetary policy to influence the overall economy. They also provide instant liquidity for both individuals and businesses requiring funds.

Banks have been consolidating in recent years with the outcome being many more very large institutions. Banks are regulated by the comptroller of the currency, the Federal Reserve, state bank regulators, and the Federal Deposit Insurance Corporation (FDIC). The comptroller of the currency, which is affiliated with the U.S. Treasury, approves new federal bank applications, federal bank closings, and mergers of federal banks. The Federal Reserve, itself a central bank, regulates certain banks, as do state regulators. The FDIC guarantees the deposits and audits the banks to identify bank difficulties.

Savings Banks and Savings and Loans

Savings banks and savings and loans (S&Ls) operate somewhat like commercial banks. They accept deposits and lend money. Deposits, which are their obligations, come from money markets, savings accounts, and certificates of deposit. Their lending consists principally of mortgages, home improvement loans, and, in some cases, commercial loans. Many of their loans, like those of commercial banks, are sold to others, in which case they get fees for originating the loans. Some also may be retained.

Along with commercial banks, many savings institutions have expanded and now offer mutual funds, insurance products, and other investment instruments.

The S&Ls are regulated by the Office of Thrift Supervision (OTS) for federal S&Ls and by the state agencies for state S&Ls. Both state and federal S&Ls also are regulated by the FDIC. Savings banks are similarly regulated by state agencies for state savings banks and by the OTS for federal savings banks. The FDIC regulates federal and state savings banks as well.

Credit Unions

Credit unions are nonprofit organizations in which all members participate in the benefits of the operations. Typically, members share some common bond such as the company worked for, profession, fraternal association, military base, union, or geographical area.

Credit union members make interest-bearing deposits that are loaned out to other members who require a source of funds. Often the loans are small personal ones, but sometimes they are for mortgages or auto loans. Because they are nonprofit and not subject to taxes, credit unions are able to effect some efficiencies in costs through a blend of lower rates on borrowings and higher interest rates on deposits.

Loans are made to individuals and, in some cases, to businesses. Excess funds are most commonly invested in U.S. government securities. Credit unions can be established by a state or federally chartered. Federal credit unions are supervised by the National Credit Union Administration, which provides guarantees for up to $100,000 for credit unions that are insured.

Insurance Companies

Insurance companies provide protection to policyholders against the possibility of a loss. They do so by absorbing part or all of the risk of that outcome for a fee. By diversifying their risk over many people, they can offer each policyholder an appealing price yet receive a required return on investment.

Insurance products are most commonly offered for losses of life and health, property, and income to both individuals and businesses. Insurance companies may be mutual companies owned by policyholders or profit-making companies owned by stockholders, with a trend for large companies to become publicly owned.

Since payouts for losses may not occur for many years while premiums are received from policyholders each year, insurance companies have excess funds. These funds are invested in government and corporate bonds, mortgages, stocks, and real estate.

Insurance companies are regulated by the states that charter them. For property and life insurance companies, supervision and examination have been grouped together under the National Association of Insurance Commissioners. States attempt to promote insurance guarantees so that when one company goes out of business, others will contribute or even assume the "book of business" of a failed company.

Brokerage Firms

Traditionally, a brokerage firm is a middleman offering to help match buyers and sellers of an asset or service for a commission. Three common brokerage areas are securities, insurance, and real estate.

The insurance broker may be affiliated with one or more insurance companies or agencies and offer their products to individuals or companies. Insurance brokers are licensed in the states in which their services are offered. The real estate broker provides services to help buy or sell a house, building, or other property.

The term *brokerage,* when referring to stocks, bonds, and other financial instruments, is rapidly becoming inadequate. Technology has rendered securities transactions, at least for smaller investors, a commodity. An increasing number of people looking for transactions alone have been utilizing discount brokerage companies.

In response, full-service brokerage companies have been offering a wider array of services, including investment management, mortgage loans, check-writing, and insurance products. An increasing amount of their income has been coming from fees, while commissions as a percentage of the total have been declining. It may be more appropriate to call them securities firms rather than brokerage firms.

Securities firms often specialize in one area such as brokerage, trading, investment management, or investment banking. Investment banking firms provide advice to businesses on financial strategies, frequently in connection with public offerings of securities, and then manage the offerings to the public. Investment banking was traditionally performed through separate firms. Although that is still true, a number of those firms have broadened their activities; most of the larger brokerage firms now offer investment banking services. Consequently, we will view them as services firms.

The Securities and Exchange Commission (SEC) is the principal regulator of the brokerage industry. It requires registration and adherence to certain practices, and it audits individual firms. The New York Stock Exchange (NYSE) and the National Association of Securities Dealers (NASD) also perform regulatory services. The NYSE does this for the companies traded on its exchange (through a live specialist), while the NASD does so for securities traded in over-the-counter markets. (Separate traders are linked by computer, which closes the trade instead of a human doing so.) The Securities Investor Protection Corporation (SIPC), funded by securities firms, provides insurance for up to $500,000 for losses from brokerage firm failures, but not against losses from financial investments.

Mutual Funds

Mutual funds are financial intermediaries between financial securities and people desiring management. They provide investment management services to individuals. The funds pool together investors' monies and manage them for a fee. They do so by forming a portfolio of investment instruments that are owned by fund shareholders. They allow investors with modest amounts of money to diversify widely, thereby reducing risk.

The fund industry has grown sharply in recent decades by offering selection advice, ongoing management, and recordkeeping services at affordable fees. The funds offer diversified or specialized portfolios of stocks, bonds, and money market instruments. They may be actively managed with the goal of outperformance relative to the market or passively managed through index funds with the objective of duplicating the market's performance.

Mutual fund organizations are regulated by the SEC. They require a prospectus that, among other things, provides disclosures of conflicts of interest and guidelines on how performance is to be reported.

Other Financial Institutions

Finance Companies

Finance companies provide capital in the form of loans to individuals and businesses. They offer consumer and business loans and mortgage loans. Unlike banks, they do not take deposits and must therefore borrow monies to finance their loan offerings to others.

Finance companies often provide monies at higher interest rates to businesses and individuals because they present greater risk of default than firms and people who borrow through bank financing. They may moderate their exposure to higher-risk loans by requiring that the lender provide assets as collateral for the loans. Some of the finance companies are parts of large corporations. For example, General Motors Acceptance Corp., which provides auto financing, is a division of General Motors. They are not closely regulated, with one exception being limitations on the maximum rate charged.

Trust Companies

Trust companies provide trustee services for individuals. As such, they act as fiduciaries that must place clients' interests first. They typically take into their possession funds in accordance with state laws on proper actions. Sometimes the trust services include investment management and possibly other activities such as tax return, bookkeeping, and bill-paying services.

Trust services may be performed for affluent individuals, children, and incapacitated people, among others. They offer perpetual operations that outlive the services of any one advisor. The services may be provided by a separate company but are often offered by commercial banks.

The characteristics of financial institutions are summarized in Table 17.10

TABLE 17.10   **Characteristics of Financial Institutions: A Summary**

Financial Institution	Deposits	Loans	Investment Services for Others	Owner Money at Risk	Most Recognized Services
Commercial bank	Yes	Yes	No[1]	Yes	Deposits and loans
Savings bank and S&L	Yes	Yes	No	Yes	Deposits and loans
Credit union	Yes	Yes	No	Yes	Deposits and loans
Brokerage company	No	No[2]	No	No	Transaction-based fees
Insurance company	No	Yes	No	Yes	Risk reduction
Mutual fund company	Yes	No	Yes	No	Investment management
Other					
Finance company	No	Yes	No	Yes	Loans
Trust company	Yes	No	Yes	No	Trustee and investment management

[1] No, traditionally; however, today may offer or have that function.
[2] Except for securities loans called margin loans.

TYPES OF BUSINESS ENTITIES

The **business** is the organizational entity for owners and workers who produce goods and services for profit. These goods and services are generally sold to consumers. The business, also called a firm or company, acquires materials, capital, and labor through the markets to enable it to produce the goods and services. In economic terms, it produces those goods where the revenue from the last item produced equals the marginal cost including the required return on the business's capital. There are a few principal structures of businesses. Included are an individual proprietorship and various types of partnerships and corporations. Each has its own method of operating, with differences in economic, legal, tax, and life span characteristics.

Individual Proprietorships

The **individual proprietorship** is the simplest form of business. One person runs the operation. Profits from the business are entered on the individual's tax return. The duration of the firm's life is the same as the individual's life. When the individual dies, the business is sold or liquidated. Among its advantages are that it is easy to form, may be less regulated by government, and has fewer taxes on operations than other formats. Its disadvantages are a lack of continuity when the owner gets sick or dies, and it may have more difficulty borrowing large sums of money. In addition, the owner has unlimited liability—all assets, not just business assets, can be available to others in the event of a suit or bankruptcy. This form is generally used for small businesses.

Partnerships

Under a **partnership,** two or more persons join their individual efforts in group activities and have liabilities for each other's actions. It can offer economic efficiencies over individual proprietorships similar to those that multiperson households have over single-person households, including specialization among partners, economies of scale, and reduced risk of income fluctuation. The profits sometimes, after fixed salaries are paid from the business, are generally assigned to each business partner based on his or her percentage ownership. The salaries and profits are then entered on each partner's income tax return.

The advantages of partnerships are that they are easy to form and often less expensive to operate than corporations. A partnership has the same disadvantages as an individual proprietorship. It has unlimited liability with the added risk of being personally liable for business mistakes of other partners. It also has a limited life. When one person leaves the firm or another person is to be admitted, a new partnership must be established. The difficulty in redrawing partnership rights, including the sharing of profits, can be somewhat burdensome. Lenders aware of the limited life of the partnership may make it more difficult to raise significant sums. Partnerships are more prevalent in small and medium-sized businesses.

Under a partnership with a limited partnership structure, partners are segregated into two groups, general and limited partners. Limited partners do not have voting rights on decisions and are only liable for partnership losses to the extent of their investment. The general partners control the business and continue to have unlimited liability. The principal advantage of this form is the ability to attract into the partnership talented individuals or those with significant resources who wish to limit their risk.

The **family limited partnership (FLP)** is a method by which a family maintains operating control and passes on financial ownership in a family business. When used under proper circumstances, it can be a sound estate planning tool. The **limited liability partnership (LLP)** combines the limited liability feature of a corporation, to be discussed in the next section, with the lower taxation of a partnership.

Corporations

The corporation is a separate organization that is established by the state and is legally separate from the individuals who form it. A major advantage of the corporation is limited liability. The owners are not personally liable for its debts and possible suits against the corporation. We can therefore define a **corporation** as a separate business entity that protects its owners against loss of personal assets. Other advantages of a corporation include ease in transferring ownership, which also gives it the potential for unlimited life. It has many of the same economic efficiencies as a partnership, but, to the extent that the corporation is larger than the partnership, it offers even more potential benefits from specialization and economies of scale.

The corporate form of ownership may be perceived by outside investors as more stable, which can make it easier to raise material sums of both debt and equity capital. If the company is publicly traded, it has the advantage of a current independently established market value and the ability for its owners to increase or decrease their ownership through transactions in the open market. The corporation's disadvantages include more complexity in establishing the business, more detailed recordkeeping in operating the business, and the possibility of being subject to more government taxation. For example, shareholders of corporations can be subject to double taxation: business profits are subject to taxes on the corporate tax return and dividends paid out to stockholders from those profits are also subject to taxation on the shareholders' tax returns.

The corporations described above are called C corporations by the IRS, referring to the way they are taxed. Under another format, the **Subchapter S corporation,** the limited liability feature is the same as for the C corporation, but the profits are taxed as if the corporation were a partnership or an individual proprietorship. Under this setup, individuals enter on their tax return their share of the profits based on percentage of ownership of the net business income or loss. An advantage of the Subchapter S corporation is the ability to deduct operating losses immediately on each individual's income tax return and to reinvest profits within the business without subjecting it to double taxation.

The **limited liability corporation (LLC),** somewhat like the Subchapter S corporation, combines the limited liability feature of a corporation with being taxed as a partnership or an individual proprietorship. It also can be taxed as a corporation. It can be somewhat more flexible than a regular corporation and may have less paperwork to do than one. It is only available in certain states.

PCs are professional service corporations whose benefit is to allow professionals to incorporate and take advantage of the limited liability feature. However, they can be sued personally for professional malpractice.

Corporations range in size from small to large along with proprietorships and partnerships, but large businesses are predominantly corporations.

An **association** is a grouping of individuals or businesses that share a common interest or goal and that generally finance an organization. It is taxed as a separate entity unless the government deems it a nonprofit association, which would then provide it with an exemption from taxes.

Of the major formats, the individual proprietorship and the corporation are the easiest to purchase. The acquisition of a proprietorship just requires the ability to persuade one person, and the corporation can generally be purchased through the vote of a majority of the shareholders. Generally, the individual proprietorship is also the easiest to liquidate because it often operates in a simpler fashion; the corporation may be the most difficult because of the complexity of its activities and assets.

A summary of characteristics of alternative business structures is shown in Table 17.11.

TABLE 17.11 Business Organizational Summary

Type of Business Organization	Characteristics			
	Economic	Taxation	Legal	Life Cycle
Individual proprietorship	Few	Income taxed on individual return	Unlimited liability	Limited to life of the proprietor
Partnership	Specialization Economies of scale Reduction in income fluctuation	Income taxed on individual return	Unlimited liability	Limited to life of first change in partnership
Limited liability partnership	Economies of scale Reduction in income fluctuation	Income taxed on individual return	Unlimited liability except for limited liability of limited partners	Unlimited
Family limited partnership	Can pass along greater assets to the next generation	Income taxed on individual return	Limited liability	Unlimited
C corporation	Specialization Economies of scale Reduction in income fluctuation	Possible double taxation: • Income taxed on separate corporate return • Dividends taxed on individual return	Limited liability	Unlimited
Subchapter S corporation	Specialization Economies of scale Reduction in income fluctuation	Income taxed on individual return	Limited liability	Unlimited
Limited liability corporation	Specialization Economies of scale	Taxed either on individual return or as C corporation	Limited liability	Unlimited

BUSINESS LAW

Law is the study of society's rules and regulations. Here we consider some fundamental concepts of business and personal law that will enable you to approach personal financial planning more effectively.

The Contract

There are three parts to a valid contract:

1. *An offer.* An offer must have intent to enter into a contract with that intent able to be verified: That offer must be communicated to the other party or parties.
2. *An acceptance.* The other party or parties to a contract must accept the offer. An acceptance must be clear and unqualified.
3. *Consideration.* Consideration refers to giving up something that has value in return for an act or promise. For example, "I will mow your lawn for $25" is a valid contract, whereas "I will mow your lawn free of charge" is not since it lacks consideration.

The contract must be lawful and engaged in by competent[2] parties adhering to the form required by law where applicable. The elements of a contract are shown in Figure 17.4.

---

[2] Being of sound mind.

FIGURE 17.4
Offer and Acceptance

Offer + Consideration + Acceptance of offer = Valid contract

Torts

A **tort** is an act of wrongdoing against a person or a business or their property for which compensation is sought. Damages must be proved. Torts generally come from intentional or negligent behavior. For example, John borrows Jack's calculator without permission and breaks it. A tort has been committed, and Jack may seek compensation to cover his loss.

Negligence

Negligence is behavior that could result in loss. It arises from not taking sufficient care to prevent the loss from occurring. There are four parts to a claim for loss because of negligence:

1. A duty was placed upon a person.
2. The duty was violated.
3. The violation caused the loss.
4. The loss resulted in damages.

For example, Arthur offered to drive Allison home. On the way home, his car slammed into the automobile in front of it because the brakes were bad. Arthur had known for months that his brakes needed repair but hadn't had a chance to take care of this. Arthur or his insurance company would be liable for damages for any injury suffered by Allison.

Negotiable Instruments

A **negotiable instrument** is a written promise to pay, without conditions, an amount of money to another person when asked or at a stated time. Checks and promissory notes are examples of negotiable instruments.

For a contract to be negotiable, it must be

1. Written.
2. Signed by the maker.
3. An unconditional promise to pay an exact amount of money.
4. Payable on demand or as agreed upon.
5. Paid to a specific person or to anyone presenting the paper (i.e., bearer).

The advantage of a negotiable instrument over a plain contract is the ease of obtaining transference to another party. For example, the contract requirement of consideration need not be demonstrated; it is assumed.

Liability

There are two types of liability that are particularly relevant in finance: professional liability and fiduciary liability.

Professional Liability

A person who is deemed to be a professional has a standard of care that must be upheld with clients. The standards may be set by what is appropriate for that profession. If that professional does not exercise due care and is in some sense negligent, he or she will be liable for the damage to a third party. The liability in that event is personal and cannot be eliminated through incorporation.

Fiduciary Liability

A **fiduciary** is a trusted party who acts as an agent for another person.[3] The agent must

1. Act with sufficient capability.
2. Comply with the terms of duties given.
3. Steer clear of conflicts of interest.
4. Refrain from revealing personal information.
5. Disclose relevant data to the principal.
6. Account for work done and its cost.

In finance, a fiduciary may handle monies for a person. A desirable fiduciary standard may be to place oneself in the shoes of the client; in other words, for the fiduciary to act as if it were the fiduciary's money, with sufficient knowledge and ability to perform the task properly.

Breaching of a fiduciary relationship can make the fiduciary liable for any losses suffered by the client.

Example 17.2

Max took care of his elderly Aunt Beatrice's estate. She gave him the right to write checks and transfer accounts. He used $10,000 of her money to support his own failing family business. That business went bankrupt anyway, and Beatrice's investment was wiped out. Max was a fiduciary who was subject to conflict of interest in investing Beatrice's money for his needs. He breached his fiduciary responsibilities and is liable for the $10,000 loss plus interest. He may be subject to sanctions by governmental and professional associations.

Arbitration and Mediation

Arbitration is the act of transferring decision making from two or more people who are in conflict to a third party. That third-party decision is generally binding and is very difficult to appeal unless the arbitrator does not follow appropriate procedures.

Mediation is a method of handling disputes in which the mediator attempts to facilitate a resolution; unlike an arbitrator, a mediator acts as an advisor and does not have the power to render a final binding decision.

Arbitration and mediation are two increasingly popular ways of resolving disputes because they are less costly than litigation. For example, many stock brokerage firms place clauses in their standard contracts calling for arbitration in the case of disputes with clients.

Summary

The topics discussed in this chapter provide important background support for handling PFP matters.

- Macroeconomics details the centrality of demand and supply for establishing prices. New equilibrium prices are an outgrowth of changes in supply and/or demand.
- Fiscal and monetary policy are government's attempts to maintain strong stable economic conditions.
- Financial institutions are intermediaries that serve as middlemen between those providing funds and individuals and institutions seeking to obtain funds for their own use.
- The way a business is established—whether in individual proprietorship or a form of partnership or corporation—has important effects on economic, taxation, legal, and life cycle matters.
- Understanding and complying with business legal matters such as contract terms, negligence issues, and general and fiduciary liability are key factors in handling household and business matters.

[3] Discussed in Chapter C on the Web site.

Key Terms

arbitration, *496*
association, *493*
business, *492*
business cycle, *482*
corporation, *493*
deflation, *482*
discount rate, *486*
disinflation, *481*
economic indicators, *483*
expansion, *482*
family limited partnership (FLP), *492*
Federal Funds rate, *486*
fiduciary, *496*

fiscal policy, *485*
gross domestic product (GDP), *484*
gross national product (GNP), *483*
individual proprietorship, *492*
inflation, *479*
limited liability corporation (LLC), *493*
limited liability partnership (LLP), *492*
macroeconomics, *478*
mediation, *496*
monetary policy, *486*

moral suasion, *487*
negligence, *495*
negotiable instrument, *495*
partnership, *492*
peak, *482*
recession (contraction), *482*
reserve ratio, *487*
Subchapter S corporation, *493*
tort, *495*
trough, *482*
yield curve, *487*

Web Sites

http://www.nber.org
National Bureau of Economic Research (NBER)
This is the home page of NBER, the nation's leading nonprofit economic research organization. The site includes links to working papers, books in progress, and various economic bulletins with analysis and statistical data.

http://www.business.gov
Businesses
Information about federal rules, regulations, guidelines, and resources that would be helpful for business users in their business activities is presented.

http://www.sba.gov
U.S. Small Business Administration
Information about starting, financing, and managing a business is given. The site includes a small business guide that serves as a roadmap for starting a business, and small business statistics.

http://www.allbusiness.com
Small Business Resources
The site provides resources for small businesses such as forms, agreements, guides, and advice. There is also a section giving a summary of key differences between various types of business entities.

http://economics.about.com/od/economicsglossary/index.htm
Economics Glossary
This link offers a glossary with definitions of economics terms.

Provided below are the official government Web sites for macro- and microeconomic data:

http://www.bls.gov
U.S. Bureau of Labor Statistics

http://www.bea.gov
Bureau of Economic Analysis

http://www.census.gov
U.S. Census Bureau

http://www.federalreserve.gov
Federal Reserve

http://www.firstgov.gov
The U.S. Government Official Web Portal

Questions

1. How are prices established in the marketplace?
2. When supply is increased, what happens to prices? Why?
3. List the causes of inflation in the economy.
4. Is inflation a good or bad thing? Explain.
5. Explain what deflation does and who benefits from it.
6. Describe a business cycle from peak to trough and back again.
7. Have there been more or fewer business cycles in recent decades? Why?
8. List four leading indicators and explain why they lead economic conditions.
9. What are the major tools to implement a change in government fiscal policy?
10. How does the Federal Reserve effect a change in monetary policy?
11. When do you think fiscal policy should principally be used and when would monetary policy be best used?
12. What is the role of a financial institution?
13. List the principal types of financial institutions.
14. Compare the operations of a commercial bank with a savings bank or savings and loan (S&L).
15. Why have brokerage firms been diversifying recently?
16. List the advantages and disadvantages of a corporation versus a partnership and an individual proprietorship.
17. Specifically, which will have the lowest taxation: a corporation, a partnership, or an individual proprietorship? Explain.
18. John vowed to paint Sarah's room because he liked to paint. Is that a legal contract? Explain.
19. Cynthia was negligent in purchasing shares for a client. She actually bought the stocks without researching them. Nonetheless, the stocks rose in price. She was sued for negligence. Will the client collect? Why?
20. List the five conditions needed for a negotiable instrument.

CFP® Certification Examination Questions and Problems

17.1 Insofar as employment and production are concerned, which two of the following industries are typically more affected by recession?

1. capital goods
2. consumer durable goods
3. consumer nondurable goods
4. services

   a. (1) and (3) only
   b. (1) and (2) only
   c. (2) and (3) only
   d. (3) and (4) only
   e. (2) and (4) only

17.2 Which of the following statements concerning supply and/or demand is/are true?

1. If demand increases and supply simultaneously decreases, equilibrium price will rise.
2. There is an inverse relationship between price and quantity demanded.
3. If demand decreases and supply simultaneously increases, equilibrium price will fall.
4. If demand decreases and supply remains constant, equilibrium price will rise.

    a. (1), (2), and (3) only
    b. (1) and (3) only
    c. (2) and (4) only
    d. (4) only
    e. (1), (2), (3), and (4)

17.3 Movement through the phases of the business cycle is initiated by shifts in aggregate demand, which create fluctuations in gross domestic product (GDP). Which combination of the following statements would be the most significant contributor to the upward shift in aggregate demand shown in the graph?

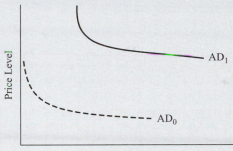

1. increase in demand for capital goods
2. increase in interest rates
3. increase in disposable income
4. increase in savings

    a. (1) and (3) only
    b. (1), (2), and (3) only
    c. (1), (3), and (4) only
    d. (2) and (4) only
    e. (3) and (4) only

17.4 The Federal Funds rate will tend to move upward under which of the following conditions?

    a. The Federal Reserve is buying government securities.
    b. The Federal Reserve lowers the discount rate.
    c. A few banks have reserve deficiencies, and the rest have ample excess reserves.
    d. A few banks have excess reserves, and the rest have significant reserve deficiencies.

17.5 Three investors wish to start a manufacturing business. The business is expected to generate a large income, which it will reinvest for many years. Investor #1 has substantial assets that he plans to contribute to the business. Investor #1 also is concerned about showing too much business income on his personal return. Which business structure(s) would be most appropriate for the business?

1. a limited partnership with Investor #1 as the limited partner
2. a business trust with all three as equal interests

    3. an S corporation with all three as equal shareholders

    4. a C corporation with all three as shareholders

       a. (1), (2), and (3) only

       b. (1) and (3) only

       c. (2) and (4) only

       d. (4) only

       e. (1), (2), (3), and (4)

17.6 Your client, a wealthy physician in the top marginal tax bracket, is interested in purchasing with some of his colleagues a franchise in a fast-growing fast food chain. After carefully reviewing the proposal, you have determined that apart from a large up-front investment, the business will *not* need to retain income and the income generated in subsequent years will be paid out to the investors.

Furthermore, your client wants to be assured that after investing so large an amount, the business would *not* be disrupted if one of his partners lost interest or encountered personal financial reversals.

What form of business makes the most sense given these circumstances?

    a. Limited partnership

    b. General partnership

    c. C corporation

    d. Professional corporation

    e. S corporation

Part Seven

Integrated Decision Making

Integration is one of the most important actions in personal financial planning. It takes decision making for all parts of the household and weighs potential moves in one area against those in another. Whenever you take the time to determine how a current decision fits within your household portfolio of resources and obligations, you are likely to have a better outcome.

Integration is often a key ingredient in distinguishing PFP from recommendations given by other professionals. They may give specific financial advice but, in their evaluations, seldom look systematically at the person as a whole. In performing comprehensive financial planning with its integration component, PFP accomplishes that task. In this section, integration is divided into its financial, human, and procedural components.

The integrated solution is expressed in financial terms in Chapter 18. In its most basic form, it is given as a simple capital needs analysis. The analysis, which incorporates all life cycle income and spending requirements, is most often used for determining retirement needs or life insurance requirements. A more sophisticated version of capital needs that explicitly includes risk is provided through Monte Carlo simulation.

Chapter 18 also presents total portfolio management (TPM), a more advanced method of integrated decision making. It includes all household assets and liabilities, risk, and correlations in decisions. Importantly, instead of handling investments separately, it integrates asset selection directly into the PFP decision-making process.

Chapter 19, on behavioral financial planning, shifts the focus from quantitative analysis to human variables. It is unwise to complete a planning project without considering human responses and behavior patterns and incorporating nonfinancial goals. In this chapter, practical ways to improve your financial performance and, in some cases, modify traditional financial goals are explored.

The final chapter, Chapter 20, describes the procedures you should follow in making integrated decisions and completing the planning process. These include reviewing preliminary decisions and procedures and assessing strengths, weaknesses, opportunities, and threats. The chapter provides a step-by-step approach to completing the financial plan.

Chapter Eighteen

Capital Needs Analysis

Chapter Goals

This chapter will enable you to:

- Understand the role of capital needs in PFP integration.
- Appreciate how risk can alter the capital needs calculation.
- Observe the advantages of a total portfolio management approach.
- Apply a retirement needs analysis.
- Appreciate how a retirement needs calculation forces choices.
- Perform an insurance needs analysis.

As the financial plan was drawing closer to its end, Dan and Laura would come in to drop off necessary and not so necessary documents. I had the feeling they were trying to influence its results, to make them rosier. At a recent meeting, Dan asked how financial planners went about reaching conclusions.

Real Life Planning

The Johnsons

For middle-aged people, retirement matters often become their number one financial concern. As people reach their 40s and 50s, many want to implement a savings plan that can provide a secure retirement.

One couple that the advisor worked with did not follow the normal path. Frank and Sarah Johnson were both in their late 40s. He was a distinguished architect in a high-paying specialty and was associated with a prominent firm. She was a lively, well-dressed woman who worked part-time. No one would suspect that these prominent people had only $35,000 in accumulated savings, all of it attributable to a recent inheritance.

When he first saw the couple, who had come from a different part of the country to consult him, they were despondent. They felt that at their stage in life, no one could help them. In fact, they had $60,000 worth of repairs and renovations that needed to be made on their home. The advisor assured them that while he couldn't produce an attractive retirement at age 65, one later on could be feasible.

The advisor went through the process of looking at assets, compiling their cost of living, incorporating returns on assets and projected inflation rates. It was clear that they would have to find a way to save more money. The wife's goals precluded a full-time job.

Therefore, they would have to cut back on expenses. Two items stood out. One was tens of thousands of dollars spent on clothing each year, mostly hers. The second was education expenses for their son, who was in graduate school.

The advisor thought about how he could best present what would be a sharp cutback in expenses and enrolled other members of his staff in the process. A carrot-and-stick approach was decided on. At the next meeting, the couple was assured that if they followed the plan, an age 67 retirement at somewhat close to their current standard of living would result. Sarah would have to cut back on her clothing expenditures. The advisor said, "All your clothes that I've seen are very attractive—so much so that they can be used for at least two years instead of one." Their son was to finance graduate school through borrowing. Their home renovation would wait and would be instituted after a fixed level of household savings was developed.

The advisor sensed they weren't fully buying into his recommendations. He decided to become more graphic. They were told that any inaction would be like playing Russian roulette, with the risk of adverse job or health circumstances placing them in a precarious situation. Savings would have to start immediately.

Two years later the couple came back, this time with only modest savings. They had implemented the expense cutbacks. However, they said there had been negative circumstances that forced them to liquidate most of the inheritance. Since little of the savings plan had been implemented, a harder line was taken. They were told that the stakes in Russian roulette had been raised and now "all the gun's chambers were loaded." They assured the advisor of their ability to comply. The advisor wanted more frequent contact but settled on a meeting in one year.

At the end of the year there were further modest additional pension savings, and the entire inheritance was spent. Once again they had failed to save. The advisor was perplexed. Why were these people coming to see him and paying money if they wouldn't follow his advice? He wondered how could two seemingly normal middle-class, well-respected people place themselves in such a vulnerable position? Other people had made the necessary adjustments fairly quickly. The advisor decided it was time to be even more blunt and graphic.

He told them that if they didn't begin material savings, their new lifestyle, which was to start when the husband retired, voluntarily or involuntarily, would be close to poverty. Without savings, if they were careful they could treat themselves once a week to a full meal at a McDonald's. Moreover, if they didn't follow the savings program, the advisor said he would resign.

The couple's request for a box of tissues and subsequent discussions indicated that the advisor had finally reached them. For the first time, Sarah said she did not believe in saving since "no one knows when it is their turn to go." However, the stark portrayal of a highly unattractive lifestyle in retirement had forced her to look at another picture—one in which the rest of her life was extremely disappointing. In fact, the Johnsons' delay had already significantly increased that risk.

In practical terms, they were now on their way to reducing the risk of an unsatisfying quality of life. They started a true savings program. From the advisor's standpoint, retirement planning had at last begun.

We will use the Johnsons' story as background for the case study later in the chapter.

OVERVIEW

Financial integration means using all assets and liabilities, all cash flows, all household activities, all future plans to arrive at decisions. Put simply, it means including all current and future resources and information in decision making. It is the opposite of making one decision at a time based strictly on the merits of that item.

Earlier in this book, you learned that the household operates as an enterprise. Let's briefly review its characteristics. The household has current and projected revenues and expenses and generates money to fund future goals. Your goals determine what future financial resources you need. These goals are expressed in a life cycle framework, generally with at least a desire for some consistency in your standard of living over time.

There are three principal ways of making integrated financial decisions: simple capital needs analysis, capital needs analysis incorporating risk, and full integration—total portfolio management.

You will learn the strengths and weaknesses of each method as well as how to do a capital needs analysis yourself. Integration will take place through a retirement needs setting that is fairly common in practice. The final part of the chapter is devoted to it. A life and disability insurance needs analysis is demonstrated in Appendix I. Both will use information on the Johnsons, whose case we have just discussed.[1]

SIMPLE CAPITAL NEEDS ANALYSIS

Capital needs analysis qualifies as a PFP integration approach because it takes into account all current and projected income, expenses, assets, and liabilities over our life cycle. It is frequently used to determine the sum needed at retirement to fund our retirement needs.

The approach taken for retirement is to estimate retirement living expenses and compare them with revenues available through Social Security and other revenue sources that we can be reasonably sure will be available. The difference, which can be called the shortfall, is typically made up through additional savings.

We compute the lump sum needed at retirement to provide cash thereafter that will meet living needs. This retirement lump sum is funded through implementation of a yearly savings figure. We need to employ a full life cycle approach in connection with the yearly savings figure to determine whether, given the costs of our current cost of living and goals, we will be able to generate that yearly savings. If the savings are not sufficient, we then determine what adjustments have to be made.

Life insurance analysis is another major use of capital needs analysis. The approach is very similar to retirement needs except life insurance is broader. The major life cycle period needs, including the retirement period, are discounted to today. The insurance needed is just the sum total of all the period's shortfalls. Life insurance is often intended to replace the cash flow from a deceased wage earner. It is discussed in Appendix I.

The simple retirement needs calculations are illustrated in a later section of this chapter.

CAPITAL NEEDS ANALYSIS—RISK-ADJUSTED

Simple capital needs analysis provides a single estimate of an outcome. For example, it attempts to tell us the amount we have to save to retire comfortably. However, virtually all projections are subject to risk. Some common risks are disappointing investment returns, longer-than-average life cycles, and higher-than-projected inflation rates.

These risks can result in your savings pattern being insufficient to meet your need, say, for retirement. Notice that our objective has now shifted from funding the single estimate[2] to one that incorporates risk. For example, the best estimate for male life span may be around age 80, but, if we funded until age 80, 50 percent of the time we would not have enough money.

---

[1] Given the complexity of the Dan and Laura case study, the simpler Johnson case was used to demonstrate the steps mathematically. Integration for the Dan and Laura case is discussed in Chapter 20.

[2] This estimate can be overly optimistic. See, for example, withdrawal risk in Chapter 12.

FIGURE 18.1
Monte Carlo
Simulation—
Probability of Having
Sufficient Assets to
Fund to Extended
Retirement Age

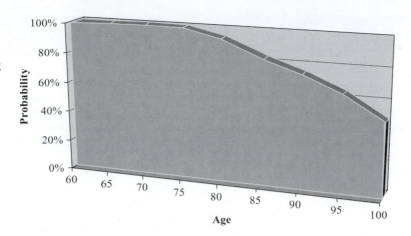

We meet that possibility by funding to an age that extends well beyond the 50 percent probability, with the exact age selected being dependent on our risk tolerance. There are two overall methods that are commonly used to adjust for that possible occurrence.

The first method is to be more conservative in our simple capital needs projections. For retirement, we may lower our assumed investment return, raise the inflation rate, and, as discussed above, provide for living well into our 90s.[3]

The advantage of this method of including risk is that it is easy to understand and to execute. The disadvantage is that you really have no benchmark to determine how much to alter each calculation. For example, to be conservative, should you take the return figure down 1, 3, or 5 percent or more? After you select a reduction in investment return, should you also raise the inflation rate and assume living to a ripe old age? You could end up being too conservative and, as a result, save too much money and forfeit a better lifestyle. Alternatively, you could not be conservative enough, thus exposing yourself to a potential negative planning outcome.

The second method used is Monte Carlo simulation. Under **Monte Carlo analysis,** selected key factors are run randomly, based on their mean figures and potential outcomes around their means. Each individual run, called a trial, provides a different combination of factor outcomes. Think of it as resembling a slot machine with many choices. Each time you press the handle, you get a different combination. Each individual combination produces a different result in money terms, telling you whether your money lasted long enough. If many of these trials are run, you receive a frequency distribution of potential outcomes. Then the probability of a favorable or unfavorable result can be estimated.

As the accompanying Figure 18.1 for Monte Carlo simulation shows, the probability of having enough money to fund retirement declines as the client's age increases. In this set of simulations, the probability declines from 100 percent at age 75 to 75 percent at age 90.

Note that Monte Carlo is run by a computer program and what is more important is an understanding of its strengths and weaknesses.

Monte Carlo allows you to combine many factors at the same time, often using their mean and standard deviations to determine the frequency of each factor's outcome. For example, running the previously mentioned investment return, age, and inflation risk together, you can get a better reading on the probability of outliving your diminishing savings. Assume the calculation indicates that there is a 75 percent chance of having sufficient funds. You can then raise the savings rate to bring that figure up to, say, 90 percent if that is the probability that you find acceptable.

---

[3] Given the withdrawal risk for many people, an investment return reduction to compensate for a poor outcome can amount to 3 percent or more.

Stanley was a liberal arts professor who had great natural curiosity. He wasn't particularly interested in money matters, but the way people made investment decisions intrigued him. He quickly learned the essence of the capital asset pricing model with its beta and alpha coefficients. He used them as input in his stock and bond purchases. When he came in to see the advisor for an overall review, he wanted to know why finance limited its analysis to publicly traded securities. He said he made his decisions based on all the assets available to him and took into account his obligations as well. From his perspective, many people used the same approach.

The advantage of Monte Carlo is a more precise calculation than the "guesstimated" risk-adjusted approach. The disadvantage is that people prefer one clear figure to probabilities. Moreover, the basic Monte Carlo approach assumes that the key factors are not correlated with each other, although they may be. On balance, Monte Carlo provides additional insight as compared with a simple capital needs analysis. Monte Carlo analysis is being used, at least in part, by a growing number of financial planners.

TOTAL PORTFOLIO MANAGEMENT

The Practical Comment above serves as an introduction to the topic.

The total portfolio management system explained below can be considered an answer to his question. Total portfolio management (TPM) is a fully integrated approach to personal financial planning. As you will see, it can provide a purer form of capital needs analysis. It does so by using all household resources in making its planning and investment decisions. The other forms of capital needs analysis we have discussed input a separately arrived-at investment return, which doesn't fully reflect individual circumstances.

Let's review what you have already learned about TPM. Unlike other models, it includes all assets and liabilities, not just financial assets alone. Assets can be separated into financial investments—stocks, bonds, mutual funds, and nonfinancial investments—real assets, human-related assets, and other assets.[4] Liabilities are made up of financial liabilities and overhead costs.[5]

Assets and liabilities include not only items that are currently marketable but those that are estimated from cash inflows and outflows using market-based discount rates. For example, a person with a U.S. government–guaranteed job for $50,000 a year indexed for inflation for 40 years, who we assume has no risk of not getting paid or being unable to work, would have a human-asset value of $2 million ($50,000 × 40). Few would argue that the cash flow from this job isn't an asset even though you cannot point to a daily traded asset figure in the newspaper since human assets are not marketable.

These assets and liabilities form a portfolio, the household portfolio. It is assumed that important decisions for the household are made on an integrated portfolio basis. That

---

[4] Sometimes we left this category out since often it is not as meaningful as the two other nonfinancial asset categories.

[5] In practice, some may wish to omit overhead costs and perhaps modest miscellaneous financial debt such as credit card obligations. This leaves only assets and debt attached to financing them to be processed—for example, mortgages paid to finance a house. If TPM is being used principally for investment allocation matters, a less exact but still beneficial approach is to drop all liabilities and concentrate on an asset-only allocation.

means decisions are made including all relevant information and activities. We call this process total portfolio management.

Example 18.1

Selena had to decide whether to go to graduate school for an MBA. She had taken a course in PFP as an undergraduate and understood that she has a proposed capital expenditure—an investment in a human asset, her own. She considered its effect on her cash balance and her need to borrow money to finance it. Importantly for her, it would cut into her leisure time and force her to postpone the purchase of both a car and a home. On the other hand, it would result in a significant increase in her income over her remaining work years.

She decided to enroll in graduate school but to postpone its date for 24 months. That would allow her to purchase the car now. She would postpone buying the home until she graduated. At the same time, she would be able to add to her financial investments. She smiled to herself when she thought about her decision, which took into account all her relevant factors, including all her assets and liabilities.

She remembered the professor calling it "total portfolio management" and saying that it was easier for her to accomplish the process than for a large organization whose owners and many workers may not always agree on actions.

The TPM method incorporates all household risks as well. Each asset and liability carries risks, as you learned in Chapter 10. The TPM approach reflects what comprehensive personal financial planning and capital analysis needs do. In fact, TPM can be thought of as a further modification of simple capital needs analysis. It uses the same basic information as inputs but employs them differently.

TPM does not depend on the validity or lack of workability of any one formula for making decisions. However, the origins of its financial solution are the Markowitz approach to modern portfolio theory (MPT). MPT is discussed in Chapter 9 and Web Appendix A, Modern Investment Theory. It uses risk-return principles to find the optimum mix of assets.

That optimum mix provides the highest return for a given level of risk.[6] When you input all assets and liabilities using the Markowitz approach, the outcome presents the net income or leisure outlays you can afford to make.[7]

Use of All Assets

TPM's use of all assets and obligations against them creates a broader and deeper analysis of a person's future requirements. It is the logical outgrowth of PFP theory discussed in Chapter 4 and more closely approximates the way financial planning practitioners think in making their recommendations to clients.

Example 18.2

There are two retirees, age 67, who have the same living costs and the same cash inflow stream including identical Social Security payments. Jack, a corporate employee without a fixed company pension, has saved in stocks and bonds currently worth $600,000 and is largely being supported by income from them and by slow withdrawals of principal. Jason, a public school teacher, receives the majority of income from a fixed government pension that has a net present value of $600,000. They have the same overall risk tolerance. Each has received a $300,000 inheritance recently. Should their allocation for that inheritance be the same?

[6] Or, less often in PFP circumstances, the lowest risk for a given level of return. A given maximum risk may approximate human behavior more closely.

[7] There are a few limitations in practice called *constraints*. The first is the assumption of flat real leisure expenditures over time as used in Modigliani's life cycle theory. The second is a budget constraint. You can only spend in early adult years as much cash flow as generated. Therefore, flat real expenditures become more appropriate over time. Finally, certain variables, including human assets and real assets such as the home, are considered separately determined and TPM may focus on the financial asset mix. These limitations are often consistent with real-life financial planning assumptions by practitioners. Where the assumption of flat real expenditures over time is not appropriate, the analysis can be modified.

TABLE 18.1
Sample Breakdown of Total Portfolio Management of Assets over the Life Cycle

	Individual Asset Categories as a Percentage of Total Assets					
Age	Human Assets	Financial Assets	House	Pension Assets	Social Security	Total
25	93%	0%	0%	2%	5%	100%
35	83	0[1]	9	2	6	100
45	74	3	13	3	7	100
55	57	12	19	3	9	100
65	18	35	29	5	13	100
75	0	45	43	3	9	100
85	0	35	65	0	0	100

[1] Financial assets at age 35 are less than 1 percent; lack of savings due to assumption of life cycle theory of level leisure expenditures throughout life span.

Although in practice some advisors might provide them with the same stock/bond mix, the answer is probably no. Jason's pension is bondlike in its payment of fixed annual sums[8] and, as a government obligation, is extremely safe. Both should view Social Security payments as bondlike as well. As it currently stands, Jason's household portfolio incorporating all assets—in this case, including human-related assets as represented by a teacher's pension—is safer than Jack's. Therefore, Jason should be provided with a greater percentage of stocks than Jack to bring their overall portfolio risks in line.

One sample breakdown of TPM assets over a life cycle is seen in Table 18.1.

Use of Correlations

The household is more than the sum of its separate assets less its liabilities. It is an operating enterprise in which the individual activities influence each other. Under TPM, the influence is partially reflected in the correlations among the assets and liabilities. The total portfolio risk is a more accurate measure of risk and makes better investment decisions. Example 18.3 illustrates the impact of including TPM.

Example 18.3

Walter was a bond buyer for a major bond firm. His strength was marketing, and he claimed no particular knack for selecting better-than-average bonds. He had his personal account managed by an independent investment advisor. Walter received the recommendations of the investment advisor from a friend, a tenured professor who was using that same person.

When the two friends were talking one day, they found they had the same asset allocation, about 50 percent invested in stocks and 50 percent in bonds. They asked the advisor why they had the same financial asset allocation. He told them each had filled out the questionnaire that provided an overall tolerance for risk in a similar way.

Walter went to a financial planner who practiced TPM. Walter was told that his human asset, his job as a bond buyer, was highly correlated with his financial assets. This correlation raised the risk of an unfavorable outcome should inflation increase sharply causing interest rates to rise materially, thereby bringing bond prices down. A sustained decline in the bond market would adversely affect both his investment portfolio and his commission income, which dropped precipitously when bond markets were weak.

The planner recommended that Walter reduce his position in traditional bonds substantially and place the monies in inflation-indexed bonds and private real estate. He said that the risk of his household portfolio would decline significantly as a result.

Integration of Investments and PFP

Investments, including asset selection and investment policy, represent one part of PFP, but often investment policy is established by itself and the return inputted into planning operations. For example, capital needs analysis runs on an assumed investment growth

[8] Of course, it is more precisely an annuity, which, unlike bonds, has no repayment of principal at death.

TABLE 18.2   Summary of Capital Needs Characteristics

	Simple Capital Needs Analysis	Simple Capital Needs Analysis Adjusted for Risk	Monte Carlo Simulation	TPM
Solves for life cycle needs	Yes	Yes	Yes	Yes
Integrates financial planning process	Yes	Yes	Yes	Yes
Tells you how much to save	Yes	Yes	Yes	Yes
Uses market-based returns as inputs	Yes	Yes	Yes	Yes
Provides a one-number savings figure	Yes	Yes	Yes	Yes
Adjusts for risk	No	Yes	Yes	Yes
Presents probability of success	No	No	Yes	Yes
Includes all assets and liabilities in investment decisions	No	No	No	Yes
Incorporates correlations of factor inputs	No	No	No	Yes
Provides full integration of planning and investing	No	No	No	Yes

rate separately decided upon. In contrast, the return on TPM is an integral part of the overall planning procedures. The asset selection and return can be combined in the planning process. Its disadvantages are that it hasn't been tested extensively and that it is somewhat more intricate to solve.

Although TPM can be used exclusively to determine asset selection alone, it is truly the end result of an overall personal financial planning process. It merits that designation because it is the implementation arm of PFP theory and approximates the goal of financial planning and practitioners.

A summary of the characteristics of alternative approaches to capital needs analysis is shown in Table 18.2.

Although TPM and Monte Carlo simulation have distinct advantages, the most popular form of analysis is the simple capital needs approach, sometimes modified to include deliberately conservative inputs to incorporate risk. It is the calculation that people taking the CFP® exam are required to be able to perform.[9] In the balance of this chapter, we will go over this method. First, we will describe the method using a retirement needs example and then we will compute its result using the Johnson case study.

SIMPLE RETIREMENT NEEDS ANALYSIS

Retirement needs analysis is broadly based on the life cycle theory of spending and saving. It is a way of mapping future cash inflows and outflows to establish resource requirements during retirement. Its objective is to ensure that enough resources are available prior to retirement to cover retirement needs. Often the retiree's goal is to maintain the standard of living in retirement that was established while working.[10]

Retirement needs analysis involves the following planning steps:

1. Review goals.
2. Establish risks and tolerance for them.
3. Determine rates and ages to be used for calculations.
4. Develop retirement income, expenses, and required capital withdrawals.
5. Calculate lump sum needed at retirement.
6. Identify current assets available at retirement.

[9] Exam takers should be familiar with the basics of the Monte Carlo method for retirement analysis as well.
[10] Often the same standard-of-living costs are less in retirement because of lower living costs.

7. Compute yearly savings needed.

8. Project income, expense, and savings during remaining working years.

9. Reconcile needs and resources.

10. Finalize plan and implement.

11. Review and update.

As you can see, retirement needs analysis is highly structured, a necessary condition to obtain the right results. We will consider each step separately.

1. Review Goals

At this point in the process, overall retirement goals already should have been established. Our role is to review them to make sure they reflect our best thinking. Key goals are the age at which retirement is to take place and the standard of living desired at that time. Are there goals to leave money to children, other individuals, or charities? If so, for what amount and are they subject to maintaining a stated minimum standard of living for household members or is a fixed amount to be provided for heirs? The answers to these questions help frame the calculations.

2. Establish Risks and Tolerance for Them

Significant risks are those occurrences that can alter retirement goals. There are many risks while working. Essentially, they were covered in previous chapters. As mentioned, retirement risks can be divided into a few major categories: longevity risk, extraordinary expenses, often health-related investment risk, and inflation risk. Our tolerance for risk helps us to determine our responses to those risks. For example, if we were to provide funds only to an average mortality date of around age 80, we would be a high-risk taker since in 50 percent of the cases we would live longer and have insufficient funds to cover the extra time. Providing funds until the early 90s would give us less than a 10 percent chance of outliving our assets, a much more conservative stance.

3. Determine Rates and Ages to Be Used for Calculations

The relevant rates required for capital needs analysis are the rate of return on investments[11] and the inflation rate. Investment returns can be calculated based on historical rates for stocks, bonds, and money market funds and the particular asset allocation used. Where different asset allocations are used before and after retirement, the assumed rate of return will change at retirement.

Rates of return should normally be expressed on an after-tax basis, which means that returns on tax-sheltered pensions would be compounding at a different rate than personal sums. Long-term inflation expectations may be estimated based on historical rates, which have averaged 3 percent over the past 20 years, or based on the current or projected time frame.

We are concerned with two ages: the retirement age and the number of years we are going to provide funds for in retirement. As already discussed, setting these ages, we combine goals and tolerance for risk.

4. Develop Retirement Income, Expenses, and Required Capital Withdrawals

Cash flow figures can change materially once retirement begins. Job-related income is replaced by Social Security and company pension payments, if any; personal investment

---

[11] The tax rate should be estimated from anticipated growth rates in revenues and deductible expenses and relevant tax-favored rates for investments. Since job-related revenues decline sharply or are eliminated in retirement, the marginal tax rate is likely to drop at that time, particularly when private pension and IRA withdrawals are not very high.

Practical Comment Withdrawals

Many people are afraid to take withdrawals of principal. They correctly perceive that declining principal increases their risk of running out of money. They prefer living on their income. Such withdrawals are often necessary, however, and in theory and fact desirable since they permit a higher standard of living in retirement. When investments are diversified and a retirement plan logically executed, much of this fear can be eliminated.

income and sometimes a part-time job are two other sources of retirement income. Returns from financial investments are excluded from this step. They are placed in step 6. Household expenses should be altered by a number of factors. Outlays for health should be examined carefully and may rise as costs for non- or partially reimbursable drugs and other charges that are not covered increase as the retiree ages. Vacation and other leisure costs also may climb, at least initially. Other costs may decline significantly. For example, job-related transportation, clothing, and food expenditures are eliminated. Household mortgage and children's educational debt are often paid off prior to retirement.

Very significantly, the household's tax bill generally declines in retirement since both the amounts subject to taxation and the marginal tax rate frequently drop. In addition, retirees have more time to focus on value-oriented shopping and, in some instances, are given senior citizen discounts to eat out and shop for food, clothing, gasoline, transportation, travel, and so on. On balance, in many cases, the cost of living declines in retirement without a perception of a decline in standard of living.

Net cash flow figures should be developed based on the decline in both revenues and costs. Most people in retirement will have to make withdrawals from investment accounts. That was the principal reason they accumulated those assets to begin with. The rate of withdrawals may rise as the cost of living can rise with inflation, but not all revenue sources are indexed for it. In addition, principal withdrawals reduce the amount of investment return, which in turn results in a greater need for further principal withdrawals.

A breakdown of income for the average retiree by source is shown in Figure 18.2.

5. Calculate Lump Sum Needed at Retirement

Once annual withdrawals and the number of years we are funding for retirement are established, we can calculate the lump sum needed at retirement to fund our retirement needs.

6. Identify Current Assets Available at Retirement

Retirement assets are those that you have on hand today. They can be brought up to the retirement date using the assumed investment return. This amount at retirement provides a partial funding of the need.

7. Compute Yearly Savings Needed

Yearly savings is the sum required to deposit annually to accumulate the shortfall between assets needed at retirement and the amount projected to be available based on existing assets.

8. Project Income, Expenses, and Savings during Remaining Working Years

Now that we know how much we need to save each year, we should compare that with our current and projected savings rate. A detailed cash flow statement incorporating income, expenses, and current savings can be developed. The method for making these pro forma statements was shown in Chapter 5. The figures are likely to be segregated by financial period since each may have its own revenues and cost structure.

FIGURE 18.2
Breakdown of Retirement Income by Source for Average Retiree, 2003

Source: Social Security Administration, *Fast Facts & Figures about Social Security* (2005), http://www.ssa.gov/policy/docs/chartbooks/fast_facts/2005/fast-facts05.html.

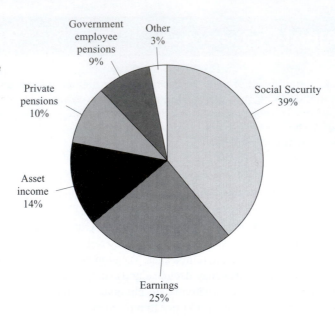

Projected savings figures should be compared with current actual savings with differences reconciled. If there are large unreconciled differences, they often come about through underestimating future expenses. When this occurs, a miscellaneous expenditure figure should be added to projections; the miscellaneous figure should generally grow at the inflation rate over time as well.

For people with less complex household operations or who best respond to saving based on need, a simpler approach of saving a fixed sum per year or a fixed percentage of salary can be feasible.

9. Reconcile Needs and Resources

The projected yearly savings needed and the anticipated yearly savings to be generated should be compared. In other words, needs should be measured against current and future resources. When resources exceed needs, no other steps have to be made. If not yet retired, household members may, if they wish, retire earlier, raise their standard of living at the current time, or increase it in retirement. Alternatively, they can use the extra money to lower their risk of insufficient funds during adverse circumstances or leave it to their heirs.

If there is a shortfall in retirement resources compared with needs, then action is called for. They may cut back expenditures today or generate additional income through changes in work-related positions or additional hours on the job. Alternatively, they may decide to work longer before retiring, work part-time during retirement, or lower their standard of living while working or in retirement.

10. Finalize Plan and Implement

Once the calculations are made and needs and resources are in balance, three questions should be asked. The first asks one last time, Is this particular plan what you want to do, given the resources available to you? The second is, Are the assumptions those that you believe in? The third is, Will you be able to carry out this plan? If the answers to all your questions are yes, then the plan can be finalized and implementation should begin.

11. Review and Update

Actual savings and accumulated investment sums should be reviewed against projected sums periodically. Major differences should be accounted for. When actual resources differ substantially from projected ones, particularly when there is a shortfall, a reappraisal

Practical Comment   Savings

Planning for retirement usually involves a sacrifice of resources to spend today for a higher quality of life in retirement. As a consequence, there often can be a difference between intended and actual savings. Rather than acknowledge to themselves or their advisor that they have spent beyond their plan, people sometimes attribute shortfalls to nonrecurring expenses. One year it can be fix-up of the house, the next an expensive variation, and so on. Of course, when nonrecurring expenditures happen frequently, even if they arise from different causes, they become, in effect, recurring.

Therefore, one nonrecurring charge may be overlooked, but a succession of them may have a significant impact on retirement plans and should be addressed. This can be done by focusing on retirement goals and acknowledging that a continuation of the preceding pattern can reduce the household's quality of life in retirement.

PROJECTIONS

Making projections is an inexact science. A 1 percent difference between actual and estimated revenues, costs, or investment returns annually can have great impact if taken over an extended period of time. Moreover, given withdrawal risk, when the possibilities of an extreme negative occurrence (particularly at the beginning of retirement) are included, the potential for a retirement planning shortfall can increase significantly. Consequently, it can be advisable to estimate all figures conservatively. If greater-than-needed savings develop, spending can be raised later on.

In making retirement projections, to be conservative, financial planners may use assumed investment returns that are a few percentage points lower than historical rates and may use higher end estimates of inflation for cost purposes. When clients are, by admission, optimists, planners may encourage moderation in projecting job-related revenues that are well in excess of inflation, particularly for extended periods of time. Similarly, consideration should be given to questioning projections of people who are unduly pessimistic—for example, when they assume flat or declining job-related revenues. If there is a spouse, he or she often can help validate these projections.

In many cases, revenue increases that are substantially different from the anticipated annual rises in the inflation rate, for more than 5 to 10 years, whether the projected differences are higher or lower, create results that may not be justified. On the other hand, the planner must take care not to influence assumptions so much that they are viewed as not being credible by household member-owners. When individuals do not believe projections are credible, they find it difficult to implement.

For example, a planner who makes too conservative an estimate of increases in wages and in investment returns, even when the prompting to do so comes from the client, can undercut the motivation for savings. The client may ignore the shortfalls as not being believable.

A more systematic method of incorporating risk in retirement planning is given in Chapter 20.

of retirement projections may be called for. Similarly, when circumstances change significantly, an overall review should be undertaken.

RETIREMENT NEEDS CASE STUDY

In this portion of our chapter, we will go over a discussion and then calculation for a retirement needs analysis. We will use the Johnson case discussed earlier. We begin that study at the point where Frank and Sarah have come to terms with their need to save money for retirement. At that time, age 50, they had $35,000 in accumulated savings.

Their steps, keyed to the previous discussion, follow.

1. Review Goals

The goal for Frank and Sarah is to live a comfortable "middle-class life" in retirement, preferably at the standard of living they enjoy today. The retirement age desired is age 67.

2. Establish Risks and Tolerance for Them

The Johnsons are subject to all the normal retirement risk exposures. Their tolerance for retirement risk has been high, as measured by their lack of saving and resultant lack of financial preparation for such exposures as health and longevity risk. There is some indication of a change to a more conservative risk tolerance, as seen in their willingness to face future expenses. They have decided to fund for living expenses through age 92, thereby reducing the longevity risk to about 10 percent.

3. Determine Investment and Inflation Rates and Time Spans to Be Used for Calculations

We decided to use a 3 percent rate for inflation and a 5 percent after-tax rate for investment both before and after retirement. They have decided to retire at age 67 and to fund for living expenses through age 92.

4. Develop Retirement Income, Expenses, and Required Capital Withdrawals

Income in retirement would come from Social Security. It was estimated at $30,000 a year combined. In addition, Frank would receive $10,000 a year as a pension. Frank grumbled that his architectural firm was cheap with its pension policy. Friends of his were receiving pensions of at least five times that amount. It didn't help that he had moved to this firm only nine years ago. Since the firm had no 401(k) plan and Sarah didn't want to put any money in IRA plans that she said "locked it up," all future savings would have to be in accounts that are not tax-advantaged.

Their retirement expenditures would be lower than the $150,000 present rate. Their tax rate in retirement would decline and the mortgage would be paid off at the anticipated retirement age of 67.

Vacation expenses, which were already sizeable, would not change and other additions and subtractions would cancel themselves out. With some additional effort when prodded by the advisor, they arrived at a figure of $95,000 for retirement expenditures including taxes.

The difference between $40,000 in income and $95,000 in expenses was a sizeable retirement need of $55,000 annually.

5. Calculate Lump Sum Needed at Retirement

The Johnson's decided they wanted to fund for a 25-year retirement that would carry them financially through age 92. Using the $55,000 annual figure, they would need $1,821,708 in lump-sum savings in retirement, as Table 18.3 shows.

6. Identify Current Assets Available at Retirement

Frank and Sarah had saved $35,000 currrently. That amount invested for 17 years would only amount to $80,221 at retirement.

7. Compute Yearly Savings Needed

The amount available at retirement of $80,221 was meager. There the lump-sum net need at retirement of $1,741,487 was almost as large as the gross need of $1,821,708. The required savings amount was $67,394 annually.

8. Project Income, Expenses, and Savings during Remaining Working Years

The Johnsons currently had household income of $150,000 per year growing at the rate of inflation. Their calculations of expenditures including taxes were about $130,000. In reality, however, they were spending every dollar that came in. A category of miscellaneous expenses was set up for $20,000. They preferred to wait until their retirement needs were calculated to establish a savings pattern.

TABLE 18.3
Retirement Needs
Statistics

	As Planned	Revised
Preretirement period	**Ages 50–67**	**Ages 50–70**
Revenues		
Household income	$150,000	$185,000
Expenses		
Household expenditures	$130,000	$134,000
Miscellaneous expenses	20,000	20,000
Total expenses	$150,000	$154,000
Cash flow	0	31,000
Postretirement period	**Ages 67–92**	**Ages 70–91**
Revenues		
Social Security income	$30,000	$33,000
Pension—Frank	10,000	12,000
Total revenues	40,000	45,000
Expenses	95,000	80,000
Cash shortfall	($55,000)	($35,000)
Lump sum needed at retirement	$1,821,708	$1,102,686
Required savings	$67,394	$30,540

9. Reconcile Needs and Resources

It was apparent that the required saving of $67,394 per year was too great. The Johnsons had waited too long to begin saving. We discussed ways of reconciling needs and resources. They decided to postpone retirement to age 70. Furthermore, the couple thought they could reduce their retirement living costs to $80,000 from $95,000. Although that level was not what they hoped for, it would meet their minimum goals.

Retiring later would add about $5,000 each year to retirement income coming from Social Security and a higher company pension payout. It also would require three years less for retirement funding. Finally, they cut back their funding date one year and assumed they would sell their house at age 91 if necessary. Consequently, retirement funding dropped by a total of four years.

When the retirement needs were recalculated, the figure came to $30,540. Sarah thought for just a minute and said she would take a full-time job. She could earn $45,000 a year pretax and $30,000 after taxes as compared with her current income of $10,000 a year pretax and $7,000 per year after-tax. Consequently, there would be a net increase of $23,000 per year in retirement funding. The final piece, then, would be a further current expense cutback of about $8,000 a year net of higher taxes due to Sarah's higher income. This would result in total additional yearly savings of $31,000, just enough to meet the need.

There are two periods in the Johnsons' retirement planning horizon: preretirement and postretirement. The retirement needs statistics for these two periods are presented in Table 18.3.

10. Finalize Plan and Implement

I summarized the parts of the revised plan. The couple would work until age 70, live on $80,000 a year in retirement, and cut back expenses by $8,000 a year. Sarah was already looking forward to the adventure of a new full-time job. The financial pieces had been agreed to.

11. Review and Update

Given the difficulty the couple had with compliance in the past, I strongly suggested meeting every quarter for the first year. I was gratified to see a new purpose and savings discipline in the follow-up meetings. The retirement plan was being implemented according to schedule.

Here we begin by presenting a retirement needs calculation format in Table 18.4 and follow it with the actual calculations for Frank and Sarah in Table 18.6. Notice that the steps are keyed to our discussion.

A summary of appropriate capital needs rates to apply under different circumstances is shown in Table 18.5.

TABLE 18.4   Retirement Needs Calculation—Described

Step	Item	Symbol	Explanation or Calculation
3	Investment rate	IR	The rate of return for investments
3	Inflation rate	ER	The rate of increase in expenses
3	Real rate	RR	The combination of the inflation and investment rates
			Formula: $RR = \left(\dfrac{1 + IR}{1 + ER} - 1 \right) \times 100$
3	Present time	t_0	Today
3	Future time	t_1	Beginning of payout period
3	Number of years for payout period	N_{t_p}	From beginning to end of payout period
3	Number of years to beginning of period	N_{t_1}	From today to start of payout period
3	Number of years to today	N_{t_0}	From beginning of payout period to today
4	Cash inflows	CI_{t_0}	Includes the total of retirement pension investment and other yearly cash inflows in current dollars
4	Cash outflows	CO_{t_0}	Discretionary and nondiscretionary expenses, capital expenditures, and other yearly retirement cash outflows in current dollars
4	Cash shortfall	CS_{t_0}	Current yearly cash inflows − cash outflows $CS_{t_0} = CI_{t_0} - CO_{t_0}$
5	Cash shortfall future	CS_{t_1}	Current yearly shortfall brought forward to beginning of payout period. The inflation rate is used to calculate the estimated future cost of the present cash shortfall.

Calculator Solution

Input:

N_{t_1}	ER	CS_{t_0}		
N	I/Y	PV	PMT	FV
Solution:				Press for CS_{t_1}

Step	Item	Symbol	Explanation or Calculation
5	Lump-sum shortfall future	LS_{t_1}	Amount of full payout period, yearly shortfalls discounted back to beginning of payout period. Since there are a series of payments occurring over a period of time, both investment and inflation rates are employed through the real rate. Use BEGIN function for beginning of the year payments.

Calculator Solution

Input:

N_{t_p}	RR		CS_{t_1}	
N	I/Y	PV	PMT	FV
Solution:		Press for LS_{t_1}		

Step	Item	Symbol	Explanation or Calculation
6	Assets accumulated	AA_{t_0}	Assets available today to help fund retirement shortfall
6	Assets accumulated future	AA_{t_1}	Assets accumulated brought forward to beginning of payout period. The investment rate is used to calculate the estimated future value of today's sum.

Calculator Solution

Inputs:

N_{t_1}	IR	AA_{t_0}		
N	I/Y	PV	PMT	FV
Solution:				Press for AA_{t_1}

Step	Item	Symbol	Explanation or Calculation
7	Additional assets required future	AR_{t_1}	Lump-sum shortfall less estimated future assets accumulated $AR_{t_1} = LS_{t_1} - AA_{t_1}$
7	Required yearly savings	$RS_{t_{0 \to 1}}$	The yearly savings required to produce the additional sum needed at the beginning of the payout period. The investment rate is used because investment return influences the amount required for the series of savings deposits.

Calculator Solution

Inputs:

N_{t_0}	IR			AR_{t_1}
N	I/Y	PV	PMT	FV
Solution:			Press for $RS_{t_{0 \to 1}}$	

TABLE 18.5
Summary of
Appropriate Capital
Needs Rate to Use

Step	Investment Rate	Inflation Rate	Real Rate
To bring current cash shortfall to future period CS_{t_0} to CS_{t_1}	No	Yes	No
To bring current investment sum to future period AA_{t_0} to AA_{t_1}	Yes	No	No
To establish lump-sum shortfall from the amount of payouts CS_{t_1} to LS_{t_1}	No	No	Yes
To bring lump-sum cash shortfall back from future period to present LS_{t_1} to LS_{t_0}	Yes	No	No
To establish yearly savings needed to fund lump-sum shortfall AR_{t_1} to $RS_{t_{0 \to 1}}$	Yes	No	No

TABLE 18.6   **Retirement Needs Calculation—Before Revision**

Step	Item	Symbol	Explanation or Calculation
3	Investment rate	IR	5% given
3	Inflation rate	ER	3% given
3	Real rate	RR	$1.9417 \quad RR = \left(\dfrac{1 + 0.05}{1 + 0.03} - 1 \right) \times 100$
3	Number of years for payout period	N_{t_p}	25 Age 67 to age 92
3	Number of years to beginning of period	N_{t_1}	17 Age 50 to age 67
3	Number of years from future period to today	N_{t_0}	17 Age 67 to age 50
4	Cash inflows	CI_{t_0}	$40,000 given
4	Cash outflows	CO_{t_0}	$95,000 given
4	Cash shortfall	CS_{t_0}	$55,000 95,000 − 40,000
5	Cash shortfall future	CS_{t_1}	*Inputs:*

Step 5 — Cash shortfall future (CS_{t_1}):

N	I/Y	PV	PMT	FV
17	3	55000		

Solution: Press **$90,907** (FV)

Step 5 — Lump-sum shortfall future (Use BEGIN function) (LS_{t_1}): *Inputs:*

N	I/Y	PV	PMT	FV
25	1.9417		90907	

Solution: Press **$1,821,708** (PV)

Step	Item	Symbol	Explanation or Calculation
6	Assets accumulated today	AA_{t_0}	$35,000 given
6	Assets accumulated future	AA_{t_1}	*Inputs:*

Step 6 — Assets accumulated future (AA_{t_1}):

N	I/Y	PV	PMT	FV
17	5	35000		

Solution: Press **$80,221** (FV)

Step	Item	Symbol	Explanation or Calculation
7	Additional assets required future	AR_{t_1}	$1,741,487
			$AR_{t_1} = LS_{t_1} - AA_{t_1} = 1{,}821{,}708 - 80{,}221$
7	Required yearly savings	$RS_{t_{0 \to 1}}$	*Inputs:*

Step 7 — Required yearly savings ($RS_{t_{0 \to 1}}$):

N	I/Y	PV	PMT	FV
17	5			1741487

Solution: Press **$67,394** (PMT)

TABLE 18.7   **Retirement Needs Calculation—After Revision**

Step	Item	Symbol	Explanation or Calculation
3	Investment rate	IR	5% given
3	Inflation rate	ER	3% given
3	Real rate	RR	$1.9417 \; RR = \left(\dfrac{1 + 0.05}{1 + 0.03} - 1\right) \times 100$
3	Number of years for payout period	N_{t_p}	21 Age 70 to age 91
3	Number of years to beginning of period	N_{t_1}	20 Age 50 to age 70
3	Number of years from future period to today	N_{t_0}	20 Age 70 to age 50
4	Cash inflows	CI_{t_0}	$45,000 given
4	Cash outflows	CO_{t_0}	$80,000 given
4	Cash shortfall	CS_{t_0}	$35,000 80,000 − 45,000
5	Cash shortfall future	CS_{t_1}	*Inputs:*

Step 5 — CS_{t_1}:

	N	I/Y	PV	PMT	FV
Inputs:	20	3	35000		
Solution:					Press **$63,214**

Step 5 — Lump-sum shortfall future (Use BEGIN function) LS_{t_1}:

	N	I/Y	PV	PMT	FV
Inputs:	21	1.9417		63214	
Solution:			Press **$1,102,686**		

Step	Item	Symbol	Explanation or Calculation
6	Assets accumulated today	AA_{t_0}	$35,000 given

Step 6 — Assets accumulated future AA_{t_1}:

	N	I/Y	PV	PMT	FV
Inputs:	20	5	35000		
Solution:					Press **$92,865**

Step	Item	Symbol	Explanation or Calculation
7	Additional assets required future	AR_{t_1}	**$1,009,820**
			$AR_{t_1} = LS_{t_1} - AA_{t_1} = 1,102,686 - 92,865$

Step 7 — Required yearly savings $RS_{t_{0 \to 1}}$:

	N	I/Y	PV	PMT	FV
Inputs:	20	5			1009820
Solution:				Press **$30,540**	

Table 18.7 provides the calculation rerun based on revised goals.

This retirement analysis and accompanying calculations for Frank and Sarah contrast with the more-involved Dan and Laura retirement case study, which takes place over three chapters—12, this one, and 20.

Back to Dan and Laura

CAPITAL NEEDS ANALYSIS

As the financial plan was drawing closer to its end, Dan and Laura would come in to drop off necessary and not-so-necessary documents. I had the feeling they were trying to influence its results, to make them rosier. At a recent meeting, Dan asked how financial planners went about reaching conclusions. He said that he, as a mathematically oriented person, could handle any simple mathematical discussion I would want to go over.

We sat down. Laura had one of those "here we go again" looks on her face. She smiled at me, took out a paperback book, and wasn't heard from for the remainder of the time together. After my explanation, Dan asked if I would summarize the discussion in writing, which I did.

Dan, there are several ways that financial planners handle integration. The first is on what I would call an ad hoc way. That is, they do it the way your grandmother might have cooked. There was no fixed recipe. She put in a little of this and that from her head, integrating all ingredients. If she was an experienced creative cook, the dish might come out well. If not, the results could be poor, each time tasting different.

Similarly, the ad hoc way is not scientific and can be off markedly from subsequent outcomes. The ad hoc way is more popular with financial advisors who aren't financial planners.

The second approach, a capital needs analysis, tells you how much money you require to fund your goals. In its simple form, it assesses the cost of your goals and compares that with the resources you are currently generating and what you expect to obtain in the future. Adjustments are made between goals and projected resources to bring them into line. The outcome is often expressed simply as the amount that is needed in savings annually to achieve your goals.

As you mentioned to me, you are familiar with Monte Carlo simulation. It can be used as a refinement of simple capital needs analysis. You are probably aware that any single amount of savings cannot predict all outcomes. What is needed is a framework that takes into account the probabilities of an outcome; for example, the probability that the savings rate given in a simple capital needs analysis will come to pass. In other words, Monte Carlo is more sophisticated than the simple method. It doesn't give the one-figure solution that you might find satisfying, but it is more realistic.

Total portfolio management is even more advanced. It takes into account all assets and obligations and their correlations in making investment decisions. It, like Monte Carlo, incorporates risk in capital needs analysis and can be looked upon in mathematical terms as a further refinement of capital needs analysis. It is a planning tool that comes directly from PFP theory and integrates PFP and investments in a way the others don't.

In performing our simple retirement calculations, often the practical reflection of capital needs analysis, we made the following assumptions:

1. An inflation rate and your costs both rising 3 percent a year.
2. Dan's salary rising 10 percent a year through 2014 and then at the rate of inflation; Laura's salary rising at the rate of inflation.
3. Stocks rising 11 percent a year. Bonds increasing 5.5 percent a year.
4. Retirement funding to age 95, as you requested, even though I prefer ages 95 and 91 for Laura and Dan, respectively, to provide an actuarially derived lower-than-10-percent chance of outliving your money.

The analysis indicates that you will have to save $60,000 in projected savings plus approximately an additional $41,000 per year beginning in year 6 to meet your goal of retiring at age 55. I consider this amount of savings difficult to achieve without further adjustments. I should mention that I have taken the investment return down 1 percent from 8.7 percent to 7.7 percent to be conservative. I recommend that we wait for the results of a risk-adjusted analysis in our final decision-making integration meeting before further discussions on retirement.

I have also promised you the outcome of a life insurance needs analysis. Based on your current living pattern, Laura needs $1,289,421 on Dan's life. If Laura passes away, the need, including the hiring of a household assistant for the children, would be $673,091.

You have no current insurance, so the entire amount will have to be purchased. Again, here I think we should wait for the risk-adjusted analysis before making specific recommendations of amounts to purchase.

We will use TPM concepts in completing your plan shortly (shown in Chapter 20).

I hope this helps in your understanding of integration. If you have any questions, let me know.

The calculations are given below.

RETIREMENT NEEDS ANALYSIS

Inputs

General

Dan's age	35
Laura's age	35
Dan's retirement age	55
Laura's retirement age	55
Dan's assumed age of death	95
Laura's assumed age of death	95
Years until retirement period 1	20
Years until retirement period 2	30
Years in retirement period 1	10
Years in retirement period 2	30

Laura

Pension at age 65, today's dollars	$40,000
After-tax pension	28,800
Current salary	0
Salary in five years, today's dollars	68,000
Annual increase thereafter	3%
Social Security benefits at age 67	$21,996

Dan

Salary	$100,000
Annual increase through 2014	10%
Annual increase beginning 2015	3%
Social Security benefits at age 67	$25,512

Expenses

Living expenses, today's dollars[1]	$83,452
15% COL reduction in retirement	($12,518)
Additional travel expenses	$10,000
Total expenses in retirement	$80,935

Economic

Inflation	3.0%
Tax rate in retirement[2]	28.0%
Investment return	7.7%
After-tax investment return	5.5%
Real return	4.6%
After-tax real return	2.5%

[1] Sum of discretionary, nondiscretionary, and capital expenses in year 6, discounted to year 1.

[2] Estimated marginal federal and state rate. Assumes flat state tax rate of 5% and blend of ordinary income and capital gains federal rates.

Step 1. Calculate the Amount Needed in Retirement

Retirement Period 1 (55–65)

Living expenses in retirement, today's dollars	$80,935
Laura's pension in today's dollars, after taxes	0
Annual shortfall, today's dollars	80,935
Annual shortfall, age 55	146,177
Lump sum needed to retire mortgage[1]	156,712
Lump sum needed at beginning of period	**$1,469,701**

Retirement Period 2 (65–95)

Living expenses in retirement, today's dollars	$80,935
Laura's pension in today's dollars, after taxes	28,800
Social Security benefits at 65 in today's dollars, after taxes	31,350
Annual shortfall, today's dollars	20,784
Annual shortfall, age 65	50,449
Lump sum needed at age 65	**$1,086,354**

[1] Amount owed after 19 years of mortgage payments at normal amortization. Assumes mortgage begins in year 2 of plan.

Step 2. Bring the Lump Sum Needed Back to the Present

Lump sum currently needed, retirement period 1	$499,526
Lump sum currently needed, retirement period 2	215,261
Lump sum needed in year 6, retirement period 1[1]	654,223
Lump sum needed in year 6, retirement period 2	281,924
Total lump sum needed now	714,787
Total lump sum needed in year 6	**$936,147**

[1] Assumes that savings cannot begin until year 6, when Laura returns to work.

Step 3. Repeat Steps for Other Needs

Lump sum needed for college in year 6	$175,665
Total other needs lump sum, year 6	**$175,665**

Step 4. Establish the Current Value of Projected Future Saving

Accumulated assets as of year 6	$100,003
Projected after-tax savings starting year 6	60,000
PV of future savings in year 6	600,498
Total existing and projected resources in year 6	**$700,500**

Step 5. Compare Resources and Needs

Total needs in year 6	$1,111,813
Total existing and projected resources in year 6	700,500
Additional resources needed	**$411,312**

Step 6. Establish Additional Annual Savings Needed

Additional savings needed beginning year 6 (level payment)	$41,097
Additional annual savings needed beginning year 6	**$41,097**

INSURANCE NEEDS ANALYSIS—DAN

Inputs

General

Dan's age	35
Laura's age	35
Laura's retirement age	55
Dan's assumed age of death	35
Laura's assumed age of death	95
Years in preretirement period 1	5
Years in preretirement period 2	15
Years in retirement period 1	10
Years in retirement period 2	30

Laura

Pension	$40,000
After-tax pension	30,000
Current salary	0
Salary in year 6	68,000
Salary after tax	51,000
Annual increase	3%
Social Security benefits	
Laura's Social Security in retirement	21,996
Survivor benefits until children grown, before tax[1]	26,250

Expenses

Current expenses	$103,032
Expense reduction at Dan's death	10%
Expenses after Dan's death	92,729
Expenses after children grown	72,841

Available Assets

Investment assets	$150,000
Liabilities	86,000
Available assets	64,000

Economic

Inflation	3.0%
Investment return	7.7%
After-tax investment return	5.5%
Real return	4.6%
After-tax real return	2.5%
Average tax rate, years 1–5	0%
Average tax rate, years 6–20	25%
Average tax rate in retirement	25%

[1] Estimate. Actual numbers will be modestly different because different benefits end in different years.

Step 1. Determine the Amount Needed to Fund the Preretirement Period

Preretirement period 1, years 1–5 (All figures in today's dollars)

Annual expenses	$92,729
Social Security survivor benefits, after taxes	26,250
Laura's salary, after taxes	0
Total income, after taxes	26,250
Annual shortfall	66,479
Lump-sum shortfall, today's dollars	**$316,754**

Preretirement period 2, years 6–20 (All figures in today's dollars)

Annual expenses	$92,729
Social Security survivor benefits, after taxes	20,672
Laura's salary, after taxes	51,000
Total income, after taxes	71,672
Annual shortfall, today's dollars	21,057
Annual shortfall, year 6	24,411
Lump-sum shortfall, year 6	310,397
Lump-sum shortfall, today's dollars	**$237,001**

Step 2. Determine the Amount Needed to Fund the Retirement Period

Retirement Period 1 (55–65)

Living expenses in today's dollars	$72,841
Income	0
Annual shortfall, today's dollars	72,841
Annual shortfall, age 55	131,559
PV lump-sum future survivor benefits	105,816
Lump-sum shortfall, age 55	1,075,874
Lump-sum shortfall, today's dollars	**$365,671**

Retirement Period 2 (65–95)

Living expenses in today's dollars	$72,841
Laura's annual pension	30,000
Social Security benefits, after taxes	15,001
Total income	45,001
Annual shortfall, today's dollars	27,840
Annual shortfall, age 65	67,576
Lump-sum shortfall, age 65	1,455,153
Lump-sum shortfall, today's dollars	**$288,338**

Step 3. Determine the Total Lump Sum Needed Today

Lump sum currently needed, preretirement period 1	$316,754
Lump sum currently needed, preretirement period 2	237,001
Lump sum currently needed, retirement period 1	365,671
Lump sum currently needed, retirement period 2	288,338
Total lump sum needed, today's dollars	**$1,207,764**

Step 4. Repeat Steps for Other Needs

Lump sum needed currently for college	$125,657
Burial expenses	20,000
Total lump sum for other needs, today's dollars	**$145,657**

Step 5. Establish Insurance Need

Total lump sump needed for all needs, today's dollars	**$1,353,421**
Available assets	**$64,000**
Total insurance needed, today's dollars	**$1,289,421**

INSURANCE NEEDS ANALYSIS—LAURA

Inputs

General

Dan's age	35
Laura's age	35
Dan's retirement age	55
Laura's assumed age of death	35
Dan's assumed age of death	95
Years in preretirement period 1	18
Years in preretirement period 2	2
Years in retirement period 1	10
Years in retirement period 2	30

Dan

Salary	$100,000
Annual increase through 2014	10%
Annual increase beginning 2015	3%
Social Security benefits	
Dan's Social Security in retirement	25,512
Survivor benefits until children grown, before tax[1]	24,150

Expenses

Current expenses	$103,032
Expense reduction at Laura's death	10%
Expenses after Laura's death	92,729
Expenses after children grown	72,841

Available Assets

Investment assets	$150,000
Liabilities	86,000
Available assets	64,000

Economic

Inflation	3.0%
Investment return	7.7%
After-tax investment return	5.5%
Real return	4.6%
After-tax real return	2.5%
Average tax rate, preretirement period	30%
Average tax rate, retirement period	28%

[1] Estimate. Actual numbers will be modestly different because different benefits end in different years.

Step 1. Determine the Amount Needed to Fund the Preretirement Period

Preretirement period 1, years 1–18

Annual expenses	$92,729
Social Security survivor benefits, after taxes	17,992
Annual shortfall	74,737
Lump-sum currently needed	1,102,088
NPV Dan's salary, after taxes	1,445,285
Lump-sum surplus, today's dollars	**$343,198**

Preretirement period 2, years 19–20

Annual expenses	$92,729
Social Security survivor benefits, after taxes	0
Annual shortfall	92,729
Annual shortfall, year 19	157,865
Lump-sum shortfall, year 19	311,925
Lump-sum shortfall, today's dollars	118,099
NPV Dan's salary years 19–20, after taxes	147,223
Lump-sum surplus, today's dollars	**$29,124**

Step 2. Determine the Amount Needed to Fund the Retirement Period

Retirement Period 1 (55–65)

Living expenses in today's dollars	$72,841
Income	0
Annual shortfall, today's dollars	72,841
Annual shortfall, age 55	131,559
PV lump-sum future survivor benefits	52,737
Lump-sum shortfall, age 55	1,128,953
Lump-sum shortfall, today's dollars	**$383,712**

Retirement Period 2 (65–95)

Living expenses in today's dollars	$72,841
Social Security benefits, after taxes	16,835
Annual shortfall, today's dollars	56,006
Annual shortfall, age 65	135,941
Lump-sum shortfall, age 65	2,927,300
Lump-sum shortfall, today's dollars	**$580,044**

Step 3. Determine the Total Lump Sum Needed Today

Lump-sum surplus, preretirement period 1	$343,198
Lump-sum surplus, preretirement period 2	29,124
Lump sum currently needed, retirement period 1	383,712
Lump sum currently needed, retirement period 2	580,044
Total lump sum needed, today's dollars	**$591,434**

Step 4. Repeat Steps for Other Needs

Lump sum needed currently for college	$125,657
Burial expenses	20,000
Total lump sum for other needs, today's dollars	**$145,657**

Step 5. Establish Insurance Need

Total lump sum needed for all needs, today's dollars	$737,091
Available assets	$64,000
Total insurance needed, today's dollars	$673,091

Summary

This chapter demonstrated how to do a simple capital needs analysis and outlined other methods. You learned that

- A simple capital needs analysis takes into account all financial cash flow factors.
- A risk-adjusted capital needs analysis provides a subjective attempt to account for uncertainty.
- Monte Carlo simulations can present the probability of achieving a certain outcome.
- Total portfolio management provides a fully integrated approach to personal financial planning. It combines PFP and the calculation of investment returns.
- TPM includes all assets, liabilities, and risk including the correlations among them.
- Retirement needs analysis is generally a very structured system that establishes the amount of cash shortfall at retirement and the sums needed to meet it.

Key Terms

financial integration, *503*	Monte Carlo analysis, *505*	retirement needs analysis, *509*

Web Site

http://www.finplan.com
Capital Needs Analysis
This site contains a section dedicated to capital needs analysis.

Questions

1. Why perform a retirement needs analysis?
2. Contrast simple and risk-adjusted capital needs analysis.
3. Identify the advantages of Monte Carlo simulation.
4. What is total portfolio management?
5. Why is overhead cost considered a liability under TPM?
6. Should a comedian and a government employee receive the same financial asset allocation if they have similar tolerances for risk? Why?
7. Provide a reason why a real estate salesperson should not have the same amount allocated to his or her home as the average person.
8. Discuss the planning steps in a simple capital needs analysis.
9. Why bring figures from today to the beginning of the retirement period?
10. When should the investment rate, the blended rate, and the inflation rate be used respectively?
11. List the steps in the retirement needs analysis.

Problems **18.1** If the investment rate of return is 7 percent after tax and the inflation rate is 4 percent, find the blended rate of return.

18.2 Eleanor needs $40,000 a year to live on in retirement net of the income she will receive. She will be retiring in 22 years and is funding for a 25-year retirement. The inflation rate is expected to be 3.5 percent a year and the after-tax return on her investments 6 percent.

   a. How much will the short fall amount to at the beginning of the retirement period?

   b. What lump sum will she need at the beginning of the retirement period?

   c. What is the required yearly savings?

18.3 Frank, age 28, wants to calculate his resources in real (inflation-adjusted) terms. Calculate the amount of resources made available by age 65 retirement if $18,000 a year is saved. Assume that outflows from ages 65 to 90 are at the rate of $27,000 a year. The projected inflation rafe is 4 percent, and the anticipated investment return is 6 percent.

   a. How much in new savings will Frank have available at age 65 before subsequent withdrawals?

   b. How much will he have left at age 90?

   c. What is the present value of that sum at age 65?

   d. How much will he have to save per year to exactly meet his need?

18.4 The Smiths had $110,000 in savings at age 51. They had a desired retirement age of 65. They want to fund through age 92. Assume a 4 percent inflation rate and a 5 percent after-tax rate for investment both pre-and postretirement. They have household income of $140,000, which is increasing at the rate of inflation. Their expenditures including taxes are $125,000 a year. They estimate that in retirement they will receive $28,000 a year together in Social Security and Mr. Smith will receive a $12,000-a-year pension, both in today's dollars. Their retirement expenditures would be $90,000 a year in today's dollars.

  1. Calculate

    a. The lump sum needed at retirement.

    b. Current assets available at retirement.

    c. Yearly savings needed.

    d. The difference between needs and resources.

  2. Analysis

    a. Is their retirement plan achievable as is?

    b. If not, what are the alternatives that could help reconcile needs and resources?

    c. What is your recommendation?

CFP®
Certification
Examination
Questions
and Problems

18.1 A client is concerned about the impact that inflation will have on her retirement income. The client currently earns $40,000 per year. Assuming that inflation averages 5.5 percent for the first five years, 4 percent for the next five years and 3.5 percent for the remaining time until retirement, what amount must her first-year retirement income be when she retires 13 years from now if she wants it to equal the purchasing power of her current earnings?

   a. $62,550

   b. $68,841

    c. $70,520

    d. $80,231

    e. $83,157

18.2 Billy's objective is to retire at age 65 with $2,000 in monthly retirement income, exclusive of Social Security benefits. He assumes a life expectancy of age 95. The union retirement plan will provide him with $1,000 monthly. (There are *no* matching contributions from Billy's employer to the plan, and his income is adequate to have the required level of contributions fall within the deferral limits of the plan. Contributions and payments, as appropriate, are made at the beginning of each month.)

    If the return in the company's plan is 10 percent, what monthly amount will Billy have to contribute to that plan for 10 years to meet his objective?

    a. $556

    b. $566

    c. $576

    d. $747

    e. $1,113

18.3 A couple wants to accumulate a retirement fund of $300,000 in current dollars in 18 years. They expect inflation to be 4 percent per year during that period. If they set aside $20,000 at the end of each year and earn 6 percent on their investment, will they reach their goal?

    a. Yes, they will accumulate $10,368 more than needed.

    b. Yes, they will accumulate $47,454 more than needed.

    c. No, they will accumulate $10,368 less than needed.

    d. No, they will accumulate $47,454 less than needed.

Appendix I

Life Insurance Needs Analysis and Case Study

Life insurance needs analysis provides the amount of life insurance that is required to help fund the household's cost of living if a wage earner were to die. The lump-sum proceeds from the policy generate the income and often the principal as well to at least partially replace the wages lost. The amount of insurance to be purchased with this approach is based on need, not income replacement. In sum, our objective is to identify the amount of capital needed—in this case, life insurance—to fund a comfortable lifestyle for remaining members of the household.

Living costs often vary over a life cycle. Therefore, it is useful to separate needs into periods that we can call financial passages. Clearly, passages differ from person to person. We will use one common life cycle period approach. The initial period can begin with the establishment of a separate household. At this time, life insurance may not be necessary. Successive periods can result in marriage, purchase of a home, and children.

At this point, life insurance needs are commonly divided into three periods. The first period is for funding until the children are out of the house. Social Security commonly provides assistance in the event of the untimely death of a spouse. The second period is the one without children while the surviving spouse is still working. Living costs may be reduced, given the lower number of household occupants. The final period is retirement, when costs may decline for reasons we have already discussed.

Each period has its own cash inflows and outflows. The approach taken is very similar to that for retirement needs. In fact, as you can see, retirement planning can be considered a subset of life insurance planning. One difference in calculation is that in the life insurance retirement calculation, the figures are adjusted for the absence of the deceased household member's income.

The steps in life insurance analysis, then, are very similar to those for retirement needs. Therefore, we will focus on differences and not repeat similar descriptions.

1. *Determine goals.* Here your goal is to fund a given living cost for the surviving spouse and any children in the event of the untimely death of a wage earner.

2. *Establish risks and tolerances for them.* The risks are provided in Chapter 10, Risk Management.

3. *Determine investment and inflation rates and time spans for calculations.* The approach is similar to the retirement one as shown on page 510.

4. *Project income, expenses, and cash savings during each financial period.* This was discussed on pages 510–512. Include amounts for major outlays, which may be handled separately. One example is educational expenditures.

5. *Calculate lump sums needed for each period and outlay.* The method is shown under retirement needs analysis on page 516. However, the approach here is to bring all figures to the current period rather than the beginning of the future period, as done for retirement.

6. *Calculate total current need.* In calculating need, include burial costs.

7. *Deduct current resources.* This step is self-explanatory.

8. *Establish total insurance need.* Add up all separate insurance needs.

9. *Deduct existing insurance.* This step is self-explanatory.

10. *Determine additional life insurance needed.*[12] Total needs less the value of existing life insurance.

11. *Implement.* Obtaining life insurance occurs in steps. One step often required is a physical exam. Procrastination can temporarily postpone or even permanently prevent the purchase of the insurance. Therefore, action should be taken as soon as it is feasible.

12. *Review and update.* Insurance is a prime example of a changing need. As you age, the amount of total wage earnings lost due to an untimely demise declines. At the same time, your financial assets generally increase. Therefore, the amount of insurance needed tends to decline over time. Of course, for people who don't save and liquidate existing investments, the opposite is true; for them, life insurance needs increase.

As you can see, the estimation of insurance needs should be updated periodically to accommodate significant changes in circumstances.

Here we turn to a practical example of the calculation of life insurance needs. It is an extension of the Johnson case already discussed. It reflects all the adjustments made in the retirement section and the change to an age-70 retirement, including the cost cutback and full-time job for Sarah.

We can now gather the key facts in the Johnson case. Frank and Sarah, currently age 50, have only $35,000 in savings and have finally decided to do something about it. They have agreed to fix their current spending including taxes at $154,000 and cut their retirement spending from $95,000 to $80,000. Sarah's decision to take a full-time job will raise her pretax income to $45,000 from $10,000 and increase her taxes from $3,000 to $15,000. The extra $12,000 in taxes is part of the current spending figure of $154,000. So actually other household spending has declined by $8,000.

The retirement age has been pushed back to age 70; the funding for retirement will be until age 91.

---

[12] Disability needs can be handled similarly to life insurance. The differences are possible Social Security payments received for the disability and the extra household costs for the disabled person. Also, disability insurance is generally linked to 60 to 70 percent of prior income, regardless of need. Companies don't want you to be tempted to profit on an after-tax basis because you are disabled. If you expect your salary to climb sharply, you will have to wait to contract for additional coverage.

TABLE 18.A1.1
Life Insurance Statistics

	As Planned	Revised	Explanation
Preretirement Period, Ages 50–70			
Revenues			
Frank work	$140,000	$0	In the event of Frank's death
Sarah work	45,000	45,000	
Total revenues	$185,000	$45,000	
Expenses	154,000	127,000	154,000 – 27,000
			Expenses attributable to Frank
Cash flow	$31,000	($82,000)	
Postretirement Period— Ages 70–91			
Revenues			
Pension—Frank	$12,000	$12,000	Sarah receives some amount if Frank dies
Social Security—Frank	22,000	—	
Social Security—Sarah	11,000	22,000	Sarah gets only Frank's pension
Total revenues	$45,000	$34,000	
Expenses	80,000	53,000	
Cash shortfall	($35,000)	($19,000)	

Let's summarize and elaborate on the Johnsons' facts. These facts are all you need to know to complete the life insurance needs analysis.

1. Determine Goals

Frank and Sarah, now age 50, finally have decided to save and plan for retirement. Frank wants Sarah to have enough insurance to maintain her current standard of living should he die. Knowing how important it is for them to save, he says to assume that the cost of the insurance will be met by further cuts in other household costs. He doesn't believe it is necessary to have insurance on Sarah's life. Should something happen to her, he will live on his salary alone.

2. Establish Risks and Tolerances for Them

The Johnsons have described themselves as moderate risk takers in investments and in other areas of their lives.

3. Determine Investment and Inflation Rates and Time Spans for Calculations

Based on risk preferences and their feelings, investment rates of 5 percent after tax and inflation rates of 3 percent were established. The couple decided to fund retirement expenses from age 70 to age 91, a 21-year life span. Their current working period is for 20 years.

4. Project Income and Expenses during Each Financial Period

There are only two periods to be concerned about since the Johnsons' children are all independent adults. The statistics for each period are shown in Table 18.A1.1. Assume burial costs of $20,000.

Steps 5 to 10 utilize the explanations provided on pages 529–530.

As we did in retirement needs analysis, we begin by presenting a life insurance needs calculation format in Table 18.A1.2, followed by the actual calculations for preretirement and postretirement periods presented in Table 18.A1.3.

11. Implement

After some further reminder, the Johnsons implemented the life insurance recommendations. They chose 20 percent whole life and 80 percent term with affordability and an optimistic assessment of working the need down over time. The advisor believed that with retirement and insurance needs on the way to being satisfied, he had accomplished something.

12. Review and Update

The advisor knew that further progress would hinge on Frank and Sarah's continued motivation and a supportive but firm attitude by him. The first follow-up meeting was set up.

TABLE 18.A1.2 Life Insurance Calculation Described

Step	Item	Symbol	Explanation and Calculation
3	Investment rate	IR	The rate of return for investments
3	Inflation rate	ER	The rate of increase in expenses
3	Real rate	RR	The combination of the inflation and investment rates Formula: $RR = \left(\dfrac{1 + IR}{1 + ER} - 1\right) \times 100$
3	Present time	t_0	Today
3	Future time	t_1	Beginning of payout period
3	Number of years for period	N_{t_p}	From beginning to end of life cycle period
3	Number of years to beginning of period	N_{t_1}	From today to start of life cycle period
3	Number of years to today	N_{t_0}	From beginning of life cycle period to today
4	Cash inflow	CI_{t_0}	Includes the total of job, investment, and other yearly cash inflows for the period in current dollars
4	Cash outflows	CO_{t_0}	Discretionary and nondiscretionary expenses, capital expenditures, and other yearly cash outflows for the period in current dollars
4	Cash shortfall	CS_{t_0}	Current yearly cash inflows minus cash outflows $CS_{t_0} = CI_{t_0} - CO_{t_0}$
5	Cash shortfall future	CS_{t_1}	Current yearly shortfall brought forward to beginning of life cycle period. The inflation rate is used to calculate the estimated future cost of the present cash shortfall. **Calculator Solution** *Inputs:*

Cash shortfall future inputs:

N_{t_1}	ER	CS_{t_0}		
N	I/Y	PV	PMT	FV

Solution: Press for CS_{t_1} (FV)

Step	Item	Symbol	Explanation and Calculation
5	Lump-sum shortfall future	LS_{t_1}	Amount of full life cycle period yearly shortfalls discounted back to beginning of life cycle period. Since there is a series of payments involving both investment and inflation factors, the real rate is employed. Use BEGIN function for beginning of year payments. **Calculator Solution** *Inputs:*

Lump-sum shortfall future inputs:

N_{t_p}	RR		CS_{t_1}	
N	I/Y	PV	PMT	FV

Solution: Press for LS_{t_1} (PV)

Step	Item	Symbol	Explanation and Calculation
5	Lump-sum shortfall today	LS_{t_0}	The shortfall for the period brought back to the present to be aggregated with other life cycle period and specific expenditure needs. The investment rate is used to tell us how much we need to receive in life insurance proceeds and invest today to meet the lump-sum shortfall at the beginning of this period. **Calculator Solution** *Inputs:*

Lump-sum shortfall today inputs:

N_{t_0}	IR			LS_{t_1}
N	I/Y	PV	PMT	FV

Solution: Press for LS_{t_0} (PV)

Step	Item	Symbol	Explanation and Calculation
6	Life cycle period		Each need requires a full separate set of calculations. Each succeeding life cycle period to be calculated is denoted by a higher time symbol, starting with t_0
6	Need period ages 50–70	$LS_{w_{t_0}}$	Life insurance need for preretirement period in current dollars
6	Need period ages 70–91	$LS_{r_{t_0}}$	Life insurance need for retirement period in current dollars
6	Need educational	$LS_{e_{t_0}}$	Life insurance need for individual expenditure in current dollars
6	Need burial	$LS_{b_{t_0}}$	Burial costs in current dollars
6	Total need	TLS_{t_0}	Gross sum of all separate life insurance needs in current dollars $TLS_{t_0} = LS_{w_{t_0}} + LS_{r_{t_0}} + LS_{e_{t_0}} + LS_{b_{t_0}}$
7	Existing investment assets	AA_{t_0}	The amount of investment assets available today
8	Total life insurance need	LIN_{t_0}	$LIN_{t_0} = TLS_{t_0} - AA_{t_0}$
9	Existing life insurance	ELI_{t_0}	The amount of life insurance available today
10	Additional life insurance required	LIR_{t_0}	The amount of life insurance recommended to purchase $LIR_{t_0} = LIN_{t_0} - ELI_{t_0}$

TABLE 18.A1.3   Life Insurance Calculation Performed for Working Years 50–70

Step	Item	Revised Symbol	Explanation or Calculation
3	Investment rate	IR	5% given
3	Inflation rate	ER	3% given
3	Real rate	RR	1.9417
			$RR = \left(\dfrac{1 + 0.05}{1 + 0.03} - 1 \right) \times 100$
3	Number of years to beginning of period	N_{t_1}	20 Age 50 to age 70
3	Number of years for payout period	N_{t_p}	21 Age 70 to age 91
3	Number of years future period to today	N_{t_0}	20 Age 70 to age 50

Preretirement Period 50–70

Step	Item	Revised Symbol	Explanation or Calculation
4	Cash inflows	$CI_{w_{t_0}}$	$45,000 given
4	Cash outflows	$CO_{w_{t_0}}$	$127,000 given
4	Cash shortfall	$CS_{w_{t_0}}$	$82,000 127,000 − 45,000
5	Lump-sum shortfall today	$LS_{w_{t_0}}$	Inputs:

Inputs (Use BEGIN function):

N	I/Y	PV	PMT	FV
20	1.9417		82000	

Solution: Press **$1,374,568** (PV)

Postretirement Period 70–91

Step	Item	Revised Symbol	Explanation or Calculation
4	Cash inflows	$CI_{r_{t_0}}$	$34,000 given
4	Cash outflows	$CO_{r_{t_0}}$	$53,000 given
4	Cash shortfall today	$CS_{r_{t_0}}$	$19,000 53,000 − 34,000
5	Cash shortfall future	$CS_{r_{t_0}}$	Inputs:

N	I/Y	PV	PMT	FV
20	3	19000		

Solution: Press **$34,316** (FV)

Step	Item	Revised Symbol	Explanation or Calculation
5	Lump-sum shortfall future	$LS_{r_{t_1}}$	Inputs:

Inputs (Use BEGIN function):

N	I/Y	PV	PMT	FV
21	1.9417		34316	

Solution: Press **$598,601** (PV)

Step	Item	Revised Symbol	Explanation or Calculation
5	Lump-sum shortfall today	$LS_{r_{t_0}}$	Inputs:

N	I/Y	PV	PMT	FV
20	5			598601

Solution: Press **$225,606** (PV)

Step	Item	Revised Symbol	Explanation or Calculation
6	Total need	TLS_{t_0}	$TLS_{t_0} = LS_{w_{t_0}} + LS_{r_{t_0}} + LS^1_{e_{t_0}} + LS_{b_{t_0}}$
			= 1,374,568 + 225,606 + 20,000
			= **$1,620,174**
7	Existing investment assets	AA_{t_0}	$35,000 given
8	Total life insurance need	LIN_{t_0}	$LIN_{t_0} = TLS_{t_0} - AA_{t_0}$
			= 1,620,174 − 35,000
			= **$1,585,174**
9	Existing life insurance	ELI_{t_0}	No existing life insurance
10	Additional life insurance required	LIR_{t_0}	$LIR_{t_0} = LIN_{t_0} - ELI_{t_0} =$ **$1,585,174**

[1] In this case, none was needed.

Chapter Nineteen

Behavioral Financial Planning

Chapter Goals

This chapter will enable you to:

- Improve upon PFP performance.
- Apply behavioral finance to PFP.
- Target human characteristics that can undermine your objectives.
- Learn how to overcome human weaknesses.
- Identify goals that differ from traditional money ones.
- Evaluate the strengths and weaknesses of behavioral finance.

Dan was feeling anxious. The process was drawing to a close and he wasn't sure I was aware of the scope of their goals or of the conflicts he and Laura were having.

Real Life Planning

Marisa was V.P. of marketing for one of the country's largest corporations. She was in charge of a worldwide staff of hundreds of financial people. She had an MBA with honors from a prestigious university paid for by her corporation. She also had a chaotic personal financial situation.

Although her salary and bonus amounted to over $1 million a year, she had trouble saving. She called it "easy money," meaning easy to spend. Each year she would set a target amount of savings and each year she would miss by a mile.

Marisa's job required that she be on top of every major consumer trend in the country. She was very successful at doing that. Her investment policy consisted of buying stocks in companies that were also in fashion at the moment. She would swap them frequently for new ones in "hot" areas of the market, almost invariably taking a loss on her initial investment.

She was fickle in her attention to her personal affairs. She paid her bills when she felt good about herself and in the mood for doing so, often less than once every three months. Consequently, she had credit card penalties even when there was enough money in her bank account to pay her debts earlier. Her credit rating was poor, and she had been rejected by more than one department store for simple credit.

Marisa told the advisor that she was aware of the contrast between her position at work as a capable executive and her shortcomings in personal affairs. The advisor thought to himself, in addition to instructions on the right way to handle financial affairs, why don't more financial textbooks discuss shortcomings in behavior? What this woman needed was someone who understood her weaknesses and found ways of helping her overcome them. Financial planners who had such an understanding of human behavior had one more tool in their arsenal.

The advisor told Marisa she could hire one or more financial people to help her with her personal difficulties on an ongoing basis. It would allow her to focus on her career, which could be the most efficient solution. He wasn't surprised when Marisa turned the idea down. He knew she was an achiever who wanted to handle her own affairs.

The advisor looked for a way to get his message across to Marisa in a way that she would understand and appreciate. He shifted gears and told Marisa to manage her household affairs as though they represented a separate business division of her corporation. By that, he said, he meant to do whatever it took to turn her financial affairs around. He advised her to have her money taken directly from her paycheck and told her to assume it was unavailable. He recommended that she use mutual funds but also told her to continue to select individual trend-setting stocks for 10 percent of her portfolio. That 10 percent would provide her with pleasure and allow the remaining 90 percent of the portfolio to grow for future goals. Marisa agreed to have a close relative come in once a month to pay her bills.

The advisor then recommended that she take a course in investments. He told her to be aware of behavioral weaknesses such as impulsive spending and investing in what the crowd is buying, which can undermine assets and PFP overall. As a motivating tool, he told her to visualize her goals and imagine her retirement lifestyle if she continued her current financial patterns versus her retirement situation if she implemented the plan that she and the advisor were now developing together.

The next time he saw Marisa, she seemed to be a changed person. No longer did she have an embarrassing private financial situation. Instead, she had developed pride in her investment capabilities. Her individual stock selections began to incorporate fundamental analysis, and she now knew more about individual mutual fund selections than almost any of the advisor's other clients.

Given her large salary, her new savings pattern had placed her close to the right path for her age and goals. Now that her financial situation seemed well in hand, she began to expand on her goals in life, what some advisors call life planning. She wanted a greater profile in her industry and also wanted to do charitable work. After further discussions with the advisor, she realized she was drawn to the option of starting a second career at age 50 with no further need for job-related income. For the first time, she was receptive to the idea of a financial plan to establish the numbers needed to make financial independence happen, to prepare the groundwork for life planning, and to protect herself against unforeseen circumstances.

The advisor reviewed her situation and his role in it. Clearly, her problem wasn't generating enough financial resources. Her salary was the envy of most people. Instead, it was her behavior patterns that were undermining her progress. Once she had gained some additional investment knowledge and learned to understand and overcome her behavioral shortcomings, and to get in touch with her goals, her progress was fine. His role in this case was as much behaviorally as financially related.

OVERVIEW

There is a great difference between the way things should be done and the way they actually are done. When we were young, our parents taught us certain rules of conduct and sometimes broke them themselves. Perhaps you've heard the expression, "Do as I say, not as I do." Textbooks often provide ideal rules, formulas, and other courses of action but ignore the fact that humans often fall short of such rules. That is unfortunate, particularly for PFP.

Practical Comment John—Part I

John was a student taking an introductory course in PFP. He wanted the information both to better his own personal affairs and because he was considering becoming a financial planner. He had never really been exposed to behavioral finance. He was aware that it was receiving more attention but also knew that there were differences of opinion about its relevance to the field. Would it provide insight into PFP, help him with his own planning, and make him a better practitioner? He decided to form his own opinion after reading about it. (To be concluded at the end of the chapter.)

Knowledge of actual human behavior is arguably more important for PFP than for any other area of finance, given its closeness to human actions and its emphasis on practicality. In fact, many people come to financial planners as much to "get structured" as for the specific recommendations. They know that structure makes it easier to implement their goals and therefore less likely they will lose control or focus.

This chapter examines behavioral finance, the study of how humans actually perform. Its objective is first to provide information on the reasons that the results of people's financial planning often fall short of maximum potential and then to address what can be done about it. Its scope is an unusually wide one for coverage of behavioral finance and it employs practical tools to improve performance, a prime objective of behavioral financial planning.

Behavioral financial planning operations can be separated into two components. The first is traditional money planning and making more efficient financial decisions. The second objective is to help clients reach their nonmonetary goals, which are incorporated under the term *life planning*. Planners vary in the degree to which they deal with this topic, which of course has a financial component. It is considered in a separate part of the chapter.

Behavioral characteristics are relevant throughout the financial planning process. However, they may be particularly important toward the end of the process, when integration and decision making occur. It is at this point that a "reality check" is in order. You must shift from what is primarily a numbers orientation to what is achievable. Knowledge and practice of behavioral financial planning can raise that achievement level. Integration, in this sense, means making sure you have folded in human characteristics.

We begin by providing an understanding of behavioral finance and what distinguishes it from traditional logical financial behavior. The chapter examines the major reasons for human weaknesses and specific human shortcomings and how to overcome them. It then discusses goals that differ from traditional money planning. Finally, it discusses how financial planners can be of assistance in modifying patterns of behavior.

The chapter has been constructed as a series of steps leading to an assessment of behavioral financial planning and its effectiveness in enhancing actual performance. The first step, determine the goal, follows.

DETERMINE THE GOAL

Our goal is to understand and evaluate the contribution of behavioral analysis to PFP. This goal is elaborated in the practical comment above.

ESTABLISH THE ROLE OF BEHAVIORAL FINANCE

To understand the role of behavioral finance, first we must recall what finance is and contrast finance theory with actual behavior.

Finance can be defined as decision making for limited resources over time. Traditional finance is logical finance; the financial person making that decision for household matters is generally assumed to have superhuman characteristics. You are assumed to act logically all the time in seeking to maximize your pleasure. You have perfect knowledge of all the information you need to make proper decisions and have full capability for recalling past experiences accurately.

You also have the intellectual capacity to make the right decisions at all times. The markets that you are exposed to are all highly competitive with no opportunity for expecting and achieving greater-than-average profits. And finally, you and all other human beings have the same tastes, preferences, beliefs, and abilities.[1]

We can sum up this superhuman person as behaving like a machine, making no errors. Of course, in reality, no such person exists. The advantage of this approach, which comes out of neoclassical economic theory, allows the testing of financial theories in a quantifiable scientific way.

Behavioral economics and behavioral finance take a different approach. Instead of looking at this "ideal" person (we use quotes here because you might disagree, finding such a person boring), they examine people as they actually are. **Behavioral finance**[2] can be defined as the study of human makeup and actions that result in deviations from logical economic and financial behavior. This broad definition allows us to examine all differences from programmed machine-like behavior so that you can improve your decision-making capability.

Behavioral finance is controversial within the discipline. Some critics believe it has no scientific underpinning. They say it can't represent all people with one analysis, much less measure them numerically. Moreover, they say, its generalizations come from laboratory experiments and questionnaires, not from how people act in real life. Those who study human behavior reply that it is difficult to argue with often similar human responses and errors and studying them can help to understand and improve human decision making. (See Appendix I.)

UNDERSTAND WHAT BEHAVIORAL FINANCIAL PLANNING IS

Behavioral financial planning is the action arm of behavioral finance. It can be defined as the analysis of individual conduct and the development of practical techniques to improve decision making. From a financial standpoint, it looks at human weaknesses and ways of overcoming them to bring you closer to your goals.

Behavioral financial planning continues the broad definition of behavioral finance. Its mandate is to focus on any behavior that provides a shortfall from ideal results and can be improved upon. We will begin by outlining the areas in which human shortcomings arise. A breakdown of human behavior into rational and irrational characteristics is provided in Appendix II.

SEPARATE HUMAN SHORTCOMINGS INTO CATEGORIES

Human shortcomings, as they relate to finance, can be thought of as differences between ideal and actual financial outcomes. They restrict our progress toward our financial planning goals. We can separate these shortcomings into two categories: cognitive errors and visceral feelings. We can identify this first grouping of shortcomings as broadly coming from the brain and its reasoning ability.

---

[1] See Richard Blundell and Thomas Stoker, "Heterogeneity and Aggregation," *Journal of Economic Literature* 43, no. 2 (June 2005), pp. 347–91.

[2] Behavioral economics and behavioral finance are very similar in approach, focusing on the person, with many of the same researchers working in both areas. Here we will combine them.

Cognitive errors come from three main areas:

1. Lack of knowledge.
2. Weakness in perception and memory.
3. Limited processing scope and speed.

Knowledge is key. Isn't that why you are reading this book? You can be highly capable, but, without the information needed to take proper actions, you will fall short of your goals.[3]

Similarly, if you cannot perceive items correctly or recall them accurately, your decision-making ability is undermined. Example 19.1 presents these weaknesses.

Example 19.1   Lana was robbed at gunpoint by a young man. She was afraid and waited two weeks before going to the police. When questioned by an officer, she couldn't be precise in identifying the car the robber drove because she had no knowledge of cars. Her perception was that he was tall—actually he was of average height—and she didn't remember key details that could have helped find him. Fortunately, the police were able to identify him and recover the money lost. These common shortfalls in knowledge, memory, and perceptions from optimal mental capabilities are very familiar to the police.

Finally, we know that the brain cannot process at the same pace or with the same range as a computer. A computer has even bested a chess champion. In addition, there are many times when we don't even want to devote the time and effort to optimal mental processing and prefer a good mental shortcut. For example, the rule of 72 discussed in Chapter 2 is a good shortcut for determining how long it takes for an investment at a given interest rate to double.

The second grouping of human shortcomings relates to **visceral feelings,** or emotions. Emotions, or feelings, can influence our actions. When emotions are thought out and stable, they reflect our preferences and lead to pleasure. On the other hand, visceral feelings can imply urges to take action that are often short term in nature and can cloud mental processing. They can be caused by biological, cultural, psychological, or other variables.

Examples of visceral feelings are rage, hunger, fear, pressure, and so on. Finance people might say that those feelings can be irrational because they can result in a very short-term level of satisfaction and long-term dissatisfaction. Full knowledge of the outcomes beforehand might not change the situation because reasoning ability may be cut off. For example, spending money through a credit card can create a temporary emotional high, but it is often followed by a more lasting feeling of depression if it results in an unneeded purchase that will have to be paid off.

In sum, all the behavioral characteristics we have discussed are weaknesses. They can still be said to broadly follow a traditional financial model because we still have the desire to maximize in financial terms. We can identify those characteristics as weaknesses since, when given the opportunity to learn or to prevent impulsive behavior, we would take it. This desire to alter our own behavior will be important in distinguishing behavioral weaknesses from nonfinancial goals. (The difference is discussed in the Life Planning part of the chapter.)

PROVIDE SELECTED BEHAVIORAL MODELS AND CHARACTERISTICS

In this section, we will examine models and characteristics of behavioral finance with the objective of better understanding human nature. The models and characteristics shown vary from emotional shortcomings to weaknesses in mental processing. Once you complete this section, you will be better able to identify common mistakes that people make and be

---

[3] Financial literacy was covered in Chapter 13.

prepared to develop ways to overcome them. In other words, you will be able to use behavioral planning to improve your financial performance.

Heuristics and Biases

Heuristics are simplified human approaches to complex tasks. Our intent in using heuristics in day-to-day situations is to reduce decision making to an approach that is easy to handle. Many mental shortcuts result in good decisions.[4] **Biases,** on the other hand, are actions based on a distorted view of reality—and are inevitably harmful in the long run. Flawed heuristics lead to biases.[5]

Example 19.2

There are a whole host of variables that can go into which television set you decide to buy. You could list them all, assign a relative weight to each based on its importance, then give each television a score for each variable. The outcome would be a weighted average overall score for each television, with the set with the highest score being selected.

Although this approach might be a rational way of handling the decision process, few people take it. Instead you use a heuristic, a shortcut to weigh the relative merits of the television set to you. The simplified analysis might include price, quality of picture, reputation of manufacturer, and recommendation of the salesman or of a magazine write-up. Heuristics such as the one for the television may be an effective way to make a good decision. Alternatively, because of a bias (for example, assuming that the reputation of the make as received through its advertising is a benchmark of TV quality), an incorrect outcome could result.

Heuristics and biases were popularized by psychologists Daniel Kahneman and Amos Tversky in their experiments in the 1970s and, as we have indicated, many researchers would probably say they had a great deal to do with the revival of interest in behavioral issues in economics and finance. Here we consider some common heuristics:

- *Anchoring.* Using an outmoded or inappropriate standard can result in making incorrect decisions when the standard is no longer appropriate. For example, "I know that John will win the basketball game for us. He always has." That model may be inappropriate now that John is 40 years old.

- *Framing.* How you communicate a thought can affect the response. For example, a security analyst writing a recommendation on a stock may be more likely to find a receptive audience by writing, "Although the company has significant problems, it is highly attractive," rather than, "The company is highly attractive, but it has significant problems."

- *Representativeness.* Judgments made on the basis of only one or two characteristics instead of embarking on a detailed analysis. For example, "I know that she is a good person; she has a kind face like all the other nice people I interact with."

- *Availability.* Believing that the likelihood that something will occur in the future is determined by how often we recall it. Some people would say, incorrectly, that airplane trips are more dangerous than car trips because they can recall more airplane accidents—clearly, a biased view.

- *Hindsight bias.* Believing, after the fact, that an outcome could have been known beforehand. For example, "It was easy to see that McDonald's would become the number-one fast food chain in the U.S." The truth is that there were many other

---

[4] See Daniel Kahneman and Amos Tversky, "On the Reality of Cognitive Illusions," *Psychological Review* 103, no. 3 (July 1996), pp. 582–88; and Gerd Gigerenzer, "On Narrow Norms and Vague Heuristics: A Reply to Kahneman and Tversky (1996)," *Psychological Review* 103, no. 3 (July 1996), pp. 592–98. In contrast to Kahneman and Tversky, Gigerenzer emphasizes favorable decisions using heuristics, although not necessarily optimal ones. What he calls "fast and frugal heuristics" include such things as rules of thumb, mental shortcuts, and adaptive learning.

[5] See Richard Thaler, "Related Disciplines," *Journal of Economic Literature* 21, no. 3 (September 1983), pp. 1046–48.

chains at the time with similar approaches who either went out of business or remained only regional businesses. Often, the observer's beliefs before an event fade in memory.

- *Salience.* Placing too much weight on recent vivid experiences. For example, believing that your favorite baseball team has improved greatly because they won their last two games by wide margins.

Loss Aversion

We will go to great lengths to avoid a loss. That is because a loss will create displeasure that is about twice as great as the pleasure from a gain of the same amount.[6]

Example 19.3

Ryan became extremely uncomfortable with losses in his portfolio. He said it made him feel "dumb." In fact, he said a loss of $10,000 on one investment would wipe out the pleasure he received from anything lower than a $60,000 gain on another. Ryan recognized that this could restrict his investment actions so he bought mutual funds where poor performance of one stock in a portfolio can be offset by gains in many others. In addition, he never looked at his funds when the stock market was weak. He was overcoming loss aversion.

Behavioral Life Cycle Theory

The behavioral life cycle theory was formulated by Richard Thaler and H. M. Shefrin,[7] two behavioral researchers, both with backgrounds in economics and finance. According to their model, people have two sides to their thinking: personality and actions, called multiple selves. They are the planner side and the doer side. Your planner side acts rationally, always in control, thinking of what is in its longer-term interests. Your doer side is more emotional, reacting impulsively to short-term pleasures without regard to their long-term consequences. Actual behavior comes from a current resolution of the conflict between the two sides, only to be repeated again in future decisions.

Satisficing

Satisficing is a term made popular by Herbert Simon, who also introduced the term *bounded rationality*.[8] Simon, a management scientist and economist, defined **satisficing** as a method by which individuals seek a satisfactory solution, not an optimal one. Once they find that satisfactory solution, they stop the process. A person who purchases apples offered in a clear bag at a store known for its fresh produce and who doesn't bother to examine each apple closely can be said to be satisficing, not optimizing.[9]

Mental Accounting

Mental accounting, as popularized by Richard Thaler,[10] is an attempt to explain the way the brain works in decision making. In this view, the brain compartmentalizes our actions, placing them into certain categories. The categories make sense to us and help motivate us

---

[6] Amos Tversky and Daniel Kahnerman, "Loss Aversion in Riskless Choice: A Reference-Dependent Model," *Quarterly Journal of Economics* 106, no. 4 (November 1991), pp. 1039–61.

[7] See Richard H. Thaler and H. M. Shefrin, "An Economic Theory of Self-Control," *Journal of Political Economy* 89, no. 2 (April 1981), pp. 392–406.

[8] For further details, see Herbert A. Simon, "A Behavioral Model of Rational Choice," *Quarterly Journal of Economics* 69, no. 1 (February 1995), pp. 99–118; and Herbert A. Simon, "Rational Decision Making in Business Organizations," *American Economic Review* 69, no. 4 (September 1979), pp. 493–513.

[9] *Satisficing* doesn't fit our definition of bounded rationality given in Appendix II because it lacks a desire for optimization—a necessary ingredient for mainstream, economically rational behavior.

[10] Richard Thaler, "Mental Accounting and Consumer Choice," *Marketing Science* 4, no. 3 (Summer 1985), pp. 199–214; and Drazen Prelec and George Loewenstein, "The Red and the Black: Mental Accounting of Savings and Debt," *Marketing Science* 17, no. 1 (1998), pp. 4–28.

so that we maintain control over our actions. The process may not be rational in the economic sense of the word, however; for example, you are more likely to save a gift of $10,000 from your parents' estate than to save $10,000 in winnings from a lottery, perhaps because your parents' gift is serious money coming from people who raised you to be responsible. The lottery winnings, on the other hand, are considered frivolous—money that came out of the blue and frees you to do what you like with it.

Additional behavioral models and characteristics are supplied in Appendix III.

LEARN ABOUT WAYS OF OVERCOMING BEHAVIORAL SHORTCOMINGS

Since weaknesses in human behavior bring about results that are less than optimal, we turn our attention to ways of overcoming or at least minimizing these weaknesses. Finding the right approach is a prime focus of behavioral financial planning.

Restricting Negative Behavioral Responses—Overall

Certain behaviors can inhibit efficient household operations and the achievement of longer-term goals. Following are some of the basic methods for limiting negative responses. Since maintaining control is a very common problem, we give it special attention.

- *Formal financial learning.* To the extent that we can become more knowledgeable about finance in general and useful financial techniques in particular, our actions can improve. Financial literacy was discussed in Chapter 13.
- *Experience.* Formal learning can be abstract. Experience with real-life financial elements can improve the way we operate. For example, you may notice the impulsive actions you display in driving a car. As a risk-management procedure, you might then practice methods such as taking deep breaths when you are thinking of displaying this behavior again.
- *Self-understanding.* The actions we have discussed and will examine further in this section can be identified. Once we understand our shortcomings, we can focus on them to obtain better results. For example, a lack of farsightedness can be helped by thinking about long-term goals and how logically they can be achieved.

Develop Effective Rules of Thumb

Keep in mind effective rules of thumb. When you find investments that have attractive operations, compare them with well-tested quantitative criteria. Examples that are given by some are limiting your stock purchases to those that have a price-earnings multiple that is no more than 25 percent higher than the average stock or saving 10 percent of your income.

Limit Reviews of Performance

People tend to overemphasize recent results, extrapolating them into the future. For example, in investments, they draw too little distinction between, say, quarterly performance and a full year's investment results. Conclusions about performance—whether related to a job, financial investment, or cost increases—should be made over longer periods of time for those susceptible to this human shortcoming.

Obtain Assistance

Sometimes others are in a better position to identify our weaknesses and offer suggestions to help overcome them. Objectivity helps. When those weaknesses are difficult to eliminate, specialists such as financial planners may be used more frequently.

Limiting reviews is one behavior that may violate the rational economic and layman's view that more information is better. In the absence of substantive reasons, resolve to ignore daily, weekly, or monthly stock price results, which can be just "noise." In the case of mutual funds, it may be best to look at results as infrequently as once a year. Controlling your impulses both to view performance frequently and to act on it can have positive effects. Advisors might consider only issuing annual results so that they do not contribute to this problem.[11]

[11] See Shlomo Bernatzi and Richard H. Thaler, "Myopic Loss Aversion and the Equity Premium Puzzle," *Quarterly Journal of Economics* 110, no. 1 (February 1995), pp. 73–92.

Savings Mechanisms and Control

Saving is a problem for many, and some believe a particular problem for our country. There can be a great disparity between planned and actual savings. We will provide a more detailed list of methods to aid in achieving planned savings. With a few modifications, these methods can be useful in establishing control in a number of other planning areas as well. Several are provided in Table 19.1.

APPLY BEHAVIORAL CHARACTERISTICS TO PFP

Table 19.2 provides practical examples of behavioral characteristics. The table presents one characteristic for each major area of personal financial planning and, where appropriate, a method for overcoming the inefficiency. For a more extensive list by PFP area, see Web Appendix C, Behavioral Finance—Applications.

SUMMARIZE "MONEY PLANNING"

In sum, we can say that the goal of behavioral financial planning is to bring actual performance as close as possible to ideal performance. The difference between the two is, of course, due to human weaknesses. There are a variety of mechanisms for overcoming these

TABLE 19.1 Methods Helpful for Maintaining Control

Method	Explanation
Visualize	Visualization can help overcome myopia. Visualize the tangible positive benefits of planned savings and the consequences of not achieving them.
Practice mental accounting	Saving in separate buckets can assist since it makes the effect of withdrawals more salient.
Restrict choices	Leaving credit cards at home can reduce impulse buying.
Reduce proximity	Going to the mall less often can reduce temptation.
Utilize commitment devices	When control is difficult, have savings wired from bank accounts. In more serious cases, purchase large-outlay whole life instead of term insurance; buy a large home with substantial mortgage payments; join Christmas clubs if that's what it takes to get you to save.
Capitalize on group influence	Announce to friends your commitment to save for the year and offer a monetary gift to those who identify a lack of fulfillment. Join with friends who have goals of their own and meet regularly to support those goals.
Think about nonessential purchases overnight	Overcome impulse buying by providing time between attraction to an item and the actual purchase of it.

TABLE 19.2 Behavioral Examples by PFP Area

PFP Topic and Behavioral Characteristic	Example
Financial Investments	
Anchoring	Undiscovered Managers Behavioral Growth Fund purchases companies that have had large positive earnings surprises. They say that securities analysts are *anchored* (wedded) to their previous opinions on the company and are slow to change them. The Behavioral Growth Fund attempts to take advantage of these sluggish reactions by buying companies that have well exceeded the market's expectations. Said succinctly, the fund seeks to outperform by taking advantage of other people's behavioral weaknesses.
	Noting this weakness, Angela, a securities analyst, vowed to be more open to changes of opinion based on new facts for the companies she follows.
Taxes	
Framing	Mason and Marston were twin brothers. Both were in need of cash to live on and told their accountants of their problem. Both had the same stocks with weak outlooks that they had large losses in. Both were told by their accountants to sell the shares. Mason's accountant said, "Mason, recognize you made a mistake; now sell the shares." Mason refused. Marston's accountant had the same request, but *framed* it differently. He said "Marston, let's 'harvest' a tax loss by selling the shares and get a significant cash benefit from the government." Marston agreed to do so.
	When the brothers had time to talk about it, they were amused by their different reactions. They decided to confer more closely in the future and to make decisions based on facts, not on the way the facts were "packaged" for them.
Nonfinancial Investments	
Hindsight bias	Shane quit her fairly interesting but low-paying job for one that was potentially more lucrative. She thought she was making an investment in her human assets by doing this. As it turned out, the job was a bust. She told everyone what a stupid decision moving was. She said anyone with a brain could see how fortunate she was having her first job. As it turned out, she was able to get her first job back.
	Six months after returning, she decided to leave for another potentially more lucrative position. The fact that she left again proved that her after-the-event comment indicating how easy it was to see her mistake in leaving was just *hindsight bias*. She would be more skeptical of this thinking in the future.
Risk Management	
Salience	Ben and Len had been close friends since they were very young. Each was highly influenced by the other's decisions, which meant that often their decisions were similar. Ben bought a long-term care policy at age 51 because another friend's mother recently had a degenerative disease diagnosis and no long-term care insurance, and his friend was going to have to contribute to her upkeep.
	Len, on the other hand, thought long-term care insurance was not productive. He said his wife would take care of him if he got ill. Ben was reacting to a *salient* event that Len hadn't witnessed. When they next met, they decided to take a more objective, less personal perspective on frequency of illness before making future purchase decisions.
Educational Planning	
Representativeness	Hillary wanted to go to a well-regarded graduate school of business in which she would be able to meet other students easily and interact with professors who had practical business experience. She visited the university campus, researched the school's ranking, and talked extensively with the recruiter. It seemed a good fit, and she accepted.
	Unfortunately, the university was large, as were the class sizes, and time with the professors was limited. Hillary's original analysis and conclusions were based on variables that weren't *representative* of her needs. She performed a more extensive analysis of other schools, transferred, and found one that exactly fit her objectives.

(continued)

(*concluded*)

PFP Topic and Behavioral Characteristic	Example
Cash-Flow Planning	
Behavioral life cycle planning	Don thought about his life cycle–planning "malfunctioning" brain. He could swear he had two inner voices giving him advice. One said plan for the future, calculate how much you can afford to spend today based on life cycle reserves and costs, and stay closely in line with a budget. The second voice said the first voice's advice was too conservative. It said, Have fun right now; the future will take care of itself; spend and enjoy as much as you can before it is too late.
	When he was occupied with doing inexpensive things he enjoyed or was distracted by work, the first voice predominated. When he was depressed or he saw something particularly alluring, the second voice usually won out. He was surprised to find that many people had mixed feelings with two opinion voices about taking spending actions. He decided to try to keep his behavior on more of an even keel.
	Don used some of the savings control mechanisms that were discussed in the previous section. As a result, he made significant progress in balancing the multiple-voice advice and in saving more money that would be needed at certain times in his life cycle, particularly retirement. To a material extent, *behavioral life cycle planning*, which subjected him to inconsistent behavior, was transformed into traditional financial life cycle planning.
Retirement Planning	
Satisficing	Alex was like other people who came from his family. Even though as a business major at college he was taught to make decisions based on doing the best he could, he retained his family's values. He took a job that was not too taxing and spent a lot of time on social activities and hobbies. He said he was young and "partying beats retirement planning." His motto was "Take it as it comes" as opposed to "Live life to the fullest."
	He was aware from college that large early savings in tax-sheltered pension plans would make his later years more enjoyable. He did save some money, but never thought of the right balance for himself between fun today and planning for the future, nor calculated how much he needed to save to reach his future goals. He read somewhere that people like him were *satisficers*, not optimizers. He smiled when he saw the article. It seemed to him that many more people were like him as opposed to those who were maximizers.
Estate Planning	
Loss Aversion	Martha was old and felt that she might not have many more years to go. On the other hand, she was still spry and mentally sharp. She did fairly well in her investments portfolio and had many gains each year that she believed were likely to continue in the future.
	She had one stock in her portfolio that she had a major loss in. Her financial planner wanted her to sell the shares and purchase something that he felt was more attractive. She believed he was right but told him she wanted to wait until the shares rebounded and she could recover her original cost. Then Martha's attorney and financial planner spoke to her together. The attorney told her that if she passed away without selling the shares, her heirs would lose her tax break on sale of a security at a loss. The planner told her the combination of tax loss benefits today, potential elimination of this benefit should she die, and more rapid gain in the new shares would result in more than twice the profit when compared with waiting until the shares recovered. She agreed to sell.
	Later Martha thought about her initial reluctance to sell and decided it was due to feeling stupid in buying the shares and having to recognize her mistake when selling. It was only the significant gain that motivated her, which was silly. The shares' attractiveness was independently determined. Aside from tax impact, the amount any stockholder paid at the time he or she bought as compared with its current price was irrelevant. She decided it wasn't too late to value securities based solely on her appraisal of their worth. Her ego could withstand any blow due to the sale at a loss. She smiled as she thought, no investor is right all the time.

FIGURE 19.1   **Behavioral Financial Planning: Money Planning**

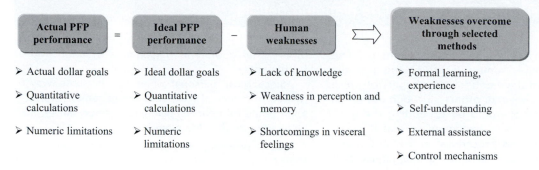

| Actual PFP performance | = | Ideal PFP performance | − | Human weaknesses | ⇒ | Weaknesses overcome through selected methods |

➤ Actual dollar goals

➤ Quantitative calculations

➤ Numeric limitations

➤ Ideal dollar goals

➤ Quantitative calculations

➤ Numeric limitations

➤ Lack of knowledge

➤ Weakness in perception and memory

➤ Shortcomings in visceral feelings

➤ Formal learning, experience

➤ Self-understanding

➤ External assistance

➤ Control mechanisms

weaknesses. The formula given at the top of Figure 19.1 reflects this approach. The explanations under the terms are selected characteristics.

The approach taken is deliberately expressed financially in order to link behavioral with ideal planning. We can call this behavioral approach money planning to distinguish it from life planning, to be discussed next. **Money planning** can be defined as planning whose goals are strictly financial and do not include life-planning objectives.

BROADEN BEHAVIORAL FINANCIAL PLANNING TO INCLUDE LIFE PLANNING

Our discussion to date has focused on human weaknesses and ways of overcoming them to bring about more efficient financial operations. **Life planning,** on the other hand, goes beyond money planning to take into account the analysis and scheduling of steps that will realize personal goals. Therefore, individual motivations cannot be measured in purely financial terms and actions that deviate from money maximization may not be human weaknesses but long-term human preferences. (See Appendix IV.)

Life planning is related to what the CFP Board calls values-driven planning or holistic planning. It deals with the personal side of the household enterprise, particularly with the goals of its members. We can use the Practical Comment by a prominent industry spokesman on the top of the next page as an introduction to the field.

Let's look at life planning more closely, the way many financial planners who practice the approach see it. They believe that what people want or need is a clearer picture of their goals. Some planners would go further and say that people are looking for meaning in their lives.[12]

Financial planners and/or other client advisors can aid in goal development and the frequent reassessment of those goals. The planners emphasize clarity of goals, thereby starting the client on the path to accomplishing them. They may ask such questions as "If you had five years to live, what would you hope to achieve in that time frame?" or "If you had one day left, what would you regret not having done?" or, more positively, "If you had three very good years, what would you have accomplished toward your goals during that time frame and how would you have done so? How would your life have been different at the end of the period?" Finally, "What additional steps do you have to take to reach your goals?"[13] Many types of alternative goals were discussed extensively in Chapter 3.

Planners can help in application of procedures to foster development toward those goals. The goals and the process for meeting them influence the planning engagement.

---

[12] See William Anthes and Shelley Lee, "Experts Examine Emerging Concept of 'Life Planning,' " *Journal of Financial Planning* 14, no. 6 (June 2001), 90–101.

[13] For an extensive discussion of this approach, see George Kinder. *Seven Stages of Money Maturity: Understanding the Spirit and Value of Money in Your Life* (New York: Dell, 2000).

Practical Comment   Life Planning Beliefs

"Today, in my view, asset management is being replaced by what some call 'life planning' as the primary top of the menu service, the service which clients value above all others—a rough definition [of life planning] would be expanding the goal-setting part of the engagement so that it covers goals that are less procedural and financial and more personal, and expanding the service part of the engagement to include the achievement of personal goals and personal satisfaction and fulfillment.

"Since most personal goals are in some way related to money, the expanded engagement is still appropriate for financial planners, but new skills will be needed to offer life planning services . . ."[14]

[14] Personal communication with Bob Veres, editor of *Inside Information,* a leading newsletter for independent personal financial planners.

Meetings may be held periodically to evaluate progress and ensure that clients are on track toward goal achievement. It is acknowledged that goals may change over time and, once goals are achieved, new ones are often established. Planners who perform these broader services intensively are sometimes called "coaches."

In sum, life planning focuses in depth upon goals and contributes ways of achieving them. It influences all steps in the financial planning process since they are based on the goals established. It extends beyond financial matters, although having money is an important ingredient. The assumptions of traditional financial analysis are questioned in such areas as philanthropy and altruism because assets and time are often given without a direct financial payback. However, life planning takes into account philanthropy and altruism because it emphasizes nonfinancial goals as well as financial ones.[15]

Life planning is a relatively new area of financial planning. Currently, planners vary greatly in their types of professional practice. Some planners restrict themselves solely to financial matters, while others provide the kind of services described here.

Life planning belongs under our definition of behavioral finance since it deals with human actions that deviate from the solitary, machine-like financial goal of making as much money as possible. Life planning can be considered a specialty area of behavioral finance. Both financial and nonfinancial goals are considered, which accentuates the search for client goals and their implementation. The essence of life planning is goal planning.

Goal planning is, at least in part, a result of a more affluent society. When people are poor, they concentrate on such basics as food, shelter, and clothing. In middle-class society in the United States today, where the basics are generally taken care of, some people seek to go beyond making as much money as possible.[16] Goal planning can be separated into two parts: satisfying basic emotions and achieving nonmonetary goals. Emotions are basic motivational factors. Some examples include feeling secure, having fun, engaging in caring relationships, and so forth. Of course, individuals have their own ranking of priorities.

The second part of goal planning is involved with the attainment of higher-level goals. These goals may be less concrete and incorporate such higher-level feelings as having completed a primary life goal, living in harmony with nature, and having achieved self-actualization.[17] Simply put, it asks such questions as "What do we want to do with our lives?" and "What are our values?"

[15] See Joel Sobel, "Interdependence Preferences and Reciprocity," *Journal of Economic Literature* 43, no. 2 (June 2005), pp. 392–436.

[16] See Chapter 3 on Maslow's hierarchy of needs.

[17] *Humanism* is defined in Webster's dictionary as a way of life centered on human interests or values. Its emphasis on human dignity and worth and capacity for self-realization through reason may best capture this approach.

FIGURE 19.2
Satisfaction with Life and Income per Capita in Japan between 1958 and 1991

Source: Bruno S. Frey and Alois Stutzer, "What Can Economists Learn from Happiness Research?" *Journal of Economic Literature* 40, no. 2 (June 2002), p. 413.

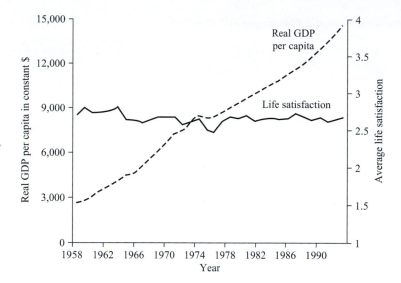

These items under goal planning are difficult or impossible to measure in financial terms. (See Appendix IV.) It is interesting to note that research on happiness by behavioral economists suggests that pleasure from earning more money is temporary. Satisfaction over the life cycle tends to stay level, perhaps regardless of the amount of money earned.[18]

Example 19.4   From the post–World War II period through the early 1990s, Japan rebuilt itself and in the process moved from a backward country to the world's second-most-prosperous nation. Yet, during this period, when personal income quadrupled, overall satisfaction in Japan did not go up; it was remarkably level. See Figure 19.2.

Behavioral financial planning is involved in both areas of goal planning. It establishes a money amount required for both basic[19] and higher-level feelings. For example, you cannot feel secure unless your elementary financial needs are taken care of. Therefore, traditional financial planning, money planning, must take place.

Basic needs should be anticipated and planned for. They necessitate an established balance between work and leisure, ideally incorporating job satisfaction as well as pleasure and caring relationships in your personal life. Knowledge and discipline may be required to establish good health and ethical behavior. Consultations with others and establishing role models can help.

Higher-level feelings can require systematic thinking and planning. First, the goals should be analyzed. Questions such as "What do I want to accomplish?" "How can I improve myself?" "What are my true values?" "How can I foster close relationships and help others?" may be asked. Then, whenever possible, concrete goals and a time frame for achieving them should be set out. Experimentation with what are true motivations can help. Identifying any career component is useful. Procrastination or sluggishness in moving toward goals can be overcome by measuring actual against projected progress. And the goals themselves must be reviewed as they can change over time.

---

[18] See Bruno S. Frey and Alois Stutzer, "What Can Economists Learn from Happiness Research?" *Journal of Economic Literature* 40, no. 2 (June 2002), pp. 402–35; and Bruno S. Frey and Alois Stutzer, *Happiness and Economics: How the Economy and Institutions Affect Human Well-Being* (Princeton, NJ: Princeton University Press, 2002). Of course, not having sufficient funds to cover basic needs might produce a different conclusion: money alone does not produce a permanently contented person.

[19] Beyond food, clothing, and shelter.

FIGURE 19.3 **Behavioral Financial Planning—Goal Planning**

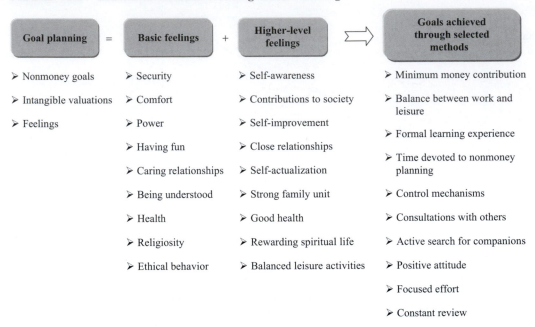

In sum, life goals are grounded in basic emotions and higher-level feelings. They extend beyond traditional finance but have a financial component. We can distinguish them from shortcomings in behavior because the actions they require are consciously planned for and we want to repeat them.

A summary of selected goal-planning characteristics is given in Figure 19.3.

BECOME FAMILIAR WITH THE FINANCIAL PLANNERS' FUNCTION IN BEHAVIORAL ANALYSIS

Financial planners have a multifaceted role in behavioral analysis in both money- and life-planning areas. In money planning and life planning, they can provide the benchmark of financial performance required by clients to achieve their goals as well as the overall planning methods for meeting them. Their role, often as the client's closest advisor in financial affairs, can provide access to both personality and motivations. They are aware of client weaknesses and can point out specific ways to overcome them. If the problem is one of control, they can establish structures such as savings "buckets" to support control procedures. They can point out unrepresentative feelings such as certain clients' belief that they are not acting responsibly in financial affairs when, in fact, they are. Many financial planners teach their clients how to understand finance and have more positive performance in the future.

As discussed, well-being does not just come from monetary rewards. Instead, there are a host of factors that people often look for. They may select an advisor not only for competence in financial matters so that they can achieve their money goals but for assistance with human-planning needs.[20] Through hard data and a reassuring manner, they can enhance positive feelings. A select number use advisor's knowledge of client's financial

[20] See Karen Altfest, *Keeping Clients for Life* (New York: John Wiley & Sons, 2001). While it is still controversial, the number doing human planning appears to be growing. On the other hand, some advisors say planning should be restricted to money matters and what they derisively call "therapy" should be left to other professions.

facts to help them with life planning. Let's look at some common nonfinancial needs of people that financial planners can help with.

- *To trust.* People seek advisors whom they feel they can trust to represent their best interests and give them straightforward advice. If there are potential conflicts between their interests and those of the advisor, they want them disclosed.

- *To find an interested person.* Talking about a problem can be therapeutic. Advisors who listen with interest to clients' problems are often viewed as good communicators, not just good listeners, and they are highly thought of even when they are not proposing a potential solution.

- *To understand.* People want simple advice that they can evaluate themselves or they at least want to understand why the advisor is making a particular comment or recommendation. Communication in easy-to-comprehend terms is part of simplicity. If advice is complicated, people may not take it all or may feel unintelligent.

- *To help establish goals.* Goals are not always immediately known. People appreciate techniques provided by advisors such as leading questions or just extensive discussions that assist in eliciting those goals. Being nonjudgmental and empathetic can help the process.

- *To feel secure.* Being financially secure and feeling secure, while synonymous in rational finance, are not always the same in practice. For example, a recommendation can be made to establish a core position in real estate investment trusts that is expected to have attractive returns, relatively low market risk, and less correlation with other equities. However, the client may feel very uneasy because of unfavorable past experiences with real estate. In general, client feelings should be taken into account and alternatives to initial recommendations may be called for.

- *To be served.* Service can be used to sum up many other factors such as competence, interest, and concern. More specifically, it includes the importance of understanding such things as timely responses, periodic meetings, specialized communications, and actions that convey to clients that their interests are being kept in mind. A person who is well served is often able to overlook shorter-term negative outcomes such as recommendations that underperform.

- *To be understood and appreciated.* People want to have someone who understands them, their problems, and their goals, both financial and nonfinancial. To be understood can be comforting in itself and is often an important step in becoming receptive to recommendations. It is often as important for a client to be as aware of his or her strong points as of his or her weak ones. In fact, a reinforcement of the client's strong points will often boost self-confidence and motivate the client to finally tackle his or her weaknesses.

- *To improve competency.* Many people want to become more knowledgeable if only with the goal of self-improvement. This is particularly true in finance, which many view as complicated. Thus, advice should be explained, even when it isn't necessary for decision-making purposes.

- *To enjoy interacting.* People want to deal with others they feel good about interacting with. The pleasure can come from the factors listed above and others such as sharing similar interests with people who are lively and empathetic.

EVALUATE THE BENEFITS OF BEHAVIORAL FINANCIAL PLANNING

In this final step, we assess the contribution of behavioral finance to PFP. To do so, we complete the Practical Comment about John begun under the first step.

Practical Comment John—Part II

John now had the benefit of going through the chapter. It was different from the other financial material he had read. Most of the other material was stated as facts, often with numerical examples. Few authors said that planning might depend on individual circumstances and individual behavior. Yet in many cases, that was just what behavioral finance did.

Behavioral finance provided a number of different theories that analyzed prominent personality traits, including many individual shortcomings when looked at from the standpoint of ideal behavior and money maximization. The trouble was that these traits, including nonmonetary goals, differed in their applicability and intensity from one person to another. He wanted hard-and-fast rules and numbers he could measure. Instead, he received soft information that required judgment to apply.

Then he thought, Isn't judgment what is required in practical business and personal situations? The chapter had outlined some basic theories that had fairly widespread applicability to people. The relevance of those theories to PFP was demonstrated by illustrating them within different areas of the planning process. In total, examples were shown for the most prominent active areas of PFP.

John appreciated the simplification of categories by separating financial shortcomings into cognitive errors and visceral feelings and the use of a model that didn't attempt to measure each individual shortcoming but only to provide the potential for quantifying the difference between ideal and present behavior.

He recognized that behavioral planning didn't promise a full explanation of people's actions. However, employing his original criteria of usefulness, John better understood the obstacles to PFP goal achievement and the tools available for overcoming them. In fact, he identified several behavior weaknesses in himself and ways of dealing with them. From a financial planner's perspective, he began to appreciate the multidimensional role that practitioners play in a client's financial life and the life-planning extension intensively employed by some professionals.

In sum, while he sometimes found behavioral financial planning less than fully satisfying, he developed a better understanding of himself and how to improve his household operations as well as of several nonquantitative methods to help others. He thought that behavioral analysis could help people realize their full potential. He became more interested in learning about how a broader range of behavioral tools can be applied to each area of the financial plan. (See the listing provided in Web Appendix C, Behavioral Finance—Applications.)

An overall evaluation of the strengths and weaknesses of behavioral versus classical finance is given in Table 19.3.

As you can see, behavioral financial planning is not so much an alternative way of looking at PFP as it is a practical supplement to it. Knowing what motivates people and finding

TABLE 19.3 Behavioral Analysis: Evaluation versus Traditional Finance

Strengths	Weaknesses
Measures what is	Can place less stress on what should be
More adaptable	More difficult to measure
More realistic portrayal of human actions	Harder to generalize
Provides a greater understanding of human motivations	Less firm conclusions
Can employ tools from other disciplines	Less satisfying financial conclusions
Permits many more individual differences	Less scientific in a financial sense
Can employ laboratory tests	Difficult to form and use aggregate data
Encourages new insight into human financial behavior	Many theories overlap
Extends beyond quantitative measurement	Can introduce bias
Allows judgment	Judgment can lead to biases
Overall	**Overall**
Can add to planning effectiveness, bringing people closer to ideal performance	No substitute for quantitative figures

ways of improving results is what behavioral planning is all about. It should be measured by its accomplishments in achieving these objectives.

Back to Dan and Laura
BEHAVIORAL ANALYSIS

Dan phoned me to say that he was feeling anxious about the financial plan. He said the process was drawing to a close and he wasn't sure I was aware of the scope of their goals or of the conflicts that he and Laura were having. I reminded him that I had tried to delve deeper into their goals originally but was told to keep to the money aspects of financial planning. I thought it was a good idea for the three of us to meet now, before the final plan was drawn up.

At the meeting, Dan started the conversation casually by showing me an article about behavioral economics and a Nobel Prize in Economics that had been awarded to researchers in the area.[21] He asked if the discipline was relevant in their situation. He mentioned that he had purchased stock in Earth Foods, as I had suggested, but the stock had lost 10 percent of its value in the following two months and he wondered whether he had made a mistake. Our time at this meeting was limited, so we decided not to deal with any issues at this meeting but to respond in writing in a subsequent communication.

I tried to learn more about their values. I asked what the word money *meant to each of them. Dan said fear. He was afraid that he would end up like his parents; the absence of money had influenced all their actions and limited their sense of well-being. Laura said she viewed money as an opportunity. Having it bought happiness in both a material and nonmaterial sense. At this point, Dan burst out in emotional terms about how Laura didn't understand what it was like to grow up poor. She always viewed the future optimistically, believing things would take care of themselves. Nor had she complied fully with the cutback in household outlays.*

Dan wondered whether they could operate as a team going forward, given their opposing views on financial matters. His parents had always agreed on money matters. All household decisions were made together, without self-interest. Throughout discussions, except for the comment on money, Laura stood by quietly. When he questioned their relationship, Laura just rolled her eyes. I mentioned that in getting to know them, I noticed that they seemed to see eye to eye on other matters and interests. Both quickly agreed.

I decided to change the subject somewhat and asked them once again what their goals were. Dan said his goal was to live a middle-class life with a house in a good neighborhood, educating his children and feeling secure that this life could not be taken away from him. If necessary, he would retire later then 55. He enjoyed being an engineer and wanted to grow in his job in both responsibility and money. When he retired, he wanted to feel that he had made a material impact on his firm's success. I asked him what he would like to do in retirement. He responded that retirement was far away, but he thought a combination of active leisure and some charity work was high on his list.

Laura's answer focused to a large extent on different factors. She said she figured Dan's fear would keep household money in balance. She wanted to make sure her children had the same opportunities she did and would grow up well-adjusted and close to their parents. She too wanted an active retirement life that included sports, vacations, and socializing. She said she wanted to improve herself in retirement, perhaps going for a master's degree in a liberal arts discipline as well as becoming a good bridge player.

I have started this section of your financial plan with Dan's question on behavioral economics. Actually, this question is very relevant to your plan and to financial planning in general. Often the questions and feelings involved are discussed orally. However, given

---

[21] To Daniel Kahnerman and Vernon Smith (2002).

your interest in the subject and your desire that I explain the reasoning behind many issues, I will detail it in writing.

Behavioral economics is the inclusion of human motivations and human weaknesses. Some of those weaknesses are truly human shortcomings. People wish they could rectify them. Others do not fall under the traditional assumptions of economics. Behavioral finance and behavioral financial planning are applications of behavioral economics. Behavioral factors are particularly relevant to financial planning because the term *goals* in finance conveys a broader meaning to most people than simply making the most money possible.

Human shortcomings include weaknesses in knowledge, memory, and mental processes. Other influences such as our friends or certain religious beliefs about controlling materialistic impulses, even if money is available, can be difficult to measure. Dan felt nonlegal obligation to help his parents, if needed, may not comply with classical economic thought. It can, however, comply with a broader view of receiving pleasure. We can call the process of identifying and achieving nonfinancial goals life planning.

So behavioral economics is just studying in a scientific way how people react in certain circumstances. The way they respond is "human," as in the expression "I am only human," implying that errors are likely. In that instance, we are not like machines, although being so could help us. In other instances, we have no desire to adhere to businesslike maximization of dollars. We are too busy having fun in our leisure pursuits and have established an equilibrium between work and leisure based on our preferences.

Let's look at the life-planning goals for both of you. Dan, yours seem to be focused on material items. Your fear of money shortages makes earning a significant amount with a low tolerance for a financial shortfall a high priority. Once you feel secure about your finances, you would like to feel that the work you are doing is worthwhile. In retirement, you would like to remain active in leisure sports and "give back" by spending more meaningful time in charitable work.

Laura, your goals seem to have more to do with relationships. You do not exhibit fear about money issues. Instead, you see it as an opportunity that is likely to present you with happy alternatives. Specifically, you want to make sure that your children have the right upbringing. It isn't surprising, then, that you have selected a teaching career. In retirement, you also would like to maintain an active and athletic life. You also would like to further yourself intellectually by pursuing a master's degree as a leisure pursuit.

Your combined goals represent a blend of materialism and noneconomic pursuit. To support both your current standard of living and your potentially costly desire to go back to school, in retirement you will need a significant cash flow. Of course, your most expensive goal is to retire at age 55 to pursue these leisure activities.

Your financial plan, to be presented soon, will indicate the feasibility of achieving those goals and, if they are not achievable given your current resources, what it will take to have them come to fruition. For now, let me handle the rest of the issues in our discussion.

It is not surprising that you do not see eye to eye on all household matters. Most people don't. It is good that you have the courage to voice your disagreements and bring them into the open. You have different personalities and backgrounds. I have found in couples that I advise that frequently people select others who are unlike them in many respects, often within a framework of shared interests and values. A psychologist once termed them "complementary dissimilarities." For example, savers seem to choose spenders and optimists often choose pessimists. I often see spouses in conflict with one another over their opposing views on several issues. When I ask them whether they would like to have married someone just like themselves, they say no. I believe you both exemplify this tendency and balance each other out well financially and otherwise. I know that I had discussed this with you early in our relationship, but I believe now, just before we complete the plan, it is worth repeating.

However, Laura, something will have to be done about your difficulty with adhering to the spending plan. This control issue is common in carrying out a financial plan. Try visualizing yourself not being able to raise your children the way you want them to be raised if you don't change your habits. Don't procrastinate; turn over a new leaf now. I recommend that you implement my previous suggestions about cash flow planning this week, including establishing separate savings accounts for each goal and writing a check to each account at the beginning of the period.

In fact, I now believe it would be better to have the money wired directly from your main account to these separate savings accounts. If that doesn't do the trick, perhaps you should leave your credit cards in a drawer and use them only on vacations. I suggest you find a hobby to at least partially replace going to the mall; it is too tempting for you.

Dan, I don't believe you have nearly begun to be able to make a judgment on Earth Foods. You have only owned that stock for two months. In that time, anything can happen to a stock. You are expressing what we sometimes call "myopic behavior"; we might call it short-term thinking. Wait and watch the fundamentals both in actual operations by visiting local markets and in examining financial results. Ask yourself whether anything fundamentally happened to alter your beliefs in the outlook for this company. If the answer is no, then ignore short-term situations. Stocks can be more representative of actual fair values over the longer term.

In sum, I think your questions and reactions are normal. I suggest that if you aren't doing so already, you try to be tolerant of each other's positions. Put yourself, as they say, in the other person's shoes. But I suspect that you are already doing this. Your common interests and balanced approach to life seem healthy to a financial person who has seen many couples.

Summary

Behavioral financial planning is a discipline intended to express finance in a way that goes beyond ideal quantitative finance. Its goal is to improve performance through use of mechanisms that humans can relate to. Among the chapter's points are

- Actual finance differs markedly from ideal finance.
- Human shortcomings come from cognitive errors and visceral feelings.
- Cognitive errors arise from lack of knowledge, weakness in perception and memory, and less-than-ideal processing scope and speed.
- Heuristics and biases are inherent human actions. Heuristics can be either good or bad, while biases can result in incorrect choice.
- There are a host of ways of overcoming behavioral weaknesses that are presented in the chapter.
- Life cycle planning goes beyond traditional financial planning to nonfinancial personal goals. PFP is involved because cash flow often, directly or indirectly, helps fund these goals.
- Financial planners can have a strong role in behavioral finance for both money planning and life planning.

Key Terms

behavioral finance, *537*
behavioral financial
planning, *537*
biases, *539*

cognitive errors, *538*
heuristics, *539*
life planning, *545*
mental accounting, *540*

money Planning, *545*
satisficing, *540*
visceral feelings, *538*

Web Sites

http://www.psychologyandmarkets.org
Institute of Behavioral Finance
A section on the Web site presents the research done by the institute. It is also a home page of the *Journal of Behavioral Finance*. The list of published articles in the journal back to 2000 is available online. There is an online information section about seminars and events.

http://www.behaviouralfinance.net
Behavioral Finance
This site offers a number of links with behavioral finance terms with definitions provided and links to related articles.

Questions

1. What is behavioral financial planning? Differentiate it from behavioral finance.
2. Indicate what a heuristic is and give four examples of it.
3. Discuss behavioral life cycle theory. Do you believe it is realistic?
4. Melinda thought about going to a dealership two hours from her location to buy a new car. She was told she might be able to save $2,000 over purchasing it locally. She decided against it. What are possible reasons for doing so?
5. How does satisficing compare with classical economic goals? Illustrate.
6. Name three behavioral weaknesses that might apply to investment analysis and give examples of them.
7. Name one behavioral characteristic in each part of active financial planning other than investments. Indicate how they can affect the financial planning process.
8. Do you believe loss aversion is practiced widely? Justify your answer.
9. Some people say that money is the only goal that counts, while others indicate that once living costs are covered, it hardly matters at all. Indicate which statement you believe to be more accurate. Justify your answer.
10. What is happiness research? Does this research indicate that money brings happiness?
11. Contrast money planning and life planning.
12. What are human weaknesses under both money planning and life planning?
13. How do basic feelings differ from higher-level feelings?
14. Indicate the mechanisms for enhancing savings practices. Are they realistic? Discuss.
15. Should goal planning be part of the financial planning process or should there just be a numbers-only approach?

Case Application
BEHAVIORAL ANALYSIS

Monica asked that we meet to see if I could help to reduce the differences between them. When the time came, she started the conversation by saying that Richard wasn't saving any money at all. They hadn't started implementing. She said he spent a good deal of time buying and selling stocks. He seemed to be influenced by the weekly ups and downs of the market. At least temporarily, however, he had raised the quality of the stocks he was buying.

Richard seemed a little annoyed and said that Monica never wanted to sell any securities. She almost always told him to wait. She said the shares would come back. When I asked what money meant to them, Richard said an opportunity to gamble and Monica replied a chance to lose what you've accumulated. As far as their long-term goals were concerned, Richard said he had no real long-term goals. The future was too fickle. He said who knew what fate had in store for them. Monica's goal was to feel secure. I had the feeling that her remark was in response to Richard's behavior. She wouldn't allow herself to think of anything beyond security until Richard's activities could be controlled.

Case Application Questions

1. What should be done about Richard's spending?
2. What kind of investment behavior is Richard demonstrating? What can be done about it?
3. What is Monica's investment behavior called? How can it be helped?
4. Contrast their two views of money. Do you have any recommendations?
5. How can Monica's fears be dealt with?

Appendix I

Behavioral versus Rational Finance

Behavioral financial planning is an alternative way of looking at finance. It makes use of approaches from psychology, sociology, and other disciplines to explain human behavior.

Many financial researchers have disagreed with its premises and conclusions. They raise the following objections:

1. Behavioral traits presented were often obtained through laboratory experiments and questionnaires, not through real-life actions of individuals. Until they are thoroughly empirically tested, they have no validity.
2. There is no overall theory of behavioral finance that explains all or most of the individual research conclusions. The separate characteristics can be identified solely through observation and have no logical basis.
3. The observations can be true only for a segment of the population and sometimes can be in conflict.
4. In market observations, overreaction and underreaction relative to fair values are split, which is what you would find in a random reaction. Therefore, since there is no bias, the results are consistent with market efficiency.[22]

[22] Eugene F. Fama, "Market Efficiency, Long-Term Returns and Behavioral Finance," *Journal of Financial Economics* 49, no. 3 (September 1998), pp. 283–306.

Practical Comment   Integrating Behavioral Finance

In practical terms, the two approaches may be able to coexist. Prevailing theories such as MPT, CAPM, and efficient markets can represent an ideal state. As Eugene Fama has said of market efficiency, "Like all models, market efficiency (the hypothesis that prices fully reflect available information) is a faulty description of price formation."[23] It is used until a better model is established and tested. Behavioral economics can provide insight into the workings of how individuals make actual decisions. Since it doesn't assume perfect rationality, it can help in finding ways to improve their performance.

In making projections, planners should take into account their own shortcomings and those of the people they are advising. These shortcomings should be compared to the ideal state, rational financial planning, with the goal of approximating it as closely as possible. Where appropriate, human planning should be reflected as well. In this way, behavioral finance can be used as a supplement to rational finance. In other words, rational finance should remain the benchmark for performing quantitative financial planning, but behavior patterns should be incorporated as well.

[23] Fama, "Market Efficiency, Long-Term Returns and Behavioral Finance."

---

5. Many seeming irrationalities, particularly in the market, are due to problems in the testing methods used and ultimately may be explained away by improved methods.

6. If irrational behavior occurs, it will be quickly eliminated by rational investors.

7. Fully embracing behavioral financial planning could involve losing the ability to measure overall economic data with a single approach.

The behaviorists say, among other things,

1. The test results indicate anomalies that are too widespread to be due to chance.

2. Financial planning requires knowledge and processing power that the average person does not have.

3. When the bias in investing is shared by many investors in the market, it can overwhelm rational players.[24]

4. What good is the ability to measure overall data with one approach when the results have so many anomalies?

To some extent, the two approaches have difficulty in reaching agreement because they use different methods. As we've seen, traditional finance employs scientific quantitative methods and seeks ways of generalizing about overall data. It values tangible results that can be expressed in money terms. Psychologists may value the process rather than the results.[25]

The results that say that characteristics vary by person but are difficult to measure may be satisfying to psychologists and behavioral economists but can be of little use to finance professors looking for generalizations on overall data that can be confirmed objectively. Many behavior-oriented researchers as well as economics and finance people consider rational economists to be closed-minded, only willing to express things in economic terms.

[24] Many would say rationality returns to the market or individual investment over the longer term. See Andrei Shleifer and Robert Vishny, "The Limits of Arbitrage," *Journal of Finance* 52, no. 1 (March 1997), pp. 35–55.

[25] See Warneryd, Karl-Erik. *The Psychology of Saving: A Study on Economic Psychology* (Cheltenham, UK: Edward Elgar, 1999), and Warneryd, Karl-Erik. *Stock-Market Psychology: How People Value and Trade Stocks* (Cheltenham, UK: Edward Elgar, 2001).

Categories of Human Behavior

There are three categories of human behavior: rational, irrational, and boundedly rational.[26] *Rational behavior* refers to logical behavior. It can be logical in a financial sense, in measurable dollars, or, more broadly, in any action we select that brings us more pleasure[27] than any alternative decision. *Irrational behavior* is illogical behavior economically or, in broader terms, behavior that results in displeasure. Robbing a general store to receive money to spend in the short term has the potential of a lengthy jail sentence, which would result in net displeasure and is therefore irrational behavior.

Boundedly rational behavior, more commonly called *bounded rationality,*[28] is conduct that resembles economically rational behavior but falls short.

Rational behavior is maximizing behavior, doing the best you can do. It represents the difference between rational economic behavior, also called ideal behavior, and actual economic behavior. We use economic behavior because it is measurable, thereby fitting in with traditional finance. Bounded rationality is where many behavioral finance theories can be placed.

Example 19.A2.1   Alfred wanted to make as much money as possible in his position as an independent accountant. He wanted to live the good life. He majored in accounting as an undergraduate and became a CPA. In promoting his career, he did all the right things except for one: he didn't finish his thesis for a master's degree in taxation. That degree would have attracted a high-paying new clientele. Rational behavior would have had him spend the time to finish the thesis. Irrational behavior would have been yelling at every client that walked through the door. Instead, he engaged in bounded rationality, pursuing rational maximization of profits but ignoring one area—completing the degree.

Additional Behavioral Models and Characteristics

In this appendix, we provide additional approaches to behavioral financial models and characteristics.

DELIBERATION COST

Deliberation cost is the mental time devoted to evaluating and making decisions; it is an attempt to present behavioral human actions in rational terms. It says that decision making incorporates many logical factors, most of which are not currently recognized in classical

---

[26] Actions can overlap and also change category depending on severity of occurrence. Each was placed into its principal or most frequently employed category.

[27] Defined as net pleasure, more pleasure than displeasure.

[28] John Conlisk, "Why Bounded Rationality?" *Journal of Economic Literature* 34, no. 2 (June 1996), pp. 669–700.

economics. There is no rigid formula used.[29] Choice may involve such variables as the cost of time, the lack of knowledge, the intensity of feeling concerning the task itself, the time period in performing the task,[30] the uncertainty about the exact time necessary to perform the task satisfactorily, and the possibility of a negative outcome. All these variables, some of which involve risk, are influenced by the knowledge and capabilities of the person performing the search.[31]

Example 19.A3.1   To finance the purchase of his new home, Seth selected a 30-year mortgage from the bank on the corner. He had been told that he could possibly save 0.5 percent per year if he performed an Internet search of all the availabilities. Seth said the bank rate he selected was generally competitive and certainly convenient since he already knew the bank's manager, who would take care of the entire process. An Internet search for the lowest rate would take many hours. It would involve detailed work that he particularly hated doing. Moreover, given his busy schedule at his job and his other commitments, he would have to do the search on weekends, which would cut into his "time off" from work worries. He wasn't sure how long it would take to find the lowest-cost reputable bank and, although it was unlikely, he was unsure that the rate of interest at the closing would not rise by more than the local bank rate. He also thought there was an outside chance that because he was a novice and did not know all the factors involved in a mortgage, he might end up with the local bank's mortgage anyway. He understood that the savings in interest would likely well exceed the cost of time as represented by his $30-per-hour charge multiplied by any reasonable estimate of the number of hours necessary to arrive at a decision.

Seth thought about all these factors for a few days, wondering which way to go, and he decided that the benefits of the local bank narrowly exceeded its cost. In other words, the deliberation cost of the search including the risks attached to an unlikely but possible lack of success exceeded its benefits. Although he knew he couldn't express his decision in a strictly quantifiable way, he was proud that he had arrived at his decision using what he learned was a logical method. Had he known about the firms that provide detailed competitive information and telephone numbers with an implied representation of at least some screening on lender reliability, he would have had a lower deliberation cost and would have made a different decision.

AGENCY THEORY

Agency theory provides an alternative approach to classical economics in household matters. As we saw in Chapter 4, classical economic theory assumes that members of a household have the same interests. Therefore, a household and the people living within it can speak as one voice in attempting to maximize. Agency theory uses a managerial-organizational approach to decision making. According to *agency theory,* owners delegate operating responsibilities including decision making to managers of activities for the businesses or household organizations.[32] As the owner's agents, these managers are supposed to act in the best interests of whichever organization they work for.

In contrast to the classical approach, however, agency theory acknowledges that individual goals can diverge from those of the organization. For example, supervisors might keep workers they like even though their output is inefficient and will not lead to profit maximization. Alternatively, one household member might want to purchase an expensive car even though it is detrimental to overall budgetary goals and household quality-of-life

---

[29] This interpretation of the term is the author's.

[30] In his original article, Becker distinguished between the cost of time during the week and the cost on the weekend. See Gary Becker, "A Theory of Allocation of Time," *Economic Journal* 75, no. 299 (1965), pp. 493–517.

[31] Stigler's search behavior is a related approach. See George Stigler, "The Economics of Information," *Journal of Political Economy* 69, no. 3 (June 1961), pp. 213–25.

[32] See Michael Jensen and William Meckling, "Theory of the Firm: Managerial Behavior, Agency Costs and Ownership Structure," *Journal of Financial Economics* 3 (October 1976), pp. 305–60.

considerations. In economic terms, under agency theory, the agents attempt to incorporate their own separate utility functions.

Households tend to be smaller units than many businesses and the participant members generally are what we have called member-owners; they work in, make overall supervisory decisions in, and share the benefits of the household they occupy. Thus, conflicts of interest tend to be concentrated among member-owners.

INTRAHOUSEHOLD ALLOCATION

An approach to household conflict related to agency theory occurs under what has been called intrahousehold allocation.[33] Intrahousehold theorists believe that the household is the organizational entity for individuals but that the traditional single-agent model of household behavior is not appropriate. They say individual household members have separate goals. Decisions are made through bargaining, during which such factors as the relative incomes of the members, their gender, and the household's overall wealth come into play.[34]

Example 19.A3.2 Sam and Martha disagreed about whether to buy a new air conditioner now. Sam, the sole wage earner, wanted one purchased on credit immediately, while Martha, concerned about their already high debt, preferred to save for it. They compromised. Martha recognized that Sam had been having difficulties sleeping on hot summer nights, which had resulted in his being late to work. And perhaps influenced by the fact that she was in a weaker position because she did not work, she agreed that they purchase an air conditioner right away. In return, Sam agreed to take $100 a month out of his account so that they could pay off the credit card debt within one year.

Conflict resolution through bargaining and other methods can be a normal and even efficient way of handling differences in interests. On the other hand, disputes, vindictiveness, and intransigent narrow-minded behavior also can lead to less-than-optimal household actions. These actions can be regarded as human weaknesses since such inefficiencies as impulsive short-term behavior can result in negative operational consequences.

Intrahousehold allocation models are more complex than the classical one-voice model. They make overall economic generalizations much more difficult than with a single-agent model since bargaining and the influence of each member can vary significantly from household to household. Clearly, intrahousehold allocation provides a similar challenge to classical economics that agency theory does for business finance's classically assumed one-voice owner and employee goal of maximization of profits.[35]

DISCOUNTING

Discounting is a basic economic operation. It assumes that we would prefer a pleasurable activity today to one in the future. In order to motivate us to postpone expenditures and save money, an attractive rate of interest must be offered. The mathematical equivalent of this process—outlays to find their present value—is basic to finance and underlies much of our discussion in this book. It is important because it places an objective numeric value,

[33] Martin Browning, Francois Bourguignon, Pierre-Andre Chiappori, and Valerie Lechene, "Income and Outcomes: A Structural Model of Intrahousehold Allocation," *Journal of Political Economy* 102, no. 6 (December 1994), pp. 1067–96.

[34] See Francine D. Blau, Marianne A. Ferber, and Anne E. Winkler, *The Economics of Women, Men, and Work,* 3rd ed. (Upper Saddle River, NJ: Prentice Hall, 1998). See also Peter Kooreman and Sophia Wunderink, *The Economics of Household Behavior* (New York: Palgrave Macmillan, 1997).

[35] The author of this text has polled his financial planning classes over time as to which predominates in marriage: overall household goals or separate individual goals. Invariably, a large majority say overall household goals.

the interest rate, on our economic actions. It therefore allows economics and finance to go forward in a rational scientific way.

Two of discounting's assumptions can be questioned. The first is that we need a positive return to delay an outlay. We often save for emergencies and for retirement, and many of us would do so even if the investment rate were 0 or even negative. In fact, those who place their money in low-interest-bearing money market accounts may earn a negative return after taxes and inflation are taken into account. Yet few people would consider the precautionary and retirement reasons for savings irrational, even in the absence of attractive returns.

The second assumption of discounting we may question is that the return we require for an action stays constant as the time to the activity date diminishes. On the contrary, it has been shown that people's preferences and therefore the discount rate are not stable but change as the activity date draws near. Specifically, the return needed to perform unpleasant tasks and to postpone pleasant ones increases as the scheduled date approaches. This has been termed *hyperbolic discounting*; the discount rate rises at an increasing rate in the period prior to performance time.[36]

Example 19.A3.3   Renee had two things she wanted to do. The first was to take her car in to be fixed. It had a loose bumper and some other items that, if handled now, would cost $1,250. If she waited more than three months, the bumper would be further damaged, and the charge would be $1,350. She found the experience unpleasant in that she would have to stay around the garage for a full day, Saturday, her day off. She decided to have the car fixed now to save the $100. She thought the amount saved was just enough to motivate her to take the repair within three months. She resolved that if she did it soon, she would spend up to $440 on a bicycle, which, if she waited until the winter to buy, nine months from then, would be available for $380.

Three months later when the last time came to bring the car in at the lower repair cost, she postponed it, saying to herself that she would do it later. She thought to herself, if the savings were $200, I would do it now. She didn't postpone the purchase of the bicycle, however. She indicated it would take a $120 savings to get her to forsake use of the new bicycle over the summer.

As you can see, her preferences for discomfort (repairs on the car) and pleasure (buying a new bicycle) changed as decision time came close. In effect, her new discount rates at the time of decision as represented by the new dollar figures were different from the original ones.

Approaches such as hyperbolic discounting are an attempt to apply a boundedly rational framework to human behavior. With time-varying discount rates, the framework for measuring preferences can still go forward.

Appendix IV

Noneconomic Behavior

The economics and finance disciplines generally assume that only money matters as an operating goal. However, many human actions are not motivated by money. Others can result in a decline in money without a tangible benefit to the person. We can call these actions noneconomic behavior. Economic measurement may be difficult or impossible to use since a different model or discipline of behavior is involved. For example, human feelings may be best analyzed using psychology.[37]

---

[36] See David Laibson, "Golden Eggs and Hyperbolic Discounting," *Quarterly Journal of Economics* 112, no. 2 (May 1997), pp. 443–77.

[37] Actions may be logical or illogical. They don't conform to the economic definition of logic but may conform to our broader definition of logical, in pleasure terms.

Or our feelings and actions may be the result of our background, how we are brought up and whom we interact with, a sociologist's specialty. Our behavior may be affected by cultural influences throughout the ages, an anthropologist's role.[38] Finally, our actions also may be affected by how our brains are "wired," a biologist's territory.

These influences may be perfectly consistent with a traditional financial view of goals. For example, the lifestyles of our parents and friends may teach us to keep up with the Joneses and buy more material goods. On the other hand, these actions may be irrational from the standpoint of traditional financial thought. Yet, the same actions can be perfectly logical from the point of view of an individual's standpoint. The criterion for affirming a perfectly logical personal goal would be that if supplied with information concerning your nonfinancially efficient actions, you would still repeat them.

Example 19.A4.1 Sherry gave $10,000 a year anonymously to a lung cancer society. She received no economic benefit from it and, in her tight current economic circumstances, it was an unpleasant gift. She did it because her father had died of lung cancer and she felt she had to show her respect for him in this way. When others told her that, given her modest income, it was not in her best interests, she just shrugged her shoulders. From a financial standpoint, her action was irrational. She had a reduction in assets without receiving enjoyment from it. From a personal standpoint, it was logical. It was her preference. The criterion of knowledge of actions was fulfilled. Whether it was custom given her family background or because, as a psychologist said, she unknowingly received pleasure from this "unpleasant gift," it was a conscious action.

Life planning further complicates traditional economic and financial analysis. Given traditional assumptions, activities can be segregated neatly into work and leisure. The amount of time we spend in work is limited to the point at which the pleasure we get from work dollars just equals the pleasure we receive from using the time in leisure pursuits (see Chapter 4, Appendix I).

The behavioral approach has been a basic assumption of PFP theory. It has allowed us to say that the household operates somewhat like a business, with hours spent at work intended to operate efficiently and maximize cash flow. Life planning can alter that separation into work and leisure by providing pleasure for work-related activities. Indeed, it is often the goal that makes that happen.

The solution can be to allocate work time and, significantly for PFP, work dollars into work and leisure. For example, a doctor making $150,000 a year who quits and becomes a teacher who works the same number of hours making $50,000 could be said to have made a yearly leisure expenditure of $100,000.

Life planning involves more than work-leisure time, however. It involves feelings and preferences. Economics and finance acknowledge preferences and a world related to feelings and tastes. However, those disciplines are more comfortable with generalizations rather than analysis that concludes, "It depends on the person." The difficulty is often in measurement. Feelings are often left to the field of psychology.[39]

We have choices with life planning and feelings in theory issues. We can define them as part of preferences, part of our objective; we can ignore them as being noneconomic choices; or we can allocate among these alternatives. To include them, we would have difficulty in measurement. For our purposes, in a practical text, we will simply refer to them as part of behavioral financial planning.

---

[38] See Kent C. Berridge, "Irrational Pursuits: Hyper-Incentives from a Visceral Brain," in *The Psychology of Economic Decisions: Rationality and Well-Being,* ed. Isabelle Brocas and Juan D. Carillo (New York: Oxford University Press, 2003).

[39] Some of those who practice life planning believe it difficult to separate feelings from intellect.

Chapter Twenty

Completing the Process

Chapter Goals

This chapter will enable you to:

- Complete the financial planning project.
- Explain the importance of planning integration.
- Demonstrate how PFP theory can improve the practice of financial planning.
- Use overall planning tools such as SWOT, scenario, and sensitivity analysis.
- List the keys to a successful plan.

The big day had finally arrived. Dan, Laura, and I were to meet and finalize the process. Unlike many other planning meetings, this one would deal almost exclusively with integration. In other words, it was decision time. As it turned out, there was a shortfall.

Real Life Planning

As soon as Walter walked in, the advisor knew that he was not an ordinary client. He had the self-assurance of someone who was used to delegating tasks to others. The easy way he combined thoughts and expressed them quickly made clear that he was unusually intelligent. It turned out he was the president of a consulting firm that specialized in financial matters.

Rather than engaging in small talk, he set the tone almost immediately by listing his needs. He wanted someone to tell him what he could spend under various alternatives for income, each involving a seven-figure sum. His cost of living was tiered according to the number of homes he would own, alternative retirement dates, and whether he could afford a yacht, an airplane, and multiple vacations each year.

He said that he wanted the work to incorporate risk and that if all we were going to give him was a one-figure estimated retirement needs analysis and some recommendations on investments and insurance, he wasn't interested. Others might be satisfied with that, but he could do that by himself. He thought for a second and said he wanted a financial plan that was as sophisticated as the plans he provided for his business clients.

He wanted all recommendations to be supported by numbers and expected his advisor to be prepared to defend assumptions and recommendations. He indicated he wanted a comprehensive plan, which included all household assets to arrive at integrated solutions. His wife, Marilyn, was very interested in the results as well. She was conservative in investment policy and life decision making about investments and personal life and was concerned about their spending pattern. She would delegate the task to him and, unlike most spouses, would not attend meetings. While she was a woman of achievement herself with a doctorate, she wanted the plan simply stated with clear conclusions and recommendations.

Walter indicated that while the conclusions would be the same, the requirements to satisfy each spouse would be different. Like his clients, he would be willing to pay a sizeable fee if it could be achieved. Did the advisor believe it to be feasible?

The first thought the advisor had was would he be able to satisfy the couple, particularly the husband. His moment of discomfort when facing the man reminded him of the first time he had a psychiatrist as a client. At the initial interview, the advisor was fearful that the psychiatrist, using his training, would analyze him and uncover some weaknesses. Instead, his client was most interested in any help the advisor could offer concerning his own problems. Moreover, in a reversal of roles, there were times when the advisor thought he bordered on being the psychiatrist's "financial shrink."

The advisor thought the amount of work involved for Walter would be well in excess of the average plan. However, he believed that he understood what motivated Walter and his concerns that he could meet them, and he accepted the invitation to do what he termed integrated financial planning.

The amount of work exceeded expectations as the number of alternatives rose. However, the possible outcomes were placed in perspective and the marketable investments portion was treated together with salary, homes, and other assets as consistent with total portfolio management. Before completing the plan, the advisor asked himself whether the plan met the couple's requirements. Was it multidimensional enough for the husband and direct enough for the wife? Did it meet their behavioral needs as well? Finally, did the conclusions make sense and were they useful, practical, and simple enough to be followed? He decided that the plan did, although it held some surprises and a limitation on Walter's expenditures, even with his mega salary. The approach would comply with the request to incorporate risk, and the recommendations would be consistent with the couple's tolerance.

Most plan presentations, in addition to the numbers, involve a behavioral theme. It can be empathy, taking control, friendship, fatherly advice, awakening to reality, and so on. This one would likely be firmness. The advisor had to be firm in his recommendations and demeanor to effectively communicate with Walter. When Walter sat down, the advisor knew that he was correct in his appraisal of the man and the meeting. The questions flew in a way that only a person who was financially sophisticated could generate. The advisor met each of Walter's questions with a specific answer and often with a reference in the written plan including numbers-laden appendixes, which virtually no other clients bothered to read. It reminded the advisor of the defense of his doctoral dissertation many years ago.

Hours later, the plan had been discussed and all questions were answered. Then Walter got up somewhat abruptly. A faint smile broke out across his otherwise tight face, and he said what all financial planners hope to hear: "Thanks, it was just what I was looking for." Then he strode out of the room.

This chapter will explain how to construct and integrate a financial plan in the manner that Walter and his wife wanted. The approach taken is relevant for most people.

OVERVIEW

Integration is the process of combining, of making something into a completed whole. In personal financial planning, it means evaluating costs and benefits over time to find the best path to our goals. Integration is often overlooked or given less emphasis than is warranted. Given limited resources, you cannot make correct choices without weighing alternatives for spending your monies.

In this book, we have looked at the household as a type of enterprise with the objective of delivering those goals. We have said that major decisions are made on an overall basis combining all household activities. In PFP terms, that becomes integration of all sources and uses of cash ranging from job-related revenues and current living costs to savings for retirement and other future household activities.

In the last two chapters, we have provided you with the building blocks for integration. Chapter 18 provided the mechanisms for ideal financial integration and Chapter 19, an approach to behavioral variables that reflect human shortcomings and nonfinancial goals.

In this chapter, we will focus more on the practical aspects of completing the planning work. We will incorporate both money planning, the bedrock of PFP and this book, and human planning. We will place a great deal of emphasis on real-life process issues. This approach is taken to achieve the chapter's planning objective of learning how to complete the PFP process in a way that provides an integrated path to your goals.

A completed financial plan for Dan and Laura is provided in Web Appendix D, Comprehensive Financial Plan—Dan and Laura.

We will begin by reexamining PFP theory and the financial ways of integrating goals. We will then detail the PFP process, which, as you will see, will be helpful in ensuring that we have covered all major factors as we move toward completion. We also will discuss three tools that are helpful in an overall planning review. In the final section of this chapter, we complete and implement the financial plan, intended to be the practical embodiment of the PFP process.

PFP THEORY

A theory is a set of concepts that unifies a body of knowledge and helps you make better decisions in practice. It helps if the theory explains things simply and provides greater insight into the area being studied.

The body of knowledge we are interested in, of course, is personal financial planning. It can be defined as the process of programming future actions to help fulfill life's goals. Put simply, PFP lays the groundwork for goal achievement. Let's summarize PFP theory discussed in Chapter 4, but in a somewhat different way, and see how it assists with understanding personal finance and leads to better decisions. We'll start with its set of concepts.

1. *The household is an enterprise that operates like a business.* It has revenues and nondiscretionary and discretionary costs. The activities for this "household firm" have a purpose: to make logical decisions and promote efficient operations. For a breakdown of the specific similarities and differences between the household and a business, see Appendix I.

2. *The goal of PFP is to provide the highest standard of living possible for household "member-owners" over their life cycle.* The standard of living is a practical way of expressing utility maximization. It consists of a blend of money outlays and time spent on pleasurable activities. This standard of living goal is not just a current one; it incorporates the entire life cycle of the household.

3. *For a given time devoted to work, the goal becomes maximization of discretionary expenditures.* The breakdown between work and leisure time is based on household values. At equilibrium, the benefits from revenues through one additional hour of work are equal to the costs in disutility of giving up one additional hour of leisure time. Consequently, each household has its own blend of work time, leisure time, and discretionary expenditures.

   Once that work-leisure equilibrium is established, the sole focus of the work side of the household is on generating the highest cash flows possible for discretionary expenditures.[1] Discretionary expenditures are the only outlays that give us pleasure.

---

[1] Over the life cycle. During interim periods, reinvestment may be made for capital expenditures and savings-investment.

Therefore, we want to maximize them for the time allocated to work. We seek to minimize nondiscretionary costs.

4. *Household finance supports the enterprise, which needs cash flow and appropriate methods for allocating its limited resources over time.* Once we discuss cash flow and decisions over time involving uncertainty, finance becomes involved. Its tools—time value of money, capital budgeting, risk-return, and portfolio management—are powerful methods for household decision making.

5. *Personal financial planning provides the strategic approach for solving household financial decisions.* PFP is the thinking and action arm of household finance. Its most significant tool is capital budgeting. PFP uses capital budgeting to help make resource decisions through evaluation and selection among alternative expenditures and then assists in implementing them.

6. *Personal financial planning decisions are made on an integrated basis that takes into account all household assets and liabilities.* Each household activity—ranging from current living (cash flow) needs to future life cycle requirements such as retirement, estate, education, and risk management—has resource requirements. The savings and other current and projected inflows are assets used for these purposes. Our obligations, legal or otherwise, are our liabilities. For example, our desire for providing funds to educate our children can be considered a liability, even though we may not have a legal obligation to do so. We include all assets and liabilities in making capital budgeting decisions for our limited resources. That is what comprehensive financial planning is all about.

7. *Total portfolio management provides the solution for personal financial planning's overall objective and the household's overall goal.* TPM's optimization model has as its payoff the asset-liability mix providing the highest return possible, given the household's tolerance for risk. This return figure is the maximum amount that can be outlaid for discretionary items. It simultaneously solves the household's maximization of discretionary expense goal and PFP's objective of helping the household reach that goal.

The distinguishing features of PFP theory in finance and its practical benefits are given in Table 20.1.

TABLE 20.1   **Distinguishing Features of PFP Theory**

Feature	Benefit
Uses household framework	Places it on par with other enterprises such as a business for improved analysis.
Highlights similarities with business	Stresses businesslike behavior—logical and efficient. Allows use of sophisticated business tools.
Expresses personal goals in money terms	Individual goals expressed in utility terms are often thought not measurable. The equilibrium approach is consistent with classical theory. It explains why household revenue and profit maximization are established, given the individual's limited time devoted to work.
Divides consumption into pleasurable and nonpleasurable expenditures	Aggregating these expenditures can lead to incorrect decisions. Discretionary and nondiscretionary expenditures (which are the financial expressions for pleasurable leisure outlays and nonpleasurable maintenance costs) are fundamentally different.
Places personal financial planning and capital budgeting at the center of household finance	Expresses what PFP does in a broader framework, links it more solidly to business finance, and leads to better financial decisions.
Uses an integrated portfolio approach for financial decision making	Improved decision making more closely parallels the way people do or should think.
Incorporates risk, return, and correlation in framework	Improved decision making by providing greater dimension in inputs and conclusions.
TPM, by using all assets and liabilities, integrates PFP and investment decisions	Better financial decisions. Use of all resources over a life cycle in arriving at conclusions. More closely resembles the way practitioners perform comprehensive financial planning.

Practical Comment PFP Theory in Simpler, More Practical Terms

As we move toward completing the plan, you should be aware of planning theory and its goals in simpler, more practical terms. People run or help run households they live in, which in many ways are operated like little businesses. Their businesses produce revenues from the human services offered. They have overhead costs from the commitments they have made and the necessities of life and profits that provide you with your standard of living. The more efficiently you operate, the higher your standard of living.

Existing finance theory in the form it is in now doesn't quite suit your needs. It tends to focus on financial assets alone, as if that were all that counts for the household. We know the household has human assets, homes, pensions, and other assets as well. We also know that the household has liabilities, not only legal ones but the obligations that arise from its living costs. Total portfolio management is a way to express this broader view of household

operations and to solve for optimal cash flows. While at first glance TPM looks like an asset management system alone, it represents all household activities and the way of planning and operating them in an integrated manner.

At this point in the financial planning process when we draw together all parts of the financial plan, we also need to think again about goals and limitations based on available cash flows. We should recognize the financial planning techniques that can be useful in integration, many of them coming directly from businesses. We should keep in mind the significance of the word *personal* in PFP. In contrast to traditional investment management, which is involved with supervision of financial assets alone, personal financial planning helps people with all their financial needs. Being conscious of PFP's broad scope and its specific planning components can help ensure that all resources and our intended uses for them have been taken into account in decision making.

In short, PFP theory highlights integration and the strong relationship PFP has with traditional business finance. Its concepts are intended to make PFP's role easier to understand and lead to improvements in the way it is practiced.

THE FINANCIAL PLAN

PFP theory explains how the PFP process should ideally be done. The financial plan, using the theory as an underpinning, is a mapping out of the practical steps through which a particular goal or goals are to be accomplished. For comprehensive financial planning, a detailed written financial plan is desirable. A financial plan has several advantages:

1. It imposes overall structure on the process through specific steps that should be taken.
2. It compels you to order your priorities and provide a specific financial solution using integrative techniques. In other words, it aids decision making.
3. It presents a document to refer back to so that you can compare actual with projected results and refresh your memory as thoughts of the original steps fade.
4. It provides a numerical base for adjustments as goals and resources change in the future.

The need for the plan to integrate all financial actions arises from the limited resources households have. Actions in one area often affect planning for other activities, as shown in Example 20.1.

Example 20.1

Liu was a successful businesswoman who earned hundreds of thousands of dollars annually but spent every dollar she made. Consequently, she had no money in her personal or pension account. Her accountant proposed that she place $100,000 in the defined benefit pension plan set up for her business. Liu recognized that her prior spending habits were extreme but still wanted to know what the $100,000 in savings would do for her as compared with continuing her previous practice. She was in the 40 percent marginal tax bracket. Her financial planner drew up a list showing the potential impact of saving $100,000 on the parts of the plan that were most likely to be affected.

Planning Area	Financial Impact	Explanation
Investment	+ $100,000	Savings immediately placed in investment vehicles.
Tax	− $40,000	Pretax dollar allocation into pension saves taxes, $100,000 × 40%.
Retirement	+ $100,000	Investment sum is available for ultimate retirement use.
Estate	+ $100,000	Investment sum not used when alive will be available for heirs.
Insurance	− $100,000	Greater assets reduce need for life and disability insurance.
Cash flow	− $60,000	Impact on current standard of living less than expected as $100,000 outlay is reduced by $40,000 in tax savings.

Note that

1. Some of this benefit is taken back due to taxation on pension distributions. On the other hand, tax deferral can reduce or even eliminate its net impact.
2. Obviously, the sum cannot be planned for both retirement and estate uses.

After seeing its impact on virtually all key financial planning functions and the effect on current lifestyle moderated by lower taxes, Liu decided to save the money.

Before making final judgments, it is advisable to examine your work by reviewing each step in the financial planning process and adding new tools that can help you in making integrated decisions. The series of questions below helps ensure that you will complete the process properly. Note that to ensure that the review process is broad in scope, the steps presented for reviewing your planning work are the same as those provided in Chapter 1 in outlining the planning process.

Establish the Scope of the Activity

Have you analyzed all areas that you intended to? Is the scope established broad enough? For example, in a comprehensive plan, if provisions have been made for retirement, has long-term care insurance been considered?

Gather the Data and Identify Goals

Has all information been gathered and is it available for use? Sometimes other information surfaces after the planning process has been completed that could change its conclusion. Two areas of data gathering sometimes omitted are the health of household members and the possibility of inheritances from parents and other relatives. Costs that are sometimes left out are purchases of cars and other durable goods, household repairs and improvements, and outlays on weddings.

Has the true goal been ascertained? Sometimes identifying the real goal may not be as simple as it appears. It may emerge only after considerable work or discussion or thought. For example, the statement "I am satisfied with my current lifestyle; my main goal is to have a roof over my head" can mask larger goals. The real goal can involve a much more elaborate lifestyle at a commensurate increase in costs.

Compile and Analyze the Data

Have all relevant data been analyzed? Have you given those data the depth of analysis they merit? Have SWOT, sensitivity, and scenario analysis been considered? (They will be explained shortly.) As you have learned, personal financial planning involves risk.

TABLE 20.2   Operating Parts of the Financial Plan

Operating Segment of the Plan	Cash Relationship[1]	Function
Revenues	Inflow	Job and investments liquidation upon retirement fund household activities
Living costs	Outflow	The costs of current overhead and pleasure-related activities
Debt	Inflow, then outflow	Supplies funds when current cash flow inadequate, followed by repayment of those funds
Capital expenditures (nonfinancial investments)	Outflow[2]	Outlays for household work-related efficiencies and pleasure-related activities
Financial investments	Outflow, then inflow	Initially invest savings held for future utilization; this segment, along with job revenues, then funds the rest of household activities
Risk management	Outflow[3]	Protects the household and brings about desired tolerance for risk
Retirement planning	Outflow	Appropriates so as to generate investment resources to be employed when working stops
Estate planning	Outflow	Used for people we care for to the extent we desire
Educational planning	Outflow[4]	Provides for household members' education
Special circumstances planning	Outflow	Outlays money for special uses

[1] At the time service is performed, except for debt and financial investments, which, as financial capital transactions, have two-part transactions, as indicated. For example, savings for retirement, which can be thought of as a multistep process with an initial outflow for the savings followed by an inflow to fund the actual expenditure when made; alternatively these two steps could be incorporated under financial investments with only the final step, the actual outflow itself, handled under retirement planning.
[2] To the extent outlays provide cash benefits, those benefits will be shown in revenues as an inflow and living costs as a deduction from outflows.
[3] Also will provide inflow if actual loss occurs.
[4] If used for spouse or other permanent member, may be covered under nonfinancial investments and provide an inflow as an outcome.

Therefore, whether for a detailed quantitative risk analysis or even for a mental "what if" process, the consequences of potentially not meeting goals should be thought through.

The evaluation process is the heart of planning integration in practice, and we therefore will discuss it in significant detail. The household is faced with many choices as to how to prorate its limited resources. The financial plan is the response. It specifies what the household intends to do with its current and future resources.

This book has presented the various parts of your financial activities over your household's life cycle. They were discussed in separate chapters that together formed household operations. Let's look again at the household as an organization that resembles a small business. Each segment of the financial plan can be viewed as a separate household operation with a separate function. Each supplies capital, requests it, or does both. These functions are shown in Table 20.2.

The household resource problem—what you should do with your current and future cash flow—can be viewed as a series of integrated capital expenditure decisions. Each part of the financial plan, each "division," competes for capital. Separate "divisions" make requests to be funded. The household has to decide which capital expenditures to fund and in what amounts. Importantly, the plan looks at these decisions not only as current ones but as those that will take place over the entire life cycle. In other words, our capital expenditures over time, to the best of our ability, are planned for today even though they take place at different points in our life cycle; for example, when you will buy a home, how often to purchase a new car, and so forth.

Figure 20.1 is a visual portrayal of the same planning process; the arrows indicate whether a given segment of the plan is a user or provider of cash. Since the household decides how much cash is to be taken in and the amount to be outlayed, we have called the centralized decision-making function PFP integration.

FIGURE 20.1
**Life Cycle Source
and Uses of Cash**

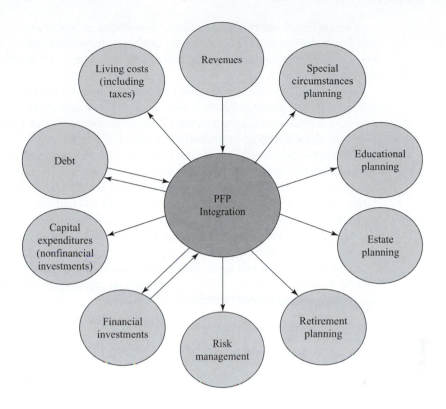

The household's decision-making function is enhanced by a few tools that are particularly relevant when the preliminary asset and liability mix, as established in each part of the financial plan, has been drawn up. These tools include SWOT analysis, sensitivity analysis, and scenario analysis.

SWOT Analysis

SWOT analysis represents an appraisal of all the major factors that can enhance or detract from the outlook for goal achievement. SWOT analysis stands for strengths, weaknesses, opportunities, threats. Strengths and weaknesses are part of the internal household analysis. Opportunities and threats are identified through an examination of the external environment. SWOT analysis provides an overall assessment of the household's situation. It is often used as a strategic tool—that is, it is for planning beyond a year or two. It goes well beyond the best estimate of savings needed.

The strengths of the household might include a conservative balance sheet that is available for borrowing; a job that holds promise for greater income in the future; or a strong household structure with two household member-owners working, thereby reducing the impact of potential revenue interruptions through layoffs or sickness.

The weaknesses in the household might include insufficient savings for goals such as retirement at an age approaching its date, an impulsive nature that leads to unnecessary spending, and an investment portfolio too concentrated in a few assets.

The external environment has an impact on the household. It includes political, legal, tax, social, economic, and technological variables closer to home as well as the industry you work in. Opportunities could arise from new regulations that result in a decline in income tax rates if you shift the way you handle household transactions, changes in industry that present the potential for higher income if you retrain, or the potential to purchase new labor-saving durable goods.

Threats could incorporate the distinct possibility of higher energy prices, which could result in a decline in your discretionary outlays; a movement toward larger houses, which could make your modest-sized home less valuable; and involvement in an industry with declining prospects.

SWOT analysis, then, is intended to uncover new information and form a realistic appraisal for the planning future. It also can lead to changes in projections or practices. For example, a prior strong accumulation of financial investments and a careful spending pattern may allow a step-up in the current standard of living.

Our first choice is to overcome our threats by changing our practices. Yet we cannot deal with all threats directly nor do we want to. For example, if we have a job that is lucrative and enjoyable, but it is in a highly risky industry, we may counter the threat by accumulating extra savings in case our income drops or we are laid off.

In any event, we will want to compare our SWOT assessment with our goals and plans. We may then provide for contingencies by taking additional risk management steps with the degree of alteration in plans dependent in part on our tolerance for risk.

In Table 20.3, you can see a representative sampling of internal and external environmental variables that affect each area of financial planning. To simplify the presentation, the items have been listed as strengths or weaknesses, or as opportunities or threats.

TABLE 20.3   SWOT Analysis by Planning Area

PFP Area	Internal Environment = Strengths or Weaknesses	External Environment = Opportunities or Threats
Balance sheet	Amount of assets Degree of liquidity	Ability to fund needed outlays arising from change in environment
Goals	Ability to ascertain deep-seated goals	Skill in matching goals with externally derived resources
Cash flow	Size of free cash flow	Ability to fund needed outlays arising from change in environment
Debt	Obligations in relation to assets and cash flow	Change in projected inflation rate
Tax planning	Availability of viable tax reduction strategies	Shift in tax rates
Investments		
Nonfinancial	Prospects for existing job Ability to invest in job-related education Productivity and enjoyment-related durable goods	Economic outlook Industry-related job opportunities Changes in technology
Financial	Degree of asset diversification Understanding of investment dynamics Ability to fund needed investments	Economic outlook Projected inflation rate Degree of speculation in markets
Risk management	State of personal health Safety practices Proper insurance coverage	Government attitude toward assistance for risk-related needs External risk-related exposures Changes in insurance policy coverage
Retirement planning	Accumulated assets Annual savings	Change in Social Security benefits Opportunity for part-time consulting
Educational planning	Money accumulated for higher education Ability to qualify for assistance	Government and college changes in assistance policy
Employee benefits	Quality of employer-funded programs Medical reimbursement policy	Changes in government-mandated assistance and tax policy Trends in overall corporate benefits
Other planning	State of physical and mental health Structure and closeness of current household relationships	Government policies toward aiding special needs Changes in society's opinion of nonmarital relationships
Estate planning	Resources accumulated relative to goals Employment of well-thought-out legal documents	Change in allowable estate tax planning strategies Society's opinion changes and estates are taxed more lightly or more heavily

Example 20.2

Doreen, a financial planner, was completing planning work for a young couple. Both spouses had jobs with a promising future. Unfortunately, the couple was significantly in debt, which was used to finance current living standards. Doreen had completed a preliminary figure of overall savings needed to fund their goals.

However, she was uncomfortable since she wondered whether there was a greater-than-average risk that they might not reach their goals. She decided she would do an assessment of their situation to see if she had handled the planning correctly. She decided to perform a SWOT analysis to aid in the review process. Following are the highlights of her analysis:

- *Strengths:* The couple had attractive jobs with a good outlook. They were young, healthy, well-educated, and flexible people.
- *Weaknesses:* Their spending pattern placed too much emphasis on living for today. They acted impulsively and sometimes regretted their wasted expenditures.
- *Opportunities:* The rapid growth in high-level jobs in their industry created a potential opportunity to raise their incomes over the next several years, which could lessen their cash squeeze. A discussion on the need to begin focusing on the goals they themselves had chosen could create the motivation to save this extra income.
- *Threats:* The main threat came from a continuation of their current spending habits. An anticipated rise in external inflation and interest rates would raise their costs and vulnerabilities. The outcome could be a severe cutback in current living expenditures or, in an extreme case, a reduction in their long-term quality of life.

Conclusion

Doreen decided that no change in projections was needed. She knew that the spending behavior was fairly common among certain types of recently married couples. She believed her clients' savings behavior would change as their goals for a home and other needs drew closer. She believed they had an understanding of the behavior that was right for them and had the flexibility to achieve it.

She decided, however, to recommend some changes in practices such as taking money directly out of their savings account to repay debt. She would suggest that they target being out of debt in two years. She also decided to present them with the summary of the SWOT analysis as part of the final meeting. If it were presented properly, it could serve as a motivating tool.

Sensitivity Analysis

Sensitivity analysis is identifying those factors that could significantly alter anticipated planning results. It may be performed as part of SWOT analysis or as a stand-alone supporting analysis. Sensitivity analysis is sometimes more quantitatively based than SWOT.

For example, retired people are highly sensitive to changes in inflation since they are often on fixed incomes.[2] In doing a sensitivity analysis for retired couples, you could raise an assumed inflation rate by 1 percent, thereby boosting costs 1 percent a year, and see what it does to outcomes and required savings. You could lower the investment return for working people and observe its effect. Most people's outcomes are highly sensitive to assumed rates of return if projected over long periods of time. Consequently, it is important to consider return projections carefully and perhaps conservatively.

Perhaps the most popular form of this type of analysis is Monte Carlo simulation. Monte Carlo, as you have learned, isolates some key planning variables such as investment return and inflation and assesses how these affect planning outcomes.

Consider Example 20.3's use of sensitivity analysis.

Example 20.3

Trina is a schoolteacher. Because of excellent employee benefits, well over half of her projected retirement revenues will come from her school pension. She went to a financial planner to see if she was on track to reach her overall goals, including funding for retirement. The planner

---

[2] Dramatic changes in inflation and interest rates have occurred over the last 20 years. Higher rates in the future could have significant effects on the elderly, as Example 20.3 demonstrates.

Practical Comment   Use of Multiple Scenario Analysis

Many financial planners who offer comprehensive financial planning are aware that clients appreciate multiple scenario analysis. In retirement planning, they may be interested in the impact of early retirement, say, at age 60 as compared with retirement at age 67. They may want to know the effect of the sale of their home and subsequent rental on the amount they have to save or spend each year. The use of scenario analysis may result in changes in planning procedures to meet risk possibilities.

did a capital needs analysis including retirement income sufficiency. He used a 5 percent after-tax return for financial investments and a 2 percent inflation rate for cost increases. The calculations showed that Trina could retire comfortably with funds to spare.

The planner was about to complete the financial plan and set up an appointment to present it when he decided to do some further analysis. He raised the inflation assumption to 3 percent and, as a believer in modern investment theory, raised the return assumption to 6 percent.

The planner figured that using the same difference between revenue and cost increases (real rate of return of 3 percent) for both cases would result in the same outcome. Instead, Trina suddenly had a shortfall in projected resources related to expense demands. The advisor was puzzled. What was the reason that the conclusion was exactly the opposite of the original one?

He then remembered the above-average importance of the pension to Trina's retirement. Although her costs and Social Security payments were going to rise steadily with inflation, her teacher's pension would not. The increase in financial investment return would not help much because investments of this type were a relatively small part of her financial picture. Over long periods of time, her pension would shrink in inflation-adjusted terms and create a serious shortfall, particularly if Trina lived into her 90s.

The advisor performed other sensitivity and scenario analyses and revised his projected outcome, saying that Trina had vulnerability. Trina instructed the planner to assume she would work a few years longer than originally anticipated and would place a little more into savings each year. The advisor made a mental note to become familiar with Monte Carlo analysis, which could shed light on the probability of that shortfall. In the meantime, he was pleased he had at least utilized a form of sensitivity analysis.

Scenario Analysis

Scenario analysis observes the effect of changes in multiple variables or in one variable that influences many situations. Its stress on creating an overall changed environment distinguishes it from one-variable scenario analysis.

For example, our projections of financial and other asset returns may be based on historical returns and the continuation of a normal economic environment. We may want to look at the impact of an alternative scenario—for example, one in which the economy is weak for an extended period of time. Given that scenario, our ability to save will be altered and we may have to consider the possibility of a temporary work layoff. In the event of such an economic outcome, the result could be a higher level of liquid savings to be drawn down.

At this point, the review process has taken place. We have applied some additional "what if" tools such as SWOT, sensitivity, and scenario analysis, which help us in making decisions on an overall household basis. This integrated look at future household plans and the reality check on what is doable often results in a modification of intended actions.

We are now ready to run the final numbers. Most often, the simple capital needs analysis or the risk-adjusted capital needs analysis is used. A growing number of financial planning practitioners are using Monte Carlo simulation alone or as a supplement to the simple method. The output tells us the amount we have to save per year or, in the case of overfunding, how much we can raise our standard of living.

Practical Comment   Reviewing Overall Decision Making

Reviewing overall decision making at this point has a number of benefits. First, it tests the decisions about to be made, which can lead to more rational outcomes. Second, by its nature it focuses on integration, which we have said is often the most overlooked part of the planning process. Finally, particularly in multi-person households, it can approximate the way the household does or should operate, which can bring about better decisions.

Along the same lines: How are we to determine quantitatively which capital expenditures are most desirable? It is not always possible to calculate returns. The answer can be through ranking based on a combination of hard numbers, sound mental shortcuts, and feelings. Often the greater the use of quantitative business techniques employing IRR and NPV, the better the result. Feelings typically serve for such things as hard-to-quantify leisure expenditures. For a discussion of one ranking procedure that discounts the cost of each goal separately to the present, see Appendix III.

Finally, for financial plans, integration by some may stop short of a quantitative capital needs analysis. There should be no doubt, however, that such an analysis is required for a realistic assessment of a household financial situation relative to its goals.[3]

[3] Retirement planning often serves as the area that presents the integration function. The feeling by many is if, after including other goals and needs, you have provided for retirement, you have covered the integration requirement.

Simple retirement needs analysis, the most popular method used by practitioners, isn't as sophisticated as TPM, with no separate provision for risk and correlation. On the other hand, it is significantly better than no integration at all, which can lead to misallocation of resources and literally running out of money. Retirement needs analysis often attempts to cover risk by using a conservative investment return and a higher inflation rate and providing for long lives.

Monte Carlo analysis provides a more precise detailing of risk. Its results are expressed in probabilities instead of the one-outcome retirement needs approach. Given the potential for negative outcomes if investment performance is poor at the beginning of the retirement payout period (withdrawal risk), Monte Carlo's role is a distinct improvement. It can be used as a stand-alone system or as support for simple retirement needs analysis. Both can be manipulated to come up with an "optimum" resource allocation, although with much more effort than TPM.

Develop Solutions and Complete the Plan

Have all feasible solutions been considered? Some solutions may not give the highest revenues or result in the lowest risk but may cost significantly less to implement and therefore be the preferred course of action. For example, the purchase of a disability policy that doesn't cover some less important benefits upon disability but costs 25 percent less may be the best choice.

Once the solutions have been completed in all areas of the plan and made to agree with current and projected resources, the plan is almost ready to be written. At this point a review of overall decision making, as discussed in the Practical Comment above, and of behavioral factors, which follows, can be particularly helpful.

Behavioral Review

As we have said many times, personal financial planning is more than a straight financial exercise. As even doctors using advanced scientific techniques to cure illness have discovered, dealing with human needs, communicating well, and ensuring that advice is being followed contribute to the success rate.

Similarly, it is often not sufficient to identify a number, a required annual savings pattern to ensure financial success. The financial plan must take into account human behavioral shortcomings. As we saw in Chapter 19, these may include an inability to recall past events accurately, limitations in processing power, and inappropriate emotional responses. It can help prospects for ultimate success if the financial plan deals with all of these factors by using the tools discussed in that chapter.

Finally, financial plans need not be restricted entirely to numbers-oriented goals but can incorporate whatever goals people may have. The steps taken toward meeting those goals

TABLE 20.4
Components of the
Financial Plan

Parts of the Plan	Key Contribution
Description and scope of plan	Indicates what a plan does overall and what this specific one is to accomplish.
Statement of goals	Sets planning focus.
	Helps establish balance between spending for today and investing for the future.
Summary of plan recommendations	Summarizes the methods for achieving the household goals.
Balance sheet	Presents current resources available.
Cash flow statement	Examines past and often projected future household sources and uses of funds, typically on a yearly basis.
Cash flow planning	Provides reality check through its role as a funder for all activities.
Debt planning	Either as part of cash flow planning or as a separate section, it can generate extra cash flow for current use.
Educational planning	Maps out funding method for improvement in household human assets.
Tax planning	Indicates how to anticipate and reduce this major operating expense.
Retirement planning	Determines amount and funding schedule for period when work ceases.
Investments	
Nonfinancial	Correct capital expenditure process yields operating efficiencies for the household.
Financial	Determines appropriate financial asset allocation. Generates the return on funds saved for future.
Risk management	Establishes appropriate level of household risk. Focuses on reducing exposures through use of insurance and other tools that adjust and make more efficient household operations.
Estate planning	Determines who gets what in the most efficient way upon our death.
Special circumstances planning	Special requirements of all types for household members.
Employee benefits	Points to approach employees should take in deciding on employer-provided benefits (sometimes this section is included in other areas).
Integration	Looks at PFP from an overall point of view, establishing priorities between goals and needs leading to appropriate decision making. The calculation and discussion is sometimes combined with retirement planning.
Summary	Provides specific steps to be taken, often with implementation dates.
Appendixes	Present additional information, both written and numerical.

often have a financial component such as being free of continuing financial concern or ability to pursue a nonfinancially rewarding career at an earlier age.

Importantly, now is the moment to ask, perhaps for the last time, Does this plan make sense? Is it feasible to do? In reality, will it be carried out? If not, what can be changed to make it more practical?

Writing the Plan

When the behavioral review has been completed, it is finally time to write the financial plan. Plans depend on the style of the writer. Some people prefer long detailed plans with explanations for each recommendation while others prefer to get right to the point.

Whatever the approach, a plan must be descriptive enough to refer back to and to be communicated to others. Recommendations should be linked to goals. The advantages and disadvantages of advice provided should be provided as well as the type of future events that could change these recommendations. The plan should provide a road map for implementation. An ideal financial plan should have a summary at the beginning, detail in each planning part, and a summary perhaps more oriented toward implementation at the end. It should have a mix of written information, numbers through tables, and figures that illustrate and enliven the text.

Delivery of Plan

Where the plan is to be presented to others, the relationship between recommendations and goals should be highlighted. An assessment of the person's understanding of the plan should be made and assistance provided when necessary. Where it is apparent that the findings have not been fully comprehended, it is often advisable to let the person read the plan and "digest it." Another face-to-face or phone meeting may be set up.

The components of a sample financial plan and their key contributions are presented in Table 20.4.

Once the plan has been written, a problem can arise in execution of it. Too often, planning conclusions and actual implementation of plans are not the same. Sometimes plans requiring great effort, even those done by professionals at great expense, lie dormant. Having an implementation schedule with specific dates can help set the required steps in motion. One such schedule is shown in Table 20.5.

Beyond the implementation schedule that begins the planning period is the problem of control. Control can be viewed as continuing to implement the plan over time. Visceral responses such as overreaction to recent information or impulsive spending regretted later can reduce household efficiency. To meet these problems, the plan may provide for specific control mechanisms discussed in Chapter 5 such as automatic savings withdrawals. It may provide for additional education to reduce or eliminate overreaction. When these weaknesses cannot be overcome or when people find it preferable to do so, financial planners can help on an ongoing basis.

TABLE 20.5
Implementation Schedule

Area	Recommendation	Timing
Cash flow	Cut back on spending by $8,000 per year	Immediately
	Save $100 per week or $5,000 per year through automatic withdrawals from paycheck	Begin next week
Debt	Repay credit card debt of $3,000	Within one year
Tax planning	Place $5,000 savings in tax-sheltered 401(k)	Begin next week
Investments	Implement a 70 percent stock, 30 percent bond allocation	Within two weeks
	Sell Low Flying Fund	This week
	Buy Rocket Man Fund	This week
Risk management	Place jewelry in safe deposit box	Within two weeks
	Increase coverage on property by $10,000	In a month
	Buy additional term insurance	In a month
	Start a liquid savings account of $20,000	Accumulate over 18 months
Retirement	Save 10 percent of salary in 401(k) each year	Begin next week
	Place additional $8,000 per year in personal savings once mortgage is repaid	Starting in four years
Other	Establish special needs trust	Contact lawyer within two weeks
Estate	Draw up a will	Contact lawyer within two weeks
	Draw up a medical power of attorney	Contact lawyer within two weeks
	Develop a statement of personal wishes	Contact lawyer within two weeks

Example 20.4   Dustin was a successful lawyer whose problems were in perception and execution. He overreacted to any change in economic circumstances. He sold at the first sign of stock market problems and bought back after he developed confidence again. In the meantime, he kept his investments in money market accounts. The upshot was substantial underperformance over a simple buy-and-hold policy.

Dustin's tendency to operate by emotion, not intellect, carried over into purchasing decisions. He always bought the latest electronic gadgets, often at $5,000 to $10,000 a clip. He "had to have" the latest status car, selling last year's preferable pick at a loss. At the beginning of each year, he would make a New Year's promise to turn over a new leaf, and before the week was over he had broken it.

He went to a financial planner for assistance. The planner drew up a financial plan that was highly specific as to what should be done. The plan was very blunt about the seriousness of noncompliance and discussed the poor investment performance in the past. The planner recommended a broad variety of index mutual funds for both stocks and bonds and told Dustin not to sell them after purchase. To cover his desire to invest frequently, he was to be given 10 percent of his savings to invest in whatever he wished.

The planner recommended many control mechanisms, one of which was having the fund management firm, which invested a preplanned amount of Dustin's money, send the planner a duplicate statement each month. He told Dustin he would be watching his monthly statement and would call if the automatic withdrawals from his paycheck were altered in any manner.

The plan provided for quarterly meetings to discuss progress. Dustin was told that veering from the steps in implementation of the financial plan without a planner's approval could jeopardize his financial future.

In addition to these requirements, as a hedge against some noncompliance, the planner reduced the projected growth rate for Dustin's blend of stocks and bonds by 1 percent as compared with market averages. He required that Dustin save additional amounts even beyond the impact of the lower investment growth rate. The planner said that after three years of following the plan, they would consider some reduction in these restrictive practices.

Dustin appreciated this "tough love" approach and said that it covered what other financial plans he had made for himself in the past had lacked. It provided structure and control.

KEYS TO A SUCCESSFUL PLAN

The guidelines below present some keys to a successful comprehensive financial plan.

1. A specific statement is made indicating whether the goals are doable and the current household course is financially consistent with those goals. Often a specific annual savings figure is presented, particularly when the household's current course is insufficient to meet the goals. It indicates that financial integration has taken place.

2. The important assumptions in the plan such as salary growth, financial investment returns, cost increases, retirement age, and longevity have been separately disclosed. Growth rates and inflation rates are coordinated. For example, usually it is not reasonable to assume a 5 percent increase in inflation and costs and only a 3 percent increase in salaries for long periods of time.

3. Steps have been taken to help with any human shortcomings and nonfinancial goals are given.

4. Where appropriate, alternative solutions have been weighed. For example, when there is a projected retirement shortfall, responses through current and retirement expense cutbacks, later retirement, and additional sources of income have all been considered and ranked by preference.

5. Before completing the plan, a review process has been undertaken that confirms that the financial figures and recommendations make sense and are attainable, given the personalities of the individuals.

MONITORING THE FINANCIAL PLAN

People's lives can undergo significant change, so financial plans should be reviewed periodically. Such changes may involve one's personal life—for example, a marriage, a divorce, having children, health problems, or the death of a loved one. Business changes may involve a job; the outlook for income; or economic, inflation, or investment assumptions. Or there may be overall changes in goals or risk tolerance.

In addition, plans should be reviewed periodically to measure actual results versus projected ones. When figures are materially different, reasons for the discrepancy should be found. If the reason stems from unrealistic plan assumptions, they should be changed.

Reviews should identify systematic, not cyclical, differences. For that reason, reexamining plans too often can be counterproductive. For example, we saw that people tend to overemphasize the impact of relatively short-term changes in asset prices[4] and that those who refrain from making frequent changes in investments may actually come out ahead.[5] On the other hand, extraordinary expenses that result in cash flow shortfalls each year as compared with projections should be considered recurring annual charges and should result in alterations in either practices or future projections for the financial plan. Appendix II provides some financial statements that can be useful for review purposes.

Back to Dan and Laura

INTEGRATION

The big day had finally arrived. Dan and Laura were to meet with me and finalize the plan. Unlike many other planning meetings, this one would be concerned almost exclusively with integration. All Dan and Laura's preferences and the costs attached to them had been gone over in separate meetings for each part of the plan. We had discussed capital needs analysis as it pertained to how much was required for retirement and insurance coverage a few meetings back. However, we really didn't get into an extended discussion of savings needed versus amounts likely to be generated by their current financial path. I had told them we would postpone such considerations for today, when I would introduce risk, probability analysis, and total portfolio management into asset selection and calculations of capital needs. I decided to devote some space in the financial plan to explaining how the system worked.

As indicated, the figures demonstrated in our capital needs analysis–retirement planning meeting showed that that there was a shortfall. Dan and Laura would not have enough money to support their living costs. This was not surprising to me given their lifestyle and desire to retire as early as age 55. I thought of the financial alternatives—a cutback in their cost of living today. That didn't seem feasible. We were already cutting back. Nor did I think they had a particularly lavish lifestyle for a middle-class family. Retirement lifestyles at such a young retirement age didn't seem amenable to cutting back either. Nor did additional work-related income seem appropriate. Both spouses were happy and committed to a full-time track in their current positions.

Usually, I didn't believe in materially upping a client's risk tolerance. Their current allocation didn't seem severely conservative, which might have prompted a different conclusion. However, I decided to wait until I used a TPM approach before coming up with a definite answer to the asset allocation question. Both had already indicated that they felt strongly about fully financing their son Brian's college education and that of the baby they were expecting.

[4] See Shlomo Bernatzi and Richard H. Thaler, "Myopic Loss Aversion and the Equity Premium Puzzle," *Quarterly Journal of Economics* 110, no. 1 (February 1995), pp. 73–92.

[5] Brad M. Barber and Terrance Odean, "Trading Is Hazardous to Your Wealth: The Common Stock Investment Performance of Individual Investors," *Journal of Finance* 55, no. 2 (April 2000). pp. 773–806.

That left two major areas. The first was the retirement date. I calculated that each additional year in which retirement was postponed would reduce preretirement savings needed by $10,000 a year in today's dollars or raise allowable discretionary expenses in retirement by $6,000 per year in today's dollars. Dan had resisted the idea that if their retirement living period was unusually long, they would have to sell the house they would live in.

I thought it was not my decision to make. I could only provide insight and an opinion if they wanted it. I gave them a choice of alternatives and asked both to rank their preferences for maintaining their current lifestyle as adjusted recently versus making further alterations. Retirement age and the house came out at the bottom of the ranking. Dan became somewhat anxious at the line of questioning. I made a mental note then to sound an extra reassuring note in the financial plan, if merited. I also decided not to burden them with a repeat of the sections of the plan that we had already gone over. I would provide a summary and integration of the key points and a detailed backup of the TPM approach and of the new capital needs analysis, including revised cash flow and tax statements if necessary.

The result of the risk analysis was a real eye opener. Whereas I thought I was being conservative in reducing their returns by one percentage point, I wasn't. Given Dan's fear of running out of money, the couple had decided they wanted a 90 percent certainty of having enough resources to last until age 95. At their present asset allocation, that would require about a 3 percent reduction in return.

I was apprehensive about telling this to Dan after having presented both of them with an already-restrictive budget. But there was no pleasant way to explain it, and I decided to present it in writing as follows.

As we discussed when we started the process, a financial plan represents the carving out of a course of action to enable you to reach your objectives. Both the objectives and the individual parts of the plan have already been worked out in our previous meetings.

As I indicated, most of these recommendations did not incorporate risk directly.

Let me explain the risk procedures: Risk is the potential for having your plans derailed by an unexpected occurrence. I have employed risk management procedures to reduce or eliminate the possibility of these occurrences. Some of the factors already discussed are diversification, insurance, and health and safety procedures. In this section of the plan, I will focus on those that still remain. To do this I will call on total portfolio management (TPM), which I explained in a previous meeting, but this time I will emphasize risk.

TPM is the method of bringing together all of your assets and liabilities into one grouping. This grouping is broader than just the marketable financial investments' portfolio, which reflects only your stocks, bonds, and mutual funds. We bring them together to develop returns and overhead expenses that are to be paid against those returns. In doing so, we are equally interested in risk. Risk is not, as you might think, adding up the risks of the individual assets and liabilities. Risk is reduced by the fact that the assets are not all affected to the same degree by an outside negative event. In effect, it is an elaboration on the term *diversification*. By solving for the return and risk on the household portfolio, we can arrive at the amount you can spend on leisure activities, according to your tolerance for risk.

Your household portfolio is presented in the attached schedule. Notice the difference between it and the balance sheet presented after our very first meeting. This balance sheet incorporates your purchase of a home. Congratulations on closing on the $250,000 purchase, financed by a mortgage of $237,500 and part of the parental gift of $65,000. Perhaps, more importantly, it incorporates all your nonmarketable assets and liabilities. Importantly, it incorporates your human-related assets. They consist of the net present value of each of your jobs and your Social Security payments. In addition, it incorporates Laura's government pension. I call this statement your broader balance sheet.

At this point, you may be asking how I am going to use this material. After all, the same information was available for projections of income and expenses, for the capital needs analysis, in the retirement planning section. The difference is in the use of the items in a TPM framework to analyze risk.

In the human-asset category, your jobs are not correlated, and, of course, Dan's job as a technology consultant possesses much more risk than Laura's essentially tenured teaching position. Dan's job correlates to some degree with overall economic variables and, specifically, the outlook for technology. Social Security and Laura's school pension can be considered low-risk investments that, in my opinion, have little chance of a material change in anything other than an extension of the effective date of a full pension to age 70 from age 67 for Social Security and three years added to the school pension before becoming eligible for it. We have assumed that you would liquidate your home to cover such an outcome or borrow against it.

Finally, the house you selected in a fast-growing part of the suburbs, attached to a broad-based metropolitan area, seems to have an outlook not related to other assets in the household portfolio. In sum, you have a broadly based grouping of largely uncorrelated assets. Noncorrelated assets, as you probably remember, diversify risk and can prevent an adverse impact on reaching your goals.

The interest on your mortgage and your other maintenance costs have grown, given your soon-to-be two children and housing outlays. Nonetheless, given Laura's relatively secure pension, two full Social Security incomes likely, and an inheritance, I would characterize your nonmarketable securities portfolio as having below-average risk.

I have attached Table 20.7 which presents a TPM balance sheet. It includes nonmarketable assets and maintenance liabilities in addition to the figures in a traditional balance sheet. As mentioned, this balance sheet, while untraditional, presents a broader view of your assets as well as providing the fixed-cost obligations that are necessary for you to support your intended standard of living.

If you had substantial financial assets, I would run the purest TPM system that takes into account all assets and liabilities and solve for the optimal asset allocation between stocks, bonds, and money market funds. But since financial assets currently account for about 2 percent of total household assets, I don't see the point. Any asset allocation for stocks and bonds right now won't make much of a difference, which will be true for the next several years as well. You won't begin meaningful savings until 2011. However, permit me to make a recommendation anyway.

In the investment section, we agreed upon a 60-40 stock-bond mix influenced by Dan's innate conservatism. My recommendation is that we raise that to 70-30. The original allocation recommendation was made based on financial assets alone. In retirement calculations, I prefer using an even more conservative return for stocks. For this reason, I assume the return on stocks to be 10 percent. The return on bonds is projected to be 5.5 percent. This revision virtually offsets the higher equity allocation and your overall investment return remains unchanged. Here is why I changed my thinking.

The new asset allocation incorporates the generally lower-risk nature of your nonfinancial assets. As you will see, even though the principal option you may want to exercise over your life cycle is in the financial area, in making decisions it is important to take into account all your assets. Incidentally, as retirement comes closer, these low-risk pension assets, which are bondlike, comprise a greater proportion of assets. The same is true of the house, whose risk is also lower than that for stocks. The result can be the ability to sustain an even greater weighting in equities over time. My final thought on financial investments is that you should consciously avoid a heavy weighting in technology shares, given their correlation with Dan's job. Your recommended asset allocation is provided in Table 20.6.

I have one final new fact for you. Unfortunately, it is not positive. I had originally thought that by reducing your investment return by 1 percent, I was being conservative about your needs. However, in performing a Monte Carlo analysis, an approach that takes into account risks in key variables such as below-average investment returns and higher-than-average inflation, I have found that figure needs to be revised. We have to take into

TABLE 20.6
Dan and Laura's
Asset Allocation

Asset Category	Current Allocation	Strategic Allocation	Tactical Allocation	Standard Deviation 10-Year
Stocks				
Small cap	10%	13%	20%	21.0
Mid cap	8%	12%	10%	20.7
Large cap	20%	22%	18%	17.8
International	17%	18%	17%	17.8
REIT	5%	5%	5%	14.1
Total Stock	**60%**	**70%**	**70%**	
Bonds				
Short term	10%	5%	8%	2.1
Intermediate	15%	8%	5%	4.1
Long term	5%	5%	5%	5.7
High yield	5%	7%	7%	7.9
Total Bond	**35%**	**25%**	**25%**	
Money market	**5%**	**5%**	**5%**	0.4
Total	**100%**	**100%**	**100%**	14.1[1]

[1] Weighted-average.

account the risks that become clear under our Monte Carlo probabilistic analysis. Specifically, the risks of below-average returns in early retirement years, called withdrawal risk, and of above-average expenses due to inflation. The upshot is a further decline of 2 percent in the assumed investment return, from 7.7 percent to 5.7 percent.

There are a number of alternatives that you have. We will provide you with the impact of a change in each alternative on your capital needs. It is called sensitivity analysis.

In addition, the amount of insurance will change to about $1,300,000 on Dan's life and approximately $700,000 on Laura's life.[6] The higher amount than indicated in our retirement meetings is due to the lower assumed return to place you at the 90 percent confidence level.

I have stated all the major alternatives except for one, but they all contain weaknesses. As it stands now, you will be unable to save any money for six years. Given your wishes, I don't believe that a cutback of the magnitude needed could be absorbed easily. And given Laura's priority on helping raise the children, extra income doesn't seem feasible. Any part-time work by Dan could hurt his progress within his field. Nor, given your retirement priorities, does a significant paring of expenses seem an option you would find attractive. Finally, I agree with your preference for holding your house for what I call longevity risk— that is, the possibility that you might live to even longer than age 90. If that were to happen, the house could be sold or borrowed against if necessary.

Based on our indicated preferences, the option I am recommending is postponement of retirement until age 60. Both of you have said you like your careers and age 55 had been selected with much strong feeling. I believe most people will be retiring later, not earlier, and an age-60 retirement will still be early relative to your peer group. It still is likely to leave plenty of time for new leisure pursuits.

Taking into account the impact of a postponement in the retirement age to 60 and the lower assumed investment return of 5.7 percent, you will need projected savings of $60,000 plus extra savings of about $8,000 per year as compared with the previous figure of $60,000 in projected savings plus $41,000 in extra savings provided in the capital needs analysis meeting. This flat yearly savings figure will average about 18 percent of your income throughout your working years.

In sum, you have many options to select from. As you can see, this meeting on integration carries great significance. To borrow a term from automobiles, Dan's great interest, it is where the "rubber meets the road." Whatever your decision, I want to stress the generally

[6] The insurance need did not change materially from the original calculation in Chapter 18; the higher income earned by the surviving spouse due to the five-year extension in working years is offset by the lower rate of return assumption.

TABLE 20.7
Dan and Laura's
TPM Balance Sheet

ASSETS		LIABILITIES	
Financial Assets		**Financial Liabilities**	
Cash	$3,000	Revolving credit	$20,000
Money market funds	7,000	Mortgage[1]	237,500
Bonds and bond funds	34,000	Other	66,000
Stocks and stock funds	96,000	**Total Financial Liabilities**	**$323,500**
Pension assets	10,000		
Total Financial Assets	**$150,000**		
Real Estate		**Maintenance Liabilities**	
Home[1]	$250,000	Fixed-cost liabilities	$4,775,894
Total Real Estate	**$250,000**	**Total Maintenance Liabilities**	**$4,775,894**
Household Assets			
Auto[2]	$42,000		
Furniture	7,000		
Other	5,000		
Total Household Assets	**$54,000**		
Nomarketable Assets		**EQUITY**	
Human	$4,050,496		
Social Security	900,782	Household equity[3]	$130,500
Pension	394,071	Nomarketable equity[4]	569,454
Total Nomarketable Assets	**$5,345,348**	**Total Equity[5]**	**$699,954**
Total Assets	**$5,799,348**	**Total Liabilities and Equity**	**$5,799,348**

[1] Projected.
[2] Includes the projected purchase of Dan's new car.
[3] Excludes nonmarketable assets and maintenance liabilities. Represents a traditional balance sheet's equity.
[4] Difference between nonmarketable assets and maintenance liabilities.
[5] Includes nonmarketable assets and maintenance liabilities.

favorable outlook you both have. Your diversity of assets enhances your prospects. Assuming you adhere to the plan and, in particular, exercise a little more control over spending, it will be difficult to throw you off course. I am confident you will move forward without too much trouble, and I will be available to continue to advise you when needed.

I was very concerned as to how Dan would take the news of the modification in the projections. Would he become fearful or cynical about the whole planning process? What would each of them think about the recommendation to postpone retirement? I had deliberately included some words of support, which I believed were true, at the end of the plan.

It turned out that my recommendation to move back the retirement date was agreed upon after only a brief discussion of the alternatives. I mentioned to them that there was no need to revise most of what transpired, given the fact that we were only changing retirement dates. I noticed that Laura kept looking over at Dan as if concerned that he take a positive view of what was going on. Finally, she asked him if the revisions were something he would worry about. He just smiled broadly and said, "I can handle it."

We made an appointment to meet next on the implementation steps.

RETIREMENT NEEDS ANALYSIS

Inputs

General	
Dan's age	35
Laura's age	35
Dan's retirement age	60
Laura's retirement age	60
Dan's assumed age of death	95
Laura's assumed age of death	95

(continued)

(*concluded*)

Years until retirement period 1	25
Years until retirement period 2	30
Years in retirement period 1	5
Years in retirement period 2	30

Laura

Pension at age 65, today's dollars	$45,000
After-tax pension	32,400
Current salary	0
Salary in five years, today's dollars	68,000
Annual increase thereafter	3%
Social Security benefits at age 67	$24,196

Dan

Salary	$100,000
Annual increase through 2014	10%
Annual increase beginning 2015	3%
Social Security benefits at age 67	$26,022

Expenses

Living expenses, today's dollars[1]	$83,452
15% COL reduction in retirement	($12,518)
Additional travel expenses	$10,000
Total expenses in retirement	$80,935

Economic

Inflation	3.0%
Tax rate in retirement[2]	28.0%
Investment return	5.7%
After-tax investment return	4.1%
Real return	2.6%
After-tax real return	1.1%

[1] Sum of discretionary, nondiscretionary, and capital expenses in year 6, discounted to year 1.
[2] Estimated marginal federal and state rate. Assumes state tax rate of 5% and blend of ordinary income and capital gains federal rates.

Step 1. Calculate the Amount Needed in Retirement

Retirement Period 1 (60–65)

Living expenses in retirement, today's dollars	$80,935
Laura's pension in today's dollars, after taxes	0
Annual shortfall, today's dollars	80,935
Annual shortfall, age 60	169,459
Lump sum needed to retire mortgage[1]	110,686
Lump sum needed at beginning of period	**$940,200**

Retirement Period 2 (65–95)

Living expenses in retirement, today's dollars	$80,935
Laura's pension in today's dollars, after taxes	32,400
Social Security benefits at 65 in today's dollars, after taxes	33,138
Annual shortfall, today's dollars	15,396
Annual shortfall, age 65	37,371
Lump sum needed at beginning of period	**964,635**

[1] Amount owed after 24 years of mortgage payments at normal amortization. Assumes mortgage begins in year 2 of plan.

Step 2. Bring the Lump Sum Needed Back to the Present

Lump sum currently needed, retirement period 1	$343,981
Lump sum currently needed, retirement period 2	288,629
Lump sum needed in year 6, retirement period 1[1]	420,602
Lump sum needed in year 6, retirement period 2	352,921
Total lump sum needed now	632,610
Total lump sum needed in year 6	**$773,523**

[1] Assumes that savings cannot begin until year 6, when Laura returns to work.

Step 3. Repeat Steps for Other Needs

Lump sum needed for college in year 6[1]	$230,488
Total other needs lump sum, year 6	**$230,488**

[1] From college planning section.

Step 4. Establish the Current Value of Projected Future Saving

Accumulated assets as of year 6	$89,479
Projected after-tax savings starting year 6[1]	60,000
PV of future savings in year 6	807,961
Total existing and projected resources in year 6	**$897,441**

[1] Assumes that saving is not possible until Laura returns to work.

Step 5. Compare Resources and Needs

Total needs in year 6	$1,004,011
Total existing and projected resources in year 6	897,441
Additional resources needed	**$106,570**

Step 6. Establish Additional Annual Savings Needed

Additional savings needed beginning year 6 (level payment)	$7,914
Additional annual savings needed beginning year 6	**$7,914**

INSURANCE NEEDS ANALYSIS—DAN

Inputs

General	
Dan's age	35
Laura's age	35
Laura's retirement age	60
Dan's assumed age of death	35
Laura's assumed age of death	95
Years in preretirement period 1	5
Years in preretirement period 2	13
Years in preretirement period 3	7
Years in retirement period 1	5
Years in retirement period 2	30

(continued)

(concluded)

Laura

Pension	$45,000
After-tax pension	33,750
Current salary	0
Salary in year 6	68,000
Salary after tax	51,000
Annual increase	3%
Social Security benefits	
Laura's Social Security in retirement	24,196
Social Security after taxes	18,147
Survivor benefits until children grown, before tax[1]	26,250
Survivor spousal benefits at age 60, before tax	10,725

Expenses

Current expenses[2]	$103,032
Reduction at Dan's death	15%
Expenses after Dan's death	87,578
Expenses after children grown[3]	68,794

Available Assets

Investment assets	$150,000
Liabilities	86,000
Available assets	64,000

Economic

Inflation	3.0%
Investment return	5.7%
After-tax return	4.1%
Real return	2.6%
After-tax real return	1.1%
Average tax rate preretirement period 1[4]	0%
Average tax rate preretirement period 2	25%
Average tax rate preretirement period 3	25%
Average tax rate retirement period 1	10%
Average tax rate in retirement	25%

[1] Estimate based on 175% of Dan's primary insurance amount at the time of his death. Actual numbers will be modestly different because different benefits end in different years.
[2] Average of living expenses over next seven years.
[3] 85 percent of what they would spend as a couple in retirement.
[4] All tax rates are estimates based on income projections.

Step 1. Determine the Amount Needed to Fund the Preretirement Period

Preretirement Period 1, Years 1–5

Annual expenses, today's dollars	$87,578
Social Security survivor benefits, after taxes	26,250
Laura's salary, after taxes	0
Total income, after taxes	26,250
Annual shortfall	61,328
Lump-sum shortfall, today's dollars	**$300,203**

Preretirement Period 2, Years 6–18

Annual expenses, today's dollars	$87,578
Social Security survivor benefits, after taxes	20,672
Laura's salary, after taxes	51,000
Total income, after taxes	71,672

Annual shortfall, today's dollars	15,906
Annual shortfall, year 6	18,439
Lump sum shortfall, year 6	225,034
Lump-sum shortfall, today's dollars	**$184,039**

Preretirement Period 3, Years 19–25

Annual expenses, today's dollars	$68,794
Laura's salary, after taxes	51,000
Total income, after taxes	51,000
Annual shortfall, today's dollars	17,794
Annual shortfall, year 19	30,294
Lump-sum shortfall, year 19	205,428
Lump-sum shortfall, today's dollars	**$99,597**

Step 2. Determine the Amount Needed to Fund the Retirement Period

Retirement Period 1 (60–65)

Living expenses, today's dollars	$68,794
Social Security spousal survivor benefits, after tax[1]	9,813
Annual shortall, today's dollars	58,981
Annual shortfall, age 60	123,493
Lump-sum shortfall, age 60	604,508
Lump-sum shortfall, today's dollars	**$221,165**

Retirement Period 2 (65–95)

Living expenses, today's dollars	$68,794
Laura's annual pension, after taxes	33,750
Social Security benefits, after taxes	16,501
Total income	50,251
Annual shortfall, today's dollars	18,544
Annual shortfall, age 65	45,010
Lump-sum shortfall, age 65	1,161,829
Lump-sum shortfall, today's dollars	**$347,632**

[1] Estimate based on Dan's primary insurance amount.

Step 3. Determine the Total Lump Sum Needed Today

Lump sum currently needed, preretirement period 1	$300,203
Lump sum currently needed, preretirement period 2	184,039
Lump sum currently needed, preretirement period 3	99,597
Lump sum currently needed, retirement period 1	221,165
Lump sum currently needed, retirement period 2	347,632
Total lump sum needed, today's dollars	**$1,152,636**

Step 4. Repeat Steps for Other Needs

Lump sum needed currently for college	$179,479
Burial expenses	20,000
Total lump sum for other needs, today's dollars	**$199,479**

Step 5. Establish Insurance Need

Total lump sump needed for all needs, today's dollars	**$1,352,116**
Available assets	**$64,000**
Total insurance needed, today's dollars	**$1,288,116**

INSURANCE NEEDS ANALYSIS—LAURA

Inputs

General

Dan's age	35
Laura's age	35
Dan's retirement age	60
Laura's assumed age of death	35
Dan's assumed age of death	95
Years in preretirement period 1	18
Years in preretirement period 2	7
Years in retirement period 1	5
Years in retirement period 2	30

Dan

Salary	$100,000
Annual increase through 2014	10%
Annual increase beginning 2015	3%
Social Security benefits	
Dan's Social Security at age 67, before tax	26,022
Social Security at age 67, after tax	19,829
Survivor benefits until children grown, before tax[1]	24,150
Survivor spousal benefits at age 60, before tax	9,867

Expenses

Current expenses[2]	$103,032
Expense reduction at Laura's death	15%
Expenses after Laura's death	87,578
Expenses after children grown[3]	68,794

Available Assets

Investment assets	$150,000
Liabilities	86,000
Available assets	64,000

Economic

Inflation	3.0%
Investment return	5.7%
After-tax investment return	4.1%
Real return	2.6%
After-tax real return	1.1%
Average tax rate, preretirement period[4]	30%
Average tax rate, retirement period 1	10%
Average tax rate, retirement period 2	28%

---

[1] Estimate based on 175% of Laura's primary insurance amount at the time of her death. Actual numbers will be modestly different because different benefits end in different years.

[2] Average of living expenses over next seven years.

[3] 85 percent of what they would spend as a couple in retirement.

[4] All tax rates are estimates based on income projections.

Step 1. Determine the Amount Needed to Fund the Preretirement Period

Preretirement Period 1, Years 1–18	
Annual expenses, today's dollars	$87,578
Social Security survivor benefits, after taxes	17,992
Annual shortfall, today's dollars	69,586
Lump-sum shortfall, today's dollars	1,145,779
NPV Dan's salary, after taxes[1]	1,612,183
Lump-sum surplus, today's dollars	**$466,404**
Preretirement Period 2, Years 19–25	
Annual expenses, today's dollars	$87,578
Dan's income[2]	118,452
Annual surplus, today's dollars	30,874
Annual surplus, year 19	52,561
Lump-sum surplus, year 19	356,428
Lump-sum surplus, today's dollars	**$172,806**

[1] Net present value calculation assumes 10 percent annual increases first eight years, 3 percent increases thereafter, and discount rate equal to rate of inflation.
[2] Calculated future salary based on assumptions in Footnote 1, then found present value based on inflation rate.

Step 2. Determine the Amount Needed to Fund the Retirement Period

Retirement Period 1 (60–65)	
Living expense, today's dollars	$68,794
Social Security survivor benefits of age 60, after taxes[1]	9,028
Annual shortfall, today's dollars	59,766
Annual shortfall, age 60	125,137
Lump-sum shortfall, age 60	612,554
Lump-sum shortfall, today's dollars	**$224,109**
Retirement Period 2 (65–95)	
Living expense, today's dollars	$68,794
Social security benefits of age 65, after taxes	16,225
Annual shortfall, today's dollars	52,569
Annual shortfall, age 65	127,599
Lump-sum shortfall, age 65	3,293,652
Lump-sum shortfall, today's dollars	**$985,497**

[1] Estimate based on Laura's primary insurance amount.

Step 3. Determine the Total Lump Sum Needed Today

Lump-sum surplus, preretirement period 1	$466,404
Lump-sum surplus, preretirement period 2	172,806
Lump sum currently needed, retirement period 1	224,109
Lump sum currently needed, retirement period 2	985,497
Total lump sum needed, today's dollars	**$570,396**

Step 4. Repeat Steps for Other Needs

Lump sum needed currently for college	$179,479
Burial expenses	20,000
Total lump sum for other needs, today's dollars	**$199,479**

Step 5. Establish Insurance Need

Total lump sump needed for all needs, today's dollars	**$769,875**
Available assets	**$64,000**
Total insurance needed, today's dollars	**$705,875**

Summary

This was the final chapter. It stressed how to complete the planning process using integration of the parts of the plan and overall completion techniques. Among its critical points were

- PFP theory helps understand and sharpen actual practices.
- Integration of all household resources as performed through TPM or other methods can improve decision making and household performance.
- SWOT, scenario, and sensitivity analyses add other dimensions to the overall review process by providing "what if" analysis.
- All steps in the process should be reviewed prior to completion of the plan with relevant questions asked in each step.
- A behavioral review at decision time can provide a reality check on what can realistically be accomplished.
- A financial plan should incorporate, among other things, clear specific recommendations made after careful review procedures, state important assumptions, and weight alternative solutions to be successful.
- Periodic review can ensure that initial plans remain relevant.

Key Terms

integration, *563*   sensitivity analysis, *571*   SWOT analysis, *569*
scenario analysis, *572*

Web Site

http://www.quickmba.com
Quick MBA Guide (SWOT analysis)
This site serves as a reference guide for people involved in the business field. It contains sections on accounting, economics, finance, business law, and so on. There is also a link with comprehensive information on SWOT analysis.

Questions

1. Detail five of the concepts that underlie PFP theory.
2. Why is a household's similarity with a business important?
3. How are we able to express the household goal in money terms when its underlying goals is to maximize utility—pleasure?
4. Why is integration so important?
5. Describe SWOT analysis.

6. What is the difference between strengths and weaknesses, on the one hand, and opportunities and threats, on the other?

7. Perform a cursory SWOT analysis for someone you are familiar with.

8. Explain the difference between sensitivity and scenario analyses.

9. Do people make integrated financial decisions? Explain.

10. Using figure 20.1 list the source and uses of cash for the household.

11. What are the reasons that a financial plan is important?

12. Outline the steps in the financial planning process and some questions under each that are significant in completing a financial plan.

13. Why is a behavioral review so relevant at this point in the planning process?

14. List five keys to a successful financial plan.

15. Why is periodic review important?

Problem 20.1

Earnestos was an accountant. He had a good job with a major accounting firm with a bright future. He also had a huge spending habit. He had $15,000 of credit card debt and was adding to it each month. His wife didn't know about it and believed that he had placed money each month into a pension plan. She had offered to go to work, but he said it wasn't necessary.

Perform a SWOT analysis and make specific recommendations for Earnestos and his wife.

CFP® 20.1

Certification Examination Questions and Problems

A young couple (both age 30) come to a financial planner with the desire for assistance in improving their family's financial position. They have two healthy children, ages three and six. The husband is a foreman for a manufacturer of auto parts. His current salary is $30,000 per year. The wife is a marketing professor for a state university. Her current salary is $40,000 per year. The couple recently purchased a riverfront home for $100,000 using their entire savings of $20,000 as a down payment. In addition to an $80,000 mortgage, the couple's only debt is an automobile loan having the balance of $12,000. Both husband and wife have very good family health insurance from their employers. The wife has employer-paid life insurance equal to two times her annual salary.

A. The couple wants to start an investment program as soon as possible. To correct the weakness in their financial planning before beginning the investment program, they should

1. Establish an emergency fund with stock mutual funds.
2. Start a college savings fund for the children.
3. Purchase disability insurance for the wife and the husband.
4. Prepare wills for the wife and the husband.
5. Secure credit life insurance for the auto loan.

   a. (5) only
   b. (1) and (2) only
   c. (1) and (3) only
   d. (3) and (4) only

B. When the couple are able to begin an investment program, they want to begin making investments for their retirement and their children's education. All of the following actions will help accomplish their goals in a tax-efficient manner *except*

   a. Investing in individual Roth IRAs.
   b. Investing through a 403(b) program for the wife.
   c. Investing in a growth and income mutual fund.
   d. Investing in education IRAs for each child.

Case Application
INTEGRATION

In working out the capital needs analysis, it became apparent that there was need for an additional $17,000 of savings annually over what was previously calculated. The first reason had to do with a recent job development that resulted in a projected moderation in Richard's raises in salary to a level 1–2 percent below the inflation rate and that made his job more risky. The second was the running of the total portfolio management approach, which indicated that the assumed investment rate needed to be lowered to 5 percent. Richard took the news in stride and said he thought I was too negative. Things would work out in the job. He would just have to invest more aggressively than originally planned.

Monica, on the other hand, was shaken. She thought that their tolerance for risk would have to be cut back. She said she would consider taking a full-time job if necessary. Richard shook his head as if to say no but didn't speak. Monica thought they could downsize by selling their house and realizing an extra $100,000. She wondered what level of insurance she could afford and whether they should cut back on the amount. Richard didn't like that idea.

Monica said disagreement on financial matters was a feature throughout their marital lives. She thought that I should make the recommendations. She pledged to follow them. Somewhat surprisingly to me, Richard agreed as well.

Case Application Questions

1. Go over the alternatives for increasing savings.
2. What do you think of Monica's offer to take a job?
3. Under the TPM approach, should the risky portion of their asset allocation be raised or lowered?
4. Should their insurance be raised or lowered?
5. Do you feel they should downsize their dwelling?
6. What are your recommendations? Incorporate savings, investing, life insurance, and other relevant areas.
7. Should there be controls set up to assist in ensuring that the recommendations were followed?
8. What kind of follow-up with the advisor would you recommend?
9. Complete the financial plan.

Appendix I

Household and Business Characteristics

A breakdown of some of the many similarities and differences between a business and a household is detailed in Tables 20.A1.1 and 20.A1.2.

On balance, the similarities appear more substantive than the differences. Therefore, the household can be characterized as an organization that in many ways resembles a business, and this has been a substantial organizing factor developed throughout this text.

TABLE 20.A1.1
**Household and
Business
Characteristics:
Similarities**

Item	Business	Household
Strategic planning	Business plan	Personal financial plan—overall approach similar to the business plan
Analytical money—decisions performed by	Internal financial planner, sometimes helped by a consultant	Internal "financial planner," sometimes helped by an external one
Organizational goal	Maximize profits	Maximization of utility approach, which uses maximization of profits
Organizational operations	Series of activities called divisions	Series of activities called functions
Production function	Products and services sold to others; some produced internally for workers	Labor services sold to others and utilized internally for benefit of member-owners
Types of capital expenditures	Machinery Plant Human capital—education and training	Machinery—auto, other durables Plant—home Human capital—education and training
Types of assets	Real, human-related, financial	Real, human-related, financial
Risk management	Practices, insurance, marketable financial instruments	Practices, insurance, marketable financial instruments
Investment tools	Time value of money NPV, IRR Portfolio management concepts	Time value of money NPV, IRR Portfolio management concepts
Use of profits—cash flow generated	Reinvested or paid out as dividends	Reinvested or paid out as dividends, called discretionary or leisure outlays

TABLE 20.A1.2
**Household and
Business
Characteristics:
Differences**

Item	Business	Household
Scope of operations	Responsibility stops at payout of dividend	Responsibility includes how dividend is spent
Centralized integrated decision making	Can be difficult in larger firms	Relatively simple to perform
Specialization of function	Done particularly in larger firms	Limited; only available in multiperson household or when specialists are retained
Life span	Theoretically unlimited	Limited by remaining life span of members
Ability to expand	Unlimited	Generally limited to two adult members
Specificity of goals	Limited to money maximization	Financial and nonfinancial goals
Separation of owner and manager	Common, particularly in larger firms	Major decisions typically made by member-owners
Role in society	To improve consumer standard of living	To improve consumer standard of living, but organization has closer function in performing that role

TABLE 20.A2.1
Cash Flow
Performance for
Period

Category	Actual	Projected	Difference	Explanation
Cash inflows				
Salary				
Business				
Investment				
Other				
Total				
Nondiscretionary expenses				
Discretionary expenses				
Operating Cash Flow				
Capital expenditures				
Financing activities				
Cash flow				
Targeted savings				
Net Cash Flow				

TABLE 20.A2.2
Statement of
Changes in Balance
Sheet Factors

Category	Amount Beginning of Period	Cash Inflows	Cash Outflows	Unrealized Appreciation/ Depreciation in Assets	Amount End of Period
Assets					
Cash					
Bond					
Stock					
Pension					
Other					
Total financial					
Home					
Auto					
Furniture and fixtures					
Jewelry					
Other					
Total real					
Total Assets					
Financial Liabilities					
Revolving credit					
Mortgage					
Other					
Total					
Total Financial Liabilities					
Net Worth					
Nonmarketable Assets					
Human					
Social Security					
Pension					
Total Nonmarketable Assets					
Fixed-Cost liabilities					
Total Net Worth Including Nonmarketable Assets					

Appendix II

Review Statements

There are two special statements that can provide insight into PFP matters. The first, a summary of cash flow considerations for the period, helps identify the differences between projected and actual performance and the reasons for them.

The second, the special balance sheet factor statement, is important because it more accurately portrays what transpired during the period. It not only incorporates traditional finance's transactional cash flow orientation but includes appreciation/depreciation in balance sheet factors not sold. Moreover, it also can include nonmarketable assets normally left off a balance sheet. This way of looking at household assets in their totality can shed some light on certain household actions. For example, many households may feel they have saved when their houses have risen in value even though they have not placed more cash into savings accounts.

Use of these statements by households can be instructive about how much of the change in net worth came about through conscious savings and the amount from market factors. These can be compared with previous projections for these factors by households and planners. The net cash flow in Table 20.A2.1 can serve as an input for or a check on the cash flow figures in Table 20.A2.2 as well as in assessing actual versus expected cash flows even when the second schedule is not employed.

Appendix III

The Money Ladder

The money ladder, discussed in a goals context in Chapter 3, is an easy-to-understand method of presenting capital needs analysis. Financial needs can be separated by activity. The activities are parts of financial planning such as current revenues, current expenses, future needs for retirement, estate, education, and so on.

Each activity's outflow or inflow is discounted to the present. Together they represent all the cash flows for the household over its life cycle. Use of this approach makes the integrative nature of PFP simple to comprehend. Actions in one area can affect the others, as shown in the Liu example on pages 566–567.

This type approach lends itself to a practical form of incorporating risk. It is an alternative to assigning a mean and standard deviation. You are asked to separately disclose not only your target goal, called the satisfactory goal, but your minimum and higher-level goals. The minimum goal is the most fundamental; if you could not obtain it, you would be profoundly disappointed. A higher-level goal is a "reach."

Each goal in each activity is translated into dollars needed to achieve the objective. The system is called a financial ladder because each rung further up the ladder represents a greater necessary expenditure for a greater reward. Based on your current practices, the system can tell you where on the ladder you are positioned now and how much saving it will take to reach a higher position.

The system can interact with risk by assuming that the difference between the satisfactory and minimum goals is equal to the standard deviation or by using the actual standard deviation not only to determine the probability of achieving the satisfactory level but also to assign a very high probability of at least reaching the minimum level, which is equivalent in ways to what is called the "downside risk" in financial investments.[7]

[7] For further discussion of the money ladder, see Lewis Altfest and Karen Altfest, *Lew Altfest Answers Almost All Your Questions about Money* (New York: McGraw-Hill, 1992), pp. 302–35.

Glossary

A

active approach to investing   The view that changes should be made in holdings over time to take advantage of new opportunities.

adjustable rate mortgage   A mortgage whose interest rate to the borrower fluctuates yearly based on overall market rates of interest at the time.

adjusted gross income (AGI)   The taxable revenue figure after adjustments are made for certain expenses.

administrator   A person who is in charge of supervising the estate. The same as an executor but takes place in the absence of a will.

adverse selection   Being negatively affected by involvement with a grouping of people who have greater knowledge of potential outcomes than you do.

affluence   Being financially independent at a high standard of living.

after-tax dollars   Dollars of income on which taxes have been paid.

alimony   The ongoing payment to the former spouse upon divorce.

alternative minimum tax (AMT)   A minimum tax that people qualify for when this alternative tax computation exceeds that for the regular calculation.

annual percentage rate (APR)   An adjusted interest rate on a loan.

annuities   A series of payments that are made or received.

annuitization   A process of converting a lump-sum asset accumulated into the payment of a fixed flow of income per year often based on life expectancy.

annuity due   Annuity payments are made at the beginning of the period.

arbitration   The act of transferring decision making from two or more people who are in conflict to a third party.

asset allocation   A planning process involving making decisions about the amount and type of securities we place our monies into.

assets   Those items that have value to the household going forward.

association   A grouping of individuals or businesses that share a common interest or goal and that generally finance an organization.

average tax bracket   The amount of tax you pay when the total tax paid is divided by the amount earned.

B

balance sheet   A statement of financial position at a given point in time.

bankruptcy   A legal way for people to eliminate or lessen the burdens of debt.

behavioral finance   The study of human makeup and actions that result in deviations from logical economic and financial behavior.

behavioral financial planning   The analysis of individual conduct and the development of practical techniques to improve financial decision making. It is the action arm of behavioral finance. It strives to understand and improve people's decision-making abilities so that they can more easily achieve the goals they set. Its goal is to educate and establish practices that close the gap between actual and ideal planning, thereby bringing people closer to their own goals.

beneficiary   The person to whom the property is given or for whom the property is being managed.

bequest   Irrevocable transfers of property to others that take place by will after the donor's death.

biases   Actions based on a distorted view of reality.

blue chips   Companies of high quality that are more likely to be large and have a strong position in their markets. They have good returns on investment and are less likely to have large noneconomic-related disappointments in earnings, which means that they generally have risk that is below overall market averages.

body language   What we reveal through facial expressions and body movements, hand gestures, eye contact, tone of voice, and so on.

bond quality   The likelihood that a bond will fulfill its obligation to pay interest and repay the amount owed at maturity.

bonds   Contracts in which an investor lends money to a borrower. As compensation for receiving the money, the borrower agrees to pay interest, often twice a year and generally of a fixed amount.

budget constraint   The limit on the amount we can consume based on our available resources.

budgeting   A method of planning current and future household cash flows.

business   The organizational entity for owners and workers who produce goods and services for profit.

business cycle   The periodic ups and downs in aggregate economic activity over time.

business plan   An outline or, more often, a detailed description of how you expect to establish and grow your firm over the next one to five years.

business risk   A risk taken for potential reward.

bypass trust (also known as a nonmarital, an exemption-equivalent, a type B, or a credit shelter trust)   A trust that is set up while the grantor is alive or provided for in the will; it must be irrevocable to qualify for tax savings. Under such a trust, funds are provided for two beneficiaries: the income beneficiary and the remainder person.

C

capital   The real, financial, and human-related assets that are generated by individuals and organizations or bought and sold in the marketplace.

capital expenditures   Cash outflows that provide household operating benefits for an extended period of time.

cash flow   (1) The amount of cash generated by household activities. (2) The financial operation of the organization based on the cash it generates.

cash flow planning   (1) A part of the financial plan in which household income and expenditures and other cash flows are compiled and analyzed. (2) The scheduling of current and future cash needs to achieve household goals.

cash flow statement   A statement that presents the financial operations for a household over a period of time. This is perhaps the single best measurement of the financial performance of the household between two periods.

charitable lead trust   Under this type of trust, the charity receives the stream of income for a designated term, and the balance thereafter goes to an heir.

charitable remainder trust   Under this type of trust, the donor receives a stream of annual income for a fixed period or for life, and the remainder is given to a charity.

child support   The series of payments that are made specifically for the support of the children in case of divorce.

closed-end mutual fund   The management company for this type of fund does not engage in any regular purchase or sales transactions after the initial offering. Consequently, pricing, purchase, and sale generally occur on a public exchange.

closed-end retail credit   A type of loan with a specific repayment schedule.

clustering   Paying and grouping two years of outlays together in one year to bring your tax-deductible expenditures above their respective floors.

cognitive errors   Human shortcomings that come from lack of knowledge, weakness in perception and memory, and less-than-ideal processing, scope, and speed.

coinsurance   Indicates that the policyholder pays a certain percentage of the outlay along with the insurance company, often subject to an overall cap on payments by the holder.

commission-only planners   Financial planners who often work for financial services firms or are independent and are compensated by commissions on products that they recommend or sell.

communication   The ability to transmit a message to another person successfully.

competency   The ability to handle a given task with the expertise necessary to provide a satisfactory outcome.

compliance   Observing all rules and conditions set up by established laws and regulatory bodies.

compounding   The mechanism that allows the amount invested, called the principal, to grow more quickly over time through the accumulation of interest on interest.

comprehensive financial plan   A financial plan in the form of a detailed written document that covers and integrates all significant areas of a person's financial life.

conservator   The person who is sometimes employed to be principally concerned with financial affairs and assets for the incapacitated.

consumption bundle   Our choice of the most attractive combination of food, clothing, shelter, and "fun" items.

conversion   Changing from one amount of tax due to a lower one.

convertible term   Allows an individual to swap a term insurance policy in the future for a whole life policy, generally offered by the same company.

corporation   A separate business entity that provides its owners with protection against loss of personal assets.

correlation coefficient   Measures the degree to which investment in a portfolio is related to other investments in that portfolio.

coupon payments   Interest payments on bonds.

coupon yield   The return that is arrived at by dividing the annual coupon payment by the face (maturity) value of a bond.

Coverdells   Special savings accounts set up with after-tax dollars for educational purposes.

credit report   The factual printout and evaluation of the creditworthiness of an individual.

current assets   Those assets that are expected to be or can be converted into cash in the current year.

current yield   The annual coupon divided by the market value of a bond.

cyclical stocks   Firms whose growth rates are at or below those for the overall economy but whose operations are highly sensitive to aggregate business conditions.

D

data gathering   Accumulating the information that is needed to perform personal financial planning objectives.

default risk   A chance of default (nonpayment) that typically results in bankruptcy.

defensive stocks   Companies that generally grow at average or below-average rates but are also less affected by business conditions.

defined benefit plans Pension structures that provide a stated stream of income, often a level amount, throughout retirement. The amount of income received generally depends on the time spent with the corporation or other organization and on your salary in the period around retirement.

defined contribution plans Pension structures that place an amount of money in the pension regularly. The amount available in retirement depends on the sum you contributed and the returns on that money.

deflation A period in which the absolute level of prices declines. In many areas of the economy, its effects are the opposite of inflation's impact.

depreciation The projected reduction in asset value due to wear and tear or obsolescence.

disabilities The factors, whether physical or mental, that make it difficult or impossible for a person to function normally in society.

disability insurance An insurance policy that provides cash flows to compensate you when you are unable to work due to an accident or illness.

discount bond A bond selling for less than its par value.

discount rate (1) The interest rate that member banks pay the Federal Reserve for borrowing from it. (2) The rate that we use to bring future cash flows to the present, generally to establish their current value.

discretionary expenses Outlays that you choose to make. In theory, they are leisure outlays.

disinflation A period in which prices are rising but at a rate of increase that is declining.

dividend discount model A security valuation method that assumes that a stock is equal to the sum of all its future dividends discounted to the present.

divorce planning The scheduling of matters in connection with the breakup of the traditional household.

documentation Written support for business practices and information provided for clients.

due diligence A legal term, often used in finance, that broadly means making an adequate investigation of the merits of an investment or other recommendation.

durable goods Within a personal financial planning context, refers to household possessions.

durable power of attorney A legal document that lets someone act on your behalf. The power survives incompetency and remains in effect over time. The amount of power and the circumstances under which it can be used are stated in the document.

E

economic indicators Those statistics that represent where our economy, or parts of it, has been, is going, or is expected to be headed.

educational planning (1) Preparing financially for the outlays for educating adult and children members of the household. (2) The process of programming direct financial and time resources that enables household members to improve their capabilities, typically through enrolling at a college or university.

educational policy statement A financial plan that sets out the goals, costs, and best method for achieving the educational objectives.

efficient market hypothesis (EMH) The theory that says that the best valuation for an individual security is its current market price, which reflects all information known about the security.

elder care planning Financial planning that involves actions taken on behalf of people, often our parents or grandparents, who are unable to adequately handle normal living matters without assistance.

empathy Attempting to place yourself in the other person's position—trying to identify with what he or she is experiencing; the thoughts, feelings, and attitudes.

employee benefits The forms of employee compensation other than salary.

engagement letter A legal contract that details the understanding between the planner and the client.

establishing goals Deciding on your priorities not only for living today but for the rest of your life.

estate planning Analyzing and deciding while you are alive how your assets are to be managed and apportioned to others in the event of your death or disability.

ethical behavior Maintaining standards of correct conduct and practice.

exchange-traded funds Portfolios of stocks and bonds that are traded on the major stock exchanges.

executor A person designated in a will who is in charge of administrating an estate, complying with legal requirements, and liquidating its assets.

expansion Defined for macroeconomic purposes as a two-quarter or longer increase in real overall economic output of a country.

F

fair value The inherent worth of nonmarketable assets based on cash flow, risk, and the time value of money principles.

family limited partnership (FLP) An organizational structure in which a family maintains operating control and passes on financial ownership in a family business.

Federal Funds rate The rate that banks borrow reserves from each other, which helps establish overall market interest rates.

fee and commission planners Financial planners who are compensated by both fees and commissions.

fee-only planners Financial planners who are compensated solely by fees paid by their clients and do not accept commissions or compensation from other sources.

fiduciary   A trusted party who acts as an agent for another person.

finance   A practical field of study that is based principally on cash flow and deals with the management of funds, which can be termed money issues.

financial advisor   A financial planner who provides financial advice to a person.

financial assets   Those assets in which ownership is represented and traded solely through pieces of paper.

financial counseling   The mechanism for assisting people in making their financial decisions.

financial difficulties   Problems in simultaneously supporting normal household operations and paying interest and principal on debt owed when due.

financial integration   Using all assets and liabilities, all cash flows, all household activities, and all future plans to arrive at decisions.

financial leverage   The amount of debt outstanding and its contribution to household fixed costs.

financial liabilities   Monies owed to others, as, for example, debt.

financial literacy   The degree to which a person is educated in financial matters.

financial plan   A structure through which you can establish and integrate all your goals and needs.

financial planner   A person with designation or educational experience, most commonly a CFP® practitioner, who practices personal financial planning.

financial ratios   A way of gauging the current state of the household's assets and operating activities.

financial risk   Comes from the amount of debt outstanding relative to assets. It also may involve the level of fixed payments in comparison with operating cash flows.

financial statements   Most commonly in PFP a balance sheet and cash flow statement, which together present a current picture of your financial condition.

financing activities   The cash flows that come from changes in debt.

firm   An organization that produces goods or services.

fiscal policy   The role played by government in attempting to favorably influence the course of economic activity through changes in government receipts and disbursements.

fixed annuities   Tax-deferred annuities that provide an interest rate that is established by the issuer and often changes annually. Frequently there is a guaranteed minimum rate that the issuer must provide.

fixed-rate mortgage   A mortgage whose interest rate remains stable over time.

floater   A rider to an insurance policy that covers the named items wherever they may be located.

fraud   Deliberately intending to deceive in order to obtain something of value.

frequency   Rate of recurrence of the losses that a household experiences.

fully marketable assets   Assets that can be sold currently in a public forum for fair value at low transaction costs.

functional cash flow statement   A cash flow statement that separates cash flows by type of household activity.

fundamental analysis   Analysis that involves looking at economic industry and company data to help determine the fair value for a company.

future value   The amount accumulated at the end of a period.

G

gifts   Irrevocable transfers of property to others that take place during the giftor's life.

grantor (trustor)   The person who sets up the trust.

grants   Outright money given in the chapter's context for educational purposes.

gross domestic product (GDP)   A measure of all activity by U.S. or foreign businesses produced solely in the United States.

gross national product (GNP)   The measure of overall U.S. economic activity produced by U.S. businesses.

growth stocks   Companies that grow more rapidly in sales and earnings than the overall economy and are less affected by cyclical business conditions.

growth style of investing   Selecting companies that are expected to have rapid growth in revenues and earnings per share.

guardian   The person who handles financial and personal affairs for people unable to care for themselves—for example, children—and for the incapacitated when there is a special needs trust.

H

hazard   A circumstance that increases the probability of a peril.

health insurance   An insurance policy that provides direct payment or reimburses you for medical expenses in connection with illness or accident.

health risk   The possibility of large unreimbursable costs.

heuristics   Simplified human approaches to complex tasks.

home equity loan   A loan that is secured by the house you own.

household   An organization of one or more individuals who live in the same dwelling and share financial and other resources intended for the well-being of its members.

household assets   (1) Those assets used in day-to-day household activities—for example, a car, furniture, and household appliances. (2) Sometimes used more broadly to include all assets that household member-owners possess.

household budget   A formal budgeting that reflects all categories of household expenditures; usually in the form of a document.

household enterprise   An organization that attempts to operate as efficiently as possible with the goal of providing as much time and money as possible for activities its members get pleasure from.

household equity (household net worth)   The difference between household assets and liabilities.

household finance   (1) The study of how a household and the people in it develop the cash flows necessary to support operations and provide for the well-being of its members. (2) The financial counterpart to the household enterprise. It is involved with making the household as efficient as possible so as to achieve its members' financial plans.

human assets   The resource that reflects the current value of all our future earnings. That is, the future income stream of a household's wage earners.

human-related assets   A term that includes human assets and other forms of resources such as pension plans, expected gifts, or inheritances that obtain their values from human assets.

hybrid ARM   A type of mortgage that offers a fixed rate for a fixed period of years and then reverts to an adjustable rate.

I

incentive stock options (IMOs)   Stock options that are not taxable to the recipient when the option is granted, even if the market price of the stock is higher at that time than the option price.

income replacement   The amount of insurance intended to cover the loss of income in full.

indemnity   Indicates that your maximum reimbursement in the event of loss of an asset you own is the value of the item.

index fund   A mutual fund that attempts to duplicate market performance and keeps costs low by using computerized programs to purchase holdings and not employing high-priced investment managers and analysts.

individual proprietorship   A business structure in which an individual and his or her company are considered a single entity for tax and liability purposes.

inflation   The increase in price for a given good or service or the growth of overall costs in the economy over time.

insurable interest   You generally can only insure against loss of items that you yourself would suffer a loss on, should they be damaged or eliminated entirely.

insurance   A method of transferring risk to a third party.

insurance risk   The risk associated with nonfinancial assets.

insurance underwriting   The process by which an insurance company agrees to assume a risk in return for a projected profit.

intangible liabilities   Less quantifiable current liabilities such as potential liabilities to third parties.

integration   The process of combining, of making something into a completed whole. In personal financial planning, connotes bringing together all financial issues and resource requirements for decision-making purposes.

interest rate   The cost for money borrowed.

internal rate of return (IRR)   The discount rate that makes the present value of cash inflows over time equal to the cash outflows.

intestate   Dying without a will.

Investment Advisers Act of 1940   An act established to protect the investment public against fraudulent and deceitful practices on the part of investment people who provide them with advice.

investment risk   The risk associated with savings placed in financial assets.

investments   Placing cash flow into assets designed to improve an organization or to provide future funds for consumption.

irregular cash flows   Differing payments over time.

irrevocable trust   A trust that cannot be altered.

J

joint tenancy with right of survivorship (JTWROS)   A joint property entity that allows a person to automatically inherit the property upon the death of the other owner.

L

lease   A way to acquire the use of an asset without purchasing it, generally through rental payments.

leisure outlays   (1) Household costs that include all non-work, nonoverhead-related items such as eating out, watching television, playing tennis, even shopping if it isn't for necessities. (2) Outlays that provide pleasure to the disburser.

letter of instruction   A supplement to a will that helps people understand your thinking and provide direction for matters to be accomplished after death.

level term   The price for term insurance that remains flat for 5, 10, 20 years, or another period of time.

liabilities   Items the household owes.

liability insurance (first-party coverage)   Liability insurance that protects you personally against having to pay for losses to you or to your property directly.

liability insurance (third-party coverage)   Insurance that protects you personally against having to pay for a variety of potential losses to others.

life cycle theory   A theory that states that individuals plan for future events using current and future financial resources with the objective of smoothing fluctuations in standard of living over time and attaining predetermined goals.

life estate   Rights to property while the spouse is alive but with no right to pass the rights on to heirs.

life insurance   A policy that provides cash to compensate for the death of a household wage earner.

life planning   A planning process that deals with the personal side of the household enterprise and goes beyond money planning for analysis and scheduling of steps for realization of personal goals.

limited liability corporation (LLC)   A corporation that combines the limited liability feature of a corporation with being taxed as a partnership or an individual proprietorship. It also can be taxed as a corporation.

limited liability partnership (LLP)   A partnership in which the partner's or investor's liability is limited to the amount he or she has invested in the company.

liquidity   The ability to convert an asset into cash quickly and at a relatively low transaction cost; that is, at a reasonable transaction cost and without loss of principal.

liquidity risk   The possibility that you will not be able to find a buyer for an asset at its current market price.

liquidity substitutes   Another way of raising cash, often in connection with unplanned-for developments. Two types of liquidity substitutes are debt and marketable securities.

living trust   A trust set up during a grantor's life.

load mutual fund   A mutual fund that provides a sales commission to the individual or brokerage firm that markets the fund, with the new fund holder paying the charge.

long-term assets   Those assets that are likely to be consumed beyond a one-year time frame.

long-term care insurance   An insurance policy that reimburses you for expenses incurred when you are unable to perform certain activities of daily living on your own.

long-term debt   Involves financial obligations whose terms call for payment to be made many years from now. While for accounting purposes it is any debt not due in the current year, it is often thought of as debt payable in four years or longer.

longevity   The remaining number of years you will live.

longevity risk   The possibility of death occurring well before or after it is expected; that is, living beyond normal expectations or dying prematurely.

M

macroeconomic risk   The risk inherent in the overall economy.

macroeconomics   The study of how our overall economy operates.

margin debt   Money generally offered by securities dealers to help finance purchase of marketable investments such as individual stocks, bonds, and mutual funds.

marginal tax bracket   The amount of tax you pay on the next dollar that you earn.

marital assets   Those that were generated or acquired during marriage.

marital property   Rights in property gained through marriage.

market structures   The economic operations of the business, the government, and the household that facilitate the purchase and sale of items.

market value   The market-established worth of a product or a financial instrument.

marketability   The capacity to find a seller or buyer of an asset at its current value.

marketable investments   Those assets that are traded publicly—for example, stocks and bonds.

markets   Places where tangible goods and financial instruments like stocks and bonds are bought and sold.

maturity   The number of years until the amount borrowed is to be repaid.

maturity date   The date that a stated sum is to be repaid to the bondholder.

maturity risk   Risk related to the time until a bond or some other financial instrument is to be repaid. The longer the period, the greater the potential for a change in the ability of a company to repay its debt.

mean reversion   The theory that returns for securities tend to move toward average historical performance when the returns are examined over longer time frames.

mediation   A method of handling disputes in which the mediator attempts to facilitate a resolution; unlike an arbitrator, a mediator acts as an advisor and does not have the power to render a final binding decision.

medical power of attorney (also called a health care power of attorney or health care proxy)   A legal document that allows someone else to make medical decisions for you when you are incapable of doing so yourself.

mental accounting   A theoretical concept that attempts to explain the way our brain works in decision making and indicates that the brain compartmentalizes our actions, placing them into certain categories.

microeconomic risk   The risk associated with an individual industry or company.

mission statement   Provides the rationale for establishing a business or a career.

modern portfolio theory (MPT)   A theory that states that we should not view investments on a one-by-one basis but overall as part of a portfolio. We should look at return in relation to risk, and that overall risk is not only influenced by the stand-alone risk but also by the degree of correlation among assets in the portfolio.

momentum investing   An approach in which stocks that have had large price movements relative to the market are purchased.

monetary policy   Government actions intended to influence the amount of money in circulation in the economy.

money planning   Planning whose goals are strictly financial and do not include life-planning objectives.

Monte Carlo analysis   A form of risk analysis in which selected key factors are run randomly, based on their mean figures and potential outcomes around their means.

moral hazard   Actions taken by the insured person with the intention of increasing the possibility of loss due to such things as an unmentioned illness or faking injury after the policy is taken out.

moral suasion   The effort by the Federal Reserve to influence the economy without actually doing anything.

morale hazard   A possibility of loss that comes not from dishonesty but from a person behaving negligently because he or she has insurance coverage.

mortality risk   The probability of dying.

mortgage   A loan secured by real property.

mutual fund   An entity that combines stock or bond assets for investors who receive centralized administration and investment management.

N

National Association of Securities Dealers (NASD)   A self-regulatory body for the securities industry.

negligence   Behavior that could result in loss. It arises from not taking sufficient care to prevent the loss from occurring.

negotiable instrument   A written promise to pay, without conditions, an amount of money to another person when asked or at a stated time.

net asset value (NAV)   The price established for the purchase or sale transaction of mutual fund shares obtained by adding up the value of all the securities owned and dividing by the number of shares of that mutual fund that are outstanding.

net cash flow   The amount of cash available after targeted investing for specific purposes such as retirement or a down payment on a home. Net cash flow is the bottom line on the cash flow statement. It is the savings available for further investing or for spending in the next period.

net present value (NPV)   The present value of all projected future cash inflows and outflows.

net working capital   A figure received by subtracting current liabilities from current assets.

no-load mutual fund   A mutual fund that does not offer sales commissions to the recommendors of the funds.

nominal return   The return on assets based on the actual number of dollars received.

nondiscretionary expenses   Fixed costs needed to sustain household activities. Also called maintenance costs.

nonfinancial assets   The assets that the household possesses aside from financial assets.

nonmarital assets   Those that were developed prior to marriage or were a result of a gift or bequest during marriage.

nonqualified plans   Pension structures that may be used for retirement but whose deposits are not eligible to receive a tax deduction.

nonqualified stock options   Stock options that are not taxable to the recipient when the option is granted but are taxed when the option is exercised.

nontraditional family   Adults other than married persons who live together in a relationship intended to be permanent.

nonverbal communication   A way of transmitting your thoughts and emotions without, or in addition to, using words. In sum, what is conveyed, intentionally or unintentionally, through facial expressions and body movements, hand gestures, tone of voice, and so on.

O

open-end credit   A type of loan that provides a loan limit that can be utilized for multiple purchases over a period of time.

open-end mutual fund   A mutual fund that is generally open to new deposits by existing or new investors and redemptions by current holders.

operating activities   Day-to-day financial functions of the household.

operating leverage   The degree to which we have fixed costs in our budget that come from household operating functions.

operating risk   Arises from uncertainties in connection with household activities.

opportunity cost of time   The amount of money we could have made if we worked instead of being involved in an alternative activity.

ordinary annuity   Annuity payments that are made at the end of the period.

ordinary income   Income taxed at normal rates based on your taxable income.

overhead costs (maintenance costs)   Those costs that directly support jobs such as commuting costs and business lunches, housing support costs such as mortgage interest and utility expenses, and personal support costs such as eating, nonbusiness clothing, and personal care.

own occupation (definition of disability)   Being unable to work in your existing occupation.

P

partnership   A business entity with two or more partners in which each partner is liable for any debts taken on by the business.

passive approach to investing   An approach to investments that makes no attempt to receive greater-than-market returns. It limits activity to maintaining constant asset allocations and strives to minimize expenses.

peak   The highest point reached during an expansion in the economic activity of a country or other entity.

pension   The savings structure into which money is deposited to generate income for retirees.

peril   Exposure to the risk of loss.

perpetual annuity   A stream of payments that is assumed to go on forever.

personal finance   The study of how people develop the cash flows necessary to support their operations and provide for their well-being.

personal financial planning   The method by which people anticipate and plot their future actions to reach their goals.

personal property   Assets that are not affixed to the land and therefore are usually portable.

personality   The sum total of all the human characteristics that distinguish you from other people.

physical hazard   A deficiency in physical property that increases the possibility of loss.

policy statements   The practices that a firm has in attempting to fulfill client engagements and in operating its business in general.

portfolio   A grouping of assets held by an individual or a business.

postnuptial agreement   An agreement that is entered into after marriage that provides the terms upon breakup due to death or divorce.

power of attorney   A legal document that lets someone act on your behalf.

practice standards   Standards that establish the appropriate level at which professional activities are conducted.

preferred stock   A type of security that has a fixed periodic payout and a lower priority on assets than bonds in the event of bankruptcy and lacks the assurance of a bond's contracted-for return of principal.

premium bond   A bond that sells for more than its par value.

prenuptial agreement   A formal form of risk management that provides, before marriage, for financial and other terms upon the divorce or death of the asset holder.

present value   A sum's worth at the beginning of the period.

pretax dollars   Dollars of income on which no taxes have been paid.

price-earnings (P/E) multiple method   A security valuation method that is based on earnings and the number of years of current earnings it takes for you to "pay off" (reach) the cost of purchasing the shares at the current price.

principal (par, maturity, or face value)   The payment due at maturity of a bond.

pro forma statements   Statements that include projections.

probate   The procedure after a person's death during which the court validates the will and/or administers certain estate assets.

profitability index (PI)   An index that relates the amount of the net present value of an asset to the size of the original investment.

property   Refers to the tangible and financial assets owned by household members.

purchasing power   The value of money as measured by the quantity and quality of products and services it can buy.

purchasing-power risk   The risk of having your money decline in what it can buy over time due to inflation.

pure risk   A risk that carries no financial reward.

Q

qualified plans   Pension structures that comply with established government regulations. They allow you to place pretax (untaxed) dollars into the plan.

R

rationed borrowers   Type of borrowers that are short of internal cash flow and would like to borrow more credit at comparable interest rates than is available.

real assets   Tangible assets—that is, items that you can see or touch—that the household owns.

real property   Dwellings and other structures that are affixed to land.

real return   The inflation-adjusted return on assets.

recession (contraction)   A two-quarter or longer decline in real overall economic output of a country.

reentry   The requirement that you pass health tests at stated times to qualify for the annual rates given in the insurance policy.

regulation   In the financial services industry, whether performed by a federal, state, or professional association, a process that is principally involved with ensuring that appropriate information and beneficial advice are provided to clients.

reinvestment risk   The possibility that cash received through payments of interest and principal will not be reinvested at the original rate on the bond.

remainder person   Under a trust, it is the person who receives the principal remaining after the death of the income beneficiary.

renewable term   Guarantees that the policy will continue in force, regardless of the health of the insured, for a stated period of time—for example, to age 65.

reporting   Presentation of material facts to the clients and regulatory bodies.

required rate of return   The return that is needed to be earned to make an investment attractive. Market factors including the investment's risk should be incorporated.

reserve ratio   The amount of money the banks have to keep in reserve for each dollar they lend.

retirement needs analysis   A way of mapping future cash inflows and outflows to establish resource requirements during retirement.

retirement planning   The process of focusing on household savings and investing decisions that allow individuals to retire at the age and lifestyle that they desire.

reverse mortgage   Borrowing money based on a house's asset value even when there is no visible means of paying it back. The amount owed compounds generally without payment of interest or principal, with repayment at time of sale.

revocable trust   A trust that can be revoked or changed by the grantor whenever desired.

risk   The uncertainty of outcomes.

risk management   The process of controlling the level of risk and consequently of loss for each significant household asset and for the entire portfolio of assets.

risk management in practical terms   The process by which we identify risks and control them so that we are able to achieve individual goals.

risk management in theory   The study of methods for controlling portfolio risk.

risk premium   The extra return that compensates you for the additional amount of risk you are taking with a particular security over a fully safe one.

risk tolerance   The amount of risk a person is willing to undertake.

S

satisficing   Method by which individuals seek a satisfactory solution, not an optimal one.

savings   The cash left over after operating, capital expenditures, and debt activities.

scenario analysis   Observing the effect of changes in multiple variables or in one variable that influences many situations.

secured debt   Borrowing that has a separated asset serving as collateral to be sold by the creditor for repayment in the event the debtor is unable to do so.

segmented financial plan   A financial plan that covers a limited specialized portion of all financial activities.

sensitivity analysis   Identifying those factors that could significantly alter anticipated planning results.

separate property   Asset owned entirely by a person.

separately managed accounts   Segregated assets that are managed personally for each individual.

severity   The level of the losses that have a material impact on the household's overall financial condition or current cash resources.

shifting income   Transferring income from a person in a higher bracket to someone in a lower bracket. Most commonly this is done by gifting money from a parent to a child.

short-term debt   Money owed that is payable in a relatively brief period. For accounting purposes it is debt due within the current year, while in finance usage it is debt payable within three years.

social insurance   Forms of insurance provided by the federal and state governments.

special circumstances planning   A miscellaneous category to handle other goals and activities such as marital or divorce planning, planning for elderly parents, and so forth.

special needs planning   Financial planning that concerns dependents who often have permanent disabilities that eliminate or limit their income-earning abilities.

special needs trust   A type of trust that provides a mechanism for presenting supplemental aid to dependents with the objective of not compromising governmental aid.

speculative investments   Generally refers to highly risky assets in which large or full loss of principal is possible. In a financial asset sense, refers to stocks or bonds of companies whose operations are less predictable; whose profitability is more precarious, with current or potential losses possible; and that often have large debt in relation to their equity.

springing power of attorney   A legal document that does not take effect until a specific event stated in the document occurs, such as an incompetency.

standard of living   Making the most money possible (in strict financial parlance); attempting to achieve an attractive balance of life's factors (in more common usage).

statement of cash flow   An alternative term for the cash flow statement when referring to personal statements.

statement of financial position   An alternative term for the balance sheet used for personal statements.

step-up in basis   New valuation for taxation purposes under which you have the option of selecting the fair market value either at the date of death or six months later for basis purposes, but the choice must be taken for the entire estate, not separately by asset.

stock option   The right to buy a stock at a specific price for a specific period of time.

Subchapter S corporation   A corporation that offers limited liability but is taxed as a partnership.

suitability   Ensuring that the advice and products provided fit the circumstances and preferences of the client.

supervisory revenues   Continuing billings for planner review and/or management of client assets, particularly financial assets, with the goal of maintaining and increasing client financial wealth.

SWOT analysis   An appraisal of all the major factors that can enhance or detract from the outlook for goal achievement. SWOT stands for strengths, weaknesses, opportunities, threats.

systematic risk   The risk of overall market factors like the economy, inflation, interest rates, and the stock market.

T

tax deferral   Postponing taxes to be paid today to some time in the future so that you can use that money in the interim.

tax-deferred annuities   Savings vehicles that allow for retirement or for other purposes and whose after-tax deposits grow tax-free until monies are withdrawn.

tax-deferred compensation   Monies that employees have earned that is not paid out by their employers until some future time.

tax elimination   Not paying taxes at all on a specific type of income being generated.

tax planning   The analysis and implementation of strategies to reduce tax expenditures to the government.

taxable income   The amount from which your tax liability is calculated.

technical analysis   Analysis that focuses exclusively on price and volume to help determine the fair value of a company.

tenancy by the entirety   A form of joint ownership that is only available to married persons; in the event of death, the surviving co-owner receives full ownership.

tenancy in common   A form of joint ownership in which each co-owner owns a specified percentage of a property and the sale of an interest is permitted. In the event of death, the property will pass to the individual's heirs, not the co-owners unless so specified.

term insurance   Life insurance providing fixed coverage for a stated period of time with policyholder premiums that vary based on the possibility of death of the insured during that time frame.

terminal illness planning   Financial planning that involves accommodating the wishes of a dying person in a way that retains as much of the financial resources as possible for the remaining household members and other intended beneficiaries.

testamentary trust   A trust that is provided for in the will and comes about after death.

theory of consumer choice   A theory that describes the method by which individuals select goods and services to satisfy their needs.

time value of money   The compensation provided for investing money for a given period.

tort   An act of wrongdoing against a person or a business or their property for which a remedy is sought.

total portfolio management (TPM)   A theory that attempts to select the best mix of assets to provide the highest return possible on the household portfolio given our resources and risk preferences.

traditional cash flow statement   A cash flow statement that groups all inflows and outflows together, with little or no distinction between flows based on operating, capital expenditures, and debt repayment.

transforming income   Changing income from a high-tax to a lower-tax status. Typically, it involves changing from being taxed at ordinary income rates to being taxed at more favorable capital gains rates.

trough   The stage of the economy's business cycle that marks the end of a period of contraction and the transition to expansion.

trust   (1) A separate legal entity generally in which a third party manages property for the benefit of another person. (2) The belief that you can rely on someone or something to perform as expected.

trustee   The person who manages trust assets for the benefit of another person.

U

umbrella insurance   Supplementary insurance that represents a broadly diversified grouping of property and liability coverages in addition to liability coverages under existing homeowners and automobile insurance policies. It is also known as excess liability insurance.

unified credit   An exemption in the form of a credit against taxes.

unit investment trusts   Portfolios that are set up at a point in time as are mutual funds but are generally unmanaged.

universal life   A life insurance policy that is more flexible than whole life. It often has a significant cash value account, but yearly payments by the policyholder may vary and under some circumstances so can insurance coverage.

unrationed borrowers   Type of borrowers that have sufficient internal cash flow and assets to be able to select the loan maturity offering the most attractive rates.

unsecured debt   Borrowing that is based solely on the full faith and credit of the debtor.

unsystematic risk   Those risks related to individual companies, such as a decline in market share, the loss of a key patent, and so forth.

utility   Satisfaction that an item or activity presents.

V

value style of investing   An approach to investments that places more emphasis on price in making purchase decisions, which means that the manager looks for companies that are out of favor or otherwise cheaply priced in relation to their outlook for earnings growth.

variable annuities   Tax-deferred annuities that offer a range of investment choices to be selected by the purchaser, often in stock and bond mutual funds. Thus, the returns are established by market factors as opposed to rates that are decided by the insurance companies on fixed annuities.

variable life   Similar to whole life insurance except that it transfers the investment function from the insurance firm to the individual.

variable universal life   Combines the payment flexibility of universal life insurance with the investment flexibility of variable life insurance.

verbal communication   A way of transmitting our thoughts and emotions through the spoken word.

verbal message   The content of the message used in verbal communication.

vesting   The point at which an employee is entitled to a stated amount of nonrevocable benefits from an employer.

viatical settlements Payouts by insurance companies or other parties on life insurance based on ascertainable terminal illnesses within a certain time frame (often two years or less).

visceral feelings Human shortcomings that come from impulses to take action that are often short term in nature and can cloud judgments.

W

whole life Life insurance providing fixed coverage for the life cycle of the insured. Level policyholder premiums are made possible by higher than pure mortality and insurance company overhead payments in early years, which bring about a cash-value savings component for the policy.

will A legal instrument that indicates who is to receive a person's assets upon death and that expresses other wishes.

withdrawal risk The uncertainty created by taking monies out to fund retirement when asset prices are depressed. The resultant larger percentage of assets withdrawn, particularly when early in the withdrawal period, can place the holder (often the retiree) in jeopardy of running out of needed resources.

wrap product One that includes advice by a broker, investment management, and transaction costs, all for one fee.

Y

yield curve The connection of individual points on a graph representing separate returns for one type of bond over all its maturity dates.

yield to maturity The return you would receive if you purchased a bond today and held it until it was repaid.

Suggested Readings

Aaron, Henry. *Behavioral Dimensions of Retirement Economics.* Washington: Brookings Institution/ New York: Russell Sage Foundation, 1999.

Abramovitz, Les. *Long-Term Care Insurance Made Simple.* Los Angeles, CA: Health Information Press, 1999.

Ackerman, Frank, David Kiron, Neva Goodwin, Jonathan Harris, and Kevin Gallagher. *Human Well-Being and Economic Goals.* Washington, DC: Island Press, 1997.

Allen, Everett T., Jerry S. Rosenbloom, Dennis Mahoney, and Joseph J. Melone. *Pension Planning: Pensions, Profit-Sharing, and Other Deferred Compensation Plans.* 8th ed. New York: McGraw-Hill, 2001.

Altfest, Karen. *Keeping Clients for Life: How to Build a Successful Financial Practice.* New York: John Wiley & Sons, 2001.

Anthony, Mitch. *Your Clients for Life: The Definitive Guide to Becoming a Successful Financial Life Planner.* Chicago, IL: Dearborn Trade Publishing, 2002.

Apolinsky, Harold, and Stewart Welch III. *New Rules for Estate and Tax Planning.* New York: John Wiley & Sons, 2001.

Beam, Burton T., Jr., and John J. McFadden. *Employee Benefits.* 6th ed. Chicago, IL: Dearborn Financial Publishing, 2000.

Beam, Burton, Jr., Barbara Poole, David Bickelhaupt, and Robert Crowe. *Fundamentals of Insurance for Financial Planning.* 4th ed. Bryn Mawr, PA: The American College, 2003.

Becker, Gary. *The Economic Approach to Human Behavior.* Chicago: University of Chicago Press, 1976.

Becker, Gary Stanley. *Human Capital: A Theoretical and Empirical Analysis, with Special Reference to Education.* 3rd ed. Chicago: University of Chicago Press, 1993.

Becker, Gary. *A Treatise on the Family.* Cambridge, MA: Harvard University Press, 1998.

Behrman, Jere R., Robert A. Pollak, and Paul Taubman. *From Parent to Child: Intrahousehold Allocations and Intergenerational Relations in the United States.* Chicago, IL: University of Chicago Press, 1995.

Bell, David, Howard Raiffa, and Amos Tversky. *Decision Making: Descriptive, Normative, and Prescriptive Interactions.* Cambridge, UK: Cambridge University Press, 1988.

Belsky, Gary, and Thomas Gilovich. *Why Smart People Make Big Money Mistakes—and How to Correct Them:*

Lessons from the New Science of Behavioral Economics. New York: Simon & Schuster, 1999.

Bernheim, B. Douglas. T*he Vanishing Nest Egg: Reflections on Saving in America.* New York: Priority Press Publications, 1991.

Bodie, Zvi, Alex Kane, and Alan Marcus. *Essentials of Investments.* 4th ed. New York: McGraw-Hill/Irwin, 2001.

Boone, Louis, David Kurtz, and Douglas Hearth. *Planning Your Financial Future.* Fort Worth, TX: Dryden Press, 1996.

Bost, John C. *Estate Planning and Taxation.* Dubuque, IA: Kendall/Hunt Publishing, 1999.

Bradford, David F. *Taxation, Wealth and Saving.* Cambridge, MA: MIT Press, 2000.

Bradford, David F. *Untangling the Income Tax.* Cambridge, MA: Harvard University Press, 1986.

Briles, Judith, Edwin Schilling III, and Carol Ann Wilson. *The Dollars and Sense of Divorce.* Chicago, IL: Dearborn Financial Publishing, 1998.

Brocas, Isabelle, and Juan Carrillo, eds. *The Psychology of Economic Decisions.* Vol. 1. *Rationality and Well-Being.* New York: Oxford University Press, 2003.

Brocas, Isabelle, and Juan Carrillo, eds. *The Psychology of Economic Decisions.* Vol. 2. *Reasons and Choices.* New York: Oxford University Press, 2004.

Browne, Marlene M. *The Divorce Process: Empowerment through Knowledge.* St. Paul, MN: West Publishing, 2001.

Bryant, W. Keith. *The Economic Organization of the Household.* New York: Cambridge University Press, 1990.

Burns, Sharon, and Raymond Forgue. *How to Care for Your Parents' Money While Caring for Your Parents.* New York: McGraw-Hill, 2003.

Campbell, John Y., and Martin Feldstein. *Risk Aspects of Investment-Based Social Security Reform.* Chicago, IL: University of Chicago Press, 2000.

Campbell, John, and Luis Viceira. *Strategic Asset Allocation.* Cambridge, MA: Oxford University Press, 2002.

Clark, Robert, Richard Burkhauser, Marilyn Moon, Joseph Quinn, and Timothy Smeeding. *The Economics of an Aging Society.* Malden, MA: Blackwell, 2004.

Clauretie, Terrence M., and G. Stacy Sirmans. *Real Estate Finance: Theory and Practice.* 3rd ed. Cincinnati, Ohio: South-Western College Publishing, 1998.

Colin F. Camerer, George Loewenstein, and Matthew Rabin. *Advances in Behavioral Economics.* Princeton, NJ: Princeton University Press, 2004.

Copeland, Thomas, and J. Fred Weston. *Financial Theory and Corporate Policy.* 3rd ed. Reading, MA: Addison-Wesley, 1992.

Cotton, Kathleen. *Financial Planning from We to Me: Divorce Strategies to Help You Get More of What You Want.* Lynnwood, WA: Wealth Books, 1996.

Crumbley, Larry, and Edward Milam. *Estate Planning: A Guide for Advisors and Their Clients.* Homewood, IL: Dow Jones-Irwin, 1986.

Doherty, Neil. *Corporate Risk Management: A Financial Exposition.* New York: McGraw-Hill, 1985.

Dorfman, Mark. *Introduction to Risk Management and Insurance.* 6th ed. Upper Saddle River, NJ: Prentice Hall, 1998.

Dreman, David. *Contrarian Investment Strategies: The Next Generation.* New York: Simon & Schuster, 1998.

Drucker, David, and Joel Bruckenstein. *Virtual Office Tools for a High Margin Practice: How Client-Centered Financial Advisors Can Cut Paperwork, Overhead, and Wasted Hours.* Princeton, NJ: Bloomberg Press, 2002.

Earl, Peter E., and Simon Kemp. *The Elgar Companion to Consumer Research and Economic Psychology.* Northampton, MA: Edward Elgar Publishing, 1999.

Eatwell, John, Murray Milgate, and Peter Newman. *The New Palgrave: The World of Economics.* London: Macmillan, 1991.

Eisner, Robert. *The Total Income System Accounts.* Chicago, IL: University of Chicago Press, 1989.

Elton, Edwin J., Martin J. Gruber, Stephen J. Brown, and William N. Goetzmann. *Modern Portfolio Theory and Investment Analysis.* 6th ed. New York: John Wiley & Sons, 2002.

Ermisch, John F. *An Economic Analysis of the Family.* Princeton, NJ: Princeton University Press, 2003.

Evensky, Harold. *Wealth Management: The Financial Advisor's Guide to Investing and Managing Your Client's Assets.* New York: McGraw-Hill, 1997.

Evensky, Harold, and Deena Katz. *The Investment Think Tank: Theory, Strategy, and Practice for Advisers.* Princeton, NJ: Bloomberg Press, 2004.

Fabozzi, Frank J. *Handbook of Portfolio Management.* New Hope, PA: Frank Fabozzi Associates, 1998.

Fabozzi, Frank, and Harry M. Markowitz. *The Theory & Practice of Investment Management.* New York: John Wiley & Sons, 2002.

Febrero, Ramon, and Pedro S. Schwartz. *The Essence of Becker.* Stanford, CA: Hoover Institution Press, 1995.

Fine, Ben, and Ellen Leopold. *The World of Consumption.* London: Routledge, 1993.

Fitzpatrick, Jon. *Money and Marriage Two: A Narrative Guide to Financial, Estate, and Retirement Planning in a Second Marriage.* Lincoln, NE: iUniverse Inc., 2004.

Fontaine, Constance J. *Fundamentals of Estate Planning.* 8th ed. Bryn Mawr, PA: American College Press, 2003.

Francis, Jack, and Roger Ibbotson. *Investments: A Global Perspective.* Upper Saddle River, NJ: Prentice Hall, 2001.

Frey, Bruno S., and Alois Stutzer. *Happiness and Economics: How the Economy and Institutions Affect the Human Well-Being.* Princeton, NJ: Princeton University Press, 2002.

Friedman, Milton. *A Theory of the Consumption Function.* Princeton, NJ: Princeton University Press, 1957.

Gates, Philimene. *Suddenly Alone: A Woman's Guide to Widowhood.* New York: Harper & Row, 1992.

Gibson, Roger C. *Asset Allocation: Balancing Financial Risk.* 3rd ed. New York: McGraw-Hill, 2000.

Gigerenzer, Gerd, and Reinhard Selten. *Bounded Rationality: The Adaptive Toolbox.* Cambridge, MA: MIT Press, 2001.

Gigerenzer, Gerd, Peter Todd, and The ABC Research Group. *Simple Heuristics That Make Us Smart.* New York: Oxford University Press, 1999.

Goodwin, Neva, Frank Ackerman, and David Kiron. *The Consumer Society.* Washington, DC: Island Press, 1997.

Graham, Benjamin. *The Intelligent Investor.* 4th rev. ed. New York: Harper Collins, 1997.

Grinblatt, Mark, and Sheridan Titman. *Financial Markets and Corporate Strategy.* 2nd ed. New York: McGraw-Hill, 2001.

Jasper, Margaret. *Consumer Rights Law.* Dobbs Ferry, NH: Oceana Publications, 1997.

Jensen, Michael. *Foundations of Organizational Management Strategy.* Cambridge, MA: Harvard University Press, 1998.

Jones, Nancy Langdon. *So You Want to Be a Financial Planner.* Sunnyvale, CA: AdvisorWorks, 2002.

Jones, Sally M. *Principles of Taxation for Business Investment Planning, 2002 Edition.* 5th ed. New York: McGraw-Hill/Irwin, 2001.

Katz, Deena. *Deena Katz on Practice Management: For Financial Advisors, Planners, and Wealth Managers.* Princeton, NJ: Bloomberg Press, 1999.

Katz, Deena. *Deena Katz's Tools and Templates for Your Practice: For Financial Advisors, Planners, and Wealth Managers.* Princeton, NJ: Bloomberg Press, 2001.

Kelvin, Jeffrey. *The Financial Planner's Handbook to Regulation and Successful Practice.* New York: Farnsworth Publishing, 1983.

Kess, Sidney, and Alan Campbell. *CCH Financial and Estate Planning Guide.* 13th rev. ed. Chicago, IL: Commerce Clearing House, 2001.

Kinder, George. *Seven Stages of Money Maturity: Understanding the Spirit and Value of Money in Your Life.* New York: Dell, 2000.

Kooreman, Peter, and Sophia Wunderink. *The Economics of Household Behavior.* New York: St. Martin's Press, 1997.

Kotlikoff, Laurence J. *Essays on Saving, Bequests, Altruism, and Life-Cycle Planning.* Cambridge, MA: MIT Press, 2001.

Krantz, Les. *Jobs Rated Almanac.* 6th ed. Fort Lee, NJ: Barricade Books, 2002.

Kritzman, Mark. *Puzzles of Finance: Six Practical Problems and Their Remarkable Solutions.* New York: John Wiley & Sons, 2000.

Lea, Stephen, Roger Tarpy, and Paul Webley. *The Individual and the Economy.* Cambridge, UK: Cambridge University Press, 1987.

Lea, Stephen, Paul Webley, and Brian Young. *New Directions in Economic Psychology: Theory, Experiment, and Application.* Cheltenham, UK: Edward Elgar, 1992.

Leimberg, Stephan, Jerry Kasner, Stephen Kandell, Ralph Gano Miller, Morey Rosenbloom, and Herbert Levy. *The Tools and Techniques of Estate Planning.* 11th ed. Cincinnati, OH: National Underwriter, 1998.

Lifson, Lawrence E., and Richard A. Geist. *The Psychology of Investing.* New York: John Wiley & Sons, 1999.

Lippett, Peter E. *Estate Planning: After the Reagan Tax Cut.* Reston, VA: Reston Pub., 1982.

Lleras, Miguel Palacios. *Investing in Human Capital: A Capital Markets Approach to Student Funding.* Cambridge, UK: Cambridge University Press, 2004.

Lo, Andrew, and Craig MacKinlay. *A Non-Random Walk Down Wall Street.* Princeton, NJ: Princeton University Press, 1999.

Loewe, Raymond. *New Strategies for College Funding: An Advisor's Guide.* New York: John Wiley & Sons, 2002.

Lord, William A. *Household Dynamics: Economic Growth and Policy.* New York: Oxford University Press, 2002.

Lustig, Harold. *4 Steps to Financial Security for Lesbian and Gay Couples.* New York: Ballantine Publishing, 1999.

Maister, David. *Managing the Professional Service Firm.* New York: Free Press, 1997.

Mandell, Lewis. *Financial Literacy: A Growing Problem.* Washington, DC: Jump$tart Coalition for Personal Financial Literacy, 2002.

Maslow, Abraham. *Motivation and Personality.* 2nd ed. New York: Harper & Row, 1970.

Michaud, Richard. *Efficient Asset Management: A Practical Guide to Stock Portfolio Optimization and Asset Allocation.* Boston, MA: Harvard Business School Press, 1998.

Mitchell, Olivia S., Anna M. Rappaport, and P. Brett Hammond, eds. *Forecasting Retirement Needs and Retirement Wealth.* Philadelphia, PA: University of Pennsylvania Press, 1999.

Modigliani, Franco. *The Collected Papers of Franco Modigliani.* Cambridge, MA: MIT Press, 1980.

Myers, Robert J., J. Robert Treanor, and Dale R. Detlefs. *Mercer Guide to Social Security and Medicare.* 28th ed. Louisville, KY: William M. Mercer Inc., 1999.

Nicolette, Parisi, and Marc Robinson. *Understanding Consumer Rights.* London: Dorling Kindersley, 2000.

Oberlin, Cliff, and Jill Powers. *Building a High-End Financial Services Practice: Proven Techniques for Planners, Wealth Managers, and Other Advisers.* Princeton, NJ: Bloomberg Press, 2004.

Palmiter, Alan. *Securities Regulation: Examples and Explanations.* 2nd ed. New York: Aspen Publishers, 2002.

Pritchett, Travis, Joan Schmit, Helen Doerpinghaus, and James Athearn. *Risk Management and Insurance.* 7th ed. St. Paul, MN: West Publishing, 1996.

Quinn, Jane Bryant. *Making the Most of Your Money.* New York: Simon & Schuster, 1997.

Ramaglia, Judith, and Diane MacDonald. *Personal Finance Tools for Decision Making.* Cincinnati: OH: South-Western College Publishing, 1998.

Rattiner, Jeffrey H. *Getting Started as a Financial Planner.* Princeton, NJ: Bloomberg Press, 2000.

Reilly, Frank, and Keith Brown. *Investment Analysis and Portfolio Management.* 7th ed. Mason, OH: South-Western, 2002.

Rich, Andrew. *How to Survive and Succeed in a Small Financial Planning Practice.* Reston, VA: Reston Publishing, 1984.

Rosen, Harvey S. *Public Finance.* 6th ed. New York: McGraw-Hill, 2001.

Ross, Stephen, Randolph Westerfield, and Jeffrey Jaffe. *Corporate Finance.* 7th ed. New York: McGraw-Hill/Irwin, 2004.

Ross, Stephen, Randolph Westerfield, and Bradford Jordan, *Essentials of Corporate Finance.* 4th ed. New York: McGraw-Hill/Irwin, 2003.

Rouse, Ken. *Putting Money in Its Place.* Dubuque, IA: Kendall/Hunt Publishing, 1994.

Rubinstein, Ariel. *Modeling Bounded Rationality.* Cambridge, MA: MIT Press, 1998.

Rutherford, Ronald. *The Complete Guide to Managing a Portfolio of Mutual Funds.* 1st ed. New York: McGraw-Hill, 1998.

Samuelson, Paul, and William Nordhaus. *Economics.* 18th ed. New York: McGraw-Hill/Irwin, 2004.

Saunders, Anthony. *Financial Institutions Management.* New York: McGraw-Hill, 2000.

Schilling, Edwin, III, and Carol Ann Wilson. *The Survival Manual for Men in Divorce.* Dubuque, IA: Kendall Hunt Publishing, 1992.

Schlesinger, Sanford J., and Barbara J. Scheiner. *Planning for the Elderly or Incapacitated Client.* Chicago, IL: Commerce Clearing House, 1993.

Scholes, Myron S., Mark A. Wolfson, Merle M. Erickson, Edward Maydew, and Terrence Shevlin. *Taxes and Business Strategy: A Planning Approach.* 2nd ed. Upper Saddle River, NJ: Prentice Hall, 2001.

Schulz, James H. *The Economics of Aging.* 7th ed. Wesport, CT: Greenwood Publishing, 2001.

Schwartz, Ronald. *Law and Aging: Essentials of Elder Law.* Upper Saddle River, NJ: Prentice Hall, 1998.

Scott, William R. *Financial Accounting Theory.* Upper Saddle River, NJ: Prentice Hall, 1997.

Sestina, John. *Fee-Only Financial Planning: How to Make It Work for You.* New York: John Wiley & Sons, 2000.

Sharpe, William, Gordon Alexander, and Jeffrey Bailey. *Investments.* 6th ed. Upper Saddle River, NJ: Prentice Hall, 1998.

Shefrin, Hersh. *Beyond Greed and Fear: Finance and the Psychology of Investing.* Boston, MA: Harvard Business School Press, 2000.

Shiller, Robert J. *Irrational Exuberance.* Princeton, NJ: Princeton University Press, 2000.

Skipper, Harold D., and Kenneth Black. *Life and Health Insurance.* 13th ed. Upper Saddle River, NJ: Prentice Hall, 1999.

Slemrod, Joel, ed. *Does Atlas Shrug? The Economic Consequences of Taxing the Rich.* Cambridge, MA: Harvard University Press, 2002.

Slemrod, Joel. *Tax Policy in the Real World.* New York: Cambridge University Press, 1999.

Slemrod, Joel, and Jon Bakija. *Taxing Ourselves: A Citizen's Guide to the Great Debate over Tax Reform.* 2nd ed. Cambridge, MA: MIT Press, 2000.

Soderlind, Steven. *Consumer Economics.* Armonk, NY: M.E. Sharpe, 2000.

Stawski, Willard. *Kids, Parents and Money: Teaching Personal Finance from Piggy Bank to Prom.* New York: John Wiley & Sons, 2000.

Stenken, Joseph. *Social Security Manual.* Cincinnati, OH: National Underwriter Company, 2002.

Stiglitz, Joseph E. *Economics of the Public Sector.* 3rd ed. New York: W.W. Norton, 2000.

Stone, Edward. *Getting Started in Financial Consulting.* New York: John Wiley & Sons, 2000.

Sulloway, Frank. *Born to Rebel: Birth Order, Family Dynamics, and Creative Lives.* New York: Vintage Books, 1997.

Swedberg, Richard. *Principles of Economic Sociology.* Princeton, NJ: Princeton University Press, 2003.

Tax Partners and Professionals of Ernst & Young LLP. *The Ernst & Young Tax Guide 2004.* New York: John Wiley & Sons, 2004.

Thaler, Richard H. *Advances in Behavioral Finance.* New York: Russell Sage, 1993.

Thaler, Richard H. *Advances in Behavioral Finance.* Vol. II. New York: Russell Sage Foundation, and Princeton, NJ: Princeton University Press, 2005.

Thaler, Richard H. *Quasi Rational Economics.* New York: Russell Sage, 1994.

Thaler, Richard H. *The Winner's Curse: Paradoxes and Anomalies of Economic Life.* Princeton, NJ: Princeton University Press, 1994.

Trieschmann, James S., Sandra Gustavson, and Robert Hoyt. *Risk Management and Insurance.* 11th ed. Cincinnati, OH: South-Western, 2000.

Tubbs, Stewart, and Sylvia Moss. *Human Communication: Principles and Contexts.* 10th ed. New York: McGraw-Hill, 2005.

Tucker, Alan, Kent Becker, Michael Isimbabi, and Joseph Ogden. *Contemporary Portfolio Theory and Risk Management.* Saint Paul, MN: West Publishing, 1994.

Twomey, David, Marianne Jennings, and Ivan Fox. *Anderson's Business Law and the Legal Environment.* 18th ed. Mason, OH: South-Western College, 2002.

Van Arsdale, Mary G. *A Guide to Family Financial Counseling.* Homewood, IL: Dow Jones-Irwin, 1982.

Vaughan, Emmett, and Therese Vaughan. *Fundamentals of Risk and Insurance.* 7th ed. New York: John Wiley & Sons, 1996.

Ventura, John. *The Credit Repair Kit.* 4th ed. Chicago, IL: Dearborn Financial Publishing, 2004.

Veres, Bob. *The Cutting Edge in Financial Services.* Cincinnati, OH: National Underwriter Company, 2002.

Vessenes, Katherine. *Protecting Your Practice.* Princeton, NJ: Bloomberg Press, 1997.

Walden, Michael. *Economics and Consumer Decisions.* Englewood Cliffs, NJ: Prentice Hall, 1992.

Wall, Ginita. *Our Money, Our Selves: Money Management for Each Stage of a Woman's Life.* New York: Consumers Union, 1992.

Warneryd, Karl-Erik. *The Psychology of Saving: A Study on Economic Psychology.* Cheltenham, UK: Edward Elgar, 1999.

Warneryd, Karl-Erik. *Stock-Market Psychology: How People Value and Trade Stocks.* Cheltenham, UK: Edward Elgar, 2001.

Weltman, Barbara. *Your Parent's Social Security.* New York: John Wiley & Sons, 1992.

Weston, Liz Pulliam. *Your Credit Score: How to Fix, Improve, and Protect the 3-Digit Number That Shapes*

Your Financial Future. Upper Saddle River, NJ: Pearson, Prentice Hall, 2005.

Williams, Arthur, Jr., Peter Young, and Michael Smith. *Risk Management and Insurance.* 8th ed. New York: McGraw-Hill/Irwin, 1998.

Wilson, Carol Ann. *The Financial Guide to Divorce Settlement.* Columbia, MD: Marketplace Books, 2000.

Zipp, Alan S. *Handbook of Tax and Financial Planning for Divorce and Separation.* Englewood Cliffs, NJ: Prentice Hall, 1985.

Provided below are some other sources of information:

Bloomberg Wealth Manager

Journal of Financial Planning

Kiplinger's Personal Finance

Index